# You Can Afford to RETIRE!

## The No-Nonsense Guide to Pre-Retirement Financial Planning

*William W. Parrott*

*&*

*John L. Parrott*

**NEW YORK INSTITUTE OF FINANCE**

NEW YORK  LONDON  TORONTO  SYDNEY  TOKYO  SINGAPORE

**Library of Congress Cataloging-in-Publication Data**

Parrott, William W.
    You can afford to retire! : the no-nonsense guide to pre-retirement financial planning / William W. Parrott and John L. Parrott.
    p.    cm.
    Includes index.
    ISBN 0-13-980160-X
    1. Retirement income—United States—Planning. 2. Retirees—United States—Finance, Personal. I. Parrott, John L.  II. Title.
HG181.P37 1992
332.024'01—dc20                    92-9499
                                   CIP

© 1992 by NYIF Corp.
Simon & Schuster
A Paramount Communications Company

**Printed in the United States of America**

10  9  8  7  6  5  4

ISBN 0-13-980160-X

New York Institute of Finance

# NOTICE TO READERS

# Introduction

To help you review this book as efficiently as possible, this special section has been prepared for your consideration.

## If You Are Retiring Soon and

A. Living on about $40,000 per year, read all the chapters except 12, 13, and 14.

B. Living on about $60,000, read all but chapters 11, 13, and 14.

C. Living on $90,000 or more, read all but chapters 11, 12, and 14.

D. An early retiree, read the entire book but skip the case studies that do not apply to your circumstances.

## If You Are Already Retired

Read the complete book but skip chapters 1, 2, and 4. Then read the case study that appears closest to your circumstances.

## In General

Retirement is a universal and very private experience. We all retire, but not everyone handles this new experience in the same fashion. Most of us have no role models to look to for guidance, as most of our parents

had no pension decisions to make since they had no pensions. Some of our friends have retired, yet we hesitate to discuss our finances with them, since we view such discussion as unseemly.

So, we have a problem, having not retired before. We sense that some preparation is essential, and the task seems daunting. It's as though each question answered begs another question. How much money will I need to maintain my lifestyle? How can I pay my taxes and still stay ahead of inflation? My company has several retirement plans, what is the best way to handle each? How much can I expect from Social Security? Should I count on this for my life? And finally, am I going to retire from my work only to have to become a full-time financial wizard?

Our objective in putting this book together is quite simple: We cannot possibly answer all of your questions, but we can answer the most commonly asked ones.

The *first part* of the book will address questions relating to income needs, taxes, inflation, retirement program options, and Social Security. The *second part* of the book will discuss investments most commonly used by people in retirement years. The *third part* will consider four case studies.

Before you begin the book, we call your attention to the distinctive features about our approach:

- We think that the best way we can help you is to be as specific as possible. Therefore, you will find current interest rates and specific investment recommendations sprinkled throughout the book.

- This time frame and its economy, world situation, value of the dollar, and the like dictated our asset allocation recommendations. They may be slightly different when you pick up the book.

- Chapter 10 (Asset Allocation) in our opinion is probably one of the most important in the book.

It will give you a relatively new, simple, and comprehensive approach to investing. Using this concept, we are comfortable with an average portfolio return of 9 to 11%.

Our unique approach will give you a real source of comfort as you deal with the major problem facing the retired person—namely, *inflation*.

### The Economy in a Nutshell (November 7, 1991)

Because this book deals in generalities, but contains concrete examples and case studies, we feel that it is important to give you a thumbnail sketch of our economy as the book goes to press.

First, some important interest rates:

### U.S. Treasury Securities

| | |
|---|---|
| 3 Month | 4.74% |
| 30 Year | 7.90% |

### Bank CDs

| | |
|---|---|
| 6 Month | 4.86% |
| 5 Year | 6.62% |

### Tax Exempt—General Obligation Bonds (Aaa)

| | |
|---|---|
| 1 Year | 4.40% |
| 25/30 Year | 6.50% |

### Economists' Thoughts*

- All expect the recovery to be slower then normal;

- Ninety percent saw little chance that the economy would slide back into recession;

---

*From the National Association of Business Economics Meeting, September 25, 1991.

- All expect inflation (CPI) to be up only 3.5% in 1991;

- All look for 2.8% growth of the U.S. economy in 1992.

We particularly like the comments of one economist, Dr. Robert Goodman, Senior Economic Advisor for the Putnam Companies. In the October 1991 issue of *Financial Planning News* he said:

> Over the next four or five years, the potential exists for the market to duplicate the performance it achieved between 1982 and 1987 when the Dow Jones Average more than tripled. Now, we're starting from a much higher level, and that would mean upwards of 8,000 on the Dow. I'm not predicting an 8,000 Dow, but at 780 on the Dow in 1982, who would have predicted five years later it would be over 2,700? Back then, the bears were getting all the attention, and those people missed the biggest bull market in stocks and bonds of this century.
>
> I think if you focus on economic fundamentals rather than on day-to-day statistics—if you act like an investor rather than a trader—then I think you stand to make a lot of money. Most people now are thinking in terms of 5, 10, and 15 minutes, as a consequence of the coup in the U.S.S.R. and the war in Kuwait. That's their time horizon, instead of thinking of 5, 10, and 15 *years*. But if they do that, they will be passed right by.
>
> If there's ever been a time to accumulate capital, perhaps in this entire century, this is it. But you've got to start now.

It is our intention to help you approach the preparation of your retirement plan with confidence and even joy as we solve problems together.

**W. W. Parrott**

**J. L. Parrott**

# Acknowledgments

We would like to express our gratitude to all those who helped us in the development of this book.

- Our wives, Aileen and Rosalie
- Our daughter and sister—Geraldine Parrott, LLB, CFP, who shared with us the experience of her numerous clients in Milwaukee, Wisconsin.
- Our friends and clients who helped with their personal experience, especially those who worked with us in reading and commenting on the book as it developd:

  Gasper Perry
  Dennis Murphy, CFP, and
  Jim and Eve Donahue

# Contents

# Part One

## *Solving the Retirement Puzzle*

# 1

# Tomorrow:
# Feast or Famine?

As we approach anything in life, we usually ask ...
"What's the cost?" The project before you is a very
sizable one. What is the cost of your retirement? How
much income do you need to live comfortably? What
about your expenses?

There are two basic and totally different approaches to resolving the budget question. One is the
*detailed method*: how much will you need for rent or
mortgage payments, taxes, utilities, food, and all the
other basic requirements of your life. This is, of course,
the best way to arrive at an accurate estimate of retirement costs and the income you will need to live
comfortably, yet it is very seldom used. Most of us are
just not into the time and effort involved. Nonetheless,
if you are interested in that type of detailed approach
see Table 1-1. It gives you a list of all the expense items
that you can incur during retirement. It also lists all
your possible sources of income.

**TABLE 1-1**

## CASH FLOW WORKSHEET

| Income | Spouse | Self |
|---|---|---|
| Pension | $ _____ | $ _____ |
| Social Security | _____ | _____ |
| IRA | _____ | _____ |
| Annuities | _____ | _____ |
| Interest and Dividends—<br>    Taxable | _____ | _____ |
| Interest and Dividends—<br>    Tax Free | _____ | _____ |
| Rent Receivable | _____ | _____ |
| Other | | |
|     Your Total | | _____ |
|     Spouse's Total | | _____ |
| (Add yours and your<br>    spouse's) | | |
|     Total Income | | [_____] |

**Expenses**

| | | |
|---|---|---|
| Income taxes (federal,<br>    state, and local) | | $ _____ |
| Housing (Rent; mortgage,<br>    and property taxes) | | _____ |
| Food | | _____ |
| Clothing (cleaning and<br>    purchases) | | _____ |
| Medical, Dental (premiums<br>    and out-of-pocket<br>    expenses) | | _____ |
| Transportation (gas,<br>    repairs, and car<br>    payments) | | _____ |
| Utilities (electric, gas, oil,<br>    and water) | | _____ |
| Insurance (auto, home, and<br>    liability) | | _____ |

**TABLE 1-1** (*Continued*)

### Expenses (Cont'd.)

| | |
|---|---|
| Loan Repayments (other than auto) | _____ |
| Entertainment (dining, theater, sports, etc.) | _____ |
| Vacation | _____ |
| Professional Fees (tax preparation and legal) | _____ |
| Gifts, Donations, (children, church/temple, and charity) | _____ |
| Miscellaneous | _____ |
| Total expenses | ☐ |
| **Net to Savings (Total income − expenses)** | $ ☐ |

## The Take-Home Approach

An easier way to determine how much money you are likely to need during retirement is the *take-home pay* approach based on your present paycheck. Start with your take-home pay. What does your pay stub show after all deductions (taxes, FICA, health insurance, savings, and so on)? The bottom line is the amount that you take home. Assuming you are married, add in your spouse's take-home pay. Subtract from the total the amount of money that you save from your paychecks. (Do not list savings that were already taken out of your salary.) The result is what you are actually living on at present. This will show the total amount you are currently spending on the items you need and want. (See Table 1-2.)

From this total you can make some additional deductions to arrive at a post-retirement budget for yourself. According to financial experts, this new budget would be anywhere from 85% to 90% of your present budget. These additional deductions are employment-

## TABLE 1-2

### POST-RETIREMENT FINANCIAL NEEDS

|                                      | Spouse        | Self          |
| ------------------------------------ | ------------- | ------------- |
| Paycheck (your take-home pay)        | _____       | _____       |
| Amount saved from paycheck           | ( _____ )   | ( _____ )   |
| Balance used to live on              | [          ]  | [          ]  |
| Costs involved with work:            |               |               |
|   Transportation           | ( _____ )   | ( _____ )   |
|   Clothing                 | ( _____ )   | ( _____ )   |
|   Business lunches         | ( _____ )   | ( _____ )   |
|   Business entertainment   | ( _____ )   | ( _____ )   |
|   Other                    | ( _____ )   | ( _____ )   |
|   Total work-related expenses | ( [      ] ) | ( [      ] ) |
| Grand total                          | [          ]  | [          ]  |
| Amount needed to live on in retirement | [          ] |             |

related expenses such as transportation to and from work, a wardrobe necessary for work, business lunches, entertainment, and other outlays that are not reimbursed by your employer. The bottom line is what you need to live on after retirement.

Now let's turn our attention to three other very important items in our planning project: life expectancy, taxes, and inflation.

## Life Expectancy

The first item that must be taken into consideration when you are deciding how much money you need is the length of time it will be needed. According to current statistics, a 65-year-old man can expect to live to the age of 79, and a 65-year-old woman will live approximately three years longer, to 82. To find out how long the average person is expected to live, see Table 1-3.

As you examine Table 1-3, you should understand that these numbers are national averages. For example, of the millions of 62-year-old females alive today, the average one will live 19.65 years. However, if you are a non-smoking female, 62 years of age and in good health and have not had a bout with cancer or heart disease, your chances of living more than 20 years are quite good. In your planning you may want to consider a life expectancy of 25 to 30 years.

We will address ourselves to the question of where the money to fund the rest of your life will come from in later chapters, but rest assured that there are many sources available.

In general, the most sensible type of retirement program should involve living off interest and dividends alone. But many people, by conserving their assets during the early part of their retirement, can, at a later date, invade principal and still not outlive all of the funds that they have accumulated.

## Taxes

Probably the greatest expense you will face in the years to come will be taxes. Because of its size (15% to 31% of our income), we would do well to examine this budget item in detail.

When you first started working years ago, you took on a partner or two who have remained with you all

## TABLE 1-3

## HOW LONG CAN YOU EXPECT TO LIVE?

| Age | Expectation in Years | |
|-----|-----|-----|
| | **Male** | **Female** |
| 50 | 25.35 | 29.53 |
| 51 | 24.51 | 28.67 |
| 52 | 23.69 | 27.82 |
| 53 | 22.88 | 26.98 |
| 54 | 22.88 | 26.98 |
| 55 | 21.28 | 23.67 |
| 56 | 20.50 | 24.49 |
| 57 | 19.73 | 23.67 |
| 58 | 18.98 | 22.86 |
| 59 | 18.23 | 22.05 |
| 60 | 17.50 | 21.25 |
| 61 | 16.77 | 20.44 |
| 62 | 16.07 | 19.65 |
| 63 | 15.37 | 18.86 |
| 64 | 14.69 | 18.08 |
| 65 | 14.03 | 17.32 |
| 66 | 13.38 | 16.57 |
| 67 | 12.75 | 15.83 |
| 68 | 12.13 | 15.10 |
| 69 | 11.53 | 14.38 |
| 70 | 10.97 | 13.67 |
| 71 | 10.40 | 12.97 |
| 72 | 9.85 | 12.28 |
| 73 | 9.32 | 11.60 |
| 74 | 8.81 | 10.95 |
| 75 | 8.32 | 10.32 |
| 76 | 7.86 | 9.71 |
| 77 | 7.41 | 9.12 |
| 78 | 6.99 | 8.55 |
| 79 | 6.59 | 8.01 |
| 80 | 6.20 | 7.48 |

*Source:* Life Insurance Commissioners of the United States.

through your life. Uncle Sam is number one and your state government is the second. In some areas, a city government is a third. No matter what job you've held, you have had to share your income with these partners. Despite the fact that you will no longer receive a paycheck, it is imperative that you include in your financial plans provisions for paying taxes and at the same time minimizing them as much as possible.

## Income Taxes

The tax system that we were used to in the recent past has changed dramatically. The 1991 tax table (see Table 1-4) has been shortened considerably to simplify our study.

Two examples should help to show how the tax table works. Take a married couple with a taxable income (after all deductions) of $47,000. They would pay $8,740 in taxes broken down as follows:

$$15\% \times \$34,000 = \$5,100$$
$$28\% \times \$13,000 = \$3,640$$

$$\text{Total} \quad \overline{\$8,740}$$

### TABLE 1-4

### FEDERAL TAX TABLE—1991

### Figures Shown Are Taxable Income (after all deductions)

| Married | Single | Tax Rate |
|---------|--------|----------|
| $0 to $34,000 | $0 to $20,350 | 15% |
| $34,001 to $82,150 | $20,351 to $49,300 | 28% |
| $82,151 and over | $49,301 and over | 31% |

Our second example is a single person with a taxable income (after all deductions) of $65,000. He or she would pay $16,025 in taxes broken down as follows:

15% × $20,350 = $ 3,052

28% × $28,950 = $ 8,106

31% × $15,700 = $ 4,867

Total Tax      $16,025

## State Income Taxes

In addition to the federal income tax, we have to take into consideration state income tax as well. Your state tax rate is listed in Table 1-5.

### TABLE 1-5

### 1991 HIGHEST MARGINAL INCOME TAX BY STATES

| State | Maximum Rate of Tax (%) | |
|-------|------------------|---|
| Alabama | 5% | on income over $3,000 |
| Arizona | 7% | on income over $150,000 |
| Arkansas | 7% | on income over $25,000 |
| California | 9.3% | on income over $55,292 |
| Colorado | 5% | on all federal taxable income |
| Connecticut | 7% | of capital gains |
| Delaware | 7.7% | on income over $40,000 |
| Georgia | 6% | on income over $7,000 |
| Hawaii | 10% | on income over $41,000 |
| Idaho | 8.2% | on income over $20,000 |
| Illinois | 3% | of federal adjusted gross income |
| Indiana | 3.4% | on adjusted gross income |
| Iowa | 9.98% | on income over $46,710 |
| Kansas | 5.15% | on income over $35,000 |

**TABLE 1-5** (Continued)

| State | Maximum Rate of Tax (%) | |
|---|---|---|
| Kentucky | 6% | on income over $8,000 |
| Louisiana | 6% | on income over $50,000 |
| Maine | 8.5% | on income over $16,200 |
| Maryland | 5% | on income over $3,000 |
| Massachusetts | 5.95% | on earned income and 12% on interest, capital gains and dividends |
| Michigan | 4.6% | on all income |
| Minnesota | 8.5% | on income over $89,500 |
| Mississippi | 5% | on income over $10,000 |
| Missouri | 6% | on income over $9,000 |
| Montana | 11% | on income over $55,000 |
| Nebraska | 6.41% | on income over $54,000 |
| New Hampshire | 5% | of interest and income dividends over $2,400 |
| New Jersey | 3.5% | on income over $50,000 |
| New Mexico | 8.5% | on income over $41,600 |
| New York | 7.875% | on income over $13,000 |
| North Carolina | 7% | on income over $12,750 |
| North Dakota | 12% | on income over $50,000 |
| Ohio | 6.9% | on income over $100,000 |
| Oklahoma | 7% | on income over $10,000 |
| Oregon | 9% | on income over $5,000 |
| Pennsylvania | 2.1% | on all income |
| Rhode Island | 22.96% | of adjusted federal income tax |
| South Carolina | 7% | on income over $10,150 |
| Tennessee | 6% | on interest and dividends |
| Utah | 7.2% | on income over $3,750 |
| Vermont | 28% | of federal income tax |
| Virginia | 5.75% | on income over $17,000 |
| Washington, D.C. | 10% | on income over $20,000 |
| West Virginia | 6.5% | on income over $60,000 |
| Wisconsin | 6.93% | on income over $20,000 |

**Note:** The following states have no personal income tax: Alaska, Florida, Nevada, South Dakota, Texas and Washington.

To add insult to injury, you may live in a city which has its own income tax.

Here are a few:

### TABLE 1-6

### SELECTED CITY MAXIMUM INCOME TAX RATES (1990)

| | |
|---|---|
| New York City | 3.91% |
| Philadelphia | 4.3% |
| Detroit | 3.0% |
| Pittsburgh | 2.1% |
| San Francisco | 1.5% |

Both the state and city taxes are deductible on the federal tax return. Thus, for example, if you are a resident of New York City and you are in the maximum bracket for both state and city, your adjusted tax rate would be as shown in Table 1-7.

Because state and city income taxes are deductible on your federal tax return, you should not simply add the respective rates together and assume that is your total tax bracket. The first thing you should do is adjust the local rates to reflect this true value.

For example, as shown in Table 1-7 the maximum tax rate in New York state is 7.875, but since it is a deductible item on your federal taxes, it is not 7.875 but rather 31% lower, namely 5.43%. A complicated concept, but as shown this New York City resident should not assume that he or she is paying 42.79% of the last dollar earned in taxes. The correct amount is 39.13%.

## How to Determine Your Taxes

Since taxes are so important, let's consider how the average retiree would arrive at a total. Under the current law, a number of changes have taken place.

## TABLE 1-7

## STATE AND LOCAL RATES—ADJUSTED

|  | Full Rate | Actual Rate Equivalent |
|---|---|---|
| Federal | 31.0% | 31.0% |
| New York State | 7.875% | 5.43% |
| New York City | 3.91% | 2.70% |
| **Total** | **42.79%** | **39.13%** |

You take your *gross income* minus special deductions. This gives you your *adjusted gross income.* Then you reduce this by either *itemized deductions* or *standard deductions* ($3,400 for singles or $5,700 for those married in 1991). *Personal exemption* ($2,150 per person) is subtracted to get your taxable income.

### Itemized Deductions

Under the current law, the following is a list of the more important deductions:

1. Mortgage interest (on your first and second home only);

2. Income taxes (state and city);

3. Property taxes (real estate);

4. Charitable gifts;

5. Medical expenses over 7.5% of your adjusted gross income; and

6. Unreimbursed business expenses and certain investment expenses in excess of 2% of your adjusted gross income.

### Personal Exemptions

In 1991, the personal exemption is $2,150 for each person. If you are more than 65 years old or are blind, you are entitled to an additional amount of standard

deduction. If you are single, you receive an extra $850, which makes your standard deduction $4,250. If you are married, each spouse over 65 receives an extra $650, which makes your standard deduction $7,000.

The current law has a major change for high-income individuals. Singles with taxable income over $100,000 and married over $150,000 have their personal exemption gradually reduced under a complicated formula. We recommend you check with your accountant if your taxable income is in excess of those amounts. High-income taxpayers may also have their itemized deductions reduced by as much as 20% under another formula.

---

### Helpful Hint

Your total tax rate is extremely important in planning your investments. For example, let's assume you have $10,000 more than you need for emergencies in your savings account and it is currently earning 5.5% interest. That would give you $550 of gross income per year, but after taxes of $193 (assuming a total tax of 35% is deducted) all you would have left is $357. If that same $10,000 were invested in a tax-free municipal at 7%, the total yield would be $700 per year, an increase of $343 ($700 − $357). That is a 96% increase in spendable income.

---

## What Will I Be Left with After Inflation?

It is a fact of financial life that the purchasing power of a 1991 dollar is greater than that of a 1993 dollar. The 1999 dollar's purchasing power will be even less. The problem is *inflation*. What will the inflation rate

### EXHIBIT 1-1 INFLATION—HISTORY & PROJECTION

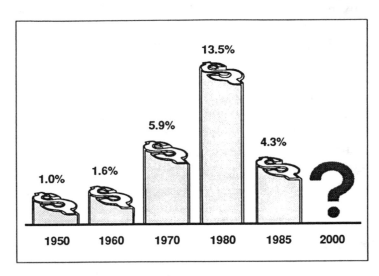

be in the future? According to Exhibit 1-1, inflation has run the gamut from a low of 1% in 1950 to a high of 13.5% in 1980. The rate for 1991 was 3.1%.

To be realistic, and somewhat hopeful, we will consider an average 5% inflation rate over the next 20 years. Let's examine what this will mean in terms of the purchasing power of your retirement dollar. We will use three examples of current (after-tax) income: $30,000, $60,000, and $110,000.

### TABLE 1-8

### BUYING POWER DECLINE 1991 to 2011

#### (Based on 5% Annual Rate of Inflation)

| Year 1991 | Buying Power of | | |
|---|---|---|---|
| | **$30,000** | **$60,000** | **$110,000** |
| 1996 | 23,213 | 46,427 | 85,116 |
| 2001 | 17,962 | 35,924 | 65,861 |
| 2006 | 13,899 | 27,797 | 50,962 |
| 2011 | $10,755 | $21,509 | $39,433 |

If your current after-tax income need is $30,000, the buying power of that $30,000 will be reduced year by year by an assumed 5%. In five years, you will be able to buy only $23,213 of goods and services with today's $30,000. In 10 years the buying power will be reduced to $17,962, in 15 years to $13,899 and in 20 years to $10,755.

Examined from a different perspective, let's look at this problem from a principal or capital point of view. Let's assume that you have $400,000 to invest; you are going to put it all into certificates of deposit and earn a steady 8% over the next 20 years. (See Table 1-9.) The value of your principal would be reduced each year by 5%.

## Look Back 30 Years

To help understand what lies ahead, let's look back in time to what we actually paid for groceries. (See Table 1-10.)

Now let's look ahead. At 5% per year, that same roughly $15 bag of groceries will cost $19 in 1996, $24 in 2001, $30 in 2006 and $39 in 2011.

One other item that should be considered as we address the inflation question is a possible annuity payment, such as a mandated pension. Let's suppose that you must take a fixed pension (we will consider the

### TABLE 1-9

### EFFECTS OF INFLATION AT 5% PER YEAR

| Year | Principal (reduced by 5% per year) | Interest at 8% |
|------|------|------|
| 1991 | $400,000 | $32,000 |
| 1996 | 309,000 | 24,761 |
| 2001 | 239,495 | 19,159 |
| 2011 | $143,394 | $11,472 |

**TABLE 1-10**

## WHAT GROCERIES IN 1961
## WOULD COST TODAY

|                    | 1961   | 1976   | 1991    |
|--------------------|--------|--------|---------|
| Bread              | $0.21  | $0.35  | $0.71   |
| Bacon              | .71    | 1.71   | 2.31    |
| Butter             | .76    | 1.26   | 1.90    |
| Chuck Roast        | .59    | .97    | 2.60    |
| Coffee             | .74    | 1.87   | 2.87    |
| Lettuce (head)     | .18    | .48    | .73     |
| Milk (½ gallon)    | .52    | .83    | 1.37    |
| Potatoes           | .06    | .15    | .39     |
| Tomatoes           | .30    | .58    | 1.67    |
|                    | $4.07  | $8.20  | $14.55  |

*Source:* Putnam research and U.S. Bureau of Labor Statistics
Retail Food Index. Prices are in dollars per pound, except as
indicated.

question of which is best in a later chapter) and that
pension is $2,000 per month. What will you be able to
buy with it 5 years from now? Assuming a 5% inflation
rate, Table 1-11 has the answer.

## How Can You Beat Inflation?

The very first consideration in determining how to
overcome the inflation problem is to understand that
every time you invest some of your money, whether it
is in a certificate of deposit (CD), a money market fund,
or any other financial instrument, inflation should be
taken into consideration.

Second, you should determine the percentage of
your assets that are to be invested in a growth instrument to counterbalance inflation. In general, our recommendation for retirees is to invest 25% to 35% of

### TABLE 1-11

## FIXED MONTHLY PENSION

### (Inflation @ 5% per year)
**Buying Power**

| | |
|---|---|
| Today | $2,000 |
| 5 years | 1,548 |
| 10 years | 1,197 |
| 15 years | 927 |
| 20 years | $ 717 |

their assets in the growth area. The larger your net worth, the higher the percentage you can allocate to growth.

Third, what type of "growth investments" should you consider? Growth investments can, and in most cases should, include common stock, both domestic and foreign, real estate, and corporate bonds. We will go into much more detail regarding these investments in later chapters.

There are two other ways to solve the inflation problem. One is to avoid spending all the income your assets produce. The majority of our clients actually live on 10% to 20% less income than their assets provide.

The other method is to spend some of your assets; that is, to invade principal. This is the least attractive of the three approaches, but if it's done properly you can outlive the depletion of your assets.

## Your Own Annuity

If you decide to invade (spend) principal, how do you go about it? You can either go to any insurance company and buy an annuity, or set up your own.

Let's assume that we are planning the payout of $200,000 for a 72-year-old widow, who does not quite have enough income to do what she wants. According

to the life expectancy table (Table 1-3), she will likely live at least 12.28 more years. Assuming she has other assets like a pension, Social Security plus another $100,000 or so, then the $200,000 under consideration could give her a regular check of $2,028 per month, including 9% of interest, and some principal paid out for a full 15 years. Her amortization schedule can be seen in Table 1-12.

As an alternative, we contacted a large insurance company in New York and were told that they would give our hypothetical widow a check for $1,936 per month over the same period of time. The reason for the lower amount is that the insurance company would only guarantee interest of 8.25%.

## TABLE 1-12

### PRIVATE ANNUITY @ 9% INTEREST

#### $200,000 Principal
#### $2,028 Monthly Payment for 15 Years

|     | Principal Remaining at End of Year | Total of Principal Paid Out | Total of Interest Paid Out |
| --- | --- | --- | --- |
| 1.  | $193,389.33 | $ 6,610.67 | $ 17,731.72 |
| 2.  | 186,158.52 | 13,841.48 | 34,843.32 |
| 3.  | 178,299.42 | 21,750.58 | 51,276.62 |
| 4.  | 169,598.39 | 30,401.61 | 66,967.99 |
| 5.  | 160,135.84 | 39,864.16 | 81,847.83 |
| 6.  | 149,785.63 | 50,214.32 | 95,840.02 |
| 7.  | 138,464.56 | 61,535.50 | 108,861.29 |
| 8.  | 126,081.37 | 73,918.63 | 120,820.56 |
| 9.  | 112,536.62 | 87,463.38 | 131,618.21 |
| 10. | 97,721.28 | 102,278.72 | 141,145.26 |
| 11. | 81,516.16 | 118,483.84 | 149,282.54 |
| 12. | 63,790.88 | 136,209.12 | 155,899,66 |
| 13. | 44,402.85 | 155,597.15 | 160,854.03 |
| 14. | 23,196.09 | 176,803.91 | 163,989.67 |
| 15. | $  -0- | $200,000.00 | $165,135.96 |

# 2

# Making the Most
# of Your Pension Plan

One of the greatest assets you own is your pension. Usually it is quite sizable, depending on how long you have worked and what income you have earned.

Most pension plans insist that a member be paid a fixed pension for life. They offer a number of variables like providing income for a spouse in case you die first or guaranteeing the income for at least 10 or 20 years. Some pensions permit their members to choose a lump sum instead of the fixed pension. Before we turn our attention to the lump-sum alternative, we will examine three of the more important pension or annuity options in some detail.

- Life income;
- Joint life; and
- Period certain.

## Life Income

The first option is the maximum or *single life income*. Monthly payments would be paid to you until you die. This would give you a fixed amount of dollars per month for the rest of your life. At your death, payments would stop completely. Your spouse or children would receive nothing. For example, let's assume that you have been in a middle-management position with a large corporation and are entitled to a payment of $2,000 per month. Under this option, you would receive a monthly check of $2,000 no matter how long you live.

However, if you died one month after starting to receive the pension, the payments would end. The remaining funds in your pension would revert to the pension trust or insurance company, whichever was making the payments. Your surviving spouse or children, if any, would receive nothing.

## Joint Life

The second option is a *joint life income* option with 50% to your spouse. In our preceding example, the $2,000 maximum would be reduced to $1,700. You and your spouse would receive $1,700 per month for the rest of your life. If you died first your spouse would receive 50% of the $1,700, or $850/month, for the balance of his or her life. If your spouse died first you would receive the $1,700 per month for the balance of your life. This is usually called *50% joint life*. Another alternative is a *100% joint life*. Here the monthly payment to you would be reduced to about $1,500 per month and, at your death, your spouse would continue to receive the same $1,500 sum for the rest of his or her life.

## Period Certain

The third major option, the *20-year certain* choice, could be selected if you wanted to take a reduced sum of money to guarantee that some survivor—a spouse, or a child, would receive some income if you died prematurely. The reduced pension would be about $1,600 per month. Thus, you would receive $1,600 per month for the balance of your life. If you died within 20 years after retirement, the same amount of money would continue to be paid to a designated beneficiary for the balance of the 20-year period. You of course would be guaranteed the $1,600 per month for the rest of your life, no matter how long you lived.

The percentage differences noted here represent those in effect in most companies. That is, there is normally a 15% drop between life income and 50% joint life, a 25% drop in the 100% joint life and a 20% differential between life income and 20-year certain.

## Life Insurance Approach

If you are married and want to protect your spouse, you would probably do what most married people do, namely choose the 50% joint life plan. But there is an

**TABLE 2-1**

**PENSION OPTIONS**

| Option | To You | Monthly Payments to Spouse at Your Death |
|---|---|---|
| Life income | $2,000 | $    0 |
| 50% joint life | 1,700 | 850 |
| 100% joint life | 1,500 | 1,500 |
| 20-year certain (for balance of 20 years) | 1,600 | 1,600 |

alternative approach to this you may wish to consider—buy a life insurance policy. It involves putting
the difference between the maximum plan, the $2,000
per month we discussed earlier and the $1,700 under
a 50% joint life plan, namely $300 per month, into life
insurance. If this idea appeals to you, you would select
the maximum $2,000 per month life income plan, use
$1,700 per month for living expenses, and pay $300 per
month for life insurance premiums. Let's assume that
you and your spouse are both 65 years of age, and that
you are a male, non-smoker, in good health. If you went
to your life insurance agent and said "How much life
insurance can I buy on my life for about $300 per month?"
You would discover that you could buy a life insurance
policy of about $82,000 for about $250 per month in
premiums and that your wife would receive about the
same protection as the 50% joint life pension plan. See
Table 2-2 for a comparison.

As you can see, the income available for both of
you to live on is just about the same; $1,700 versus

## TABLE 2-2

### SPOUSAL BENEFITS
*(Joint and 50% Pension vs. Life Insurance)*

|  | Joint and 50% Pension | Life Insurance |
|---|---|---|
| Monthly pension | $1,700 | $2,000 |
| Cost of insurance | 0 | 243 |
| Available income | 1,700 | 1,757 |
| Death benefit (net after tax) | 850 | 850 |
| Cost if spouse dies first | 300 | 0 |
| Savings (10 years) | 0 | 27,755 |
| Stop payments | Never | About 10 years |

$1,757. The after-tax death benefit should you die first, is also the same, $850 per month for the rest of your wife's life. However, on the saving side of the ledger, you would be far better off using the life insurance approach if your wife dies first. Under the pension plan, you would continue to lose $300 per month for the rest of your life because your pension has been permanently reduced from $2,000 to $1,700 per month. Under the insurance plan, you would cancel the policy because there would be no further need for it, pick up the cash value and dividends and save the $300 per month that you were paying for the policy. For example, if your wife died in the tenth year and you cancelled the insurance policy, you would receive a check from the life insurance company of $27,755, assuming the dividends came in as the insurance company projected. There is also a large difference in saving under the two plans. There is absolutely no saving under the pension plan while there is a saving of about $27,755 under the insurance approach. The $27,755 is the total amount of guaranteed cash value and accumulated dividends built up in the policy in the tenth year.

Another difference between the two approaches is a *paid-up* feature in the insurance policy. Under the pension plan approach, the program is never paid up. Once you agree that you will receive a lower benefit to protect your wife, you can never change the payment. If, however, you choose to receive the $2,000 per month and put $243 of it into life insurance, that $243 per month could stop in approximately 10 years. It would be unnecessary to make further payments, because of the buildup of cash values and dividends. That sum would be sufficient to pay all premiums for the policy after approximately 10 years.

## Is Insurance Always Necessary?

Before making your final decision on which pension option to choose and, for that matter, whether or not you should use the life insurance approach at all,

we recommend that you thoroughly review your assets. It is quite possible that your best pension option may be the maximum one, even though you are married. In many cases, where we have done the planning for married couples with a net worth of about $500,000 there is no need for additional life insurance coverage, and our recommendation has been to choose the maximum pension option the corporation or union offers, despite the fact that the pension payment stops at the death of the retiree. This assumes of course that the retiring employee is in good health.

The reasoning behind this recommendation is two-fold: first, assuming you are 65 and in good health, you will live until age 80. (See the life expectancy table, Table 1-3). Thus, in our example, you and your wife would give up $300 per month for a period of about 15 years (that's $54,000). This assumes you would die at age 80. Secondly, and most important, there are usually enough assets around other than life insurance to assure a good income to your spouse for the balance of her life. Take a good look at "Abe and Bernice Cooper" in Chapter 11. Assume that Abe died before Bernice. She would lose his pension of $18,753 per year and Social Security of $9,247 but would be left with a fairly dependable $43,943 gross income per year and a paid-up home. Her net worth would still be $485,127. Do keep in mind that Abe and Bernice said that all they needed to live on together was $40,000 per year after taxes. Bernice should be able to make do with about $37,000 net after taxes. Therefore, our recommendation in their case was for Abe to take the maximum pension offered by his firm.

Knowing your net worth and the individual components that make it up will give you the ability to make these critical decisions. If you don't have enough assets to protect your spouse, indeed your best choice may be the joint and 50% plan or, assuming good health, you could choose the maximum plan and put the difference into a new life insurance policy.

## Why Not Take It All at Once? Is Lump-Sum Distribution the Better Way to Go?

The figures presented in the previous section of this chapter assume that you are locked into receiving a fixed pension. Some of the more progressive corporations, however, are permitting employees to choose a lump-sum distribution of their pension plan funds. This generally is a better way to go. If you are a person who will not spend your money loosely, but will invest it wisely and consume only the interest or dividends that your investments produce, you will be far better off with a lump-sum distribution.

The reason, quite simply, is that you will continue to own the principal and will always be able to deal, in your own way, with inflation and other economic problems that might arise. If you must opt for an annuity or pension option, the principal is spent and your heirs will never receive anything after you die. At your death, except in the case of the 50% joint life option or the 20-year certain program, the monthly income would cease. Under a lump-sum distribution, the principal would always be there for beneficiaries.

Let's look at two examples: first let's assume that you are a married man and that you are offered the pension numbers shown in Table 2-1. Further let's assume you worked for a progressive corporation and they offered you a lump-sum distribution option. That number would be about $220,000 (depending entirely on what interest rate and longevity assumption your corporation used). Assuming that you took the $220,000 to a knowledgeable and experienced financial planner or stockbroker, who could get a fairly conservative return of 9.5%. This would produce an income of $20,900 per year or $1,742 per month. Not only is that higher than the $1,700 per month offered for the joint and 50% pension, but you and your wife would own the $220,000 of principal and would be able to deal with the inflation problem far more effectively. Our strong recommen-

dation would be to take the lump-sum distribution of $220,000 and run.

A second example assumes that you are a single female. Your choice is a little harder to make, because you would expect to receive $2,000 per month from the pension as opposed to the $1,742 from the lump sum. Our recommendation would be to take the lump sum and seek a higher yield.

In any case, you should consider inflation. We feel that it is the biggest problem that you will face in retirement. Table 2-3 shows the ravaging effect inflation has on a fixed pension using a 3%, 5% and 8% inflation factor.

## Lump-Sum Distribution

Let's now look at what a lump-sum distribution is and how it will be taxed.

In our previous example of $2,000 per month as a maximum pension, the lump-sum distribution equivalent would be approximately $220,000. Other lump-sum sources are:

- Owners of small companies. Quite often they permit their employees to take a lump-sum distribution.

### TABLE 2-3

### BUYING POWER OF A FIXED
### MONTHLY PENSION

*(At various inflation factors)*

|          | 3%      | 5%      | 8%      |
|----------|---------|---------|---------|
| Today    | $2,000  | $2,000  | $2,000  |
| 5 Years  | 1,717   | 1,546   | 1,318   |
| 10 Years | 1,475   | 1,197   | 869     |
| 15 Years | 1,267   | 927     | 573     |
| 20 Years | 1,088   | 717     | 377     |

- Sole proprietors, partnerships, and closely held corporations with 1 to 50 employees.

- Profit-sharing plans. They must provide a lump-sum distribution option.

- Corporations where a thrift plan, savings plan or 401(k) plan is in effect allow lump-sum distribution options. A savings or thrift plan is one in which you are permitted to set aside a certain percentage of your pay check in a special corporate savings plan. Quite often, the corporation will match a portion of it, anywhere from 10% to 100%. At retirement time, the employee's accumulated savings, including the corporation's matching funds and interest, are available as a lump-sum.

## Taxes and the Lump-Sum Distribution

The question then arises, "How shall these funds be received?" They can be taken in one of three ways:

- As a lump sum (one total payment);

- As an annuity through a life insurance company, or

- Transferred into an individual retirement account (IRA).

The next question is, "How is each option taxed?" Some plans allow you to contribute both pre-tax and after-tax dollars. *Pre-tax dollars* are contributions that have not had any taxes withheld. *After-tax dollars* have had taxes withheld. According to Internal Revenue Service rules and regulations, your after-tax contribution to the plan is subtracted from the total amount available. This amount, of course, is returned to you. It is separated from the balance which has never been

taxed. Since taxes have already been paid on this portion of your contribution, it is not subject to tax again.

Let's use an example of a lump-sum distribution of
$92,145 from a 401(k) (corporate saving plan). When
you receive the check, your employer is required by
law to indicate the amount you contributed to the plan
with after-tax dollars. Let's assume that it was $16,586.
This would leave $75,559 taxable ($92,145 minus $16,586).
It can be taxed using one of four methods:

- 10-year average;

- 5-year average;

- Rolled over into an IRA; or as an

- Annuity.

The 10-year average is only available to you if you
were 50 years of age on January 1, 1986 (born before
January 1, 1936).

If you want to take the lump sum and use the after-
tax proceeds to invest in real estate, a business or some
other investment which requires a large sum of money,
you should consider the 10-year average or 5-year average tax. Table 2-4 will help you see the differences.

As you can see the 10-year average cost is lower
until the lump-sum amount becomes quite large. Note
that with the $500,000 amount the 5-year average tax
is less than the 10-year average tax. Thus, if you want
the distribution in after-tax cash (as opposed to an IRA
rollover) your best bet is the 10-year or 5-year average
tax method.

## Who Qualifies for Averaging?

- If you were age 50 before January 1, 1986, you
  can use both 10-year averaging or 5-year averaging and choose the one that results in a lower
  tax.

## TABLE 2-4

## TAXABILITY OF LUMP-SUM DISTRIBUTION USING THE SPECIAL 10-YEAR AND 5-YEAR METHODS

| Amount of Distribution | 10-year Avg. Tax | Effective Rate | 5-year Avg. tax | Effective Rate |
|---|---|---|---|---|
| $    30,000 | $    2,521 | 8.4% | $    3,300 | 11.0% |
| 50,000 | 5,874 | 11.7% | 6,900 | 13.8% |
| 70,000 | 9,505 | 13.6% | 10,500 | 15.0% |
| 90,000 | 12,706 | 14.1% | 13,500 | 15.0% |
| 100,000 | 14,471 | 14.5% | 15,000 | 15.0% |
| 150,000 | 24,570 | 16.4% | 28,773 | 19.2% |
| 250,000 | 50,770 | 20.3% | 56,878 | 22.8% |
| 500,000 | 143,682 | 28.7% | 134,378 | 26.9% |
| $1,000,000 | $382,210 | 38.2% | $289,378 | 28.9% |

- If you were younger than 50 on January 1, 1986, you can only use the 5-year average approach (or the IRA rollover).

- Teachers and others involved in "qualified" tax deferred annuities cannot use the 5- or 10-year tax averaging. They must pay "ordinary income" tax, use the IRA rollover, or take an annuity.

### Other Rules

- If you use either 5- or 10-year averaging you must pay your tax by the April 15th due date of the following year.

- The assets must come from a qualified retirement plan (pension, profit-sharing, 401(k), stock bonus, Keogh or ESOP (Employer Stock Ownership Plan).

- The lump-sum distribution must be 100% of your interest in the plan and it must be paid to you in one taxable year.

- Your reason for receving it must be one of the following:
    Retiring;
    Resigning;
    Being terminated;
    Disability;
    Death; or
    Age 59-1/2 and still employed (if your plan allows it).

- You must have been in the plan for 5 years.

- 5-year or 10-year averaging is not available unless you are at least age 59-1/2. If you were age 50 by January 1, 1986, the age 59-1/2 requirement does not apply.

- You can only use 10-year averaging once in a lifetime.

- You are required to use the same tax treatment if you receive more than one lump-sum distribution in the same year.

- If you use one of the averaging approaches and you were age 50 by January 1, 1986, you may take advantage of the long-term capital gains (assuming you participated in the retirement plan prior to 1974). Your company will inform you if any of your assets qualify.

- If you qualify to use the 10-year averaging method you must use 1986 tax rates for the calculations. The 5-year averaging method uses the tax rates that are in effect in the year that you receive the distribution. Both 5- and 10-year methods use the single taxpayer rates whether or not you are married.

## IRA Rollover

Now let's examine the pros and cons of the IRA rollover. We find that the vast majority of people are

better off using the IRA rollover approach for the following reasons:

- A greater amount of spendable net after-tax income.

- The possibility of tax deferral.

- An on-going tax shelter for growth investments.

- Some states do not tax IRA proceeds (New York for example does not tax the first $20,000 of IRA and pension income).

A lump-sum distribution analysis should be done before you make your decision. This can be done by your accountant, financial planner or broker. Table 2-5 is a simple example.

A few pointers to help you understand the analysis:

- If you use the 5- or 10-year tax averaging approach you can use the lower of the two. In this example, the 10-year average method results in less tax.

- After taxes were paid on the lump sum, we simply invested the balance in tax-free municipal bonds at 7%. Of course, you could invest it in growth instruments, but our effort here is to compare so-called safe investments.

- The full amount ($100,000) would be rolled into your IRA.

- Here, we put it all into a Government National Mortgage Association (GNMA, familiarly known as a "Ginnie Mae" to be explained in a later chapter) at 9.5%.

- Our next assumption is that you took the $9,500 out of the IRA to live on. You were in a 28% tax bracket leaving a net after-tax amount of $6,840.

Obviously, in this example, the IRA rollover is the better way to go.

## TABLE 2-5

## LUMP-SUM DISTRIBUTION ANALYSIS

| | |
|---|---:|
| Lump sum | $110,000 |
| Your contribution | 10,000 |
| Taxable | 100,000 |

**5-year Average**

| | |
|---|---:|
| Tax | 15,000 |
| Percentage | 15.0% |

**10-year Average**

| | |
|---|---:|
| Tax | 14,471 |
| Percentage | 14.5% |
| Balance available for investment | 85,529 |
| Invested (tax free) @ | 7.0% |
| After-tax income | $5,987 |

**IRA Rollover**

| | |
|---|---:|
| Lump sum | $100,000 |
| Invested @ | 9.5% |
| Gross income | 9,500 |
| Withdrawn @ assumed tax rate | 28.0% |
| Net after-tax income | $6,840 |

**Comparison of Net After-Tax Income**

| | |
|---|---:|
| 10-year average | $5,987 |
| IRA rollover | 6,840 |

---

### Helpful Hint

In general on larger lump sum amounts (over $70,000) IRA rollover is the best way unless you need or want large sums of money to invest in a business, real estate or some other worthwhile venture right now. For smaller lump sums you might be better off using 5- or 10-year averaging because the effective tax rate is a lot lower than ordinary income tax rates. (See Table 2-4).

## Other Considerations if You Use IRA Rollovers

- You may want to keep separate your regular contribution IRA from the lump-sum IRA (to permit you to transfer it to a pension plan at a later date, if you go to work at another company and want to roll it into the new company's plan). Every one of our older clients have commingled the two.

- If you want to roll over only part of the lump sum, you will have to pay ordinary income tax rates on the part that you do not roll over, and you may not use 5- or 10-year averaging on it.

- If you are under 59-1/2 and take distribution out of your IRA you will be subject to a 10% penalty tax unless:

    You are totally and permanently disabled; or You take distributions in regular scheduled installments over your life expectancy. (See Chapter 14 on early retirement for an explanation of this procedure.)

- You do not have to take a distribution until you turn 70-1/2. If you wait until then, you must take a minimum distribution based upon either a federal life expectancy table or a life insurance table. If you are single the minimum distribution in the year you become 70-1/2 is 1/16 of the total value of your IRA. If you are married the distribution depends on both your age and your spouse's age. If you were both age 70-1/2 your minimum first year distribution would be 1/20.6 of your IRA's value.

- If you decide to roll over your lump sum, you must do it within 60 days of receipt of the lump sum or you will be forced to pay tax on it using another method.

- If you do not take out the required amount at age 70-1/2, you will be subject to a penalty of 50% of

the amount that you should have withdrawn. That's right—50%.

## Special Considerations on Larger Distributions

If you are fortunate enough to have very sizable sums available at retirement, you should be aware of the following:

- There is an excise tax, regardless of your age, equal to 15% of the amount of "excess" retirement plan distributions.

- For an IRA, "excess" distributions are any distributions that exceed $150,000 in one tax year.

- If you use 5- or 10-year averaging, the excise tax begins when your lump sum is larger than $750,000.

- There is a transition rule which says that if you had accrued retirement benefits over $562,500 as of August 1, 1986 you could have elected (no later than your 1988 tax return) to exclude your "accrued" amount from the excise tax. If you made this election, the excise tax calculation is more complicated.

Needless to say, you should consult your accountant regardless of the size of your lump-sum distribution. His or her comments become even more important with extra large ones.

# 3

# What Will Social Security Provide?

We will approach this subject on the assumption that you have been paid maximum Social Security wages over the years. Further we are assuming that you are retiring tomorrow. We will cover those Social Security subjects which in our opinion are of greatest importance to you.

If you are 65 years of age and fully covered, and have paid maximum Social Security taxes during your working years, you would receive $12,264 per year in Social Security benefits. If your spouse was also fully covered and paid maximum Social Security taxes, he or she would receive an equal amount (i.e., $12,264 for a total of $24,528). If your spouse never worked and, therefore, paid nothing into the system, he or she would be entitled to one-half of the amount that you receive, assuming that you are both the same age. Your spouse would receive $6,132 for a total between the two of you

of $18,396. The amount that a retiree is entitled to is dependent upon his or her earnings record.

## Who Is Covered?

Generally speaking, almost all employees in private industry, self-employed persons, and members of the Armed Forces are covered.

Some groups are excluded:

- Federal employees hired before 1984.

- Railroad employees (who are under the Railroad Retirement System).

- Employees of state and local governments who have chosen not to be covered.

The above list covers the majority of those who are not covered, however, this is not meant to be a complete list.

## Insured Status

In all probability, you are covered for Social Security. Simply put, if you have worked and contributed to the Social Security system for 10 years then you are covered for benefits. If you do not have 10 years (40 quarters as Social Security regulations, put it) you will not qualify for retirement benefits. This is an important point for many wives, who returned to work after the children were grown. The Social Security "Personal Earnings and Benefit Estimate Statement" will answer the question for you. You may obtain a copy of this form from your local Social Security office.

## What Will Your Social Security Benefit Be?

Determining your actual pension benefits is a bit difficult. The Social Security Administration, of course, will give you the exact amount. Table 3-1 will help you arrive at an approximation of what you can expect,

## TABLE 3-1

### APPROXIMATE SOCIAL SECURITY BENEFITS AT RETIREMENT
*(For Ages 55 to 65)*

| Year of Birth | Maximum Monthly Benefit | |
| --- | --- | --- |
| | At 65 | At 62 |
| 1926 | $1,022 | $691 |
| 1927 | 1,049 | 739 |
| 1928 | 1,056 | 780 |
| 1929 | 1,045 | 836 |
| 1930 | 1,066 | 852 |
| 1931 | 1,087 | 869 |
| 1932 | 1,109 | 887 |
| 1933 | 1,130 | 904 |
| 1934 | 1,152 | 921 |
| 1935 | 1,174 | 939 |

*Source:* National Underwriter Company.

assuming again that you had earned the maximum Social Security covered salary each year.

Let's assume for example that you were born in 1927. If you wait for retirement until age 65, you will receive $1,049 per month. If you took retirement at 62, your Social Security benefit would be $739 per month.

Your Social Security benefits will increase each year as the cost of living rises. The amount of each year's increase will be the same as the increase in the Consumer Price Index (CPI).

## Should You Take Benefits at 62?

As you can see from Table 3-1, the drop in benefits is 20%. This begs the question, "Should I wait 'till 65?" Let's take a look at an example. Assume you just turned 62 in 1991 (born in 1929) and are entitled to maximum benefits which would be $836 per month. If you take

the benefits now, you would receive $10,032 for 3 years, a total of $30,096.

If you waited until 65, you would have received $1,045 per month, an extra $209 per month. How long would you have to live to catch up with the $30,096 you would receive if you take benefits at 62? Using simple math and ignoring the time value of money the answer is just about 12 years. In other words, you would have to live until you were 77 before you would be ahead waiting until 65 to take your Social Security benefits.

Our recommendation is to take it at 62, unless you intend to work. Your spouse's benefit, if taken at age 62, would be reduced slightly more than yours. It would be 75% of the age 65 amount.

---

### Helpful Hint

Assuming your earned income is under $7,440 in 1992: Take your Social Security benefit at 62—Don't wait for the higher amount at age 65.

---

## Working While Collecting Social Security

If you decide to work after retirement, there is a limit to the amount of income that you can receive without causing a reduction in Social Security benefits. In 1992, assuming you are age 65 or over, you could earn up to $10,200 and still collect all of your benefits. If you earned more than that, a dollar would be deducted for every $3 above $10,200.

If you are under age 65, the maximum amount you could earn in 1992 without losing benefits would be $7,440. If earnings exceed that amount $1 in benefits would be deducted for each $2 above the $7,440 figure.

This information applies to earned income, that is, income received from your labor. Income received from investments (dividends, interest, capital gains, rent, and the like) does not affect Social Security benefits.

If you are 70 years or over and want to work, you can earn any income you wish and it will have no impact on your Social Security payments. The full benefit will be paid regardless of what you earn.

## Suppose You Don't Take Benefits Until 70

If you decide to continue working until age 70, what impact will that have on your monthly Social Security check? Again, more complicated computations. However, let's simply examine Table 3-2 and look for our answer. As you can see, Uncle Sam would like us to work after 65.

Again an example: Let's assume that you turn 62 in 1993. The Social Security rules say that you will increase your Social Security check by 5% for each and every year after 65 that you continue to work. So, if you work until age 70, your check would be 25% bigger.

### TABLE 3-2

**DELAYED RETIREMENT CREDIT RATES**
*(For Ages 55 to 65)*

| Attain Age 62 | Yearly Percentage |
|---|---|
| 1991 – 1992 | 4.5% |
| 1993 – 1994 | 5.0% |
| 1995 – 1996 | 5.5% |
| 1997 – 1998 | 6.0% |
| 1999 – 2000 | 6.5% |
| 2001 – 2002 | 7.0% |
| 2003 – 2004 | 7.5% |
| 2005 or after | 8.0% |

## Taxes on Social Security Payments

In 1983, Congress made a major change in the Social Security law. It permitted the taxation of up to one-half of an individual's Social Security benefits. This change went into effect on January 1, 1984. The formula used to determine your tax is as follows:

1. Take your total income (pension, interest, dividends, rental, and so on).

2. Add in your tax-exempt interest from say, municipal bonds, and one-half of your total Social Security benefit. If this number exceeds $25,000 for single or $32,000 for a married couple, then one-half of the amount that exceeds $25,000 (single) or $32,000 (married) will be subject to tax. The maximum amount of your Social Security that can be taxed is one-half of what you are receiving, regardless of how high your income goes.

Here's an example of how this works for a married couple:

| | |
|---|---:|
| Gross Income | $28,000 |
| 50% of Social Security income | 6,000 |
| Total income | 34,000 |
| Deduct the maximum amount | 32,000 |
| Excess income | 2,000 |
| 50% of excess income | $ 1,000 |

The amount of your Social Security income subject to tax would be $1,000. Therefore, in our example, you must add that $1,000 to your gross income of $28,000. The new total of $29,000 is your adjusted gross income.

A second example shows the computation for a single person with an adjusted gross income of $35,000 and $10,000 in Social Security retirement benefits.

| | |
|---|---:|
| Gross income | $35,000 |
| 50% of the Social Security income | 5,000 |
| Total | 40,000 |

| | |
|---|---|
| Maximum allowance (single) | 25,000 |
| Excess income | 15,000 |
| 50% of excess income | $ 7,500 |
| | |
| Maximum taxable amount of | |
| Social Security (50%) | $ 5,000 |
| Adjusted gross income | 35,000 |
| New adjusted gross income | 40,000 |

The $40,000 is arrived at by dividing the gross income of $35,000 and one half of Social Security ($10,000 divided by 2 = $5,000) for a total of $40,000. The portion of Social Security subject to taxes in this example is $5,000. Remember, the most that can be taxed is 50% of the amount of Social Security received.

## What Will Your Spouse Receive?

We have already covered the living benefits for your spouse. But what if you die first? What will your spouse be entitled to? Answer—a Widow's or Widower's benefit.

Assuming the surviving spouse is age 65 or over, the benefit would be equal to *your* benefit. Let's assume that you are a 69-year-old male married to a 67-year-old woman, that your Social Security check is $886 per month and your wife's is $623 per month (she worked for 21 years, was fully covered but did not have maximum coverage). At your death, she could choose to receive your widow's benefit. Her income would be $886 per month. She would stop receiving her previous $623 benefit.

If she had not worked prior to retirement and was receiving half of your benefit, or $443 per month, she would still jump up to $886 per month because she is your widow and is entitled to the widow's benefit. A reduced benefit is available for younger widows beginning at age 60.

In addition a death benefit of $255 is payable to a spouse or child. That's a one-time payment. Additional payments may be available for disabled spouses, spouses caring for children under 16 years old, and for dependent children and parents.

## How to File

Social Security payments are not automatic, you must file an application. This should be done 3 months before you expect to retire. You can apply by telephone or by going to a Social Security office. You will need your birth certificate and if applying for spousal benefits, proof of marriage, and your spouse's birth certificate.

## Medicare

A federal health insurance program for persons 65 or older will provide:

1. **Part A**—hospital insurance:
   - inpatient hospital care;
   - skilled nursing facility; and
   - home health care.

   It is financed by Social Security taxes.

2. **Part B**—medical insurance
   A voluntary supplemental medical-insurance plan that helps pay for:
   - physician's services;
   - outpatient hospital care;
   - physical therapy;
   - ambulance trips (under certain conditions);
   - medical equipment and prosthesis; and
   - a number of other services.

It is financed partly by a premium paid by those who enroll, and partly by general revenue of the federal government.

## Part A (Hospital Insurance)

In 1992, for hospital insurance (Part A) coverage, you pay a deductible of $652 for the first 60 days of continuous hospitalization. You would then pay $163 per day in co-insurance for days 61 to 90. After that, unless you have lifetime reserve days (call Social Security regarding this) you pay the entire bill. For skilled nursing home care, you must be hospitalized for at least three days prior to admission in order for Medicare to contribute part of the cost. Medicare then pays for *all* covered services for the first 20 days. For days 21 to 100, you will be required to pay $81.50 per day in co-insurance. After that you must pay the entire daily cost.

Home health care is covered for post-hospital home health care services such as part-time nursing care, physical therapy, and speech therapy. There is no deductible and no limit on the number of visits allowed up to a maximum of 5 days per week. You must be homebound and services must be ordered by a doctor.

Hospice care is covered up to 210 days and can be extended longer.

## Part B (Voluntary Supplemental Medical Insurance Plan)

In 1992, the voluntary supplemental medical insurance plan (Part B) is voluntary and available to anyone 65 years of age or older who is willing to pay the monthly premium of $31.80. After you meet an annual $100 deductible, Medicare will pay 80% of the Medicare-approved charge for doctor and other services. You would be responsible for the remaining 20% plus the balance of what Medicare considers unreasonable. On prescription drugs, Medicare helps pay only for drugs that cannot be self-administered.

For a detailed explanation of Medicare coverage, write for the booklet *All About Medicare* put out by the National Underwriter at 505 Gest St., Cincinnati, OH 45203 or call 800-543-0874. (The cost is $7.95.) You

can also contact the Social Security Administration directly for free information and booklets.

## Nursing Home Care and Medicaid

As some writers put it, we are in the sunset of our lives. Our eventual need for long-term care and possibly a nursing home should be part of our planning. As we all know, this can be quite expensive. What will become of our assets?

First of all, let's examine the Medicaid law and see what we are allowed to keep. The guidelines for Medicaid eligibility are set by the federal government, however each state sets the qualifying amounts of assets and income for that states' residents within the federal guidelines. Effective January 1, 1991 the federal government set the amount of assets that the healthy spouse can keep between $13,296 and $66,480. The income allowance for the healthy spouse was set at $1662 per month. These amounts are indexed for cost-of-living changes and have therefore risen each year since 1989. The amount of assets that the spouse filing for Medicaid can own is extremely low. For example in New York state in 1991 the filing spouse can have only about $4,500 in assets and $500 in monthly income. While these numbers for both spouses are quite low it does necessarily mean that all additional assets owned must be spent on medical treatment before the ill spouse qualifies for Medicaid. There are strategies available with the potential for saving substantial additional assets. We recommend that you seek the services of an attorney who is well versed in the relatively new practice called *elder law*.

## Long-Term Care Insurance

Nursing homes are expensive. A long stay in one can devastate the assets you've worked a lifetime to accumulate. One answer to the problem is insurance.

There are a number of insurance companies that offer this type of protection. At the end of this section we will list a few. However, in an effort to help you find a dependable one we will list the benefits offered by one such worthwhile policy. You can use this to get comparison information from other companies.

First of all, look at an A or A+ rated company such as A.M. Best, to do the rating. As an example, AMEX Life Assurance Company, owned by American Express is rated A+ (Superior). It pioneered the development of long-term care insurance back in 1974.

Coverage is available under these policies if you are, say, from age 50 through 84 and meet such policies' underwriting standards, which are not too hard to meet.

Such policies pay a daily cash benefit when you are in an approved nursing home. This benefit is paid regardless of the type of care you need:

- Skilled;

- Intermediate; and

- Custodial.

They do not pay if you are in a rest home, home for the aged, a sheltered living accommodation, or residence homes. They do not require a prior hospital stay to receive benefit. In other words, you can go directly from your home into a nursing home. They do, of course, require a doctor's certificate that your admission is necessary. Alzheimers disease is also covered and there are no exclusions or limitations for pre-existing conditions.

You can select the benefit you want from $30 to $150 per day, and include a 5% inflation factor.

You also must decide how long you want to be paid:

- 2 years;

- 3 years;

- 4 years; or

- As long as you live.

There is also a deductible (initial days for which you will pay before insurance kicks in). This can be for 20 days or 100 days. Also you are guaranteed the right to renew your coverage for life and premiums will not increase because of your age or health.

They do include a *waiver-of-premium clause*. This means that after you have received benefits for 90 days, your premium is waived and not due again for as long as that nursing home stay lasts.

Benefits are paid regardless of any other insurance you may have, including Medicare.

Here are examples of the cost assuming you are:

- Age 62

- Lifetime coverage

- 20-day deductible

- Inflation protection included

- $100 per day

- Cost $1,417 per year.

Assume you are 72 with the same coverage—the premium would be $2,893 per year.

For further information you can write to:

AMEX Life Assurance Co.
Long Term Care
1650 Los Gamos Drive
San Rafael, CA 94903-1899
(415) 492-7300

Continental Casualty Company
CNA Plaza
Chicago, Illinois 60685
(312) 822-5000

John Hancock Mutual Life
John Hancock Plaza
PO Box 111
Boston, Massachusetts 02117
1 (800) 922-5050

These are just three examples of many excellent long-term care providers. There are many more.

# 4

# Your
# Financial Assets

## Where Are They Invested Now?

You want to improve your financial plan. Your first step should be to look at where you are right now. For your benefit, we have printed a blank Balance Sheet and Income Statement (see Table 4-1).

A few pointers will help you complete your personal balance sheet and income statement.

## Savings Accounts

List all your savings accounts here including money market accounts. The interest rate is 5.25% or 5.5% depending upon the type of bank you use. Money market accounts usually pay higher rates. In November of 1991, the average money market rate was about 5.0%. Broker/dealers (like Merrill Lynch or Prudential) pay a little higher.

**TABLE 4-1**

## BALANCE SHEET AND INCOME STATEMENT

| Assets | Description | Current Value | Interest or Yield | Annual Income |
|---|---|---|---|---|
| **Savings Account** | ——— ——— ——— | ——— ——— | ——— ——— | ——— ——— |
| **Checking Account** | ——— ——— | ——— | ——— | ——— |
| **Certificates of Deposit** Date Due ——— ——— | ——— ——— | ——— ——— | ——— ——— | ——— ——— |
| **Common Stock** Number of Shares ——— ——— ——— | ——— ——— | ——— ——— | ——— ——— | ——— ——— |

**Bonds**
Due Date

**Mutual Funds**
Shares

**Real Estate**

**Corp. Savings**
(401(k) and
Profit Sharing)

**Deferred
Annuities**

**TABLE 4-1** (*Continued on next page*)

**TABLE 4-1** (*Continued*)

| Assets | Description | Current Value | Interest or Yield | Annual Income |
|---|---|---|---|---|
| **Social Security** | Yours at Age ___ | | | |____| |
| | Spouse's at Age ___ | | | |____| |
| **Pension** (Annual Income or Lump Sum) | _____ _____ | |____| |____| | |____| |____| | |____| |____| |
| **Miscellaneous** | _____ _____ | |____| |____| | |____| |____| | |____| |____| |
| **Total Assets and Income** | | | □ | | □ |

**Name**

**Balance Due**

**Liabilities**

Mortgages _____

Auto Loans _____

Personal Loans _____

Other Debts _____

Total Liabilities _____

Total Assets _____
Total Liabilities (Minus) ( _____ )

**Net Worth** _____

You should also list your credit union funds here. The rate will depend on how generous your credit union is. Multiply the interest rate times the current value to get your annual income.

## Checking Accounts

List all your checking accounts here and their approximate balance. More often than not the interest rate is zero. Some banks do pay interest depending on the balance you keep.

## Certificates of Deposit (CDs)

Next all certificates of deposit (CDs) should be posted, indicating first the date due, then the name of the bank or brokerage house, and the interest rate you are earning. Your IRA/CDs should be posted here.

## Common Stocks

In this section, you should list the number of shares of each stock, its correct name and current value (price times number of shares), the dividend yield and the total amount of dividends that you receive from that particular company's stock each year. A convenient way to do this is to use your latest broker/dealer monthly statement.

## Bonds

List the date your bond is due, first, then list an accurate description of the bond and its current value. This amount is generally listed on your brokerage house's monthly statement. Then post the interest rate.

All your municipal bonds, corporate, and U.S. Treasury, and government agency bonds such as Ginnie Maes, Fannie Maes, Freddie Macs, and the like should be posted here. Also include U.S. savings bonds and unit investment trusts that invest in bonds. (The common types are: municipal investment trusts, which buy municipal bonds, corporate income funds, which buy corporate bonds, government securities income funds which buy both U.S. government bonds and government agency bonds.)

## Mutual Funds

You should list here the number of shares of each fund you own. The full name of the fund and its current value go next, followed by the yield. An immediate problem arises with any growth fund—what yield should you use last year's or the 5- or 10-year average? We recommend that you call your fund's 800 telephone number and find out what its average total return was for the past 10 years (or 5 years, if you prefer). Total return is the annual income paid by the fund, added to the change in its share price during the course of the year. For example, if a fund paid out 7% in income and the share price rose by 4%, the total return for that year would be 11%. Whatever that number is, discount it by two or three percentage points. Then post the discounted number. Remember, you are trying to project future income. Yield times current value will give you a rough idea of how much income you could draw without using principal.

## Real Estate

Your residence should be listed along with a rough estimate of its value. Since you live there, the interest or yield is zero. If it's a multiple residence, check with

your accountant and establish a net, after expense, annual income. If you own a second home, that should
be listed. Investment real estate goes next along with
its yield. Finally, all real estate limited partnerships should
be listed along with their estimated yield.

## Corporate Savings Plans

Here is where you post your 401(k) plans and profit-
sharing plans. If you work for a school district or nonprofit organization you may be investing in a tax deferred annuity, that gets posted here along with your
estimate of its yield.

## Deferred Annuities and Life Insurance

Any and all annuities should be reported here. Single premium deferred annuities are purchased from life
insurance companies and generally have a fixed or
guaranteed rate of interest.

Tax deferred annuities are often provided for employees of school districts, hospitals, municipalities and
nonprofit organizations.

All of your life insurance policies should be listed
here. Do not post the death benefit. Look up the cash
value. If you don't know how, call your life insurance
agent. At the same time find out how much dividends
you have on deposit with the company. Don't forget to
subtract any loans you may have against them. Under
the current value column, you should indicate both the
guaranteed cash value and the dividends. Your agent
will be able to give you the dividend rate.

## Social Security

Your *annual* Social Security income is posted next. Do not list the monthly rate. Use the amount you expect to receive at the age you will be at retirement.

## Pension

Pension plans are generally paid out as an annuity. Your employer is required to give you an annual statement showing the amount of pension you are currently entitled to. Quite often they will extrapolate the number to show what you could expect to receive at age 65. This number can be put in the income column. Remember to use the *annual* income. If your corporation offers you the opportunity to take a lump sum, you should post that amount next to the words lump sum under the heading, "current value," and use a conservative interest rate like 7.5% in the yield column to approximate the amount of annual income that the lump sum could reasonably produce.

Profit-sharing plans always offer you a lump-sum option or an annuity. Post the lump sum in the current value column and list the actual yield currently being earned or use a conservative yield that can be earned in today's market (like 7.5%).

Keogh plan assets (for self-employed persons) should actually be posted in the correct investment sections with the word Keogh after the investment. For example, suppose you have accumulated $100,000 in your Keogh plan and the $100,000 is invested as follows:

| | |
|---|---|
| Money Market | $27,000 |
| CD | 46,000 |
| IBM Stock | 27,000 |

Post each item in its respective section. Under money market, post—State Bank (Keogh)—27,000 @ 5.0%. Under

CD, post—7/14/92—State Bank (Keogh)—46,000 @ 5.65%. Under stock, post—240 shares of IBM (Keogh) $23,490 (97.875 per share) @ 4.9%.

## Miscellaneous

This is the place to list any businesses you may own. A very difficult question to resolve is the business' value and yield.

Boats, automobiles, art, and jewelry can be posted here as well.

## Liabilities

This section does not need explanation except for the use of parentheses. In the accounting field, all liabilities are posted in parentheses to emphasize that they are subtracted from the assets.

## Taxes

On the figures in the income column, you must take into consideration the taxable nature of the income. You may want to place an (X) next to all municipal bonds, municipal investment trusts, and municipal mutual funds.

A (Q) can be placed next to the following items indicating that the income is tax-deferred and only taxed when the funds are taken out of the account:

- IRA;
- 401(k);
- Profit sharing;
- Keogh;

- Tax deferred annuities;
  Single premium deferred annuities and life insurance cash value and dividends

This is the method that we use in the case studies in Chapters 11, 12, 13, and 14.

## Investment Concerns

Next you should determine your investment concerns. How important, for example, is safety in your investment program? But safety of what, principal or buying power? What amount of risk, if any, should you take? What percentage of your income should be liquid? These questions are vital to proper planning.

Table 4-2 includes a list of investment concerns. You should decide which of these items is most important to you and list that as number 1. The second most important item receives number 2, and so forth.

To help you decide the safety of principal or buying power question, we refer you to the section on inflation in Chapter 1. Our feeling is that stability of buying power should be carefully considered given the inflation rate during the 1970s and the 1980s—and the erosion of buying power that this inflation has caused retirees.

### TABLE 4-2

### INVESTMENT CONCERNS

*(Rate yourself: 1 is most important; 6 is least important)*

| | |
|---|---|
| _____ | Safety of principal |
| _____ | Stability of buying power |
| _____ | Income |
| _____ | Taxes |
| _____ | Growth |
| _____ | Liquidity |

## TABLE 4-3

### LIQUIDITY/SAFETY VS. RISK

How many months of income should you have available in liquid investments?

> 3      6      9      12      (circle one)

What percentage of your net worth should be in:

Growth investments ＿＿ %
Safe investments      ＿＿ %
Total                        100%

Next, you should estimate how many months of income you should keep liquid for emergencies and then decide the percentage of your assets that should be in growth investments to counter inflation.

As to the number of months of spendable income you should have available for emergencies, (funds held in liquid assets such as money market, savings, or checking accounts) financial planners, in general, recommend six months for the average person, during their *working* years.

When you retire, you do not need quite as much money in liquid assets as you did before retirement. Prior to retirement, you had to safeguard against losing your job or being out of work because of illness. Both of these concerns cease to be a problem once retirement is reached. However, the cost of health-related expenses increases. This question was dealt with in Chapter 3. When you retire, the concern about unemployment is over. As a result we recommend that an amount equal to three months' living expenses should be kept in quickly available funds.

## Comfort Zone

Your "comfort zone" (ability to take risks) is of utmost importance. Bob, a client of ours, for example, kept $100,000 in a day of deposit to day of withdrawal

regular savings account. This represented approximately 40% of his net worth. The average person might think this too conservative and we would agree.

For this particular client, however, it was correct because he felt "safer" with the funds in a savings bank, as opposed to any other type of investment. His "comfort zone" required that he keep a sizable portion of his assets in very short-term investments. In this case, that meant a savings account in his local bank.

However, let's assume, that all Bob really needed available for possible emergencies was $10,000. The remaining $90,000 would have earned, in today's market in a fairly safe municipal bond fund investment, 6.84% for a total annual return of $6,156 instead of $4,950 at 5.5%. That is an increase of $1,206 a year, a 24% higher yield. And that does not take into consideration the tax free savings of the municipal bond fund. Assuming no "comfort zone" problem, that's a sizable increase. In our opinion the $90,000 was "lazy" money. It was just not working hard enough.

## Safety vs. Growth

The next issue involves determining the percentage of one's remaining assets that should be kept in "safe" investments versus the amount that should be put into growth investments to fight inflation. Most people have 100% of their assets in so-called "safe" investments while others have 50% in safe investments and 50% in growth investments. It depends entirely upon the circumstances and your feelings about the risk associated with growth investments. Next, let's estimate how to decide how much should be allocated to "safe" and how much to "growth" investments. As a general guide, if you have a net worth of $300,000, and you're 65 years old, we would recommend that approximately 25% to 35% of your assets be kept in growth investments, (common stock and/or real estate). Therefore, the balance of 65%

to 75% would be in safe investments, such as Treasuries or Ginnie Maes. The reason for the high percentage of safe investments is very simple. After retirement, there is no longer time to correct errors in one's investment program. The money-making machine, namely you, has stopped producing income. Safety of principal, therefore, is extremely important. However, as we've already discussed, inflation is one of the biggest problems you will face in the future. Therefore, there must be some prudent "growth" investments in your portfolio to insure an adequate rate of return on your total estate.

---

### Helpful Hint

What percentage of your assets should be in growth investments?

| Net Worth | Safe | vs. | Growth |
|---|---|---|---|
| $ 300,000 | 65 to 75% | | 25 to 35% |
| 600,000 | 60 to 70% | | 30 to 40% |
| 1,000,000 | 50 to 60% | | 40 to 50% |

---

## The Pyramid Approach

A helpful approach in trying to determine one's best investment strategy is the use of the investment pyramid (see Exhibit 4-1). This will help to show how your assets are allocated among the different levels of risk.

The first level, or foundation, of the pyramid is for *safe* investments, including (as noted) savings accounts, money market funds, CDs, Treasury bills, bonds, and notes, U.S. savings bonds, Government National Mortgage Association securities, and other government agency bonds, equity in one's home, cash value in life insurance, and annuities.

## EXHIBIT 4-1   INVESTMENT PYRAMID

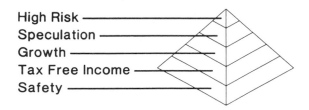

High Risk
Speculation
Growth
Tax Free Income
Safety

The second level is for *tax-sheltered investments*. This includes: single premium deferred annuities, municipal bonds, and investment real estate.

The third level is *growth* investments. Here we include corporate bonds, high-quality common stock, investment real estate, precious metals, and collectibles.

The fourth level, *speculation*, includes such investments as *new* stock issues (corporations going public for the first time), turn around cases (corporations that were doing badly and appear to be moving up in value), and other higher risk situations.

The fifth level, *high risk*, involves concepts such as raw or unimproved land, futures, and options. We will not deal with either the fourth or fifth level in this book. Except for very high net worth people, investments in the bottom three levels should be the only ones considered by retired people.

Annuities and investment real estate are both mentioned in two levels on the investment pyramid because they fit into both categories. For example, annuities can be both safe and tax-sheltered. Investment real estate offers both tax shelter and growth potential.

# Part Two

## Individual Investments

# 5

# The Homestead—
# What to Do?

## Should You Sell or Borrow?

Like most retirees, you want your future to be comfortable and fun filled. To accomplish this, you need to
have money available for the things you enjoy. You
probably also want to minimize the work involved in
home ownership and maintenance. As retirement approaches, your decisions about housing basically come
down to staying where you are or selling your home
and moving. Each choice offers advantages and disadvantages.

Whatever your eventual decision, it should be made
carefully. Buying a home was probably your greatest
single investment. Today your home is likely to be your
largest single asset. Housing expenses usually become
a major concern for retirees living on a fixed income,
especially during inflationary times when the cost of
housing can increase at a higher rate than you expected
when you were planning for your retirement.

As you evaluate all of the factors that should go into your decision, keep this in mind: because the life changes that come with retirement are stressful in themselves, experts recommend that you make *no* changes in your housing situation until at least one year after you retire. That way you will have time to adjust to your new life before making the very important decision about where to live.

After that first year, when you are ready to make your decision, proceed with caution. The first thing you want to do is dispel any romantic myths you may have developed about the retirement home of your dreams.

Many retirees, for example, have fantasized for years about relocating to their favorite vacation spot, perhaps by winterizing a summer home. But a vacation spot is not the same in the off-season as it is during vacation time. The weather can be bad, and social and cultural events may slow to a crawl. Try it out first. Move to your vacation spot in the off-season, renting if necessary, to determine whether it is really a place you want to live year-round.

Take the same cautious approach even if you want to remain in your area but move to a smaller place. If possible, try renting before you invest in that condominium, cooperative, or mobile home. Or perhaps house-sit to get the feel of apartment living and a sense of the neighborhood. Although you think you want to get away from the maintenance demands of a large home, you may end up feeling cramped and confined in a smaller place.

---

### Helpful Hint

- Do not make changes in your housing situation until about one year after you retire
- Seriously consider renting for about one year before moving permanently to a new area

## Non-Financial Considerations

Although this chapter focuses primarily on the financial aspects of retirement housing, non-financial considerations also enter into your decision. These will be discussed here briefly. To choose the right type and location of housing for you, think about the following:

### Location

If you have developed roots in a community over many years, you may be taking for granted some important personal and neighborhood associations. These may become more valuable to you as you get older. In fact, about 90% of retirees choose to remain in the area where they have been living.

Among the most important of these associations is proximity to children, grandchildren, other relatives, friends, and neighbors. Also important is the availability of recreational facilities, religious institutions, civic groups, and professional services such as physicians, attorneys, stockbrokers, and the like. Many or all of these connections could be severed or drastically limited if you moved far away from your present location.

### Climate

Although many residents of northern states dream about escaping from cold winters, heavy snows, and dreary springtimes, southern and southwestern locations typically have hot summers and high humidity. What overall climate would best suit your health and lifestyle?

### Type of Dwelling

Among your options are a smaller home, or possibly a condominium, cooperative, retirement community, mobile home, moving in with other people, or having

someone move in with you. Try to imagine yourself
in the option that most appeals to you. Also talk with
friends and acquaintances who have chosen that
option.

## Size

Now that your children are on their own, is your
house or apartment too big? On the other hand, do you
still need room for entertaining overnight visitors? When
picturing your ideal residence, think about the number
of bedrooms and bathrooms, along with dining room
and outdoor space. How much privacy do you prefer,
both within your own living unit and from neighbors?

## Layout and Amenities

If you or your spouse have back or leg problems,
would a one-floor housing unit make life easier? Is a
large kitchen a must because cooking is your favorite
hobby? Are you sick of mowing the lawn and long for
a condominium or cooperative to handle it for you?
Would remodeling rather than moving be the answer?
Now is the time to list your "druthers" and figure out
a way to have, if not all of them, at least most of them.

## Staying in Your Home

According to census statistics, about three out of
four householders 65 years of age or older own their
homes, and about 85 percent of these have paid off
their mortgages. In most parts of the country, living in
a mortgage-free home is cheaper than paying rent. But
staying put has to be weighed against the loss of interest
or dividends you would earn if you sold your home and

invested the proceeds. A good idea is to calculate the difference based on rental costs in the area where you want to live.

Another consideration is the cash bind you may find yourself in each month. If you bought your home years ago, you may have a very low-interest mortgage or none at all, and the value of your home has gone up substantially. But inflation has reduced the buying power of your pension, and even if you should want to sell your home, you may not find an affordable housing alternative.

To alleviate your cash-bind dilemma you can use the equity you have in your home as collateral to borrow money. But remember to treat that equity as part of your overall retirement savings. Except in an emergency, borrowing against your equity is actually spending your savings unless you invest the borrowed money and live off the interest. There are four common ways of raising income from your home without having to sell it.

## Home Equity Loans

This is really just a second mortgage at an adjustable rate. It has also been compared to a credit card. The lender gives you an open line of credit, usually up to about 75% of the total value of your house, and charges interest based on prime rate plus 1% or 2%. This rate changes frequently. It goes up or down depending upon increases or decreases in the prime rate or the Treasury Index.

## Refinancing Your Current Mortgage

With this method, you pay off your existing mortgage and take out a new, larger mortgage based on the current higher value of your home. This new mortgage

may have a higher interest rate, but you can use the additional money for your cash needs.

For example, your home is appraised at $125,000, the current mortgage is $5,000 and you presently have $120,000 equity in the home. This is $120,000 that is *not* working for you. The bank will loan you up to 80 percent of the home's appraised value, that is, $100,000 (assuming you can, in the viewpoint of the bank, make the higher monthly payment). You then use this money to pay off your first mortgage of $5,000, and the remaining $95,000 is yours to invest at a rate presumably higher than the interest charged by the bank on the $100,000. Recent tax law changes have put limits on the amount of mortgage interest that you can deduct for both home equity loans and refinancings. You should, therefore, check with your tax advisor before borrowing.

## Reverse Mortgage

A new program of the Federal Housing Administration (FHA) permits anyone over age 62 to pick up a reverse mortgage at any of the 10,000 banks across the country that handle FHA mortgages. Seventy percent of Americans who are over 62 own their own homes. This can be a sizable help if they need money. Eighty-five percent of these owners have no mortgages and the vast majority of the owners prefer to live in them as opposed to selling and moving elsewhere.

With a reverse mortgage you simply approach the proper bank and ask for what amounts to an annuity. Your house is put up as collateral and you start receiving monthly checks for the rest of your life or until you decide to sell.

The minimum amount is $67,500 and the maximum is $124,875. When you sell or die the outstanding loan is deducted from the value or sale price. If you are house rich but cash poor, this may be worth looking into.

## Charitable Remainder Trust

With this plan you donate your property to a charitable institution in exchange for a lifetime annuity and the right to remain in your home for the rest of your life.

## Conclusions

Each of these options has advantages and disadvantages, depending upon your situation. The advantages of the home equity loan are:

(a) that it is fairly easy to receive the credit line;

(b) most banks do not charge points (a point is one percent of the full amount of the mortgage);

(c) the application fee is nominal; and

(d) you are only charged for the money you use.

The disadvantage is that the interest rate can go up or down monthly, which makes financial planning and budgeting difficult.

Home equity loans are also popular with younger people who use the money for vacations or investments. But for most retirees this constitutes living beyond their means and is not the best choice.

The advantages of refinancing your current mortgage are that:

(a) you get cash to invest for income;

(b) you are removing some of the equity in your home to use for investment purposes; and

(c) the interest on the mortgage loan may be tax deductible.

The disadvantages are that you will have a bigger monthly payment and you may not be able to invest at a rate higher than you will be paying to the bank.

The advantage of a reverse mortgage is that it allows you to tap into the appreciation on your home by providing monthly income. The disadvantages are that the bank may not provide the best annuity available for you, and that this *is* a loan, so you again have to figure in monthly mortgage payments.

The advantage of a charitable remainder trust is that you get a present current charitable tax deduction, based on a percentage of the appraised value of your home. The disadvantages are that the charity may not provide the best annuity available for you, and there is no cost-of-living increase structured into the annuity payments.

A final word about the financial aspects of staying in your home: Many retiring homeowners are tempted to remodel to make their homes comfortable for their retirement years. While certain changes make a great deal of sense—for example, adding a bathroom on the main floor to cut down on having to use the stairs— be careful about undertaking any major expenditures. When it eventually becomes time to sell the home, your remodeling choices may not appeal to prospective buyers and this will not have increased the value of your home.

---

### Helpful Hint

- If you intend to live in your present home—don't borrow at all
- If however you need additional income we recommend you consider (in this order)

    A reverse mortgage, or
    A charitable remainder trust.

## Selling Your Home

Selling your home can free up money to buy a retirement home that may better suit your needs and lifestyle. It may also give you the cash you need for monthly expenses and the mortgage interest on the new home is fully deductible.

If you are 55 years or older and your home has been your principal residence for at least three of the last five years, you can sell your house, profit up to $125,000 from the sale and not pay any federal taxes on the gain.

The market, however, is not always advantageous for sellers. As this is being written, the entire country is experiencing substantial real estate slowdowns.

Ideally, you want to sell your home the day before the slowdown and buy in an area the day before a boom is just starting. Unfortunately, most of us have never been terribly accurate at economic forecasting. And neither, it should be pointed out, have most professional forecasters.

Once you have decided to sell your home, it is essential to price it so that it will sell. To you it's a home and that concept is priceless. But your prospective buyers see your concept as a monthly payment. So be realistic. Also, be mindful that most buyers expect to bargain over the price, so avoid setting it at your lowest acceptable amount.

## Your New Home

Now that the house is sold, do you buy a new one or rent? The first thing to do is to check in the area you have chosen for rentals. Could you rent the house or condo for less than it would cost to buy?

Your computation of the cost to buy should include the following items:

| | |
|---|---|
| Mortgage payments | $ _____ |
| Taxes (real estate) | _____ |
| Insurance | _____ |
| Maintenance (periodic painting and the like) | _____ |
| Replacement costs (roof, furnace, siding, and the like) | _____ |
| Interest lost on your down payment | _____ |
| Total | $ |

One other factor that must be considered is the *growth* of your investment. Will your new home appreciate in value? As you know the real estate market in general is down. But will it stay down in your area or will it get back on a growth track? One area that has been sluggish for many years is Florida. Here the answer to the question of growth may well be "none."

Let's assume however that you are looking in an area that has had a good growth record in the past (except for the last year or two). We think its fair to assume a 5% to 10% growth factor. Thus, if your comparison shows rental at $1,000 per month and buying at the same monthly amount, the potential of 5% to 10% growth in value could very well tip the scale in the direction of buying.

## Mortgage Versus Cash

Another major factor for your consideration is whether to take out a mortgage or pay cash (assuming you have enough money to do so). We are of the opinion that taking out a mortgage is, in general, a good idea. The interest is fully tax deductible.

Let's assume that you can get a 10% mortgage and that you are in the 28% tax bracket. The real cost of the mortgage is only 7.2%. If you can invest your money and earn more than 7.2% after tax you should opt for a mortgage instead of paying all cash.

What kind of mortgage should you use is the next question. Our answer is a *fixed-rate mortgage*. The rate is set and, for a change, inflation will work for you not against you. Assume your mortgage payment is $672.27 per month and inflation averages 5% per year. In 14 years you will still be paying the same $672.27 but the buying power of that sum will be cut in half namely $336.14. We do not recommend you consider any of the new type mortgages such as:

- Variable rate;

- Graduated pay-out; or

- Renegotiable rate.

However, a *shared appreciation mortgage*, assuming you can get one, is worthy of consideration. Here the bank trades off a low interest rate for a share of the future appreciation of your property. You buy your house at an interest rate about one-third below the prevailing cost of money. However, when you sell your house you must pay about one-third of the gross profit to the lender (assuming that was the agreement you negotiated with the bank).

# 6

# Guaranteed Investments

## Savings Accounts

Savings accounts are held by your bank at an interest rate of approximately 5.5%. This is usually a day-of-deposit to day-of-withdrawal account. You could compare rates to determine which bank offers the best return. However, convenience is probably the more important factor here. Proximity to your home, parking facilities, and the friendliness of personnel are important considerations. The amount that should be kept in the savings account should be relatively small. Enough, for example, to cash checks conveniently.

## Money Market Funds

The greater portion of your liquid or immediately available assets should be kept in money market funds. Savings accounts and most money market accounts are

insured by the Federal Deposit Insurance Corp. (FDIC) and Savings Association Insurance Fund (SAIF). The federal government guarantees that, should the bank fail, your funds will be fully returned by the federal government up to a maximum of $100,000 per account.

An excellent place to keep liquid assets is in money market funds, which usually pay a higher rate than savings accounts. A money market fund is a special form of mutual fund that invests in short-term securities, such as CDs, Treasury bills, government debt securities, and occasionally commercial paper (IOUs of large corporations). The average interest rate or yield on these in November 1991 was about 5.0%.

There are many institutions offering money market funds. Banks and savings and loan associations will gladly accept your funds, which are fully insured up to $100,000. Funds invested in a money market are completely liquid, and most money market funds offer check-writing privileges. Your funds can be cashed by wire, telephone, or mail.

An important question for some investors is government-backed guarantees. If that's the case with you, these funds should be kept in a savings bank or a federal savings and loan association. If, however, you are looking for the highest possible yield, other institutions should be considered. Brokerage houses, mutual funds and some insurance companies can be contacted. They usually do not have the backing of FDIC and SAIF. However the interest rate is generally higher.

## Cash Management Accounts

A number of brokerage houses offer cash management accounts. These allow you to combine a money market account, a Visa cash withdrawal card, and the ability to buy, sell, and hold stocks, bonds, mutual funds, CDs, and many other kinds of investments.

This service permits you to put a lot of your assets (cash, stocks, bonds, mutual funds, and so on) into one

account and receive interest from the day of deposit to the day of withdrawal at money market rates, and to be able to go into most commercial banks in the country and withdraw cash based upon the balance in your account.

## Certificates of Deposit (CDs)

Certificates of deposit, or as they are commonly called, CDs, are issued by banks and guaranteed by the federal government up to a maximum of $100,000. Their term is from 3 months to 10 years. When an investor places funds in such an instrument, the funds must be kept there for the designated term or you pay a penalty to get out early. In general, it is wise to weigh thoroughly the term of one's investment. Some funds could be invested for a short period of time, for example 3 months. Other funds could be invested for an intermediate term of 3 to 5 years, and still others could be earning a higher rate for a longer term, from 5 to 15 years.

Some people who make extensive use of CDs follow a staggered maturity plan to help them with their cash flow and to offset interest rate changes. Let's say you want to put $90,000 into CDs. You would invest them as in Table 6-1.

If you insist on maximum safety of principal you can place all your funds in CDs backed by the federal government. This, however, is not the wisest approach. Recall what happened to the buying power of the funds we discussed on page 15 with a 3.1% inflation factor.

In considering how to invest emergency funds, you should decide whether to put your money in money market funds or short-term CDs. This can be done by comparing the rates being offered by banks or brokerage houses on each of these instruments. On December 1, 1991, the average 6-month CD was 5.05 percent whereas the average money market rate was 5.0 percent.

## TABLE 6-1

## STAGGERED MATURITY PLAN

*$90,000 in Certificates of Deposit*

| | |
|---|---|
| $10,000—3 month | @ 5.00% |
| $10,000—6 month | @ 5.05% |
| $10,000—1 year | @ 4.45% |
| $10,000—2 years | @ 5.00% |
| $10,000—3 years | @ 5.70% |
| $10,000—4 years | @ 6.05% |
| $10,000—5 years | @ 6.70% |
| $10,000—7 years | @ 7.15% |
| $10,000–10 years | @ 7.50% |

Rates effective 11/29/91

Most brokerage houses offer CDs that are fully backed by the federal government. They operate in this fashion: The brokerage house goes to the banking industry and asks for bids on very sizable sums of money, for example, $1 billion of 1-year CDs. They are in general able to get higher rates of interest than most local banks. They in turn offer them to their clients without charge. The investor is usually able to receive a higher yield on longer term CDs than he would get from a local bank, primarily because of the volume of business that the brokerage house does with the bank or savings and loan with which the house deals. The only drawback is that the banks the brokerage houses use are usually out of state.

The investor should also do some shopping to determine which bank or brokerage house offers the best overall investment in CDs. A few phone calls will provide the answer. One must, however be aware of the "comfort zone" problem. The location of the bank may be extremely important to some people. For them, it may be better to give up a little yield to have their funds closer to home.

---

### Helpful Hint

In Chapter 1, we discussed the amount of your *monthly* spendable income needs. Normally, only three times that amount is needed for most emergencies. This is the amount we recommend be kept in savings accounts, money market accounts, or 3-month CDs.

---

## Treasury Bills, Notes, and Bonds

The Treasury of the United States issues IOUs to those who are willing to lend money to the federal government. These IOUs are, in fact, Treasury bills, notes, and bonds. Bills have a term of 3 months, 6 months, and 1 year. Notes run 2 to 10 years, and bonds run 10 to 30 years. All of these are fully backed by the U.S. government and are the safest possible investments available. Along with safety there is a tax advantage. States and cities do not tax the income on federal instruments. In general, Treasury bills, notes, and bonds have a slightly lower yield than CDs of comparable terms, but their tax-free advantage at the state

### TABLE 6-2

### TREASURY INTEREST RATES

|                          | 11/14/91 | One Year Previous |
|--------------------------|----------|-------------------|
| 3-Month Treasury Bills   | 4.74     | 7.32              |
| 6-Month Treasury Bills   | 4.86     | 7.41              |
| 10-Year Treasury Notes   | 7.34     | 8.38              |
| 30-Year Treasury Bonds   | 7.81     | 8.53              |

and local levels more than makes up for this. Treasury bills require a $10,000 minimum investment. Treasury notes and bonds have a minimum of $5,000. They can be purchased directly from the Federal Reserve Board's local office or from a bank or brokerage house. However, banks and brokerage houses often charge a nominal fee for providing this service, usually about $50.

## Term of Investment

When you are considering the amount of time you are willing to lock up your money, a very important *market risk* should be considered, namely, the direction interest rates are going. Are they moving up or down? For example, if you purchased a 30-year Treasury bond with an interest rate of 10.5% on 8/27/85, you were faced with two problems. (See Table 6-3)

Interest rates can go up or down. Since your investment has a fixed rate, namely, 10.5%, the paper value of your asset will increase or decrease depending on the direction of rates.

As Table 6-3 shows, if rates went up to 12.5% the value of your bond would decrease to $8,850. Why? Because the person buying the bond that you own can

### TABLE 6-3

### MARKET RISK

- The value of your Treasury bond will vary with the market.

- Example: 30-Year $10,000 Treasury bond bought on 8/27/85 with a yield of 10.5%.

- If interest rates *increase* to 12.5% anytime, the value of your bond would decrease to $8,850 if you were to sell it.

- If interest rates *decrease* to 8.5% and you decide to sell, the value of your bond would increase to $12,290.

go to the open market and get 12.5% on a new bond. The buyer of your bond would insist on getting a discount from you.

Let's make this clearer with a hypothetical example. The potential buyer of your bond could buy a $10,000 bond at the open market with a 12.5% rate and expect to get $1,250 in interest every year. If the buyer paid you $10,000 for your old bond he or she would only receive $1,050. That's $200 per year less. Obviously, the only way he or she would buy your bond would be at a discount. Because of sales and other cost the actual price would be $8,850.

If interest rates went down to 8.5% you could sell your bond for $12,290. That's called selling *at a premium*. However if you don't sell it you continue to get $1,050 per year.

## Ginnie Maes

The U.S. government has a number of other financial instruments available to the investing public. Some are fully insured by the government itself. Others are insured by sub-divisions of the government. This instrument, commonly called a Ginnie Mae, is basically a mortgage insured by the Federal Housing Authority (FHA) and the Veterans Administration (VA).

All Ginnie Maes are backed by the federal government. If an individual borrower fails to make his or her mortgage payments, the federal government steps in and makes that payment. Thus, an investor can feel completely secure in knowing that his or her Ginnie Maes investment is safe.

This very useful and effective investment is a mortgage-backed security issued by the Government National Mortgage Association (GNMA).

Anyone who meets the government's requirements is entitled to borrow money for their mortgage from a bank and qualify for the approval of the FHA or VA.

The bank, in turn, sells such mortgages to the Government National Mortgage Association, which in turn sells them through other financial institutions (for example brokerage houses) to corporations, pension plans, insurance companies, and individuals like you. The major reason for buying a Ginnie Mae is its higher yield.

Ginnie Maes can be purchased in one of three ways:

1. An *individual Ginnie Mae*. This requires a minimum investment of $25,000 and was yielding 8.03% on November 27, 1991. Ginnie Mae yields are fixed at a set percent for the life of the Ginnie Mae (usually about 12 years).

2. A *Ginnie Mae trust*. A pool of Ginnie Maes from various locations throughout the country. The minimum investment is $1,000 and the yield is fixed for the life of the trust (about 12 years). The yield on November 27, 1991 was 8.13%.

3. A *managed Ginnie Mae mutual fund*. This kind of mutual fund is like the Ginnie Mae trust except that the yield is not fixed. For instance, Kemper's U.S. Government Securities was paying 8.54% on November 27, 1991. It will increase if future interest rates go higher and it will decrease if they go lower.

The payout to you in the two fixed investments (1 and 2 in our list) consists of two parts: interest and principal. We recommend that you specify monthly checks for accrued interest only, and reinvest the principal. This can be done easily enough by your broker.

While, as we noted, the term of the investment is generally about 12 years, it is important to understand that under a FHA or VA mortgage, the borrower has the right to pay off the mortgage ahead of time without incurring a penalty. In times of declining interest rates, this is done quite often. Thus, a Ginnie Mae investor

might find that the investment is repaid in 6 or 8 years instead of the normal 12.

The major difference among the three Ginnie Mae instruments is whether the interest rate is fixed or variable. Mutual funds are controlled by expert managers who first decide which Ginnie Maes throughout the country offer the highest possible yield to the investor. Secondly, they determine which have the least likelihood of being repaid ahead of time. The principal payment they receive from the mortgages are automatically reinvested for you. Simply put, they buy and sell Ginnie Maes to keep your interest rate as high as possible.

Another factor that must be considered in choosing which type of Ginnie Mae to buy is the basic value or selling price of your investment at any given date in the future. In the case of the fixed Ginnie Maes, the interest rate is set (fixed) and, therefore, the value of the basic instrument will fluctuate in direct proportion to the changing interest rate market (exactly like Treasury bonds). If interest rates rise, the value of your trust or individual Ginnie Mae will decrease.

The mutual fund will move in the same direction. However, it will not vary quite as much because it is a managed portfolio. The manager will buy, sell, and swap his/her portfolio to keep the net asset value (sales value) of your share as level as possible. If the managers do a good job, the net asset value should not move up or down more than 15% from the amount you originally invested. Assuming they perform well, you should be able to stay in the fund for a considerable length of time, possibly for the rest of your life.

There are other government-backed investments, for example, Fannie Maes (issued by the Federal National Mortgage Association) and Freddie Macs (issued by the Federal Home Loan Mortgage Corp.). They too are worthy of your consideration but will not be treated in any detail in this book. In our opinion, the way to invest in these is through mutual funds specializing in government instruments.

> ### Helpful Hint
>
> Balance your Ginnie Mae portfolio. Act like a bank lending mortgage money. They would prefer that all or most of their mortgages have a variable rate so that they can't get hurt if interest rates skyrocket like they did in the early 1980s.
>
> Therefore, our recommendation for your *Ginnie Mae* portfolio is:
>
> 75%—Mutual funds
> 25%—Ginnie Mae trusts
>         and individual Ginnie Maes

Some brokerage houses and mutual funds have entered the field of federal agency issues, bundling these accounts and selling them as trusts. All brokerage houses and some banks sell individual Ginnie Maes and trusts. Mutual funds invested in Ginnie Maes can be purchased from hundreds of institutions. Here are a few:

- AARP (American Association of Retired Persons)
  1909 K Street NW
  Washington, D.C. 20049

- Dreyfus
  767 Fifth Avenue
  New York, NY 10022

- Kemper Financial Services, Inc.
  120 South LaSalle Street
  Chicago, IL 60603

- Putnam Investors Services
  99 High Street
  Boston, MA 02110

- T. Rowe Price Reserve
  100 East Pratt Street
  Baltimore, MD 21202

Your broker will know of others; discuss not just these but other options as well.

# 7

# Tax-Wise
# Investments

As we begin to consider the area of tax saving investments, remember that we are approaching your possible investments in a descending order of safety. All of the investments covered in the previous chapter have the backing, in one way or another, of the federal government and are extremely safe investments.

A tax-wise investment is one which avoids taxes altogether or defers them to a later date. The first tax-wise investment to consider is the annuity. Instead of the government backing the instrument, a large insurance company performs that function, namely, guaranteeing that principal and interest will be paid when due. Prudential Life Insurance Company, for example, has $153 billion in assets and has been in business for over 115 years. When they, or any equally well established, well-known firm, promise to pay a given amount on a given day, you can rest assured that the money will be there when you expect it.

## Annuities

An annuity is an instrument which guarantees that a fixed amount of money will be paid by an insurance company to an individual for a given period of time, usually the life of the individual. Annuities are offered by insurance companies in two basic forms, immediate and deferred. An example of the immediate annuity would be if a male purchases, for $10,000, an annuity of $82 per month for the rest of his life. The amount to be received would be dependent upon the person's age and sex.

As we said in Chapter 2, we do not favor fixed-rate immediate annuities for two reasons:

1. The principal must be paid up front and is gone forever;

2. The purchasing power of the monthly payment decreases every year because of inflation.

### Variable Annuity

The second type of immediate annuity is the *variable annuity*. Here your money is invested in 4 to 10 different funds and your payment varies with the market. The actual monthly check you receive is generally based on the portfolio results of the fund you choose. As you can see by studying Table 7-1, the monthly payments can vary considerably, however, with just a few exceptions the return, was uniformly higher than a fixed rate annuity for the same person with the same investment—namely, $100,000 on 12/1/82.

If the fixed annuity were chosen the monthly payment would have been $849 and the annual total would have been $10,188.

Over the 8-year period the total amount you would have received had you chosen the guaranteed $849 per month would have been $82,353. Had you decided on

## TABLE 7-1

### VARIABLE VS. FIXED ANNUITY PAYMENTS

*Compass II (Sun Life of Canada/MFS) Capital Appreciation Fund—$100,000—Male—Age 65—Life Income*

| Date Paid | Monthly Variable Payment | Fixed Rate Payment |
|---|---|---|
| Dec 1982 | $     645.92 | $    849 |
| Dec 1983 | 1,032.38 | 849 |
| Dec 1984 | 812.39 | 849 |
| Dec 1985 | 926.33 | 849 |
| Dec 1986 | 1,030.91 | 849 |
| Dec 1987 | 908.48 | 849 |
| Dec 1988 | 1,036.02 | 849 |
| Dec 1989 | 1,426.39 | 849 |
| Dec 1990 | 1,224.72 | 849 |
| Total Payments | $103,432 | $82,353 |

*Source:* Planco,™ Paoli, PA.

the variable rate and chosen the Sun Life of Canada/ MFS Capital Appreciation Fund, for example, your checks would have been different each month but with the exception of the first and third years—the overall increase would have been $21,079. The Capital Appreciation Funds total payments for 8 years was $103,432.

The specific numbers we work with make it easier to understand our point. We are not saying that you should use this company. Do some shopping! Other important factors to keep in mind with the variable annuity:

- The principal is still spent (you no longer own the principal).

- The monthly minimum payment was only *$645.92* (it can never go below this).

- Each month your payment will be different.

- You can choose any one or more of the following funds:
    Money market;
    Government securities;
    World governments;
    High yield;
    Total return;
    Capital appreciation;
    Managed sectors; and
    Fixed account.

---

### Helpful Hint

We don't recommend the immediate annuity. With it, your principal is spent and, therefore, gone forever. However, if you prefer a guaranteed equal monthly payment, our recommendation is to invest in both the fixed and variable annuities as follows:

    Fixed      66%
    Variable    34%

---

## Deferred Annuity

There is still another annuity, and we do recommend it, namely, the *the single premium deferred annuity* (SPDA). This is an investment in which an insurance company guarantees the safety of the principal and will, at a deferred date, for example age 80, give you an immediate annuity. During the deferral period, you can withdraw 10% of the investment each year without penalty. If you leave all of the accrued interest inside the annuity, there is no income tax on it (federal or state). The tax savings can be considerable. Examine Exhibit 7-1 to see what that could mean to you.

## EXHIBIT 7-1  THE POWER OF TAX DEFERRAL

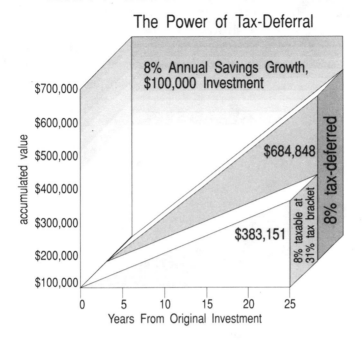

The Power of Tax-Deferral

The exhibit illustrates the difference in return between $100,000 invested in a tax-deferred investment and $100,000 invested in an instrument (e.g., a bond) taxed at a 31% rate (both examples are illustrated at an 8% investment rate). After 25 years, your tax-deferred $100,000 has grown to $684,848, compared with $383,151 in the vehicle taxed annually at 31%.

Earnings from the SPDA are subject to taxation only when withdrawn. And there is an added tax benefit. That portion of each annuity payment you receive after retirement is, by IRS rules, considered part of your initial investment and is also tax free.

With a 10-year guaranteed rate of 6.9% on 11/19/91 your SPDA would double in 10½ years. Thus, if you put $50,000 in a SPDA at 6.9% per year and you made no withdrawals, in 10½ years you would have $100,000 in the plan (and you would have paid no taxes).

Also, there is no sales charge when you purchase an SPDA. However, there is a penalty for early withdrawal. This factor should be examined carefully when considering which company to buy from. Here's an example of one insurance companies' withdrawal penalty:

## TABLE 7-2

## TYPICAL SPDA PENALTY FOR EARLY WITHDRAWAL

| First Year | 7% | Fifth Year | 3% |
|---|---|---|---|
| Second Year | 6 | Sixth Year | 2 |
| Third Year | 5 | Seventh Year | 1 |
| Fourth Year | 4 | Eight & Later | 0 |

Seven percent of the first year, declining by 1% each contract year to zero at the end of the seventh year.

You can, however, withdraw 10% per year without penalty. If you had invested $100,000 3 years ago at a fixed rate of 8%, the SPDA would have grown to about $125,000 today. If you wanted to withdraw the full $125,000 the penalty would be 4% of $112,500 or $4,500 (see Table 7-2). The $112,500 is the net amount subject to the penalty, arrived at by subtracting the 10% or $12,500 from the $125,000 available.

## Single Premium Variable Annuity

There is a new type of SPDA. It offers the basic fixed rate as well as a number of different investment funds. Thus, a buyer could instruct the insurance company to invest, for example, one-third of the assets in the stock fund, one-third in the aggressive growth fund and the remaining third in a balanced fund.

One variable annuity produced the following results:

**TABLE 7-3**

**PHOENIX MUTUAL SINGLE PREMIUM
VARIABLE ANNUITY AS OF
SEPTEMBER 1991**

|                  | 5-year Average | 3-year Average |
| ---------------- | :------------: | :------------: |
| Growth Fund      |     16.9%      |     17.1%      |
| Total-Vest Fund  |     11.5%      |     11.5%      |
| Corporate Bond   |     10.9%      |      7.5%      |

*Source:* Financial Planning Magazine, September 1991.

These are excellent results, particularly when you consider that they are tax-sheltered. There are no federal, state or local taxes on the growth until the assets are withdrawn from the annuity. Another important benefit is that there are no taxes levied when you change from one fund to another, which can be done 12 times each year. It is not considered a taxable event. If this were a regular mutual fund (as opposed to a single premium deferred annuity), switches *are* considered a taxable event. For example, if you invested $10,000 in a growth and income fund and it grew to $15,000, and for some reason you wanted to change to a tax-exempt fund, you would have to pay a tax on the $5,000 gain.

The *single premium variable annuity* has no sales charges. However, there is an annual fee. One company charges $25 for an annual maintenance fee and an annual mortality and expense risk fee of 1.25% of the fund's current value. The money manager's fee is .75%. Thus, the total annual cost is 2.0% of the value of the fund plus $25.

The 1.25% mortality expense covers your life in case you die and the market is lower than it was when you

made your original investment. Your beneficiary would receive the full amount you invested.

The following are a few of the financial institutions offering SPVA:

- AEtna Life Insurance & Annuity Co.
  1-203-273-2131

- Anchor National Life
  1-800-922-0876

- Fidelity Investments Life Insurance
  1-800-343-2430

- Guardian Insurance and Annuity Co.
  1-800-221-3253

You may wish to investigate others as well.

## Municipal Bonds

To avoid taxes and still remain fairly safe in their investments, many people turn to *municipal bonds*. These are IOUs issued by states, cities, counties, towns, villages, and the like. The bonds are of varying terms, ranging anywhere from 30 months to 40 years. The major advantage of a municipal bond is that it is totally income tax-free at the federal level. If it is purchased by a resident of the state issuing it, there is no state or city income tax.

Municipal bonds are stable and safe. The number of municipals that have defaulted in payment has been infinitesimally small. For an individual whose major concern is safety of principal, a review of the municipal failure rates can be quite assuring. For example, the state of New York has never experienced a municipality that defaulted on its bonds. New York City came quite close, but never did actually default. Every dollar of principal and interest has been paid on all municipals issued by or in the State of New York since 1776.

There are three ways you can invest in municipal bonds:

1. Individual municipal bonds;

2. Municipal investment trusts; and

3. Mutual funds.

## Individual Municipal Bonds

A municipal bond is a fixed instrument. The purchaser buys a specific bond for a set term, paying a set interest rate. For example, there is the short-term (money market) tax-free bond which offered an interest rate of 3.1% on April 1, 1991. An intermediate-term bond (10 to 15 years) had an interest rate of 6.4%, while long-term bond (15 to 30 years) rates were 7%. Interest is paid semi-annually. The minimum investment is $5,000.

Ratings are an important factor in the purchase of any bond, whether municipal or corporate. There are two rating organizations: Standard & Poor's Corporation and Moody's Investor Service. See Table 7-4 for their ratings.

### TABLE 7-4

### BOND RATES

| Moody's | S&P | Definition |
|---------|-----|------------|
| Aaa | AAA | *High-grade investment bonds.* The highest rating assigned, extremely strong capacity to pay principal and interest. |
| Aa | AA | *High-grade investment bonds.* High quality by all standards, but rated lower because the margins of protections are not quite as strong. |

**TABLE 7-4** (*Continued*)

| Moody's | S&P | Definition |
|---|---|---|
| A | A | *Medium-grade investment bonds*. Many favorable investment attributes, but susceptibility to adverse economic changes. |
| Baa | BBB | *Medium-grade investment bonds*. Adequate capacity to pay principal and interest but lacking protective elements against adverse economic conditions. |
| Ba | BB | *Speculative issues*. Only moderate protection of principal and interest. |
| B | B | *Speculative issues*. Assurance of principal and interest may be small. |
| Caa | CCC | *Default*. Poor-quality issues that may be in default or in danger of default. |
| Ca | CC | Default. Highly speculative issues, often in default. |
| C |  | Default. Extremely poor investment quality. |
|  | C | Default. Income bonds on which no interest is paid. |
|  | D | Default. Issues actually in default. |

*Source:* Moody's Bond Record and Standard & Poor's Bond Guide.


A Triple A rating (AAA), the highest rating, is an indication that the buyer of that bond has an excellent chance of receiving repayment of principal and interest. The rating organization, from their study of the bond, has given this specific bond its highest rating. The AAA rating tells the purchaser that this is the safest bond available for purchase. AA rating is the second safest and so on down to unsafe C or D ratings. There are a

considerable number of unrated bonds, sometimes called "Junk" bonds.

Ratings of Triple B (BBB) and above are considered investment grade. Many states permit banks or trusts to invest in BBB and above rated bonds for widows and orphans funds. Your stock broker should be questioned about the rating level best for you and other matters to help you decide which bond to buy.

In the purchase of bonds the market factor, (previously discussed in Chapter 6 under the section "Treasury Bills, Notes, and Bonds") is operative. If interest rates go up, the value of one's bonds decrease. This, however, is not significant if the investor intends to hold the bond to term and receive the income annually, on a long-term investment basis.

### Tax Savings

The savings equivalent that an individual receives by purchasing municipal bonds is shown in Table 7-5.

Assuming a 7% yield on a municipal bond, a person in the 28% tax bracket would have to earn 9.72% from an equally safe, but taxable, corporate or government bond in order to equal the after-tax yield on a 7% tax-exempt bond. Remember, you are taxed by the federal, state, and some cities. These taxes add up and can be

### TABLE 7-5

### SEVEN PERCENT TAX-EXEMPT
### YIELD EQUIVALENT

| If Your Tax Bracket Is | Equivalent Taxable Yield Must Exceed |
|---|---|
| 31.0% | 10.14% |
| 28.0% | 9.72% |
| 15.0% | 8.24% |

*Source:* Creative Retirement Planning, Inc., New York, NY.

saved by investing in munis. For those who live in a city which has an income tax, that rate should be considered as well. Don't forget to discount the state and city rates since they are deductible on the federal rate.

There are three ways that bonds can be purchased: the *regular way*, at a *discount*, or at a *premium*.

### Regular Way

The *regular way* involves paying no premium and receiving no discount for the bond. For example you pay $10,000, and you receive a $10,000 bond. With a coupon rate of 7%, the return would be $700 per year.

### Discount Bonds

The second way is to buy the bond at a *discount*. If the bond is purchased at a discount rate the purchase price might be $9,000 with the same coupon rate of 7% for a return of $700 per year. The actual yield, therefore, has changed from 7.0% to 7.8% ($700 divided by 9,000 = 7.8%). When the bond is redeemed at its due date, ex. 7/1/2000, the full amount of $10,000 is received for an additional profit of $1,000. The yield to maturity is then a total of 8.66%.

### Premium

Finally, bonds can also be purchased at a *premium*. For a $10,000 bond with a 7.5% coupon, an individual might pay $11,000 (in order to get a higher interest rate or a safer bond). The premium (or extra price) paid in this example is $1,000. The actual annual yield is only 6.36% (the $700 dividend divided by $11,000). The yield to maturity is only 6.0%, because an extra $1,000 was paid.

If you wish to take the time to study this thoroughly, you will see that there are definite advantages to purchasing bonds at a discount. If you are planning to buy individual bonds it is important to know precisely what

you are paying for. That is, are you paying the regular amount, a discount price, or a premium price?

Another factor to be considered when purchasing individual bonds is the *call* provision. The municipality may "call" in or buy back the bond before the stated term has expired. Call provisions are set forth in the bond instrument itself. Your broker should bring it to your attention. The disadvantage to certain "call" provisions is that you may not be able to get your original interest rate on a new bond if your existing bond is "called" early and interest rates have fallen.

## Municipal Investment Trusts

A second approach to the purchase of municipal bonds is a *municipal investment trust* (MIT). This is a fixed instrument of approximately 12 to 16 individual municipal bonds bundled together by a given corporation and sold to individuals. It is exactly like individual municipals except that the minimum price of an MIT is $1,000. Interest is paid monthly instead of semi-annually.

The buyer is assured of a diversified portfolio. For example, an investor with $10,000 to put into bonds would have a maximum of 2 individual bonds ($5,000 each, that's the minimum size), with an MIT the investment would include 12 to 16 bonds. On November 27, 1991 a federal tax-free municipal investment trust (MIT) was offering about a 6.5% yield.

A major consideration in purchasing an MIT is that it is a fixed instrument. Its interest rate will not change for the duration of the trust. However, they are subject to call and you should check this provision before you purchase.

## Municipal Mutual Funds

A mutual fund consisting of *municipal bonds* is the equivalent of a municipal investment trust except that it is managed on a day to day basis. The managers of

the municipal bond fund, buy, sell, and swap bonds whenever it is appropriate, to improve the overall yield of the fund.

If you purchased a Federal Tax-Free Income Fund from Franklin Distributors on November 29, 1991 with a yield of 7.06% and the interest rate 5 years later for the same type of municipals was 8.5%, the purchaser should expect to see that the Franklin Fund yield is not locked in at 7.06%, but rather has increased to approximately 8%. Thus, when purchasing a managed fund, you should anticipate that its payout will in general keep up with current interest rates. You should also understand however that interest rates of the fund will lag slightly behind because of certain technical considerations. If interest rates are declining you should also expect that your yield will decline similarly.

Using the mutual fund approach, you generally are assured of even greater diversification. Instead of the 12 to 16 bonds in an MIT (Municipal Investment Trust), a mutual fund might include 2 to 3 times that many.

---

### Helpful Hint

A combination of individual bonds, municipal investment trusts, and managed mutual funds should be considered, depending upon your desire for safety, diversification, and interest rates. Our recommendation is to invest your bond money as follows:

Fixed-rate municipal bonds   25% (Individual bonds and municipal investment trusts)

Variable-rate municipal bonds   75% (Mutual funds)

Buy BBB or better-rated bond funds

---

As examples of mutual bond funds, we have listed the following five:

- Franklin Fund, 777 Mariners Island Boulevard, San Mateo, CA 94404.

- Scudder Managed Municipal Bond Fund, 175 Federal Street, Boston, MA 02110.

- Putnam—New York, 99 High Street, Boston, MA 02110.

- Sun America, 11601 Wilshire Boulevard, Los Angeles, CA 90025-1748

- Vanguard Group, Drummers Lane, Valley Forge, PA 19482.

## Real Estate

All of the investments we have considered thus far have been stable in nature. That is to say, there is no substantial growth or loss in the principal amounts involved. You put your $10,000 down and you expect to get $10,000 back if you decide to sell plus you get a monthly income.

The first investment to consider for growth potential is *real estate*. This investment is considered by many experienced investors to be relatively safe. That is provided you pay strict attention to three important items when you are deciding which real estate to purchase: Location, Location, Location. Know the area in which you are buying.

As we will discuss in a later chapter, 7.3% of the world's wealth is invested in real estate. It can be safely said that a heavy percentage of real estate investors have done quite well. Your own residence is a good example of that. The growth in value of real estate has been estimated at 11.6% per year over the last 15 years. The last few years, however, have been unkind to the real estate market.

Those individuals who wish to consider this investment in their retirement years should look for two

major benefits: income and growth. In addition to these, there are, under current law, some very important advantages to investing in real estate.

1. *Depreciation*—Improved property, run as a business has a very important feature, namely *depreciation*. The federal government permits you to depreciate the value of this type of investment over a fixed number of years. We will not go into details, but simply give you an example. Assume that you purchased a two-family house at a cost of $120,000 and placed a value on the land of $20,000 and the building, $100,000. Assume that you're renting out both apartments. You could depreciate the building, using a straight-line 27.5-year depreciation factor of 3.636%. You would show, therefore, a $3,636 paper loss for each of the 27.5 years. Thus, regardless of the amount of income that you might receive annually from this real estate, you can reduce that income by the depreciation of $3,636 each year, giving you a far lower tax to pay.

2. *Interest deduction*—The interest on any mortgage you pay on the property is deductible.

3. *Taxes and other expenses*—All expenses paid in operating your business real estate are deductible against the income produced. However, if income is less than expenses your loss can be carried back to other income. The maximum deduction allowed is $25,000 provided your other "adjusted gross income" does not exceed $100,000. A partial deduction is permitted up to an *adjusted gross income* (AGI) of $150,000. If your AGI exceeds $150,000 losses from a real estate business are not deductible at all.

## Limited Partnerships

If you are not interested in the management of your own real estate investments, you might consider purchasing a *limited partnership* through one of the large

brokerage houses. For an investment as low as $5,000, you can enter into a number of different types of real estate investments. For the sake of brevity and clarity, we will limit our consideration here to the type of investment that may be of value to some retirees, namely, an investment that will produce income and, probably, growth.

Once you have made your $5,000 or more investment, you are in a position to sit back and not have to be involved in the decisions of management. You are considered solely a "limited partner"—limited to your financial investment—and indeed you have entered into a partnership relationship with the general partner. Your money is locked up from 5 to 15 years. There is no regular market for the sale of limited partnerships.

Because you are setting aside the funds invested in this instrument for a relatively long period of time, it is imperative that you thoroughly check the "track record" of the general partner. What has been the yield on previous investments? You should purchase it through a reputable dealer, who has completed what is known as a *due diligence investigation* of the firm itself so that you are protected as much as possible. Brokerage houses, before they can sell a limited partnership are required, by law, to investigate a general partnership thoroughly.

You should also look for one other important feature in a limited partnership. You should receive your benefits before the general partners receive theirs.

Your personal objectives in investing in this type of an instrument should be income and capital gain. However, you should understand that under current law, losses from limited partnerships are generally not deductible from other income.

As you know, action in the real estate market has been quite low for the last few years. Prices have gone down as well. On the positive side, many feel that the bottom has been hit and this may be a good time to buy. It does, however, require a good bit of courage and research.

# 8

# Growth Investments

Growth investments are those made with an eye to beating inflation—the idea is to invest in things that produce income faster than inflation rises. Among these investment areas are common stock, preferred stock, and bonds. Their relative merits, methods of analysis, including the use of investment newsletters, and how to choose a broker are detailed below.

## Stock—What is it?

A *stock* represents a share of ownership in a corporation. Each stockholder owns a fraction of the corporation, the size of which depends upon the number of shares owned. As an owner, you reap the benefit of the company's success and bear the ultimate burden of loss. You actually own a part of every building, piece of machinery, or whatever the company owns. Forty million people currently own stock in public corporations. Through stock ownership, you make money two ways:

- Income, in the form of dividend payments; and
- Capital gains, the selling of stock for more than you paid.

## Common Stocks—Can they make you money?

Common stocks are the cheapest, most plentiful shares made available by a corporation. The vast majority of stocks are common stocks. How well have stockholders done?

Let's look at the record: One dollar invested in *common stock* in 1925 with dividends reinvested, grew to $517 by the end of the year 1990. (See Exhibit 8-1.) This chart is based on Standard & Poor's (S&P) Composite Index (Standard & Poor's publishes several indexes—the Composite Index is the most all-inclusive). This 65-year period includes the Great Depression, World War II, Korea, Vietnam, and numerous economic cycles. Simply put, the record shows that common stocks are a good investment. The problem is picking the right ones.

### EXHIBIT 8-1   COMMON STOCK TOTAL RETURNS (1926–1990)

*Source:* Ibbotson Associates. Ibbotson, Roger G., and Rex A. Sinquefield, *Stocks, Bonds, Bills, and Inflation* (SBBI), 1982, updated in *Stocks, Bonds, Bills, and Inflation 199_ Yearbook*™ [or in the (month or quarter) 199_ update], Ibbotson Associates, Chicago. All rights reserved.

According to Ibbotson Associates, an independent organization that tracks financial information, common stock did considerably better than other forms of investment during the lifetime of the average reader. Exhibit 8-2 shows that funds invested in the Standard & Poor's 500 listing of average common stock would have grown at a rate of 10.1% per year during your lifetime. By contrast, most people have their funds invested in the equivalent of U.S. Treasury bills, which averaged only 3.7% per year.

## Preferred Stock

*Preferred stock* is a unique form of ownership that has features both of corporate stocks and of bonds. Preferred stock is like a company's IOU. Like common stock, the corporation promises to pay a "specified" dividend to the shareholder, if the firm has the money. Your safety net here, though not guaranteed is that, after bondholders, the corporation must pay your dividend before it pays dividends to its common stockholders. As with bonds, if the company goes broke,

**EXHIBIT 8-2   ANNUAL RETURNS 1926–1990**

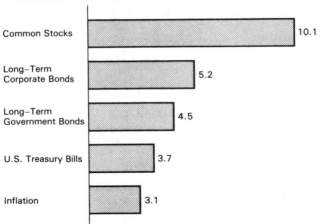

Source: Ibbotson Associates. Ibbotson, Roger G., and Rex A. Sinquefield, *Stocks, Bonds, Bills, and Inflation* (SBBI), 1982, updated in *Stocks, Bonds, Bills, and Inflation 199_ Yearbook™* [or in the (month or quarter) 199_ update]. Ibbotson Associates, Chicago. All rights reserved.

preferred stockholders receive their share before common stockholders do. Fewer preferred stocks are offered than common stocks, and they are pricier.

## Stock Exchanges

Stocks are traded primarily on two national exchanges, the largest, the New York Stock Exchange (NYSE), and the American Stock Exchange (AMEX), and *over-the-counter*, or OTC. Although over-the-counter sounds a bit like do-it-yourself, a broker is needed for OTC stock too. The difference between OTC stock and NYSE or AMEX stock is the size and seasoning of the companies involved: national exchange-listed companies are by and large the biggest and the best.

There are 6 regional exchanges:

- Pacific Stock Exchange;

- Philadelphia Stock Exchange;

- Boston Stock Exchange;

- Spokane Stock Exchange;

- Intermountain Stock Exchange; and

- Cincinnati Stock Exchange.

The over-the-counter (OTC) market is the largest exchange in terms of the number of companies' stocks that are traded. This market handles about 40,000 securities. Most small and unseasoned companies are listed, and most government and corporate bonds are traded here.

### Types of Stock

*Blue Chip Stocks* are stocks offered by nationally known companies with long histories of growth and dividend payments. Some examples are General Electric, IBM, and DuPont. Most people associate blue chip

stocks with the 30 stocks that make up the *Dow Jones Industrial Average* (DJIA). The term "blue chip stock," which started around the turn of the century, refers to the chips used in poker—blue is the most valuable chip.

*Growth Stocks* are stocks of companies with consistent growth patterns or with potential for significant growth. Usually they provide little immediate dividend income. These are found in each exchange, but more frequently in the over-the-counter market.

*Cyclical Stocks* are very responsive to business cycles. Their prices and earnings rise and fall dramatically as the economy strengthens and weakens. Examples of cyclical industries are aluminum, steel, autos, and housing.

*Defensive Stocks* are stocks in companies that are relatively immune to the rise and fall of the economy. Food and drug companies are examples of such industries, for the need for their products never abates.

*Speculative Stocks* offer very large possibilities for gain or loss. They are offered by relatively new corporations without long-term records of profitability. *Penny stocks* fall in this category.

---

### Helpful Hint

If you are interested in owning individual stocks, we recommend that you limit yourself to *blue chip* and *defensive stocks*.

---

## How to Decide Which Stock to Buy

With about 1,600 stocks listed on the New York Stock Exchange and tens of thousands more on the other exchanges, how do you go about making a choice?

## Fundamental Analysis

*Fundamental analysis* is one approach that experts use to rate stock. Their aim is to assess the real value of the company that is issuing the stock, based on such factors as net worth (assets minus liabilities), earnings, dividends, and prospects of future dividends. Industry trends and management capabilities are also factored by these experts into such an analysis. Essentially, what is being decided here is what the company would sell for if put on the market today—for these analysts, that is the fundamental factor.

An example of such an analysis is shown in Exhibit 8-3. This is a partial reprint of *Value Line*'s rating and report on AT&T. You can study the report carefully and learn the importance of all the figures or simply go to the bottom line (actually the top line, left side). Here you will get the analyst's opinion of the stock. On October 18, 1991, Steven P. Halper, *Value Line*'s analyst for this stock, gave AT&T a No. 2 for *timeliness*, meaning that he felt that this stock was above average in comparison with all the rest. He also gave it a No. 1 for *safety*, declaring it one of the safest stocks to own at that time.

## Technical Analysis

*Technical analysis* is another approach; one in which analysts try to predict future stock movements by analyzing and charting past sequences of stock prices, and the force of supply and demand. This approach analyzes factors external to particular companies. Technical analysts use a wide variety of methods. Some technical advisers focus on investor psychology, others watch the actions of mutual fund managers and other such sophisticated investors. Other indicators technical analysts follow are advances versus declines in the Dow Jones Industrial Average Index, moving average analysis, sentiment indicators, Barron's Confidence Index, and similar statistics and charts.

# EXHIBIT 8-3  VALUE LINE'S RATING AND REPORT ON AT&T

| AT&T NYSE-T | RECENT PRICE 37 | P/E RATIO 14.0 (Trailing: 14.2 / Median: NMF) | RELATIVE P/E RATIO 0.98 | DIV'D YLD 4.1% | VALUE LINE 752 |
|---|---|---|---|---|---|

TIMELINESS **2** Above Average (Relative Price Performance Next 12 Mos.)

SAFETY **1** Highest (Scale: 1 Highest to 5 Lowest)

BETA .85 (1.00 = Market)

**1994-96 PROJECTIONS**

| | Price | Gain | Ann'l Total Return |
|---|---|---|---|
| High | 70 | (+90%) | 20% |
| Low | 55 | (+50%) | 14% |

**Insider Decisions**

| | D | J | F | M | A | M | J | J | A |
|---|---|---|---|---|---|---|---|---|---|
| to Buy | 0 | 0 | 0 | 0 | 0 | 0 | 0 | 0 | 0 |
| Options | 0 | 0 | 0 | 0 | 0 | 0 | 0 | 0 | 0 |
| to Sell | 0 | 0 | 0 | 1 | 0 | 0 | 0 | 0 | 0 |

**Institutional Decisions**

| | 4Q90 | 1Q91 | 2Q91 |
|---|---|---|---|
| to Buy | 172 | 214 | 216 |
| to Sell | 218 | 187 | 176 |
| Hld(000) | 249998 | 258580 | 266026 |

Percent shares traded: 6.0 / 4.0 / 2.0

Relative Price Strength

Target Price Range 1994 1995 1996

Shaded areas indicate recessions

Options: CBOE

AT&T, in its present configuration, came into being on January 1, 1984, as a result of a Court-ordered division of the Bell System's telecommunications business into Bell operating companies (owned by seven regional holding companies) and AT&T. Shares began trading on a when-issued basis on November 21, 1983. Data in 1981, 1982, and 1983 are pre-divestiture and are not comparable with subsequent information.

**CAPITAL STRUCTURE as of 6/30/91**
Total Debt $14485 mill. Due in 5 Yrs $7991 mill.
LT Debt $9036 mill. LT Interest $775 mill.
Incl. $367 mill. capitalized leases.
(LT interest earned: 6.4x; total interest coverage: 5.5x)   (34% of Cap'l)

| | 1981 | 1982 | 1983 | 1984 | 1985 | 1986 | 1987 | 1988 | 1989 | 1990 | 1991 | 1992 | 94-96 |
|---|---|---|---|---|---|---|---|---|---|---|---|---|---|
| High: | | | 21.3 | 20.3 | 25.4 | 27.9 | 35.9 | 30.4 | 35.9 | 47.0 | 46.6 | 40.4 | |
| Low: | | | 17.4 | 14.9 | 19.0 | 20.9 | 22.3 | 24.1 | 22.3 | 28.1 | 29.0 | 29.0 | |
| © VALUE LINE PUB, INC. | | | | | | | | | | | | 1992 | 94-96 |
| Revenues per sh^A | -- | -- | -- | 31.98 | 32.65 | 31.80 | 31.29 | 32.79 | 33.57 | 34.14 | 32.00 | 35.55 | 45.10 |
| "Cash Flow" per sh^A | -- | -- | -- | 3.89 | 4.38 | 5.30 | 5.34 | 5.55 | 5.64 | 5.61 | 5.20 | 6.00 | 6.20 |
| Earnings per sh^B | -- | -- | -- | 1.25 | 1.43 | 1.64 | 1.88 | 2.11 | 2.50 | 2.51 | 2.80 | 3.00 | 4.50 |
| Div'ds Decl'd per sh^C ■ | -- | -- | -- | 1.20 | 1.20 | 1.20 | 1.20 | 1.20 | 1.20 | 1.32 | 1.40 | 1.52 | 2.25 |
| Cap'l Spending per sh | -- | -- | -- | 3.34 | 3.91 | 3.39 | 3.41 | 3.75 | 3.15 | 4.07 | 3.10 | 2.65 | 3.40 |
| Book Value per sh^B | -- | -- | -- | 13.26 | 13.68 | 12.64 | 13.46 | 10.68 | 11.84 | 12.90 | 12.80 | 14.85 | 21.00 |
| Common Shs Outst'g^D | -- | -- | -- | 1037.7 | 1069.3 | 1072.0 | 1073.7 | 1073.7 | 1075.8 | 1092.1 | 1300.0 | 1315.0 | 1320.0 |
| Avg Ann'l P/E Ratio | -- | -- | -- | 14.0 | 15.3 | 14.7 | 14.9 | 13.0 | 14.8 | 14.9 | Bold figures are Value Line estimates | | 14.0 |
| Relative P/E Ratio | -- | -- | -- | 1.30 | 1.24 | 1.00 | 1.00 | 1.08 | 1.12 | 1.11 | | | 1.15 |
| Avg Ann'l Div'd Yield | -- | -- | -- | 6.8% | 5.5% | 5.0% | 4.3% | 4.4% | 3.2% | 3.5% | | | 3.6% |
| Revenues ($mill)^A | 58066 | 65093 | 67599 | 33188 | 34910 | 34087 | 33598 | 35210 | 36112 | 37285 | 41650 | 46780 | 60000 |
| Operating Margin | 45.8% | 44.2% | 43.8% | 14.7% | 17.4% | 21.0% | 21.4% | 22.9% | 21.2% | 22.0% | 21.5% | 22.5% | 24.5% |
| Depreciation ($mill) | 7900.3 | 8734.5 | 9188.5 | 2777.9 | 3231.6 | 3925.0 | 3724.0 | 3690.0 | 3366.0 | 3396.0 | 3615 | 4000 | 4950 |
| Net Profit ($mill) | 6822.9 | 7278.8 | 7187.9 | 1369.9 | 1556.8 | 1843.0 | 2044.0 | 2266.0 | 2697.0 | 2735.0 | 3120 | 3920 | 5965 |
| Income Tax Rate | 55.6% | 57.4% | 58.2% | 24.7% | 35.9% | 39.4% | 35.6% | 43.9% | 32.4% | 35.3% | 38.0% | 37.0% | 37.5% |

7.5x "Cash Flow" p'sh

The vast majority of our readers will not have the background to use any of these methods themselves. However, if you enjoy the activity of buying and selling stocks and you'd like some guidance other than that from your broker, you might consider subscribing to an investment newletter or two. These newsletters provide such technical or fundamental analysis in an accessible, understandable way.

## Investment Newsletters

There are hundreds of *investment newsletters*— some are good, some not-so-good. If you are interested in finding out about a newsletter service for yourself, you may want to refer to *The Hulbert Guide to Financial Newsletters*. This guide evaluates the performance of about 100 investment newsletters. The guide's editor, Mark Hulbert, writes a column in *Forbes* magazine on the subject of rating newsletters.

One highly rated newsletter is *The Zweig Forecast*, edited by Dr. Martin Zweig, who predicted the October 19, 1987 drop. *The Zweig Forecast* is an example of technical analysis. Assuming Zweig's readers followed his recommendations, sold their stocks in time, and got back into the market when he so suggested, they would have made a very substantial gain. Two other examples of investment newsletters are *the Value Line Investments Survey* and Standard & Poor's *The Outlook*, which are based on fundamental analysis. Over a million investors subscribe to newsletters which can cost from $50 to about $1,000 per year. To give you an idea of how successful newsletter services can be Exhibit 8-4 shows how effective one—namely *Value Line*—has been.

This exhibit shows that if you had invested a sum of money, say, $10,000, on July 19, 1965, and purchased shares of all the stocks that *Value Line* gave a timeliness rating of No. 1 and held those stocks for a full year, and the next year sold them and bought all those stocks that *Value Line* then considered No. 1, and did

the same thing each and every year, by July 19, 1991, your portfolio would have been worth $362,000. However, this does not take into consideration two important items—taxes on these transactions and brokers' fees. Nonetheless, the net amount even after these expenses is very substantial. If you had purchased the stocks in an IRA account, taxes would not have to be considered.

One other important bit of information to be gleaned from Exhibit 8-4 is that the same $10,000 invested in all the Group 4 stocks over the same period of time would have only grown to $25,000. Hardly worth the effort!

Two other factors are your willpower and your discipline. Once in, would you stay in regardless of what happens in the market? And, secondly, would you stay with it and make the required swaps at the end of each year? Both these factors are crucial to success, and no

**EXHIBIT 8-4   RECORD OF VALUE LINE'S RANKINGS FOR TIMELINESS (WITHOUT ALLOWING FOR CHANGES IN RANK (1965– 1991))**

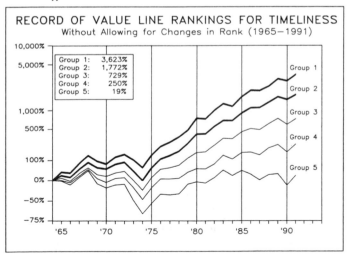

RECORD OF VALUE LINE RANKINGS FOR TIMELINESS
Without Allowing for Changes in Rank (1965–1991)

| Group 1: | 3,623% |
| Group 2: | 1,772% |
| Group 3: | 729% |
| Group 4: | 250% |
| Group 5: | 19% |

newsletter can substitute for them. The willpower and discipline have to be yours.

This example shows the result of one investment newsletter service. You might do as well or better with others. An example of a good newsletter that rates other newsletters heads the list.

- *Hulbert Guide to Financial Newsletters*
  New York Institute of Finance
  2 Broadway
  New York, NY 10004
  212-344-2900
  $24.95
- *Zweig Forecast*
  Dr. Martin Zweig—Editor
  P.O. Box 2900
  Wantagh, NY 11793
  516-785-1300
  $265 per year
  Frequency—Once every 3 weeks
- *The Value Line Investment Survey*
  711 Third Avenue
  New York, NY 10017
  212-687-3965
  $525 per year
- *The Prudent Speculator*
  Al Frank—Editor
  P.O. Box 1767
  Santa Monica, CA 90436
  213-315-9888
  $225 per year
  Frequency—Once every 3 weeks

---

**Helpful Hint**

If you are interested in owning individual stocks and are not extremely capable in the area of stock selection, we recommend that you find a good investment newsletter and follow its suggestions.

---

## Market Timing vs. Buy and Hold

When is the best time to buy? One very successful millionaire answered this question simply: "When you have available funds." This is basically a buy and hold approach. Not everyone agrees, though—some feel that you can and should *time* the market, that is, get in when the market is moving up and out when it's going down. "Buy low and sell high," they advise. Not everyone, however, is able to agree on *how* to time the market. A considerable amount of time and effort could be spent on this subject, however, let's get to the point: we do not recommend that you invest short term (to try to time the market) but quite the opposite—you should invest *long term*. Buy and hold is our philosophy.

## Foreign Stocks

With all the changes taking place in the world, it may be time to turn your attention to *foreign stocks*. About half of the world's publicly traded stocks are registered outside the United States. During the 1980s alone, a dollar invested in the world markets appreciated by 515% in contrast to a return of 223% in the U.S. market.

Foreign stock can provide a profit or loss in two ways:

1. The price of the stock in local currency can rise or fall; or

2. The value of the foreign currency can rise or fall relative to the U.S. dollar.

There are two ways to invest in foreign stocks:

1. Individual stocks can be purchased using *American depository receipts* (ADRs); or

2. Mutual funds.

For the unsophisticated investor, the only way to go, in our opinion, is with mutual funds (more about this in our next chapter).

## Corporate Bonds

Like government and municipal bonds, *corporate bonds* are simply IOUs of corporations. When a corporation wants to raise money, it can do so by selling shares of ownership through common or preferred stock (the equity approach). If the corporation prefers to raise money by borrowing, it does so through an offering of its corporate bonds (the debt approach).

A bond has a *fixed-interest rate*, for example 11-⅜% for its entire term, and a set date of redemption, for example March 1, 2010. The bond's fixed interest rate is printed on the bond itself. Like treasury and municipal bonds, the price of a corporate bond will rise and fall depending on prevailing interest rates. Corporate bond certificates have a *par value* that is, a face value printed right on them, usually $1,000. In the past, bonds were issued with coupons attached; they were called *bearer* bonds—the owner's name was not printed on them. Today almost all bonds are *registered*; they bear the name of their owner and do not have coupons attached. However, what is really important about a corporate bond is its *yield*. This is determined by dividing the amount of money a bond will pay in interest by the price you pay for the bond. The *yield* is posted daily in *The New York Times*, *The Wall Street Journal*, and in many other large daily local newspapers.

Another important factor, and a more precise measure of the bond's real value, is its *yield-to-maturity*. This reflects the interest rate in relation to the actual price paid (not the par value), and the number of years left to maturity. If you buy a bond for $950 with a par value of $1,000, the $50 difference will add to your actual yield when the bond is received at maturity.

Bond prices fluctuate considerably, along with interest rates. Recently, bonds have been as volatile, if not more so, than stocks.

If a corporation goes bankrupt, bondholders have first claim on any remaining assets. Preferred stockholders are next and, last, holders of common stock. This is additional protection for bond investors.

---

### Helpful Hint

If you are interested in buying individual bonds, we recommend:

- Ratings of AAA, AA, A, and BBB.
- Staggered maturities (buy bonds with various maturity dates).
- Call protection of at least 10 years. Make sure your broker finds out if the bond can be called in before the stated maturity dates.
- General obligation as opposed to revenue bonds if you're buying municipals.
- Ask your broker for the following:
  yield;
  yield-to-maturity; and
  yield-to-call.

---

## Convertible Bonds

These are corporate bonds with a special feature — *convertibility*. These bonds are convertible into the common stock of the corporation. Many consider it to be a conservative approach to the stock market.

Basically, you buy a convertible bond for the interest it pays. The kicker lies in the fact that if the price

of the common stock of the corporation rises, you may convert the bond into stock at a specified ratio and realize the gain in the stock price. The yield on convertible bonds is less than that on a nonconvertible bond because of this conversion privilege.

## Junk Bonds

Corporate bonds with very low or no S&P and Moody's ratings are called *junk bonds*. Believe it or not, most U.S. firms have issued bonds of this classification. However, only a few hundred of the larger corporations receive good or investment grade ratings.

Why do people buy them? High yields! On average, these bonds pay about 13% to 15%. They are, however, quite volatile, and many financial advisors feel that this is not the best bet for the average retiree today.

A recent Harvard study found that 34% of all high-yield (junk) bonds issued in 1977 and 1978 had defaulted by 1988. The problem with high-yield bonds started around 1985 with leveraged buyouts, because such buyouts involved borrowing entirely too much. More than half of all high-yield bonds in existence today were issued after 1985. Some corporations must pay 50% to 70% of earnings in interest on this type of debt. Prices for junk bonds have been very volatile. In 1989 the junk bond market dropped dramatically only to recover just as dramatically in 1991.

## Gold and Other Tangible Investments

Should you consider putting some money in gold or other tangible assets? The answer depends upon how conservative you are, your opinion on the future of our economy, and your degree of expectation of a worldwide calamity—when all money systems fail, gold and other tangible investments retain an intrinsic value. If

**TABLE 8-1**

**GOLD**

*1968–1990 New York spot price; $ per troy ounce; year-end*

**How a $1,000 investment performed over**

| 5 years | 10 years | 15 years | 20 years | 25 years | 30 years |
|---|---|---|---|---|---|
| 1986–1990 $1,191.23 (3.76%)^ | | | | | |
| | 1981–1990 $670.22 (−3.72%) | | | | |
| | | 1976–1990 $2,798.36 (7.10%) | | | |
| | | | 1971–1990 $10,431.61 (12.44%) | | |
| | | | | 1966–1990 $11,221.43 (10.15%) | |
| | | | | | 1961–1990 $11,221.43 (8.39%) |

annual compound rate of return for that period.

*Source:* American Metal Market, Handy & Harman; U.S. Bureau of Mines. © 1991 Chase Global Data & Research, 289 Great Road, Acton, MA 01720.

you are considering such investments strictly from an investment point of view, a lot can be learned from past history. Gold went from $35 an ounce in 1967 to $586 an ounce in 1980. This huge jump was caused in part by the ending of a legal prohibition on gold ownership. Gold was free to float in value on the open market. But Table 8-1 shows that gold was a *bad* investment in the 1980s. Gold averaged *minus* 4.3% per year, whereas in the 1970s and 1980s (20 years), it averaged a nice 12.37% gain per year.

### TABLE 8-2

## FINANCIAL AND TANGIBLE ASSETS—COMPOUND ANNUAL RATES OF RETURN

|                        | 20 Years | 10 Years | 5 Years | 1 Year |
| ---------------------- | -------- | -------- | ------- | ------ |
| U.S. Coins             | 17.3     | 7.3      | 15.0    | 14.6   |
| Chinese Ceramics[a]    | 14.4     | 7.6      | 14.6    | 18.0   |
| Stocks[b]              | 12.7     | 17.3     | 17.7    | 15.4   |
| Old Masters[a]         | 12.7     | 12.3     | 23.9    | 44.5   |
| Gold                   | 12.3     | −4.3     | 3.0     | 0.5    |
| Diamonds[c]            | 10.7     | 6.4      | 11.8    | 5.5    |
| Bonds[b]               | 9.6      | 12.6     | 12.0    | 7.5    |
| Oil                    | 9.0      | −3.8     | −7.0    | −0.7   |
| 3-Mos. Treasury Bills[b] | 8.6    | 9.5      | 7.0     | 8.3    |
| Housing                | 7.4      | 4.7      | 5.0     | 2.4    |
| U.S. Farmland          | 6.5      | −0.6     | −0.6    | 3.9    |
| CPI                    | 6.2      | 4.8      | 3.8     | 4.4    |
| Silver                 | 5.4      | −10.2    | −4.0    | −2.9   |
| Foreign Exchange       | 4.4      | 1.5      | 11.9    | 10.5   |

[a]Source: Sotheby's.
[b]Stock returns assume quarterly reinvestment of dividends. Bond returns assume monthly reinvestment.
[c]Source: The Diamond Registry.
CPI Consumer Price Index.
Note: All returns are for the period ended June 1, 1990, based on latest available data.
*Table 8-2 Source:* Salomon Bros. Inc., New York, NY.

Many feel that gold is a good inflation hedge, but that is not necessarily true. In 1988, inflation rose by 4.1% and gold fell 14.5%. But when inflation topped 13% in 1979, the upward spiral of gold prices really took off. It hit $825 per ounce on January 1, 1980 and fell back to $625 only 5 days later.

In the past decade, gold ore has been discovered in a number of new locations and, consequently, prices have been driven lower. Future prospects for gold are not very bullish. Some experts are saying that the prices could go as low as $250 per ounce. (On June 6, 1991, gold was $364.85 per ounce.)

Although many financial planners advocate that you keep 5% to 10% of your assets in gold, it is probably best to put your money elsewhere, because there is no income from gold. Unpredictable price fluctuations and the probability of a bearish future for gold are other reasons to avoid it.

Regarding other tangible investments, such as coins, oil, silver, stamps, ceramics, diamonds and art, it's best to leave them to the experts in those fields. Table 8-2 shows that, although rates of return on tangible investments may be great, their fluctuations are extreme. Tangible investments are too erratic for those relying on investment for income stability, and they require in-depth, insider knowledge to stay on top of. Brokers are money-experts, not art, coin, diamond, or silver experts.

## Choosing a Broker

Assuming you are interested in investing in individual stocks and bonds, need expert guidance, and have $50,000 or more to invest, here are some suggestions about choosing and working with a broker. Start by getting referrals from friends, your financial planner, or accountant. Call those referred and ask about the following:

- Experience—how long are they in the business?

- Specialties—do they work with retirees?

- Complaints—with NASD, SEC, or state agencies.

- Education—bachelors degree, masters degree and so on.

- Clients—how many? What net worth?

- Contacts—how often will you be called?

- Operating style—buy and hold or heavy trader?

When you have narrowed down your potential list of brokers to one or two, you should pay each a personal visit. Listen carefully to the questions they ask. Do they start pitching for business right away or are they anxious to find out about you and your goals? Ask them for a few references and check them carefully.

Once you have selected your broker, you should say how much you want to invest and give him or her some idea of what percentage of your assets this amount represents. You should discuss commissions charged, and if you are an unsophisticated investor you should never give your broker complete discretion (control) over your account. That's another way of saying don't let your broker buy and sell in your account without your permission and without presenting a good rationale for a transaction.

If you are using an investment newsletter and are qualified to make your own investment decisions, you may want to consider using a discount broker. This is because the discount broker simply acts on your orders and provides no research.

Generally, the gains involved with stock investment give every evidence of outweighing the risk. Moreover, by being patient with yourself, availing yourself of an investment newsletter or two, and carefully choosing your broker, you can minimize risk, further ensuring overall gains over the long haul.

# 9

# Mutual Funds

## Mutual Funds—What Are They?

*Mutual funds* are pools of individuals' commingled assets in one big account. When you invest in a mutual fund, you don't have your own portfolio; you have a share of, and derive income from, a *large*, pooled portfolio. Individuals invest their assets together with others' to get (a) professional management, (b) diversification, and (c) liquidity. There are about 3,000 mutual funds available today. They aim for such investment objectives as capital gains, or regular dividends, or a higher yield, or a combination thereof. (See Table 9-1.)

**TABLE 9-1**

**TYPES OF MUTUAL FUNDS
(A FEW EXAMPLES).**

*Aggressive Growth*—These mutual funds aim for capital gain as their goal. These funds invest in new companies, in those that have fallen on hard times but are expected to bounce back, and in currently out-of-favor industries. Many use option-writing programs.

*Growth*—These funds buy common stock in less volatile companies. These too focus on capital gains as opposed to dividends.

*Growth and Income*—These invest in common stock in established corporations with good track records. Dividends are paid regularly and capital gains are also an aim.

*International*—These have common stock investments in corporations located outside the United States. They focus on equity and capital gains.

*Global*—These are invested in both U.S. and foreign corporations. Capital gains is their goal.

*Income equity*—These are funds in which good dividend-paying corporations make up the portfolio, with some equity exposure.

*Option/Income*—These funds have a higher yield as their objective. Call options are traded on dividend-paying common stock.

*Balanced*—These mutual funds are a combination of common stock, bonds, money market, and other debt securities. They aim for dividends with some equity exposure.

**TABLE 9-1** (*Continued*)

*U.S. Government Income*—These invest in a variety of government securities, including treasuries and government-backed mortgages. The goal is income with an emphasis on stability.

*Ginnie Mae*—These mutual funds invest in Government National Mortgage Association bonds only. They are a specialized type of U.S. government income funds.

*Municipal Bond*—These are special funds that invest only in municipal bonds of one state or all states. Some are long term. Other are intermediate or short term. Still others are insured. They are another specialized type of government income funds.

*Source:* Investment Company Institute, Washington D.C.

---

**Helpful Hint**

If you are an average or unsophisticated investor our recommendation is to focus on the following types of funds:

GNMA and U.S. government income funds;
Municipal bond funds;
Growth funds; and
Global or international funds.

If you have an above-average to high net worth, you may want to add to this list the following:

Aggressive growth funds; or
Option/income funds.

## Why Invest in Mutual Funds?

Over the years, individual investors have come to realize that they are up against sizable competition when it comes to investing in stocks and bonds. With all the professionals out there—corporations, pension funds, insurance companies, unions, wealthy investors, full-time traders, and brokerage houses—the little guy, the small investor, doesn't stand much of a chance. But by combining their assets with those of other small investors in mutual funds, the little guys are able to obtain the considerable advantages offered by investing in a broad range of stocks, bonds, and government securities.

### Professional Management

When you decide to invest in equities (equity is a corporation's value after all its liabilities are discharged), you can do so by buying individual stocks. But which ones? And when should you buy? And the toughest of all, when should you sell?

These questions are answered for you when you invest in a mutual fund. The professional manager of the fund makes these decisions for you. But first you should study the track records of the funds you want. Their past five-year or ten-year record can be a good guide. Though it is no guarantee of future performance, a recent research study by Professors Roger Ibbotson and William Goetzmann of Columbia University found "strong evidence that both winners and losers are likely to repeat" their performance in subsequent years.

The fund manager and staff invests your money along with that of the thousands if not hundreds of thousands of others in the fund. The manager and staff will decide what to buy, when to buy it, and when to sell it. Their track record defines their success.

## Diversification

Diversification is a basic investment principle. Moreover, government regulations require mutual funds to diversify a portfolio. Diversification is a most reliable method of reducing the risk inherent in all investing. It can take different forms:

- The diversification of a specific company's fund is reflected in the wide range of common stocks the fund manager has in the fund portfolio. Some funds also include corporate bonds and even government bonds.

- Diversification can be widened by investing in two or three different families of funds in the same asset class. For example—split up your government bond investments by putting some of your money with Company A, some with Company B, and some with Company C.

## Liquidity and Income

A very important advantage of mutual funds for a retiree who needs to receive regular income is the systematic withdrawal plan. Most, if not all, growth funds offer such a feature. Each month, for example, you can instruct your mutual fund to send you a regular check. Table 9-2 shows you how this worked with the Phoenix Growth Fund, which we will use for our example, keeping in mind that there are many excellent funds we could have used as well.

As shown in Table 9-2, assuming you invested $25,000 in this fund on May 31, 1981, you would have purchased 2,475 shares of the Phoenix Growth Fund. Had you instructed the fund to send you a monthly check of $208.33 each and every month regardless of what happened in the stock market, the fund would have sent you that check on a regular basis by selling some shares or paying you the dividends and/or capital gains earned by the fund.

## TABLE 9-2

## SYSTEMATIC WITHDRAWAL PLAN PHOENIX GROWTH FUND

| Date | Initial Investment | Shares Purchased |
|------|--------------------|------------------|
| 5/31/81 | $25,000 | 2475 |

Monthly Withdrawals of 10% of Fund. ($208.33) Beginning 6/30/81.

| Date | Amounts Withdrawn | Shares Held | Value of Remaining Shares* |
|------|-------------------|-------------|----------------------------|
| 12/31/81 | $1,458 (7 mo.) | 2,470 | $22,329 |
| 12/31/82 | 2,500 | 2,334 | 28,643 |
| 12/31/83 | 2,500 | 2,744 | 34,114 |
| 12/31/84 | 2,500 | 2,639 | 34,857 |
| 12/31/85 | 2,500 | 2,633 | 43,254 |
| 12/31/86 | 2,500 | 2,988 | 49,000 |
| 12/31/87 | 2,500 | 3,433 | 52,109 |
| 12/31/88 | 2,500 | 3,360 | 53,157 |
| 12/31/89 | 2,500 | 3,393 | 64,973 |
| 12/31/90 | 2,500 | 3,514 | 66,270 |
| 12/31/91 | 1,042 (5 mo.) | 3,465 | 77,655 |

Total Withdrawn     $25,000

Shares Still Held                           3,465

Remaining Value                                                    $77,655

*Includes increase in value, dividends, and capital gains.

*Source:* Phoenix Mutual Life Insurance Company, Enfield, CT.

At the end of this very favorable 10-year period you would still have owned 3,465 shares valued at $77,655. Your immediate question may be, is this what I can expect in the future? The answer is no. You may be fortunate enough to match these numbers, you may even exceed them, but you may also suffer a loss. There

is always a risk in investing in common stock. You are the one who has to make the decision—should I invest?

You can, of course, sell any or all of your shares in a fund at any time. The price will depend on the market at the time. You can also add to your investment any time you wish.

## How Do You Choose a Fund?

Recommendations from friends and relatives is one method, your stockbroker's recommendation is another. Some people study the analysis of experts in such publications as *Money Magazine, Barron's, The New York Times* and *The Wall Street Journal*. Others refer to mutual fund comparison services. For those who are interested here is the basic information on the major ones:

> *CDA Mutual Fund Report*
> 800-232-2285
> Cost—$275 per year
> Service—monthly

> *Morningstar, Inc.*
> 800-876-5005
> Cost—$395/A
> Service—Bi-weekly complete analytical report on all mutual funds

> *S&P/Lipper Mutual Fund Profiles*
> 212-208-8000
> Cost—$125 per year
> Service—Quarterly

> *Wiesenberger Investment Comp. Services*
> 800-950-1201
> Cost—$69/A
> Service—Monthly comparison performance

We recommend that our average reader ask his or her broker/financial planner for the analytical report from one of these services, or from some other service of which he or she might know. That way you will have a dispassionate opinion on the fund being recommended to you. You may wish to investigate some of the many other excellent investment service newsletters as well. *Hulbert Guide to Financial Newsletters*, as mentioned in Chapter 8, can help you choose.

Mutual fund comparison services help us to determine which funds have been performing best in the recent past. For example, we posed this question to our CDA computer program, one of many special computer programs used by brokers and other money specialists. How did the following U.S. government funds compare during the past 6 years? (We could, of course, have included any of the other 30 or so funds in this area.) The results are shown in Table 9-3. The funds in question include:

Franklin U.S. Government Securities

Kemper U.S. Government Securities

Putnam U.S. Government Income

Studying the table, it appears that the best fund is Kemper. However, that is not necessarily the case. It depends upon your objective. If you are retired and

### TABLE 9-3

**MUTUAL FUND PERFORMANCE RATES OF RETURN INCLUDING INCOME: 12/31/84–12/31/90 ANNUALIZED**

| Kemper U.S. Government Securities | 11.6% |
| Franklin U.S. Government Securities | 10.9% |
| Putnam U.S. Government Income | 10.3% |

*Source:* CDA Investment Technologies, Inc.

looking for the highest current income, your choice could be Putnam. Its dividend payout was 9.17%. Kemper was second with 8.99%.

If you are looking for total return, that is, income *plus* the value of your basic investment (or net asset value), Kemper was far better than Putnam (60.5% as opposed to 46.1%) over the 6-year period.

## Net Asset Value

*Net asset value* basically represents the value of your shares on any given day, that is, the price one share could be sold for on that day. The net asset value is arrived at by dividing the total value of the fund's holdings by the total number of shares of the fund.

When you buy government funds (U.S. and municipals), the net asset value is of secondary importance because government bond funds usually vary very little. If you have chosen your fund well, you should be able to stay in it for a considerable number of years, possibly for life. However, this is not guaranteed.

Let's examine the net asset value history of Kemper U.S. Government Securities as an example, over the past 5 years. Table 9-4 gives you the details.

A thorough study of these numbers shows that the net asset value of this particular government fund fluctuation is slight. Thus, if you had invested $10,000 on March 31, 1986, you would have purchased 956 shares with a net asset value of $9,560. Adding the sales charge of $440 brings the total to $10,000. Had you sold all your shares on December 31, 1990, you would have received a check of $8,623, a loss of $1,377.

But why sell? Your reason for buying is to receive income.

During the past 10 years your income stream would have been considerable as Table 9-5 shows.

The monthly checks fluctuate with interest rates. In general, the amount will increase if interest rates rise and decrease if interest rates decline. The fund man-

## TABLE 9-4

### NET ASSET VALUE (NAV)—KEMPER U.S. GOVERNMENT SECURITIES FUND

| Date | | NAV |
|------|-----------|-------|
| 1986 | March 31 | 10.00 |
|      | June 31 | 9.86 |
|      | Sept 30 | 9.81 |
|      | Dec 31 | 9.90 |
| 1987 | March 31 | 9.79 |
|      | June 31 | 9.49 |
|      | Sept 30 | 8.97 |
|      | Dec 31 | 9.14 |
| 1988 | March 31 | 9.20 |
|      | June 31 | 9.07 |
|      | Sept 30 | 8.96 |
|      | Dec 31 | 8.78 |
| 1989 | March 31 | 8.64 |
|      | June 31 | 9.09 |
|      | Sept 30 | 8.95 |
|      | Dec 31 | 9.05 |
| 1990 | March 31 | 8.72 |
|      | June 31 | 8.78 |
|      | Sept 30 | 8.66 |
|      | Dec 31 | 9.02 |

Source: Kemper Financial Services.

ager's objective is to keep the pay-out rate as stable as possible without affecting the net asset value too much.

It is best if, once purchased, you are able to stay in the fund for a considerable number of years and receive an above-average income.

A good mutual fund is a very good investment indeed, considerably better than CDs. For example, on November 27, 1991, a 1-year CD was paying 4.45% at a local New York City bank, as opposed to 8.54% on one of the better U.S. Government mutual funds.

If $10,000 had been invested in the New York bank's 1-year CD, the income would have been $37.08 per month.

## TABLE 9-5

## INCOME FROM KEMPER U.S.
## GOVERNMENT SECURITIES FUND

*(Purchased 1140 shares on 3/31/81 for $10,000)*

| Payble Date | Payout/ Share | Monthly Check |
|---|---|---|
| 4/30/81 | 8.5 cents | $ 96.90 |
| 4/30/82 | 9.0 | 102.60 |
| 4/29/83 | 8.5 | 96.90 |
| 4/27/84 | 8.75 | 99.75 |
| 4/29/85 | 9.0 | 102.60 |
| 5/2/86 | 9.0 | 102.60 |
| 4/30/87 | 8.5 | 96.90 |
| 4/29/88 | 8.0 | 91.20 |
| 4/28/89 | 7.5 | 85.50 |
| 4/30/90 | 7.0 | 85.50 |

*Source:* Kemper Financial Services.

Compare that with the same investment at the same time with Kemper U.S. Government Securities when the pay-out rate was 8.54%. Kemper's check would have been $71.17 per month.

There are many similar funds, whose variations suit them to each individual investor's particular circumstance. Any sound mutual fund will, over all, pay you more than CDs. You may want to review the prospectuses of several such firms in order to decide which one suits your specific investment needs best, or refer to a good investment newsletter. As an example, we have highlighted the important factors concerning Kemper U.S. Government Securities in Exhibit 9-1.

Yield—9.1%.

Performance— 5-year average annual total return = 9.27%.

Load—4.5%.

## EXHIBIT 9-1   KEMPER U.S. GOVERNMENT SECURITIES

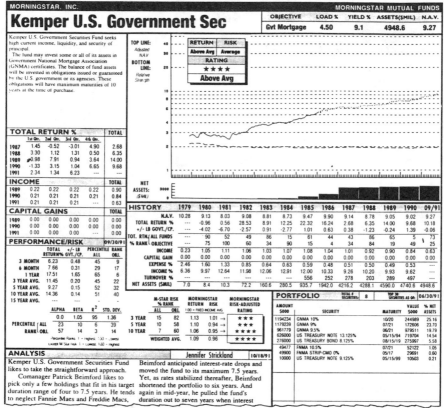

Source: Morningstar, Inc., Chicago, IL.

Summary—Upper left corner.

Portfolio—Middle right column.

## Prospectus

A *prospectus* is the official document that describes a mutual fund in detail. The fund company must provide you with a copy before you invest. It is dated and must be renewed every 16 months. It contains information required by the Securities and Exchange Commission (SEC) on subjects including the fund's objectives and services. The prospectus tells you how you can buy and

sell shares, explains its fee structure, and contains its financial statement. A full description of past performance is included as is the fund's level of risk. The prospectus contains a list of such features as trading over the phone, check writing, transferability to other funds within the same company, and automatic reinvestment of your dividends.

## Fees

When you are dealing with stockbrokers and most financial planners, you should expect to be encouraged to invest in mutual funds that have a sales charge built in. This charge runs from 1% to 8.5%. These charges are less if you invest larger sums. For example Oppenheimer Funds has the following fee schedule:

|  | Equity Funds | Fixed-Income Funds |
|---|---|---|
| Less than $25,000 | 5.75% | 4.75% |
| $25,000 but under $50,000 | 5.50% | 4.75% |
| $50,000 but under $100,000 | 4.75% | 4.50% |
| $100,000 but under $250,000 | 3.75% | 3.5% |

To keep your sales charges down consider using:

- A letter of intent; and/or
- A right of accumulation.

## Letter of Intent

Your *letter of intent* is a simple statement on a company form or a plain piece of paper that you intend to invest $x$ amount of dollars, say $50,000, in an Oppenheimer Equity fund sometime during the next 13 months. Thus, if you are currently only investing, say,

$13,000, your sales charge will be at the third break point—namely, 4.75% instead of 5.75%.

## Right of Accumulation

The *right of accumulation* involves purchasing additional shares of, for instance, the Oppenheimer U.S. Government Trust. Let's say you have owned $30,000 of the fund for a number of years and you decide to buy $70,000 more. If you exercise your right of accumulation your sales charge should be 3.5%, not 4.5%. All you have to do is notify your broker that you have already invested $30,000 in the fund.

## No-Load Funds

Instead of using a stockbroker or commissionable financial planner, you can choose one or more of the 740 *no-load mutual funds*. "No-load" means no sales charge, because you are on your own, with no broker-dealer to pay. If you go this route, using the sources we have already mentioned would be helpful.

## 12b-1 Fees

Instead of the front-end sales charge common to broker/dealers, some funds charge an annual *12b-1 fee* which can run as high as 1.25% for each year you are in the fund. Many such funds also charge a deferred sales charge if you sell your shares during the first few years of ownership. The name "12b-1" comes from a 1980 SEC rule that permitted these fees to help so-called no-load funds pay for distribution costs, such as advertising or for commissions paid to brokers.

## Management Fees

There is an annual fee on most funds for managing your assets. On average, it's 1.26% of the current assets under investment. Some funds have no or very low management fees and others charge as high as 2.0%.

---

### Helpful Hint

*Load Funds versus No-Load Funds— Which Way to Go?*

If you are an average to unsophisticated investor, your best bet is to use the load funds for the following reasons:

- *Fund selection*—There are 3,000 funds on the market today. Which one is best for you? Your broker or planner can be of considerable help, for which he or she is paid a portion of the "load" or sales charge.

- *Buy and Hold*—If you do not sell your shares but, rather, hold them for a 10-year period the sales charge is, so to speak, spread out over those 10 years and is, therefore, equal to about .45% per year.

- *Panic Selling*—This is avoidable if you have a knowledgeable and honest broker. 50% more people sold their no-load funds after the October 1987 Black Monday than did those who had load funds. Presumably their brokers wisely told

them to "hold." As we now
know the paper loss (for those
who did not sell) was re-
covered.

- *Brokers know the score and
  do the work*—Most people do
  not want to be bothered with
  all the work involved in choosing a no-load mutual fund.
  According to the Investment
  Company Institute, 75% of all
  funds purchased in 1988 were
  done through a broker.

## How Is Your Fund Doing?

Once you have purchased your mutual fund, you
can find out its value on any given day by looking in
the "Mutual Funds" section of your newspaper. Most
of the larger dailies have such a section. We have re-
produced part of the September 13, 1991 section of *The
Wall Street Journal* to help analyze its various parts.
(See Exhibit 9-2.)

Let's assume that you have purchased $10,000 of,
say, Fidelity Magellan fund on September 12, 1991. The
next day's paper will show its value.

As you can see, the *buy* price per share on the
Fidelity Magellan fund was $69.71 per share on Sep-
tember 12, 1991 when you bought $10,000 of this fund.
Simple arithmetic shows that you purchased 143.45
shares of the fund. The net asset value of your shares
is shown as $67.62 per share. This means that if you
sold your shares on the same day you would only receive $9,700. The difference of $300 represents your
sales charge. You will note that those funds which have
no sales charge do not have a buy price. You can buy
or sell at that one price (NAV).

## EXHIBIT 9-2 FIDELITY MAGELLAN MUTUAL FUND CLOSING PRICE AS REPORTED IN *THE WALL STREET JOURNAL*, SEPTEMBER 13, 1991

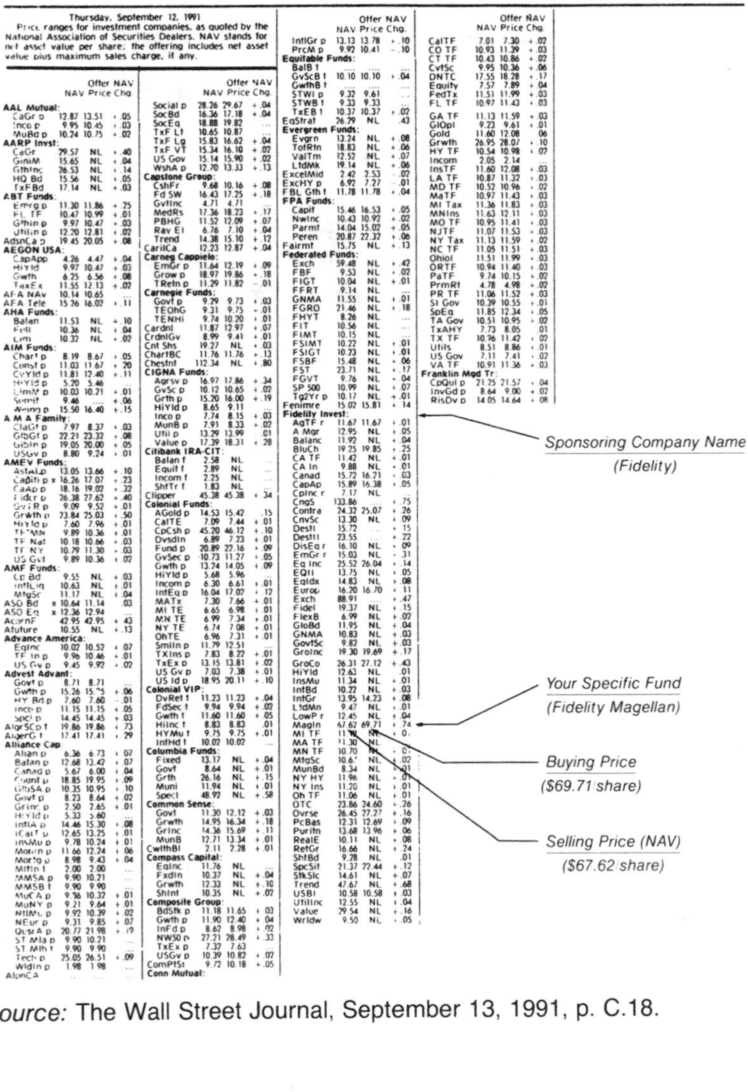
Sponsoring Company Name
(Fidelity)
Your Specific Fund
(Fidelity Magellan)
Buying Price
($69.71/share)
Selling Price (NAV)
($67.62/share)

Thursday, September 12, 1991

Price ranges for investment companies, as quoted by the National Association of Securities Dealers. NAV stands for net asset value per share; the offering includes net asset value plus maximum sales charge, if any.

| | NAV | Offer Price | NAV Chg. |
|---|---|---|---|
| **AAL Mutual:** | | | |
| CaGr p | 12.87 | 13.51 | +.05 |
| Inco p | 9.95 | 10.45 | +.03 |
| MuBd p | 10.24 | 10.75 | +.02 |
| **AARP Invst:** | | | |
| CaGr | 29.57 | NL | +.40 |
| GiniM | 15.65 | NL | +.04 |
| GthInc | 26.53 | NL | +.14 |
| HQ Bd | 15.56 | NL | +.05 |
| TxFBd | 17.14 | NL | +.03 |
| **ABT Funds:** | | | |
| Emrg p | 11.30 | 11.86 | +.25 |
| FL TF | 10.47 | 10.99 | +.01 |
| GthIn p | 9.97 | 10.47 | +.03 |
| UtilIn p | 12.20 | 12.81 | +.02 |
| AdsnCa p | 19.45 | 20.05 | +.08 |
| **AEGON USA:** | | | |
| CapApp | 4.26 | 4.47 | +.04 |
| HiYld | 9.97 | 10.47 | +.03 |
| Gwth | 6.25 | 6.56 | +.08 |
| TaxEx | 11.55 | 12.13 | +.02 |
| AFA NAv | 10.14 | 10.65 | ... |
| AFA Tele | 15.26 | 16.02 | +.11 |
| **AHA Funds:** | | | |
| Balan | 11.53 | NL | +.10 |
| Full | 10.36 | NL | +.04 |
| Lim | 10.32 | NL | +.02 |
| **AIM Funds:** | | | |
| Chart p | 8.19 | 8.67 | +.05 |
| Const p | 11.03 | 11.67 | +.20 |
| CvYld p | 11.81 | 12.40 | +.11 |
| HiYld p | 5.20 | 5.46 | ... |
| LimM p | 10.03 | 10.21 | +.01 |
| Sumit | 9.46 | .... | +.06 |
| Weing p | 15.50 | 16.40 | +.15 |
| **A M A Family:** | | | |
| ClaGt p | 7.97 | 8.37 | +.03 |
| GlbGt p | 22.21 | 23.32 | +.08 |
| GlbIn p | 19.05 | 20.00 | +.05 |
| USGv p | 8.80 | 9.24 | +.01 |
| **AMEV Funds:** | | | |
| AstAl p | 13.05 | 13.66 | +.10 |
| Capiti p x | 16.26 | 17.07 | +.23 |
| CaAp p | 18.16 | 19.02 | +.32 |
| Fidcr p | 26.38 | 27.62 | +.40 |
| GvtR p | 9.09 | 9.52 | +.01 |
| Grwth p | 23.84 | 25.03 | +.50 |
| HiYld p | 7.60 | 7.96 | +.01 |
| TF MN | 9.89 | 10.36 | +.01 |
| TF Nat | 10.18 | 10.66 | +.03 |
| TF NY | 10.79 | 11.30 | +.03 |
| US Gvt | 9.89 | 10.36 | +.02 |
| **AMF Funds:** | | | |
| Cp Bd | 9.55 | NL | +.03 |
| IntlLiq | 10.63 | NL | +.01 |
| MtgSc | 11.17 | NL | +.04 |
| ASO Bd x | 10.64 | 11.14 | .03 |
| ASO Eq x | 12.36 | 12.94 | ... |
| AcornF | 42.95 | 42.95 | +.43 |
| Afuture | 10.55 | NL | +.13 |
| **Advance America:** | | | |
| EqInc | 10.02 | 10.52 | +.07 |
| TF In p | 9.96 | 10.46 | +.01 |
| US Gv p | 9.45 | 9.92 | +.02 |
| **Advest Advant:** | | | |
| Govt p | 8.71 | 8.71 | ... |
| Gwth p | 15.26 | 15.75 | +.06 |
| HY Bd p | 7.60 | 7.60 | -.01 |
| Inco p | 11.15 | 11.15 | +.05 |
| Spcl p | 14.45 | 14.45 | +.03 |
| AlgrSCp t | 19.86 | 19.86 | +.73 |
| AlgerG t | 17.41 | 17.41 | +.29 |
| **Alliance Cap:** | | | |
| Alian p | 6.36 | 6.73 | +.07 |
| Balan p | 12.68 | 13.42 | +.07 |
| Canad p | 5.67 | 6.00 | +.04 |
| Count p | 18.85 | 19.95 | +.09 |
| GlbSA p | 10.35 | 10.95 | +.10 |
| Govt p | 8.23 | 8.64 | +.02 |
| GrInc p | 2.50 | 2.65 | +.01 |
| HiYld p | 5.33 | 5.60 | ... |
| IntlA p | 14.46 | 15.30 | +.08 |
| ICalT p | 12.65 | 13.25 | +.01 |
| InsMu p | 9.78 | 10.24 | +.01 |
| Monin p | 11.66 | 12.24 | +.06 |
| Mortg p | 8.98 | 9.43 | +.04 |
| MitIn t | 2.00 | 2.00 | ... |
| MMSA p | 9.90 | 10.21 | ... |
| MMSB t | 9.90 | 9.90 | ... |
| MuCA p | 9.36 | 10.32 | +.01 |
| MuNY p | 9.21 | 9.64 | +.01 |
| NtlMu p | 9.92 | 10.39 | +.02 |
| NEur p | 9.31 | 9.85 | +.07 |
| QusrA p | 20.77 | 21.98 | +.19 |
| ST Mla p | 9.90 | 10.21 | ... |
| ST Mlb t | 9.90 | 9.90 | ... |
| Tech p | 25.05 | 26.51 | +.09 |
| Wldln p | 1.98 | 1.98 | ... |
| AlonCA | .... | .... | ... |
| Social p | 28.26 | 29.67 | +.04 |
| SocBd | 16.36 | 17.18 | +.04 |
| SocEq | 18.88 | 19.82 | ... |
| TxF Lt | 10.65 | 10.87 | ... |
| TxF Lg | 15.83 | 16.62 | +.04 |
| TxF VT | 15.34 | 16.10 | +.02 |
| US Gov | 15.14 | 15.90 | +.02 |
| WshA p | 12.70 | 13.33 | +.13 |
| **Capstone Group:** | | | |
| CshFr | 9.68 | 10.16 | +.08 |
| Fd SW | 16.43 | 17.25 | +.18 |
| GvtInc | 4.71 | 4.71 | ... |
| MedRs | 17.36 | 18.23 | +.17 |
| PBHG | 11.52 | 12.09 | +.07 |
| Rav EI | 6.76 | 7.10 | +.04 |
| Trend | 14.38 | 15.10 | +.12 |
| CarilCa | 12.23 | 12.87 | +.04 |
| **Carneg Cappielo:** | | | |
| EmGr p | 11.64 | 12.19 | +.09 |
| Grow p | 18.97 | 19.86 | +.18 |
| TRetn p | 11.29 | 11.82 | -.01 |
| **Carnegie Funds:** | | | |
| Govt p | 9.29 | 9.73 | +.03 |
| TEOhG | 9.31 | 9.75 | -.01 |
| TENHi | 9.74 | 10.20 | +.01 |
| Cardnl | 11.87 | 12.97 | +.07 |
| CrdnlGv | 8.99 | 9.41 | +.01 |
| Cnt Shs | 19.27 | NL | +.03 |
| ChartBC | 11.76 | 11.76 | +.13 |
| Chestnt | 112.34 | NL | +.80 |
| **CIGNA Funds:** | | | |
| Agrsv p | 16.97 | 17.86 | +.34 |
| GvSc p | 10.12 | 10.65 | +.02 |
| Grth p | 15.20 | 16.00 | +.19 |
| HiYld p | 8.65 | 9.11 | ... |
| Inco p | 7.74 | 8.15 | +.03 |
| MunB p | 7.91 | 8.33 | +.02 |
| Util p | 13.29 | 13.99 | .01 |
| Value p | 17.39 | 18.31 | +.28 |
| **Citibank IRA-CIT:** | | | |
| Balan f | 2.58 | NL | ... |
| Equit f | 2.89 | NL | ... |
| Incom f | 2.25 | NL | ... |
| ShtTr f | 1.83 | NL | ... |
| Clipper | 45.38 | 45.38 | +.34 |
| **Colonial Funds:** | | | |
| AGold p | 14.53 | 15.42 | .15 |
| CalTE | 7.09 | 7.44 | +.01 |
| CpCsh p | 45.20 | 46.12 | +.10 |
| DvsdIn | 6.89 | 7.23 | +.01 |
| Fund p | 20.89 | 22.16 | +.09 |
| GvSec p | 10.73 | 11.27 | +.05 |
| Gwth p | 13.74 | 14.05 | +.09 |
| HiYld p | 5.68 | 5.96 | ... |
| Incom p | 6.30 | 6.61 | +.01 |
| IntEq p | 16.04 | 17.02 | +.12 |
| MATx | 7.30 | 7.66 | +.01 |
| MI TE | 6.65 | 6.98 | +.01 |
| MN TE | 6.99 | 7.34 | +.01 |
| NY TE | 6.74 | 7.08 | +.01 |
| OhTE | 6.96 | 7.31 | +.01 |
| SmlIn p | 11.79 | 12.51 | ... |
| TXIns p | 7.83 | 8.22 | +.01 |
| TxEx p | 13.15 | 13.81 | +.02 |
| US Gv p | 7.03 | 7.38 | +.01 |
| US Id p | 18.95 | 20.11 | +.10 |
| **Colonial VIP:** | | | |
| DvRet t | 11.23 | 11.23 | +.04 |
| FdSec t | 9.94 | 9.94 | +.02 |
| Gwth t | 11.60 | 11.60 | +.05 |
| HiInc t | 8.83 | 8.83 | .01 |
| HYMu t | 9.75 | 9.75 | +.01 |
| IntHd t | 10.02 | 10.02 | ... |
| **Columbia Funds:** | | | |
| Fixed | 13.17 | NL | +.04 |
| Govt | 8.64 | NL | +.01 |
| Grth | 26.16 | NL | +.15 |
| Muni | 11.94 | NL | +.01 |
| Specl | 48.92 | NL | +.58 |
| **Common Sense:** | | | |
| Govt | 11.30 | 12.12 | +.03 |
| Grwth | 14.95 | 16.34 | +.18 |
| GrInc | 14.36 | 15.69 | +.11 |
| MunB | 12.71 | 13.34 | +.01 |
| CwlthBI | 2.11 | 2.28 | +.01 |
| **Compass Capital:** | | | |
| EqInc | 11.76 | NL | ... |
| FxdIn | 10.37 | NL | +.04 |
| Grwth | 12.33 | NL | +.10 |
| ShInt | 10.35 | NL | +.02 |
| **Composite Group:** | | | |
| BdStk p | 11.18 | 11.65 | +.03 |
| Gwth p | 11.90 | 12.40 | +.04 |
| InFd p | 8.62 | 8.98 | +.02 |
| NW50 p | 27.21 | 28.49 | +.33 |
| TxEx p | 7.32 | 7.63 | ... |
| USGv p | 10.39 | 10.82 | +.02 |
| ComPtSt | 9.72 | 10.18 | +.05 |
| **Conn Mutual:** | | | |
| IntlGr p | 13.13 | 13.78 | +.10 |
| PrcM p | 9.92 | 10.41 | -.10 |
| **Equitable Funds:** | | | |
| BalB t | .... | .... | ... |
| GvScB t | 10.10 | 10.10 | +.04 |
| GwthB t | .... | .... | ... |
| STWI p | 9.32 | 9.61 | ... |
| STWB t | 9.33 | 9.33 | ... |
| TxEB t | 10.37 | 10.37 | +.02 |
| EqStrat | 26.29 | NL | .43 |
| **Evergreen Funds:** | | | |
| Evgrn | 13.24 | NL | +.08 |
| TotRtn | 18.83 | NL | +.06 |
| ValTm | 12.52 | NL | +.07 |
| LtdMk | 19.14 | NL | +.06 |
| ExcelMid | 2.42 | 2.53 | -.02 |
| ExcHY p | 6.92 | 7.27 | -.01 |
| FBL Gth t | 11.78 | 11.78 | +.04 |
| **FPA Funds:** | | | |
| Capit | 15.46 | 16.53 | +.05 |
| NwInc | 10.43 | 10.92 | +.02 |
| Parmt | 14.04 | 15.02 | +.05 |
| Peren | 20.87 | 22.32 | +.06 |
| Fairmt | 15.75 | NL | +.13 |
| **Federated Funds:** | | | |
| Exch | 59.48 | NL | +.42 |
| FBF | 9.53 | NL | +.02 |
| FIGT | 10.04 | NL | +.01 |
| FFRT | 9.14 | NL | ... |
| GNMA | 11.55 | NL | +.01 |
| FGRO | 21.46 | NL | +.18 |
| FHYT | 8.26 | NL | ... |
| FIT | 10.56 | NL | ... |
| FIMT | 10.15 | NL | ... |
| FSIMT | 10.22 | NL | +.01 |
| FSIGT | 10.23 | NL | +.01 |
| FSBF | 15.48 | NL | +.06 |
| FST | 23.71 | NL | +.17 |
| FGVT | 9.76 | NL | +.04 |
| SP 500 | 10.99 | NL | +.07 |
| Tg2Yr p | 10.17 | NL | +.01 |
| Fenimre | 15.02 | 15.81 | +.14 |
| **Fidelity Invest:** | | | |
| AgTF r | 11.67 | 11.67 | +.01 |
| A Mgr | 12.95 | NL | +.05 |
| Balanc | 11.92 | NL | +.04 |
| BluCh | 19.25 | 19.85 | +.25 |
| CA TF | 11.42 | NL | +.01 |
| CA In | 9.88 | NL | +.01 |
| Canad | 15.72 | 16.21 | -.03 |
| CapAp | 15.89 | 16.38 | +.05 |
| CpInc r | 7.17 | NL | ... |
| CngS | 133.86 | .... | +.75 |
| Contra | 24.32 | 25.07 | +.26 |
| CnvSc | 13.30 | NL | +.09 |
| DestI | 15.72 | .... | +.15 |
| DestII | 23.55 | .... | +.22 |
| DisEq r | 16.10 | NL | +.09 |
| EmGr r | 15.03 | NL | -.31 |
| Eq Inc | 25.52 | 26.04 | +.14 |
| EQII | 13.75 | NL | +.05 |
| EqIdx | 14.83 | NL | +.08 |
| Europ | 16.20 | 16.70 | +.11 |
| Exch | 88.91 | .... | +.47 |
| Fidel | 19.37 | NL | +.15 |
| FlexB | 6.99 | NL | +.02 |
| GloBd | 11.95 | NL | +.04 |
| GNMA | 10.83 | NL | +.03 |
| GovtSc | 9.82 | NL | +.03 |
| GroInc | 19.30 | 19.69 | +.17 |
| GroCo | 26.31 | 27.12 | +.43 |
| HiYld | 12.63 | NL | .01 |
| InsMu | 11.34 | NL | +.01 |
| IntBd | 10.22 | NL | +.03 |
| IntGr | 13.95 | 14.23 | +.08 |
| LtdMn | 9.47 | NL | +.01 |
| LowP r | 12.45 | NL | +.04 |
| Magln | 67.62 | 69.71 | +.74 |
| MI TF | 11.[illegible] | NL | +0.[illegible] |
| MA TF | 11.30 | NL | [illegible] |
| MN TF | 10.70 | NL | -.0[illegible] |
| MtgSc | 10.6[illegible] | NL | +.02 |
| MunBd | 8.34 | NL | +.01 |
| NY HY | 11.96 | NL | +.0[illegible] |
| NY Ins | 11.20 | NL | +.01 |
| Oh TF | 11.06 | NL | +.01 |
| OTC | 23.86 | 24.60 | +.26 |
| Ovrse | 26.45 | 27.27 | +.16 |
| PcBas | 12.31 | 12.69 | +.09 |
| Puritn | 13.68 | 13.96 | +.06 |
| RealE | 10.11 | NL | +.08 |
| RetGr | 16.66 | NL | +.24 |
| ShtBd | 9.28 | NL | .01 |
| SpcSit | 21.37 | 22.44 | +.12 |
| StkSlc | 14.61 | NL | +.07 |
| Trend | 47.67 | NL | +.68 |
| USBI | 10.58 | 10.58 | +.03 |
| UtilInc | 12.55 | NL | +.04 |
| Value | 29.54 | NL | +.16 |
| Wrldw | 9.50 | NL | +.05 |
| CalTF | 7.01 | 7.30 | +.02 |
| CO TF | 10.93 | 11.39 | +.03 |
| CT TF | 10.43 | 10.86 | +.02 |
| CvtSc | 9.95 | 10.36 | +.06 |
| DNTC | 17.55 | 18.28 | +.17 |
| Equity | 7.57 | 7.89 | +.04 |
| FedTx | 11.51 | 11.99 | +.03 |
| FL TF | 10.97 | 11.43 | +.03 |
| GA TF | 11.13 | 11.59 | +.03 |
| GlOpl | 9.23 | 9.61 | +.01 |
| Gold | 11.60 | 12.08 | .06 |
| Grwth | 26.95 | 28.07 | +.10 |
| HY TF | 10.54 | 10.98 | +.07 |
| Incom | 2.05 | 2.14 | ... |
| InsTF | 11.60 | 12.08 | +.03 |
| LA TF | 10.87 | 11.32 | +.03 |
| MD TF | 10.52 | 10.96 | +.02 |
| MaTF | 10.97 | 11.43 | +.03 |
| MI Tax | 11.36 | 11.83 | +.03 |
| MNIns | 11.63 | 12.11 | +.03 |
| MO TF | 10.95 | 11.41 | +.03 |
| NJTF | 11.07 | 11.53 | +.03 |
| NY Tax | 11.13 | 11.59 | +.02 |
| NC TF | 11.05 | 11.51 | +.03 |
| OhioI | 11.51 | 11.99 | +.03 |
| ORTF | 10.94 | 11.40 | +.03 |
| PaTF | 9.74 | 10.15 | +.02 |
| PrmRt | 4.78 | 4.98 | +.02 |
| PR TF | 11.06 | 11.52 | +.03 |
| SI Gov | 10.39 | 10.55 | +.01 |
| SpEq | 11.85 | 12.34 | +.05 |
| TA Gov | 10.51 | 10.95 | +.02 |
| TxAHY | 7.73 | 8.05 | .01 |
| TX TF | 10.96 | 11.42 | +.02 |
| Utils | 8.51 | 8.86 | +.01 |
| US Gov | 7.11 | 7.41 | +.02 |
| VA TF | 10.91 | 11.36 | +.03 |
| **Franklin Mgd Tr:** | | | |
| CpQul p | 21.25 | 21.57 | +.04 |
| InvGd p | 8.64 | 9.00 | +.02 |
| RisDv p | 14.05 | 14.64 | +.08 |

*Source:* The Wall Street Journal, September 13, 1991, p. C.18.

Anytime you want to figure what you can sell your shares for, look up the net asset value and multiply that by the number of shares you own. This computation is done for you by the sponsoring company, usually at the end of each month, and is included in your statement.

## An Example of a Growth Fund

We could show a comparison with all *growth* funds, but our objective here is not to make an exhaustive study but, rather, to give you an overview of the fund selection process—that is, how one goes about selecting a fund. The *Morningstar* report on Phoenix Growth fund gives a good representative example of how one good growth fund is rated.

We have selected Phoenix Growth because of its excellent track record over the past 10 years. (See Exhibit 9-3.) It is also part of an exceptionally fine family of funds. This is important should you want to move out of the growth area with all or part of your investment. This can be done at any time. In our *asset allocation* approach to investing, as shown in Chapter 10, the feature of transferability from one fund to another is shown to be quite important.

We highlight what we consider to be the most important features of Phoenix Growth Fund:

### Average Annual Total Return

(Total return includes both income and growth)

|         |        |
|---------|--------|
| 1 Year  | 13.45% |
| 5 Year  | 12.62% |
| 10 Year | 19.46% |

These are average annual returns for this fund for the respective number of years, counting back from June 30, 1991.

### Total Return (Year by Year)

|      |                   |
|------|-------------------|
| 1991 | 13.56 (to 7/1/91) |
| 1990 | 6.05              |
| 1989 | 27.47             |

## EXHIBIT 9-3  PHOENIX GROWTH FUND

MORNINGSTAR, INC.                                                                                          MUTUAL FUND VALUES

# Phoenix Growth

| OBJECTIVE | LOAD % | YIELD % | ASSETS($MIL) | N.A.V. |
|---|---|---|---|---|
| Growth | 4.75 | 2.5 | 906.1 | 21.26 |

Phoenix Growth Fund Series seeks long-term appreciation of capital. Any income will be incidental.
The fund invests primarily in common stocks of companies believed to have appreciation potential. However, any amount of its assets may be designated for any type of security, as long as these investments will further the fund's investment objective. The fund may also write covered call options on certain securities in its portfolio.

**TOP LINE:** Adjusted N.A.V.  **BOTTOM LINE:** Relative Strength

| RETURN | RISK |
|---|---|
| High | Low |

RATING
★★★★★ Highest

### TOTAL RETURN %

| | 1st Qtr. | 2nd Qtr. | 3rd Qtr. | 4th Qtr. | TOTAL |
|---|---|---|---|---|---|
| 1987 | 17.93 | 2.84 | 5.43 | -13.04 | 11.19 |
| 1988 | 1.84 | 2.66 | 1.08 | 1.20 | 6.95 |
| 1989 | 4.99 | 6.38 | 9.12 | 4.59 | 27.47 |
| 1990 | -1.72 | 7.98 | -7.44 | 7.97 | 6.05 |
| 1991 | 15.69 | -1.84 | — | — | — |

### INCOME

| | | | | | TOTAL |
|---|---|---|---|---|---|
| 1989 | 0.00 | 0.34 | 0.00 | 0.33 | 0.67 |
| 1990 | 0.00 | 0.29 | 0.00 | 0.39 | 0.68 |
| 1991 | 0.00 | 0.16 | — | — | 0.16 |

### CAPITAL GAINS

| | | | | | TOTAL |
|---|---|---|---|---|---|
| 1989 | 0.00 | 0.00 | 0.00 | 0.28 | 0.28 |
| 1990 | 0.00 | 0.00 | 0.00 | 0.77 | 0.77 |
| 1991 | 0.00 | 0.00 | — | — | 0.00 |

### PERFORMANCE/RISK 04/30/91

| | TOTAL RETURN % | +/- S&P 500 | PERCENTILE ALL | RANK OBL. |
|---|---|---|---|---|
| 3 MONTH | -1.84 | -1.56 | 77 | 66 |
| 6 MONTH | 13.56 | -0.71 | 42 | 70 |
| 1 YEAR | 13.49 | 6.08 | 6 | 6 |
| 3 YEAR AVG. | 16.23 | 1.56 | 7 | 15 |
| 5 YEAR AVG. | 12.62 | 0.71 | 8 | 13 |
| 10 YEAR AVG. | 19.46 | 3.96 | 1 | 3 |
| 15 YEAR AVG. | 17.92 | 4.33 | 9 | 18 |

| | ALPHA | BETA | R² | STD. DEV. |
|---|---|---|---|---|
| | 2.8 | 0.77 | 92 | 3.35 |
| PERCENTILE ALL | 8 | 69 | 17 | 82 |
| RANK OBL. | 9 | 92 | 22 | 94 |

Percentile Ranks: 1 = Highest, 100 = Lowest
Except MFV Risk: 1 = Lowest, 100 = Highest

| | MFV RISK % RANK | | MFV RETURN | MFV RISK | MFV RISK-ADJUSTED |
|---|---|---|---|---|---|
| | ALL | OBL. | 1.00 = EQUITY AVG. | | RATING |
| 3 YEAR | 35 | 4 | 1.61 | 0.59 → | ★★★★★ |
| 5 YEAR | 45 | 7 | 1.50 | 0.72 → | ★★★★★ |
| 10 YEAR | 38 | 5 | 1.67 | 0.65 → | ★★★★★ |
| WEIGHTED AVG. | | | 1.61 | 0.66 | ★★★★★ |

### HISTORY

| | 1979 | 1980 | 1981 | 1982 | 1983 | 1984 | 1985 | 1986 | 1987 | 1988 | 1989 | 1990 | 06/91 |
|---|---|---|---|---|---|---|---|---|---|---|---|---|---|
| N.A.V. | 9.47 | 9.46 | 9.04 | 12.27 | 12.43 | 13.21 | 16.43 | 16.40 | 15.18 | 15.82 | 19.15 | 18.86 | 21.26 |
| TOTAL RETURN % | 33.05 | 46.24 | 1.79 | 42.51 | 28.41 | 10.15 | 32.32 | 19.24 | 11.19 | 6.95 | 27.47 | 6.05 | 13.56 |
| +/- S&P 500 INDEX | 14.75 | 14.02 | 6.87 | 21.05 | 5.95 | 4.02 | 0.68 | 0.61 | 5.97 | -9.56 | -4.20 | 9.15 | -0.71 |
| TOT. RTN/ALL FUNDS | 22 | 14 | 46 | 10 | 15 | 24 | 18 | 25 | 12 | 82 | 25 | 21 | 42 |
| % RANK OBJECTIVE | 40 | 24 | 36 | 12 | 18 | 8 | 29 | 20 | 12 | 85 | 46 | 3 | 70 |
| INCOME | 0.27 | 0.78 | 0.59 | 0.62 | 0.49 | 0.42 | 0.62 | 0.34 | 0.57 | 0.41 | 0.67 | 0.68 | 0.16 |
| CAPITAL GAIN | 0.00 | 3.05 | 0.00 | 0.00 | 2.86 | 0.00 | 0.32 | 2.91 | 2.56 | 0.00 | 0.28 | 0.77 | 0.00 |
| EXPENSE % | 0.97 | 0.96 | 0.98 | 1.06 | 0.90 | 0.88 | 0.82 | 0.78 | 0.71 | 0.85 | 1.06 | 1.01 | — |
| INCOME % | 3.97 | 4.19 | 6.24 | 6.18 | 3.80 | 4.83 | 3.87 | 2.68 | 2.64 | 2.48 | 3.79 | 3.37 | — |
| TURNOVER % | 56 | 90 | 179 | 213 | 208 | 150 | 151 | 170 | 185 | 221 | 180 | 203 | — |
| NET ASSETS ($MIL) | 24.1 | 25.2 | 37.6 | 47.1 | 66.1 | 76.2 | 112.3 | 271.9 | 523.4 | 587.2 | 715.8 | 743.5 | 906.1 |

### PORTFOLIO

TOTAL # STOCKS: 63   TOP 30 EQUITY HOLDINGS AS OF: 03/31/91

| SHARE CHANGE | AMOUNT | STOCK | VALUE $000 | % NET ASSETS |
|---|---|---|---|---|
| 0 | 400000 | PFIZER | 42800 | 4.72 |
| 150000 | 600000 | GENERAL ELECTRIC | 41850 | 4.62 |
| 500000 | 500000 | HEWLETT-PACKARD | 25000 | 2.76 |
| 400000 | 700000 | BAXTER INTERNATIONAL | 23275 | 2.57 |
| 100000 | 300000 | WARNER-LAMBERT | 22388 | 2.47 |
| -25000 | 225000 | AMERICAN INTERNATIONAL GROUP | 21684 | 2.39 |
| -25000 | 275000 | BRISTOL-MYERS SQUIBB | 21484 | 2.37 |
| -90000 | 150000 | AMGEN | 19688 | 2.17 |
| 90000 | 490000 | WASTE MANAGEMENT | 19355 | 2.14 |
| 425000 | 425000 | LIZ CLAIBORNE | 18222 | 2.01 |
| -50000 | 250000 | CHUBB | 17909 | 1.98 |
| 0 | 300000 | MELVILLE | 15863 | 1.75 |

### ANALYSIS

Strickland/Gillis  07/26/91

It's hard to think up any complaints about Phoenix Growth Fund.
Comanager Robert Chesek has mastered whose price multiples are cheap relative to their current and projected growth rates.)
As of now, the fund is highly concentrated

*Source:* Morningstar, Inc., Chicago, IL.

## Total Return (Year by Year) (*Continued*)

| | |
|---|---|
| 1988 | 6.95 |
| 1987 | 11.19 |
| 1986 | 19.24 |
| 1985 | 32.32 |
| 1984 | 10.15 |
| 1983 | 28.41 |
| 1982 | 42.51 |
| 1981 | 1.79 |
| 1980 | 46.24 |

Notice that there were only 3 out of the 10 years which had low total returns. The return in 1981 was 1.79%, in 1988 it was 6.95, and in 1990 it was 6.05. Notice, too, in the crash year of 1987 there was a gain of 11.19%. The other years as you can see had sizable growth.

## Global Investing

Having examined the question of global investing in some detail in the previous chapter, we will now turn our attention to how the average investor can get into the act without worrying about which stock to buy, when to buy, and when to sell.

Both CDA and *Morningstar* give priority to such funds as Oppenheimer Global, Putnam Global Growth, G.T. International Growth, Templeton Foreign, and Dreyfus Strategic World Investing to name a few. Remember, there are others, but we cannot spend time on all the excellent choices here, now.

For simplicity sake we will again examine one fund— Oppenheimer Global. *Morningstar's* partial report is shown in Exhibit 9-4.

Let's examine Oppenheimer's total return record:

### EXHIBIT 9-4   OPPENHEIMER GLOBAL

**MORNINGSTAR, INC.**                                                          **MORNINGSTAR MUTUAL FUNDS**

# Oppenheimer Global

| OBJECTIVE | LOAD % | YIELD % | ASSETS($MIL) | N.A.V. |
|---|---|---|---|---|
| Intl Stock | 5.75 | 0.3 | 913.0 | 30.14 |

Oppenheimer Global Fund seeks capital appreciation. Current income is not an objective. Using a global approach, the fund emphasizes investment in common stocks or convertible securities of growth-type companies. The fund may also invest in securities of cyclical industries and special situations.

In its operations, the fund may use special investment techniques, such as hedging, borrowing money for investment in securities, short-term trading, and placement of up to 10% of its assets in restricted securities.

Prior to February 1, 1987, the fund was named Oppenheimer A.I.M. Fund.

TOP LINE: Adjusted NAV
BOTTOM LINE: Relative Strength

| RETURN | RISK |
|---|---|
| Above Avg | Average |

**RATING**
★★★★
**Above Avg**

**TOTAL RETURN %**

| | 1st Qtr. | 2nd Qtr. | 3rd Qtr. | 4th Qtr. | TOTAL |
|---|---|---|---|---|---|
| 1987 | 16.56 | 6.64 | 14.13 | -31.95 | -3.46 |
| 1988 | 8.82 | 6.08 | -4.73 | 11.84 | 22.99 |
| 1989 | 10.08 | 3.51 | 12.12 | 5.71 | 35.05 |
| 1990 | 4.55 | 8.75 | -16.15 | 4.18 | -0.68 |
| 1991 | 8.71 | -3.72 | — | — | — |

**INCOME**

| | 1st Qtr. | 2nd Qtr. | 3rd Qtr. | 4th Qtr. | TOTAL |
|---|---|---|---|---|---|
| 1989 | 0.00 | 0.00 | 0.00 | 0.11 | 0.11 |
| 1990 | 0.00 | 0.00 | 0.00 | 0.08 | 0.08 |
| 1991 | 0.00 | 0.00 | 0.00 | — | — |

**CAPITAL GAINS**

| | 1st Qtr. | 2nd Qtr. | 3rd Qtr. | 4th Qtr. | TOTAL |
|---|---|---|---|---|---|
| 1989 | 0.00 | 0.00 | 0.00 | 3.00 | 3.00 |
| 1990 | 0.00 | 0.00 | 0.00 | 1.69 | 1.69 |
| 1991 | 0.00 | 0.00 | 0.00 | — | — |

NET ASSETS

**PERFORMANCE/RISK** 07/31/91

| | TOTAL RETURN % | +/- S&P 500 | +/- EAFE | PERCENTILE RANK ALL | RANK OBJ |
|---|---|---|---|---|---|
| 3 MONTH | 4.25 | 0.11 | 6.03 | 21 | 9 |
| 6 MONTH | 11.42 | -3.17 | 8.20 | 36 | 22 |
| 1 YEAR | -8.63 | -21.42 | -0.15 | 95 | 57 |
| 3 YEAR AVG. | 17.48 | 0.93 | 16.89 | 8 | 3 |
| 5 YEAR AVG. | 14.09 | -0.17 | 3.84 | 10 | 20 |
| 10 YEAR AVG. | 15.00 | -1.02 | -2.70 | 23 | 55 |
| 15 YEAR AVG. | 17.53 | 3.55 | 0.88 | 12 | 8 |

| | ALPHA | BETA | R² | STD. DEV. |
|---|---|---|---|---|
| | 3.6 | 0.76 | 41 | 5.07 |
| PERCENTILE ALL | 7 | 70 | 88 | 31 |
| RANK OBJ. | 6 | 54 | 61 | 40 |

Percentile Ranks: 1 = Highest, 100 = Lowest
Except MMF Risk: 1 = Lowest, 100 = Highest

**HISTORY**

| | 1979 | 1980 | 1981 | 1982 | 1983 | 1984 | 1985 | 1986 | 1987 | 1988 | 1989 | 1990 | 07/91 |
|---|---|---|---|---|---|---|---|---|---|---|---|---|---|
| N.A.V. | 15.75 | 22.44 | 15.73 | 17.58 | 19.50 | 14.33 | 21.25 | 26.99 | 20.86 | 23.82 | 28.98 | 26.99 | 30.14 |
| TOTAL RETURN % | 56.51 | 55.82 | -11.13 | 14.12 | 26.12 | -21.77 | 49.11 | 46.54 | -3.46 | 22.99 | 35.05 | -0.68 | 11.67 |
| +/- S & P 500 INDEX | 38.21 | 23.60 | -6.05 | -7.34 | 3.66 | -27.90 | 17.47 | 27.91 | -8.68 | 6.48 | 3.38 | 2.42 | -8.03 |
| +/- EAFE INDEX | 51.76 | 33.24 | -8.85 | 15.98 | 2.43 | -29.16 | -7.05 | -22.90 | -28.09 | -5.28 | 24.51 | 22.77 | 5.11 |
| TOT. RTN: ALL FUNDS | 4 | 7 | 91 | 87 | 21 | 97 | 2 | 3 | 82 | 11 | 10 | 40 | 61 |
| % RANK: OBJECTIVE | 7 | 13 | 95 | 32 | 74 | 100 | 27 | 44 | 88 | 19 | 17 | 6 | 35 |
| INCOME | 0.31 | 0.25 | 0.33 | 0.32 | 0.17 | 0.06 | 0.10 | 0.11 | 0.07 | 0.09 | 0.11 | 0.08 | 0.00 |
| CAPITAL GAIN | 0.00 | 1.64 | 3.73 | 0.00 | 2.50 | 0.93 | 0.00 | 3.87 | 5.62 | 1.73 | 3.00 | 1.69 | 0.00 |
| EXPENSE % | 1.09 | 1.11 | 1.20 | 1.02 | 1.00 | 1.48 | 1.21 | 1.60 | 1.49 | 1.89 | 1.90 | 1.68 | — |
| INCOME % | 2.39 | 1.46 | 1.55 | 2.10 | 0.82 | 0.35 | 0.81 | 0.47 | 0.16 | 0.15 | 0.73 | 0.16 | — |
| TURNOVER % | 143 | 199 | 150 | 102 | 91 | 50 | 29 | 25 | 37 | 27 | 63 | 27 | — |
| NET ASSETS ($MIL) | 164.4 | 220.0 | 190.9 | 189.0 | 285.6 | 245.7 | 231.7 | 387.6 | 370.7 | 414.9 | 566.8 | 805.0 | 913.0 |

| M-STAR RISK % RANK | | MORNINGSTAR RETURN RISK | | MORNINGSTAR RISK-ADJUSTED RATING |
|---|---|---|---|---|
| | ALL | OBJ. | | |
| 3 YEAR | 66 | 24 | 1.39  0.92 → | ★★★★ |
| 5 YEAR | 66 | 45 | 1.29  0.92 → | ★★★★ |
| 10 YEAR | 82 | 74 | 1.16  1.09 → | ★★★ |
| WEIGHTED AVG. | | | 1.24  1.01 | ★★★★ |

**PORTFOLIO**   TOTAL # STOCKS: 111   TOP 30 EQUITY HOLDINGS AS OF: 03/30/91

| SHARE CHANGE | AMOUNT | STOCK | VALUE $000 | % NET ASSETS |
|---|---|---|---|---|
| 0 | 330000 | AMGEN | 43313 | 4.69 |
| 74200 | 364000 | ASTRA CL A | 32414 | 3.51 |
| 0 | 1914000 | BOMBARDIER CL B | 28703 | 3.11 |
| 26150 | 395300 | NOVO NORDISK | 24545 | 2.66 |
| 350400 | 791700 | GAMBRO CL B | 23115 | 2.50 |
| -4000 | 1346000 | SAGA PETROLEUM CL A | 21175 | 2.36 |
| 0 | 125000 | CANAL PLUS | 20940 | 2.27 |
| -280 | 34500 | BBC BROWN BOVERI | 19714 | 2.13 |
| 4665 | 44665 | GOLDSCHMIDT | 18572 | 2.01 |
| 0 | 137250 | KONE-OY CL B | 17688 | 1.91 |

**ANALYSIS**                                    Jennifer Strickland   08/23/91

Oppenheimer Global Fund is betting that blondes have more fun.   telecommunications, and construction/engineering as prime investment sectors. In

*Source:* Morningstar, Inc., Chicago, IL.

## AVERAGE ANNUAL TOTAL RETURN
## (INCLUDES DIVIDENDS AND
## CAPITAL GAINS)

| 3 Year  | 17.48% |
|---------|--------|
| 5 Year  | 14.09% |
| 10 Year | 15.00% |

### YEAR BY YEAR—TOTAL RETURN

| Year | Total Return |
|------|--------------|
| 1991 | 11.67 (to 7/31/91) |
| 1990 | (0.68) |
| 1989 | 35.05 |
| 1988 | 22.99 |
| 1987 | (3.46) |
| 1986 | 46.54 |
| 1985 | 49.11 |
| 1984 | (21.77) |
| 1983 | 26.12 |
| 1982 | 14.12 |
| 1981 | (11.13) |
| 1980 | 55.82 |

Notice that the returns on the global fund are much more volatile than the domestic stock fund (Phoenix Growth).

## Municipals

In the municipal (tax-free) mutual fund category, *Morningstar*, for instance, gives a list of "above-average" funds. A few good ones are Nuveen Municipal Bond Fund, MFS Managed Municipal Bond Trust, Colonial Tax-Exempt Fund, and Calvert Tax-Free Reserve Limited Term, for example. These are free of federal taxes. There are numerous other good examples, but your broker can fill you in. Nuveen Municipal Bond Fund is one of the best, Morningstar's analysis is shown in Exhibit 9-5.

## EXHIBIT 9-5   NUVEEN MUNICIPAL BOND FUND

MORNINGSTAR, INC.     MORNINGSTAR MUTUAL FUNDS

### Nuveen Municipal Bond

| OBJECTIVE | LOAD % | YIELD % | ASSETS($MIL) | N.A.V. |
|---|---|---|---|---|
| Muni General | 4.75 | 6.5 | 1550.8 | 9.04 |

Nuveen Municipal Bond Fund seeks as high a level of federally tax-exempt, current interest income as is consistent with capital preservation.

The fund intends to invest at least 80% of its assets in municipal bonds rated BBB or higher. The fund plans to emphasize municipals with long-term maturities.

Besides investing in general obligation and revenue bonds, the fund may also invest in lease obligations or installment purchase contract obligations. But, the fund will not invest more than 10% of its assets in those that contain "non-appropriation" clauses.

TOP LINE: Adjusted N.A.V.   BOTTOM LINE: Relative Strength

| RETURN | RISK |
|---|---|
| Average | Below Avg |

RATING ★★★★ Above Avg

### TOTAL RETURN %

| | 1st Qtr. | 2nd Qtr. | 3rd Qtr. | 4th Qtr. | TOTAL |
|---|---|---|---|---|---|
| 1987 | 2.25 | -3.88 | -2.26 | 6.36 | 2.17 |
| 1988 | 2.24 | 2.40 | 2.80 | 2.58 | 10.41 |
| 1989 | 1.04 | 5.98 | 0.21 | 3.33 | 10.87 |
| 1990 | 0.22 | 2.30 | 0.10 | 3.57 | 6.29 |
| 1991 | 2.38 | 2.34 | 3.35 | --- | --- |

### INCOME

| | | | | | TOTAL |
|---|---|---|---|---|---|
| 1989 | 0.15 | 0.15 | 0.15 | 0.15 | 0.60 |
| 1990 | 0.15 | 0.15 | 0.15 | 0.15 | 0.60 |
| 1991 | 0.15 | 0.15 | 0.15 | 0.05 | 0.49 |

### CAPITAL GAINS

| | | | | | TOTAL |
|---|---|---|---|---|---|
| 1989 | 0.00 | 0.00 | 0.03 | 0.00 | 0.03 |
| 1990 | 0.00 | 0.00 | 0.00 | 0.04 | 0.04 |
| 1991 | 0.00 | 0.00 | 0.00 | --- | 0.00 |

### PERFORMANCE/RISK

09/30/91

| | TOTAL RETURN% | +/- LB GVT./CP. | PERCENTILE RANK ALL | PERCENTILE RANK OBJ. |
|---|---|---|---|---|
| 3 MONTH | 3.35 | -2.40 | 86 | 83 |
| 6 MONTH | 5.77 | -1.58 | 59 | 62 |
| 1 YEAR | 12.15 | -3.71 | 82 | 63 |
| 3 YEAR AVG. | 9.39 | -1.86 | 58 | 20 |
| 5 YEAR AVG. | 8.36 | -0.76 | 57 | 11 |
| 10 YEAR AVG. | 12.82 | -1.40 | 73 | 58 |
| 15 YEAR AVG. | --- | --- | --- | --- |

| | ALPHA | BETA | R² | STD. DEV. |
|---|---|---|---|---|
| | -0.4 | 0.65 | 64 | 1.02 |
| PERCENTILE ALL | 28 | 69 | 69 | 76 |
| RANK OBL | 10 | 71 | 73 | 65 |

Percentile Ranks: 1 = Highest, 100 = Lowest
Except M-Star Risk: 1 = Lowest, 100 = Highest

### HISTORY

| | 1979 | 1980 | 1981 | 1982 | 1983 | 1984 | 1985 | 1986 | 1987 | 1988 | 1989 | 1990 | 09/91 |
|---|---|---|---|---|---|---|---|---|---|---|---|---|---|
| N.A.V. | 8.60 | 7.04 | 5.93 | 7.15 | 7.28 | 7.31 | 8.24 | 8.96 | 8.38 | 8.59 | 8.87 | 8.77 | 9.04 |
| TOTAL RETURN % | 0.00 | -11.60 | -7.15 | 32.40 | 9.90 | 8.75 | 21.39 | 19.19 | 2.17 | 10.41 | 10.87 | 6.29 | 8.28 |
| +/- LB GOVT./CP. | -2.29 | -14.66 | -14.41 | 1.31 | 1.91 | -6.27 | 0.08 | 3.57 | -0.13 | 2.83 | -3.37 | -1.99 | -1.96 |
| TOT. RTN/ALL FUNDS | 89 | 95 | | 78 | 32 | 79 | 32 | 62 | 24 | 40 | 57 | 65 | 28 |
| % RANK OBJECTIVE | 30 | 35 | 43 | 74 | 37 | 44 | 18 | 21 | 10 | 61 | 9 | 46 | 43 |
| INCOME | 0.53 | 0.59 | 0.64 | 0.61 | 0.57 | 0.58 | 0.58 | 0.60 | 0.60 | 0.60 | 0.60 | 0.60 | 0.44 |
| CAPITAL GAIN | 0.00 | 0.00 | 0.00 | 0.00 | 0.00 | 0.00 | 0.00 | 0.00 | 0.21 | 0.04 | 0.03 | 0.04 | 0.00 |
| EXPENSE % | 0.75 | 0.75 | 0.75 | 0.75 | 0.75 | 0.74 | 0.73 | 0.71 | 0.68 | 0.65 | 0.64 | 0.62 | 0.60 |
| INCOME % | 5.65 | 7.11 | 9.12 | 9.99 | 7.81 | 7.91 | 7.68 | 6.95 | 6.85 | 7.11 | 6.85 | 6.78 | 6.61 |
| TURNOVER % | 37 | 47 | 32 | 42 | 78 | 44 | 28 | 39 | 16 | 8 | 12 | 8 | 14 |
| NET ASSETS ($MIL) | 85.0 | 119.6 | 122.9 | 183.8 | 272.2 | 337.6 | 459.5 | 668.1 | 764.0 | 993.4 | 1183.5 | 1399.5 | 1550.8 |

| | M-STAR RISK % RANK | MORNINGSTAR RETURN RISK 1.00 = MUNI AVG | | MORNINGSTAR RISK-ADJUSTED RATING |
|---|---|---|---|---|
| 3 YEAR | 13 | 22 | 0.94 | 0.86 → ★★★★ |
| 5 YEAR | 13 | 19 | 1.04 | 0.87 → ★★★★ |
| 10 YEAR | 9 | 20 | 1.03 | 0.86 → ★★★★ |
| WEIGHTED AVG. | | | 1.01 | 0.86 ★★★★ |

### PORTFOLIO

TOTAL # SECURITIES: 166    TOP 20 SECURITIES AS OF: 03/31/91

| AMOUNT $000 | SECURITY | MATURITY | VALUE % NET $000 ASSETS |
|---|---|---|---|
| 41635 | MI HOSP FIN AUTH HARPER-GRACE 10% | 10/01/16 | 47040   3.19 |
| 43330 | NE CONSUMERS PUB PWR DIST 5.1% | 01/01/03 | 38961   2.65 |
| 34500 | FL ALACHUA HLTH FAC AUTH SHANDS HOSP 8% | 12/01/15 | 35939   2.44 |
| 31900 | IL HLTH FAC AUTH RUSH PRESBYTERIAN 8% | 10/01/25 | 33306   2.26 |
| 33935 | MA STATE GO 6.5% | 08/01/00 | 32645   2.22 |
| 27700 | FL ORLANDO UTIL COM 8.5% | 01/01/09 | 30506   2.07 |
| 27600 | CA HLTH FAC FIN AUTH DAUGHTERS 9.25% | 03/01/15 | 30501   2.07 |
| 31130 | WA COLUMBIA STORAGE PWR EXCHANGE 3.875% | 04/01/03 | 30352   2.06 |
| 28775 | UT INTERMOUNTAIN PWR AGCY 7.875% | 07/01/14 | 29906   2.03 |
| 26950 | FL NORTH BROWARD HOSP DIST 8% | 01/01/14 | 27744   1.88 |
| 25990 | IL DU PAGE GO WTR COM 7.875% | 03/01/11 | 27206   1.85 |
| 28075 | PA PHILADELPHIA HOSP & HIGHER EDUC 7.25% | 07/01/14 | 27090   1.84 |

### ANALYSIS

Jennifer Strickland   11/01/91

Nuveen Municipal Bond Fund walks on a different side of the track.

Unlike yield-driven vehicles, this fund bond prices. Spalding hopes that his near 20% housing play will behave similarly. Restrictive mortgage legislation could

Source: Morningstar, Inc., Chicago, IL.

Here we feel that income is more important than total return, so we've focused on that column. It shows an income stream for each investment of $10,000 as follows:

| Year | % | Monthly Tax-Free Income |
|---|---|---|
| 1991 | 6.61 | $55.08 |
| 1990 | 6.78 | 56.50 |
| 1989 | 6.85 | 57.08 |
| 1988 | 7.11 | 59.25 |
| 1987 | 6.85 | 57.08 |
| 1986 | 6.95 | 57.92 |

The second area of importance with municipal bond funds is volatility of net asset values (NAV). Here we find the following:

| Year | NAV |
|------|------|
| 1991 | $9.04 |
| 1990 | 8.77 |
| 1989 | 8.87 |
| 1988 | 8.59 |
| 1987 | 8.38 |
| 1986 | 8.96 |

If you had purchased, for instance, the Nuveen Municipal Bond Fund on December 31, 1986, your net asset value would have been $8.96 per share. At the end of 1991, the value would have been $9.04 per share, a gain of only 8 cents, or 1%. That is considered quite stable.

## Load Versus No-Load

There is in each of us a strong desire to avoid sales charges. Whether we are selling a house or buying a car, most of us would like to do without a salesperson. In the real world, that is seldom possible.

Since we feel that mutual funds are the best investment for the average retiree, let's examine the merits of sales charges in greater detail.

### Fund Selection

Assuming that you will need about 6 funds to satisfy your investment objectives, you are confronted with the awesome task of choosing them from the 3,000+ funds available. You can, of course, subscribe to one of the analytical services we mentioned earlier in this chapter or you can seek guidance from a publication such as *The New York Times*, *The Wall Street Journal*, *Barron's*, or *Money Magazine*. However, your best bet,

in our opinion, is to seek the expertise of a reputable financial planner.

For a fee, the planner will recommend specific no-load funds tailored to your requirements. Most people, however, choose to use a commissionable financial planner or a regular stockbroker. Assuming they chose their counselor well, they can use a buy-and-hold approach (avoiding unnecessary sales charges) and keep their fund for well beyond the 10-year average holding period for mutual funds.

Had you invested $50,000 in, for example, a Kemper U.S. Government Bond Fund, your sales charge would have been 4.5% or $2,250. Not a small sum of money; but if you keep the fund for 10 or more years, you could assume your sales charge to be only $225 per year or $150 per year for 15 years. The full amount is, however, deducted from your $50,000 at the time of the investment.

### Performance

In many cases, load funds can, and, do outperform the no-load funds. For example, in the U.S. government category we have already covered, let's add two no-load funds to the list and see how they compare. We will use Fidelity and Scudder as examples (this is an American Association of Retired People fund). Table 9-6 shows the comparison.

Notice that the dividend payout is higher for the three load funds. So too is the total return.

### Panic Selling

When panic sets in, such as after Black Monday (October 19, 1987), there was a 117% higher redemption rate by people who had no-load growth funds than those who used brokers and bought load funds. (See Table 9-7.) The losses suffered by those who did not have a broker or planner to counsel them at this perilous time was measured in billions of dollars.

## TABLE 9-6

### RATES OF RETURN

*12/31/84 to 12/31/90 (Annualized)*

| Name of Fund | Dividend Payout 6/28/91 | Total Return Percent |
|---|---|---|
| Kemper U.S. Government Securities | 9.0 | 11.6 |
| Putnam U.S. Government Income | 9.1 | 10.9 |
| Franklin U.S. Government Securities | 8.9 | 10.3 |
| Fidelity Government Securities | *7.6 | 10.2 |
| Scudder GNMA (AARP) | *8.2 | 9.9 |

*No-load fund.

*Source:* CDA Investment Technologies, Inc.

## TABLE 9-7

### GROWTH AND INCOME FUND REDEMPTIONS

*Load vs. No-Load—1987*

| | Load (Through Broker) | No-Load (No Broker) |
|---|---|---|
| October | 1.6% | 3.7% |
| November | 1.0% | 1.6% |
| December | 1.0% | 2.3% |

A total of 7.6% of all no-load growth funds were re-
deemed during the 3 months after "Black Monday" as
opposed to only 3.6% for load funds. In our opinion, these
statistics confirm the importance of an honest sales person. *Buy, hold, and don't panic* is our recommendation.

We will close this section on load versus no-load
funds, with a quotation from Don Phillips, the editor of
*Mutual Fund Values*, an investment service that com-
pares all mutual funds on a regular basis:

> More important than considering the penalty of a
> sales charge, however, is to consider the gain an
> investor receives from paying such charges. If an
> investor receives good advice, these fees can be a
> tremendous bargain. As one financial planner puts
> it, if it's worth paying a waiter 15% to 20% to bring
> food to a table, isn't it worth paying a 5% premium
> to get sound financial advice? The danger, of course,
> is that an investor may pay the same charge to an
> uninformed salesperson that is paid to a dedicated
> financial planner. Moreover, while the quality of
> the meal is known immediately, the merits of an
> investment portfolio take considerably longer to
> show. Still, sales charges are well-spent money for
> investors working with a good broker or financial
> planner.

# 10

# Asset Allocation

Now it's time to turn our attention to one reliable method of investment. It's called *asset allocation*. Regarding asset allocation, the first and most important question is, what overall yield should you set for your entire portfolio? For example, should you settle for the prevailing rate of short-term CDs (4.45% on November 27, 1991 for a 1-year CD) or should you set your goal at 8.5%, 10.5%, or whatever? Having set this goal, your next question is, how do you assemble your portfolio to reach the objective you have set? Do you follow the path set by the large, nationally-known broker/dealers or is there a better way?

When learning about investing, you are bombarded by advice from many sources. The daily newspapers contain articles and advertisements that suggest this or that approach. Magazines, radio, and TV programs add their comments. This is all to the good, but also very confusing. It seems to us that what you should be looking for is a *plan*, or a *method* to follow. Our recommendation is that you adopt an asset allocation approach to assembling your retirement portfolio.

## Types of Asset Allocation

Previously, asset allocation has meant limiting asset categories to stocks, bonds, or cash. This remains the method of choice for most large brokerage houses. Of late, however, a new, academic approach to asset allocation, using a broader, more detailed list of categories, has been developed. This new approach is quite different from the usual asset allocation you are used to reading about or receiving from one or more of the brokers. They limit themselves to 3 asset classes— stocks, bonds and cash. And they all have slightly different recommendations. Table 10-1 shows the various asset allocation recommendations made by a few large brokerage houses for October 1991.

The Merrill-Lynch Research Department, for example, said that in October 1991, the average person should have 60% of their investable assets in stocks, 35% in bonds, and 5% in cash. This, of course, is a general asset allocation, but somehow or other you kind of get the feeling that that is where you should have your assets regardless of your age or net worth. And that is not necessarily so.

### TABLE 10-1

### ASSET ALLOCATION RECOMMENDATIONS

*October 1991*

| Firm | Stocks | Bonds | Cash |
|---|---|---|---|
| Shearson Lehman Hutton | 60 | 35 | 5 |
| Donaldson, Lufkin & Jenrette | 50 | 40 | 10 |
| Merrill Lynch | 60 | 35 | 5 |
| Kidder Peabody | 70 | 30 | 0 |

*Source: Stanger's Investment Advisor.*

One other problem with following the broker/ dealers' recommendations is that their asset allocation recommendations change frequently (4 or 5 times per year). A third problem is that they place considerable emphasis on individual stocks and bonds. Market timing—when should you buy and when should you sell—is also very important to them.

## The Academic Approach

A recent academic study[1] shows us a far better method. The new (academic) approach to asset allocation is the better way to go for those interested in stable, growth and income.

With this new, academic approach, the first step is to organize the various investments into such broadened asset categories as treasury bills, corporate bonds, U.S. common stocks, international stocks, small stocks, international bonds, and real estate—not just stocks, bonds, and cash. The second step is to decide which of those categories should be included in your portfolio. The third step is to decide what percentage of your assets should be assigned to each category and, finally, the fourth step, deciding which individual securities you should have within each of the categories.

They studied the performance of 91 large pension plans over the previous 10 years. The major reason found for their having reached their objectives was asset allocation, not individual stock or bond selection or market timing. Specifically, 93.6% of their results was attributed to asset allocation and only 2.5% to individual stock and bond selection and another 1.7% to market timing. (The remaining 2.2% was not determined.)

---

[1]Brinson, Gary P., Hood, L. Randolph, and Beebower, Gilbert L. "Determinants of Portfolio Performance," *Financial Analysis Journal*, July–August 1986, pp. 39–44.

Roger C. Gibson in his book, *Asset Allocation* (Dow Jones-Irwin), tells us further that we should increase the categories and not limit ourselves to stock, bonds, and cash, but rather open our horizons to some of the following: treasury bills, corporate bonds, U.S. common stocks, international stocks, small stocks, international bonds, equity real estate investment trusts (REITS), and real estate. It will not be long before you see the large brokerage houses increasing their categories from the old-fashioned three classes to include some or even most of these. The compound annual returns of these assets categories during the past 15 years shows why they should be considered.

As you examine Table 10-2, the first thing that meets your eye is that you don't see the asset class listed where most of your money is likely invested right now, namely, savings accounts, money markets, and CDs. They are there, however, included under the heading "treasury bills." Treasury bills are considered by financial planners to be surrogates for these short-term instruments.

## TABLE 10-2

### INVESTMENT PERFORMANCE (1975–1990)

*Asset Class*

| | Compound Annual Return |
|---|---|
| Treasury bills | 8.1% |
| Corporate bonds | 10.0% |
| Common stock | 13.0% |
| Small stocks | 17.4% |
| International stocks | 17.0% |
| Real estate | 11.1% |

*Source:* CDA Investment Technologies, Inc.

An average of 8.1% over this 15-year period is what would have been earned by a reasonable combination of these assets. Thus, when you see the word treasury bills, remember that you can substitute the words savings accounts, money market, and short-term CDs.

Now let's translate some of these numbers into more meaningful terms. Take common stock, for example, as opposed to treasury bills, and let's examine how they compare over the past 65 years. We will add one other item in our comparison, namely, inflation. This addition will help us to compare the "buying power" of the dollar over the years.

## Inflation

First of all, let's start with the cost of a breakfast in the year 1925. Many of us were born around that time. Let's assume breakfast cost $1 then. What would it cost today? Exhibit 10-1 shows us that it is $7.46. The cost of living increased about 7-½ times over the lifetime of a 65-year-old person.

## Treasury Bills

Now let's examine how our money would have fared if we had invested $1 in Treasury bills. Remember, this is the rough equivalent of CDs, money market, and savings accounts. Exhibit 10-2 shows that it would have grown to $10.43. Yes, we would have done better than inflation, but only a little. Hardly enough to live on, if we were consuming the interest.

## Common Stock

Instead of investing in Treasury bills, say that we had invested the $1 in U.S. common stock. Our $1 would have grown to $517.50 as if by some magic we invested $1 in 500 stocks representing the Standard & Poor's

# EXHIBIT 10-1   INFLATION: RATES OF CHANGE (1925–1990)

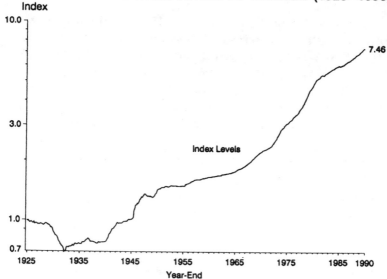

# EXHIBIT 10-2   U.S. TREASURY BILLS: RETURNS (1925–1990)

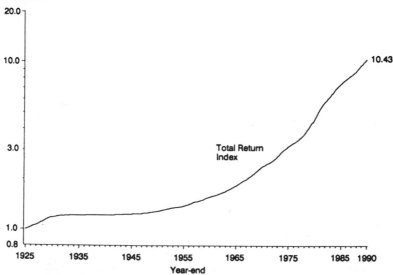

Composite Index. See Exhibit 10-3. This is far better than the Treasury bills or inflation. But what a roller-coaster ride. Four years after we started, we were hit with the Great Depression. We went through a world war and two limited wars, not to mention a few recessions. Was it worth it? The numbers speak for themselves ($517.50 as opposed to $10.43 using the Treasury bill route). Do we have to put all of our assets in common stock? Definitely not. But we should certainly consider a portion in common stock.

Even though you may consider yourself a financially conservative person you should consider these facts of life:

● We have always had inflation with us and we must provide for it in the future.

● Treasury bills stayed ahead of inflation in the past, but only barely. If you will be drawing down

**EXHIBIT 10-3   COMMON STOCKS: RETURNS (1925–1990)**

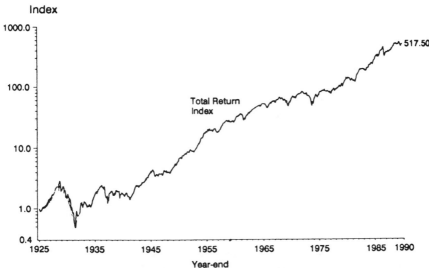

*Source:* Ibbotson Associates, Chicago. Ibbotson, Roger G., and Rex A. Sinquefield, *Stocks, Bonds, Bills, and Inflation* (SBBI), 1982, updated in *Stocks, Bonds, Bills, and Inflation 199_ Yearbook*™ [or in the (month or quarter), 199_ update], Ibbotson Associates, Chicago. All rights reserved.

income from your assets in the future and you are heavily invested short-term (CDs, Treasury bills, and money market funds), you will not be able to retain the purchasing power of your money.

- Common stock did much better than Treasury bills ($517.50 versus $10.43). But watch the time horizon. Exhibits 10-2 and 10-3 covered a 65-year period. Your time limit is about 20 to 30 years. Further, you will be drawing down some or all of the interest and dividends your assets are earning to live on.

## Correlation

Before we start to select the asset class we want to use, we should consider the possible impact from the economy, the value of the dollar, world events, and other forces that can effect your assets. Economic conditions, for example, can help increase the value of common stocks at a given time and at another time will cause those same stocks to fall. The impact on bonds or real estate may be quite different.

College professors tell us that if two investments move in the same direction at the same time, the volatility of our portfolio is not helped. What we should do is look for a portfolio that is balanced so that when one asset class goes up, another one will go down, but not equally. Exhibit 10-4 shows how the principal of balance or correlation works. Notice when stocks go down, bonds may go up and make your portfolio less volatile. This is a very complicated area and gets more complicated as you add a third, fourth, and fifth asset category. Your financial advisor should be consulted in this area. Diversification is essential in your portfolio, and it's imperative for you to keep in mind that the correlation of these assets is also of considerable importance.

## EXHIBIT 10-4    BENEFITS OF DIVERSIFICATION

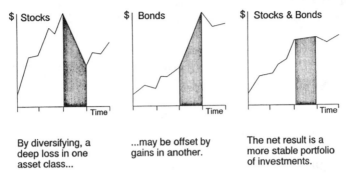

By diversifying, a deep loss in one asset class...

...may be offset by gains in another.

The net result is a more stable portfolio of investments.

*Source:* Ibbotson Associates, Chicago.

# What Variations Can We Expect?

## Standard Deviation

Another question we have to ask as we get closer to making a choice of asset classes is, what variations can we expect in the future from these groups? Here we will introduce another concept. It's called *standard deviation*. Simply put, standard deviation means the range of how high or low we can expect our return to be on a specific asset. (See Table 10-3.)

If you knew nothing at all about these asset classes and you wanted the highest return possible you would surely choose the small stock group and expect a nice return of 17.4% on your money each and every year.

However, you do have some knowledge about financial matters. For one thing, you know that there is a good deal of risk with an investment in small stocks. It can go up sizably, but it can also go down sizably as well. The row headed "standard deviation" gives us a number showing approximately how much it can move from its expected return and how, to some extent, each asset class relates to the other.

## TABLE 10-3

## INVESTMENT PERFORMANCE STATISTICS
## FOR MAJOR ASSET CLASSES (1975–1990)

| Asset Class | Compound Annual Return | Standard Deviation |
|---|---|---|
| Treasury bills | 8.1% | 2.0% |
| Corporate bonds | 10.0% | 1.9% |
| Common stock | 13.0% | 5.5% |
| Small stocks | 17.4% | 6.8% |
| International stocks | 17.0% | 4.9% |
| Real estate | 11.1% | 3.9% |

Source: CDA Investment Technologies, Inc.

We see that Treasury bills deviated (moved up or down) by 2.0%. During the 15-year period from 1975 to 1990, Treasury bills had an average 8.1% compound annual return with a high of 10.1% and a low of 6.1%. In other words, although we were looking for an 8.1% yield on Treasury bills during the past 15 years, we could have received a low of 6.1% or a high of 10.1% in any given year.

Now let's take a look at one of the other assets—*common stock*. We see that the average was 13% and the standard deviation was 5.5%. This tells us that during the 15-year period from 1975 to 1990 we could have received a high of 18.5% on our common stock investments, (13% plus 5.5%) or a low of 7.5% (13% minus 5.5%).

## Percentage Allocation

Next we should decide what percentage of our funds should be allocated to each asset class. It may be help-

ful at this point to tell you about the average client who comes to us for counseling. (See Table 10-4.)

As you can see, this portfolio may look a bit like yours. That may make you feel comfortable, but this type of portfolio will be devastated by inflation. It must be changed, but how?

The experts tell us that the starting point for a good portfolio is to match yours against the entire world's wealth distribution. The basic assumption here is that the entire wealth of the world is invested as we see in Exhibit 10-5. This includes all the big investors: millionaires, pension plans, corporate funds, and insurance companies. It includes not only the assets in the United States but also those of the entire world. If, somehow or other, we could match those percentages in our own portfolios, the assumption is that we too could be wealthy. However, we doubt very much that you are ready, for example, to invest 28.3% of your assets in foreign stocks.

Now, let's take a closer look at our average client portfolio and see what kind of return they would receive today with their old portfolios. (See Table 10-5.)

(These rates of return are those anticipated by CDA Investment Technologies over the next 3 years. The numbers are published in CDA's Mutual Fund Optim-

## TABLE 10-4

### AVERAGE CLIENT PORTFOLIO

*(Before Recommendations)*

| Asset Class | Percentage |
|---|---|
| Money market, Treasuries, and CDs | 76% |
| Municipal bonds | 6 |
| Government bonds and GNMAs | 11 |
| Growth and income stock | 7 |

*Source:* Creative Retirement Planning, New York.

**EXHIBIT 10-5   TOTAL INVESTABLE CAPITAL
MARKET (DECEMBER 31, 1990)**

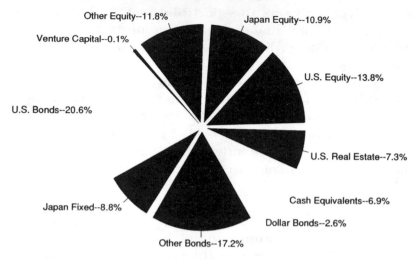

**$24.2 Trillion**

*Source:* Brinson Partners, Inc.

**TABLE 10-5**

**AVERAGE CLIENT'S PORTFOLIO**

*(Before Recommended Changes)*

| Current Holdings Percentage | Asset Class | Annual Rate of Return |
|---|---|---|
| 76 | Money market and CDs | 6.0% |
| 6 | Municipal bonds (tax equivalent) | 8.5% |
| 11 | Government and GNMAs | 8.5% |
| 7 | Growth stock | 13.3% |
| 100 | | |

Average expected return      6.9%
Portfolio standard deviation      1.7

*Source:* CDA Investment Technologies, Inc. and Creative
Retirement Planning Inc.

izer program. The standard deviation is for a three-year period.)

The average anticipated return over the next 3 years for the entire portfolio is 6.9%. As the result of a complicated mathematical formula we were able to determine the overall portfolio standard deviation of 1.7%.[2] Then our client's problem was to understand that if they use the entire 6.9% to live on, they will have trouble overcoming the problem of inflation.

After applying the principles of asset allocation and considering a reasonable risk tolerance of 20 (on a scale of "0 to 100" with "0" being the lowest risk), we were able to get their average expected return up to 10.0% by changing their holdings as shown in Table 10-6.

## TABLE 10-6

### AVERAGE CLIENT'S PORTFOLIO

*(After Recommended Changes)*

| Recommended Holdings Percentage | Asset Class | Annual Rate of Return |
|---|---|---|
| 6.0 | Money market and CDs | 6.0% |
| 26.0 | Growth and income stocks | 13.3 |
| 54.0 | Government and GNMAs | 8.5 |
| 10.0 | International equities | 12.8 |
| 4.0 | Municipal bonds (tax equivalent) | 8.5 |
| 100.0% | | |

Average return          10.0%
Portfolio standard deviation     2.4%

*Source:* CDA Investment Technologies, Inc. and Creative Retirement Planning Inc.

[2]CDA Investment Technologies Optimizer.

Please note that the average portfolio return has increased from 6.9% to 10.0%, while the standard deviation went from 1.7 to 2.4. You will recall that this translates into a yearly possible portfolio return on the high side of 12.4% (10.0 plus 2.4) and on the low side of 7.6% (10.0 minus 2.4).

The final step in our process is to choose specific investments. You will see how that works in the upcoming four case studies. For your use, Table 10-7 shows an Investment Portfolio Design form you can put to use in considering your present asset allocation. Fill it in as best you can and you will get a good idea of how many asset categories you are invested in now.

## TABLE 10-7

### YOUR CURRENT INVESTMENT PORTFOLIO

Name _____

Date _____

| *Short-Term Debt Investments* | | **Percentage** |
|---|---|---|
| Saving accounts | $ _____ | |
| | _____ | |
| Money market funds | _____ | |
| | _____ | |
| CDs        · | _____ | |
| Treasury bills | _____ | |
| Guaranteed investment contracts (401k)  · | _____ | |
| Annuities/pensions (multiply annual pension by .08) | _____ _____ _____ | |
| A.                          Total | _____ | _____ % |

*Long-Term Debt Investments*

*Government issues*
    Treasury notes and          $ _____
        bonds                      _____

**TABLE 10-7** (*Continued*)

Ginnie Maes                           _____

Fannie Maes                           _____

B.                    Total           _____  _____ %

*Corporate Issues (Domestic)*

Corporate bonds             $ _____

_____

C.                    Total           _____  _____ %

*Corporate Issues (Foreign)*

Foreign Corporate bonds     $ _____

_____

D.                    Total           _____  _____ %

*Common Stock*

*Aggressive growth*          $ _____
(Small cap, recovery)        _____

E.                    Total           _____  _____ %

*Growth and income*          $ _____
(Utility and high yield)     _____

F.                    Total           _____  _____ %

*Growth*                     $ _____

_____

_____

G.                    Total           _____  _____ %

*Foreign*                    $ _____

_____

H.                    Total           _____  _____ %

*Investment Real Estate*

Limited partnerships         $ _____
Joint ownership (rentals)    _____

## TABLE 10-7 (*Continued*)

Individually owned (rent-
als)                                           _____

I.                              Total    _____   _____ %

*Precious Metals/collectibles*

    Gold                                $ _____
    Silver                                _____
    Stamps                                _____
    Other                                 _____

J.                              Total    _____   _____ %

# Part Three

---

# *Individual Case Studies*

## How to Use the Case Studies

We are now ready to consider 4 case studies. They were prepared, for your consideration, as an aid in preparing your own plan. You can do it alone, but you will probably do far better with the assistance of a good financial planner and/or stockbroker.

We suggest you examine the table of contents and find the case study that is closest to your *income needs*. For example, let's say that you have determined that you need $43,000 of income per year to live on, then turn your attention first to Case Study I (Abe and Bernice Cooper). Suppose you are retiring early, then you should first look at Case Study IV (Christine DeSanto). If you own a small business, Case Study III (Hank and Irene Young) should be read first. Finally, Case Study II (Carol Wright) is an example of a single professional retiring after 65.

Once you have studied carefully the case study that is closest to your situation, then the others should be reviewed. It should be pointed out that none of these are actual case studies, rather, they are a compilation of facts garnered from a number of different actual cases.

We have used the names of several well-known stocks and mutual funds as examples of types to buy. These are examples only, there are, and would be at any time, equally rewarding alternatives. Also, your broker's or fund manager's job is to keep these stocks up to date. If you are reading this in a year or two after publication different styles of examples might have been used.

# 11

## Case Study I— Abe and Bernice Cooper

**Net Worth $485,127**

**Income Needs $40,000 per year**

Abe and Bernice Cooper live in a busy part of New York City called Forest Hills. Abe, age 64, worked for Pfizer for the last 33 years. His current salary is $38,400 per year. He expects to get a comparatively generous pension of $1,563 per month starting October 15, 1992. He will have saved $106,410 in the company's matching savings and investment plan.

Bernice, now 63, reentered the work force at age 48 after their two children completed most of their education. She works as a clerk in a mid-size accounting firm and is paid $22,300 per year. The firm started a

pension plan about 12 years ago and Bernice is looking forward to receiving a lump sum of $53,622 in October 1992, when she will retire at age 65.

Both Abe and Bernice are in good health, as are Mark and Sarah, their two children. Both of the kids are doing well. Sarah graduated from Queens College with a degree in English. She is single and works for a large advertising agency. Her career path looks good and she is of no financial concern to her parents. Mark, also a college graduate majoring in computer science, is working toward a masters degree. He is happily married and presented Abe and Bernice with their first grandchild who is now two years of age. Mark and his family moved to Atlanta, Georgia where he works for a *Fortune 500* firm.

Although Abe and Bernice have their roots in Forest Hills, they are seriously considering a move to a warmer climate. They feel that they can live comfortably on $40,000 per year. Their vital statistics and investment objectives are as follows:

## INVESTMENT OBJECTIVES AND VITAL STATISTICS
### Abe and Bernice Cooper

#### Vital Statistics

*Ages*

| Abe's | 64 |
| Bernice's | 63 |

*Retiring*

| Abe | 10/15/92 |
| Bernice | 10/1/92 |

*1991 Salaries*

| Abe | $38,400 |
| Bernice | $22,300 |

*Post-Retirement Income Needs*

| (After Taxes) | $40,000 |

## Investment Objectives

1. Consistency of buying power
2. Safety of principal
3. Income
4. Tax avoidance
5. Growth

They agreed that all they need in short-term (money market) assets is 3 months worth of income. Since $40,000 is what they will need for an entire year, short-term fund requirements will total only $10,000. Having lived a fairly frugal life, Abe and Bernice were able to accumulate significant assets. A $45,000 inheritance from Bernice's parents about 5 years ago when her mother died helped to bring their net worth up to $485,127. Our problem then is to determine how to follow their investment priorities and still provide them with the income they require today and *tomorrow*. Their assets and our recommendations as to how they should be invested are set forth in the next few pages. We will examine their situation in detail to show how their retirement income was assured, even increased, by using some of the principles we have already discussed in previous chapters.

## Current Assets and Liabilities

Our financial planning procedure for Abe and Bernice is as follows. First, we compile all of a client's assets on a *projected balance sheet and income statement.* (See Table 11-1.) Then we do an *asset allocation.* Finally, we recommend investment changes on the *projected balance sheet and income statement.* This reflects our best effort to reach Abe's and Bernice's overall goals by using an optimum plan.

The corporation and bank names used here and throughout are used strictly as a few of many sound, stable firms. There are many other excellent institu-

**TABLE 11-1**

**PROJECTED BALANCE SHEET AND INCOME STATEMENT
FOR ABE AND BERNICE COOPER**

*(Values at July 1991)*

| Due Dates | Asset Description | Current Value | Interest Rate | Income | Tax Status* |
|---|---|---|---|---|---|
| | **Savings Accounts** | | | | |
| | Chase Bank | $6,500 | 5.50% | $358 | |
| | Chase Bank—Checking | $1,000 | 5.50% | $55 | |
| | Credit Union | $12,000 | 6.00% | $720 | |
| | Citibank—Money Market | $9,000 | 3.75% | $338 | |
| | **CDs** | | | | |
| 8/1/92 | Chase Bank IRA (Abe) | $17,400 | 6.54% | $1,138 | Q |
| 11/17/93 | Apple Bank IRA (Bernice) | $12,100 | 6.40% | $774 | Q |

| Shares | Common Stock | Current Value | Yield | Income | |
|---|---|---|---|---|---|
| 27 | Abbott Labs | $1,596 | 2.00% | $32 | |

| | | | | | |
|---|---|---|---|---|---|
| 50 | Exxon | $2,875 | 4.70% | $135 | |
| 100 | GTE Corporation | $2,975 | 5.30% | $158 | |
| 75 | Minnesota Mining | $6,806 | 3.40% | $231 | |
| 847 | Pfizer | $57,384 | 2.00% | $1,148 | |
| 11/1/92 | Treasury Bill | $50,000 | 4.96% | $2,480 | |
| 7/1/2015 | Nassau County G.O. | $20,000 | 8.35% | $1,670 | X |

**Funds**

| **Shares** | | | | | |
|---|---|---|---|---|---|
| 361 | Dreyfus NY TX Exempt | $5,464 | 6.58% | $360 | X |

**Real Estate**

| | | | | | |
|---|---|---|---|---|---|
| | Residence | $125,000 | | | |

**Thrift Plan**

| | | | | | |
|---|---|---|---|---|---|
| | Corp. Savings Plan | $106,410 | 9.00% | $9,577 | Q |

**Life Ins. C.V.**

| | | | | | |
|---|---|---|---|---|---|
| | Metropolitan Life | $5,282 | 6.00% | $317 | Q |

**TABLE 11-1** (*Continued*)

| Asset Description | Current Value | Interest Rate | Income |
|---|---|---|---|
| **Social Security** | | | |
| Abe's | | | $12,275 |
| Bernice's | | | $9,247 |
| **Pension** | | | |
| Abe's Pension | | | $18,753 |
| Bernice's Lump Sum | $53,622 | 8.25% | $4,424 |
| **Totals** | $495,415 | | $64,189 |
| **Loans** | | | |
| Mortgages | $3,500 | | |
| Margin | $0 | | |
| Other Loans | $6,788 | | |

**Net Worth**     $485,127

Salary (After retirement)     $0

**Tax Computation:**

Adjusted Gross Income     $64,189

**Non-Taxable Items:**

Total Qualified Income     ($16,230)
   (if not withdrawn)

Social Security (amount     ($18,923)
   not taxed)

Tax Exempts     ($2,030)

**Gross Taxable**     $27,006

Deductions (Personal)     ($4,300)
Deductions (Standard)     ($6,350)

**TABLE 11-1** (*Continued*)

| Net Taxable | | | $16,356 |
| --- | --- | --- | --- |

| | **Taxes** | **Rate** | |
| --- | --- | --- | --- |
| | Federal | 15.0% | ($2,453) |
| | State | 4.30% | ($136) |
| | City | 2.25% | ($71) |

**Net Income After Taxes**
(Leaving $16,230 of
qualified income inside
IRAs and Corporate
Savings Plans)                                         $45,299

*Letters in the "Tax Status" column indicate the following: X = Tax-free; Q = Tax-deferred

tions, funds, and corporations to choose from. By staying in contact with your broker and/or financial planner you can get an idea of which are best for you at a given time.

## Inflation Analysis

Assuming the net after-tax income need of $40,000 remained constant and inflation averaged 5% per year, the buying power of the Cooper's income would decrease each year of their lives. Table 11-2 shows what the buying power would be every 5 years.

They can, of course, dip into the IRA funds for additional income, but inflation will have an impact on that as well. Assuming the Coopers made no changes in their investments, after a number of years they would be forced to invade principal.

In our opinion, they should make some changes in their investments to increase their total yield. The asset allocation approach to determining what changes to make is our next step.

### TABLE 11-2

### BUYING POWER vs. 5% INFLATION

*A & B Cooper $40,000*

| Year | Buying Power |
|------|-------------|
| 1992 | $40,000 |
| 1997 | $30,951 |
| 2002 | $23,949 |
| 2007 | $18,532 |
| 2012 | $14,339 |

## Asset Allocation

Using the Mutual Fund Optimizer asset allocation program of CDA we found that the total return of all the Coopers' investments would be only 7.0%. The Coopers' current portfolio consists of 83% *short-term and guaranteed instruments* (money market, saving accounts, CDs, treasury bonds, pension annuities, and corporate saving plan), 13% growth (domestic common stock) and 4% *Muni* (municipal bonds). Graphically, their portfolio (Exhibit 11-1) consists of only 3 asset classes. As we saw in the inflation analysis, their portfolio is just not adequate for their future needs.

Abe could have received a lump-sum distribution of about $196,000 instead of the annual pension of $18,753, however the Coopers felt it was essential that they have a guaranteed pension. Thus in our asset allocation analysis we assumed that they had invested the $196,000 in a conservative immediate annuity. This represented about 35% of their total assets.

Assigning a low risk tolerance of "20" (on a scale of "1" to "100") we found that we could increase their portfolio expected return to 9.2% by adding two asset

### EXHIBIT 11-1   COOPER'S CURRENT PORTFOLIO HOLDINGS

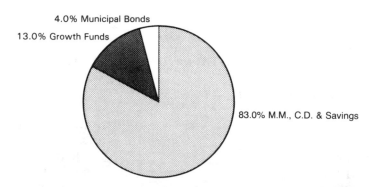

Total Portfolio:  Expected Annual Return 7.0%

*Source:* CDA Investment Technologies, Inc.

categories—government agencies and international funds—and changing the percentages as shown in Exhibit 11-2.

## Recommendations

Armed with the asset allocation information, we then studied the Coopers' individual investments and recommended the changes shown in the Creative Retirement Planning analysis in Table 11-3. (Our discussion of the Cooper's retirement planning through the end of the chapter systematically refers to the various sections of Table 11-3.)

### EXHIBIT 11-2 COMPARATIVE PORTFOLIO HOLDINGS—CURRENT VS. OPTIMUM (RISK TOLERANCE IS 20)

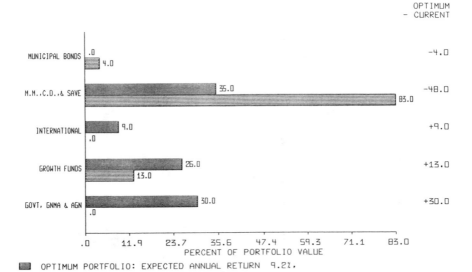

PREPARED BY: CREATIVE RETIREMENT PLANNING
NEW YORK, NY 10020

PREPARED FOR: ABE & BERNICE COOPER 12/8/91
BASED ON 9/30/91 DATA

OPTIMUM
– CURRENT

MUNICIPAL BONDS .0 / 4.0 — -4.0

M.M.,C.D.,& SAVE 35.0 / 83.0 — -48.0

INTERNATIONAL 9.0 / .0 — +9.0

GROWTH FUNDS 26.0 / 13.0 — +13.0

GOVT, GNMA & AGN 30.0 / .0 — +30.0

.0    11.9    23.7    35.6    47.4    59.3    71.1    83.0
PERCENT OF PORTFOLIO VALUE

OPTIMUM PORTFOLIO: EXPECTED ANNUAL RETURN  9.2%.
CURRENT PORTFOLIO: EXPECTED ANNUAL RETURN  7.0%.

*Source:* CDA Investment Technologies, Inc.

## TABLE 11-3

### CREATIVE RETIREMENT PLANNING—PROJECTED BALANCE SHEET AND INCOME STATEMENT FOR ABE AND BERNICE COOPER

*November 1991*

| Due Date or Shares | Assets Description | Before Current Value | Before Interest or Yield | Before Income | Before Tax Status | After | After Current Value | After Interest or Yield | After Income | After Tax Status | Asset To Be Bought |
|---|---|---|---|---|---|---|---|---|---|---|---|
| **Savings Accounts** | | | | | | **Savings Accounts** | | | | | |
| | Chase Bank | $6,500 | 5.50% | $358 | | H | $6,500 | 5.50% | $358 | | |
| | Chase Bank—Checking | $1,000 | 5.50% | $55 | | H | $1,000 | 5.50% | $55 | | |
| | Credit Union | $12,000 | 6.00% | $720 | | S | $4,000 | 6.00% | $240 | | Hold $4,000 |
| | Citibank Money Market | $9,000 | 3.75% | $338 | | S | | | | | |
| | | | | | | B | $17,000 | 8.54% | $1,452 | | Kemper U.S. Government |
| **CDs** | | | | | | **CDs** | | | | | |
| Aug 92 | Chase Bank IRA (Abe) | $17,400 | 6.54% | $1,138 | Q | S | | | | | |
| | | | | | | B | $17,400 | 8.66% | $1,507 | Q | Sun America U.S. Government |
| Nov 93 | Apple Bank IRA (Bernice) | $12,100 | 6.40% | $774 | Q | S | | | | | |
| | | | | | | B | $12,100 | 8.66% | $1,048 | Q | Sun America U.S. Government |

## Common Stocks

| | | | | |
|---|---|---|---|---|
| 27 | Abbot Labs | $1,596 | 2.00% | $32 |
| 50 | Exxon | $2,875 | 4.70% | $135 |
| 100 | GTE Corp. | $2,975 | 5.30% | $158 |
| 75 | Minnesota Mining | $6,806 | 3.40% | $231 |
| 847 | Pfizer | $57,384 | 2.00% | $1,148 |

## Bonds

| | | | | | |
|---|---|---|---|---|---|
| Nov 92 | Treasury Bill | $50,000 | 4.96% | | $2,480 |
| Jul 2015 | Nassau County G.O. | $20,000 | 8.35% | X | $1,670 |

## Funds

| | | | | | |
|---|---|---|---|---|---|
| 361 | Dreyfus NY Tax Exempt | $5,464 | 6.58% | X | $360 |

## Real Estate

| | |
|---|---|
| Residence | $125,000 |

## Common Stocks

| | | | | | |
|---|---|---|---|---|---|
| H | Abbot Labs | $1,596 | 2.00% | | $32 |
| S | Exxon | | | | |
| S | GTE Corp. | | | | |
| S | Minnesota Mining | | | | |
| P | Pfizer | $6,775 | 2.00% | | $136 | Hold 100 shares Pfizer |
| B | | $4,316 | 2.00% | | $86 | Round to 100 SH Abbott |
| B | | $48,950 | 13.00% | | $6,364 | Phoenix Growth |
| | | $10,000 | 0.00% | | $0 | Capital Gains Tax |

## Bonds

| | | | | | |
|---|---|---|---|---|---|
| S | Treasury Bill | | | | |
| B | Nassau County | $50,000 | 6.15% | | $3,075 |
| H | | $20,000 | 8.35% | Q X | $1,670 | Hartford SPDA |

## Funds

| | | | | | |
|---|---|---|---|---|---|
| H | Dreyfus NY Tax | $5,464 | 6.58% | X | $360 |

## Real Estate

| | |
|---|---|
| H | Residence | $125,000 |

**TABLE 11-3** (Continued)

| | Before | | | | After | | | | | |
|---|---|---|---|---|---|---|---|---|---|---|
| Assets Description | Current Value | Interest or Yield | Income | Tax Status | | Current Value | Interest or Yield | Income | Tax Status | Asset To Be Bought |
| **Thrift Plan** | | | | | **Thrift Plan** | | | | | |
| Corp. Savings Plan | $106,410 | 9.00% | $9,577 | Q | S | | | | | |
| | | | | | B | $30,000 | 12.00% | $3,600 | Q | Oppenheimer Global |
| | | | | | B | $22,410 | 8.66% | $1,941 | Q | Sun America U.S. Government |
| | | | | | B | $54,000 | 8.54% | $4,612 | Q | Kemper U.S. Government |
| **Life Ins. C.V.** | | | | | **Life Ins. C.V.** | | | | | |
| Metropolitan Life | $5,282 | 6.00% | $317 | Q | S | | | | | |
| | | | | | B | $5,282 | 11.00% | $581 | Q | Hartford SPVA Stock |
| **Social Security** | | | | | **Social Security** | | | | | |
| Abe's | | | $12,276 | | H | | | $12,276 | | |
| Bernice's | | | $9,247 | | H | | | $9,247 | | |
| **Pension** | | | | | **Pension** | | | | | |
| Abe's Pension | | | $18,753 | | H | | | $18,753 | | |
| Bernice's Lump-Sum Distribution | $53,622 | 8.25% | $4,424 | Q | S | | | | | |

| | Column A | Column B |
|---|---:|---:|
| **Total** | $495,415 | $64,189 / $71,943 |
| **Loans** | | |
| Mortgages | $3,500 | $3,500 |
| Margin | $0 | $0 |
| Other | $6,788 | $6,788 |
| **Net Worth** | $485,127 | $485,127 |
| **Salary** | $0 | $0 |
| **Adjusted Gross Income** | $64,189 | $71,943 |
| **Non-Taxable Items** | | |
| Social Security (amt. not taxed) | ($18,923) | ($17,389) |
| Tax Exempts | ($2,030) | ($2,030) |
| Qualified Funds | ($16,230) | ($20,916) |
| **Gross Taxable** | $27,006 | $31,608 |
| Deductions (Personal) | $4,300 | $4,300 |
| Deductions (Standard) | $6,350 | $6,350 |

Investment holdings:

| Security | Type | Amount | | Rate | Income |
|---|---|---:|---|---:|---:|
| Kemper U.S. Government | Q | $30,000 | B | 8.54% | $2,562 |
| Merrill Lynch GNMA | Q | $23,622 | B | 8.43% | $1,991 |
| | | | | | $71,943 |

## TABLE 11-3 (Continued)

|  |  | Before | After |
|---|---|---|---|
| Net Taxable |  | $16,356 | $20,958 |
| Federal | 15% | $2,453 | $3,144 |
| State Tax | 4.30% | $136 | $375 |
| New York City | 2.25% | $71 | $196 |
| Total Tax |  | ($2,660) | ($3,715) |
| Net After Tax |  | $45,299 | $47,312 |

*You will notice letters in the dividing column between the "Before" and "After" section, they indicate the following:

H    Hold (keep investment as is).
P    Partial hold (hold the amount indicated).
S    Sell (sell or swap this investment).
B    Buy (buy this investment).

The letters in the "Tax Status" column indicate the following: X = Tax-free; Q = Tax-deferred. Assumes no withdrawals are taken from IRAs. Additional income available from IRAs approximately $20,916. (Will be taxed when withdrawn.)

## Cash

Starting with the "cash" segment (savings, checking, money markets, and CDs) of their assets in Table 11-3, you will notice that the Coopers' first problem was that they have entirely too much money in savings banks. They have a total of $58,000 in short-term investments ($6,500 savings, $1,000 checking, $12,000 credit union, $9,000 money market, and $29,500 in CDs), producing $3,382 of taxable income. For emergencies, Abe and Bernice decided they only needed 3 months income or a total of $10,000. We recommend they keep $6,500 in a cash management account, $1,000 in a checking account, and $4,000 in Abe's credit union for a total liquid position of $11,500. The balance of $46,500 should be put into higher income-producing instruments [Kemper U.S. Government Bond Fund ($17,000) and Sun America U.S. Government Bond Fund ($29,500)]. Notice the Q in the tax column indicating that this income, if not withdrawn, is tax-deferred.

## Common Stock

Abe and Bernice dabbled in the stock market in a limited way. He purchased Pfizer stock through a salary deduction program. The plan was not *qualified*, meaning there is no tax protection. Any income or gain is subject to taxes. Abe simply had a specific amount of money taken out of his weekly check to purchase shares of his company's stock. Thus, his Pfizer holdings represented a substantial portion of his stock portfolio. Pfizer is an excellent stock for safety and has an "above average" recommendation by *Value Line* (see the alphabetical listing in Appendix A). Our recommendation is to hold only 100 shares of it and invest the balance in the Phoenix Growth fund. It averaged 19.46% per year for the past 10 years. (See the alphabetical listing in Appendix B.) Since the past 10 years were excellent

for common stock, we lowered the projected growth rate to 13%.

We also recommended that the Coopers increase their holdings of Abbott Labs. to 100 shares. *Value Line* also rated this firm No. 2 "above average" for timeliness and No. 1 for safety.

Since Exxon was rated only No. 3, "average," for timeliness, we recommend that it be sold.

*Value Line* considered GTE No. 4 "below average" for timeliness, we therefore recommended it too be sold, along with Minnesota Mining which had a rating of No. 3, the same rating. This left Abe and Bernice with 100 shares of two above-average stocks and $48,950 invested in an above-average growth fund. The fund can provide them with an income stream if they so choose. They simply notify the fund to mail them say 10% of their initial investment. In this example they would ask for a check of $400 per month. The risk, of course, is that the fund may not grow as projected.

With these changes, they were able to diversify their stock portfolio to a far greater degree after setting aside an estimated $10,000 for capital gains tax.

## Bonds

The bond portfolio consisted of a Treasury bill of $50,000 due November 1, 1992, earning 4.96% and a Nassau County General Obligation Bond due July 1, 2015 earning 8.35% [the income from the Nassau Bond is triple tax-free (no federal, state, or city tax on its income)]. Our recommendation was to hold the Nassau County General Obligation Bond. Notice the $x$ in the tax status column indicating that it is tax-free. We recommended that the Treasury bill be sold and the proceeds invested in a tax-deferred single premium deferred annuity (SPDA) earning a relatively safe tax-deferred 6.15%. The Q indicates that there is no tax until income is withdrawn.

## Other Assets

Abe and Bernice had $5,464 invested in a Dreyfus tax-exempt fund yielding 6.58% tax-free. Our recommendation was to hold it.

The Coopers lived in an apartment that went co-op a few years ago. They were able to purchase it, as "insiders," for about $40,000. The approximate value when we made the analysis was $125,000. They were considering the possibility of moving to Florida, where they could get what they considered a comfortable condo for about $60,000. If they finally decided to sell and move this would give them, after expenses, an additional $60,000 of investable funds. If it were invested at 9% it could give them $5,400 a year in additional income.

Their corporate saving and investment plan of $106,410 was the next item to be considered. The first thing we did was to examine what the tax bite would be. This analysis is set forth in detail in Table 11-4 under the heading *Lump-Sum Distribution Tax Analysis*. Our suggestion was that it would be best to roll it into an IRA. This income, which if not needed for current living expenses, can then grow, tax-deferred, and help protect from inflation down the line. Secondly, this IRA fund could be invested in a combination of global stock funds and government bond funds. Thirty thousand dollars was allocated in this case study for Oppenheimer Global, which averaged 15.0% per year for the past 10 years. In our calculation we assume only 12% per year for the future. $22,410 was to be invested in Sun America U.S. Government Bond Funds paying 8.66%. The remaining $54,000 was to be invested in Kemper U.S. Government paying a fairly safe 8.54%. One major advantage of investing IRA rollover funds in growth instruments is that the growth is sheltered from taxes until withdrawn.

Abe also had an old $10,000 Metropolitan life insurance policy. It had accumulated $5,282 in cash value and dividends, earning approximately 6% per year. Like

### TABLE 11-4

## LUMP-SUM DISTRIBUTION TAX ANALYSIS
## FOR ABE COOPER, NOVEMBER 1991

### 10-Year Average

| | | |
|---|---|---|
| Total L.S.D. | $106,410 | |
| Divided By 10 | $10,641 | |
| Add Back | $2,570 | |
| Total | $13,211 | |
| Tax* | $1,563 | |
| Total Tax | | ($15,630) |
| Balance Available After Tax | | $90,780 |
| Invested Tax-Free @ | | 6.5% |
| After-Tax Income | | **$5,901** |

### 5-Year Average

| | | |
|---|---|---|
| Total L.S.D. | $106,410 | |
| Divided by 5 | $21,282 | |
| Tax** | $3,313 | |
| Total Tax | | ($16,565) |
| Balance Available After Tax | | $89,845 |
| Invested Tax-Free @ | | 6.5% |
| After-Tax Income | | **$5,840** |

### IRA Rollover

| | | |
|---|---|---|
| L.S.D. | $106,410 | |
| Invested @ | 8.5% | |
| Gross Income | $9,045 | |
| Clients Tax Rate | 15% | |
| Tax | $1,357 | |
| Net Income After Tax | | **$7,688** |

### Comparison

| | |
|---|---|
| 10-Yr. Averaging Net A/T | $5,901 |
| 5-Yr. Averaging Net A/T | $5,840 |
| IRA Rollover Net A/T | $7,688 |

*Tax—Use 1986 single rates for 10 yr. average.
**Tax— Use current single rates for 5 yr. average.

*Source:* Creative Retirement Planning, Inc., New York, NY.

all life insurance policies, the buildup of cash values and dividends is sheltered from taxes—thus the Q in the tax column. Our recommendation was to cancel the policy and put the $5,282 proceeds in a Hartford single premium variable annuity (SPVA) which earns a higher yield (the stock fund averaged 12.85 per year for 10 years) and is sheltered from taxes. Assuming good health and average longevity, the Coopers will be better off with such a switch. In 15 years (life expectancy for a 65-year-old male) the cash value of the single premium deferred annuity would be much greater than the death benefit in the old policy. What is more important is that Abe and Bernice can use the income from the SPVA while they are alive.

## Social Security

Abe's Social Security income amounts to $1,023 per month ($12,276 per year) and Bernice, when she retires will receive her entitlement of $770 per month ($9,247 per year).

## Pensions

One of the major decisions the Coopers have to make involves their pensions. Both have the option to take a lump sum instead of the annual annuity. Although our initial recommendation was for them both to take a lump-sum payment, they are very conservative and feel they would prefer to take Abe's as an annuity of $1,562 per month ($18,753 per year). They did agree to take Bernice's $53,622 as a lump sum instead of the monthly annuity offered of $438 ($5,265 per year). Even though they will receive a lower monthly income from her IRA, they agreed that having the $53,622 in her IRA more than made up for the small loss in income.

We completed a lump sum distribution calculation on her $53,622 and decided that the IRA was the better

way to go. Thirty thousand dollars was to be invested in the Kemper U.S. government fund earning 8.54% and the balance of $23,622 in a Merrill Lynch GNMA unit investment trust at 8.43%.

## What's the Bottom Line?

How well did the Coopers do with the proposed changes? Net after Taxes, they increased their income from $45,299 to $47,312 for a gain of $2,013 in spendable income. They also increased their sheltered income (IRA's and deferred annuities) from $16,230 to $20,916 a gain of $4,686. Their total percentage increase was 10.1%.

Other benefits they received were:

• Better diversification

• A balanced portfolio and hopefully

• The inflation problem solved.

## What's Left if Abe Dies Before Bernice?

One of Abe's main concerns was what Bernice would have to live on if he died before her. Their combined income with both living would amount to $71,943 per year. If Abe died first, Bernice would lose $28,000 per year in income (his pension $18,753 and her $9,247 Social Security. She would continue to receive his $12,276 Social Security payment). This would mean her income would be $43,943 per year, with $485,127 in total assets.

They both agreed that this was more than enough to take care of her needs for the rest of her life. They agreed that Abe, whose health is very good, should choose the maximum pension plan that his employer offered, knowing that Bernice would not be left wanting, if he died first. Since funds were invested in both domestic and foreign stocks the buying power of the Cooper's income should remain somewhat level. There is indeed a risk in investing in equities but there is, in our opinion, a far greater risk in ignoring inflation.

# 12

# Case Study II— Carol M. Wright

> Net Worth $1,191,894
>
> Income Needs $50,000

Carol Wright, a single attorney, lives in Libertyville, Illinois. She practiced alone in Chicago for 23 years and then received an attractive offer from a large, very successful law firm. Now, after 21 years with the firm, she is ready to retire at age 69.

Having been single all her life, she was able to spend her considerable free time on her favorite interests. A devout Episcopalian, Carol gave freely of her time and income to religious causes. Evangelism and ecumenism are her special concerns. She looks forward in retirement to spending 3 or 4 days a month in this work.

Her younger brother's 3 children are dear to her and live near by. She expects to leave the bulk of her estate to them. Her church will receive a large bequest as well.

A few years back Carol suffered a stroke, but was able to return to work shortly thereafter. At age 69, she decided to quit work altogether and spend her remaining years pursuing her church work and travel.

## Investments

As a single person, Carol has been able to amass a fairly sizable estate over the years (see Table 12-1). She owns two homes. Her Libertyville residence has been valued, in this weak real estate market, at $142,000. She owns it free and clear of mortgages.

About 10 years ago she purchased a small country house. Its current value is $57,000 and has a mortgage balance of $14,379. She likes both houses and intends to keep them in retirement.

As a private practitioner, Carol was able to set up a Keogh pension plan for her retirement. However, for economic reasons she was not able to start it until her practice was well established and, therefore, accumulated only about $30,000. When she entered her present law firm, she rolled over the Keogh plan into an IRA. It grew slowly in her local bank and 3 years ago she transferred it to a large brokerage house IRA. She now has $88,327 with the brokerage house and $19,380 with her bank.

Despite her generosity toward her church, other charities, and her nieces and nephews, she was able to save about $117,000 in CDs and money market accounts. She invested on a buy and hold basis in common stock. Her stocks have a current value of about $200,000. She has a Treasury bill worth $127,000 and a Ginnie Mae trust valued at about $37,000. One municipal bond was purchased a year ago and is currently valued at

$53,000. Finally, she invested about $13,000 9 years ago in a single premium deferred annuity with Aetna Life. Its current value is $27,355. A brief summary of her vital statistics, investment objectives and projected balance sheet and income statement follow.

## INVESTMENT OBJECTIVES AND VITAL STATISTICS

Carol M. Wright

| | |
|---|---|
| Age | 69 |
| Retiring | 11/1/92 |
| Salary (1991) | $95,000 |
| Post-Retirement Income Needs After taxes | $50,000 |

### Investment Objectives
1. Income
2. Safety of principal
3. Growth
4. Tax reduction
5. Stability of buying power

## Asset Allocation

Currently Carol has 62% of her assets in so-called safe investments (savings, money markets, CDs and Treasuries), 20% in growth, 4% in government agencies, 9% in corporate bonds, and 5% in muni bonds. According to the CDA Optimizer Program, this type of portfolio would produce an expected return of 7.4% per year. Graphically, her present investment portfolio is shown in Exhibit 12-1.

Giving Carol a risk tolerance of "30" on a scale of "1 to 100" (with "100" being the gambler type), we found that her overall expected annual return could be increased from 7.4% before these changes to 9.5% after. The 28% increase in yield should go a long way to solve the inflation problem.

**TABLE 12-1**

## PROJECTED BALANCE SHEET AND INCOME STATEMENT—
## CAROL M. WRIGHT, JULY 1991
### Current Holdings

| Due Date | Asset Description | Current Value | Interest Rate or Dividend | Income | Tax* Status |
|---|---|---|---|---|---|
| | **Savings Account** | | | | |
| | Dreyfus Liquid Assets | $25,460 | 5.03% | $1,281 | |
| | Fidelity M.M. | $16,419 | 5.40% | $887 | |
| | **Checking** | | | | |
| | Great Western | $4,733 | 0.00% | $0 | |
| | **CDs** | | | | |
| Feb 92 | Great Western | $12,769 | 6.25% | $798 | |
| Mar 92 | Dime | $17,298 | 6.30% | $1,090 | |
| Dec 92 | Finstar | $40,777 | 6.55% | $2,671 | |
| Mar 93 | Lincoln IRA | $19,380 | 6.90% | $1,337 | Q |

## Common Stock

| | | | | | |
|---|---|---|---|---|---|
| 1123 | Anheuser-Busch | $62,884 | 2.00% | $1,258 | |
| 927 | Lilly (Eli) | $68,813 | 2.80% | $1,926 | |
| 1336 | Pepsico | $40,418 | 1.70% | $687 | |
| 480 | McGraw-Hill | $28,980 | 3.60% | $1,043 | |

## Bonds

| | | | | | |
|---|---|---|---|---|---|
| Mar 92 | Treasury Bill | $127,000 | 4.51% | $5,728 | |
| Nov 04 | IBM-IRA | $46,544 | 9.38% | $4,364 | Q |
| Sept 98 | Texaco-IRA | $41,783 | 8.65% | $3,614 | Q |
| | GNMA UIT | | | | |
| | Brown #57 | $37,093 | 9.10% | $3,375 | |
| Jan 07 | Rockford IL. Gen. Ob. | $53,077 | 6.60% | $3,503 | X |

## Real Estate

| | | | | | |
|---|---|---|---|---|---|
| | Residence | $142,000 | | | |
| | Country House | $57,000 | | | |

**Life Ins. C.V.**

| | | | | | |
|---|---|---|---|---|---|
| | AEtna Deferred Annuity | $27,355 | 7.60% | $2,079 | Q |

## Social Security

| | | | | | |
|---|---|---|---|---|---|
| | Carol (age 69) | | | $14,018 | |

**TABLE 12-1** (*Continued*)

| Asset Description | Current Value | Interest Rate | Income | Tax* Status |
|---|---|---|---|---|
| **Pension** | | | | |
| Lump Sum Dist. | $336,491 | 7.50% | $25,237 | |
| **Totals** | $1,206,273 | | $74,896 | |
| **Loans** | | | | |
| Mortgages | $14,379 | | | |
| Margin | $0 | | | |
| Other Loans | $0 | | | |
| **Net Worth** | $1,191,894 | | | |
| Salary (after retirement) | | | $0 | |
| **Tax Computation:** | | | | |
| Adjusted Gross Income | | | $74,896 | |

**Non-Taxable Items**

| | |
|---|---|
| Social Security (amount not taxed) | ($7,009) |
| Tax Exempts | ($3,503) |
| Qualified Funds (if not withdrawn) | ($11,394) |

**Gross Taxable**     $52,990

| | |
|---|---|
| Deductions (Personal) | ($2,150) |
| Deductions (Other) | ($8,366) |

**Net Taxable**     $42,474

| Taxes | Rate | |
|---|---|---|
| Federal | 28% | ($9,247) |
| State | 2.3% | ($381) |

**Net Income After Taxes**
(Leaving $11,394 of IRA income unused)     $53,874

*Letters in the "Tax Status" column indicate the following: X = Tax-free; Q = Tax-deferred.

## EXHIBIT 12-1  WRIGHT'S CURRENT PORTFOLIO HOLDINGS

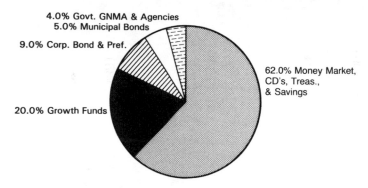

4.0% Govt. GNMA & Agencies
5.0% Municipal Bonds

9.0% Corp. Bond & Pref.

62.0% Money Market, CD's, Treas., & Savings

20.0% Growth Funds

Total Portfolio:  Expected Annual Return 7.4%

*Source:* CDA Investment Technologies, Inc.

As Exhibit 12-2 shows, her risk-oriented investments did increase a fair amount (growth funds from 20% to 25% and international funds from 0% to 5%), but the sizable increase in yield made it worthwhile.

## Recommendations

Now let's turn our attention to the specific recommendations we made to Carol. (See Table 12-2, the before and after balance sheet and income statement.) Remember, the companies used here are only examples. It is up to you to discuss this with your broker, or financial planner, as to whether these or other highly rated companies would suit your needs best.

First of all, we kept about $21,000 in short-term savings, for emergencies. ($16,419 in Fidelity money market and $4,733 in Great Western checking account). Our first investment was to the Rochester Fund, a tax-free bond for $25,460. One CD (due December, 1992) of $40,777 was to be left on hold rather than incur an early withdrawl penalty. However, when it comes due,

**EXHIE** **EXHIBIT 12-2   COMPARATIVE PORTFOLIO**
**HOLC** **HOLDINGS (CURRENT VS. OPTIMUM)**
**TOLE** **(RISK TOLERANCE IS 30)**

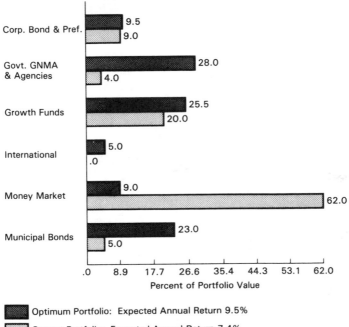

Percent of Portfolio Value

■ Optimum Portfolio: Expected Annual Return 9.5%
□ Current Portfolio: Expected Annual Return 7.4%

*Source:* CDA Investment Technologies, Inc.

it could be put in one of the growth funds or the government agency funds.

We put $30,067 in a *Value Line* Tax-Exempt High-Yield Fund earning 6.70%. Also, $19,380 was to be invested in Growth Fund of America which averaged 15.17% per year for the past 10 years.

The stock analysis showed us that three stocks received "above average" ratings for Timeliness by *Value Line.* (See Appendix A.) We recommended a hold on these. McGraw-Hill, however, received a "below average" rating and we recommended selling. Since it was purchased in 1979 at $12 per share, we allowed for a capital gains tax of $8,000. The balance, $20,980, was

## TABLE 12-2

## PROJECTED BALANCE SHEET AND INCOME STATEMENT— CAROL M. WRIGHT, JULY 1991

| Due Dates | Assets Description | Before | | | | After | | | | | Asset To Be Bought |
|---|---|---|---|---|---|---|---|---|---|---|---|
| | | Current Value | Interest Rate or Dividends | Income | Tax Status | | Current Value | Interest Rate or Dividends | Income | Tax Status | |
| | **Savings Accounts** | | | | | **Savings Accounts** | | | | | |
| | Dreyfus Liquid Assets | $25,460 | 5.03% | $1,281 | | S | | | | | |
| | | | | | | B | $25,460 | 6.90% | $1,757 | X | Rochester Fund |
| | Fidelity M.M. | $16,419 | 5.40% | $887 | | H | $16,419 | 5.40% | $887 | | |
| | **Checking** | | | | | **Checking** | | | | | |
| | Great Western | $4,733 | 0.00% | $0 | | H | $4,733 | 0.00% | $0 | | |
| | **CDs** | | | | | **CDs** | | | | | |
| Feb 92 | Great Western | $12,769 | 6.25% | $789 | | S | | | | | |
| Mar 92 | Dime | $17,298 | 6.30% | $1,090 | | S | | | | | |
| | | | | | | B | $30,067 | 6.70% | $2,014 | X | Value Line Tax-Exempt High Yield |
| Dec 92 | Finstar | $40,777 | 6.55% | $2,671 | | H | $40,777 | 6.55% | $2,671 | | |
| Mar 93 | Lincoln IRA | $19,380 | 6.90% | $1,337 | Q | S | | | | | |
| | | | | | | B | $19,380 | 13.00% | $2,519 | Q | Growth Fund of America |

## Common Stock

| Shares | Common Stock | Value | Rate | Income | | Owner | Value | Rate | Income | | Notes |
|---|---|---|---|---|---|---|---|---|---|---|---|
| 1123 | Anheuser-Busch | $62,884 | 2.00% | $1,258 | | H | $62,884 | 2.00% | $1,258 | | |
| 927 | Lilly (Eli) | $68,813 | 2.80% | $1,926 | | H | $68,813 | 2.80% | $1,926 | | |
| 1336 | Pepsico | $40,418 | 1.70% | $687 | | H | $40,418 | 1.70% | $687 | | |
| 480 | McGraw-Hill | $28,980 | 3.60% | $1,043 | | S | $8,000 | | | | Capital Gains Tax Due |
| | | | | | | B | | | | | Quest for Value |
| | | | | | | B | $20,980 | 13.00% | $2,727 | | |

## Bonds

| | Bonds | Value | Rate | Income | | Owner | Value | Rate | Income | | Notes |
|---|---|---|---|---|---|---|---|---|---|---|---|
| Mar 92 | Treasury Bill | $127,000 | 4.51% | $5,728 | | S | $77,000 | 6.10% | $4,697 | X | Calvert T/F LTD Term |
| | | | | | | B | $50,000 | 6.59% | $3,295 | X | Nuveen Ins #225 |
| Nov 04 | IBM IRA | $46,544 | 9.38% | $4,364 | Q | H | $46,544 | 9.38% | $4,364 | Q | |
| Sep 98 | Texaco IRA | $41,783 | 8.65% | $3,614 | Q | H | $41,783 | 8.65% | $3,614 | Q | |
| | GNMA UIT(UC) Brown #57 | $37,093 | 9.10% | $3,375 | | H | $37,093 | 9.10% | $3,375 | | |
| Jan 07 | Rockford IL. Gen. Ob. | $53,077 | 6.60% | $3,503 | X | H | $53,077 | 6.60% | $3,503 | X | |

## Real Estate

| | Real Estate | Value | | | | Owner | Value |
|---|---|---|---|---|---|---|---|
| | Residence | $142,000 | | | | H | $142,000 |
| | Country House | $57,000 | | | | H | $57,000 |

## Life Ins. Cash Value

| | Life Ins. Cash Value | Value | Rate | Income | | Owner | Value | Rate | Income | |
|---|---|---|---|---|---|---|---|---|---|---|
| | Aetna Deferred Ann. | $27,355 | 7.60% | $2,079 | Q | H | $27,355 | 7.60% | $2,079 | Q |

## Social Security

| | Social Security | Value | | | | Owner | Value |
|---|---|---|---|---|---|---|---|
| | Carol @69 | $14,018 | | | | H | $14,018 |

**TABLE 12-2** *(Continued)*

| Assets Description | Before Current Value | Interest Rate | Income | Tax Status | After Current Value | Interest Rate | Income | Tax Status | Asset To Be Bought |
|---|---|---|---|---|---|---|---|---|---|
| **Pension** | | | | | **Pension** | | | | |
| Lump Sum Dist. | $336,491 | 7.50% | $25,237 | | | | | S | Rollover IRA |
| | | | | | $100,000 | 8.60% | $8,600 | B | Alliance Mortgage Securities |
| | | | | | $100,000 | 8.45% | $8,450 | B | Merrill Lynch Federal Securities |
| | | | | | $50,000 | 13.00% | $6,500 | B | G.T. International Growth |
| | | | | | $50,000 | 8.20% | $4,100 | B | Eaton Vance Government Obligations |
| | | | | | $36,491 | 12.0% | $4,379 | B | Guardian Park Avenue |
| **Total** | $1,206,273 | | $74,896 | | $1,206,273 | | $87,421 | | |
| Loans Mortgages | ($14,379) | | | | ($14,379) | | | | |
| **Net Worth** | $1,191,894 | | | | $1,191,894 | | | | |

|  | | |
|---|---|---|
| Salary | $0 | $0 |
| Adjusted Gross Income | $74,896 | $87,421 |
| **Non-Taxable Items** | | |
| Social Security | ($7,009) | ($7,009) |
| Tax Exempts | ($3,503) | ($15,266) |
| Qualified Funds | ($11,394) | ($12,576) |
| **Gross Taxable** | $52,990 | $52,570 |
| Deductions (Personal) | ($2,150) | ($2,150) |
| Deductions (Other) | ($8,366) | ($8,366) |
| **Net Taxable** | $42,474 | $42,054 |
| **Taxes** | | |
| Federal 28% | ($9,247) | ($9,130) |
| State 3.0% | ($1,162) | ($1,168) |
| **Net After Tax** | $56,763 | $68,218 |

(Leaving $11,394 of qualified income in IRAs)

(Leaving $12,576 of qualified income in IRAs and annuities)

*The letters stand for:

H   Hold current asset (no change recommended).
S   Sell current asset (now or at maturity).
B   Buy (for each Sell there is a buy recommendation).
X   Tax-free or tax-deferred assets.
Q   Qualified funds (i.e., IRA rollovers, profit-sharing plans, T.D.A. plans, 403-B plans, and the like).

to be invested in a Quest for Value Fund which averaged 17.99% per year in total return for the past 10 years.

We recommended the sale of the Treasury bill and investment of $77,000 in a short-term municipal bond fund called Calvert Tax-Free Limited-Term Fund. It paid 6.1% in November, 1991. The bonds in this fund had an average term of one year. Fifty thousand dollars was placed in a Nuveen Municipal Bond Fund paying 6.59% per year tax-free.

After studying her lump-sum distribution analysis (see Table 12-3), we recommended that Carol's pension lump-sum distribution of $336,491 be rolled over into an IRA and $250,00 invested in safe government agency bond funds and *unit* investment trusts paying from 8.2% to 8.6%.

Fifty thousand dollars was invested in G.T. International Growth, whose total return was 16.49% per year for the past 5 years. Another $36,491 was put in Guardian Park Avenue Fund which averaged 16.97% per year in total return for the past 10 years.

## What's the Bottom Line?

The bottom line on these changes, after allowing reasonable reductions in yields, was an increase in the income stream before taxes of $12,525 ($87,421 − $74,896)—a 17% increase.

Of course, there is no guarantee that any of the growth funds will perform as well as we indicate. That's the risk we all must take if we are trying to maintain the buying power of our current income.

## Health Considerations

Carol had a stroke about 3 years ago and is concerned about a possible reoccurrence. After considering this at length, she decided that in light of the possibility of spending a fair amount of time in a nursing

## TABLE 12-3

## LUMP-SUM DISTRIBUTION TAX ANALYSIS
## FOR CAROL M. WRIGHT,
## NOVEMBER 15 1991

### 10-Year Average

| | | |
|---|---|---|
| Total L.S.D. | $336,491 | |
| Divided by 10 | $33,649 | |
| Add back | $2,570 | |
| Total | $36,219 | |
| Tax* | $7,874 | |
| Total Tax | | ($78,740) |
| Balance Available | | $257,751 |
| After Tax | | |
| Invested Tax-Free @ | | 6.5% |
| After-Tax Income | | **$16,754** |

### 5-Year Average

| | | |
|---|---|---|
| Total L.S.D. | $336,491 | |
| Div. by 5 | $67,298 | |
| Tax** | $16,738 | |
| Total Tax | | ($83,690) |
| Balance Available | | $252,801 |
| After Tax | | |
| Invested Tax-Free @ | | 6.5% |
| After-Tax Income | | **$16,432** |

### IRA Rollover

| | | |
|---|---|---|
| L.S.D. | $336,491 | |
| Invested @ | 8.5% | |
| Gross Income | $28,602 | |
| Clients Tax Rate | 28% | |
| Tax | $8,008 | |
| Net Income A/T | | **$20,593** |

### Comparison

| | |
|---|---|
| 10-Yr. Averaging Net A/T | $16,754 |
| 5-Yr. Averaging Net A/T | $16,432 |
| IRA Rollover Net A/T | $20,593 |

*Tax—You must use 1986 single rates for 10-yr. average.
**Tax—Use the current tax rate for the 5-yr. average.

home that her favorite people be protected by setting up two *living trusts*.

The first would receive $500,000 of her assets, invested as we recommended. The income stream would be paid to Carol during her lifetime and would be available to pay part of her costs at a nursing home. The principal ($500,000) could not be touched by the government or nursing home because it would go to those individuals she included in her trust as "remaindermen" (her nieces and nephews).

A second trust would be set up with $100,000 of assets. Again, income to Carol during her life and the principal would go to her church and other favorite charities at her death.

# 13

# Case Study III— Hank and Irene Young

Net Worth $1,386,078

Income Needs $70,000

Henry and Irene Young own a large store called Young's Hardware in Modesto, California, a mid-size city about 100 miles west of San Francisco. They opened the store 36 years ago with some financial help from Irene's parents. Its current value is about $250,000, and it is debt free, except for the usual small short-term inventory loans. The business pays Hank $78,000 per year and Irene $31,000.

The target date for their retirement is August 1, 1992. Since they established a defined benefit pension

plan 14 years ago, they expect to receive lump-sum distributions of $267,000 for Hank and $65,000 for Irene.

In addition to their pensions, Hank entered into a deferred compensation agreement with his corporation. It was funded by a $150,000 life insurance policy and a growth-oriented side fund. At retirement time, Hank expects the total will be worth $150,000. By agreement, Hank is to be paid $15,000 per year for 10 years.

A number of years ago, Hank started a 401(k) plan at the store and expects that his account will be worth $49,000 on August 1, 1992. Irene's 401(k) will be worth about $21,000.

The Young's have 3 children: Lawrence 39 years old, Elizabeth 36, and Jennifer 29. Larry joined the hardware store 12 years ago and has made a sizable contribution to its growth. He is married and has 1 child. Elizabeth lives in Princeton, New Jersey, with her husband, Philip. They are expecting their first child in a few months. Jennifer, Hank, and Irene's youngest child, is single and works for a small accounting firm in San Francisco.

Since Hank is approaching 68 years of age and Irene is almost 65, they decided to sell their business to Larry for $200,000 ($50,000 less than its probable value). The terms of the agreement included payments over 10 years at 10% interest. The numbers were arrived at after considering Larry's ability to run the business profitably and at the same time to provide Hank and Irene with a reasonable return on their years of time and effort in building the business. The income would be $2,643 per month or $31,716 per year. Hank and Larry's agreement included a provision to delay payments in case of poor business conditions.

### INVESTMENT OBJECTIVES AND VITAL STATISTICS—HANK AND IRENE YOUNG

Ages
| | |
|---|---|
| Hank | 68 |
| Irene | 65 |

**INVESTMENT OBJECTIVES AND VITAL STATISTICS—HANK AND IRENE YOUNG**
*(Continued)*

| | |
|---|---|
| Retiring | 8/1/92 |
| 1991 Salaries | |
| Hank | $78,000 |
| Irene | $31,000 |
| Post-Retirement Income Needs | |
| After taxes | $70,000 |

Investment Objectives
1. Stability of buying power
2. Income
3. Growth
4. Safety of principal
5. Tax avoidance

Their projected current balance sheet and income statement is shown in Table 13-1. We suggest you read this before continuing with the text.

The names of firms used below as examples are, indeed, only examples. Your broker, financial planner, and/or investment service newsletters will provide many other excellent options.

## Spendable Income

Hank and Irene would have $75,193 of spendable income without touching their IRAs at all. Since they indicated that they wanted $70,000 to live on, it seems that they are in pretty good shape. However, there are a few problems facing them. In 10 years, they will lose the income from the deferred compensation plan ($15,000), and the business buyout ($31,716) will be completed. However, their untapped IRA income (currently $33,754 per year), may be able to replace the loss. The biggest problem facing them, however, is inflation.

## TABLE 13-1

## PROJECTED BALANCE SHEET AND INCOME STATEMENT— HANK AND IRENE YOUNG, JULY 1991

### Current Holdings

| Due Date | Asset Description | Current Value | Interest Rate or Dividends | Income | Tax* Status |
|---|---|---|---|---|---|
| | **Savings Account** | | | | |
| | Bank of America | $12,000 | 5.50% | $660 | |
| | Wells Fargo | $6,000 | 5.50% | $330 | |
| | **Checking** | | | | |
| | Bank of America | $7,000 | 5.50% | $385 | |
| | Wells Fargo | $2,000 | 5.50% | $110 | |
| | **Money Market** | | | | |
| | Bank of America | $44,000 | 4.75% | $2,090 | |
| | Wells Fargo | $29,000 | 4.48% | $1,299 | |
| | Great Western | $68,000 | 4.70% | $3,196 | |

|  | CDs |  |  |  |
|---|---|---|---|---|
| 6/92 | Bank of America (IRA) | $12,500 | 7.30% | Q |
| 4/93 | Wells Fargo (Keogh) | $38,000 | 6.50% | Q |

| Shares | Common Stocks |  |  |  |
|---|---|---|---|---|
| 100 | Automatic Data | $3,325 | 1.30% | $43 |
| 200 | Bell Atlantic | $9,300 | 5.40% | $502 |
| 300 | Federal Realty | $5,738 | 7.70% | $442 |
| 200 | IBM | $19,900 | 4.90% | $975 |
| 200 | Ohio Edison | $3,625 | 8.30% | $301 |
| 1000 | Young's Hardware Inc. (Closely Held Corp.) | $200,000 | (By contract) | $31,716 |

| Bonds |  |  |  |  |
|---|---|---|---|---|
| Jul 93 | NYS Power Authority | $49,450 | 9.70% | $4,797 | X |
| Mar 02 | Calif. State GO | $45,740 | 7.30% | $3,339 | X |

| Real Estate |  |  |  |
|---|---|---|---|
| Residence | $225,000 | 0.00% | $0 |
| Summer House | $110,000 | 0.00% | $0 |
| Investment Real Estate | $67,000 | 5.00% | $3,350 |
| Real Estate Ltd Partnership | $25,000 | 1.75% | $438 |

**TABLE 13-1** (*Continued*)

| Asset Description | Current Value | Interest Rate or Dividends | Income | Tax* Status |
|---|---|---|---|---|
| **Corporate Savings Plans** | | | | |
| Deferred Comp. (10 yrs.) | | | $15,000 | |
| 401(k) Plan (Hank) | $49,000 | 8.25% | $4,043 | Q |
| 401(k) Plan (Irene) | $21,000 | 8.25% | $1,733 | Q |
| **Life Ins. C.V.** | | | | |
| Nat'l Service Life | $6,000 | 6.00% | $360 | Q |
| **Social Security** | | | | |
| Hank's | | | $13,196 | |
| Irene's | | | $6,138 | |
| **Pension** | | | | |
| Lump-Sum Dist. (Hank) | $267,000 | 7.30% | $19,491 | Q |
| Lump-Sum Dist. (Irene) | $65,000 | 7.30% | $4,745 | Q |
| **Totals** | $1,390,578 | | $122,060 | |

## Loans

| | |
|---|---|
| Mortgages | $0 |
| Margin | $0 |
| Other Loans | $4,500 |

**Net Worth** $1,386,078

**Salary (after retirement)** $0

**Tax Computation:**

**Adjusted Gross Income** $122,060

## Non-Taxable Items

| | |
|---|---|
| Social Security (50%) | ($9,667) |
| Tax Exempt Income | ($8,136) |
| Qualified Income (if not withdrawn) | ($33,754) |

**Gross Taxable** $70,504

| | |
|---|---|
| Deductions (Personal) | ($4,300) |
| Deductions (Itemized) | ($11,500) |

**Net Taxable** $54,704

**TABLE 13-1** (*Continued*)

| Taxes | Rate | Income |
|---|---|---|
| Federal | 28% | ($10,897) |
| State | 3.9% | ($2,216) |
| **Net Income After Tax** (With $33,754 of income left in IRAs) | | $75,193 |

*Letters in the "Tax Status" column indicate the following: X = Tax-free; Q = Tax-deferred.

## Inflation Analysis

Assuming inflation averages 5% per year over the next 20 years and Hank and Irene's $75,193 net after-tax income remains constant, the buying power of that income would decrease every year. Table 13-2 shows us how much they need in income to equal the buying power of the $70,000 of 1992 income they say they need.

This is simple arithmetic. In 1997, they will need $89,340 of spendable income to replace the buying power of today's $70,000, assuming the inflation rate stays at a steady 5% per year. In 10 years, when Hank's deferred compensation and buyout income ends, in addition to losing $46,716 of income they will still need $114,023 to live on. Assuming they leave their IRAs untouched and that they earn 8% per year in income and inflation stays at 5%, the $452,500 in their IRAs would have grown to $608,122 at the rate of 3% (8% − 5%). At 8%, that principal would then produce $48,650 in gross income. That would be just enough to keep their standard of living the same. But they should be *planning* to live another 10 years (to Hank's 88th and Irene's 85th birthdays). With a long life in mind, changes must be made in their approach to investments. They must seek a higher return on their assets. 8% will not be adequate.

## Asset Allocation

According to our asset allocation program, the annual return on the Youngs' present program is not 8%, but, rather, 6.3%. With 81% of their assets invested in

### TABLE 13-2

**BUYING POWER VS 5% INFLATION**

| | |
|---|---|
| 1992 | $70,000 |
| 1997 | $89,340 |
| 2002 | $114,023 |
| 2007 | $145,525 |
| 2012 | $185,731 |

short-term savings, money market, and CDs, 8% in municipal bonds, 8% in investment real estate and REITS, and 3% in growth stock, they will not be able to cover their income needs for the next 20 to 25 years. Graphically, their holdings can be seen in the pie chart in Exhibit 13-1.

Since the Youngs are a low-risk tolerance couple, they were assigned a rate of "30" on a scale of "0 to 100." We added 3 new asset classes (see Exhibit 13-2):

1. government agencies;

2. small capitalization funds; and

3. international funds.

This new configuration should produce, over a long-term investment period, a 50% increase in yield from their current average annual return of 6.3% as opposed to the 9.6% their new investments should provide. Keep in mind that these projections are based on past history and are not guaranteed.

### EXHIBIT 13-1   THE YOUNG'S CURRENT PORTFOLIO HOLDINGS

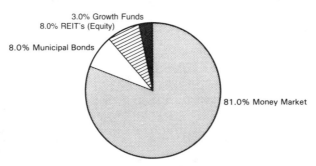

Total Portfolio: Expected Annual Return 6.3%

*Source:* CDA Investment Technologies, Inc.

The bar chart on the following page shows the changes that we suggest take place in their asset allocation.

Knowing their current assets, future plans, and objectives and having agreed on a long-term asset allocation plan, we recommended the investment changes shown in the before and after balance sheet and income statement in Table 13-3.

## Recommendations

Noticeable here was a very common tendancy of most investors—the Youngs had entirely too much money in short-term assets (savings accounts, checking, money market, and CDs): $218,500, to be exact. They agreed that all they needed for emergencies in money market and checking accounts was $15,000 to $20,000. We recommended that $118,000 be invested in a single premium variable annuity with Prudential Discovery Plus. The full amount would be invested in the Stock Index fund which has averaged 16.79% per year for the past 3 years. We project 10% per year. As we pointed out in Chapter 7, there are no taxes on the income until it is withdrawn. Thus the Q in the tax status column.

Thirty-one thousand dollars would be invested in the T. Rowe Price High Yield Tax-Free Bond Fund which pays 6.3% per year tax-free, and $50,500 in the Phoenix Growth Fund, which earned 19.2% per year for the past 10 years.

A study of *Value Line's* analysis of their stock portfolio (see Appendix A) indicated that two of the stocks had a number "4"—"below average" rating and two a number "3"—"Average" rating for timeliness and, therefore, in our opinion should be sold. Automatic Data was rated 2 and should be held. We estimated a capital gains tax on the sale of these stocks at $6,000, leaving $32,563 to be invested in a Franklin California Tax-Free Bond fund paying 7.06% (free of both federal and state taxes).

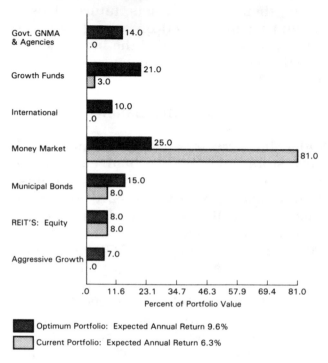

**EXHIBIT 13-2   COMPARATIVE PORTFOLIO HOLDINGS (CURRENT VS. OPTIMUM, RISK TOLERANCE IS 30)**

Govt. GNMA & Agencies: 14.0 / .0
Growth Funds: 21.0 / 3.0
International: 10.0 / .0
Money Market: 25.0 / 81.0
Municipal Bonds: 15.0 / 8.0
REIT'S: Equity: 8.0 / 8.0
Aggressive Growth: 7.0 / .0

.0   11.6   23.1   34.7   46.3   57.9   69.4   81.0
Percent of Portfolio Value

Optimum Portfolio: Expected Annual Return 9.6%
Current Portfolio: Expected Annual Return 6.3%

*Source:* CDA Investment Technologies, Inc.

Since Hank will retire August 1, 1992 and would receive both his 401(k) funds ($49,000) and his lump-sum pension ($267,000), in the same year, we recommend that they both be rolled over into an IRA. This way, $49,000 would be invested in Oppenheimer Global fund, which averaged 15.07% per year for the past 5 years.

We recommend that Irene delay the reception of her 401(k) funds until 1993, when she can use the 10-year average plan and pay only 5.8% in federal taxes ($1,232). The balance would be invested in the Franklin California Tax-Free Fund, paying 7.06% per year totally tax-free.

## TABLE 13-3

## CREATIVE RETIREMENT PLANNING—PROJECTED BALANCE SHEET AND INCOME STATEMENT FOR HANK AND IRENE YOUNG

*November 1991*

| | | Before | | | | After | | | | | |
|---|---|---|---|---|---|---|---|---|---|---|---|
| Due Date | Assets Description | Current Value | Interest or Dividends | Income | Tax Status | | Current Value | Interest or Dividends | Income | Tax Status | Asset To Be Bought |
| | **Savings Accounts** | | | | | **Savings Accounts** | | | | | |
| | Bank of America | $12,000 | 5.50% | $660 | | S | | | | | |
| | Wells Fargo | $6,000 | 5.50% | $330 | | S | | | | | |
| | | | | | | B | $18,000 | 10.00% | $1,800 | Q | Prudential SPVA "Discovery Plus" |
| | **Checking** | | | | | **Checking** | | | | | |
| | Bank of America | $7,000 | 5.50% | $385 | | H | $7,000 | 5.50% | $385 | | |
| | Wells Fargo | $2,000 | 5.50% | $110 | | H | $2,000 | 5.50% | $110 | | |
| | **Money Market** | | | | | **Money Market** | | | | | |
| | Bank of America | $44,000 | 4.75% | $2,090 | | P | $10,000 | 4.75% | $475 | | |
| | Wells Fargo | $29,000 | 4.48% | $1,299 | | S | | | | | |
| | Great Western | $68,000 | 4.70% | $3,196 | | S | | | | | |
| | | | | | | B | $100,000 | 10.00% | $10,000 | Q | Prudential SPVA |
| | | | | | | B | $31,000 | 6.30% | $1,953 | X | T. Rowe Price Tax-Free High Yield |

# TABLE 13-3 (Continued)

| | | Before | | | | After | | | | | |
| | Assets Description | Current Value | Interest or Dividends | Income | Tax Status | | Current Value | Interest or Dividends | Income | Tax Status | Asset To Be Bought |
|---|---|---|---|---|---|---|---|---|---|---|---|
| **CDs** | | | | | | **CDs** | | | | | |
| Jun 92 | Bank of America (IRA) | $12,500 | 7.30% | $913 | Q | S | | | | | |
| Apr 93 | Wells Fargo (Keogh) | $38,000 | 6.50% | $2,470 | Q | S | | | | | |
| | | | | | | B | $50,500 | 13.00% | $6,565 | Q | Phoenix Growth |
| **Common Stocks** | | | | | | **Common Stocks** | | | | | |
| 100 | Automatic Data | $3,325 | 1.30% | $43 | | H | $3,325 | 1.30% | $43 | | |
| 200 | Bell Atlantic | $9,300 | 5.40% | $502 | | S | | | | | |
| 300 | Federal Realty | $5,738 | 7.70% | $442 | | S | | | | | |
| 200 | IBM | $19,900 | 4.90% | $975 | | S | | | | | |
| 200 | Ohio Edison | $3,625 | 8.30% | $301 | | S | | | | | |
| | | | | | | B | $6,000 | | | | Capital Gains Tax |
| 1000 | (Closely Held Corp.) 200.00 | $200,000 | (Per contract) | $31,716 | | B | $32,563 | 7.06% | $2,299 | X | Franklin Cal. Tax-Free |
| | | | | | | H | $200,000 | 0.00% | $31,716 | | |
| **Bonds** | | | | | | **Bonds** | | | | | |
| Jul 93 | Power Authority | $49,450 | 9.70% | $4,797 | X | H | $49,450 | 9.70% | $4,797 | X | |
| Mar 2002 | Calif. State GO | $45,740 | 7.30% | $3,339 | X | H | $45,740 | 7.30% | $3,339 | X | |

## Real Estate & Corp. Plans

| | Value | % | Amount | | | Value | % | Amount | | Fund |
|---|---|---|---|---|---|---|---|---|---|---|
| **Residence** | $225,000 | 0.00% | | | H | $225,000 | 0.00% | $0 | | |
| **Summer House** | $110,000 | 0.00% | | | H | $110,000 | 0.00% | $0 | | |
| **Investment Real Estate** | $67,000 | 5.00% | $3,350 | | H | $67,000 | 5.00% | $3,350 | | |
| **Real Estate Ltd Partnership** | $25,000 | 1.75% | $438 | | H | $25,000 | 1.75% | $438 | | |
| **Deferred Comp. (10 Yrs.)** | $15,000 | | | | H | $15,000 | | | | |
| **401(k) Plan (Hank)** | $49,000 | 8.25% | $4,043 | Q | S / B | $49,000 | 12.00% | $5,880 | Q | Oppenheimer Global |
| **401(k) Plan (Irene)** | $21,000 | 8.25% | $1,733 | Q | S / B | $1,232 / $19,768 | 0.00% / 7.06% | $0 / $1,396 | X | 10 Yr. Avg. Tax Franklin Cal. Tax-Free |

### Life Ins. C.V.

| | Value | % | Amount | | | Value | % | Amount | | |
|---|---|---|---|---|---|---|---|---|---|---|
| **Nat'l Service Life** | $6,000 | 6.00% | $360 | Q | H | $6,000 | 6.00% | $360 | Q | |

### Social Security

| | Value | | | | | Value | | | | |
|---|---|---|---|---|---|---|---|---|---|---|
| **Hank's** | $13,196 | | | | H | $13,196 | | | | |
| **Irene's** | $6,138 | | | | H | $6,138 | | | | |

### Pension

| | Value | % | Amount | | | Value | % | Amount | | Fund |
|---|---|---|---|---|---|---|---|---|---|---|
| **Lump-Sum Dist. (Hank)** | $267,000 | 7.30% | $19,491 | Q | S | | | | | |
| | | | | | B | $50,000 | 12.00% | $6,000 | Q | Putnam Global Growth |
| | | | | | B | $50,000 | 8.40% | $4,200 | Q | Scudder GNMA—AARP |
| | | | | | B | $67,000 | 9.11% | $6,104 | Q | Putnam U.S. Government |
| | | | | | B | $100,000 | 12.00% | $12,000 | Q | IDEX Fund |
| **Lump-Sum Dist. (Irene)** | $65,000 | 7.30% | $4,745 | Q | B / S | $65,000 | 11.00% | $10,400 | Q | Alger Small Cap. |
| **Total** | $1,390,578 | | $122,060 | | | $1,390,578 | | $147,943 | | |

**TABLE 13-3** (*Continued*)

| Assets Description | Before | | | | After | | | | Asset To Be Bought |
|---|---|---|---|---|---|---|---|---|---|
| | Current Value | Interest or Yield | Income | Tax Status | Current Value | Interest or Yield | Income | Tax Status | |
| **Loans** | | | | | | | | | |
| Mortgages | $0 | | | | $0 | | | | |
| Margin | $0 | | | | $0 | | | | |
| Other | $4,500 | | | | $4,500 | | | | |
| **Net Worth** | $1,386,078 | | | | $1,386,078 | | | | |
| **Salary** | | | | $0 | | | | $0 | |
| **Adjusted Gross Income** | | | $122,060 | | | | $147,943 | | |
| **Non-Taxable Items** | | | | | | | | | |
| Social Security | | | ($9,667) | | | | ($9,667) | | |
| Tax Exempts | | | ($8,136) | | | | ($13,783) | | |
| Qualified Funds | | | ($33,754) | | | | ($63,309) | | |
| **Gross Taxable** | | | $70,504 | | | | $61,184 | | |
| Deductions (Personal) | | | ($4,300) | | | | ($4,300) | | |
| Deductions (Itemized) | | | ($11,500) | | | | ($11,500) | | |

**Net Taxable**
**Taxes**

|  |  | ($54,704) |  | ($45,384) |
|---|---|---|---|---|
| Federal | 28% | ($12,213) | 28% | ($9,603) |
| State | 9.3% | ($5,654) | 9.3% | ($4,666) |

**Net After Tax**                $70,439                                    $70,365*

(Leaving $33,754 of qualified income)        (Leaving $63,309 of qualified income)

You will notice letters in the dividing column between the "Before" and "After" section, they indicate the following:

H   Hold (keep investment as is).
P   Partial hold (hold the amount indicated).
S   Sell (sell or swap this investment).
B   Buy (buy this investment).

The letters in the "Tax Status" column indicate the following: X = Tax-free; Q = Tax-deferred.

On Hank's pension lump-sum distribution, we recommended $50,000 to Putnam Global Growth which averaged 16.33% per year for the last 10 years, $50,000 to Scudder GNMA (through the AARP) paying about 8.4%, $67,000 to Putnam U.S. Government paying 9.11% (note that the total invested in Putnam Funds is over $100,000 and therefore receives a lower sales charge) and $100,000 to the Idex Fund which averaged 16.39% per year for the past 5 years.

Finally, Irene's lump sum of $65,000 would be invested in Alger Small Cap. Fund, which has averaged 33.18% per year for the past 3 years.

Although Hank and Irene have increased their gross income by $25,883 ($147,943 vs. $122,060) they have not increased the risk of loss appreciably. According to our asset allocation program their current expected annual return of 6.3% could have gone up or down by 1.7%. The new investment program would give them an expected annual return of 9.6% with a 2.5% up or down possibility. In our opinion, the addition of $25,883 per year in anticipated income far outweighs the additional risks they will be taking.

# 14

## Case Study IV— Christine DeSanto, Early Retirement

> **Net Worth $309,261**
>
> **Income Needs $30,000**

Early retirement programs are now quite common. Municipal governments have offered them to police and firemen for years. Teachers and other municipal workers are also included. The federal government started offering early retirement decades ago for the military and many unions have won it in collective bargaining. In recent years, corporations have started a real push to encourage their older employees to take the big step and retire early.

Early retirement programs have become quite popular with companies that are trying to reduce costs by trimming what they consider to be excess workers and layers of management. In order to avoid layoffs that can have a demoralizing effect on the remaining workers, corporate America has tried to encourage workers to leave voluntarily through "retirement incentive" programs. There are many different packages offered to employees as inducements. In general, however, the

retirement incentive increases the employees' retirement benefits in one or more of the following ways:

- *Paying a Cash Bonus*—This is a flat, one-time payment—the employee receives, for example, one week's pay for each year he or she worked for the company.

- *Adding Years of Service and Increasing Employees Age* (for the purpose of computing the annual pension)—This increases the pension amount that will be received annually.

- *Paying a Pension Supplement to Age 62*—This extra monthly payment is meant to provide additional income until Social Security begins at age 62.

- *Ensuring Enhanced Medical Benefits*—This ensures that when the company is changing to a less favorable medical plan, the employee is allowed to keep the old plan.

Some pension plans actually encourage retirement well before age 65 by limiting the maximum monthly pension benefit that a worker can receive. The formula for computing the pension might state that once the employee has 25 years of service and has attained the age of 55, he or she will receive the maximum pension. If the employee chooses to continue working, the pension will not be increased. This type of plan is common among unions if an increase in the maximum pension has to be negotiated every few years when a new contract is settled with the employer. Certain jobs, such as police, firemen and teachers, have allowances for early retirement.

During the early 1980s, there were tremendous changes in America's corporate structure. Leveraged buyouts, both friendly and unfriendly, resulted in the breakup of many established corporations and the loss of many jobs. Corporate mergers quite often result in

layoffs or retirement incentives. When 2 companies merge, an initial result is the duplication of many jobs (*e.g.*, two payroll departments, two personnel departments, and the like).

Clearly then, if you are planning to retire well before the age of 65, there are some very important considerations to analyze. For example, because of advances in medical treatments, people today live longer and are in better health than were previous generations. According to the tables used by life insurance companies (see page 8), a 55-year-old man today has a life expectancy of 21.28 years, and a 55-year-old woman has one of 23.67 years. Therefore, you have to plan on stretching your assets over a longer period. Another way to look at this problem is that a person retiring at age 55 has fewer years of saving and more years of spending compared to a person who retires at 65.

Inflation will also have a far greater impact on the person who chooses to retire early. There will be more years for the cost of living to increase and more years for the purchasing power of your income to decrease. If inflation were to remain at the 4.5% level for the next 10 years, today's dollar would be worth only 63 cents. In 20 years, the dollar value would be worth only 40 cents! In order to counter the increased effect of inflation, we strongly believe a significant portion of the investment portfolio should be allocated to growth investments.

## Leisure Time

Do you plan to devote more time to an existing hobby or take up a new avocation? Perhaps you're looking forward to playing lots of golf or tennis or maybe learning a new hobby. You may not want to stop working at all, but instead plan a change from your current high-stress job to one that is less demanding and have more time for yourself.

Just as you plan for your finances in retirement, you should also give serious thought to what you'll do with all that free time.

Psychologists demonstrate that we derive a lot more from our jobs than just the salary that is paid to us. We get a great deal of satisfaction from finishing a challenging project or solving a difficult problem. Achieving career goals provides a great feeling of accomplishment. We also get a sense of belonging when we work alongside others at our jobs.

Some experts believe that in order to successfully make the emotional transition to retirement, a person should plan for some leisure activities that will continue to challenge the mind as well as others that will challenge the body and spirit. Therefore, a variety of activities are recommended. You might want to take some classes in a subject that has always interested you or do some sort of volunteer work that will give you a sense of accomplishment.

As you won't be seeing your friends on the job on a daily basis anymore, you may want to target certain social activities that will give you a chance to make new friends, such as joining a club or some service organization. Church, temple, or community-orientated activities can fill a great need for many retirees.

Some choose to work part time. In doing so, they are able to make social contacts, challenge themselves on the job, and supplement their income at the same time. For example, if you plan to retire at age 57, you might want to work part time to give you extra income until age 62 when Social Security begins. This should allow you to put a larger part of your assets in growth investments that do not generate much current income but will help to counter the effects of inflation later on.

## IRA Distributions

If you find that you need extra income to carry you from your date of retirement until you reach age 62 when Social Security begins, you can now tap your IRA

before you're 59½ without paying the 10% penalty. The Tax Reform Act of 1986 changed the law to allow for premature IRA distributions without penalty if the distributions qualify as "substantially equal periodic payments."

What qualifies as "substantially equal periodic payments?" First of all, the payments must be made at least annually and continue for at *least* 5 years *or* until you reach the age of 59½, whichever comes later. The IRS now allows 3 different methods for computing the amount of each payment, which result in 3 different allowable distribution levels.

The first method is the simplest and is the same as that used for figuring your minimum IRA distribution at age 70½. First, determine your life expectancy from an actuarial table. Your current IRA account balance is then divided by this number to figure the amount of your first withdrawal. Each year you recalculate your life expectancy (using the tables), or you can lock in your first-year life expectancy and reduce this number by one digit for each year thereafter. Recalculating your life expectancy each year will result in a slightly smaller distribution.

*Example:* A 50-year-old male with a $100,000 IRA would divide $100,000 by 33.1 (his life expectancy) resulting in a first-year distribution of $3,021.

The second, more complicated method amortizes the IRA over your life expectancy using a "reasonable" interest rate. The IRS provides the following example: a 50-year-old male with $100,000 in his IRA using an 8.0% interest rate would take out $8,037 each year.

The third, also more complicated, method involves dividing your IRA account by an "annuity factor" that takes into account your life expectancy combined with a "reasonable" interest rate. The IRA example for this method uses an annuity factor of 11.109 for our 50-year-old man. The $100,000 IRA divided by 11.109 results in a yearly distribution of $8,335.

Remember, the method that you choose to use must be continued for the greater of five years or until you reach age 59½. At that age you can change or even stop taking payments. If you break this rule, *ALL* of the payments taken will be hit with the 10% penalty retroactively: Once you reach age 62 and Social Security begins, you can cut back on your IRA distributions and let this money grow again to help fight inflation in your later years.

Now let's turn our attention to a case study.

Christine DeSanto is 58 years old and lives in Miami, Florida. She is divorced and has two children, Rosemarie and Jean. Christine has been a teacher in the Dade County School System for 33 years and is planning to retire at the end of the current school year. She is eligible for the full pension benefit, having taught for more than 30 years and being over age 55. Christine expects to receive $21,500 as an annual pension. Her salary in this, her final year of teaching, is $43,000.

Her two children are fully independent and she does not expect to have to aid either of them financially. Rosemarie, age 32, is an assistant vice president at a local bank and is in charge of one of the data processing departments. Jean, age 28, has followed in her mother's footsteps and entered the teaching profession. She teaches special education and enjoys the challenge of working with children who have learning disabilities. Neither Rosemarie nor Jean is marrried and both live within an hour's drive of Miami.

Christine is eagerly anticipating retirement and has plans to spend a good deal of her time pursuing her two favorite pastimes: listening to classical music and playing golf. She has plans to combine both of these hobbies on future trips to cities that have both highly regarded symphony orchestras and challenging golf courses! Christine is also planning a trip to Europe to visit the birthplaces of some of the great classical composers. Other plans include becoming more active in her church and donating six hours per week to Project

Literacy U.S. to help disadvantaged children learn to read.

Christine plans on remaining in her apartment, which she rents for $850 per month in Miami. She always rented and never bought investment real estate. She likes the climate in south Florida, which allows her to play golf all year round and remain near her children.

As is common with many school systems around the country, Dade County has a provision for a tax-deferred annuity (403-B) plan to supplement her pension. Using this plan, Christine was able to contribute a certain portion of her salary each month, before taxes, to her own tax-deferred annuity. These contributions, plus interest earned over the years, has grown to $121,000. The money has never been taxed and Christine has a choice: a monthly distribution for the rest of her life (like a second pension) or a lump sum that she can roll over to an IRA. There it would grow and remain tax-deferred until she decides to withdraw it.

Christine has old IRAs totalling $27,015 that are invested in CDs. Christine expects to receive $9,200 per year from Social Security beginning in 1996. Her other assets include various bank savings accounts, EE bonds, and some utility stocks inherited from her father's estate in 1988. A list of these other assets are shown in the projected balance sheet and income statement in Table 14-1.

### CHRISTINE DeSANTO

| | |
|---|---|
| Age | 58 |
| Retiring | 7/1/92 |
| 1991 Salary | $43,000 |
| Post-Retirement After-Tax Income Needs | $30,000 |

**Investment Objectives:**

1. Safety of principal.
2. Income.

**TABLE 14-1**

## PROJECTED BALANCE SHEET AND INCOME STATEMENT— CHRISTINE DeSANTO (VALUES AT NOVEMBER 1991)

### Current Holdings

| Due Dates | Asset Description | Current Value | Interest Rate or Dividends | Income | Tax* Status |
|---|---|---|---|---|---|
| | **Savings Account** | | | | |
| | Citibank | $26,600 | 5.50% | $1,463 | |
| | Amerifirst | $20,860 | 5.30% | $1,106 | |
| | Dade County Credit Union | $22,300 | 5.50% | $1,227 | |
| | **Checking** | | | | |
| | Barnett Bank | $5,000 | 0.00% | $0 | |
| | **CDs** | | | | |
| Dec 92 | Barnett Bank | $30,425 | 6.55% | $1,993 | |
| Aug 92 | Barnett Bank IRA | $14,100 | 6.30% | $888 | Q |
| Jan 93 | Amerifirst Bank IRA | $5,450 | 6.55% | $357 | Q |
| Apr 93 | Citibank IRA | $4,775 | 6.70% | $320 | Q |
| Jun 93 | Barnett Bank IRA | $2,690 | 6.90% | $186 | Q |

## Common Stock

| | | | | |
|---|---|---|---|---|
| 240 | AT&T | $9,360 | 3.50% | $328 |
| 72 | Ameritech | $4,284 | 5.70% | $244 |
| 108 | Bellsouth | $5,157 | 5.20% | $268 |
| 96 | Bell Atlantic | $4,464 | 5.00% | $223 |
| 200 | FPL Group | $6,075 | 8.00% | $486 |
| 48 | NYNEX | $3,540 | 6.10% | $216 |
| 96 | Pacific Telesis | $3,912 | 4.80% | $188 |
| 72 | Southwestern Bell | $3,825 | 5.30% | $203 |
| 96 | U.S. West | $3,444 | 5.60% | $193 |

## Bonds

| | | | | |
|---|---|---|---|---|
| | U.S. (EE) Bonds | $12,000 | 6.75% | $810 |

## Thrift Plan

| | | | | |
|---|---|---|---|---|
| | Tax-Deferred Annuity | $121,000 | 7.50% | $9,075 |

## Social Security

| | | |
|---|---|---|
| | Begins in 1996 | $0 |

## Pension

| | | |
|---|---|---|
| | Teachers Annual Pension | $21,500 |

**TABLE 14-1** (*Continued*)

|  | Current Value | Income |
|---|---|---|
| **Totals** | $309,261 | $41,272 |
| **Loans** | | |
| Mortgages | $0 | |
| Margin | $0 | |
| Other Loans | $0 | |
| **Net Worth** | $309,261 | |
| **Salary (after retirement)** | | $0 |
| **Tax Computation:** | | |
| **Adjusted Gross Income** | | $41,272 |

## Non-Taxable Items

| | |
|---|---:|
| Social Security | ( $0) |
| Tax Exempts | ( $0) |
| Qualified Funds | ($10,826) |

**Gross Taxable**      $30,446

| | |
|---|---:|
| Deductions (Personal) | ($2,150) |
| Deductions (Standard) | ($3,400) |

**Net Taxable**      $24,896

| **Taxes** | **Rate** | |
|---|---|---:|
| Federal | 28.0% | ($4,325) |
| State | | ($24) |
| Total Tax | | $4,349 |

**Net Income After Taxes**      $26,097
(Leaving $10,826 of Qualified income
inside IRAs and Thrift Plans)

*The letter Q in the "Tax Status" column indicates tax-deferred.

3. Stability of buying power.
4. Growth.
5. Tax reduction.

Christine feels that she will need $30,000 in after-tax income to maintain her present lifestyle. The big problem facing her is how to generate this income while, at the same time, ensuring enough growth in her assets. to keep up with inflation over her longer than average retirement years. According to life expectancy tables, Christine must plan for the next 25.9 years and quite possibly longer if she beats the averages.

An additional problem that Christine faces is that her Social Security income of approximately $9,200 per year will not begin until 1996.

In order to fight inflation, her plan is to try not to draw income from her tax-deferred annuity and her IRAs, thereby allowing this money to continue to grow. The value of her tax-deferred annuity is $121,000 and of her old IRAs another $27,015, for a total of $148,015. If she is able to get by on her pension plus the dividends and interest earned on her stocks and savings accounts, then the $148,015 in her tax-deferred accounts will form the lion's share of her inflation hedge.

Since Christine needs $30,000 to live on after taxes, we note that the $26,097 of after-tax income produced by her current investments will not do it. She, therefore, must start withdrawing right away from her IRAs. As we have already noted this can be done without penalty (see pages 233 and 234 for a full explanation). If she were to withdraw the full $10,826 she is earning in her existing IRAs she would pay income tax on that sum— $3,031—leaving her with a net spendable amount of $7,795. This added to her $26,097 would total $33,892, a little more than she needs. Of course, she does not have to withdraw the full $10,826 from her IRAs. She could leave three or four thousand in the IRAs and thus defer the taxes on the balance. Yes, she could live nicely on her $30,000 and have a few thousand left over. But, what about the future? Will she, say in 5 years, be able

to live on the $30,000 she needs today? Inflation says
no. Table 14-2 shows why.

As you can see, her income needs will increase each
year because of inflation. For example, in the year 2002
when she will be only 68, she will need $48,867 to equal
the buying power of todays $30,000.

In her current portfolio, the only items that will
increase in value will be her stocks and Social Security.
That will start in 4 years and bring in approximately
$9,200 per year. In our opinion, investment changes will
have to be made. To help us decide where to make
these changes we turn our attention to asset allocation.

## Asset Allocation

Using our asset allocation program, we find that
Christine's current portfolio has only 2 asset classes.
She has 92% in the Money Market category (including
CDs, annuities, and money markets) and 8% in the *growth*
category (stocks and bonds). The expected annual return for this total portfolio is 6.1% as shown on the pie
chart in Exhibit 14-1.

By reallocating the amounts in each of these categories and by adding two new categories, we find that
the expected annual return can be increased to 9.0%.
Since Christine is looking for a relatively low-risk in-

## TABLE 14-2

### INFLATION IMPACT (AT 5% PER YEAR)

| | |
|---|---|
| 1992 | $30,000 |
| 1997 | $38,288 |
| 2002 | $48,867 |
| 2007 | $62,368 |
| 2012 | $79,599 |

### EXHIBIT 14-1    DeSANTO'S CURRENT PORTFOLIO HOLDINGS

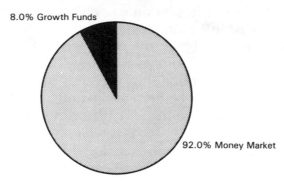

8.0% Growth Funds

92.0% Money Market

Total Portfolio: Expected Annual Return 6.1%

*Source:* CDA Investment Technologies, Inc.

vestment portfolio, on a scale of "1 to 100," with "1" being the lowest risk tolerance, we consider her a "20."

Her graph of the comparative portfolio holdings (see Exhibit 14-2) shows how the amounts allocated to each of the four categories are either increased or decreased to reach the optimum portfolio generating 9.0%. The Money Market category is reduced to 45%, which is made up almost exclusively by her $21,500 pension. (We assumed its Lump Sum equivalent to be about $25,000.) The international stock category, a new category for her, is set at 9.5%. The growth category is increased from 8% to 30.5%. The GNMA and government agencies, the other new category, would be 15%.

Knowing that her present portfolio was quite inadequate for the future and that sizeable changes would have to be made in her investments, we did an item-by-item analysis. We came up with the following before and after balance sheet and income statement (see Table 14-3). The reasons for our recommendations will be explained in the next few pages. As always, keep in mind that there are a vast number of equally good, profitable corporations, funds, and other instruments to choose from. The ones we choose are just examples.

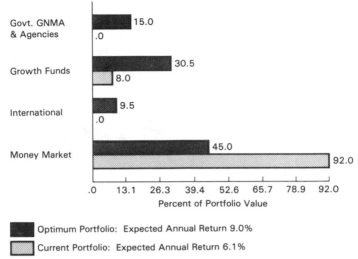

**EXHIBIT 14-2   COMPARATIVE PORTFOLIO HOLDINGS (CURRENT VS. OPTIMUM, RISK TOLERANCE IS 10)**

Optimum Portfolio: Expected Annual Return 9.0%

Current Portfolio: Expected Annual Return 6.1%

*Source:* CDA Investment Technologies, Inc.

# Recommendations

## Cash Section

Our first step is to decide on an amount to be kept liquid for emergencies. Christine felt $10,000 would be sufficient. We suggested that she keep $5,000 in one of her money market accounts and $5,000 in a checking account. We also suggested that she open an interest-bearing checking account instead of her current one which pays no interest. Looking at the balance sheet, we see that Christine has far too much of her money in relatively low-interest savings accounts and CDs.

The balance of Christine's savings accounts should be invested as follows: $30,000 to be invested in the Growth Fund of America, which had an average total return of 15.17% per year for the past 10 years, $34,760 in a U.S. government bond mutual fund offered by Sun

# CREATIVE RETIREMENT PLANNING

## TABLE 14-3

## PROJECTED BEFORE AND AFTER BALANCE SHEET AND INCOME STATEMENT— CHRISTINE DeSANTO, NOVEMBER 1991

### Creative Retirement Planning

| Due Date | Asset Description | Before Current Value | Interest Rate or Dividends | Income | Tax Status | After Current Value | Interest Rate or Dividends | Income | Tax Status | Assets To Be Bought |
|---|---|---|---|---|---|---|---|---|---|---|
| | **Savings Accounts** | | | | | | | | | |
| | Citibank | $26,600 | 5.50% | $1,463 | | $5,000 | 5.50% | $275 | P | Savings Account |
| | Amerifirst | $20,860 | 5.30% | $1,106 | | | | | S | |
| | Dade County Credit Union | $22,300 | 5.50% | $1,227 | | | | | S | |
| | | | | | | $34,760 | 8.26% | $2,871 | B | Sun America U.S. Government |
| | | | | | | $30,000 | 13.00% | $3,900 | B | Growth Fund of America |
| | **Checking** | | | | | | | | | |
| | Barnett Bank | $5,000 | 0.00% | $0 | | | | | S | |
| | | | | | | $5,000 | 5.50% | $275 | B | Interest Checking |
| | **CDs** | | | | | | | | | |
| Dec 92 | Barnett Bank | $30,425 | 6.55% | $1,993 | | | | | S | |
| | | | | | | $30,425 | 8.10% | $2,464 | B | Fund For U.S. Government |

| | | | | | | | | | | | |
|---|---|---|---|---|---|---|---|---|---|---|---|
| Aug 92 | Barnett Bank IRA | $14,100 | 6.30% | $888 | Q | H | $14,100 | 6.30% | $888 | Q | Hold until due |
| Jan 93 | Amerifirst IRA | $5,450 | 6.55% | $357 | Q | H | $5,450 | 6.55% | $357 | Q | Invest in Growth |
| Apr 93 | Citibank IRA | $4,775 | 6.70% | $320 | Q | H | $4,775 | 6.70% | $320 | Q | Funds when due |
| Jun 93 | Barnett Bank IRA | $2,690 | 6.90% | $186 | Q | H | $2,690 | 6.90% | $186 | Q | |

**Shares  Common Stocks**

| | | | | | | | | | | | |
|---|---|---|---|---|---|---|---|---|---|---|---|
| 240 | AT&T | $9,360 | 3.50% | $328 | | H | $9,360 | 3.50% | $328 | | |
| 72 | Ameritech | $4,284 | 5.70% | $244 | | S | | | | | |
| 108 | Bellsouth | $5,157 | 5.20% | $268 | | S | | | | | |
| 96 | Bell Atlantic | $4,464 | 5.00% | $223 | | S | | | | | |
| 200 | FPL Group | $6,075 | 8.00% | $486 | | H | $6,075 | 8.00% | $486 | | |
| 48 | Nynex | $3,540 | 6.10% | $216 | | S | | | | | |
| 96 | Pacific Telesis | $3,912 | 4.80% | $188 | | S | | | | | |
| 72 | Southwestern Bell | $3,825 | 5.30% | $203 | | S | | | | | |
| 96 | U.S. West | $3,444 | 5.60% | $193 | | H | $3,444 | 5.60% | $193 | | |
| | | | | | | B | $3,500 | | | | Capital Gains Tax Due |
| | | | | | | B | $21,682 | 13.00% | $2,819 | | Templeton Foreign |

**Bonds**

| | | | | | | | | | | | |
|---|---|---|---|---|---|---|---|---|---|---|---|
| | U.S. (EE) Bonds | $12,000 | 6.75% | $810 | | S | | | | | |
| | | | | | | B | $12,000 | 6.75% | $810 | | Savings Bonds (HH) |

**Thrift Plan**

| | | | | | | | | | | | |
|---|---|---|---|---|---|---|---|---|---|---|---|
| | Tax-Deferred Annuity | $121,000 | 7.50% | $9,075 | Q | S | | | | | Rollover to IRA |
| | | | | | | B | $60,000 | 11.00% | $6,600 | Q | Met Life Capital Appreciation |
| | | | | | | B | $31,000 | 14.00% | $4,340 | Q | Fidelity Magellan |
| | | | | | | B | $30,000 | 8.87% | $2,661 | Q | Lord Abbett U.S. Government |

**TABLE 14-3** (Continued)

| Asset Description | Before Current Value | Before Income | After Current Value | After Income |
|---|---|---|---|---|
| **Social Security** | | | | |
| Begins in 1994 | | $0 | H | $0 |
| **Pension** | | | | |
| Teachers Annual Pension | | $21,500 | H | $21,500 |
| **Totals** | $309,261 | $41,272 | $309,261 | $51,273 |
| **Loans** | | | | |
| Mortgages | $0 | | $0 | |
| Margin | $0 | | $0 | |
| Other Loans | $0 | | $0 | |
| **Net Worth** | $309,261 | | $309,261 | |
| **Salary** | | $0 | | $0 |
| **Adjusted Gross Income** | | $41,272 | | $51,273 |

**Non-Taxable Items**

| | | |
|---|---:|---:|
| Qualified Funds | ($10,826) | ($15,352) |
| **Gross Taxable** | $30,446 | $35,921 |
| Deductions (Personal) | ($2,150) | ($2,150) |
| Deductions (Standard) | ($3,400) | ($3,400) |
| **Net Taxable** | $24,896 | $30,371 |
| Taxes — Rate | 28% | 28% |
| Federal | $4,325 | $5,858 |
| State | $24 | $24 |
| **Net Income After Tax** | $26,097 | $30,039 |

(Leaving income inside IRAs & TDAs of $10,826)

(Leaving income inside IRAs of $15,352)

*The letters dividing the columns represent:

H    Hold current asset (no change recommended).

S    Sell current asset (now or at maturity).

B    Buy (for each sell there is a buy recommendation).

Q    Qualified funds (i.e., IRA rollovers, profit-sharing plans, T.D.A. plans, 403-B plan, and the like).

America. This fund paid a monthly income of about $239 in November of 1991 (about $2,871 per year).

Her $30,425 CD due in December 1992 was to be kept until due then invested in the Fund For U.S. Government which paid 8.10%. The other IRA-CD investments were to be held until due then invested in "growth" funds.

## Common Stock

Christines' stock holdings were inherited from her fathers' estate as mentioned earlier. They are all utilities which pay dividends ranging from a low of 3.50% for AT&T to a high of 8.0% from FPL GROUP. The current value of the stock portfolio is $44,061 and the annual income from dividends totals $2,348.

Christine's common stock problems are two-fold: first, the income is relatively low (5%) and, second, she has no easily organized way to take the growth in value of her stocks.

Using *Value Line*'s analysis, we recommend that she sell all stocks rated number 4—below average (see Appendix A.), pay her taxes (estimated at $3,500), and invest the balance $21,682 in Templeton Foreign which averaged 18.26% per year in total return for the last 5 years. Our estimate for Christine was only 13% per year with a further recommendation that she use her right to receive a systematic withdrawal of for example 10% per year.

## Bonds

Christine's only bond holdings are her $12,000 in matured U.S. savings bonds (EE). The tax-deferred nature of these bonds was good for her while she was working, but now she needs income. We therefore recommended that she convert these to (HH) bonds, which are another type of U.S. savings bond that pay income.

The $12,000 will now generate an annual income of approximately $810.

## Tax-Deferred Annuity

Christine's other retirement benefit is her tax-deferred annuity. It has grown to $121,000 and earns 7.5% per year. She has two choices facing her with this money. One, she could choose to "annuitize" (take an immediate and fixed annuity). This money would then be paid to her as a fixed monthly income (of $950) for the rest of her life. Christine agreed that this would *not* be a good idea because she would have no growth potential (to offset inflation) and would be using up her principal. Christine's second choice is to roll over the entire $121,000 into an IRA account and invest it in accordance with her overall asset allocation program. This would also allow her to choose when to begin to draw income from the IRA where the money will grow, tax-deferred, until she needs it. In fact, Christine plans to defer this IRA income for four years. As noted earlier, she hopes to be able to get by on her pension and the income from her other assets until Social Security begins in 1996.

Our recommendations for the investment of her IRA assets are as follows: $60,000 to Met Life Capital Appreciation Fund whose total return averaged 17.20% per year for the past 5 years. $31,000 to Fidelity Magellan which averaged 21.19% for the same 10 years. And $30,000 to Lord Abbett U.S. government bond fund that paid 8.87% in income.

Christine's other IRAs, which are all at local banks in CDs, can be added to her large IRA rollover account when they mature in order to consolidate her holdings and reduce the number of IRA statements she will receive.

When Christine's annual pension of $21,500 is added to the income generated by her other assets, invested as we have recommended, she will have a total income

of $51,273 before taxes. This includes $15,352 generated by her IRA accounts. As noted earlier, she plans to let this $15,352 continue to grow in her IRA accounts and not use it for current income.

After subtracting the estimated federal tax, she will have $30,039 of spendable income.

## What's the Bottom Line?

By implementing our recommendations, Christine has increased her net after-tax income by $3,942 ($30,039 − $26,097). And this does not include the $15,352 additional income and growth from her IRAs.

It should be noted, however, that along with her increase in income, there has also been an increase in risk. Nonetheless, the changes recommended in Christine's investment portfolio are prudent, and will meet her income needs now and in the future.

Other benefits she received were:

• Greater diversification

• A balanced portfolio, and hopefully

• A solution to the inflation problem

# Appendix A

## Value Line's Ratings

This appendix represents the Value Line report (evaluation) of each stock mentioned in the case studies. We feel that it would be helpful to you to see in detail how we arrived at our opinion to Buy, Hold, or Sell a stock. They are alphabetized for easy researching and are cut in half to keep the type size reasonably large. The major information of value to you is:

- *Timeliness?*—Value Line's recommendation as to whether or not this was a good stock to own in the fall of 1991 when the case studies were written. Value Line rates stock as follows:

    1—Highest
    2—Above Average
    3—Average
    4—Below Average
    5—Lowest

- *Safety* and
- *Stock Price* chart

In our opinion any stock with a timeliness rating of 4 to 5 should not be held by a retired person. Depending on how much stock an individual owns, how they obtained it (inherited, purchased through a broker or at work), what percentage of their assets are in equities, and a few other factors helps us to decide to the #3 rated stocks should be held or sold.

# ABBOTT LABS. NYSE-ABT

| | | |
|---|---|---|
| **RECENT PRICE** 54 | **P/E RATIO** 20.7 (Trailing: 22.7) (Median: 15.0) | **RELATIVE P/E RATIO** 1.44 | **DIV'D YLD** 2.0% | **VALUE LINE** 199 |

**TIMELINESS** 2 Above Average (Relative Price Perform-ance Next 12 Mos.)

**SAFETY** 1 Highest
(Scale: 1 Highest to 5 Lowest)

**BETA** 1.05 (1.00 = Market)

| | High: | 7.1 | 8.1 | 10.3 | 13.3 | 12.2 | 18.0 | 27.5 | 33.5 | 26.2 | 35.2 | 46.4 | 55.6 |
|---|---|---|---|---|---|---|---|---|---|---|---|---|---|
| | Low: | 4.3 | 5.9 | 6.3 | 9.0 | 9.2 | 10.0 | 15.8 | 20.0 | 21.4 | 23.1 | 31.3 | 39.3 |

**1994-96 PROJECTIONS**
| | Price | Gain | Ann'l Total Return |
|---|---|---|---|
| High | 100 | (+85%) | 18% |
| Low | 80 | (+50%) | 12% |

**Insider Decisions**
| | N | D | J | F | M | A | M | J | J |
|---|---|---|---|---|---|---|---|---|---|
| to Buy | 1 | 1 | 1 | 1 | 1 | 0 | 2 | 1 | 0 |
| Options | 2 | 1 | 1 | 0 | 0 | 0 | 2 | 0 | 1 |
| to Sell | 3 | 0 | 0 | 0 | 0 | 3 | 1 | 0 | 1 |

**Institutional Decisions**
| | 4Q90 | 1Q91 | 2Q91 |
|---|---|---|---|
| to Buy | 171 | 171 | 192 |
| to Sell | 202 | 218 | 179 |
| Hld's(000) | 220023 | 216778 | 212988 |

2-for-1 split • 2-for-1 split • 14.0 x "Cash Flow" p sh • 2-for-1 split • Relative Price Strength

Target Price Range 1994 1995 1996

**CAPITAL STRUCTURE as of 6/30/91**
Total Debt $719.5 mill. Due in 5 Yrs $689.3 mill.
LT Debt $134.7 mill. LT Interest $10.5 mill.
Includes $83.6 mill. capitalized leases.
(Long-term interest earned: 127x; total interest coverage: 15.8x) (4% of Cap'l)

Pension Liability None

Pfd Stock None

Common Stock 426,542,117 shs. (96% of Cap'l)
as of 7/31/91

**Options: PHLE**

| | 1975 | 1976 | 1977 | 1978 | 1979 | 1980 | 1981 | 1982 | 1983 | 1984 | 1985 | 1986 | 1987 | 1988 | 1989 | 1990 | 1991 | 1992 | © VALUE LINE PUB., INC. | 94-96 |
|---|---|---|---|---|---|---|---|---|---|---|---|---|---|---|---|---|---|---|---|---|
| | 2.15 | 2.30 | 2.62 | 3.01 | 3.49 | 4.13 | 4.78 | 5.33 | 6.04 | 6.45 | 7.02 | 8.32 | 9.68 | 10.98 | 12.16 | 14.35 | 16.30 | 18.30 | Sales per sh | 27.50 |
| | .16 | .25 | .31 | .38 | .45 | .53 | .63 | .76 | .93 | 1.10 | 1.30 | 1.62 | 1.93 | 2.27 | 2.64 | 3.08 | 3.50 | 4.05 | "Cash Flow" per sh | 6.50 |
| | .16 | .20 | .25 | .31 | .37 | .43 | .50 | .59 | .72 | .84 | .97 | 1.16 | 1.39 | 1.67 | 1.93 | 2.22 | 2.55 | 2.95 | Earnings per sh A | 4.75 |
| | .05 | .06 | .07 | .10 | .13 | .15 | .18 | .21 | .25 | .30 | .35 | .42 | .50 | .60 | .70 | .84 | 1.00 | 1.16 | Div'ds Decl'd per sh B■ | 1.75 |
| | .12 | .11 | .13 | .18 | .23 | .33 | .40 | .47 | .62 | .67 | .57 | .77 | .89 | 1.16 | 1.30 | 1.49 | 1.70 | 1.80 | Cap'l Spending per sh | 2.00 |
| | .92 | 1.20 | 1.38 | 1.61 | 1.86 | 2.08 | 2.35 | 2.68 | 2.93 | 3.33 | 3.91 | 3.89 | 4.62 | 5.48 | 6.16 | 6.60 | 7.80 | 8.95 | Book Value per sh C | 14.50 |
| | 436.92 | 471.67 | 474.33 | 480.62 | 482.36 | 494.10 | 490.10 | 488.41 | 484.39 | 480.94 | 478.38 | 457.68 | 453.46 | 449.69 | 442.48 | 429.14 | 426.50 | 425.00 | Common Shs Outst'g D | 410.00 |
| | 13.9 | 14.3 | 11.9 | 12.8 | 11.8 | 13.0 | 14.0 | 13.5 | 15.9 | 12.9 | 14.1 | 18.9 | 20.7 | 14.1 | 15.3 | 17.2 | Bold figures are Value Line estimates | Avg Ann'l P/E Ratio | 19.0 |
| | 1.85 | 1.83 | 1.56 | 1.74 | 1.71 | 1.73 | 1.70 | 1.49 | 1.34 | 1.20 | 1.14 | 1.28 | 1.38 | 1.17 | 1.16 | 1.28 | | | Relative P/E Ratio | 1.60 |
| | 2.1% | 2.0% | 2.4% | 2.5% | 2.8% | 2.7% | 2.5% | 2.6% | 2.2% | 2.8% | 2.6% | 1.9% | 1.7% | 2.6% | 2.4% | 2.2% | | | Avg Ann'l Div'd Yield | 2.0% |
| | | | | | | | 2342.5 | 2602.4 | 2927.9 | 3104.0 | 3360.3 | 3807.6 | 4387.9 | 4937.0 | 5379.8 | 6158.7 | 6960 | 7785 | Sales ($mill) | 11300 |
| | | | | | | | 20.5% | 22.1% | 24.1% | 25.9% | 26.6% | 28.3% | 28.5% | 27.8% | 28.4% | 28.6% | 29.0% | 29.0% | Operating Margin | 30.5% |
| | | | | | | | 63.8 | 84.0 | 100.6 | 128.7 | 155.8 | 199.5 | 243.7 | 270.9 | 307.3 | 355.9 | 400 | 460 | Depreciation ($mill) | 650 |
| | | | | | | | 247.3 | 289.1 | 347.6 | 402.6 | 465.3 | 540.5 | 632.6 | 752.0 | 859.8 | 965.8 | 1085 | 1260 | Net Profit ($mill) | 1965 |
| | | | | | | | 37.0% | 38.9% | 39.5% | 37.7% | 33.0% | 34.0% | 32.5% | 28.8% | 28.0% | 28.5% | 29.5% | 28.0% | Income Tax Rate | 29.5% |
| | | | | | | | 10.6% | 11.1% | 11.9% | 13.0% | 13.8% | 14.2% | 14.4% | 15.2% | 16.0% | 15.7% | 15.6% | 16.2% | Net Profit Margin | 17.4% |
| | | | | | | | 192.7 | 230.8 | 616.0 | 743.3 | 891.9 | 585.4 | 668.7 | 913.3 | 719.3 | 460.0 | 625 | 800 | Working Cap'l ($mill) | 1225 |
| | | | | | | | 205.6 | 190.9 | 483.9 | 470.2 | 443.0 | 297.4 | 271.0 | 146.7 | 134.8 | 125 | 135 | Long-Term Debt ($mill) | 200 |
| | | | | | | | 1152.1 | 1310.9 | 1417.9 | 1602.7 | 1870.7 | 1778.9 | 2093.5 | 2464.7 | 2726.4 | 2833.6 | 3325 | 3795 | Net Worth ($mill) | 5900 |
| | | | | | | | 18.9% | 19.8% | 19.4% | 20.6% | 21.1% | 26.7% | 27.3% | 27.2% | 30.3% | 32.7% | 32.0% | 32.5% | % Earned Total Cap'l | 32.5% |
| | | | | | | | 21.5% | 22.1% | 24.5% | 25.1% | 24.9% | 30.4% | 30.2% | 30.5% | 31.5% | 34.1% | 33.0% | 33.0% | % Earned Net Worth | 32.5% |
| | | | | | | | 13.8% | 14.2% | 15.9% | 16.1% | 15.9% | 19.5% | 19.3% | 20.0% | 20.5% | 21.7% | 20.0% | 20.0% | % Retained to Comm Eq | 21.0% |
| | | | | | | | 36% | 35% | 35% | 36% | 36% | 36% | 36% | 35% | 35% | 36% | 39% | 39% | % All Div'ds to Net Prof | 37% |

**Percent shares traded**
| | 8.0 | 6.0 | 4.0 | 2.0 |
|---|---|---|---|---|

| CURRENT POSITION ($MILL) | 1989 | 1990 | 6/30/91 |
|---|---|---|---|
| Cash Assets | 48.7 | 53.2 | 203.3 |
| Receivables | 892.7 | 1070.1 | 1051.4 |
| Inventory (FIFO) | 696.0 | 777.6 | 816.7 |
| Other | 465.5 | 560.3 | 659.7 |
| Current Assets | 2102.9 | 2461.2 | 2731.1 |
| Accts Payable | 309.8 | 351.2 | 372.8 |
| Debt Due | 300.5 | 653.8 | 584.8 |
| Other | 773.3 | 986.2 | 1112.4 |
| Current Liab. | 1383.6 | 2001.2 | 2070.0 |

| ANNUAL RATES of change (per sh) | Past 10 Yrs. | Past 5 Yrs. | Est'd '88-'90 to '94-'96 |
|---|---|---|---|
| Sales | 13.5% | 14.0% | 14.0% |
| "Cash Flow" | 19.5% | 19.0% | 16.0% |
| Earnings | 18.0% | 19.0% | 16.0% |
| Dividends | 19.0% | 18.0% | 16.0% |
| Book Value | 12.5% | 12.5% | 15.5% |

| Cal-endar | QUARTERLY SALES ($ mill) | | | | |
|---|---|---|---|---|---|
| | Mar.31 | Jun.30 | Sep.30 | Dec.31 | Full Year |
| 1988 | 1188.4 | 1229.9 | 1212.4 | 1306.3 | 4937.0 |
| 1989 | 1295.5 | 1318.4 | 1310.3 | 1455.6 | 5379.8 |
| 1990 | 1438.4 | 1503.4 | 1506.8 | 1710.1 | 6158.7 |
| 1991 | 1653.6 | 1683.0 | 1695 | 1919.4 | 6950 |
| 1992 | 1835 | 1880 | 1885 | 2120 | 7785 |

| Cal-endar | EARNINGS PER SHARE A | | | | |
|---|---|---|---|---|---|
| | Mar.31 | Jun.30 | Sep.30 | Dec.31 | Full Year |
| 1988 | .38 | .41 | .38 | .50 | 1.67 |
| 1989 | .44 | .48 | .44 | .57 | 1.93 |
| 1990 | .51 | .55 | .51 | .65 | 2.22 |
| 1991 | .59 | .63 | .60 | .73 | 2.55 |
| 1992 | .65 | .73 | .70 | .85 | 2.95 |

| Cal-endar | QUARTERLY DIVIDENDS PAID B■ | | | | |
|---|---|---|---|---|---|
| | Mar.31 | Jun.30 | Sep.30 | Dec.31 | Full Year |
| 1987 | .105 | .105 | .125 | .125 | .48 |
| 1988 | .125 | .125 | .15 | .15 | .58 |
| 1989 | .15 | .15 | .175 | .175 | .68 |
| 1990 | .175 | .175 | .21 | .21 | .81 |
| 1991 | .21 | .21 | .25 | .25 | |

(A) Primary earnings. Next earnings report due late Oct. (B) Next dividend meeting about Dec 13 Goes ex div. 'end about Oct 8 Div- dend payment dates February 15, May 15, August 15, November 15. ■ Dividend reinvestment plan available. (C) Includes intangibles In 1990 $412.2 million, 96¢ a share (D) In millions adjusted for stock splits.

BUSINESS: Abbott Laboratories makes health care products including drugs, diagnostic tests, intravenous solutions, laboratory and hospital instruments, prepared infant formulas, and nutritional products. Also makes agricultural and chemical products. Brand names include Erythrocin, Similac, Isomil, Sucaryl, Murine, and Selsun Blue. 1990 sales (operating profits) by segment: Drug & nutritional, 51% (60%); Hosp. & lab, 49% (40%). Int'l business: 37% of sales, 25% of pretax profits. 1990 R&D: 9.2% of sales; depreciation rate: 8.4%. Estimated plant age: 5 years. Has 43,770 employees; 49,827 stockholders Insiders control .3% of stock. Retirement Plan, 6.9%. Chairman: D.L. Burnham. Inc.: Illinois. Address: One Abbott Park Road, North Chicago, IL 60064. Tel.: 708-937-6100.

It's steady as she goes for Abbott Labs, as earnings should continue to grow about 15% annually in 1991 and 1992. Through the first six months, sales rose 13.4%, with international business and hospital/lab products leading the advance. This, plus wider gross margins and fewer shares outstanding, more than made up for larger expenditures on R&D and product promotion, lower non-operating income, and a higher effective tax rate. Going forward, new drugs will probably play a more important role. We note that two antibiotics are being introduced worldwide and sales of a treatment for endometriosis should accelerate. Their contribution will probably help lift volume in the drug/nutritional product segment 12%, to $4 billion, in 1992, while widening margins. The hospital/lab group should achieve a similar sales gain, thanks to the launch of such offerings as the TDxFLx, which can randomly assay patient samples for up to 13 drugs. Higher selling expenses will probably limit profit growth, but not enough to prevent share earnings from rising 15%-16% in 1992, from an estimated $2.55 this year.

Hytrin should be generating sizable profits in the 1994-96 period. As an anti-hypertensive agent, this drug will probably contribute $125 million in sales this year. While considerable, this sum is but a fraction of what it may achieve as a treatment for non-cancerous enlargement of the prostate, a condition that afflicts 60% of men over the age of 50. Clinical trials have shown the drug improves urine flow, and Abbott plans to file a petition with the FDA by year end for this use. Yet, studies will continue in an effort to determine whether Hytrin and a Merck drug can act synergistically in treating the problem. (The two compounds work via different mechanisms.) The results might prove helpful in promoting Hytrin for the new use. Given the size of the market and the present need for pharmaceutical therapy, we've assumed Hytrin sales reach $500 million by mid-decade.

This investment-grade stock is on our recommended list, thanks to solid fundamental support. Then, too, we think it's attractive for the 3- to 5-year pull on a risk-adjusted basis.

Keith A. Markey        September 20, 1991

| | |
|---|---|
| Company's Financial Strength | A++ |
| Stock's Price Stability | 85 |
| Price Growth Persistence | 80 |
| Earnings Predictability | 100 |

# AMERITECH NYSE-AIT

| | | | |
|---|---|---|---|
| RECENT PRICE | 22.3 | P/E RATIO 60 | (Trailing: 13.4) (Median: NMF) |
| | | P/E RATIO 12.9 | RELATIVE P/E RATIO 0.90 | DIV'D YLD 5.7% |

**TIMELINESS 5** Lowest
(Relative Price Perform-ance Next 12 Mos.)

**SAFETY 1** Highest
(Scale: 1 Highest to 5 Lowest)

**BETA .85** (1.00 = Market)

**1994-96 PROJECTIONS**

| | Price | Gain | Ann'l Total Return |
|---|---|---|---|
| High | 90 | (+50%) | 15% |
| Low | 75 | (+25%) | 11% |

**Insider Decisions**

| | D | J | F | M | A | M | J | J | A |
|---|---|---|---|---|---|---|---|---|---|
| to Buy | 0 | 0 | 0 | 1 | 0 | 0 | 1 | 2 | 0 |
| Options | 0 | 0 | 2 | 0 | 0 | 0 | 1 | 0 | 0 |
| to Sell | 1 | 0 | 1 | 0 | 0 | 0 | 0 | 0 | 0 |

**Institutional Decisions**

| | 4Q90 | 1Q91 | 2Q91 |
|---|---|---|---|
| to Buy | 135 | 112 | 104 |
| to Sell | 119 | 148 | 161 |
| Hld'000 | 76258 | 73110 | 79045 |

| Percent shares traded | 6.0 / 4.0 / 2.0 | |

American Information Technologies Corp. (Ameritech), is one of the seven regional holding companies resulting from the breakup of the American Telephone & Telegraph Co. on January 1, 1984. One share of Ameritech stock was exchanged for 10 shares of AT&T (pre-divestiture) common stock. The stock began trading on a when-issued basis on November 21, 1983. "Regular" trading of Ameritech shares began on February 16, 1984.

**CAPITAL STRUCTURE as of 6/30/91**
Total Debt $6981.6 mill. Due in 5 Yrs $2500.0 mill.
LT Debt $5185.1 mill. LT Interest $409.6 mill.
Incl. $32.9 mill. capitalized leases.
(LT interest earned: 5.1x; total interest coverage: 4.1x)

Leases, Uncapitalized: Annual rentals $86.0 mill.

Pension Liability None
Pfd Stock None

Common Stock 265,487,000 shs.

| | Hight: Low: | 22.3 20.7 | | | | | | | | | | | | |

| | 1981 | 1982 | 1983 | 1984A | 1985 | 1986 | 1987 | 1988 | 1989 | 1990 | 1991 | 1992 | ©VALUE LINE PUB., INC. | 94-96 |
|---|---|---|---|---|---|---|---|---|---|---|---|---|---|---|
| Revenues per sh | 8070.5 | 8723.8 | 8900.8 | 8346.8 | 9021.1 | 9362.1 | 9536.0 | 9903.3 | 10211 | 10663 | 10850 | 11350 | Revenues ($mill) | 51.50 |
| Net Profit ($mill) | 848.7 | 892.7 | 1037.1 | 990.6 | 1077.7 | 1138.4 | 1188.1 | 1203.4 | 1238.2 | 1253.8 | 1200 | 1330 | Net Profit ($mill) | 15.10 |
| Income Tax Rate | 60.5% | 61.7% | 60.8% | 44.2% | 43.2% | 44.9% | 37.8% | 33.8% | 30.6% | 30.7% | 30.0% | 30.5% | Income Tax Rate | 6.25 |
| Net Profit Margin | 10.5% | 10.2% | 11.7% | 11.9% | 11.9% | 12.2% | 12.5% | 12.2% | 12.1% | 11.8% | 11.7% | 11.7% | Net Profit Margin | 4.40 |
| Long-Term Debt Ratio | | | 42.4% | 40.4% | 37.8% | 37.1% | 36.9% | 36.4% | 39.7% | 39.6% | 40.5% | 34.5% | Long-Term Debt Ratio | 8.69 |
| Common Equity Ratio | | | 57.6% | 59.6% | 62.2% | 62.9% | 63.1% | 63.6% | 60.3% | 60.4% | 59.5% | 61.5% | Common Equity Ratio | 35.40 |
| Total Capital ($mill) | | | 11475 | 11887 | 11967 | 12106 | 12052 | 12331 | 12755 | 12807 | 13260 | 13850 | Total Capital ($mill) | 252.00 |
| Net Plant ($mill) | | | 14410 | 15024 | 15362 | 15789 | 15933 | 16078 | 16296 | 16652 | 16800 | 17100 | Net Plant ($mill) | 14525 |
| % Earned Total Cap'l | | | 9.0% | 10.1% | 10.7% | 10.9% | 11.4% | 11.3% | 11.1% | 11.2% | 10.5% | 11.0% | % Earned Total Cap'l | 18000 |
| % Earned Net Worth | | | 15.7% | 14.0% | 15.0% | 15.0% | 15.6% | 15.3% | 16.1% | 16.2% | 15.5% | 15.5% | % Earned Net Worth | 12.5% |
| % Earned Comm Equity | | | 15.7% | 14.0% | 15.0% | 15.0% | 15.6% | 15.3% | 16.1% | 16.2% | 15.5% | 15.5% | % Earned Comm Equity | 18.0% |
| % Retained to Comm Eq | | | 15.7% | 5.7% | 5.8% | 5.9% | 6.3% | 5.9% | 5.9% | 5.3% | 4.0% | 4.5% | % Retained to Comm Eq | 5.5% |
| % All Div'ds to Net Prof | | | | 59% | 60% | 61% | 60% | 61% | 63% | 67% | 75% | 72% | % All Div'ds to Net Prof | 71% |

Target Price Range 1994 1995 1996

Relative Price Strength

1 for 2 x Dividends p sh divided by Interest Rate

2-for-1 split

3-for-2 split

Options: CBOE

Shaded areas indicate recessions

| CURRENT POSITION ($mill.) | 1989 | 1990 | 6/30/91 |
|---|---|---|---|
| Cash Assets | 520.2 | 119.2 | 65.3 |
| Other | 2250.8 | 2358.8 | 2437.3 |
| Current Assets | 2771.0 | 2478.0 | 2502.6 |
| Accts Payable | 1351.5 | 1396.6 | 1400.0 |
| Debt Due | 512.9 | 1694.8 | 1796.5 |
| Other | 1362.8 | 1515.5 | 1361.4 |
| Current Liab. | 3227.2 | 4606.9 | 4557.9 |
| Fix. Chg. Cov. | 537% | 461% | 377% |

| ANNUAL RATES of change (per sh) | Past 10 Yrs. | Past 5 Yrs. | Est'd '88-'90 to '94-'96 |
|---|---|---|---|
| Revenues | -- | 5.5% | 5.0% |
| "Cash Flow" | -- | 5.5% | 5.0% |
| Earnings | -- | 5.5% | 5.5% |
| Dividends | -- | 7.5% | 6.5% |
| Book Value | -- | 3.0% | 3.5% |

| Cal-endar | QUARTERLY REVENUES ($ mill.) Mar.31 | Jun.30 | Sep.30 | Dec.31 | Full Year |
|---|---|---|---|---|---|
| 1988 | 2416 | 2476 | 2507 | 2504 | 9903 |
| 1989 | 2500 | 2552 | 2555 | 2604 | 10211 |
| 1990 | 2619 | 2680 | 2669 | 2695 | 10663 |
| 1991 | 2628 | 2742 | 2705 | 2775 | 10850 |
| 1992 | 2725 | 2855 | 2850 | 2920 | 11350 |

| Cal-endar | EARNINGS PER SHARE (B) Mar.31 | Jun.30 | Sep.30 | Dec.31 | Full Year |
|---|---|---|---|---|---|
| 1988 | 1.08 | 1.13 | 1.06 | 1.15 | 4.42 |
| 1989 | 1.12 | 1.19 | 1.06 | 1.22 | 4.59 |
| 1990 | 1.13 | 1.33 | 1.18 | 1.09 | 4.73 |
| 1991 | 1.07 | 1.15 | 1.18 | 1.15 | 4.55 |
| 1992 | 1.17 | 1.28 | 1.30 | 1.25 | 5.00 |

| Cal-endar | QUARTERLY DIVIDENDS PAID (C) Mar.31 | Jun.30 | Sep.30 | Dec.31 | Full Year |
|---|---|---|---|---|---|
| 1987 | 625 | 625 | 625 | 625 | 2.50 |
| 1988 | 675 | 675 | 675 | 675 | 2.70 |
| 1989 | 73 | 73 | 73 | 73 | 2.92 |
| 1990 | 79 | 79 | 79 | 79 | 3.16 |
| 1991 | 85 | 85 | 85 | | |

(A) Figures from before divestiture (1/1/84) are not comparable to post-divestiture estimates and results. (B) Based on average shares outstanding. Excludes nonrecurring gain: 1988.

13¢ Includes nonrecurring loss: 1990, 12¢. Next earnings report due early Dec. (C) Next dividend meeting about Dec. 15. Goes ex about Dec. 20. Dividend payment dates about the 1st of February, May, August, and November ■ Dividend reinvestment plan available (D) In millions, adjusted for stock splits

Factual material is obtained from sources believed to be reliable, but the publisher is not responsible for any errors or omissions contained herein. For the confidential use of subscribers. Reprinting, copying, and distribution by permission only. Copyright 1991 by Value Line Publishing, Inc. ® Reg TM—Value Line, Inc.

BUSINESS: Ameritech is a holding co. for the ILL., IND., MICH., OH, and WIS Bells & other subs. Provides communications services directly to about 75% of the population in these states. In 10/83 Ameritech became first regional holding company to offer cellular telephone service (17.5 million POPS, 366,000 customers). Access lines: 16.4 million; 44% of switching is digital. 90 rev. breakdown: local service, 45%; long-distance, 13%; network access, 24%; other, 18%. Purchased 49.9% stake in Telecom Corp. of New Zealand on 9/90. Customer lines/Bell employee: 238. '90 dep. rate: 6.9%. Has 75,765 employees, 1.1 million shareholders. Chairman/C.E.O.: William L. Weiss. Inc.: DE. Address: 30 South Wacker Drive, Chicago, IL 60606. Tel.: 312-750-5000.

**Ameritech will probably report lower earnings for 1991.** Weakness in the Michigan and Ohio economies, brought on by the ailing auto industry, is responsible for abnormally low usage growth in Ameritech's phone network. Added to this, the company is incurring high upfront expenses resulting from significant investments in operations. Starting in the third quarter, earnings comparisons should become progressively better as cost savings from these investments are realized. For now, though, these shares are not timely.

**Efficiency gains in Ameritech's phone network point to an earnings rebound in 1992.** As mentioned above, lower expenses should result from the company's current investment program. In addition, payroll expenses should fall as a result of an early retirement incentive package being offered to most of its managers. Its goal is to reduce the workforce by about 4% before yearend. Finally, as the economy recovers, usage in Ameritech's networks should pick up and spread fixed operating costs over a larger sales base. Note that our 1992 earnings estimate doesn't factor in the CyberTel deal, which will probably take 20 cents off share net once that deal is closed (probably by yearend).

**A couple of factors should boost earnings growth over the long-term.** Ameritech's cellular segment continues to grow rapidly. Currently, the company subscriber base is expanding by more than 40% yearly. By 1997, we expect market penetration to triple from current levels. Such revenue gains should also result in wider margins as fixed costs remain flat and as lower-margin equipment sales keep declining as an overall portion of revenues. And, as exemplified by recent forays into New Zealand and Poland, the company is investing in international telecommunications projects. The growth and regulatory aspects of these ventures appear to be relatively attractive. However, it remains to be seen whether Ameritech's international operations will be large enough by mid-decade to significantly boost profit growth.

**These shares feature a high yield and merit top marks for Safety.** Total return prospects look better for some of the other stocks within the group of regional bell operating companies, however.
Philip S. Mulqueen      *October 18, 1991*

| | |
|---|---|
| Company's Financial Strength | A+ |
| Stock's Price Stability | 95 |
| Price Growth Persistence | 95 |
| Earnings Predictability | 100 |

# ANHEUSER-BUSCH NYSE-BUD

| | | |
|---|---|---|
| RECENT PRICE | 55 | |
| P/E RATIO | 16.7 | (Trailing: 17.2 / Median: 12.0) |
| RELATIVE P/E RATIO | 1.09 | |
| DVD YLD | 2.0% | |
| VALUE LINE | 1531 | |

**TIMELINESS** 2 (Relative Price Performance Next 12 Mos.) — Above Average

**SAFETY** 1 Highest (Scale: 1 Highest to 5 Lowest)

**BETA 1.00** (1.00 = Market)

High: 5.2 / Low: 3.5
High: 7.4 / Low: 4.8
High: 11.8 / Low: 8.4

## 1994-96 PROJECTIONS

| | Price | Gain | Ann'l Total Return |
|---|---|---|---|
| High | 70 | (+25%) | 8% |
| Low | 60 | (+10%) | 5% |

### Insider Decisions

| | J | F | M | A | M | J | J | A | S |
|---|---|---|---|---|---|---|---|---|---|
| to Buy | 0 | 0 | 0 | 0 | 0 | 0 | 0 | 0 | 0 |
| Options | 0 | 0 | 0 | 3 | 0 | 0 | 2 | 2 | 4 |
| to Sell | 2 | 0 | 3 | 2 | 0 | 0 | 2 | 5 | 4 |

### Institutional Decisions

| | 4Q'90 | 1Q'91 | 2Q'91 |
|---|---|---|---|
| to Buy | 174 | 177 | 158 |
| Options | 129 | 147 | 164 |
| to Sell | 147607 | 151808 | 151394 |

Percent shares traded: 8.0 / 6.0 / 3.0

Target Price Range 1994 | 1995 | 1996

Shaded areas indicate recessions

Options: PHLE

9.0 x "Cash Flow"p sh

Relative Price Strength

2-for-1 split

3-for-2 split

| | 1975 | 1976 | 1977 | 1978 | 1979 | 1980 | 1981 | 1982 | 1983 | 1984 | 1985 | 1986 | 1987 | 1988 | 1989 | 1990 | 1991 | 1992 | © VALUE LINE PUB., INC. | 94-96 |
|---|---|---|---|---|---|---|---|---|---|---|---|---|---|---|---|---|---|---|---|---|
| Sales per sh [A] | 6.08 | 5.33 | 6.79 | 8.34 | 10.22 | 12.16 | 14.10 | 15.80 | 20.78 | 23.02 | 25.27 | 28.55 | 28.19 | 31.49 | 33.50 | 38.06 | 38.65 | 42.10 | | 52.65 |
| "Cash Flow" per sh | .50 | .40 | .57 | .65 | .81 | 1.00 | 1.19 | 1.41 | 1.74 | 2.01 | 2.36 | 2.86 | 3.11 | 3.79 | 4.16 | 4.74 | 5.15 | 5.65 | | 7.25 |
| Earnings per sh [B] | .31 | .21 | .34 | .41 | .53 | .63 | .80 | .93 | 1.08 | 1.24 | 1.42 | 1.69 | 2.04 | 2.45 | 2.68 | 2.95 | 3.25 | 3.60 | | 4.60 |
| Div'ds Decl'd per sh [C] | .11 | .11 | .12 | .14 | .15 | .17 | .19 | .23 | .27 | .32 | .37 | .46 | .57 | .69 | .80 | .94 | 1.00 | 1.10 | | 1.40 |
| Cap'l Spending per sh | .57 | .74 | .58 | .84 | 1.59 | 2.18 | 1.54 | 1.23 | 1.47 | 1.84 | 2.17 | 2.89 | 2.81 | 3.35 | 3.80 | 3.18 | 3.15 | 3.15 | | 3.15 |
| Book Value per sh [D] | 2.20 | 2.29 | 2.51 | 2.79 | 3.35 | 3.83 | 4.42 | 5.22 | 6.04 | 6.66 | 7.80 | 8.56 | 9.87 | 10.95 | 10.95 | 13.03 | 15.15 | 17.65 | | 26.60 |
| Common Shs Outst'g [E] | 270.41 | 270.41 | 270.83 | 270.83 | 271.57 | 271.10 | 272.93 | 289.75 | 290.37 | 282.47 | 277.04 | 268.87 | 293.00 | 283.41 | 282.99 | 282.31 | 285.00 | 285.00 | | 265.00 |
| Avg Ann'l P/E Ratio | 18.2 | 24.4 | 11.1 | 9.5 | 7.4 | 7.0 | 7.7 | 9.3 | 10.2 | 8.7 | 10.9 | 14.7 | 16.7 | 12.3 | 14.4 | 13.4 | *Bold figures are Value Line estimates* | 14.0 | | 14.0 |
| Relative P/E Ratio | 2.43 | 3.12 | 1.45 | 1.29 | 1.07 | .93 | .94 | 1.02 | .86 | .81 | .89 | 1.00 | 1.12 | 1.02 | 1.09 | 1.00 | | 1.15 | | 1.15 |
| Avg Ann'l Div'd Yield | 1.9% | 2.3% | 3.1% | 3.5% | 3.8% | 3.7% | 3.1% | 2.6% | 2.4% | 3.0% | 2.4% | 1.8% | 1.7% | 2.2% | 2.1% | 2.4% | | 2.2% | | 2.2% |

### CAPITAL STRUCTURE as of 6/30/91
Total Debt $3066.6 mill. Due in 5 Yrs $1925.4 mill.
LT Debt $3066.6 mill. LT Interest $270.0 mill.
Includes $241.4 million 8% debentures (due 1996) each convertible into a 5% convertible preferred stock at a price of $47.60 per preferred share.
Includes $89.5 million capitalized leases.

(43% of Cap'l)

(LT interest earned: 8.5x;
total interest coverage: 8.2x)

Pension Liability None

Pfd Stock None
Common Stock 282,306,253 shs.
(290 million fully diluted shares)

(57% of Cap'l)

| | 1975 | 1976 | 1977 | 1978 | 1979 | 1980 | 1981 | 1982 | 1983 | 1984 | 1985 | 1986 | 1987 | 1988 | 1989 | 1990 | 1991 | 1992 | | 94-96 |
|---|---|---|---|---|---|---|---|---|---|---|---|---|---|---|---|---|---|---|---|---|
| Sales ($mill) [A] | | | | | | | 3647.2 | 4576.6 | 6034.2 | 6501.2 | 7000.3 | 7677.2 | 8258.4 | 8924.1 | 9481.3 | 10744 | 11100 | 12000 | | 15000 |
| Operating Margin | | | | | | | 12.1% | 13.7% | 14.7% | 14.7% | 15.3% | 16.7% | 17.5% | 18.2% | 18.3% | 19.5% | 20.0% | 20.0% | | 20.0% |
| Depreciation ($mill) | | | | | | | 108.7 | 133.6 | 187.3 | 203.4 | 236.1 | 277.5 | 315.5 | 359.0 | 410.3 | 495.7 | 500 | 575 | | 750 |
| Net Profit ($mill) | | | | | | | 217.4 | 274.0 | 348.0 | 391.5 | 443.7 | 518.0 | 614.7 | 715.9 | 767.2 | 842.4 | 900 | 1030 | | 1220 |
| Income Tax Rate | | | | | | | 33.1% | 42.2% | 43.5% | 43.2% | 43.2% | 45.0% | 41.8% | 38.3% | 37.5% | 37.7% | 38.0% | 38.0% | | 38.0% |
| Net Profit Margin | | | | | | | 5.7% | 6.0% | 5.8% | 6.0% | 6.3% | 6.7% | 7.4% | 8.0% | 8.1% | 7.8% | 8.0% | 8.6% | | 8.0% |
| Working Cap'l ($mill) | | | | | | | 45.9 | 45.8 | 175.1 | 80.3 | 127.7 | 5.0 | 82.9 | 15.2 | d25.7 | 14.4 | 270 | 535 | | 2110 |
| Long-Term Debt ($mill) | | | | | | | 817.3 | 969.0 | 961.4 | 835.8 | 861.3 | 1126.8 | 1396.5 | 1615.3 | 3307.3 | 3147.1 | 3010 | 2675 | | 2510 |
| Net Worth ($mill) | | | | | | | 1206.8 | 1811.6 | 2052.5 | 2237.9 | 2460.6 | 2600.6 | 2892.2 | 3102.9 | 3099.9 | 3679.1 | 4260 | 5020 | | 7560 |
| % Earned Total Cap'l | | | | | | | 12.8% | 11.4% | 13.3% | 13.3% | 15.3% | 15.2% | 15.3% | 16.6% | 13.3% | 14.4% | 14.5% | 14.5% | | 14.0% |
| % Earned Net Worth | | | | | | | 18.0% | 15.1% | 17.0% | 17.5% | 18.0% | 19.9% | 21.3% | 23.1% | 24.7% | 22.9% | 21.5% | 20.5% | | 17.5% |
| % Retained to Comm Eq | | | | | | | 13.6% | 13.8% | 13.7% | 14.2% | 14.5% | 16.1% | 15.4% | 17.0% | 17.5% | 15.7% | 15.0% | 14.0% | | 12.0% |
| % All Div'ds to Net Prof | | | | | | | 24% | 24% | 31% | 30% | 29% | 28% | 27% | 26% | 29% | 31% | 31% | 31% | | 31% |

November 22, 1991

## CURRENT POSITION ($MILL.)

| CURRENT POSITION ($MILL.) | 1989 | 1990 | 6/30/91 |
|---|---|---|---|
| Cash Assets | 36.4 | 95.3 | 137.5 |
| Receivables | 527.8 | 562.6 | 768.5 |
| Inventory (LIFO) | 531.7 | 567.2 | 599.8 |
| Other | 181.0 | 201.2 | 231.8 |
| Current Assets | 1276.9 | 1426.3 | 1737.6 |
| Accts Payable | 608.0 | 711.2 | 655.4 |
| Debt Due | 104.0 | 16.6 | - - |
| Other | 590.6 | 684.1 | 784.3 |
| Current Liab. | 1302.6 | 1411.9 | 1439.7 |

| ANNUAL RATES of change (per sh) | Past 10 Yrs. | Past 5 Yrs. | Est'd '88-'90 to '94-'96 |
|---|---|---|---|
| Sales | 13.0% | 8.5% | 7.5% |
| "Cash Flow" | 18.0% | 16.0% | 9.5% |
| Earnings | 18.0% | 17.0% | 9.0% |
| Dividends | 18.5% | 20.5% | 9.5% |
| Book Value | 13.5% | 11.0% | 14.5% |

| QUARTERLY SALES ($ mill.) A Cal-endar | Mar.31 | Jun.30 | Sep.30 | Dec.31 | Full Year |
|---|---|---|---|---|---|
| 1988 | 2075 | 2332 | 2340 | 2187 | 8924 |
| 1989 | 2205 | 2480 | 2486 | 2310 | 9481 |
| 1990 | 2393 | 2779 | 2889 | 2683 | 10744 |
| 1991 | 2541 | 2845 | 2943 | 2771 | 11100 |
| 1992 | 2750 | 3000 | 3200 | 3300 | 12200 |

| EARNINGS PER SHARE B Cal-endar | Mar.31 | Jun.30 | Sep.30 | Dec.31 | Full Year |
|---|---|---|---|---|---|
| 1988 | .51 | .72 | .78 | .44 | 2.45 |
| 1989 | .58 | .82 | .83 | .45 | 2.68 |
| 1990 | .64 | .90 | .91 | .50 | 2.95 |
| 1991 | .70 | .99 | 1.01 | .55 | 3.25 |
| 1992 | .75 | 1.00 | 1.10 | .75 | 3.60 |

| QUARTERLY DIVIDENDS PAID C■ Cal-endar | Mar.31 | Jun.30 | Sep.30 | Dec.31 | Full Year |
|---|---|---|---|---|---|
| 1987 | .12 | .12 | .15 | .15 | .54 |
| 1988 | .15 | .15 | .18 | .18 | .66 |
| 1989 | .18 | .18 | .22 | .22 | .80 |
| 1990 | .22 | .22 | .25 | .25 | .94 |
| 1991 | .25 | .25 | .28 | | |

(A) Excludes excise taxes. Includes Campbell Taggart as of 11/82. (B) Fully diluted earnings beginning 1990. Prior years based on average shares outstanding. Excludes special gains: 79, 38¢, 82, 9¢ Next earnings report due late Jan. (C) Next dividend meeting about Jan. 25th Goes ex-dividend about February 1st. Dividend payment dates first week of March, June, September, December. December ■ Dividend reinvestment plan available. (D) Includes intangibles. In 90, $533.6 million, $1.89/share. (E) In millions, adjusted for stock splits

BUSINESS: Anheuser-Busch Companies, Inc. is the nation's largest brewer (1990 shipments: 86.5 million barrels, an estimated 43.7% of industry total). Brands: Budweiser, Michelob, and Busch families of beer. Also, Natural Light, Classic Dark, and O'Doul's. Has 12 breweries with about 87 million barrels of capacity. Non-beer businesses include: baked goods, edible oils, and frozen prepared foods (Campbell Taggart), snack foods (Eagle Snacks), metal containers, and theme parks. Has 45,432 employees, 65,991 shareholders. Officers and directors own 2.2% of common stock; Boatman's Bancshares owns 8.3%. Chairman and President: August A. Busch, III. Incorporated in Missouri. Address: One Busch Place, St. Louis, Missouri 63118. Telephone: 314-577-2000.

**Anheuser-Busch continues to gain domestic market share in brewing.** The company's stated goal is to attain a 50% share by the mid-90s versus its current low-to-mid-40% range, a somewhat lofty target given the difficulties of growing from a position of dominance. However, the financial difficulties of competitors Stroh and Heilemann are working to A-B's advantage. The company has been able to gain about one share point per year so far this decade.

**Global market share may prove more elusive.** Anheuser-Busch has had some success licensing its beer for production in Asia. We think this success is due in part to the similarity of A-B's lighter, rice-based beers to Asian beers, and in part to the appeal of American products in that region of the world. In Europe, however, the beers are heavier, darker, and served warmer than their stateside counterparts. Moreover, brewing there has a long history, and things American may not have any added appeal. Consequently, expanding the distribution of A-B's existing product line to the Continent may be a lengthy process.

**Getting a meaningful contribution from Eagle Snacks and the entertainment operations might also be difficult.** The snack food unit continues to lose money, due to intense industrywide price competition and insufficient volumes. Meanwhile, the theme parks have been hurt by recession-related declines in tourism and a heavy debt burden. **The stock should appeal only to performance-minded investors.** Anheuser-Busch common earns high marks for Price Stability and Growth Persistence, as well as our highest rank for Safety. In addition, our Timeliness model pegs this issue as a relative outperformer in the coming six to 12 months. Longer term, though, due to the factors described above, A-B's growth may well slow. And the current quotation appears to richly discount the profit growth we project for A-B over the pull to 1994-96. However, if the company were to acquire a foreign brewer in its quest for international growth, its earnings and share-price performance might well outstrip our current projections.

*Deborah Schondorf*    November 22, 1991

| | |
|---|---|
| Company's Financial Strength | A+ |
| Stock's Price Stability | 90 |
| Price Growth Persistence | 90 |
| Earnings Predictability | 100 |

# AT&T NYSE-T

| | | |
|---|---|---|
| RECENT PRICE | 37 | |
| P/E RATIO | 14.0 | (Trailing: 14.2 / Median: NMF) |
| RELATIVE P/E RATIO | 0.98 | |
| DVD YLD | 4.1% | |
| VALUE LINE | 752 | |

**TIMELINESS 2** Above Average (Relative Price Perform-ance Next 12 Mos.)

**SAFETY 1** Highest (Scale: 1 Highest to 5 Lowest)

**BETA .85** (1.00 = Market)

| | High: | Low: |
|---|---|---|
| | 21.3 | 17.4 |
| | 20.3 | 14.9 |
| | 25.4 | 19.0 |
| | 27.9 | 20.9 |
| | 35.9 | 22.3 |
| | 30.4 | 24.1 |
| | 47.0 | 28.1 |
| | 46.6 | 29.0 |
| | 40.4 | 29.0 |

Target Price Range 1994 | 1995 | 1996

Options: CBOE

**1994-96 PROJECTIONS**

| | Price | Gain | Ann'l Total Return |
|---|---|---|---|
| High | 70 | (+90%) | 20% |
| Low | 55 | (+50%) | 14% |

**Insider Decisions**

| | D | J | F | M | A | M | J | J | A |
|---|---|---|---|---|---|---|---|---|---|
| to Buy | 0 | 0 | 0 | 0 | 0 | 1 | 0 | 0 | 0 |
| Options | 0 | 0 | 0 | 0 | 0 | 0 | 0 | 0 | 0 |
| to Sell | 0 | 0 | 0 | 1 | 0 | 0 | 0 | 0 | 0 |

**Institutional Decisions**

| | 4Q'90 | 1Q'91 | 2Q'91 |
|---|---|---|---|
| to Buy | 172 | 216 | 201 |
| to Sell | 218 | 214 | 176 |
| Hld's(000) | 249998 | 256580 | 266026 |

Percent shares traded: 6.0 / 4.0 / 2.0

AT&T, in its present configuration, came into being on January 1, 1984, as a result of a Court-ordered division of the Bell System's telecommunications business into Bell operating companies (owned by seven regional holding companies) and AT&T. Shares began trading on a when-issued basis on November 21, 1983. Data in 1981, 1982, and 1983 are pre-divestiture and are not comparable with subsequent information.

**CAPITAL STRUCTURE as of 6/30/91**

Total Debt $14485 mill.  Due in 5 Yrs $7991 mill.
LT Debt $9036 mill.  LT Interest $775 mill.
Incl. $367 mill. capitalized leases.
(LT interest earned: 6.4x; total interest coverage: 5.5x)  (34% of Cap'l)

Leases, Uncapitalized Annual rentals $695 mill.

Pension Liability None

Pfd Stock None

Common Stock 1,285,012,000 shs. (66% of Cap'l)

| | 1981 | 1982 | 1983 | 1984 | 1985 | 1986 | 1987 | 1988 | 1989 | 1990 | 1991 | 1992 | 94-96 | © VALUE LINE PUB., INC. |
|---|---|---|---|---|---|---|---|---|---|---|---|---|---|---|
| Revenues per sh[A] | -- | -- | -- | 31.98 | 32.65 | 31.80 | 31.29 | 32.79 | 33.57 | 34.14 | 32.00 | 35.55 | 45.10 | |
| "Cash Flow" per sh | -- | -- | -- | 3.89 | 4.38 | 5.30 | 5.34 | 5.55 | 5.64 | 5.61 | 5.20 | 6.00 | 8.20 | |
| Earnings per sh[B] | -- | -- | -- | 1.25 | 1.43 | 1.64 | 1.88 | 2.11 | 2.50 | 2.51 | 2.60 | 3.00 | 4.50 | |
| Div'ds Decl'd per sh[C] | -- | -- | -- | 1.20 | 1.20 | 1.20 | 1.20 | 1.20 | 1.20 | 1.32 | 1.40 | 1.52 | 2.25 | |
| Cap'l Spending per sh | -- | -- | -- | 3.34 | 3.91 | 3.39 | 3.41 | 3.75 | 3.15 | 4.07 | 3.10 | 2.85 | 3.40 | |
| Book Value per sh | -- | -- | -- | 13.26 | 13.68 | 12.64 | 13.46 | 10.68 | 11.84 | 12.90 | 12.80 | 14.65 | 21.00 | |
| Common Shs Outst'g[D] | -- | -- | -- | 1037.7 | 1069.3 | 1072.0 | 1073.7 | 1073.7 | 1075.8 | 1092.1 | 1300.0 | 1315.0 | 1330.0 | |
| Avg Ann'l P/E Ratio | -- | -- | -- | 14.0 | 15.3 | 14.7 | 14.9 | 13.0 | 14.8 | 14.9 | Bold figures are | | 14.0 | |
| Relative P/E Ratio | -- | -- | -- | 1.30 | 1.24 | 1.00 | 1.00 | 1.08 | 1.12 | 1.11 | Value Line | | 1.15 | |
| Avg Ann'l Div'd Yield | -- | -- | -- | 6.8% | 5.5% | 5.0% | 4.3% | 4.4% | 3.2% | 3.5% | estimates | | 3.6% | |
| Revenues ($mill)[A] | 58066 | 65093 | 67599 | 33188 | 34910 | 34087 | 33598 | 35210 | 36112 | 37285 | 41650 | 46760 | 60000 | |
| Operating Margin | 45.8% | 44.2% | 43.8% | 14.7% | 17.4% | 21.0% | 21.4% | 22.9% | 21.2% | 22.0% | 21.5% | 22.5% | 24.5% | |
| Depreciation ($mill) | 7900.3 | 8734.5 | 9188.5 | 2777.9 | 3231.6 | 3925.0 | 3724.0 | 3690.0 | 3366.0 | 3396.0 | 3615 | 4000 | 4650 | |
| Net Profit ($mill) | 6822.9 | 7278.8 | 7187.9 | 1369.9 | 1556.8 | 1843.0 | 2044.0 | 2266.0 | 2697.0 | 2735.0 | 3120 | 3920 | 5965 | |
| Income Tax Rate | 55.6% | 57.4% | 58.2% | 24.7% | 35.9% | 39.4% | 35.6% | 43.9% | 32.4% | 35.3% | 38.0% | 37.0% | 37.5% | |
| Net Profit Margin | 11.8% | 11.2% | 10.6% | 4.1% | 4.5% | 5.4% | 6.1% | 6.4% | 7.5% | 7.3% | 7.5% | 8.4% | 9.9% | |
| Working Cap'l ($mill) | -- | -- | -- | 6089.4 | 5430.1 | 4355.0 | 4395.0 | 4377.0 | 3054.0 | 2687.0 | 3580 | 4235 | 5690 | |
| Long-Term Debt ($mill) | -- | -- | 45320 | 8745.4 | 7716.6 | 7309.0 | 7243.0 | 8128.0 | 8144.0 | 9118.0 | 9225 | 9065 | 9085 | |
| Net Worth ($mill) | -- | -- | 66962 | 15257 | 16090 | 14462 | 14537 | 11465 | 12738 | 14093 | 16725 | 19560 | 27325 | |
| % Earned Total Cap'l | -- | -- | 6.4% | 6.6% | 7.6% | 9.6% | 10.6% | 13.2% | 14.5% | 13.4% | 12.0% | 15.0% | 17.5% | |
| % Earned Net Worth | -- | -- | 10.7% | 9.0% | 9.7% | 12.7% | 14.1% | 19.8% | 21.2% | 19.4% | 18.5% | 20.0% | 21.5% | |
| % Retained to Comm Eq | -- | -- | -- | 3% | 1.2% | 3.4% | 5.0% | 8.5% | 11.0% | 9.5% | 8.0% | 10.0% | 10.5% | |
| % All Div'ds to Net Prof | -- | -- | 97% | 97% | 88% | 75% | 65% | 57% | 48% | 51% | 50% | 51% | 50% | |

| CURRENT POSITION (\$MILL.) | 1989 | 1990 | 6/30/91 E |
|---|---|---|---|
| Cash Assets | 1183 | 1389 | 1944 |
| Receivables | 4555 | 12290 | 14887 |
| Other | 4553 | 4097 | 5221 |
| Current Assets | 15291 | 17776 | 22352 |
| Accts Payable | 4763 | 4566 | 4989 |
| Debt Due | 2426 | 4804 | 5449 |
| Other | 5048 | 5719 | 6707 |
| Current Liab. | 12237 | 15089 | 17145 |

| ANNUAL RATES of change (per sh) | Past 10 Yrs. | Past 5 Yrs. | Est'd 88-90 to 94-96 |
|---|---|---|---|
| Revenues | -- | 0.5% | 5.0% |
| "Cash Flow" | -- | 6.5% | 6.5% |
| Earnings | -- | 8.5% | 11.5% |
| Dividends | -- | 0.5% | 10.5% |
| Book Value | -- | -2.5% | 10.0% |

| QUARTERLY REVENUES (\$ mill) Cal-endar | Mar.31 | Jun.30 | Sep.30 | Dec.31 | Full Year |
|---|---|---|---|---|---|
| 1988 | 8349 | 8759 | 8746 | 9356 | 35210 |
| 1989 | 8659 | 9256 | 8896 | 9301 | 36112 |
| 1990 | 8904 | 9038 | 9379 | 9964 | 37285 |
| 1991 | 9192 | 9525 | 11000 | 11533 | 41650 |
| 1992 | 11500 | 11750 | 12000 | 11510 | 46760 |

| EARNINGS PER SHARE B Cal-endar | Mar.31 | Jun.30 | Sep.30 | Dec.31 | Full Year |
|---|---|---|---|---|---|
| 1988 | .46 | .55 | .55 | .55 | 2.11 |
| 1989 | .55 | .65 | .65 | .65 | 2.50 |
| 1990 | .62 | .60 | .65 | .64 | 2.51 |
| 1991 | .65 | .68 | .62 | .65 | 2.60 |
| 1992 | .70 | .75 | .75 | .80 | 3.00 |

| QUARTERLY DIVIDENDS PAID B Cal-endar | Mar.31 | Jun.30 | Sep.30 | Dec.31 | Full Year |
|---|---|---|---|---|---|
| 1987 | 30 | 30 | 30 | 30 | 1.20 |
| 1988 | 30 | 30 | 30 | 30 | 1.20 |
| 1989 | 30 | 30 | 30 | 33 | 1.20 |
| 1990 | 30 | 33 | 33 | 33 | 1.20 |
| 1991 | 33 | 33 | 33 | | 1.29 |

**BUSINESS:** AT&T, which resulted from a Court-ordered breakup of the Bell System, received about 23% of the former company's assets. Operates the interstate and international toll networks, and portions of the intrastate networks. Also owns local on-premise equipment, Western Electric, and Bell Laboratories. 1990 revenue breakdown: telecommunications services (net of access charges), 53%, product and system sales, 33%, rentals and other, 12%, financial services and leases, 2%. '90 depreciation rate: 8.8%. Estimated plant age 7 years. Has 273,700 employees, about 2.6 million shareholders. Insiders own less than 1%. Chairman, C.E.O., & President: Robert E. Allen. Incorporated: New York. Address: 550 Madison Avenue, New York, NY 10022. Telephone: 212-605-5500.

**Life after the NCR deal is getting under way at AT&T.** AT&T recently acquired NCR for $110.74 per share, or about $7.2 billion in AT&T stock. (184.5 million AT&T shares were issued and we have restated all estimates and projections to reflect the merger.) The company estimates that integration charges and restructuring costs (to fold its existing computer business into NCR) associated with the merger would be near $4.0 billion ($2.4 billion after taxes or $1.85 a share, which is excluded from our earnings presentation.) Based on proforma results and statements that NCR's revenues and net income for the remainder of this year would be below previous estimates (due to the recession), we now think that AT&T will earn $2.60 a share in 1991, down only 10¢ from our pre-merger estimate.
**The long distance business is holding up.** Despite lower calling volume in recent months, AT&T has all but stabilized its leading share of the long distance market. A recent AT&T network failure in the Northeast United States has brought negative press reports and attacking advertisements from competitors, but it's not likely to cause any significant fall in market share. Assuming some recovery in unit volume of calls, higher computer sales from NCR next year, and continuing progress with the *Universal Card*, 1992 share earnings may well reach $3.00.
**Recent FCC actions might help in the long run.** Although the 800-portability and price-discrimination rulings were negatives, the FCC reduced regulation on AT&T's offerings to major business customers. Most importantly, the FCC extended its study to allow local exchange access rate charges to be based on volume, rather than the current flat fees that put no emphasis on the actual cost of services. Eventually, we feel the FCC will allow the local carriers to give some sort of volume discounts, thus benefiting AT&T.
**These timely and high-quality shares are suitable for most investors.** Although with the NCR acquisition, AT&T becomes more exposed to the business cycle, its long-term profit prospects remain well defined, in our opinion. Factoring in expected dividend growth, AT&T equity is a solid total return vehicle to 1994-96.
*Steven P. Halper        October 18, 1991*

| Company's Financial Strength | A+ |
|---|---|
| Stock's Price Stability | 90 |
| Price Growth Persistence | 75 |
| Earnings Predictability | 100 |

(A) Calendar year (except 83, 12 months ended 6/30). (B) Primary earnings. Excludes unusual items: 85, 36¢; 86, (35); 88, (35). Next earnings report due late Oct. 1991 includes six month contribution by NCR. (C) Next dividend meeting about Dec 20. Goes ex about Dec. 26. Dividend payment dates: 1st day of Feb, May, Aug, and Nov. ■ (D) In millions. (E) Based on proforma results of merged companies at 6/30/91. Dividend reinvestment plan available.

# AUTO. DATA PROC. NYSE-AUD

| RECENT PRICE | 34 | P/E RATIO | 20.0 (Trailing: 20.9 / Median: 17.0) | RELATIVE P/E RATIO | 1.30 | DIV'D YLD | 1.2% | VALUE LINE | 2118 |

**TIMELINESS 2** (Relative Price Performance Next 12 Mos.) Above Average
**SAFETY 2** Above Average
(Scale: 1 Highest to 5 Lowest)
**BETA 1.10** (1.00 = Market)

**1994-96 PROJECTIONS**

| | Price | Gain | Ann'l Total Return |
|---|---|---|---|
| High | 60 | (+75%) | 16% |
| Low | 45 | (+30%) | 9% |

**Insider Decisions**

| | N | D | J | F | M | A | M | J | J |
|---|---|---|---|---|---|---|---|---|---|
| to Buy | 0 | 0 | 0 | 1 | 0 | 0 | 0 | 0 | 0 |
| Options | 0 | 0 | 1 | 0 | 3 | 0 | 0 | 2 | 1 |
| to Sell | 2 | 3 | 3 | 2 | 7 | 3 | 0 | 2 | 1 |

**Institutional Decisions**

| | 4Q90 | 1Q91 | 2Q91 |
|---|---|---|---|
| to Buy | 97 | 111 | 116 |
| to Sell | 106 | 109 | 123 |
| Hld(000) | 90118 | 98660 | 91421 |

| Percent shares traded | 9.0 / 6.0 / 3.0 |

Relative Price Strength

13.0 x "Cash Flow" p sh

2-for-1 split (multiple)

**Target Price Range 1994 | 1995 | 1996** (scale: 80 50 40 32 24 20 16 12 10 8 6 4)

**Options: PHLE**

| | 1975 | 1976 | 1977 | 1978 | 1979 | 1980 | 1981 | 1982 | 1983 | 1984 | 1985 | 1986 | 1987 | 1988 | 1989 | 1990 | 1991 | 1992 | ©VALUE LINE PUB., INC. | 94-96 |
|---|---|---|---|---|---|---|---|---|---|---|---|---|---|---|---|---|---|---|---|---|
| Revenues per sh (A) | 1.39 | 1.67 | 2.06 | 2.50 | 3.06 | 3.67 | 4.15 | 4.90 | 5.39 | 6.25 | 7.17 | 8.20 | 8.93 | 10.03 | 11.53 | 11.61 | 12.80 | 13.35 | | 18.10 |
| "Cash Flow" per sh | .18 | .23 | .30 | .37 | .48 | .57 | .66 | .79 | .89 | 1.06 | 1.31 | 1.47 | 1.51 | 1.80 | 2.14 | 2.20 | 2.45 | 2.70 | | 3.85 |
| Earnings per sh (B) | .12 | .16 | .20 | .23 | .28 | .31 | .38 | .43 | .47 | .54 | .62 | .73 | .88 | 1.10 | 1.27 | 1.44 | 1.63 | 1.85 | | 2.90 |
| Div'ds Decl'd per sh (C) | .01 | .03 | .04 | .06 | .07 | .08 | .10 | .12 | .13 | .15 | .16 | .18 | .20 | .24 | .28 | .33 | .38 | .40 | | .65 |
| Cap'l Spending per sh | .12 | .13 | .36 | .36 | .50 | .51 | .70 | .77 | .69 | .90 | .82 | .50 | .51 | 1.08 | .55 | .55 | .50 | .60 | | .95 |
| Book Value per sh (D) | .72 | .87 | 1.05 | 1.23 | 1.45 | 1.71 | 2.34 | 2.66 | 3.01 | 3.34 | 3.89 | 4.52 | 5.64 | 6.36 | 6.53 | 7.63 | 7.55 | 7.90 | | 13.05 |
| Common Shs Outst'g (E) | 111.37 | 112.78 | 118.94 | 119.63 | 121.22 | 123.96 | 134.64 | 136.48 | 139.79 | 142.32 | 143.65 | 146.96 | 155.04 | 154.52 | 145.50 | 147.66 | 130.30 | 132.00 | | 130.00 |
| Avg Ann'l P/E Ratio | 18.5 | 23.5 | 17.7 | 15.1 | 14.2 | 14.7 | 16.8 | 15.4 | 17.6 | 16.6 | 16.5 | 20.7 | 19.9 | 19.9 | 15.1 | 16.9 | 17.7 | | | 10.0 |
| Relative P/E Ratio | 2.47 | 3.01 | 2.32 | 2.06 | 2.05 | 1.95 | 2.04 | 1.70 | 1.49 | 1.55 | 1.34 | 1.40 | 1.52 | 1.65 | 1.14 | 1.26 | 1.23 | | | 1.50 |
| Avg Ann'l Div'd Yield | .5% | .7% | 1.0% | 1.5% | 1.8% | 1.8% | 1.6% | 1.7% | 1.6% | 1.6% | 1.6% | 1.2% | 1.0% | 1.0% | 1.5% | 1.3% | 1.3% | | | 1.2% |
| Revenues ($mill) (A) | 558.4 | 669.3 | 752.8 | 886.9 | 1030.0 | 1204.2 | 1384.2 | 1549.2 | 1677.7 | 1714.0 | 1771.8 | | | | | | | 1840 | | 2350 |
| Operating Margin | 24.8% | 24.0% | 23.7% | 24.2% | 25.5% | 25.7% | 24.9% | 24.5% | 24.7% | 24.0% | 24.0% | | | | | | | 24.0% | | 26.0% |
| Depreciation ($mill) | 41.9 | 49.6 | 59.6 | 75.9 | 99.8 | 110.6 | 102.2 | 107.1 | 123.6 | 113.5 | 110 | | | | | | | 105 | | 120 |
| Net Profit ($mill) | 47.4 | 57.8 | 64.5 | 75.1 | 87.9 | 106.0 | 132.0 | 170.3 | 187.6 | 211.7 | 227.7 | | | | | | | 250 | | 380 |
| Income Tax Rate | 47.3% | 46.1% | 44.0% | 43.7% | 43.4% | 42.3% | 40.5% | 33.2% | 31.0% | 25.8% | 24.0% | | | | | | | 25.0% | | 27.0% |
| Net Profit Margin | 8.5% | 8.6% | 8.6% | 8.5% | 8.5% | 8.8% | 9.5% | 11.0% | 11.2% | 12.4% | 12.9% | | | | | | | 13.6% | | 16.2% |
| Working Cap'l ($mill) | 102.8 | 84.2 | 57.0 | 103.6 | 222.7 | 496.2 | 470.1 | 493.2 | 351.8 | 352.9 | 370 | | | | | | | 330 | | 1050 |
| Long-Term Debt ($mill) | 67.2 | 57.0 | 60.1 | 68.2 | 162.0 | 312.1 | 205.7 | 244.7 | 259.9 | 82.1 | 75.0 | | | | | | | 65.0 | | 45.0 |
| Net Worth ($mill) | 314.5 | 363.5 | 420.8 | 475.6 | 558.2 | 664.8 | 875.1 | 982.3 | 949.5 | 1127.0 | 1045 | | | | | | | 1045 | | 1600 |
| % Earned Total Cap'l | 13.2% | 14.1% | 13.8% | 14.3% | 12.8% | 11.6% | 13.0% | 14.5% | 16.2% | 18.1% | 20.5% | | | | | | | 23.0% | | 20.5% |
| % Earned Net Worth | 15.1% | 15.9% | 15.3% | 15.8% | 15.7% | 15.9% | 15.1% | 17.3% | 19.8% | 18.8% | 22.0% | | | | | | | 24.0% | | 21.0% |
| % Retained to Comm Eq | 11.1% | 11.7% | 11.1% | 11.7% | 12.1% | 11.7% | 11.7% | 13.7% | 15.6% | 14.7% | 16.5% | | | | | | | 19.0% | | 16.5% |
| % All Div'ds to Net Prof | 27% | 27% | 27% | 26% | 26% | 24% | 22% | 21% | 21% | 22% | 23% | | | | | | | 22% | | 22% |

**CAPITAL STRUCTURE as of 3/31/91**
Total Debt $106.1 mill. Due in 5 Yrs $54.9 mill.
LT Debt $76.2 mill. LT Interest $8.0 mill.
Includes $41.3 mill. capitalized leases.
(Total interest coverage: 37.6x) (7% of Cap'l)

Leases, Uncapitalized Annual rentals $94.0 mill.

Pension Liability None

Pfd Stock None

Common Stock 139,048,206 shs. (93% of Cap'l)
as of 4.26.91

| CURRENT POSITION ($MILL) | 1989 | 1990 | 3/31/91 |
|---|---|---|---|
| Cash Assets | 372.8 | 396.3 | 391.7 |
| Receivables | 240.7 | 261.9 | 248.0 |
| Inventory (FIFO) | 38.6 | 35.7 | 31.8 |
| Other | 76.3 | 41.2 | 53.3 |
| Current Assets | 728.4 | 735.1 | 724.8 |
| Accts Payable | 41.5 | 43.2 | 20.1 |
| Debt Due | 22.3 | 33.6 | 29.9 |
| Other | 312.8 | 305.4 | 299.1 |
| Current Liab. | 376.6 | 382.2 | 349.1 |

| ANNUAL RATES of change (per sh) | Past 10 Yrs. | Past 5 Yrs. | Est'd '88-'90 to '94-'96 |
|---|---|---|---|
| Revenues | 13.5% | 12.0% | 8.5% |
| "Cash Flow" | 16.0% | 13.5% | 11.0% |
| Earnings | 16.5% | 18.5% | 15.0% |
| Dividends | 15.0% | 14.0% | 16.0% |
| Book Value | 16.5% | 15.0% | 12.5% |

| Fiscal Year Ends | QUARTERLY REVENUES ($ mill) (A) | | | | Full Fiscal Year |
|---|---|---|---|---|---|
| | Sep.30 | Dec.31 | Mar.31 | Jun.30 | |
| 1988 | 361.3 | 376.7 | 418.0 | 393.2 | 1549.2 |
| 1989 | 396.1 | 409.5 | 454.0 | 418.1 | 1677.7 |
| 1990 | 403.4 | 414.0 | 470.8 | 425.8 | 1714.0 |
| 1991 | 414.3 | 425.1 | 490.9 | 441.5 | 1771.8 |
| 1992 | 420 | | 510 | 465 | 1840 |

| Fiscal Year Ends | EARNINGS PER SHARE (A)(B) | | | | Full Fiscal Year |
|---|---|---|---|---|---|
| | Sep.30 | Dec.31 | Mar.31 | Jun.30 | |
| 1988 | .20 | .26 | .33 | .31 | 1.10 |
| 1989 | .23 | .29 | .38 | .37 | 1.27 |
| 1990 | .26 | .34 | .44 | .40 | 1.44 |
| 1991 | .29 | .39 | .50 | .45 | 1.63 |
| 1992 | .32 | .43 | .57 | .53 | 1.85 |

| Calendar | QUARTERLY DIVIDENDS PAID (C) | | | | Full Year |
|---|---|---|---|---|---|
| | Mar.31 | Jun.30 | Sep.30 | Dec.31 | |
| 1987 | .048 | .048 | .055 | .055 | .21 |
| 1988 | .055 | .055 | .065 | .065 | .24 |
| 1989 | .065 | .065 | .075 | .075 | .28 |
| 1990 | .075 | .075 | .088 | .088 | .33 |
| 1991 | .088 | .10 | | | |

In spite of continued economic sluggishness, Automatic Data Processing should again post double-digit earnings growth in fiscal 1992 (ends June 30, 1992). The Employer Services unit (just over half of total revenues) should continue to grow through the year, albeit at a slightly slower rate than the historical norm – about 12% versus 15%-17% during healthier economic times. Business in the low-end segment (small employers) has been weak, as the recent recession pushed some clients into bankruptcy, dragging down ADP's usually high client retention rate. Low-end customers account for only around 15% of Employer Services' business, however. Results at the mid-sized and large business segments have stayed solid and will likely grow through this year. ADP's Brokerage Service business should also yield positive earnings comparisons this year, since fiscal 1991 was not especially good, with lackluster trading volumes and a flat terminal count. We expect results there to improve in fiscal '92 as trading volume on Wall Street picks up and the unit's proxy service expands. Overall, we think earnings per share will climb by 14%, to $1.85 this year.

We're projecting solid growth through 1994-96. Corporate outsourcing of data and accounting needs will probably continue to expand as firms look to trim their payrolls and slash costs, boosting revenues for firms like ADP. Also, the company's bottom line will likely benefit from expanding margins, as ADP automates more of its own business functions. Stock repurchases should give a further lift to per share figures over the 3 to 5 years ahead (management is authorized to buy back over 6 million more shares). We're looking for share net advances of better than 15% annually through 1994-96.

This good-quality issue looks like a good selection for the year ahead. Conservative accounts may find this stock to be an especially appealing choice: ADP's revenue stream is fairly stable, since a large portion of its business is of a recurring nature. Also, the company's financial condition is top notch, with cash currently exceeding $400 million, and debt comprising only 7% of capital (ADP's Financial Strength rating is A+).

Stuart Novick          September 13, 1991

(A) Fiscal year ends June 30th of calendar year. Incl. interest income through fiscal 90.
(B) Primary earnings. Next earnings report due late October. Excl. extraordinary gain: 81, 48¢; July, October.
(C) Next dividend meeting about November 5. Goes ex about December 15. Dividend payment dates about the 1st of January, April.
(D) Includes intangibles. In 1990 $201.6 million $1.41/share.
(E) In millions, adjusted for stock splits.

| | |
|---|---|
| Company's Financial Strength | A+ |
| Stock's Price Stability | 70 |
| Price Growth Persistence | 80 |
| Earnings Predictability | 100 |

# BELL ATLANTIC NYSE-BEL

| | | |
|---|---|---|
| RECENT PRICE **44** | P/E RATIO **11.8** (Trailing: 13.0)(Median: NMF) | RELATIVE P/E RATIO **0.83** DIV'D YLD **6.0%** |

VALUE LINE **754**

TIMELINESS **4** Below Average (Relative Price Performance Next 12 Mos.)
SAFETY **1** Highest (Scale: 1 Highest to 5 Lowest)
BETA .90 (1.00 = Market)

**1994-96 PROJECTIONS**

| | Price | Gain | Ann'l Total Return |
|---|---|---|---|
| High | 70 | (+60%) | 17% |
| Low | 60 | (+35%) | 13% |

**Insider Decisions**

| | D | J | F | M | A | M | J | J | A |
|---|---|---|---|---|---|---|---|---|---|
| to Buy | 0 | 0 | 0 | 0 | 0 | 0 | 1 | 0 | 0 |
| Options | 1 | 2 | 0 | 0 | 0 | 1 | 0 | 0 | 1 |
| to Sell | 0 | 0 | 0 | 1 | 0 | 1 | 0 | 0 | 1 |

**Institutional Decisions**

| | 4Q90 | 1Q91 | 2Q91 |
|---|---|---|---|
| to Buy | 135 | 143 | 127 |
| to Sell | 155 | 162 | 178 |
| Hld's(000) | 118555 | 116073 | 114333 |

Options: CBOE

Shaded areas indicate recessions.

Target Price Range 1994 1995 1996

Bell Atlantic is one of the seven regional holding companies resulting from the breakup of the American Telephone & Telegraph Company on January 1, 1984. Each AT&T shareholder received one share of Bell Atlantic common for every 10 shares of AT&T (pre-divestiture) common stock held. The stock began trading on a when-issued basis on November 21, 1983. "Regular" trading of Bell Atlantic shares began on February 16, 1984.

| | High: / Low: | 1983 | 1984 | 1985 | 1986 | 1987 | 1988 | 1989 | 1990 | 1991 |
|---|---|---|---|---|---|---|---|---|---|---|
| Price High | | 17.8 | 20.8 | 26.8 | 38.5 | 39.9 | 37.3 | 56.1 | 57.1 | 54.1 |
| Price Low | | 16.3 | 16.4 | 19.4 | 25.0 | 30.3 | 31.1 | 34.7 | 39.5 | 43.0 |

(Notes on chart: 1.48 x Dividends p sh — divided by Interest Rate; 2-for-1 split; 2-for-1 split; Relative Price Strength)

© VALUE LINE PUB., INC.

| | 1981 | 1982 | 1983 | 1984 | 1985 | 1986 | 1987 | 1988 | 1989 | 1990 | 1991 | 1992 | 94-96 |
|---|---|---|---|---|---|---|---|---|---|---|---|---|---|
| Revenues per sh (A) | | | | 20.30 | 22.74 | 24.93 | 25.99 | 27.61 | 29.02 | 31.28 | 31.90 | 34.45 | 41.00 |
| "Cash Flow" per sh | | | | 5.44 | 6.45 | 7.77 | 8.47 | 9.32 | 9.06 | 9.38 | 9.40 | 10.25 | 12.25 |
| Earnings per sh (B) | | | | 2.49 | 2.74 | 2.93 | 3.12 | 3.33 | 3.34 | 3.38 | 3.70 | 3.95 | 5.00 |
| Div'ds Decl'd per sh (C) | | | | 1.60 | 1.70 | 1.80 | 1.92 | 2.04 | 2.20 | 2.36 | 2.52 | 2.72 | 3.30 |
| Cap'l Spending per sh | | | | 4.80 | 5.41 | 5.76 | 5.97 | 6.23 | 6.55 | 6.41 | 6.35 | 6.70 | 7.25 |
| Book Value per sh | | | | 18.84 | 19.83 | 20.91 | 22.07 | 23.29 | 21.78 | 22.71 | 23.90 | 25.00 | 29.25 |
| Common Shs Outst'g (D) | | | | 398.46 | 399.49 | 397.94 | 396.19 | 394.03 | 394.45 | 393.19 | 395.00 | 395.00 | 400.00 |
| Avg Ann'l P/E Ratio | | | | 7.3 | 8.2 | 11.1 | 11.2 | 10.5 | 13.4 | 14.5 | *Bold figures are Value Line estimates* | | 13.0 |
| Relative P/E Ratio | | | | .68 | .67 | .75 | .75 | .87 | 1.01 | 1.07 | | | 1.10 |
| Avg Ann'l Div'd Yield | | | | 8.8% | 7.6% | 5.5% | 5.5% | 5.8% | 4.9% | 4.8% | | | 5.1% |
| Revenues ($mill) | 7500.3 | 8367.7 | 8883.4 | 8090.1 | 9084.2 | 9920.8 | 10298 | 10880 | 11449 | 12298 | 12600 | 13600 | 16400 |
| Net Profit ($mill) | 839.3 | 928.1 | 1026.1 | 973.1 | 1092.9 | 1167.1 | 1240.4 | 1316.8 | 1319.3 | 1312.5 | 1465 | 1550 | 2000 |
| Income Tax Rate | 57.1% | 39.8% | 42.7% | 42.9% | 42.6% | 43.7% | 36.5% | 28.7% | 29.9% | 33.8% | 34.0% | 34.0% | 34.0% |
| Net Profit Margin | 11.2% | 11.1% | 11.6% | 12.0% | 12.0% | 11.8% | 12.0% | 12.1% | 11.5% | 10.7% | 11.6% | 11.4% | 12.2% |
| Long-Term Debt Ratio | | | 41.1% | 38.7% | 38.2% | 37.3% | 37.3% | 41.7% | 47.3% | 47.8% | 46.5% | 46.0% | 43.0% |
| Common Equity Ratio | | | 58.9% | 61.3% | 61.8% | 62.7% | 62.7% | 58.3% | 52.7% | 52.2% | 53.5% | 54.0% | 57.0% |
| Total Capital ($mill) | | | 11794 | 12254 | 12812 | 13278 | 13941 | 15734 | 16311 | 17101 | 17639 | 18205 | 20530 |
| Net Plant ($mill) | | | 15084 | 15789 | 16537 | 16932 | 17245 | 18174 | 18874 | 19447 | 19735 | 20260 | 21930 |
| % Earned Total Cap'l | | | 8.7% | 9.6% | 10.1% | 10.3% | 10.3% | 9.8% | 9.5% | 9.2% | 10.0% | 10.0% | 11.0% |
| % Earned Net Worth | | | 14.8% | 13.0% | 13.8% | 14.0% | 14.2% | 14.3% | 15.4% | 14.7% | 15.5% | 15.5% | 17.0% |
| % Earned Comm Equity | | | 14.8% | 13.0% | 13.8% | 14.0% | 14.2% | 14.3% | 15.4% | 14.7% | 15.5% | 15.5% | 17.0% |
| % Retained to Comm Eq | | | .6% | 4.6% | 5.2% | 5.4% | 5.5% | 5.7% | 5.4% | 4.5% | 5.0% | 5.0% | 6.0% |
| % All Div'ds to Net Prof | 87% | 88% | 96% | 65% | 62% | 61% | 61% | 60% | 65% | 69% | 60% | 69% | 66% |

**CAPITAL STRUCTURE as of 6/30/91**

Total Debt $10986.0 mill. Due in 5 Yrs $5022.3 mill.
LT Debt $8033.7 mill. LT Interest $525.0 mill.
Incl. $153.2 mill. capitalized leases.
(LT interest excludes interest due to finance sub. operations)
(LT interest earned: 5.3x; total interest coverage: 4.1x)
Leases, Uncapitalized Annual rentals $120.8 mill.
Pension Liability None
Pfd Stock None

Common Stock 393,100,000 shs.

| CURRENT POSITION | 1989 | 1990 | 6/30/91 |
|---|---|---|---|
| (\$MILL) | | | |
| Cash Assets | 443.1 | 109.7 | 189.9 |
| Other | 3325.8 | 3717.9 | 3651.3 |
| Current Assets | 3768.9 | 3827.6 | 3841.2 |
| Accts Payable | 2157.7 | 2171.0 | 1866.3 |
| Debt Due | 1731.2 | 2597.0 | 2952.3 |
| Other | 1164.1 | 1197.0 | 1233.9 |
| Current Liab. | 5053.0 | 5965.0 | 6052.5 |
| Fix. Chg. Cov. | 433% | 396% | 304% |

| ANNUAL RATES | Past | Past | Est'd '88-'90 |
|---|---|---|---|
| of change (per sh) | 10 Yrs. | 5 Yrs. | to '94-'96 |
| Revenues | .. | .. | 5.0% |
| "Cash Flow" | .. | .. | 6.0% |
| Earnings | .. | .. | 7.0% |
| Dividends | .. | .. | 7.0% |
| Book Value | .. | .. | 4.5% |

| Cal- | QUARTERLY REVENUES (\$ mill.) | | | | Full |
|---|---|---|---|---|---|
| endar | Mar.31 | Jun.30 | Sep.30 | Dec.31 | Year |
| 1988 | 2634 | 2719 | 2755 | 2772 | 10880 |
| 1989 | 2768 | 2882 | 2910 | 2889 | 11449 |
| 1990 | 3018 | 3077 | 3098 | 3105 | 12298 |
| 1991 | 2996 | 3081 | 3200 | 3323 | 12600 |
| 1992 | 3200 | 3350 | 3450 | 3600 | 13600 |

| Cal- | EARNINGS PER SHARE(B) | | | | Full |
|---|---|---|---|---|---|
| endar | Mar.31 | Jun.30 | Sep.30 | Dec.31 | Year |
| 1988 | .83 | .87 | .86 | .77 | 3.33 |
| 1989 | .84 | .87 | .86 | .77 | 3.34 |
| 1990 | .90 | .92 | .91 | .65 | 3.38 |
| 1991 | .91 | .91 | 1.00 | .88 | 3.70 |
| 1992 | .95 | .95 | 1.10 | .95 | 3.95 |

| Cal- | QUARTERLY DIVIDENDS PAID (C)■ | | | | Full |
|---|---|---|---|---|---|
| endar | Mar.31 | Jun.30 | Sep.30 | Dec.31 | Year |
| 1987 | .45 | .48 | .48 | .48 | 1.89 |
| 1988 | .48 | .51 | .51 | .51 | 2.01 |
| 1989 | .51 | .55 | .55 | .55 | 2.16 |
| 1990 | .55 | .59 | .59 | .59 | 2.32 |
| 1991 | .59 | .63 | | | |

**BUSINESS:** Bell Atlantic Corp. is a holding company for the Chesapeake & Potomac Telephone Cos., N.J. Bell, Diamond State Tel., and Bell Co. of PA. Bell Atlantic is a major supplier of telephone services in DE, MD, NJ, VA, West Virginia, and Washington, D.C. Owns 10.7% of the assets of the former AT&T. 50% of joint acquisition of Telecom Corp. Access lines in service: 17.6 mil. About 98% of switching is electronic. '90 revenue breakdown: local service, 38%; access charges, 24%; toll, 13%; other, 25%. Telco depr. rate: 7.7%. Est. plant age: 5 years. Has 81,277 employees, 1.2 million shareholders. Chairman & C.E.O.: Raymond W. Smith. Inc.: DE. Address: 1600 Market Street, Philadelphia, PA 19103. Tel.: 215-963-6000.

**Bell Atlantic's investment in New Zealand is already contributing to the bottom line.** Last year's joint venture with Ameritech to purchase Telecom Corp. of New Zealand is paying off better than expected. Telecom is New Zealand's leading supplier of international and domestic telecommunications services. According to the agreement with New Zealand, the partners were committed to sell a majority interest in the franchise to the public and two New Zealand companies. In the initial public offering, which took place in July, investor interest exceeded the initial allotment so that underwriters increased their offering and exercised their option for additional shares. All told, the partnership sold about 725 million shares, or 77% of the shares that are needed to meet their agreement with New Zealand. Also, the sale resulted in a capital gain of about $75 million in the current quarter, or about 19¢ a share and will allow management to reduce outstanding debt by $375-$400 million. Although management has indicated that it expects to use this gain to offset other corporate charges, it will still bolster results during this recessionary period.

**The regional economy is starting to show some signs of improvement.** However, business conditions in New Jersey are still feeling the impact of the steep economic recession that hit the area and are restricting the possibility of a significant rebound in earnings. Bell Atlantic has been able to increase revenues due to some growth in access lines, a pick-up in cellular use and 20%-30% growth in cellular customers. In addition, the company recently announced plans to acquire Metro Mobile CTS for about $1.6 billion in a stock-for-stock merger agreement. Also, Bell will assume about $825 million in Metro debt. At closing, it is expected that Metro will own or control about 11.5 million 'pops' (units of population). We expect the merger to initially dilute share earnings by about 10%-12%, which is not currently factored into our estimates. **Bell Atlantic stock, although ranked to underperform the year-ahead market, offers above-average total-return potential to 1994-96.** We note, too, the company's high Safety ranking and the company's well-defined earnings prospects.

*Jerome D. Fischer*          *October 18, 1991*

| | |
|---|---|
| Company's Financial Strength | A+ |
| Stock's Price Stability | 90 |
| Price Growth Persistence | 95 |
| Earnings Predictability | 100 |

# BELLSOUTH NYSE-BLS

| | RECENT PRICE | 47 | P/E RATIO | 15.1 | (Trailing: 18.8) (Median: NMF) | RELATIVE P/E RATIO | 1.06 | DIVD YLD | 5.9% | VALUE LINE | 755 |

**TIMELINESS 5** Lowest
(Relative Price Performance Next 12 Mos.)

**SAFETY 1** Highest
(Scale: 1 Highest to 5 Lowest)

**BETA .90** (1.00 = Market)

**1994-96 PROJECTIONS**

| | Price | Gain | Ann'l Total Return |
|---|---|---|---|
| High | 80 | (+70%) | 19% |
| Low | 65 | (+40%) | 13% |

**Insider Decisions**

| | D | J | F | M | A | M | J | J | A |
|---|---|---|---|---|---|---|---|---|---|
| to Buy | 0 | 0 | 0 | 0 | 0 | 0 | 0 | 0 | 0 |
| Options | 0 | 0 | 0 | 0 | 0 | 0 | 0 | 0 | 0 |
| to Sell | 0 | 0 | 0 | 0 | 0 | 0 | 0 | 0 | 0 |

**Institutional Decisions**

| | 4Q90 | 1Q91 | 2Q91 |
|---|---|---|---|
| to Buy | 158 | 139 | 125 |
| Options | 155 | 199 | 202 |
| to Sell | 123755 | 124804 | 123812 |

BellSouth Corporation is the largest regional telephone company resulting from the breakup of the American Telephone & Telegraph Company on January 1, 1984. Each AT&T shareholder received one share of BellSouth common for each 10 shares of AT&T (pre-divestiture) held. The stock began trading on a when-issued basis on November 21, 1983. "Regular" trading of BellSouth shares began on February 16, 1984.

**CAPITAL STRUCTURE as of 6/30/91**
Total Debt $9153.7 mill. Due in 5 Yrs $1815.1 mill.
LT Debt $7840.3 mill.   LT Interest $645.0 mill.

Incl. $413.1 million capitalized leases.

(LT interest earned: 3.5x; total interest coverage: 3.0x)

Pension Liability None
Pfd Stock None

Common Stock 483,500,000 shs.

| | Highest | Lowest |
|---|---|---|
| High | 20.1 | 23.9 |
| Low | 18.6 | 18.2 |

| | Percent shares traded | 6.0 / 4.0 / 2.0 |

Options: ASE

| | 1981 | 1982 | 1983 | 1984 | 1985 | 1986 | 1987 | 1988 | 1989 | 1990 | 1991 | 1992 | ©VALUE LINE PUB., INC. | 94-96 |
|---|---|---|---|---|---|---|---|---|---|---|---|---|---|---|
| | -- | -- | | 21.47 | 23.29 | 23.99 | 25.50 | 29.30 | 29.07 | 30.06 | 29.90 | 32.30 | Revenues per sh(A) | 40.75 |
| | -- | -- | | 6.23 | 7.03 | 7.39 | 8.65 | 9.37 | 9.36 | 9.50 | 9.30 | 9.90 | "Cash Flow" per sh | 12.75 |
| | -- | -- | | 2.85 | 3.13 | 3.39 | 3.46 | 3.51 | 3.48 | 3.38 | 3.15 | 3.55 | Earnings per sh(B) | 5.40 |
| | -- | -- | | 1.72 | 1.88 | 2.04 | 2.20 | 2.36 | 2.52 | 2.68 | 2.76 | 2.96 | Div'ds Decl'd per sh(C)■ | 3.72 |
| | -- | -- | | 5.07 | 5.73 | 5.94 | 6.25 | 6.91 | 6.69 | 6.69 | 6.60 | 6.25 | Cap'l Spending per sh | 7.00 |
| | -- | -- | | 20.98 | 22.27 | 23.61 | 24.89 | 25.51 | 27.21 | 26.54 | 26.60 | 27.45 | Book Value per sh | 32.50 |
| | -- | -- | | 448.68 | 457.90 | 476.97 | 481.22 | 464.04 | 481.55 | 477.30 | 465.00 | 480.00 | Common Shs Outst'g(D) | 465.00 |
| | -- | -- | | 7.2 | 8.4 | 11.0 | 11.4 | 11.5 | 14.0 | 15.8 | Bold figures are Value Line estimates | | Avg Ann'l P/E Ratio | 13.5 |
| | -- | -- | | .67 | .68 | .75 | .76 | .95 | 1.06 | 1.17 | | | Relative P/E Ratio | 1.10 |
| | -- | -- | | 8.4% | 7.1% | 5.4% | 5.6% | 5.9% | 5.2% | 5.0% | | | Avg Ann'l Div'd Yield | 5.1% |
| 9206.3 | 10354 | 10724 | 9631.4 | 10664 | 11444 | 12269 | 13597 | 13996 | 14345 | 14600 | 15500 | Revenues ($mill)(A) | 18975 |
| 1164.3 | 1351.8 | 1371.5 | 1257.2 | 1417.8 | 1588.7 | 1664.8 | 1665.5 | 1642.2 | 1631.5 | 1535 | 1725 | Net Profit ($mill) | 2505 |
| 55.4% | 41.7% | 43.1% | 43.0% | 42.9% | 45.1% | 38.4% | 31.5% | 30.9% | 32.3% | 33.0% | 33.0% | Income Tax Rate | 34.0% |
| 12.6% | 13.1% | 12.8% | 13.1% | 13.3% | 13.9% | 13.6% | 12.2% | 11.7% | 11.4% | 10.8% | 11.0% | Net Profit Margin | 13.2% |
| | -- | -- | 43.5% | 38.8% | 35.7% | 34.5% | 37.3% | 35.0% | 38.1% | 38.0% | 38.0% | Long-Term Debt Ratio | 36.0% |
| | -- | -- | 56.5% | 61.2% | 64.3% | 65.5% | 62.7% | 65.0% | 61.9% | 62.0% | 62.0% | Common Equity Ratio | 64.0% |
| | -- | -- | 14574 | 16669 | 17517 | 18299 | 18870 | 20157 | 20447 | 20425 | 21260 | Total Capital ($mill) | 23640 |
| | -- | -- | 19082 | 21234 | 22169 | 22678 | 23455 | 23742 | 23907 | 24130 | 24080 | Net Plant ($mill) | 23750 |
| 11.4% | | 11.4% | 9.8% | 10.3% | 10.7% | 10.6% | 10.4% | 9.6% | 9.5% | 9.0% | 9.5% | % Earned Total Cap'l | 12.0% |
| | -- | -- | 16.6% | 13.4% | 13.9% | 13.9% | 14.1% | 12.5% | 12.9% | 12.0% | 13.0% | % Earned Net Worth | 16.5% |
| | -- | -- | 16.6% | 13.4% | 13.9% | 14.1% | 13.9% | 14.1% | 12.5% | 12.9% | 12.0% | 13.0% | % Earned Comm Equity | 16.5% |
| | | 3.2% | 5.2% | 5.6% | 5.6% | 5.1% | 4.7% | 3.5% | 2.8% | 1.5% | 2.2% | % Retained to Comm Eq | 5.0% |
| 81% | 75% | 81% | 61% | 60% | 60% | 64% | 66% | 72% | 78% | 87% | 83% | % All Div'ds to Net Prof | 69% |

**Target Price Range 1994 | 1995 | 1996**

180 / 120 / 100 / 80 / 64 / 48 / 40 / 32 / 24 / 20 / 16 / 12 / 8

3-for-2 split

3-for-1 split

1.40 x "Dividends p sh" divided by "Interest Rate"

Relative Price Strength

Shaded areas indicate recessions

BUSINESS: BellSouth Corp. is the largest telephone holding company resulting from the AT&T breakup (owns 14% of the former AT&T's assets). Through Southern Bell and South Central Bell subsidiaries serves customers in Alabama, Florida, Georgia, Kentucky, Louisiana, Mississippi, North Carolina, South Carolina, and Tennessee. Access lines in service: 17.5 million; 90 telco revenue breakdown: local service, 40%; access charges, 26%; toll, 11%; other, 23%. Telephone company employees per 10,000 access lines: 48.4. '90 depreciation rate: 7.9%. Estimated plant age: 5 yrs. Has 100,111 employees, about 1.4 mill. shareholders. Chairman, C.E.O. & President: John L. Clendenin. Inc.: GA. Address: 1155 Peachtree St., N. E., Atlanta, GA 30367. Tel.: 404-249-2000.

**Results at BellSouth remain depressed due to the unfavorable economic conditions in its operating region.** The recession is still taking its toll on BellSouth's revenues. Although access lines continue to grow at about 1% and telephone usage is increasing, the decline in rates due to the initial effects of incentive regulations are offsetting much of the gains. Furthermore, the economic outlook in the region remains gloomy. But if the economy begins to recover by yearend, as Value Line expects, revenues are likely to move up before long.

**Earnings appear to be on the decline.** The protracted poor operating conditions in the Southeast, costs related to recent acquisitions, and corporate restructuring charges are having a negative effect on profits. In particular, third-quarter earnings are expected to be significantly below our earlier expectations. As a result, we have reduced our '91 share earnings estimate to $3.15. In addition, we have lowered our '92 earnings estimate by 20¢ to $3.55 a share.

**BellSouth's cellular network continues to grow.** The company recently completed its purchase of McCaw Cellular Communications' interest in seven Indiana markets, ten in Wisconsin, and one in Illinois for $360 million in cash and turned over its non-wireline service in Rochester, N.Y. All told, this transaction will add about 2.4 million equity 'POPs' (units of population) to its cellular system. Also, BellSouth completed the purchase of Graphic Scanning Corp. ($102 million in fiscal 1990 sales), a supplier of cellular telephone services in Indiana and Wisconsin and paging and wireless cable television properties in the U.S. and U.K., for about $170 million. In addition, BellSouth recently entered into an agreement with Ram Broadcasting Corp. to jointly own and operate mobile data communications networks worldwide, as well as radio paging and cellular assets in the U.S. **High-quality BellSouth stock is a good total-return choice,** assuming the company's earnings benefit from the incentive regulations that have been put in force over the last several years. Also, we expect its good earnings results to lead to above-average dividend growth to 1994-96.
*Jerome D. Fischer*          *October 18, 1991*

| CURRENT POSITION ($MILL.) | 1989 | 1990 | 6/30/91 |
|---|---|---|---|
| Cash Assets | 500.4 | 469.1 | 567.8 |
| Other | 3213.4 | 3180.4 | 3195.9 |
| Current Assets | 3713.8 | 3649.5 | 3763.7 |
| Accts Payable | 1266.7 | 1037.9 | 860.5 |
| Debt Due | 1178.2 | 1122.5 | 1313.4 |
| Other | 1821.7 | 2116.0 | 2110.4 |
| Current Liab. | 4266.6 | 4276.4 | 4284.3 |
| Fix Chg Cov. | 379% | 391% | 340% |

| ANNUAL RATES of change (persh) | Past 10 Yrs. | Past 5 Yrs. | Est'd '88-'90 to '94-'96 |
|---|---|---|---|
| Revenues | -- | -- | 5.5% |
| "Cash Flow" | -- | -- | 5.0% |
| Earnings | -- | -- | 8.0% |
| Dividends | -- | -- | 8.0% |
| Book Value | -- | -- | 3.5% |

| Cal-endar | QUARTERLY REVENUES ($ mill.) | | | | Full Year |
|---|---|---|---|---|---|
| | Mar.31 | Jun.30 | Sep.30 | Dec.31 | |
| 1988 | 3112 | 3213 | 3456 | 3816 | 13597 |
| 1989 | 3367 | 3468 | 3545 | 3615 | 13996 |
| 1990 | 3524 | 3619 | 3551 | 3651 | 14345 |
| 1991 | 3540 | 3583 | 3650 | 3727 | 14500 |
| 1992 | 3700 | 3800 | 3900 | 4100 | 15500 |

| Cal-endar | EARNINGS PER SHARE | | | | Full Year |
|---|---|---|---|---|---|
| | Mar.31 | Jun.30 | Sep.30 | Dec.31 | |
| 1988 | .90 | .83 | .88 | .90 | 3.51 |
| 1989 | .82 | .87 | .89 | .90 | 3.48 |
| 1990 | .88 | .91 | .84 | .75 | 3.38 |
| 1991 | .83 | .76 | .65 | .91 | 3.15 |
| 1992 | .80 | .85 | .90 | 1.00 | 3.55 |

| Cal-endar | QUARTERLY DIVIDENDS PAID | | | | Full Year |
|---|---|---|---|---|---|
| | Mar.31 | Jun.30 | Sep.30 | Dec.31 | |
| 1987 | 50 | 55 | 55 | 55 | 2.16 |
| 1988 | 55 | 59 | 59 | 59 | 2.32 |
| 1989 | 59 | 63 | 63 | 63 | 2.48 |
| 1990 | 63 | 67 | 67 | 67 | 2.64 |
| 1991 | 67 | 69 | | | |

(A) Historical figures (pre-1984) are not comparable to post-divestiture estimates and re-sults. (B) Based on average shares outstand-ing. Next earnings report due mid-Jan. Ex-cludes extraordinary loss: 89.5¢. Excludes nonrecurring gain: 89, 21¢. (C) Next dividend meeting about Nov. 23. Goes ex-dividend about Jan 5.
Dividend payment dates: Feb 1, May 1, Aug. 1, Nov 1. ■ Dividend reinvestment plan available. (D) In millions, adjusted for stock splits.

| Company's Financial Strength | A+ |
|---|---|
| Stock's Price Stability | 95 |
| Price Growth Persistence | 90 |
| Earnings Predictability | 100 |

# EXXON CORP. NYSE-XON

| RECENT PRICE | 59 | P/E RATIO | 14.3 (Trailing: 12.6, Median: 8.5) | RELATIVE P/E RATIO | 0.99 | DIV'D YLD | 4.8% | VALUE LINE | 410 |
|---|---|---|---|---|---|---|---|---|---|

TIMELINESS (Relative Price Performance Next 12 Mos.) **3** Average

SAFETY **1** Highest (Scale: 1 Highest to 5 Lowest)

BETA .75 (1.00 = Market)

| | 1980 | 1981 | 1982 | 1983 | 1984 | 1985 | 1986 | 1987 | 1988 | 1989 | 1990 | 1991 |
|---|---|---|---|---|---|---|---|---|---|---|---|---|
| High: | 22.2 | 20.5 | 16.1 | 19.9 | 22.8 | 27.9 | 37.1 | 50.8 | 47.8 | 51.6 | 55.1 | 61.4 |
| Low: | 13.0 | 14.8 | 12.4 | 14.3 | 18.1 | 22.1 | 24.2 | 30.9 | 36.8 | 41.5 | 44.9 | 49.6 |

**1994-96 PROJECTIONS**

| | Price | Gain | Ann'l Total Return |
|---|---|---|---|
| High | 70 | (+20%) | 9% |
| Low | 55 | (-5%) | 4% |

**Insider Decisions**

| | D | J | F | M | A | M | J | J | A |
|---|---|---|---|---|---|---|---|---|---|
| to Buy | 0 | 0 | 0 | 0 | 0 | 0 | 1 | 0 | 0 |
| Options | 1 | 4 | 1 | 0 | 0 | 0 | 5 | 1 | 2 |
| to Sell | 1 | 0 | 0 | 0 | 2 | 0 | 4 | 0 | 1 |

**Institutional Decisions**

| | 4Q'90 | 1Q'91 | 2Q'91 |
|---|---|---|---|
| to Buy | 211 | 229 | 201 |
| to Sell | 241 | 244 | 269 |
| Hld's(000) | 462075 | 484984 | 459338 |

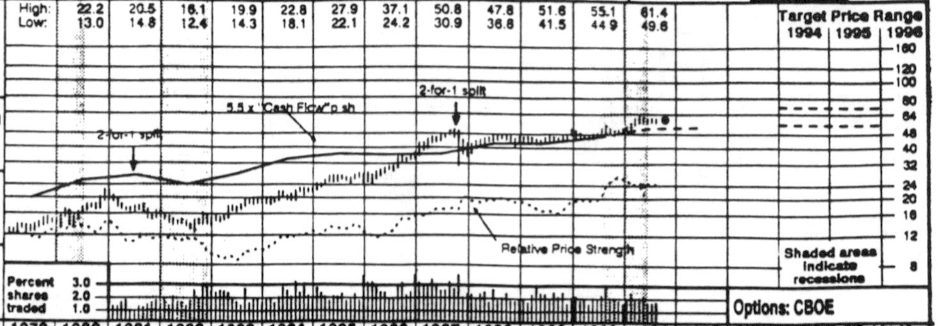

Target Price Range
1994 | 1995 | 1996
160
120
100
80
64
48
40
32
24
20
16
12
8
2-for-1 split
5.5 x "Cash Flow" p sh
2-for-1 split
Relative Price Strength
Shaded areas indicate recessions
Percent shares traded
3.0
2.0
1.0


Options: CBOE

| 1975 | 1976 | 1977 | 1978 | 1979 | 1980 | 1981 | 1982 | 1983 | 1984 | 1985 | 1986 | 1987 | 1988 | 1989 | 1990 | 1991 | 1992 | © VALUE LINE PUB., INC. | 94-96 |
|---|---|---|---|---|---|---|---|---|---|---|---|---|---|---|---|---|---|---|---|
| 25.07 | 27.13 | 30.20 | 34.00 | 45.07 | 59.68 | 62.25 | 56.10 | 52.33 | 58.02 | 59.28 | 48.69 | 55.40 | 61.72 | 69.32 | 84.75 | *84.70* | *93.10* | Sales per sh [A] | *125.00* |
| 2.25 | 2.28 | 2.22 | 2.50 | 3.60 | 4.59 | 4.90 | 4.32 | 5.03 | 6.13 | 6.63 | 6.55 | 6.58 | 7.68 | 7.70 | 8.42 | *9.50* | *9.65* | "Cash Flow" per sh | *12.50* |
| 1.40 | 1.48 | 1.35 | 1.55 | 2.44 | 3.25 | 3.22 | 2.41 | 2.89 | 3.39 | 3.72 | 3.45 | 3.43 | 3.84 | 3.65 | 3.96 | *4.70* | *4.45* | Earnings per sh [B] | *5.75* |
| .63 | .68 | .75 | .83 | .98 | 1.35 | 1.50 | 1.50 | 1.55 | 1.68 | 1.73 | 1.80 | 1.90 | 2.15 | 2.30 | 2.47 | *2.75* | *3.00* | Div'ds Decl'd per sh [C] ■ | *3.75* |
| 1.99 | 2.29 | 2.01 | 2.36 | 3.05 | 3.74 | 5.18 | 5.22 | 4.21 | 5.01 | 6.05 | 3.78 | 4.20 | 4.59 | 5.05 | 5.26 | *5.50* | *5.75* | Cap'l Spending per sh | *6.00* |
| 9.51 | 10.31 | 10.89 | 11.40 | 12.85 | 14.70 | 16.42 | 16.42 | 17.40 | 18.42 | 19.90 | 22.30 | 24.38 | 24.64 | 24.20 | 26.55 | *27.80* | *29.15* | Book Value per sh [D] | *35.00* |
| 1789.8 | 1792.4 | 1792.4 | 1774.5 | 1755.3 | 1728.3 | 1736.7 | 1732.0 | 1692.2 | 1566.0 | 1462.0 | 1435.3 | 1379.4 | 1289.0 | 1250.0 | 1245.0 | *1240.0* | *1235.0* | Common Shs Outst'g [E] | *1200.0* |
| 7.4 | 8.5 | 9.3 | 7.7 | 5.5 | 5.3 | 5.2 | 5.9 | 6.0 | 6.1 | 6.9 | 8.9 | 12.7 | 11.5 | 12.3 | 12.3 | *Bold figures are* | | Avg Ann'l P/E Ratio | *11.0* |
| .99 | 1.09 | 1.22 | 1.05 | .80 | .70 | .63 | .65 | .51 | .57 | .56 | .60 | .85 | .95 | .93 | .92 | *Value Line* | | Relative P/E Ratio | *.90* |
| 6.0% | 5.4% | 6.0% | 6.9% | 7.3% | 7.9% | 8.9% | 10.5% | 8.9% | 8.1% | 6.8% | 5.9% | 4.4% | 4.9% | 5.1% | 5.1% | *estimates* | | Avg Ann'l Div'd Yield | *5.5%* |

**CAPITAL STRUCTURE as of 6/30/91**
**Total Debt** $12150 mill. **Due in 5 Yrs** $8427 mill.
**LT Debt** $7974 mill. **LT Interest** $600 mill.
Includes $383 mill. capitalized leases.
(LT interest earned: 17.1x; total interest coverage: 8.1x) (20% of Cap'l)

**Leases, Uncapitalized** Annual rentals $460 mill.

**Pension Liability:** None
**Pfd Stock** None
**Common Stock** 1,243,838,125 shares (80% of Cap'l)

| 1981 | 1982 | 1983 | 1984 | 1985 | 1986 | 1987 | 1988 | 1989 | 1990 | 1991 | 1992 | | 94-96 |
|---|---|---|---|---|---|---|---|---|---|---|---|---|---|
| 108108 | 97173 | 88561 | 90854 | 86673 | 69888 | 76416 | 79557 | 86656 | 105519 | *105000* | *115000* | Sales ($mill) [A] | *150000* |
| 10.9% | 10.7% | 14.6% | 15.3% | 16.6% | 17.0% | 14.7% | 16.4% | 15.0% | 13.4% | *14.0%* | *14.0%* | Operating Margin | *15.0%* |
| 2947.9 | 3333.5 | 3527.8 | 4073.0 | 4274.0 | 4415.0 | 4239.0 | 4790.0 | 5002.0 | 5545.0 | *6000* | *6500* | Depreciation ($mill) | *8000* |
| 5567.5 | 4155.9 | 4978.0 | 5528.0 | 5415.0 | 4991.0 | 4840.0 | 5108.0 | 4655.0 | 5010.0 | *5850* | *5500* | Net Profit ($mill) | *7000* |
| 42.5% | 45.6% | 48.2% | 46.9% | 47.4% | 36.6% | 34.6% | 36.7% | 37.0% | 37.5% | *38.0%* | *38.0%* | Income Tax Rate | *38.0%* |
| 5.2% | 4.3% | 5.6% | 6.1% | 6.2% | 7.1% | 6.3% | 6.4% | 5.4% | 4.7% | *5.6%* | *4.8%* | Net Profit Margin | *4.7%* |
| 6104.9 | 3328.0 | 3556.8 | 1974.0 | d1734 | 1100.0 | 95.0 | d2633 | d5408 | d5689 | *d4000* | *d6500* | Working Cap'l ($mill) | *d6500* |
| 5153.4 | 4555.6 | 4668.9 | 5105.0 | 4820.0 | 4294.0 | 5021.0 | 4689.0 | 9275.0 | 7687.0 | *7800* | *7900* | Long-Term Debt ($mill) | *9500* |
| 28517 | 28440 | 29443 | 28851 | 29096 | 32012 | 33626 | 31767 | 30244 | 33055 | *34500* | *36000* | Net Worth ($mill) | *42000* |
| 17.3% | 13.4% | 15.3% | 17.1% | 17.3% | 14.5% | 13.0% | 14.5% | 12.8% | 13.0% | *15.0%* | *13.5%* | % Earned Total Cap'l | *14.5%* |
| 19.5% | 14.6% | 16.9% | 19.2% | 18.6% | 15.6% | 14.4% | 16.1% | 15.4% | 15.2% | *17.0%* | *15.5%* | % Earned Net Worth | *16.5%* |
| 10.4% | 5.5% | 7.3% | 9.7% | 9.7% | 7.5% | 6.4% | 7.0% | 5.7% | 5.6% | *7.0%* | *5.0%* | % Retained to Comm Eq | *6.0%* |
| 47% | 63% | 54% | 50% | 48% | 52% | 55% | 56% | 63% | 63% | *59%* | *67%* | % All Div'ds to Net Prof | *65%* |

## CURRENT POSITION (MILL.)

| | 1989 | 1990 | 6/30/91 |
|---|---|---|---|
| Cash Assets | 2016.0 | 1379.0 | 1088.0 |
| Receivables | 7787.0 | 9574.0 | 7681.0 |
| Inventory (LIFO) | 5622.0 | 6386.0 | 5753.0 |
| Other | 1151.0 | 997.0 | 989.0 |
| **Current Assets** | 16576.0 | 18336.0 | 15511.0 |
| Accts Payable | 13581.0 | 15611.0 | 12560.0 |
| Debt Due | 6757.0 | 6090.0 | 4176.0 |
| Other | 1646.0 | 2324.0 | 1727.0 |
| **Current Liab** | 21984.0 | 24025.0 | 13463.0 |

## ANNUAL RATES

| of change (per sh) | Past 10 Yrs. | Past 5 Yrs. | Est'd '88-'90 to '94-'96 |
|---|---|---|---|
| Sales | 4.5% | 5.0% | 9.5% |
| "Cash Flow" | 6.5% | 6.0% | 8.0% |
| Earnings | 4.5% | 6.0% | 7.0% |
| Dividends | 8.5% | 7.0% | 8.5% |
| Book Value | 7.0% | 6.0% | 6.0% |

## QUARTERLY SALES ($ mill.)A

| Calendar | Mar.31 | Jun.30 | Sep.30 | Dec.31 | Full Year |
|---|---|---|---|---|---|
| 1988 | 20045 | 19614 | 19465 | 20433 | 79557 |
| 1989 | 20115 | 19928 | 21473 | 25140 | 86656 |
| 1990 | 24457 | 23444 | 23432 | 34196 | 105519 |
| 1991 | 26383 | 25669 | 25000 | 27500 | 105000 |
| 1992 | 25000 | 30000 | 30000 | 30000 | 115000 |

## EARNINGS PER SHARE B

| Calendar | Mar.31 | Jun.30 | Sep.30 | Dec.31 | Full Year |
|---|---|---|---|---|---|
| 1988 | .95 | .90 | .93 | 1.06 | 3.84 |
| 1989 | .99 | .80 | .87 | .99 | 3.65 |
| 1990 | 1.01 | .87 | .85 | 1.23 | 3.96 |
| 1991 | 1.71 | .90 | .95 | 1.14 | 4.70 |
| 1992 | 1.15 | 1.00 | 1.05 | 1.25 | 4.45 |

## QUARTERLY DIVIDENDS PAID Ca

| Calendar | Mar.31 | Jun.30 | Sep.30 | Dec.31 | Full Year |
|---|---|---|---|---|---|
| 1987 | .45 | .45 | .50 | .50 | 1.90 |
| 1988 | .50 | .55 | .55 | .55 | 2.15 |
| 1989 | .55 | .55 | .60 | .60 | 2.30 |
| 1990 | .60 | .60 | .60 | .67 | 2.47 |
| 1991 | .67 | .67 | | | |

**BUSINESS:** Exxon Corp. is the world's largest integrated oil company. Net production/day 90: oil & liquids, 1.7 mill. barrels; nat. gas, 5.3 bill. cu. ft. Reserves: 6.3 bill. bbls. crude and liquids, 24.9 trill. cu. ft. gas. Est. pretax pres. value of world res.: $54.5 bill. in 90 vs. $39.5 bill. in 89 Est. 5-yr. avg. finding costs (worldwide): $4.52/bbl. (ex-'86 writedown and vs. indus. avg. $4.60). 5-year reserve replacement ratio: 101% (vs. indus. avg. 100%). Daily refinery runs, 3.3 mill. bbls.; product sales, 4.7 mill. bbls. Owns 70% of Imperial Oil. Employs 104,000: has 709,455 shareholders. Insiders own less than 1% of stock. Chairman: L.G. Rawl. President: L.R. Raymond. Inc.: New Jersey. Add.: 225 East John W. Carpenter Freeway. Irving, TX 75062-2298 Telephone: 214-444-1000.

**Exxon's overseas presence is a major blessing.** This is particularly true with regard to natural gas, for which the company has been able to raise volumes in Europe. And while prices are retreating, (lagging oil price movements of earlier this year), they haven't collapsed as has been the case in the United States. Refining is also more profitable abroad than at home.

**The company isn't doing badly stateside.** Exxon didn't suffer as much as its peers from the collapse of the U.S. natural gas prices, because a large proportion of its sales is contract gas, which commands a premium to spot. And with its refining and marketing concentration in the Gulf and East coasts, the company has largely avoided the pricing wars that are taking place on the West Coast. With June-quarter results right in line with our earlier forecast, we're maintaining our earnings estimates of $4.70 a share for 1991, and $4.45 a share for 1992.

**Exxon has a tough act to follow.** Despite its strong overseas presence overall, the company isn't particularly well-represented in oil-producing frontier areas such as West Africa, and Southeast Asia (with the exception of Malaysia). These less-developed regions offer greater possibilities for large finds than more mature foreign areas such as the United Kingdom and Canada. Even so, a somewhat higher oil price (which probably will be realized by 1994-96) would do wonders toward improving the economics of the company's extensive current holdings. But the earnings that we project for 3 to 5 years hence already seem largely discounted in the current stock price, so appreciation potential to that time is limited. And with its high base, a given find would make less of an impact on the company's bottom line than it would for a smaller concern. Moreover,

**Exxon is still on the hook for the 1989 Alaska Valdez oil spill.** One court awarded a number of plaintiffs several million dollars for damage to fishing grounds (a verdict that is being appealed). This may send a signal to other plaintiffs and juries. Continuing litigation won't help Exxon's chances of participating fully if and when highly prospective areas onshore Alaska are made available for drilling.

Thomas P. Au        *October 4, 1991*

88.11¢, .89 .26¢, 91.7¢. Next earnings report due June Oct. (C) Next dividend meeting about Oct. 28 Goes ex about Nov. 5 Approximate dividend payment dates March 10 June 10. September 10. December 10 ■ Dividend reinvestment plan available (D) Includes deferred charges. In 90 $2.3 billion. $1.85/share. (E) In millions, adjusted for splits.

| | |
|---|---|
| Company's Financial Strength | A++ |
| Stock's Price Stability | 100 |
| Price Growth Persistence | 90 |
| Earnings Predictability | 80 |

# FEDERAL REALTY NYSE-FRT

| | | |
|---|---|---|
| RECENT PRICE | 20 | |
| P/E RATIO | 64.5 | (Trailing: 74.1 / Median: NMF) |
| RELATIVE P/E RATIO | 4.36 | |
| DIV'D YLD | 7.6% | |
| VALUE LINE | 1173 | |

**TIMELINESS 3** Average
(Relative Price Perform-
ance Next 12 Mos.)

**SAFETY 2** Above Average
(Scale: 1 Highest to 5 Lowest)

**BETA .80** (1.00 = Market)

**High / Low:** 7.5 / 4.9 · 8.0 / 5.9 · 10.5 / 6.5 · 12.0 / 8.7 · 14.2 / 10.7 · 17.1 / 13.3 · 23.3 / 16.1 · 25.8 / 17.3 · 22.3 / 19.0 · 26.0 / 20.8 · 22.0 / 12.5 · 21.0 / 13.6

## 1994-96 PROJECTIONS

| | Price | Gain | Ann'l Total Return |
|---|---|---|---|
| High | 40 | (+100%) | 24% |
| Low | 30 | (+50%) | 17% |

### Insider Decisions

| | D | J | F | M | A | M | J | J | A |
|---|---|---|---|---|---|---|---|---|---|
| to Buy | 0 | 1 | 0 | 0 | 0 | 0 | 0 | 0 | 0 |
| Options | 0 | 0 | 2 | 0 | 0 | 0 | 0 | 0 | 0 |
| to Sell | 0 | 0 | 0 | 0 | 0 | 0 | 1 | 0 | 0 |

### Institutional Decisions

| | 4Q91 | 1Q91 | 2Q91 |
|---|---|---|---|
| to Buy | 20 | 16 | 10 |
| to Sell | 16 | 14 | 15 |
| Hld'(000) | 6124 | 5931 | 5854 |

**Target Price Range 1994 | 1995 | 1996**

Options: None

Shaded areas indicate recessions

Relative Price Strength

1.5 x Dividends p sh divided by Interest Rate

2-for-1 split

| 1975 | 1976 | 1977 | 1978 | 1979 | 1980 | 1981 | 1982 | 1983 | 1984 | 1985 | 1986 | 1987 | 1988 | 1989 | 1990 | 1991 | 1992 | ©VALUE LINE PUB., INC. | 94-96© |
|---|---|---|---|---|---|---|---|---|---|---|---|---|---|---|---|---|---|---|---|
| 3.12 | 3.23 | 3.23 | 3.29 | 3.14 | 3.56 | 3.46 | 4.60 | 5.08 | 6.29 | 6.31 | 7.26 | 7.32 | 6.90 | 8.75 | 7.73 | 6.40 | 5.30 | Book Value per sh | 8.05 |
| .43 | .43 | .47 | .45 | .45 | .56 | .67 | .69 | .92 | 1.11 | 1.15 | 1.21 | 1.20 | 1.56 | 1.43 | 1.37 | 1.55 | 1.65 | "Cash Flow" per sh | 2.10 |
| .44 | .39 | .43 | .38 | .29 | .31 | .46 | .55 | .88 | 1.03 | .87 | 1.26 | .47 | .68 | .82 | .35 | .30 | .45 | Earnings per sh A | .95 |
| .34 | .41 | .42 | .45 | .46 | .56 | .62 | .69 | .77 | .92 | 1.00 | 1.06 | 1.14 | 1.26 | 1.38 | 1.44 | 1.50 | 1.55 | Div'ds Decl'd per sh B■ | 1.85 |
| 9.58 | 5.73 | 6.79 | 8.86 | 8.72 | 10.35 | 9.86 | 7.95 | 10.38 | 9.10 | 13.92 | 20.89 | 20.97 | 29.58 | 28.53 | 29.55 | 28.00 | 29.15 | Loans & Real Est per sh | 29.25 |
| 2.34 | 4.05 | 4.08 | 4.29 | 4.29 | 5.67 | 5.82 | 7.92 | 8.93 | 11.22 | 11.48 | 12.23 | 13.71 | 13.86 | 16.70 | 16.72 | 17.25 | 18.00 | Common Shs Outst'g C | 20.50 |
| -43% | 33% | -24% | -15% | -17% | -9% | 1% | 86% | 118% | 91% | 138% | 164% | 202% | 199% | 167% | 142% | Bold figures are Value Line estimates | | Premium Over Book | 105% |
| 3.6 | 11.0 | 11.3 | 14.7 | 18.2 | 19.6 | 15.5 | 13.8 | 12.0 | 11.7 | 17.3 | 15.2 | 47.4 | 53.6 | 28.6 | 53.4 | | | Avg Ann'l P/E Ratio | 35.0 |
| .48 | 1.41 | 1.48 | 2.00 | 2.63 | 2.60 | 1.88 | 1.52 | 1.01 | 1.09 | 1.41 | 1.01 | 3.14 | 2.52 | 2.15 | 3.95 | | | Relative P/E Ratio | 2.90 |
| 9.5% | 9.7% | 8.6% | 8.1% | 8.6% | 9.3% | 8.8% | 9.2% | 7.3% | 7.6% | 6.7% | 5.5% | 5.2% | 6.1% | 5.9% | 7.7% | | | Avg Ann'l Div'd Yield | 5.6% |

## CAPITAL STRUCTURE as of 6/30/91

**ST Debt** None **Due in 5 Yrs** $31.2 mill.
**LT Debt** $391.7 mill. **LT interest** $37.0 mill.
Incl. $127.7 mill. capitalized leases.
(Total interest coverage in '90: 1.1x) (77% of Cap'l)
Incl. $4.4 mill. 8¾% conv. sub. debentures ('10)
each conv. into 62.5 shs. at $16.00. $96.0 mill.
5¼% conv. sub. debs. ('02) each conv. into 32.6
shs. at $30.63.
**Pfd Stock** None
**Common Stock** 17,179,613 shs. (23% of Cap'l)
as of 8/8/91 (20.6 mill. fully diluted shs.)

| | 1981 | 1982 | 1983 | 1984 | 1985 | 1986 | 1987 | 1988 | 1989 | 1990 | 1991 | 1992 | | 94-96© |
|---|---|---|---|---|---|---|---|---|---|---|---|---|---|---|
| | 15.1 | 15.7 | 23.8 | 30.3 | 35.6 | 52.1 | 60.4 | 72.0 | 90.1 | 91.9 | 96.0 | 110 | Gross Income ($mill) | 140 |
| | 2.7 | 3.4 | 8.0 | 10.3 | 9.9 | 14.9 | 6.0 | 9.3 | 12.0 | 5.8 | 5.0 | 8.0 | Net Profit ($mill) | 19.0 |
| | 17.7% | 21.3% | 33.8% | 34.0% | 27.8% | 28.6% | 10.0% | 12.9% | 13.3% | 6.3% | 5.2% | 7.3% | Net Profit Margin | 13.6% |
| | 57.4 | 63.0 | 92.7 | 102.2 | 159.8 | 255.4 | 287.4 | 410.1 | 476.3 | 494.0 | 500 | 525 | Loans & Real Est ($mill) | 600 |
| | | | | | | | | | | | NMF | NMF | Cash Reserve ($mill) | NMF |
| | 9.3% | 8.2% | 8.4% | 9.7% | 9.5% | 9.6% | 9.3% | 8.0% | 9.0% | 9.0% | 9.5% | 9.5% | Avg Interest Paid | 9.0% |
| | .6 | | | | | | | | | | NMF | NMF | Short-Term Debt ($mill) | NMF |
| | 36.9 | 45.9 | 57.4 | 53.7 | 116.9 | 203.3 | 284.0 | 356.3 | 389.8 | 389.1 | 400 | 450 | Long-Term Debt ($mill) | 450 |
| | 20.1 | 36.4 | 45.3 | 70.6 | 72.4 | 88.8 | 100.3 | 95.7 | 146.1 | 129.3 | 110 | 95.0 | Net Worth ($mill) | 165 |
| | 96.9% | 44.2% | 44.1% | 56.8% | 59.5% | 44.0% | 57.0% | 54.4% | 47.0% | 45.0% | 41.0% | 36.5% | % Cap Funds to Tot Cap | 27.0% |
| | 3.2% | 3.1% | 3.3% | 3.4% | 3.4% | 2.9% | 2.6% | 3.2% | 3.4% | 3.5% | 4.5% | 4.0% | % Expenses to Assets | 3.5% |
| | 26.4% | 10.5% | 13.4% | 14.3% | 9.6% | 12.7% | 8.4% | 8.4% | 9.3% | 7.7% | 6.5% | 6.5% | % Earned Total Cap'l | 10.5% |
| | 13.3% | 15.1% | 19.1% | 19.0% | 13.7% | 18.5% | 6.2% | 9.5% | 9.9% | 4.2% | 4.0% | 8.0% | % Earned Net Worth | 15.5% |

FINANCIAL POSITION, FUNDS FLOW tables and Value Line report

| FUNDS FLOW ($mill.) | 1988 | 1989 | 1990 |
|---|---|---|---|
| Net Profit Plus Noncash charges | 21.4 | 28.7 | 27.4 |
| Investments Repaid | -- | .1 | 1.8 |
| Net New Debt | 5.4 | 33.3 | (7) |
| New Equity | 1.0 | 47.9 | .2 |
| Investments Funded | 38.0 | 48.2 | 33.3 |
| Dividends Declared | 16.8 | 19.2 | 23.7 |

| FINANCIAL POSITION | 12/31/90 | 6/30/91 |
|---|---|---|
| Senior Debt | $284.5 mill. | $285.3 mill. |
| Subordinated Debt | $104.6 mill. | $104.6 mill. |
| Sr Debt/Cap'l Funds | 1.22:1 | 1.32:1 |
| Total Debt/Equity | 3.0:1 | 3.6:1 |

| PORTFOLIO CONDITION | Year Ago | Latest |
|---|---|---|
| Mtges Repaid in Quarter | Nil | Nil |
| Loss Reserve – %/Invests. | NA | NA |
| Non-Earn Assets – %/Invests. | NA | NA |

| LOANS & REAL ESTATE ($mill.) | | | | |
|---|---|---|---|---|
| Cal-endar | Mar.31 | Jun.30 | Sep.30 | Dec.31 |
| 1988 | 301.6 | 302.8 | 304.1 | 410.1 |
| 1989 | 409.9 | 437.3 | 443.0 | 476.3 |
| 1990 | 478.5 | 463.1 | 488.3 | 494.0 |
| 1991 | 496.2 | 496.7 | 498 | 500 |
| 1992 | 505 | 510 | 515 | 525 |

| EARNINGS PER SHARE A | | | | | |
|---|---|---|---|---|---|
| Cal-endar | Mar.31 | Jun.30 | Sep.30 | Dec.31 | Full Year |
| 1988 | .16 | .09 | .05 | .38 | .68 |
| 1989 | .11 | .55 | .11 | .05 | .82 |
| 1990 | .10 | .14 | .08 | .03 | .35 |
| 1991 | .08 | .07 | .06 | .09 | .30 |
| 1992 | .09 | .10 | .12 | .14 | .45 |

| QUARTERLY DIVIDENDS PAID B | | | | | |
|---|---|---|---|---|---|
| Cal-endar | Mar.31 | Jun.30 | Sep.30 | Dec.31 | Full Year |
| 1987 | .27 | .27 | .27 | .30 | 1.11 |
| 1988 | .30 | .30 | .30 | .33 | 1.23 |
| 1989 | .33 | .33 | .33 | .35 | 1.36 |
| 1990 | .35 | .35 | .35 | .37 | 1.42 |
| 1991 | .37 | .37 | .37 | .38 | |

(A) Based on average shares outstanding. Next earnings report due mid-Nov. (B) Next dividend meeting about Nov. 28. Goes ex about Dec. 20. Dividend payment dates about the 15th of Jan., April, July, and Oct. ■ Dividend reinvestment plan available. (C) In millions adjusted for stock splits. (D) Fully diluted 3 to 5 years hence.

Factual material is obtained from sources believed to be reliable, but the publisher is not responsible for any errors or omissions contained herein.
For the confidential use of subscribers. Reprinting, copying, and distribution by permission only. Copyright 1991 by Value Line Publishing Inc. ● Reg. TM—Value Line, Inc.

BUSINESS: Federal Realty Investment Trust is a self-administered, real estate investment trust with an emphasis on the ownership and renovation of income-producing shopping malls in mid-Atlantic states. At 6/30/91, 97% of invested assets were in real estate (based on original cost); mortgage loans, 3%. Revenues in '90: shopping center rents, 91%; apartment rents, 2%; other, 7%. Major retail lessees include Peoples Drug, J. C. Penney, Loehmann's, Kids "R" Us, Annie Sez, Burlington Coat Factory, Winn Dixie, and T.J. Maxx. Has about 3,300 shareholders. Insiders own about 4% of stock. Organized: District of Columbia. President & Chief Executive Officer: Steven J. Guttman. Address: 4800 Hampden Lane, Suite 500, Bethesda, Maryland 20814. Telephone: 301-652-3360.

**Federal Realty has experienced some recession-related vacancies, but we're not overly concerned just yet.** The recession has not been kind to the retail sector, and this, in turn, has put pressure on a number of FR's tenants. Several large tenants were unable to keep up their lease payments and had to vacate their premises. Turning adversity into advantage, however, FR's top-notch leasing team has, in a number of instances, been able to re-rent a significant percentage of the vacated space, with total rent receipts coming in higher than what was previously being earned. Additionally, although FR has several anchor tenants whose parent companies are going through bankruptcy reorganizations, so far, it appears that their Federal store locations will remain open. This can be taken as a testament to the high regard that retailers have for Federal's top-quality centers. If the economy continues to limp along, however, further difficulties could crop up that might not lend themselves so readily to easy resolution.

**We urge investors not to be discouraged by FR's string of negative share earnings comparisons.** For property-owning trusts, with their large depreciable asset bases, cash flow from operations (equal to net income plus noncash charges for depreciation and amortization) is the most relevant gauge of performance. Despite a very unaccomodating economic environment, share cash flow is up about 4% so far this year. The board recently showed its confidence in the trust's prospects by voting a 5.4% increase in the quarterly dividend.

**Leverage has risen, but the added interest should be easily handled by cash flow gains.** Stricter bank postures on real estate lending forced FR's credit line to be renegotiated at a higher interest rate, and on a secured basis. Also, the trust took out five new mortgages on existing properties, resulting in a net increase in debt of just over $30 million. Although we don't expect this equity to match the year-ahead market, the value that FR has added, and continues to add to its holdings, will likely promote respectable total reutrns to patient investors over the pull to the middle of the decade.

*William Acheson* *November 8, 1991*

# FPL GROUP, INC. NYSE-FPL

| RECENT PRICE | P/E RATIO | | | RELATIVE P/E RATIO | DIV'D YLD | VALUE LINE |
|---|---|---|---|---|---|---|
| 33 | 11.3 | Trailing: 11.4 | Median: 9.0 | 0.78 | 7.3% | 177 |

**TIMELINESS** 3 Average (Relative Price Performance Next 12 Mos.)

**SAFETY** 1 Highest (Scale: 1 Highest to 5 Lowest)

**BETA** .65 (1.00 = Market)

### 1994-96 PROJECTIONS

| | Price | Gain | Ann'l Total Return |
|---|---|---|---|
| High | 40 | (+20%) | 11% |
| Low | 35 | (+5%) | 9% |

**Insider Decisions**

| | N | D | J | F | M | A | M | J | J |
|---|---|---|---|---|---|---|---|---|---|
| to Buy | 0 | 0 | 0 | 0 | 0 | 3 | 2 | 1 | 0 |
| Options | 0 | 0 | 0 | 3 | 2 | 1 | 0 | 0 | 2 |
| to Sell | 0 | 0 | 0 | 0 | 0 | 1 | 0 | 0 | 2 |

**Institutional Decisions**

| | 4Q90 | 1Q91 | 2Q91 |
|---|---|---|---|
| to Buy | 127 | 128 | 95 |
| to Sell | 86 | 112 | 129 |
| Hld(000) | 69249 | 66421 | 62381 |

High / Low price:

| 14.1 | 16.0 | 18.8 | 21.1 | 22.8 | 29.0 | 38.0 | 34.9 | 32.5 | 36.8 | 36.5 | 34.0 |
|---|---|---|---|---|---|---|---|---|---|---|---|
| 9.9 | 11.9 | 14.1 | 17.5 | 17.6 | 20.5 | 26.4 | 24.4 | 27.8 | 29.0 | 26.1 | 28.1 |

Legend notes on chart: 1.25 x Dividends p sh, divided by Interest Rate; Relative Price Strength; 2-for-1 split.

Options: PHLE

### © VALUE LINE PUB., INC. — Per-Share Data

| | 1975 | 1976 | 1977 | 1978 | 1979 | 1980 | 1981 | 1982 | 1983 | 1984 | 1985 | 1986 | 1987 | 1988 | 1989 | 1990 | 1991 | 1992 | 94-96 |
|---|---|---|---|---|---|---|---|---|---|---|---|---|---|---|---|---|---|---|---|
| Revenues per sh | 15.96 | 14.85 | 18.28 | 20.43 | 23.69 | 26.87 | 34.11 | 29.16 | 29.75 | 33.32 | 35.93 | 31.47 | 34.14 | 44.64 | 46.35 | 39.05 | 33.85 | 33.85 | 34.60 |
| "Cash Flow" per sh | 2.80 | 2.30 | 3.59 | 4.19 | 4.08 | 3.80 | 4.22 | 4.47 | 4.72 | 5.43 | 6.40 | 5.90 | 6.93 | 7.78 | 8.76 | 6.35 | 5.95 | 6.00 | 7.20 |
| Earnings per sh | 1.74 | 1.20 | 1.91 | 2.27 | 2.11 | 1.97 | 2.13 | 2.39 | 2.51 | 2.62 | 3.11 | 2.90 | 3.10 | 3.10 | 3.12 | 2.65 | 2.90 | 2.90 | 3.25 |
| Div'd Decl'd per sh | .72 | .78 | .83 | 1.00 | 1.16 | 1.32 | 1.48 | 1.64 | 1.77 | 1.86 | 1.94 | 2.02 | 2.10 | 2.18 | 2.26 | 2.34 | 2.39 | 2.43 | 2.70 |
| Cap'l Spending per sh | 6.77 | 5.96 | 4.85 | 6.04 | 7.40 | 8.29 | 8.45 | 9.40 | 8.06 | 6.15 | 5.96 | 4.95 | 5.41 | 5.11 | 6.44 | 6.45 | 8.13 | 8.95 | 7.75 |
| Book Value per sh | 13.60 | 13.91 | 14.98 | 16.25 | 17.15 | 17.45 | 17.95 | 18.80 | 19.47 | 20.14 | 21.38 | 22.99 | 23.82 | 24.90 | 25.89 | 19.63 | 19.25 | 20.00 | 22.45 |
| Common Shs Outst'g | 74.10 | 80.10 | 80.63 | 81.54 | 87.35 | 90.54 | 100.86 | 112.69 | 118.28 | 121.05 | 130.03 | 131.03 | 131.12 | 133.34 | 161.07 | 165.00 | 172.00 | | 183.00 |
| Avg Ann'l P/E Ratio | 6.5 | 10.5 | 6.9 | 6.5 | 6.3 | 6.5 | | | | | | | | | 10.2 | 11.5 | | | 11.5 |
| Relative P/E Ratio | .87 | 1.34 | .90 | .80 | .91 | .86 | | | | | | | | | .77 | .86 | | | .95 |
| Avg Ann'l Div'd Yield | 6.3% | 6.2% | 6.3% | 7.5% | 7.5% | 10.3% | | | | | | | | | 7.1% | 7.7% | | | 7.2% |

### Financial Data

| | 1981 | 1982 | 1983 | 1984 | 1985 | 1986 | 1987 | 1988 | 1989 | 1990 | 1991 | 1992 | 94-96 |
|---|---|---|---|---|---|---|---|---|---|---|---|---|---|
| Revenues ($mill) | 3088.6 | 2940.8 | 3352.5 | 3940.9 | 4348.8 | 4091.5 | 4439.2 | 5853.5 | 6179.8 | 6289.0 | 5650 | 5775 | 6700 |
| Net Profit ($mill) | 224.1 | 266.7 | 314.0 | 349.9 | 418.7 | 413.1 | 451.2 | 450.3 | 454.2 | 405.9 | 530 | 555 | 660 |
| Income Tax Rate | 43.0% | 38.3% | 41.7% | 44.1% | 43.9% | 43.3% | 34.6% | 28.2% | 27.5% | 20.0% | 27.0% | 25.0% | 30.0% |
| AFUDC % to Net Profit | 31.3% | 48.1% | 36.2% | 18.5% | 16.8% | 18.4% | 6.8% | 3.6% | 4.8% | 6.3% | 10.5% | 17.0% | 7.5% |
| Long-Term Debt Ratio | 52.5% | 52.0% | 49.4% | 50.6% | 50.6% | 48.4% | 47.7% | 47.3% | 46.6% | 51.2% | 51.0% | 51.0% | 51.0% |
| Common Equity Ratio | 37.6% | 38.7% | 40.9% | 40.7% | 40.2% | 45.1% | 44.5% | 45.3% | 46.4% | 41.9% | 40.5% | 40.0% | 41.0% |
| Total Capital ($mill) | 4318.3 | 4900.3 | 5359.8 | 5854.8 | 6435.5 | 6633.2 | 6963.7 | 7212.5 | 7436.8 | 7545.8 | 7650 | 8540 | 9990 |
| Net Plant ($mill) | 5415.3 | 6104.6 | 6561.4 | 6872.4 | 7124.7 | 7331.5 | 7573.1 | 7940.2 | 8078.8 | 8455.9 | 9280 | 10270 | 12610 |
| % Earned Total Cap'l | 7.8% | 8.0% | 8.5% | 8.5% | 8.8% | 8.6% | 8.6% | 8.3% | 8.3% | 7.5% | 9.0% | 9.0% | 9.0% |
| % Earned Net Worth | 10.9% | 11.3% | 11.6% | 12.1% | 13.5% | 11.7% | 12.4% | 11.8% | 11.4% | 11.0% | 14.0% | 13.0% | 13.0% |
| % Earned Comm Equity | 11.6% | 12.1% | 12.2% | 12.7% | 14.4% | 12.2% | 13.0% | 12.4% | 11.9% | 11.5% | 15.0% | 14.0% | 14.0% |
| % Retained to Comm Eq | 3.5% | 3.8% | 3.6% | 3.7% | 5.4% | 4.2% | 4.2% | 3.7% | 3.3% | 1.0% | 2.5% | 2.5% | 2.5% |
| % All Div'ds to Net Prof | 74% | 73% | 75% | 75% | 66% | 73% | 71% | 73% | 75% | 90% | 84% | 86% | 85% |

Bold figures are Value Line estimates.

### CAPITAL STRUCTURE as of 6/30/91

Total Debt $3760.9 mill. Due in 5 Yrs $303.7 mill.
LT Debt $3756.4 mill. LT Interest $327.4 mill.
Includes $287.1 in capital leases
(LT interest earned: 2.8x)

Leases Uncapitalized Annual rentals $30.0 mill.

Pension Liability None

Pfd Stock $505.2 mill. Pfd Div'd $42.1 mill.
5,052,000 shs 4.32% to 11.32% all $100 par and cum., call. from 101 to 108.63 per sh. incl.
1,589,500 shs 6.84% to 11.32% cum $100 par. call. 104.00 to 108.63, sinking fund began 4/1/80.

Common Stock 162,921,236 as of 8/31/91

Target Price Range 1994 | 1995 | 1996

## ELECTRIC OPERATING STATISTICS

| | 1988 | 1989 | 1990 |
|---|---|---|---|
| % change Sales (KWH) | +5.8 | -7.1 | +1.6 |
| Avg. Resid Use (KWH) | 11490 | 11895 | 11955 |
| Avg. Resid Revs. per KWH (¢) | 8.32 | 8.05 | 8.01 |
| Capacity at Peak (Mw) | 13629 | 16173 | 16293 |
| Peak Load, Summer (Mw) | 12382 | 13425 | 13754 |
| Annual Load Factor (%) | 60 | 59 | 59 |
| % Change Customers yr-end | -3.8 | -3.8 | -2.7 |

| ANNUAL RATES of change (per sh) | Past 10 Yrs. | Past 5 Yrs. | Est'd '88-'90 to '94-'96 |
|---|---|---|---|
| Revenues | 6.0% | 5.5% | .5% |
| "Cash Flow" | 6.5% | 6.5% | .5% |
| Earnings | 3.5% | 1.5% | .5% |
| Dividends | 7.0% | 4.0% | 3.0% |
| Book Value | 3.5% | 3.0% | Nil |

Fixed Charge Cov. (%): 218  213  173

| Cal-endar | QUARTERLY REVENUES ($ mill.) Mar.31 | Jun.30 | Sep.30 | Dec.31 | Full Year |
|---|---|---|---|---|---|
| 1988 | 1345.4 | 1463.6 | 1652.8 | 1391.7 | 5853.5 |
| 1989 | 1365.8 | 1530.1 | 1812.5 | 1471.4 | 6179.8 |
| 1990 | 1357.4 | 1575.3 | 1774.5 | 1581.8 | 6289.0 |
| 1991 | 1163.1 | 1386.7 | 1600 | 1400.2 | 5550 |
| 1992 | 1200 | 1450 | 1675 | 1450 | 5775 |

| Cal-endar | EARNINGS PER SHARE A Mar.31 | Jun.30 | Sep.30 | Dec.31 | Full Year |
|---|---|---|---|---|---|
| 1988 | .70 | .73 | 1.33 | .34 | 3.10 |
| 1989 | .54 | .85 | 1.20 | .53 | 3.12 |
| 1990 | .29 | .72 | 1.35 | .29 | 2.65 |
| 1991 | .44 | .81 | 1.27 | .38 | 2.90 |
| 1992 | .45 | .75 | 1.30 | .40 | 2.90 |

| Cal-endar | QUARTERLY DIVIDENDS PAID B■ Mar.31 | Jun.30 | Sep.30 | Dec.31 | Full Year |
|---|---|---|---|---|---|
| 1987 | .51 | .53 | .53 | .53 | 2.10 |
| 1988 | .53 | .55 | .55 | .55 | 2.18 |
| 1989 | .55 | .57 | .57 | .57 | 2.26 |
| 1990 | .57 | .59 | .59 | .59 | 2.34 |
| 1991 | .59 | .60 | | | |

(A) Based on avg. shares out. Next earnings report due late Oct. Excl. nonrecur. losses/gains: '91, (11¢); '90, ($5.50); '88, 32¢; '83, 3¢; '82, 72¢. (B) Next div'd meeting about Nov. 11 Goes ex about Nov 22. Div'd payment dates Mar 15, June 17, Sept 16, Dec 15 ■ Div'd reinvestment plan available. (C) Incl. deferred items in '89 $416.3 mill., $3.12/sh. (D) Rate base net original cost. Rate allowed on com. equity in '90 11.8%-13.9%, earned on '90 average com. eq. 10.9%. Reg. Climate Above Avg. (E) In millions, adj. for stock split.

Factual material is obtained from sources believed to be reliable but the publisher is not responsible for any errors or omissions contained herein. For the confidential use of subscribers. Beginning... Copyright 1991 by Value Line Publishing, Inc. ® Reg. TM—Value Line, Inc.

**FPL Group is doing some restructuring.** The company is reviewing its operations to identify areas where savings can be made. For example, since last October, 1,500 of its 19,500 workers have been eliminated. This and other cost cutting measures should enable FPL Group to be more competitive in the future as the utility industry becomes less regulated and more driven by market forces.

**Another charge against earnings has been taken,** however. FPL incurred a $56 million (35¢ a share) aftertax write-off in the second quarter to cover severance pay and restructuring costs. This followed one-time charges of $689 million in 1990 and $135 million in 1991's first quarter, both of which were related to the sale of FPL's Colonial Penn insurance subsidiary.

**Florida Power & Light operates in a healthy service area that is regulated by constructive authorities.** Economic growth in Florida is outpacing the national average as the state's population continues to increase steadily. Moreover, a large portion of the utility's sales are to residential customers, which are very predictable and leave Florida P&L less exposed to the business cycle. Another positive is that Florida regulators have a history of working with utilities. This is very important considering that the company will need rate relief in late 1992 or early 1993.

**Capital spending will be heavy in the years ahead.** Florida Power & Light will need roughly 3,500 megawatts of capacity by 1995 to meet its service area's growing demand for power. The company will have to depend upon external funds to finance about 50% of its estimated $1.5 billion annual capital budget. Thus, FPL Group's earnings might be diluted as more shares are issued to prevent the company's equity-to-total capital ratio from slipping.

**Dividend growth prospects are subpar for a utility.** Even without the drain of Colonial Penn, and assuming the company can earn a high 13%-14% return on equity because of robust demand for electricity, FPL Group will still have a high payout ratio. This will leave very little room for dividend hikes. True, FPL Group stock carries a generous current yield. But on a potential total return basis, we think the equity is not particularly attractive.

James A. Flood
September 20, 1991

| | |
|---|---|
| Company's Financial Strength | A |
| Stock's Price Stability | 100 |
| Price Growth Persistence | 55 |
| Earnings Predictability | 90 |

# GTE CORP. NYSE-GTE

| | | |
|---|---|---|
| RECENT PRICE | **31** | |
| P/E RATIO | **15.5** | (Trailing: 16.2 / Median: 10.0) |
| RELATIVE P/E RATIO | **1.08** | |
| DIV'D YLD | **5.7%** | |
| VALUE LINE | **762** | |

**TIMELINESS 4** Below Average (Relative Price Perform-ance Next 12 Mos.)

**SAFETY 1** Highest
(Scale: 1 Highest to 5 Lowest)

**BETA .95** (1.00 = Market)

### 1994-96 PROJECTIONS

| | Price | Gain | Ann'l Total Return |
|---|---|---|---|
| High | 55 | (+75%) | 19% |
| Low | 45 | (+45%) | 14% |

### Insider Decisions

| | D | J | F | M | A | M | J | J | A |
|---|---|---|---|---|---|---|---|---|---|
| to Buy | 0 | 0 | 0 | 0 | 0 | 1 | 0 | 2 | 0 |
| Options | 0 | 0 | 0 | 0 | 0 | 1 | 0 | 0 | 1 |
| to Sell | 0 | 0 | 0 | 0 | 0 | 1 | 0 | 1 | 0 |

### Institutional Decisions

| | 4Q'90 | 1Q'91 | 2Q'91 |
|---|---|---|---|
| to Buy | 194 | 248 | 221 |
| to Sell | 156 | 200 | 204 |
| Hld's(000) | 361384 | 460240 | 452209 |

**CAPITAL STRUCTURE as of 6/30/91**
Total Debt $17273 mill. Due in 5 Yrs $6374 mill.
LT Debt $14583 mill. LT Interest $1200 mill.
(LT interest earned: 3.0x; total interest
coverage: 2.8x)

**Pension Liability** None

Pfd Stock $679.0 mill. Pfd Div'd $44.0 mill.
Incl. 518,828 shs. cv. pfd. stocks with various div'd
and cv. rates.

**Common Stock** 884,773,718 shs.
as of 7/31/91

Options: ASE

Shaded areas indicate recessions

| Target Price Range 1994 | 1995 | 1996 |
|---|---|---|

| | 1975 | 1976 | 1977 | 1978 | 1979 | 1980 | 1981 | 1982 | 1983 | 1984 | 1985 | 1986 | 1987 | 1988 | 1989 | 1990 | 1991 | 1992 | © VALUE LINE PUB., INC. | 94-96 |
|---|---|---|---|---|---|---|---|---|---|---|---|---|---|---|---|---|---|---|---|---|
| | 15.64 | 17.34 | 18.78 | 20.48 | 21.48 | 22.18 | 22.28 | 22.63 | 23.74 | 24.76 | 22.90 | 23.68 | 25.22 | 26.38 | 24.67 | 25.00 | 26.20 | Revenues per sh | 30.75 |
| | 2.63 | 2.94 | 3.26 | 3.51 | 3.45 | 3.98 | 4.21 | 4.68 | 4.86 | 4.17 | 5.10 | 5.48 | 5.73 | 6.04 | 5.70 | 5.70 | 6.10 | "Cash Flow" per sh | 7.50 |
| | .91 | 1.03 | 1.22 | 1.33 | .94 | 1.37 | 1.46 | 1.58 | 1.78 | 1.72 | 1.69 | 1.62 | 1.77 | 2.08 | 1.93 | 1.95 | 2.25 | Earnings per sh^A | 3.35 |
| | .60 | .63 | .71 | .79 | .87 | .93 | .96 | .99 | 1.01 | 1.04 | 1.11 | 1.24 | 1.30 | 1.40 | 1.52 | 1.64 | 1.75 | Div'ds Decl'd per sh^B | 2.25 |
| | 3.39 | 3.79 | 4.10 | 4.38 | 5.74 | 5.83 | 5.33 | 4.78 | 5.75 | 5.59 | 4.73 | 4.83 | 4.73 | 4.88 | 4.80 | 4.50 | 4.25 | Cap'l Spending per sh | 4.00 |
| | 7.56 | 8.05 | 8.72 | 9.20 | 9.63 | 9.94 | 10.50 | 11.30 | 12.03 | 10.75 | 11.61 | 11.92 | 12.45 | 12.01 | 11.84 | 12.50 | 13.00 | Book Value per sh^C | 15.75 |
| | 380.28 | 389.37 | 409.06 | 428.06 | 442.76 | 497.10 | 541.49 | 571.94 | 612.71 | 535.52 | 559.92 | 651.10 | 552.58 | 660.50 | 367.00 | 585.00 | 890.00 | Common Shs Outst'g^D | 905.00 |
| | 8.3 | 8.9 | 8.5 | 7.3 | 9.5 | 7.1 | 7.3 | 9.1 | 9.0 | 8.1 | 10.6 | 12.1 | 11.2 | 13.3 | 15.5 | Bold figures are Value Line estimates | | Avg Ann'l P/E Ratio | 14.5 |
| | 1.11 | 1.14 | 1.11 | 1.00 | 1.26 | .96 | .90 | .77 | .68 | .66 | .72 | .81 | .93 | 1.01 | 1.14 | | | Relative P/E Ratio | 1.20 |
| | 8.0% | 6.9% | 6.8% | 8.0% | 9.2% | 10.1% | 9.0% | 6.9% | 7.8% | 7.5% | 6.1% | 6.3% | 6.6% | 5.1% | 5.1% | | | Avg Ann'l Div'd Yield | 4.6% |
| | 11026 | 14401 | 15521 | 16803 | 17470 | 18024 | 18965 | 20002 | 15421 | 15732 | 15112 | 16024 | 16460 | 17424 | 21393 | 22150 | 23000 | Revenues ($mill) | 27365 |
| | 722.0 | 6927 | 18235 | 19708 | 21069 | 21128 | 22002 | 22987 | 1134.2 | 486.7 | 1091.5 | 1091.5 | 1224.7 | 1417.3 | 1715.0 | 1775 | 2025 | Net Profit ($mill) | 3070 |
| | 31.3% | 7.7% | 8.0% | 8.4% | 9.0% | 8.6% | 8.6% | 8.9% | 33.6% | -- | 42.9% | 8.6% | 33.5% | 31.3% | 30.7% | 34.5% | 34.0% | Income Tax Rate | 34.0% |
| | 6.5% | 12.5% | 12.3% | 12.9% | 13.0% | 13.2% | 13.7% | 13.7% | 7.4% | 3.1% | 7.2% | 13.2% | 7.4% | 8.1% | 8.0% | 8.0% | 8.7% | Net Profit Margin | 11.0% |
| | 55.8% | 14.0% | 13.7% | 14.1% | 14.1% | 13.8% | 14.1% | 14.5% | 48.8% | 50.3% | 50.2% | 13.8% | 49.8% | 52.8% | 53.8% | 55.0% | 54.5% | Long-Term Debt Ratio | 50.5% |
| | 34.3% | 5.0% | 5.0% | 5.6% | 6.0% | 4.4% | 3.6% | 4.0% | 42.2% | 40.8% | 42.5% | 4.4% | 41.7% | 38.4% | 39.6% | 42.5% | 43.0% | Common Equity Ratio | 47.0% |
| | | 66% | 65% | 62% | 59% | 69% | 75% | 74% | 17470 | 21168 | 21128 | 69% | 19500 | 20658 | 29234 | 26060 | 30200 | Total Capital ($mill) | 30225 |
| | | | | | | | | | 21069 | 21658 | 21128 | | 22987 | 23700 | 29234 | 29580 | 30200 | Net Plant ($mill) | 30200 |
| | | | | | | | | | 9.0% | 5.7% | 8.8% | | 8.6% | 9.6% | 9.3% | 7.0% | 7.5% | % Earned Total Cap'l | 10.0% |
| | | | | | | | | | 13.0% | 6.4% | 13.2% | | 13.2% | 16.3% | 15.7% | 15.0% | 16.5% | % Earned Net Worth | 20.5% |
| | | | | | | | | | 14.1% | 6.6% | 13.6% | | 14.1% | 17.3% | 16.3% | 16.0% | 17.5% | % Earned Comm Equity | 21.5% |
| | | | | | | | | | 6.0% | NMF | 4.4% | | 3.6% | 5.6% | 6.0% | 2.9% | 3.3% | % Retained to Comm Eq | 7.5% |
| | | | | | | | | | 59% | NMF | 69% | | 75% | 69% | 64% | 62% | 73% | % All Div'ds to Net Prof | 66% |

BUSINESS: GTE Corporation owns the largest non-Bell telecommunications system. Acquired Contel Corp. 3/91. Serves 17.7 million access lines in 31 states, British Columbia and Dominican Republic. Has cellular interests in about 25 states. Other operations include government systems, telecommunications prods., directory publishing. Sylvania lighting prods. and precision materials. Owns 19.9% interest in US Sprint; Purchase by United Tel. expected in 1991 or 1992. '90 depreciation rate: 7.1%. Estimated plant age: 5 yrs. Has about 175,000 employees, 474,000 stockholders. Directors own 1% of stock. Chairman & Chief Executive Officer: James L. Johnson. President: Charles Lee. Inc.: New York. Address: 1 Stamford Forum Stamford, Connecticut 06904 Tel.: 203-965-2789.

GTE is looking to exit the lighting and precision materials business. After purchasing Contel and some cellular properties in 1990, GTE concluded that its Electrical Products Group (EPG) does not fit its long-range telecommunications strategy. (Sales from this segment were about 11% of the parent's 1990 total and 14% of net profit.) Recently, EPG's profits have suffered due to muted economic growth in the U.S. and slowing economies in Europe, where EPG has significant exposure. Management has stated that it is exploring several options for EPG: divestiture, a tax-free spin-off to shareholders, or maybe a joint venture with another lighting supplier. We expect the unit would fetch in the range of $1.5 billion to $2.0 billion. We view this step as a positive for GTE, as it would remove some degree of cyclicality from its earnings, although a sale isn't likely until next year. GTE would likely use the proceeds to pay down long-term debt, fund continuing businesses, or to add more telcos and cellular properties. We feel the market for international cellular services is particularly attractive to GTE. Our estimates and projections are based on GTE's current configuration and will not be restated until after the sale.)

Meanwhile, access line growth at the telco operations remains sluggish. Due to the weak economy, access line growth will probably come in at only 3% this year. Too, cellular revenues per average subscriber are likely to be lower. Even though GTE continues to work hard at cost cutting and integrating Contel, 1991 full-year earnings will probably be flat versus last year's combined results.

1992 profit prospects look more promising. As we expect gradual economic growth next year, access line growth should rebound to 4%. Benefits from the Contel merger are also likely to flow through to the bottom line, helping earnings rise to $2.25 a share.

Conservative investors might want to consider high-yielding, high-quality GTE stock. We feel the 3- to 5-year profit picture is well defined, given the stability of the telcos and the growing use of cellular phones. Factoring in expected good dividend growth, these untimely shares offer good total return potential to 1994-96.
*Steven P. Halper* *October 18, 1991*

(A) Based on primary shares outstanding. Excl. nonrecurring loss: '84, 6¢; '85, $1.97; '86, 7¢; '87, 2¢; '90, 23¢; '91, 30¢; nonrecurring gain: '88, 3¢. Next earnings report due late Jan. Ex-
Excludes Contel prior to 1990. (B) Next dividend meeting about Nov. 25. Goes ex about Nov. 25. Divd. payment dates Jan 1, April 1, July 1, Oct. 1. ■ Dividend reinvestment plan available.
Factual material is obtained from sources believed to be reliable but the publisher is not responsible for any errors or omissions contained herein.
For the confidential use of subscribers. Reprinting, copying and distribution by permission only. Copyright 1991 by Value Line Publishing, Inc.
(C)
Incl. intangibles. In '90 $2221.0 mill. $2.56/sh.
(D) In millions, adjusted for stock splits.
® Reg. TM—Value Line, Inc.

| CURRENT POSITION (MILL.) | 1989 | 1990 | 6/30/91 |
|---|---|---|---|
| Cash Assets | 396 | 462 | 356 |
| Other | 5201 | 5984 | 5753 |
| Current Assets | 5597 | 6446 | 6109 |
| Accts Payable | 1919 | 2246 | 2019 |
| Debt Due | 1049 | 3124 | 2690 |
| Other | 2735 | 2854 | 2984 |
| Current Liab. | 5703 | 8224 | 7693 |
| Fix. Chg. Cov. | 273% | 269% | 226% |

| ANNUAL RATES of change (per sh) | Past 10 Yrs. | Past 5 Yrs. | Est'd '88-'90 to '94-'96 |
|---|---|---|---|
| Revenues | 1.5% | 1.5% | 3.0% |
| "Cash Flow" | 5.0% | 5.0% | 4.5% |
| Earnings | 5.0% | 5.0% | 9.5% |
| Dividends | 5.0% | 7.0% | 8.0% |
| Book Value | 2.5% | 1.5% | 4.5% |

| Calendar | QUARTERLY REVENUES ($ mill.) | | | | Full Year |
|---|---|---|---|---|---|
| | Mar.31 | Jun.30 | Sep.30 | Dec.31 | |
| 1988 | 3943 | 4207 | 4000 | 4310 | 16460 |
| 1989 | 4124 | 4323 | 4353 | 4624 | 17424 |
| 1990 | 5219 | 5323 | 5327 | 5524 | 21393 |
| 1991 | 5224 | 5367 | 5700 | 5859 | 22150 |
| 1992 | 5800 | 5850 | 5800 | 5850 | 23300 |

| Calendar | EARNINGS PER SHARE A | | | | Full Year |
|---|---|---|---|---|---|
| | Mar.31 | Jun.30 | Sep.30 | Dec.31 | |
| 1988 | .42 | .43 | .45 | .47 | 1.77 |
| 1989 | .49 | .49 | .53 | .57 | 2.08 |
| 1990 | .46 | .46 | .49 | .52 | 1.93 |
| 1991 | .45 | .47 | .50 | .53 | 1.95 |
| 1992 | .50 | .55 | .60 | .60 | 2.25 |

| Calendar | QUARTERLY DIVIDENDS PAID ■ | | | | Full Year |
|---|---|---|---|---|---|
| | Mar.31 | Jun.30 | Sep.30 | Dec.31 | |
| 1987 | 305 | 305 | 305 | 315 | 123 |
| 1988 | 315 | 315 | 315 | 335 | 128 |
| 1989 | 335 | 335 | 335 | 365 | 137 |
| 1990 | 365 | 365 | 365 | 395 | 149 |
| 1991 | 395 | 395 | 395 | 425 | |

| | A |
|---|---|
| Company's Financial Strength | 90 |
| Stock's Price Stability | 65 |
| Price Growth Persistence | 95 |
| Earnings Predictability | |

# INT'L BUS. MACH. NYSE-IBM

| RECENT PRICE | P/E RATIO | RELATIVE P/E RATIO | DIV'D YLD | VALUE LINE |
|---|---|---|---|---|
| 99 | 21.2 (Trailing: 17.3, Median: 12.0) | 1.43 | 4.9% | 1098 |

**TIMELINESS 4** Below Average (Relative Price Perform-ance Next 12 Mos.)
**SAFETY 1** Highest
**BETA .95** (1.00 = Market)

**1994-96 PROJECTIONS**

| | Price | Gain | Ann'l Total Return |
|---|---|---|---|
| High | 200 | (+100%) | 23% |
| Low | 160 | (+60%) | 17% |

**Insider Decisions**

| | D | J | F | M | A | M | J | J | A |
|---|---|---|---|---|---|---|---|---|---|
| to Buy | 0 | 0 | 0 | 0 | 0 | 0 | 0 | 0 | 0 |
| Options | 0 | 0 | 0 | 0 | 0 | 0 | 0 | 0 | 0 |
| to Sell | 1 | 0 | 2 | 0 | 1 | 1 | 0 | 0 | 0 |

**Institutional Decisions**

| | 4Q89 | 1Q91 | 2Q91 |
|---|---|---|---|
| to Buy | 272 | 245 | 339 |
| to Sell | 248 | 275 | 339 |
| Hld'000 | 283609 | 292591 | 273913 |

Options: CBOE

Relative Price Strength — 6.0 x "Cash Flow" p sh — 4-for-1 split

Target Price Range 1994 1995 1996: 400, 300, 250, 200, 180, 160, 120, 100, 80, 90, 60, 50, 40, 30, 20

Shaded areas indicate recessions

High:/Low: prices by year

| | 1975 | 1976 | 1977 | 1978 | 1979 | 1980 | 1981 | 1982 | 1983 | 1984 | 1985 | 1986 | 1987 | 1988 | 1989 | 1990 | 1991 | 1992 | ©VALUE LINE PUB., INC. 94-96 |
|---|---|---|---|---|---|---|---|---|---|---|---|---|---|---|---|---|---|---|---|
| High | | | | | | | 72.8 | 71.5 | 98.0 | 134.3 | 128.5 | 158.8 | 161.9 | 175.9 | 129.5 | 123.1 | 139.8 | | |
| Low | | | | | | | 50.4 | 48.4 | 55.8 | 92.3 | 99.0 | 117.4 | 119.3 | 102.0 | 104.5 | 94.5 | 92.0 | | |
| Revenues per sh F | 24.09 | 27.05 | 30.74 | 36.14 | 39.18 | 44.90 | 49.08 | 57.04 | 65.79 | 74.98 | 81.34 | 84.49 | 90.77 | 100.78 | 109.10 | 120.79 | 114.50 | 127.70 | 181.00 |
| "Cash Flow" per sh | 6.12 | 6.83 | 7.67 | 8.88 | 9.14 | 10.83 | 11.21 | 13.23 | 15.43 | 15.99 | 15.61 | 14.47 | 16.15 | 17.94 | 18.57 | 19.82 | 15.20 | 20.65 | 28.05 |
| Earnings per sh A | 3.34 | 3.99 | 4.58 | 5.32 | 5.16 | 6.10 | 5.63 | 7.39 | 9.04 | 10.77 | 10.67 | 7.81 | 8.72 | 9.83 | 9.05 | 10.51 | 4.25 | 6.75 | 15.00 |
| Div'ds Decl'd per sh B ■ | 1.63 | 2.00 | 2.50 | 2.88 | 3.44 | 3.44 | 3.44 | 3.44 | 3.71 | 4.10 | 4.40 | 4.40 | 4.40 | 4.40 | 4.73 | 4.84 | 4.90 | 5.25 | 7.00 |
| Cap'l Spending per sh | 3.83 | 3.94 | 5.43 | 6.51 | 9.66 | 10.61 | 11.56 | 11.10 | 8.07 | 8.93 | 10.45 | 7.62 | 7.21 | 9.14 | 11.16 | 11.39 | 11.50 | 12.50 | 16.35 |
| Book Value per sh | 19.06 | 21.15 | 21.39 | 23.14 | 25.64 | 28.18 | 30.66 | 33.13 | 38.02 | 43.23 | 51.98 | 56.67 | 64.06 | 66.96 | 67.00 | 74.96 | 74.80 | 77.65 | 95.40 |
| Common Shs Outst'g C | 599.38 | 602.78 | 589.98 | 583.24 | 583.59 | 583.81 | 592.29 | 602.41 | 610.72 | 612.69 | 615.42 | 606.61 | 597.33 | 590.04 | 574.78 | 571.39 | 565.00 | 560.00 | 550.00 |
| Avg Ann'l P/E Ratio | 15.3 | 16.6 | 14.5 | 12.7 | 13.9 | 10.4 | 10.3 | 9.4 | 12.7 | 10.8 | 12.3 | 18.0 | 16.6 | 11.9 | 12.3 | 10.4 | | | 12.0 |
| Relative P/E Ratio | 2.04 | 2.12 | 1.90 | 1.73 | 2.01 | 1.38 | 1.25 | 1.04 | 1.07 | 1.01 | 1.00 | 1.22 | 1.11 | .99 | .93 | .77 | | | 1.00 |
| Avg Ann'l Div'd Yield | 3.2% | 3.0% | 3.8% | 4.3% | 4.8% | 5.4% | 5.9% | 5.0% | 3.2% | 3.5% | 3.4% | 3.1% | 3.0% | 3.8% | 4.2% | 4.4% | | | 3.9% |

Bold figures are Value Line estimates

**Percent shares traded:** 9.0 / 6.0 / 3.0

| | 1980 | 1981 | 1982 | 1983 | 1984 | 1985 | 1986 | 1987 | 1988 | 1989 | 1990 | 1991 | 1992 | 94-96 |
|---|---|---|---|---|---|---|---|---|---|---|---|---|---|---|
| Revenues ($mill) F | 29070 | 34364 | 40180 | 45937 | 50056 | 51250 | 54217 | 59461 | 62710 | 69018 | 64700 | 71500 | | 100000 |
| Operating Margin | 32.2% | 33.8% | 33.7% | 31.4% | 28.5% | 23.1% | 22.4% | 23.8% | 23.5% | 22.7% | 17.5% | 22.5% | | 22.5% |
| Depreciation ($mill) D | 3329.0 | 3562.0 | 3938.0 | 3215.0 | 3051.0 | 3988.0 | 4390.0 | 4764.0 | 5425.0 | 6020.0 | 6175 | 6625 | | 7725 |
| Net Profit ($mill) | 3308.0 | 4409.0 | 5485.0 | 6582.0 | 6555.0 | 4789.0 | 5258.0 | 5824.0 | 5251.0 | 6020.0 | 2425 | 4930 | | 8255 |
| Income Tax Rate | 44.8% | 44.4% | 44.8% | 43.4% | 43.6% | 42.9% | 38.9% | 39.2% | 41.9% | 41.0% | 44.0% | 42.0% | | 42.0% |
| Net Profit Margin | 11.4% | 12.8% | 13.7% | 14.3% | 13.1% | 9.3% | 9.7% | 9.8% | 8.4% | 8.7% | 4.0% | 6.9% | | 8.3% |
| Working Cap'l ($mill) | 2983.0 | 4805.0 | 7763.0 | 10735 | 14637 | 15006 | 17643 | 17956 | 14175 | 13644 | 11150 | 10725 | | 12250 |
| Long-Term Debt ($mill) | 2669.0 | 2851.0 | 2674.0 | 3269.0 | 3955.0 | 4169.0 | 3858.0 | 8518.0 | 10825 | 11943 | 11960 | 11960 | | 12000 |
| Net Worth ($mill) | 18161 | 19960 | 23219 | 26489 | 31990 | 34374 | 38263 | 39509 | 38509 | 42832 | 42160 | 43600 | | 52475 |
| % Earned Total Cap'l | 16.5% | 20.0% | 21.7% | 22.7% | 18.8% | 12.9% | 12.9% | 12.9% | 11.3% | 11.7% | 5.5% | 10.0% | | 13.5% |
| % Earned Net Worth | 18.2% | 22.1% | 23.6% | 24.8% | 20.5% | 13.9% | 13.7% | 14.7% | 13.6% | 14.1% | 6.0% | 11.5% | | 15.5% |
| % Retained to Comm Eq | 7.1% | 11.8% | 13.9% | 15.4% | 12.0% | 6.1% | 6.8% | 8.1% | 6.5% | 7.6% | Nil | 4.5% | | 8.5% |
| % All Div'ds to Net Prof | 61% | 47% | 41% | 38% | 41% | 56% | 50% | 45% | 52% | 46% | 115% | 60% | | 47% |

**CAPITAL STRUCTURE as of 6/30/91**
Total Debt $20755 mill. Due in 5 Yrs $17065 mill.
LT Debt $11991 mill. LT Interest $810.0 mill.
Incl. $2004 mill. 7 7/8% sub. debs. ('04) cv. into
6.51 com. shs. at $153 6563. Redeemable at
103.150% at 11/90 and at decreasing prices there-
after. Sinking fund pmts. begin 1994.
(Total interest coverage: 6.0x)          (24% of Cap'l)
Leases, Uncapitalized: Annual rentals $1558.0 mill.

Pension Liability None

Pfd Stock None
Common Stock 572,137,849 shs.          (76% of Cap'l)
(585.1 mill. fully diluted shs.)

November 1, 1991
George A. Niemond

| CURRENT POSITION | 1989 | 1990 | 6/30/91 |
|---|---|---|---|
| Cash Assets | 3700 | 3853 | 4700 |
| Receivables | 20164 | 22644 | 18391 |
| Inventory (Avg Cst) | 9463 | 10108 | 10157 |
| Other | 2548 | 2315 | 2268 |
| Current Assets | 35875 | 38920 | 35516 |
| Accts Payable | 3167 | 3367 | 680 |
| Debt Due | 5892 | 7602 | 8764 |
| Other | 12641 | 14307 | 7041 |
| Current Liab. | 21700 | 25276 | 22285 |

| ANNUAL RATES of change (per sh) | Past 10 Yrs. | Past 5 Yrs. | Est'd 88-90 to 94-96 |
|---|---|---|---|
| Revenues | 10.5% | 8.5% | 8.5% |
| "Cash Flow" | 7.0% | 3.5% | 7.5% |
| Earnings | 6.0% | -.5% | 7.5% |
| Dividends | 3.5% | 2.5% | 7.0% |
| Book Value | 10.5% | 9.5% | 5.5% |

| Cal-endar | QUARTERLY REVENUES ($ mill.) Mar.31 | Jun.30 | Sep.30 | Dec.31 | Full Year |
|---|---|---|---|---|---|
| 1988 | 12058 | 13907 | 13714 | 19782 | 59461 |
| 1989 | 12730 | 15213 | 14305 | 20462 | 62710 |
| 1990 | 14185 | 16495 | 15277 | 23061 | 69018 |
| 1991 | 13545 | 14732 | 14433 | 21990 | 64700 |
| 1992 | 14500 | 16500 | 16000 | 24500 | 71500 |

| Cal-endar | EARNINGS PER SHARE Mar.31 | Jun.30 | Sep.30 | Dec.31 | Full Year |
|---|---|---|---|---|---|
| 1988 | 1.57 | 2.14 | 2.10 | 4.02 | 9.83 |
| 1989 | 1.61 | 2.31 | 1.51 | 3.62 | 9.05 |
| 1990 | 1.81 | 2.45 | 1.95 | 4.30 | 10.51 |
| 1991 | .93 | .20 | .30 | 2.82 | 4.25 |
| 1992 | 1.35 | 1.75 | 1.75 | 3.90 | 8.75 |

| Cal-endar | QUARTERLY DIVIDENDS PAID Mar.31 | Jun.30 | Sep.30 | Dec.31 | Full Year |
|---|---|---|---|---|---|
| 1987 | 1.10 | 1.10 | 1.10 | 1.10 | 4.40 |
| 1988 | 1.10 | 1.10 | 1.10 | 1.10 | 4.40 |
| 1989 | 1.10 | 1.10 | 1.21 | 1.21 | 4.73 |
| 1990 | 1.21 | 1.21 | 1.21 | 1.21 | 4.84 |
| 1991 | 1.21 | 1.21 | 1.21 | 1.21 | 1.84 |

BUSINESS: International Business Machines Corporation is the world's largest supplier of advanced information processing technology and communication systems and services, and program products. 1990 revenue breakdown: Sales, 64%; support services, 16%; software, 14%; rentals and financing, 6%. Foreign business accounted for 52% of 1990 revenues and 77% of pretax earnings. Research, development and engineering costs equaled 9.5% of revenues. '90 depreciation rate: 9.9%. Estimated plant age: 5 years. Has 373,816 employees, 789,050 shareholders. Insiders control 6% of stock. Chairman and Chief Executive Officer: John Akers. President: J.D. Kuehler. Incorporated: New York. Address: Armonk, NY 10504. Telephone: 914-765-1900.

IBM's painful mainframe transition should be finished. Big Blue announced its new generation of mainframes in the fall of 1990, but the largest models in the line only started to ship in late September of this year. In the meantime, many potential customers chose to make do with their existing machines, or opted for used computers. Those decisions, coupled with the economic slowdown, were mainly responsible for the weak earnings in the first nine months of this year. Pent up demand for the new models is strong, though. IBM has already booked orders for all the computers it can produce this year, and we think production for much of 1992's March quarter is also spoken for.

We expect to see earnings improvement starting in the current quarter. The product line has also been enhanced by updated mid-range members of the AS/400 family and aggressively priced, more powerful PS/1 personal computers aimed at the home and small business markets. And the RS/6000 workstations are still selling well. The company continues to chip away at its expenses, too. Employment probably will fall by 20,000

this year, and shrink further in 1992. Over the longer term, benefits are likely to flow from IBM's plan to position its mainframes at the center of enterprises' computer networks, providing security and insuring the integrity of data. Too, Big Blue's moves to work with other companies in the field, such as a deal with Apple to develop software that will be easier to use and that will run on a number of platforms, should be pluses. Finally, we think IBM will gain further business from companies that decide to "outsource" their data processing operations. Thus, share earnings may well rebound to $8.50-$9.00 in 1992, and rise to $14.00-$16.00 by 1994-96.

These shares have some appeal, in our opinion. The issue is ranked Below Average for year-ahead relative performance. However, the earnings gains we project for the 3- to 5-year haul probably will allow this equity to outperform the market averages by a bit over that span. The issue's dividend yield is attractive, too, and the payout appears safe, unless the company's earnings slump continues longer than we forecast.

George A. Niemond                November 1, 1991

(A) Based on average shares outstanding. Excludes nonrecurring gain (losses): '88, 86¢; (89¢); '89, ($2.58); '91 ($3.96). Next earnings report due mid-Jan.

(B) Next dividend meeting about Jan 28 Goes ex about Feb 3. Dividend payment dates: about March 10, June 10, Sept. 10, Dec. 10. ■ Dividend reinvestment plan available (no bro-

kerage fee). (C) In millions, adjusted for stock split. (D) Depreciation on accelerated basis. (E) Fully diluted 3- to 5-years here. (F) Includes financial subsidiary.

| Company's Financial Strength | A++ |
|---|---|
| Stock's Price Stability | 95 |
| Price Growth Persistence | 15 |
| Earnings Predictability | 80 |

# LILLY (ELI) & CO. NYSE-LLY

| | | |
|---|---|---|
| RECENT PRICE | **76** | |
| P/E RATIO | **16.3** | (Trailing: 17.5 / Median: 14.0) |
| RELATIVE P/E RATIO | **1.10** | |
| DIV'D YLD | **2.8%** | |
| VALUE LINE | **1268** | |

**TIMELINESS 2** Above Average (Relative Price Perform'ance Next 12 Mos.)
**SAFETY 1** Highest (Scale: 1 Highest to 5 Lowest)
**BETA 1.10** (1.00 = Market)

High: 15.9  Low: 11.4

**1994-96 PROJECTIONS**

| | Price | Gain | Ann'l Total Return |
|---|---|---|---|
| High | 170 | (+125%) | 24% |
| Low | 140 | (+85%) | 19% |

**Insider Decisions**

| | D | J | F | M | A | M | J | J | A |
|---|---|---|---|---|---|---|---|---|---|
| to Buy | 0 | 0 | 0 | 0 | 1 | 0 | 1 | 0 | 0 |
| Options | 0 | 0 | 2 | 0 | 1 | 0 | 1 | 0 | 0 |
| to Sell | 2 | 1 | 1 | 0 | 1 | 0 | 1 | 2 | 0 |

**Institutional Decisions**

| | 4Q90 | 1Q91 | 2Q91 |
|---|---|---|---|
| to Buy | 194 | 219 | 218 |
| to Sell | 188 | 168 | 183 |
| Hld(000) | 187624 | 191667 | 185937 |

Percent shares traded: 9.0 / 6.0 / 3.0

**Target Price Range 1994 | 1995 | 1996**
Scale: 200, 180, 128, 96, 80, 64, 48, 40, 32, 24, 16, 12
Shaded areas indicate recessions
Relative Price Strength
2-for-1 split
Options: ASE

## Annual Per-Share Statistics

| | 1975 | 1976 | 1977 | 1978 | 1979 | 1980 | 1981 | 1982 | 1983 | 1984 | 1985 | 1986 | 1987 | 1988 | 1989 | 1990 | 1991 | 1992 | ©VALUE LINE PUB., INC. 94-96 |
|---|---|---|---|---|---|---|---|---|---|---|---|---|---|---|---|---|---|---|---|
| Sales per sh A | 4.46 | 4.85 | 5.38 | 6.35 | 7.56 | 8.44 | 9.12 | 9.77 | 10.32 | 10.86 | 11.72 | 13.38 | 13.07 | 14.84 | 14.98 | 19.43 | 19.65 | 22.20 | 33.15 |
| "Cash Flow" per sh B | .77 | .85 | .92 | 1.11 | 1.30 | 1.32 | 1.46 | 1.63 | 1.89 | 2.13 | 2.34 | 2.65 | 2.91 | 3.52 | 4.19 | 5.15 | 5.30 | 6.10 | 9.53 |
| Earnings per sh B | .66 | .73 | .78 | .95 | 1.13 | 1.13 | 1.23 | 1.36 | 1.53 | 1.68 | 1.85 | 2.01 | 2.15 | 2.67 | 3.20 | 3.90 | 4.50 | 5.25 | 8.25 |
| Div'ds Decl'd per sh C | .28 | .31 | .36 | .41 | .59 | .55 | .60 | .65 | .69 | .75 | .80 | .90 | .90 | 1.15 | 1.35 | 1.64 | 2.00 | 2.30 | 3.50 |
| Cap'l Spending per sh | .39 | .24 | .28 | .31 | .59 | .76 | .78 | .78 | .68 | .72 | .74 | 1.02 | 1.23 | 1.36 | 1.99 | 3.77 | 4.10 | 3.25 | 4.50 |
| Book Value per sh D | 3.46 | 3.90 | 4.28 | 4.75 | 5.39 | 5.73 | 6.21 | 6.78 | 7.22 | 7.76 | 8.56 | 9.85 | 10.92 | 11.76 | 13.48 | 12.98 | 16.60 | 19.50 | 31.00 |
| Common Shs Outst'g D | 276.50 | 276.52 | 282.33 | 291.56 | 291.63 | 303.12 | 303.92 | 303.35 | 293.96 | 286.19 | 279.00 | 278.11 | 278.74 | 274.24 | 278.82 | 267.14 | 292.55 | 292.60 | 294.00 |
| Avg Ann'l P/E Ratio | 25.1 | 17.8 | 12.5 | 11.9 | 11.8 | 11.8 | 10.5 | 9.0 | 10.2 | 9.0 | 11.5 | 17.5 | 20.5 | 15.6 | 17.7 | 18.4 | | | 19.0 |
| Relative P/E Ratio | 3.35 | 2.28 | 1.64 | 1.62 | 1.77 | 1.57 | 1.43 | 1.16 | .86 | .84 | .93 | 1.19 | 1.37 | 1.30 | 1.34 | 1.36 | | | 1.60 |
| Avg Ann'l Div'd Yield | 1.7% | 2.4% | 3.7% | 3.6% | 3.5% | 4.1% | 4.1% | 4.6% | 4.4% | 4.9% | 3.8% | 2.6% | 2.3% | 2.8% | 2.4% | 2.3% | | | 2.5% |

Bold figures are Value Line estimates

## Financial Statistics

| | 1981 | 1982 | 1983 | 1984 | 1985 | 1986 | 1987 | 1988 | 1989 | 1990 | 1991 | 1992 | 94-96 |
|---|---|---|---|---|---|---|---|---|---|---|---|---|---|
| Sales ($mill) A | 2773.2 | 2962.7 | 3033.7 | 3109.2 | 3270.6 | 3720.4 | 3643.8 | 4069.7 | 4175.6 | 5191.6 | 5750 | 6500 | 9750 |
| Operating Margin | 24.7% | 25.4% | 27.1% | 27.8% | 27.5% | 27.9% | 28.5% | 30.7% | 33.4% | 34.4% | 35.0% | 35.5% | 38.0% |
| Depreciation ($mill) | 69.2 | 83.1 | 98.3 | 120.7 | 136.2 | 177.7 | 184.3 | 204.0 | 229.3 | 247.5 | 235 | 255 | 365 |
| Net Profit ($mill) | 374.5 | 411.8 | 457.4 | 490.2 | 517.6 | 558.2 | 626.5 | 761.0 | 939.5 | 1127.3 | 1315 | 1535 | 2425 |
| Income Tax Rate | 42.0% | 39.8% | 39.4% | 36.4% | 35.0% | 36.3% | 32.8% | 31.8% | 29.4% | 29.5% | 29.5% | 30.0% | 31.0% |
| Net Profit Margin | 13.5% | 13.9% | 15.1% | 15.8% | 15.8% | 15.0% | 17.2% | 18.7% | 22.5% | 21.7% | 22.9% | 23.6% | 24.9% |
| Working Cap'l ($mill) | 847.6 | 806.8 | 841.8 | 760.3 | 894.4 | 909.7 | 1275.9 | 1125.9 | 945.6 | d316.3 | 125 | 200 | 950 |
| Long-Term Debt ($mill) | 53.8 | 49.4 | 90.7 | 116.6 | 238.6 | 395.3 | 365.7 | 387.7 | 269.5 | 277.0 | 700 | 725 | 600 |
| Net Worth ($mill) | 1888.3 | 2055.5 | 2121.0 | 2221.2 | 2387.7 | 2739.6 | 3042.6 | 3225.3 | 3757.1 | 3467.5 | 4655 | 5705 | 9100 |
| % Earned Total Cap'l | 19.4% | 19.7% | 20.9% | 21.2% | 20.1% | 18.3% | 18.8% | 21.5% | 23.6% | 30.4% | 24.0% | 24.0% | 25.0% |
| % Earned Net Worth | 19.8% | 20.0% | 21.6% | 22.1% | 21.7% | 20.4% | 20.6% | 23.6% | 25.0% | 32.5% | 27.0% | 27.0% | 26.5% |
| % Retained to Comm Eq | 10.0% | 10.4% | 11.7% | 12.3% | 11.3% | 11.2% | 11.4% | 13.8% | 15.1% | 19.5% | 15.0% | 15.0% | 15.0% |
| % All Div'ds to Net Prof | 50% | 48% | 46% | 44% | 43% | 45% | 44% | 42% | 40% | 40% | 44% | 44% | 43% |

**CAPITAL STRUCTURE as of 9/30/91**

Total Debt $1194.3 mill. Due in 5 Yrs $698.1 mill.
LT Debt $496.2 mill. LT Interest $37.9 mill.
(Total interest coverage: 33.3x)   (9% of Cap'l)

Leases, Uncapitalized Annual rentals $56.0 mill.

Pension Liability None

Pfd Stock None

Common Stock 292,341,284 shs.   (91% of Cap'l)

| CURRENT POSITION (mill.) | 1989 | 1990 | 9/30/91 |
|---|---|---|---|
| Cash Assets | 652.0 | 750.8 | 861.1 |
| Receivables | 732.1 | 770.7 | 804.9 |
| Inventory (LIFO) | 599.5 | 673.0 | 793.0 |
| Other | 290.8 | 306.8 | 306.5 |
| Current Assets | 2274.4 | 2501.3 | 2765.5 |
| Accts Payable | 196.2 | 259.9 | 171.9 |
| Debt Due | 134.0 | 1239.5 | 698.1 |
| Other | 998.6 | 1318.2 | 1035.7 |
| Current Liab. | 1328.8 | 2817.6 | 1905.7 |

| ANNUAL RATES of change (per sh) | Past 10 Yrs. | Past 5 Yrs. | Est'd '88-'90 to '94-'96 |
|---|---|---|---|
| Sales | 8.0% | 13.0% | 12.5% |
| "Cash Flow" | 13.0% | 15.0% | 14.5% |
| Earnings | 12.0% | 14.0% | 17.0% |
| Dividends | 11.0% | 13.0% | 17.0% |
| Book Value | 9.0% | 10.0% | 16.0% |

| QUARTERLY SALES ($ mill.) A | | | | | |
|---|---|---|---|---|---|
| Cal-endar | Mar.31 | Jun.30 | Sep.30 | Dec.31 | Full Year |
| 1988 | 1072.1 | 1014.7 | 940.6 | 1042.3 | 4069.7 |
| 1989 | 1052.0 | 986.6 | 991.0 | 1146.0 | 4175.6 |
| 1990 | 240.6 | 1225.4 | 1281.8 | 1443.8 | 5191.6 |
| 1991 | 1435.5 | 1376.3 | 1596.9 | | 5750 |
| 1992 | 1570 | 1525 | 1615 | 1790 | 6500 |

| EARNINGS PER SHARE B | | | | | |
|---|---|---|---|---|---|
| Cal-endar | Mar.31 | Jun.30 | Sep.30 | Dec.31 | Full Year |
| 1988 | .82 | .64 | .60 | .61 | 2.67 |
| 1989 | .99 | .75 | .73 | .73 | 3.20 |
| 1990 | 1.16 | .93 | .90 | .91 | 3.90 |
| 1991 | 1.35 | 1.08 | 1.01 | 1.06 | 4.50 |
| 1992 | 1.50 | 1.27 | 1.21 | 1.27 | 5.25 |

| QUARTERLY DIVIDENDS PAID C■ | | | | | |
|---|---|---|---|---|---|
| Cal-endar | Mar.31 | Jun.30 | Sep.30 | Dec.31 | Full Year |
| 1987 | .25 | .25 | .25 | .25 | 1.00 |
| 1988 | .288 | .288 | .288 | .288 | 1.15 |
| 1989 | .337 | .337 | .337 | .337 | 1.35 |
| 1990 | .41 | .41 | .41 | .41 | 1.64 |
| 1991 | .50 | .50 | | | |

**We're lowering our 1991 earnings per share target for Lilly by 15¢ to $4.50.** The anti-depressant *Prozac,* Lilly's single biggest product (accounts for 15%-20% of corporate sales), is witnessing a slowdown in prescriptions due to patient concerns about allegations linking the drug to an increased risk of suicidal tendencies and violent behavior. Additionally, growth in Advanced Cardiovascular System's (ACS) balloon angioplasty catheters has slowed due to competition. Foreign operations, meanwhile, are suffering from negative currency effects. These factors, along with a 3% increase in shares outstanding, restrained share net growth in the third quarter and will likely hold Lilly's full-year 1991 net to a gain of only 15%, still respectable, but shy of the increases likely to be registered by many of its peers.

**Profit growth should pick up a bit in 1992.** We expect prescriptions for *Prozac* to pick up as patients' fears are allayed in the wake of the FDA's assertion that there appears to be no link between the anti-depressant and suicidal behavior; sales should rise 10% or so to nearly $1 billion, despite the expected launch of a similar drug (*Zoloft*) from Pfizer. The introduction of *Lovan* (for obesity control) should also help bolster profits. Sales of medical instruments are expected to pick up with the introduction of new, more competitive angioplasty devices from ACS. All in all, we estimate that Lilly's bottom line will move up 15%-20% in '92 to $5.25 a share.

**Healthy double-digit earnings growth remains in prospect for 1994-96.** True, the company's big-selling oral antibiotic, *Ceclor* ($900 million in annual sales), is scheduled to lose its U.S. patent protection in December of 1992. But we believe the threat of generic competition to the lucrative franchise will be ameliorated as a result of the difficulty of the manufacturing process, plus the launch of a sustained-release formulation of the drug called *Ceclor SR.* In any event, Lilly has other promising new drugs waiting in the wings, including *Lorabid,* an antibiotic.

**High-quality Lilly stock is expected to outleg the year-ahead market.** Moreover, with solid profit growth projected through 1994-96, this issue's appreciation potential appears good and well defined.
*Rudolph C. Carryl*          *November 8, 1991*

| | |
|---|---|
| Company's Financial Strength | A + + |
| Stock's Price Stability | 80 |
| Price Growth Persistence | 95 |
| Earnings Predictability | 100 |

(A) Incl. IVAC from '77; Cardiac Pacemakers from '78; Physio-Control from '80; Advanced Cardiovascular Systems from '84; Hybritech from '86. Excl. Elanco's agri business from '89  (B) Fully diluted. Primary egs. prior to '87. Excl. nonrecurring items: '87, $1.58/sh. Next earnings report due late January. (C) Next dividend meeting about December 17  Goes ex about February 7. Dividend payment dates: March 10, June 9, September 10, December 10 ■ Dividend reinvestment plan available. (D) In millions adjusted for stock splits & divds

Factual material is obtained from sources believed to be reliable, but the publisher is not responsible for any errors or omissions contained herein. Copyright 1991 by Value Line Publishing, Inc. ■ Reg. TM--Value Line, Inc.
For the confidential use of subscribers. Reprinting, copying, and distribution by permission only.

# McGRAW-HILL NYSE-MHP

| RECENT PRICE | 52 | P/E RATIO | 15.8 (Trailing: 16.5 Median: 16.0) | RELATIVE P/E RATIO | 1.07 | DIV'D YLD | 4.3% | VALUE LINE | 1799 |
|---|---|---|---|---|---|---|---|---|---|

**TIMELINESS** 4 Below Average (Relative Price Performance Next 12 Mos.)

**SAFETY** 2 Above Average (Scale: 1 Highest to 5 Lowest)

**BETA** 1.15 (1.00 = Market)

**1994-96 PROJECTIONS**

|  | Price | Gain | Ann'l Total Return |
|---|---|---|---|
| High | 105 | (+100%) | 22% |
| Low | 80 | (+55%) | 15% |

**Insider Decisions**

|  | J | F | M | A | M | J | J | A | S |
|---|---|---|---|---|---|---|---|---|---|
| to Buy | 0 | 0 | 0 | 0 | 1 | 0 | 0 | 0 | 0 |
| Options | 0 | 0 | 0 | 0 | 0 | 0 | 0 | 0 | 0 |
| to Sell | 0 | 0 | 0 | 0 | 1 | 0 | 0 | 0 | 1 |

**Institutional Decisions**

|  | 2Q91 | 3Q91 | 4Q91 |
|---|---|---|---|
| to Buy | 84 | 84 | 67 |
| to Sell | 86 | 71 | 92 |
| Hld(000) | 28453 | 28877 | 28950 |

Percent shares traded: 12.0 / 8.0 / 4.0

2-for-1 split (1983)

Relative Price Strength

Shaded areas indicate recessions

Options: PHLE

Target Price Range 1994 | 1995 | 1996

**CAPITAL STRUCTURE as of 9/30/91**

Total Debt $624.4 mill. Due in 5 Yrs $114.7 mill.
LT Debt $511.5 mill. LT Interest $50.0 mill.
Incl. $246,000 3¾% sub. debs. ('92) conv. into 7,872 com. shs. at $31.25.
(Total interest coverage 6.4x)  (35% of Cap'l)

Leases, Uncapitalized Annual rentals $35.1 mill.
Pension Liability None

Pfd Stock None
Common Stock 49,046,901 shs.  (65% of Cap'l)

© VALUE LINE PUB., INC.

| | 1975 | 1976 | 1977 | 1978 | 1979 | 1980 | 1981 | 1982 | 1983 | 1984 | 1985 | 1986 | 1987 | 1988 | 1989 | 1990 | 1991 | 1992 | 94-96 |
|---|---|---|---|---|---|---|---|---|---|---|---|---|---|---|---|---|---|---|---|
| Sales per sh | 11.61 | 12.66 | 13.67 | 15.53 | 17.84 | 20.22 | 22.32 | 23.94 | 25.82 | 27.85 | 29.99 | 31.22 | 36.32 | 37.44 | 36.75 | 39.62 | 39.55 | 43.10 | 55.60 |
| "Cash Flow" per sh | .88 | 1.03 | 1.26 | 1.53 | 1.86 | 2.16 | 2.43 | 2.70 | 3.07 | 3.40 | 3.78 | 4.07 | 4.61 | 4.81 | 4.81 | 4.89 | 4.60 | 5.30 | 7.25 |
| Earnings per sh | .68 | .82 | 1.04 | 1.29 | 1.55 | 1.74 | 1.97 | 2.20 | 2.52 | 2.86 | 2.92 | 3.04 | 3.11 | 3.45 | 3.40 | 3.53 | 3.15 | 3.70 | 5.40 |
| Div'ds Decl'd per sh | .28 | .32 | .40 | .50 | .64 | .76 | .84 | 1.08 | 1.24 | 1.40 | 1.52 | 1.68 | 1.84 | 2.00 | 2.16 | 2.16 | 2.20 | 2.29 | 2.54 |
| Cap'l Spending per sh | .16 | .16 | .28 | .37 | .42 | .51 | .76 | .84 | .98 | .99 | .97 | .84 | 1.08 | .92 | 1.19 | 1.96 | 1.10 | 1.25 | 1.80 |
| Book Value per sh | 4.55 | 5.13 | 6.01 | 6.81 | 7.82 | 8.46 | 9.95 | 10.84 | 12.28 | 13.86 | 15.40 | 17.05 | 17.11 | 19.00 | 18.08 | 19.50 | 20.45 | 21.95 | 29.40 |
| Common Shs Outst'g | 46.21 | 46.58 | 48.22 | 49.01 | 49.32 | 49.46 | 49.73 | 49.86 | 50.16 | 50.33 | 50.40 | 50.50 | 48.22 | 48.56 | 48.69 | 48.93 | 48.95 | 48.95 | 49.00 |
| Avg Ann'l P/E Ratio | 8.1 | 9.1 | 8.7 | 8.6 | 8.4 | 9.6 | 12.1 | 12.7 | 17.6 | 14.4 | 15.7 | 18.5 | 21.1 | 17.4 | 20.4 | 14.8 | | | 17.0 |
| Relative P/E Ratio | 1.08 | 1.16 | 1.14 | 1.17 | 1.22 | 1.28 | 1.47 | 1.40 | 1.49 | 1.34 | 1.27 | 1.25 | 1.41 | 1.44 | 1.54 | 1.10 | | | 1.40 |
| Avg Ann'l Div'd Yield | 5.1% | 4.3% | 4.4% | 4.5% | 4.9% | 4.6% | 3.5% | 3.4% | 2.4% | 3.0% | 3.1% | 2.7% | 2.6% | 3.1% | 2.9% | 4.1% | | | 2.8% |
| Sales ($mill) | | | | | | | 1110.1 | 1193.6 | 1295.2 | 1401.8 | 1491.1 | 1576.8 | 1751.2 | 1818.0 | 1789.0 | 1938.6 | 1935 | 2110 | 2725 |
| Operating Margin | | | | | | | 18.2% | 18.6% | 19.7% | 20.2% | 20.5% | 21.0% | 19.1% | 18.7% | 19.1% | 20.2% | 19.0% | 19.0% | 20.0% |
| Depreciation ($mill) | | | | | | | 22.5 | 24.8 | 27.7 | 26.8 | 43.3 | 51.5 | 65.6 | 66.2 | 68.9 | 66.8 | 72.0 | 80.0 | 90.0 |
| Net Profit ($mill) | | | | | | | 98.1 | 110.0 | 126.5 | 144.2 | 147.4 | 154.0 | 156.8 | 167.4 | 165.3 | 172.5 | 155 | 180 | 265 |
| Income Tax Rate | | | | | | | 48.8% | 48.8% | 48.8% | 48.8% | 48.2% | 47.9% | 44.3% | 40.4% | 42.1% | 43.0% | 42.0% | 40.0% | 40.0% |
| Net Profit Margin | | | | | | | 8.8% | 9.2% | 9.8% | 10.3% | 9.9% | 9.8% | 9.0% | 9.2% | 9.2% | 8.9% | 8.0% | 8.5% | 9.7% |
| Working Cap'l ($mill) | | | | | | | 151.9 | 175.4 | 230.2 | 227.8 | 277.3 | 246.1 | 116.8 | 157.4 | 47.2 | 116.4 | 115 | 125 | 165 |
| Long-Term Debt ($mill) | | | | | | | 14.5 | 11.2 | 3.6 | 2.3 | 6.4 | 3.9 | 3.9 | 1.9 | 377.6 | 507.6 | 400 | 350 | 350 |
| Net Worth ($mill) | | | | | | | 496.1 | 541.6 | 616.6 | 698.0 | 776.7 | 861.4 | 825.3 | 922.8 | 880.2 | 954.3 | 1000 | 1075 | 1440 |
| % Earned Total Cap'l | | | | | | | 19.4% | 20.0% | 20.4% | 20.6% | 18.9% | 17.7% | 18.9% | 18.1% | 14.2% | 13.4% | 12.5% | 14.0% | 16.0% |
| % Earned Net Worth | | | | | | | 19.8% | 20.3% | 20.5% | 20.7% | 19.0% | 17.9% | 19.0% | 18.1% | 18.8% | 18.1% | 15.5% | 17.0% | 18.5% |
| % Retained to Comm Eq | | | | | | | 11.4% | 11.7% | 11.8% | 11.7% | 9.9% | 9.0% | 8.8% | 8.5% | 7.5% | 7.0% | 4.5% | 6.5% | 10.0% |
| % All Div'ds to Net Prof | | | | | | | 43% | 43% | 43% | 43% | 48% | 50% | 54% | 53% | 60% | 61% | 70% | 62% | 47% |

Bold figures are Value Line estimates

| CURRENT POSITION | 1989 | 1990 | 9/30/91 |
|---|---|---|---|
| ($MILL.) | | | |
| Cash Assets | 34.6 | 20.6 | 17.3 |
| Receivables | 498.1 | 568.9 | 488.7 |
| Inventory (FIFO) | 166.5 | 188.0 | 211.7 |
| Other | 140.5 | 183.6 | 140.8 |
| Current Assets | 839.7 | 961.1 | 858.5 |
| Accts Payable | 30.0 | 30.2 | 86.5 |
| Debt Due | 124.8 | 114.7 | 112.9 |
| Other | 637.7 | 699.8 | 551.8 |
| Current Liab. | 792.5 | 844.7 | 751.2 |

| ANNUAL RATES of change (per sh) | Past 10 Yrs. | Past 5 Yrs. | Est'd '88-'90 to '94-'96 |
|---|---|---|---|
| Sales | 8.0% | 6.5% | 6.5% |
| "Cash Flow" | 11.0% | 7.0% | 7.0% |
| Earnings | 9.0% | 4.5% | 7.5% |
| Dividends | 12.5% | 10.0% | 4.0% |
| Book Value | 9.0% | 6.5% | 7.5% |

| Cal-endar | QUARTERLY SALES ($ mill.) | | | | Full Year |
|---|---|---|---|---|---|
| | Mar.31 | Jun.30 | Sep.30 | Dec.31 | |
| 1988 | 395.7 | 443.7 | 471.2 | 507.4 | 1818.0 |
| 1989 | 390.3 | 428.4 | 452.2 | 518.1 | 1789.0 |
| 1990 | 420.0 | 457.8 | 502.8 | 558.0 | 1938.6 |
| 1991 | 428.5 | 456.9 | 489.5 | 560.1 | 1935 |
| 1992 | 440 | 500 | 560 | 610 | 2110 |

| Cal-endar | EARNINGS PER SHARE A | | | | Full Year |
|---|---|---|---|---|---|
| | Mar.31 | Jun.30 | Sep.30 | Dec.31 | |
| 1988 | .49 | .88 | 1.08 | 1.00 | 3.45 |
| 1989 | .48 | 1.04 | 1.31 | .57 | 3.40 |
| 1990 | .34 | .76 | 1.38 | 1.05 | 3.53 |
| 1991 | .26 | .71 | 1.13 | 1.05 | 3.15 |
| 1992 | .40 | .90 | 1.25 | 1.15 | 3.70 |

| Cal-endar | QUARTERLY DIVIDENDS PAID | | | | Full Year |
|---|---|---|---|---|---|
| | Mar.31 | Jun.30 | Sep.30 | Dec.31 | |
| 1987 | .42 | .42 | .42 | .42 | 1.68 |
| 1988 | .46 | .46 | .46 | .46 | 1.84 |
| 1989 | .50 | .50 | .50 | .50 | 2.00 |
| 1990 | .54 | .54 | .54 | .54 | 2.16 |
| 1991 | .55 | .55 | .55 | .55 | |

(A) Primary earnings. Excludes nonrecurring gains, (loss): '87, 16¢; '88, 38¢; '89, ($2.59). Excludes accounting gain: '89, 16¢. Next earnings report due late January. (B) Next div'd meeting about Dec. 26. Goes ex about Jan. 23 Approximate dividend payment dates: 12th of March, June, Sept, Dec. ■Div'd reinvestment plan available. (C) Includes intangibles. In '90 \$588.3 mill., \$12.01/share. (D) In millions, adjusted for stock split. (E) '89 results restated to include Macmillan/McGraw-Hill joint venture (formed 7/1/89) for full twelve months.

Factual material is obtained from sources believed to be reliable, but the publisher is not responsible for any errors or omissions contained herein. For the confidential use of subscribers. Reprinting, copying and distribution by permission only. Copyright 1991 by Value Line Publishing Inc. ® Reg. TM – Value Line, Inc.

BUSINESS: McGraw-Hill, Inc. is a multimedia publishing and information services company. Publishes textbooks, technical and popular books, and business and industrial periodicals (*Business Week, Aviation Week, ENR*, et al). Owns 50% of Macmillan/McGraw Hill School Publishing Co., formed in mid-89. Markets information services for the financial and construction fields (*Stan-*

*dard & Poor's, F.W. Dodge, Data Resources, Platt's*). Owns 4 TV stations. Labor costs: est'd 33% of sales. 1990 deprec. rate: 6.2%. Has 15,250 employees; 7,372 stockholders. Insiders control 6% of shares. Chairman and President: Joseph L. Dionne. Chairman Emeritus: Harold W. McGraw Jr. Incorp.: NY. Address: 1221 Avenue of the Americas, New York, NY 10020. Tel.: 212-512-2000.

**McGraw-Hill has been stuck in a rut.** The publishing and information services company was slowed down for several years by a top-heavy management and repeated restructurings. This year, McGraw-Hill was supposed to show evidence that it had found the right formula with the elimination of a whole layer of corporate management at the end of 1990. But sluggish revenues have overwhelmed any efficiency gains. The recession has been especially harsh for McGraw-Hill's crown jewel, *Business Week*, with advertising pages down 23% from last year's pace in the first nine months. The F.W. Dodge unit is also suffering from a sharp slowdown in its construction markets. McGraw-Hill will probably earn no more than \$3.15 a share in 1991, its weakest performance in four years. **The automation of F.W. Dodge is complete.** The company has replaced its eighteen paper-intensive regional offices with five new technologically-advanced facilities during the past year; the last of the obsolete offices was shut down in the third quarter. As a result, Dodge has been able to cut its work force by 20%. Equally im-

portant, the division has a greater ability to develop new on-line services. Although its depreciation charges will be bumped up, F.W. Dodge is likely to show considerably higher profits next year. **The company has other reasons to be optimistic about 1992.** The company's broadcast TV stations should get an advertising boost in the national election year and *Business Week* should also do considerably better if the economy picks up. McGraw-Hill also has a strong line of college textbooks slated for introduction next year. We expect the company to make a double-digit rebound, with 1992 earnings hitting \$3.70 a share. **McGraw-Hill is searching for new applications for its technology.** For example, the company now offers some customized college textbooks, with professors able to select chapters and sequences. McGraw-Hill's technological prowess and financial flexibility give it the ability to significantly increase shareholder value over the pull to 1994-96. But this stock is likely to remain in the doldrums until the company can get its earnings growth on track.

*Ben Sharav*      *December 6, 1991*

| Company's Financial Strength | A++ |
|---|---|
| Stock's Price Stability | 65 |
| Price Growth Persistence | 65 |
| Earnings Predictability | 90 |

# MINNESOTA MNG. NYSE-MMM

| RECENT PRICE | P/E RATIO | RELATIVE P/E RATIO | DIV'D YLD | VALUE LINE |
|---|---|---|---|---|
| 88 | 16.3 (Trailing: 15.7) (Median: 13.0) | 1.05 | 3.5% | 1894 |

**TIMELINESS 3** (Relative Price Performance Next 12 Mos.) — Average
**SAFETY 1** Highest (Scale: 1 Highest to 5 Lowest)
**BETA 1.05** (1.00 = Market)

| | High | Low |
|---|---|---|
| 1981 | 31.4 | 22.9 |
| 1982 | 32.5 | 24.0 |
| 1983 | 39.7 | 24.4 |
| 1984 | 45.3 | 38.3 |
| 1985 | 42.8 | 34.6 |
| 1986 | 45.8 | 38.8 |
| 1987 | 59.4 | 43.0 |
| 1988 | 67.5 | 55.3 |
| 1989 | 81.9 | 60.1 |
| 1990 | 91.4 | 73.6 |
| 1991 | 97.5 | 78.3 |

**1994-96 PROJECTIONS**

| | Price | Gain | Ann'l Total Return |
|---|---|---|---|
| High | 150 | (+70%) | 17% |
| Low | 120 | (+35%) | 11% |

Insider Decisions / Institutional Decisions
Hld's(000) 138870 139609 139348

Target Price Range 1994 | 1995 | 1998
(scale: 200 180 160 128 96 80 64 48 40 32 24 16 12)

Options: CBOE

© VALUE LINE PUB, INC.  94-96

## Annual Per-Share Data

| | 1975 | 1976 | 1977 | 1978 | 1979 | 1980 | 1981 | 1982 | 1983 | 1984 | 1985 | 1986 | 1987 | 1988 | 1989 | 1990 | 1991 | 1992 | '94-96 |
|---|---|---|---|---|---|---|---|---|---|---|---|---|---|---|---|---|---|---|---|
| Sales per sh | 13.62 | 15.23 | 17.15 | 19.82 | 23.19 | 25.91 | 27.70 | 28.00 | 30.02 | 33.13 | 34.24 | 37.64 | 41.45 | 47.17 | 53.85 | 59.23 | 62.08 | 67.00 | 85.79 |
| "Cash Flow" per sh | 1.81 | 2.22 | 2.62 | 3.26 | 3.74 | 3.97 | 4.07 | 4.05 | 4.41 | 4.88 | 5.08 | 5.63 | 6.51 | 7.96 | 8.73 | 9.50 | 9.40 | 10.25 | 14.35 |
| Earnings per sh | 1.15 | 1.47 | 1.79 | 2.42 | 2.80 | 2.89 | 2.87 | 2.69 | 2.84 | 3.14 | 3.01 | 3.40 | 4.02 | 5.09 | 5.50 | 5.91 | 5.40 | 5.90 | 9.00 |
| Div'ds Decl'd per sh | .68 | .73 | .85 | 1.00 | 1.19 | 1.40 | 1.50 | 1.66 | 1.80 | 1.92 | 2.12 | 2.24? | — | — | 2.60 | 2.92 | 3.12 | 3.24 | 4.50 |
| Cap'l Spending per sh | 1.37 | .96 | 1.08 | 1.31 | 1.92 | 2.23 | 2.39 | 2.58 | 2.38 | 3.01 | 3.56 | 3.41 | 3.62 | 3.75 | 5.33 | 6.08 | 6.10 | 6.25 | 7.00 |
| Book Value per sh | 7.94 | 8.86 | 9.75 | 11.02 | 12.58 | 14.04 | 14.68 | 15.05 | 15.77 | 16.40 | 17.49 | 19.53 | 22.24 | 24.58 | 24.15 | 27.79 | 29.30 | 31.30 | 41.25 |
| Common Shs Outst'g | 229.56 | 235.14 | 230.90 | 232.08 | 234.59 | 234.61 | 234.93 | 235.78 | 234.47 | 232.60 | 229.14 | 228.53 | 227.49 | 224.33 | 224.15 | 222.66 | 219.83 | 217.00 | 215.00 |
| Avg Ann'l P/E Ratio | 24.6 | 20.3 | 14.0 | 9.9 | 9.5 | 9.8 | 9.9 | 9.5 | 11.1 | 11.4 | 12.4 | 13.3 | 15.5 | 16.8 | 12.0 | 12.9 | 13.9 | | 15.0 |
| Relative P/E Ratio | 3.28 | 2.60 | 1.83 | 1.43 | 1.26 | 1.19 | 1.22 | 1.22 | 1.15 | 1.08 | 1.05 | 1.12 | 1.00 | .98 | 1.00 | 1.03 | | | 1.25 |
| Avg Ann'l Div'd Yield | 2.4% | 2.4% | 3.4% | | | 5.1% | 5.4% | 5.4% | 4.4% | 4.0% | 4.4% | 4.4% | 3.4% | 2.8% | 3.5% | 3.6% | 3.6% | | 3.2% |

2-for-1 split (1987)
Relative Price Strength
Bold figures are Value Line estimates

## Capital Structure as of 6/30/91

Total Debt $1703 mill.  Due in 5 Yrs $906.0 mill.
LT Debt $879.0 mill.  LT Interest $75.0 mill.
(Total interest coverage: 20.5x)  (13% of Cap'l)

Pension Liability None
Pfd Stock None
Common Stock 219,934,855 shs.  (87% of Cap'l)

## Financial Data ($mill)

| | 1981 | 1982 | 1983 | 1984 | 1985 | 1986 | 1987 | 1988 | 1989 | 1990 | 1991 | 1992 | '94-96 |
|---|---|---|---|---|---|---|---|---|---|---|---|---|---|
| Sales ($mill) | 6508.0 | 6601.0 | 7039.0 | 7705.0 | 7846.0 | 8602.0 | 9429.0 | 10581 | 11990 | 13021 | 13469 | 14460 | 18009 |
| Operating Margin | 22.3% | 20.6% | 21.4% | 21.9% | 21.3% | 22.3% | 22.7% | 23.8% | 23.8% | 22.8% | 21.5% | 21.5% | 23.5% |
| Depreciation ($mill) | 282.0 | 325.0 | 366.0 | 403.0 | 471.0 | 507.0 | 564.0 | 632.0 | 700.0 | 781.0 | 865 | 900 | 1130 |
| Net Profit ($mill) | 673.0 | 631.0 | 667.0 | 733.0 | 689.0 | 779.0 | 918.0 | 1154.0 | 1244.0 | 1308.0 | 1175 | 1270 | 1500 |
| Income Tax Rate | 41.6% | 37.8% | 40.0% | 41.5% | 39.9% | 42.2% | 41.3% | 38.7% | 39.3% | 37.4% | 37.2% | 37.5% | 37.5% |
| Net Profit Margin | 10.3% | 9.6% | 9.5% | 9.5% | 8.8% | 9.1% | 9.7% | 10.9% | 10.4% | 10.0% | 8.7% | 8.8% | 10.5% |
| Working Cap'l ($mill) | 1744.0 | 1710.0 | 1911.0 | 1954.0 | 1894.0 | 2138.0 | 2298.0 | 2370.0 | 2661.0 | 2390.0 | 2440 | 2440 | 3575 |
| Long-Term Debt ($mill) | 327.0 | 340.0 | 358.0 | 330.0 | 431.0 | 436.0 | 435.0 | 406.0 | 885.0 | 760.0 | 800 | 800 | 500 |
| Net Worth ($mill) | 3449.0 | 3548.0 | 3698.0 | 3814.0 | 4008.0 | 4463.0 | 5060.0 | 5514.0 | 5378.0 | 6110.0 | 6035 | 6725 | 8695 |
| % Earned Total Cap'l | 19.5% | 16.6% | 16.8% | 18.2% | 16.0% | 16.2% | 17.0% | 19.8% | 20.5% | 19.5% | 17.0% | 17.5% | 21.0% |
| % Earned Net Worth | 19.5% | 17.8% | 18.0% | 17.2% | 17.5% | 17.5% | 18.1% | 20.9% | 23.1% | 21.4% | 18.5% | 19.0% | 22.0% |
| % Retained to Comm Eq | 9.3% | 7.2% | 7.5% | 8.8% | 7.1% | 8.2% | 9.7% | 12.2% | 12.4% | 10.8% | 8.5% | | 11.0% |
| % All Div'ds to Net Prof | 52% | 60% | 58% | 54% | 56% | 53% | 46% | 42% | 46% | 49% | 50% | 53% | 50% |

| CURRENT POSITION ($MILL) | 1989 | 1990 | 6/30/91 |
|---|---|---|---|
| Cash Assets | 887 | 591 | 429 |
| Receivables | 2075 | 2367 | 2481 |
| Inventory (FIFO) | 2120 | 2355 | 2255 |
| Other | 300 | 416 | 456 |
| Current Assets | 5382 | 5729 | 5621 |
| Accts Payable | 724 | 811 | 692 |
| Debt Due | 455 | 736 | 824 |
| Other | 1542 | 1792 | 1646 |
| Current Liab. | 2721 | 3339 | 3162 |

| ANNUAL RATES of change (per sh) | Past 10 Yrs. | Past 5 Yrs. | Est'd '88-'90 to '94-'96 |
|---|---|---|---|
| Sales | 9.0% | 10.5% | 8.0% |
| "Cash Flow" | 9.0% | 13.0% | 8.5% |
| Earnings | 7.5% | 13.0% | 8.5% |
| Dividends | 8.0% | 8.5% | 10.0% |
| Book Value | 7.5% | 9.0% | 8.5% |

| Cal-endar | QUARTERLY SALES ($ mill) Mar.31 | Jun.30 | Sep.30 | Dec.31 | Full Year |
|---|---|---|---|---|---|
| 1988 | 2602 | 2711 | 2689 | 2579 | 10581 |
| 1989 | 3017 | 3025 | 2994 | 2954 | 11990 |
| 1990 | 3164 | 3234 | 3343 | 3280 | 13021 |
| 1991 | 3389 | 3349 | 3370 | 3352 | 13460 |
| 1992 | 3500 | 3600 | 3700 | 3600 | 14400 |

| Cal-endar | EARNINGS PER SHARE Mar.31 | Jun.30 | Sep.30 | Dec.31 | Full Year |
|---|---|---|---|---|---|
| 1988 | 1.22 | 1.36 | 1.30 | 1.21 | 5.09 |
| 1989 | 1.43 | 1.49 | 1.37 | 1.31 | 5.60 |
| 1990 | 1.51 | 1.54 | 1.52 | 1.34 | 5.91 |
| 1991 | 1.37 | 1.36 | 1.35 | 1.32 | 5.40 |
| 1992 | 1.45 | 1.50 | 1.50 | 1.45 | 5.90 |

| Cal-endar | QUARTERLY DIVIDENDS PAID ■ Mar.31 | Jun.30 | Sep.30 | Dec.31 | Full Year |
|---|---|---|---|---|---|
| 1987 | .465 | .465 | .465 | .465 | 1.96 |
| 1988 | .53 | .53 | .53 | .53 | 2.12 |
| 1989 | .65 | .65 | .65 | .65 | 2.60 |
| 1990 | .73 | .73 | .73 | .73 | 2.92 |
| 1991 | .78 | .78 | | | |

(A) Primary earnings. Next earnings report due late October. Excludes nonrecurring gain in 85, 13¢.

(B) Next dividend meeting about Nov. 14. Goes ex about Nov. 18. Dividend payment dates: about March 10, June 10, Sept. 10, and Dec. 10. ■ Dividend reinvestment plan available

(C) In millions, adjusted for stock split.

**BUSINESS:** Minnesota Mining & Manufacturing Co. is a diversified manufacturer. Products include tapes, adhesives, coatings, sealants, abrasives, elastomers, fasteners, plastic films, floor coverings, fabric and paper protectors, cleaning agents, roofing granules, firefighting agents, electrical connectors, insulating and conductive materials, graphic arts and photographic supplies, magnetic media,

medical and dental products, and office supplies. Foreign sales, 49% of total. Research and development, 6.6%. 1990 depreciation rate: 8.3%. Est'd plant age: 5.7 yrs. Has 89,600 employees, 113,000 stkhldrs. Insiders hold 1% of stock. Chairman & C.E.O.: Allen F. Jacobson. Incorporated: Delaware. Address: 3M Center, St. Paul, Minnesota 55144-1000. Telephone: 612-733-1110.

Minnesota Mining's 1991 earnings will likely fall short of last year's tally. A combination of the U.S. economic recession and slow growth abroad resulted in a 9% decline in 3M's first-half share net, despite fewer 3M shares outstanding and moderate currency translation gains. Weakness in demand was most evident in the U.S. market, in which 3M had zero unit growth — a trend that may well persist for the full year. Although unit sales growth abroad will likely remain around the 7% level witnessed in the first half, this pace is down from the double-digit gains of recent years. And while currency translation gains boosted share earnings by about 20¢ in the first half, losses of roughly the same magnitude should be a drag on share net for the remainder of the year. All in all, we expect that 3M's 1991 share earnings will fall to $5.40, an 8.5% decline from 1990's tally. But . . .

3M's earnings should rebound to last year's level in 1992, assuming the resumption of U.S. economic growth and stronger demand for the company's products beyond our borders. We expect that the domestic economy is emerging from its downturn, and anticipate gradually improving, economic conditions extending into 1992. If so, demand for 3M's extensive line of products should pick up, especially at the company's presently depressed automotive segment. And since 3M's sales abroad are nearly 50% of its total, the company should benefit from the low double-digit growth it has typically achieved in less-saturated markets outside the U.S. Thus, we estimate that 3M's share net will reach the $5.90 level next year.

These neutrally-ranked shares possess solid longer-term prospects. The company spends a considerable 6.6% of sales on research & development. The pursuit of this strategy — as well as 3M's encouragement of intra-corporate entrepreneurship — has resulted in roughly 30% of current sales emanating from products less than five years old. These high-quality shares (ranked 1, Highest, for Safety) offer a decent dividend yield of 3.5%, and are appropriate for conservative accounts stressing total return over the 3- to 5-year time frame.

*Robert M. Egan*     *September 6, 1991*

| Company's Financial Strength | A++ |
|---|---|
| Stock's Price Stability | 90 |
| Price Growth Persistence | 80 |
| Earnings Predictability | 95 |

# NYNEX CORP. NYSE-NYN

| | | |
|---|---|---|
| RECENT PRICE | 75 | |
| P/E RATIO | 12.7 | (Trailing: 12.8 Median: NMF) |
| RELATIVE P/E RATIO | 0.89 | |
| DIV'D YLD | 6.1% | |
| VALUE LINE | 766 | |

**TIMELINESS** 4 Below Average (Relative Price Perform-ance Next 12 Mos.)

**SAFETY** 1 Highest
(Scale: 1 Highest to 5 Lowest)

**BETA** .85 (1.00 = Market)

**1994-96 PROJECTIONS**
| | Price | Gain | Ann'l Total Return |
|---|---|---|---|
| High | 115 | (+55%) | 16% |
| Low | 95 | (+25%) | 11% |

**Insider Decisions**
| | D J F M A M J J A |
|---|---|
| to Buy | 0 0 0 0 0 0 0 0 0 |
| Options | 0 0 0 0 0 0 0 0 0 |
| to Sell | 1 0 0 0 0 0 0 0 0 |

**Institutional Decisions**
| | 4Q90 | 1Q91 | 2Q91 |
|---|---|---|---|
| to Buy | 142 | 120 | 113 |
| to Sell | 136 | 136 | 149 |
| Hld'000s | 72753 | 72795 | 74982 |

| | High: | Low: |
|---|---|---|
| 1981 | | |
| 1982 | | |
| 1983 | 32.1 | 30.1 |
| 1984 | 37.9 | 29.3 |
| 1985 | 49.3 | 36.4 |
| 1986 | 73.3 | 46.4 |
| 1987 | 78.4 | 58.0 |
| 1988 | 70.9 | 60.9 |
| 1989 | 92.0 | 65.3 |
| 1990 | 91.0 | 67.1 |
| 1991 | 77.8 | 67.0 |

1.45-for-Dividends-p-sh
divided by Interest Rate

2-for-1 split

Relative Price Strength

Shaded areas indicate recessions

Options: NYSE

Target Price Range
1994 | 1995 | 1996

Percent shares traded
6.0
4.0
2.0

NYNEX Corporation is one of the seven regional holding companies resulting from the breakup of American Telephone & Telegraph Company on January 1, 1984. Each AT&T shareholder received one share of NYNEX common for every ten shares of AT&T (pre-divestiture) common stock held. The stock began trading on a when-issued basis on November 21, 1983. Regular trading of NYNEX shares began on Febru-ary 16, 1984.

**CAPITAL STRUCTURE as of 6/30/91**
Total Debt $8541.5 mill. Due in 5 Yrs 2420.8 mill.
LT Debt $7366.8 mill. LT Interest $615.0 mill.

(LT interest earned: 3.9x; total interest coverage: 3.4x)

Pension Liability None

Pfd Stock None

Common Stock 202,003,833 shs.

| | 1981 | 1982 | 1983 | 1984 | 1985 | 1986 | 1987 | 1988 | 1989 | 1990 | 1991 | 1992 | © VALUE LINE PUB., INC. | 94-96 |
|---|---|---|---|---|---|---|---|---|---|---|---|---|---|---|
| Revenues per sh[A] | -- | -- | -- | 47.63 | 51.01 | 55.95 | 59.12 | 64.29 | 67.05 | 67.88 | 67.35 | 71.10 | | 85.25 |
| "Cash Flow" per sh | -- | -- | -- | 10.89 | 12.51 | 14.16 | 16.18 | 17.62 | 17.51 | 16.42 | 16.70 | 18.00 | | 22.25 |
| Earnings per sh[B] | -- | -- | -- | 5.05 | 5.43 | 6.01 | 6.26 | 6.63 | 5.75 | 6.08 | 5.80 | 6.20 | | 8.20 |
| Div'ds Decl'd per sh[C]■ | -- | -- | -- | 3.00 | 3.20 | 3.48 | 3.72 | 4.04 | 4.36 | 4.56 | 4.55 | 4.72 | | 5.20 |
| Cap'l Spending per sh | -- | -- | -- | 9.22 | 10.32 | 11.85 | 13.48 | 14.13 | 12.29 | 12.46 | 13.35 | 13.75 | | 14.75 |
| Book Value per sh | -- | -- | -- | 39.08 | 41.29 | 43.75 | 44.99 | 47.83 | 47.55 | 45.72 | 46.95 | 47.40 | | 54.75 |
| Common Shs Outst'g[D] | -- | -- | -- | 201.00 | 202.20 | 202.70 | 204.40 | 196.94 | 197.03 | 200.12 | 202.00 | 204.00 | | 205.00 |
| Avg Ann'l P/E Ratio | -- | -- | -- | 6.5 | 7.8 | 10.3 | 10.9 | 9.9 | 13.3 | 12.8 | Bold figures are Value Line estimates | | | 13.0 |
| Relative P/E Ratio | -- | -- | -- | .61 | .63 | .70 | .73 | .82 | 1.01 | .95 | | | | 1.10 |
| Avg Ann'l Div'd Yield | -- | -- | -- | 9.1% | 7.6% | 5.6% | 5.4% | 6.1% | 5.7% | 5.9% | | | | 4.9% |
| Revenues ($mill)[A] | 8541.4 | 9686.3 | 10270 | 9573.3 | 10314 | 11342 | 12084 | 12661 | 13211 | 13585 | 13600 | 14500 | | 17400 |
| Net Profit ($mill) | 899.9 | 973.1 | 982.7 | 986.4 | 1095.3 | 1215.3 | 1276.5 | 1315.0 | 1132.5 | 1208.1 | 1170 | 1270 | | 1675 |
| Income Tax Rate | 38.0% | 39.5% | 41.1% | 39.2% | 42.1% | 42.3% | 34.7% | 22.1% | 28.5% | 28.0% | 32.0% | 32.0% | | 32.0% |
| Net Profit Margin | 10.4% | 10.0% | 9.6% | 10.3% | 10.6% | 10.7% | 10.6% | 10.4% | 8.6% | 8.9% | 8.6% | 8.8% | | 8.6% |
| Long-Term Debt Ratio | -- | -- | 43.2% | 40.9% | 39.3% | 38.2% | 39.8% | 39.9% | 40.8% | 43.2% | 43.0% | 42.5% | | 39.5% |
| Common Equity Ratio | -- | -- | 56.8% | 59.1% | 60.7% | 61.8% | 60.2% | 60.1% | 59.2% | 56.8% | 57.0% | 57.5% | | 60.5% |
| Total Capital ($mill) | -- | -- | 12588 | 13297 | 13752 | 14344 | 15273 | 15661 | 15834 | 16094 | 16420 | 16825 | | 18570 |
| Net Plant ($mill) | -- | -- | 15196 | 16377 | 17107 | 17904 | 18531 | 18370 | 19465 | 19729 | 20120 | 20520 | | 21245 |
| % Earned Total Cap'l | -- | -- | 9.7% | 9.2% | 9.6% | 10.2% | 10.0% | 10.4% | 9.0% | 9.3% | 9.0% | 9.0% | | 10.5% |
| % Earned Net Worth | -- | -- | 13.7% | 12.6% | 13.1% | 13.7% | 13.9% | 14.0% | 12.1% | 13.2% | 12.5% | 13.0% | | 15.0% |
| % Earned Comm Equity | -- | -- | 13.7% | 12.6% | 13.1% | 13.7% | 13.9% | 14.0% | 12.1% | 13.2% | 12.5% | 13.0% | | 15.0% |
| % Retained to Comm Eq | -- | -- | 1.2% | 5.0% | 5.4% | 5.8% | 5.5% | 5.6% | 3.1% | 4.3% | 2.5% | 3.0% | | 5.5% |
| % All Div'ds to Net Prof | 80% | 86% | 91% | 60% | 59% | 58% | 61% | 60% | 74% | 70% | 79% | 76% | | 64% |

BUSINESS: NYNEX Corporation is a holding company for New York Telephone Company and New England Telephone Company. NYNEX is a major supplier of telephone service in New York, Maine, Massachusetts, New Hampshire, Rhode Island, Vermont and parts of Connecticut. The company owns 11.4% of the assets of the former AT&T. Access lines in service: 15.3 million. 1990 revenue breakdown: local service, 42%; network access, 24%; toll service, 10%; other, 24%. Telephone company employees per 10,000 access lines: 46.0. '90 depreciation rate: 7.7%. Has 93,300 employees, about 1.1 mill. shareholders. Chairman & Chief Executive Officer: William Ferguson. Incorporated: DE. Address: 335 Madison Ave. New York, NY 10017. Telephone 212-370-7400.

The economic scenario in NYNEX's operating region continues to be weak. All aspects of NYNEX's operations are being hurt by the severe economic crunch that has taken hold in the Northeast. To date, there are few signs that the regional economy is ready to turn around. Indeed, we expect the Northeast economy to lag the rest of the nation (Value Line thinks the national economy has already begun to recover).

Revenues are barely holding above last year's levels. Although part of the slump in sales is due to the elimination of the money-losing NYNEX Business Centers, the recession is seriously reducing growth in access lines, limiting the amount of usage by existing customers, and is restricting expansion of its cellular network. Also, its directory business is slumping.

Earnings are likely to remain under pressure. Although the company's cost-containment program is beginning to show some promise, earnings are being restricted by poor revenue results. Thus, we have reduced our earnings estimate for this year by 10¢ a share, to $5.80. In addition, since we expect the Northeast's economy to lag the rest of the country, we don't look for a meaningful recovery in operating earnings until mid-1992. Therefore, we have lowered our '92 share-earnings estimate by 30¢, assuming that the New England and New York economies begin to recover by early next year.

A new dawn is shinning on NYNEX's labor relations. The company's poor reputation with regards to its labor relations is well-documented by lengthy labor strikes in the past. However, new management is conscientiously setting out to avoid similar conflicts in the future and has recently announced an agreement with its unions to extend its existing contracts through August, 1995. Also, the company is instituting an early retirement program as a part of this agreement.

NYNEX stock is ranked to lag the year-ahead market averages. However, we think these shares offer worthwhile total-return potential, based on the earnings and dividend growth that we foresee to 1994-96, assuming the regional economy begins to recover before long.
*Jerome D. Fischer* — *October 18, 1991*

| CURRENT POSITION ($MILL) | 1989 | 1990 | 6/30/91 |
|---|---|---|---|
| Cash Assets | 155.0 | 121.7 | 106.2 |
| Other | 3513.6 | 3791.7 | 3432.7 |
| Current Assets | 3668.6 | 3913.4 | 3538.9 |
| Accts Payable | 2748.2 | 2979.4 | 2478.8 |
| Debt Due | 946.3 | 1467.7 | 1147.7 |
| Other | 855.7 | 1044.5 | 1230.0 |
| Current Liab. | 4550.2 | 5491.6 | 4676.5 |
| Fix. Chg. Cov. | 328% | 298% | 326% |

| ANNUAL RATES of change (per sh) | Past 10 Yrs. | Past 5 Yrs. | Est'd '88-'90 to '94-'96 |
|---|---|---|---|
| Revenues | -- | 6.0% | 4.5% |
| "Cash Flow" | -- | 8.0% | 4.5% |
| Earnings | -- | 3.0% | 5.0% |
| Dividends | -- | 7.0% | 3.0% |
| Book Value | -- | 3.0% | 2.5% |

| Cal-endar | QUARTERLY REVENUES ($ mill.) Mar.31 | Jun.30 | Sep.30 | Dec.31 | Full Year |
|---|---|---|---|---|---|
| 1988 | 3070 | 3165 | 3181 | 3245 | 12661 |
| 1989 | 3235 | 3299 | 3309 | 3368 | 13211 |
| 1990 | 3315 | 3442 | 3390 | 3438 | 13585 |
| 1991 | 3356 | 3361 | 3400 | 3483 | 13600 |
| 1992 | 3500 | 3550 | 3650 | 3800 | 14500 |

| Cal-endar | EARNINGS PER SHARE (B) Mar.31 | Jun.30 | Sep.30 | Dec.31 | Full Year |
|---|---|---|---|---|---|
| 1988 | 1.55 | 1.64 | 1.70 | 1.74 | 6.63 |
| 1989 | 1.44 | 1.42 | 1.47 | 1.42 | 5.75 |
| 1990 | 1.46 | 1.52 | 1.50 | 1.60 | 6.08 |
| 1991 | 1.34 | 1.44 | 1.47 | 1.55 | 5.80 |
| 1992 | 1.45 | 1.50 | 1.60 | 1.65 | 6.20 |

| Cal-endar | QUARTERLY DIVIDENDS PAID (C) ■ Mar.31 | Jun.30 | Sep.30 | Dec.31 | Full Year |
|---|---|---|---|---|---|
| 1987 | .87 | .95 | .95 | .95 | 3.72 |
| 1988 | .95 | 1.01 | 1.01 | 1.01 | 3.98 |
| 1989 | 1.01 | 1.09 | 1.09 | 1.09 | 4.28 |
| 1990 | 1.09 | 1.14 | 1.14 | 1.14 | 4.51 |
| 1991 | 1.14 | 1.14 | | | |

(A) Calendar years (except 83, 12 months ending 6.30). (B) Based on average shares outstanding. Excludes nonrecurring loss sh: 89 $1.64, '90 $1.30. Next earnings report due late-Oct. (C) Next dividend meeting about Dec. 19. Goes ex about Jan 3. Dividend payment dates Feb 1, May 1, Aug 1, Nov 1. ■ Dividend reinvestment plan available (D) In mill. ions. adjusted for split.

| | |
|---|---|
| Company's Financial Strength | A+ |
| Stock's Price Stability | 95 |
| Price Growth Persistence | 95 |
| Earnings Predictability | 95 |

# OHIO EDISON NYSE-OEC

| RECENT PRICE | 20 | P/E RATIO | 12.3 (Trailing: 14.2)(Median: 7.5) | RELATIVE P/E RATIO | 0.86 | DIV'D YLD | 7.5% | VALUE LINE | 733 |

**TIMELINESS 3** Average (Relative Price Performance Next 12 Mos.)

**SAFETY 4** Below Average (Scale: 1 Highest to 5 Lowest)

**BETA .80** (1.00 = Market)

**1994-96 PROJECTIONS**

| | Price | Gain | Ann'l Total Return |
|---|---|---|---|
| High | 25 | (+25%) | 12% |
| Low | 15 | (-25%) | 2% |

Insider Decisions

Institutional Decisions

Relative Price Strength

0.88 × Dividends p sh divided by Interest Rate

Options: PACE

Target Price Range 1994 | 1995 | 1996

Shaded areas indicate recessions

© VALUE LINE PUB., INC.

## Per-share data

| | 1975 | 1976 | 1977 | 1978 | 1979 | 1980 | 1981 | 1982 | 1983 | 1984 | 1985 | 1986 | 1987 | 1988 | 1989 | 1990 | 1991 | 1992 | 94-96 |
|---|---|---|---|---|---|---|---|---|---|---|---|---|---|---|---|---|---|---|---|
| Revenues per sh | 16.62 | 16.18 | 15.55 | 16.56 | 16.68 | 15.77 | 16.26 | 14.88 | 13.98 | 13.39 | 12.80 | 11.63 | 11.68 | 14.05 | 14.12 | 14.59 | 15.40 | 15.65 | 16.70 |
| "Cash Flow" per sh | 3.18 | 3.47 | 3.07 | 2.66 | 3.13 | 2.73 | 3.12 | 2.75 | 3.16 | 3.54 | 3.59 | 3.61 | 3.70 | 3.23 | 3.97 | 3.66 | 3.80 | 3.80 | 4.10 |
| Earnings per sh A | 1.95 | 2.14 | 1.97 | 1.19 | 1.80 | 1.52 | 2.10 | 1.89 | 2.22 | 2.50 | 2.45 | 2.47 | 2.40 | 1.22 | 2.18 | 1.67 | 1.60 | 1.70 | 1.50 |
| Div'd Decl'd per sh B | 1.66 | 1.67 | 1.72 | 1.76 | 1.76 | 1.76 | 1.76 | 1.80 | 1.80 | 1.84 | 1.88 | 1.92 | 1.96 | 1.96 | 1.96 | 1.73 | 1.50 | 1.50 | 1.60 |
| Cap'l Spending per sh | 7.93 | 8.17 | 6.99 | 7.58 | 8.00 | 7.52 | 7.22 | 8.06 | 6.88 | 7.10 | 6.03 | 5.18 | 4.63 | 1.26 | 1.45 | 1.68 | 1.80 | 1.70 | 2.40 |
| Book Value per sh C | 15.39 | 15.93 | 16.93 | 16.33 | 16.26 | 15.57 | 15.61 | 15.49 | 15.78 | 15.93 | 16.30 | 16.97 | 17.40 | 16.60 | 16.82 | 16.68 | 16.80 | 17.00 | 17.20 |
| Common Shs Outst'g D | 35.70 | 39.86 | 51.21 | 52.12 | 59.62 | 68.53 | 78.68 | 96.08 | 108.46 | 122.24 | 137.09 | 149.81 | 152.40 | 152.51 | 152.57 | 152.57 | 152.57 | 152.57 | 152.57 |
| Avg Ann'l P/E Ratio | 8.0 | 8.6 | 10.1 | 14.9 | 8.5 | 8.8 | 5.8 | 7.1 | 6.7 | 4.8 | 6.1 | 7.8 | 8.7 | 15.4 | 9.8 | 11.5 | | | 10.0 |
| Relative P/E Ratio | 1.07 | 1.10 | 1.32 | 2.03 | 1.23 | 1.17 | .70 | .78 | .57 | .45 | .50 | .53 | .58 | 1.28 | .74 | .86 | | | .85 |
| Avg Ann'l Div'd Yield | 10.7% | 9.0% | 8.6% | 9.9% | 11.5% | 13.1% | 14.4% | 13.2% | 12.1% | 15.3% | 12.5% | 9.9% | 9.4% | 10.4% | 9.2% | 9.0% | | | 8.4% |

Bold figures are Value Line estimates

## Financial data

| | 1981 | 1982 | 1983 | 1984 | 1985 | 1986 | 1987 | 1988 | 1989 | 1990 | 1991 | 1992 | 94-96 |
|---|---|---|---|---|---|---|---|---|---|---|---|---|---|
| Revenues ($mill) | 1279.7 | 1429.6 | 1515.8 | 1637.1 | 1754.8 | 1741.9 | 1779.6 | 2142.6 | 2155.0 | 2225.5 | 2350 | 2415 | 2550 |
| Net Profit ($mill) | 183.0 | 195.6 | 272.4 | 339.3 | 370.7 | 410.8 | 412.9 | 218.9 | 361.0 | 281.7 | 270 | 285 | 310 |
| Income Tax Rate | 13.0% | 15.2% | 20.5% | 16.6% | 17.6% | 17.6% | 21.1% | 33.4% | 29.5% | 37.8% | 40.7% | 40.0% | 40.0% |
| AFUDC % to Net Profit | 69.8% | 82.0% | 74.8% | 75.7% | 77.6% | 78.1% | 78.6% | 11.5% | 7.3% | 7.3% | 5.0% | 4.5% | 6.0% |
| Long-Term Debt Ratio | 51.1% | 57.2% | 55.6% | 56.1% | 54.4% | 53.6% | 51.0% | 51.8% | 50.5% | 51.2% | 51.0% | 52.5% | 50.0% |
| Common Equity Ratio | 35.7% | 32.0% | 33.4% | 33.4% | 35.4% | 37.4% | 40.6% | 40.9% | 42.2% | 42.0% | 42.5% | 43.0% | 44.0% |
| Total Capital ($mill) | 3444.2 | 4657.3 | 5125.1 | 5633.1 | 6309.7 | 6799.6 | 6533.8 | 6190.6 | 6083.5 | 6067.5 | 6025 | 5995 | 6000 |
| Net Plant ($mill) | 3867.8 | 4522.7 | 5150.9 | 5945.6 | 6609.2 | 7216.1 | 6336.1 | 6048.0 | 6081.7 | 6049.2 | 5380 | 5915 | 6220 |
| % Earned Total Cap'l | 7.7% | 7.3% | 8.3% | 8.9% | 9.0% | 8.9% | 8.9% | 6.1% | 8.7% | 7.1% | 6.5% | 7.0% | 7.0% |
| % Earned Net Worth | 10.9% | 9.8% | 12.0% | 13.2% | 14.2% | 13.0% | 12.9% | 7.3% | 12.0% | 9.5% | 9.0% | 9.5% | 10.0% |
| % Earned Comm Equity | 12.2% | 10.8% | 13.3% | 14.9% | 14.2% | 13.0% | 12.9% | 7.4% | 13.0% | 10.0% | 9.5% | 10.0% | 11.0% |
| % Retained to Comm Eq | 1.9% | .7% | 2.4% | 3.9% | 3.3% | 3.1% | 2.6% | NMF | 1.3% | NMF | -.5% | 1.0% | 1.5% |
| % All Div'ds to Net Prof | 87% | 95% | 85% | 78% | 80% | 81% | 84% | NMF | 90% | 102% | 94% | 90% | 65% |

**CAPITAL STRUCTURE as of 6/30/91**

Total Debt $3688.1 mill. Due in 5 Yrs $1480.8 mill.
LT Debt $3175.7 mill. LT Interest $360.3 mill.
(LT interest earned: 2.5x)

Leases, Uncapitalized Annual rentals $123.1 mill.
Pension Liability None

Pfd Stock $398.9 mill. Pfd Div'd $24.1 mill.
5,815,815 shs. 3.9% to 15.0%, $25 to $100 par, cum, callable $25.75 to $113.66; 9,000 shs. 10.25%, no par, cum, callable $1040.00.

Common Stock 152,569,437 shs.

## ELECTRIC OPERATING STATISTICS

| | 1988 | 1989 | 1990 |
|---|---|---|---|
| % Change Sales (KWH) | +20.1 | -10.7 | -1.8 |
| Avg. Resid'l Use (KWH) | 8425 | 8336 | 8159 |
| Avg. Resid'l Revs. per KWH (¢) | 9.40 | 9.69 | 10.23 |
| Capacity at Peak (Mw) | 5964 | 5964 | 5964 |
| Peak Load, Summer (Mw) | 5027 | 5152 | 5394 |
| Annual Load Factor (%) | 65.6 | 67.8 | 65.0 |
| % Change Customers (Yr-end) | +1.0 | +1.0 | +1.0 |

| | Past 10 Yrs. | Past 5 Yrs. | Est'd '88-'90 to '94-'96 |
|---|---|---|---|
| Fixed Charge Cov. (%) | 171 | 172 | 180 |

**ANNUAL RATES** of change (per sh)

| | Past 10 Yrs. | Past 5 Yrs. | Est'd '88-'90 to '94-'96 |
|---|---|---|---|
| Revenues | -1.5% | 1.5% | 2.5% |
| "Cash Flow" | 2.5% | 1.0% | 2.0% |
| Earnings | 1.0% | -6.5% | 2.0% |
| Dividends | .5% | .5% | -2.5% |
| Book Value | .5% | 1.0% | 1.0% |

| Cal-endar | QUARTERLY REVENUES ($ mill.) | | | | Full Year |
|---|---|---|---|---|---|
| | Mar.31 | Jun.30 | Sept.30 | Dec.31 | |
| 1988 | 526.8 | 515.7 | 567.1 | 533.0 | 2142.6 |
| 1989 | 546.7 | 512.6 | 550.0 | 545.7 | 2155.0 |
| 1990 | 559.7 | 522.9 | 572.8 | 570.1 | 2225.5 |
| 1991 | 588.4 | 564.2 | 602.4 | 595 | 2350 |
| 1992 | 600 | 580 | 620 | 615 | 2415 |

| Cal-endar | EARNINGS PER SHARE A | | | | Full Year |
|---|---|---|---|---|---|
| | Mar.31 | Jun.30 | Sept.30 | Dec.31 | |
| 1988 | .54 | .42 | .51 | .25 | 1.22 |
| 1989 | .60 | .50 | .59 | .49 | 2.18 |
| 1990 | .59 | .50 | .41 | .17 | 1.67 |
| 1991 | .43 | .40 | .41 | .36 | 1.60 |
| 1992 | .45 | .40 | .45 | .40 | 1.70 |

| Cal-endar | QUARTERLY DIVIDENDS PAID B ■ | | | | Full Year |
|---|---|---|---|---|---|
| | Mar.31 | Jun.30 | Sept.30 | Dec.31 | |
| 1987 | .49 | .49 | .49 | .49 | 1.96 |
| 1988 | .49 | .49 | .49 | .49 | 1.96 |
| 1989 | .49 | .49 | .49 | .49 | 1.96 |
| 1990 | .49 | .49 | .375 | .375 | 1.96 |
| 1991 | .375 | .375 | .375 | .375 | 1.73 |

(A) Next earnings report due mid-Feb. Excl. extraordinary gains: '81, 20¢; '82, 24¢; Incl. non-recurring charge: '88, 84¢. (B) Next dividend meeting about Nov. 19. Goes ex about Dec. 3

Dividend payment dates: March 31, June 30, Sept. 30, Dec. 31. ■ Dividend reinvestment plan available. (C) Incl. intangibles. In '90: $11.52 6 mill. (D) Rate base original

cost, rate allowed on common '90: 13.2%; earn. average common equity '90: 9.9%. Regulatory Climate Average (E) in millions.

BUSINESS: Ohio Edison Company serves central and northeastern Ohio (87% of revenues) and western Pennsylvania (13%) through a subsidiary, Pennsylvania Power Company. Electric revenue mix: residential, 35%; commercial, 27%; industrial, 26%; other, 12%. Largest load centers: Akron, Youngstown-Warren, Lorain-Elyria, and Springfield account for about 50% of population served.

Principal industries: agriculture, steel, automotive, metal fabrication, rubber. Fuel costs: 21% of revenues; labor costs, 18%. '90 depreciation rate: 3.2%. Estimated plant age: 9 years. Fuels in 1990; coal, 77%; nuclear, 23%. Has 6,792 employees; 177,900 stockholders. Chrm'n: J. Rogers. Pres.: W. Holland. Inc.: Ohio. Address: 76 South Main Street, Akron, OH 44308. Tel.: 800-633-4766.

**Abnormally warm weather buoyed Ohio Edison's second-quarter results.** As we'd expected, earnings were down from the year before (40¢ a share vs. 50¢) but the early heat caused customers to turn on air conditioners sooner than usual. As a result, kwh sales to residential and commercial classes rose 5.1% and 5.3% respectively above 1990 results, carrying the bottom line some 20%-25% higher than Wall Street had expected.

**But we're sticking to our $1.60-a-share estimate for 1991.** For one thing, important factors in OE's service territory, have continued to post very poor sales figures. For another, while the Midwest has held up better than other sections of the country during the tough times that started to hit the nation about midyear 1990, more recent statistics suggest that the economy in the central states has been slipping recently at a somewhat faster pace than previously. Our conservative stance comes also from the fact that . . . **Ohio Ed is still operating under a disappointing rate order** — handed down in August 1990 by The Public Utilities Commission of Ohio. PUCO allowed only $142 million of the $218 million requested by OE to cover the capital and operating costs of the company's interest in 833-mw nuclear generator, Beaver Valley #2. Oral arguments before the Ohio Supreme Court in the utility's appeal of the rate case are scheduled to begin on October 22nd with a decision expected in early 1992.

**OE has issued "market auction" preferred stock for the first time.** In August, the company sold 500,000 shares at $100 a share. For this breed of stock, buyers — usually corporations — make a dividend rate bid for the offered shares. The lowest bids that would purchase all the available shares becomes the dividend rate for all outstanding shares until the next auction period. The rate was set at 5.25% in August. It rose to 5.39% at the next auction on September 23rd, and will be reset in 49-day intervals. These shares replaced a $50-million issue of adjustable rate preferred last paying a 9.45% dividend.

**This stock might be attractive to income-oriented investors,** able to live with a 4 (Below Average) rank for Safety.
Raymond S. Cowen    October 18, 1991

| | |
|---|---|
| Company's Financial Strength | C++ |
| Stock's Price Stability | 95 |
| Price Growth Persistence | 40 |
| Earnings Predictability | 55 |

# PACIFIC TELESIS NYSE-PAC

| | | |
|---|---|---|
| RECENT PRICE **41** | P/E RATIO **14.3** (Trailing:14.6 / Median:NMF) | RELATIVE P/E RATIO **1.00** |
| DIV'D YLD **5.2%** | VALUE LINE **767** | |

**TIMELINESS 4** Below Average (Relative Price Perform-ance Next 12 Mos.)

**SAFETY 1** Highest (Scale: 1 Highest to 5 Lowest)

**BETA .90** (1.00 = Market)

**1994-96 PROJECTIONS**

| | Price | Gain | Ann'l Total Return |
|---|---|---|---|
| High | 65 | (+60%) | 16% |
| Low | 55 | (+35%) | 12% |

**Insider Decisions**

| | D | J | F | M | A | M | J | J | A |
|---|---|---|---|---|---|---|---|---|---|
| to Buy | 0 | 0 | 1 | 0 | 0 | 0 | 0 | 0 | 0 |
| Options | 0 | 0 | 1 | 0 | 0 | 0 | 0 | 0 | 0 |
| to Sell | 0 | 0 | 0 | 0 | 0 | 0 | 0 | 0 | 0 |

**Institutional Decisions**

| | 4Q90 | 1Q91 | 2Q91 |
|---|---|---|---|
| to Buy | 129 | 137 | 141 |
| to Sell | 177 | 190 | 193 |
| Hld'000 | 144393 | 145660 | 143323 |

Percent shares traded: 6.0 / 4.0 / 2.0

**Target Price Range 1994 | 1995 | 1996**

Scale markers: 100 80 64 48 40 32 24 20 16 12 8 6

Shaded areas indicate recessions

Relative Price Strength

2-for-1 split / 2-for-1 split

1.33 x Dividends p sh divided by Interest Rate

Options: PACE

Pacific Telesis Group is one of the seven regional holding companies that resulted from the breakup of American Telephone & Telegraph on January 1, 1984. One share of Pacific Telesis stock was exchanged (for every 10 shares of AT&T common (pre-divestiture). PacTel shares began trading on a when-issued basis on November 21, 1983. "Regular" trading began on February 16, 1984.

**CAPITAL STRUCTURE as of 6/30/91**
Total Debt $6566 mill. Due in 5 Yrs $1900.0 mill.
LT Debt $5400 mill. LT Interest $567.0 mill.
(LT interest earned: 4.1x; total interest coverage: 3.5x)

Leases, Uncapitalized None

Pension Liability None

Pfd Stock None

Common Stock 399,129,322 shs. as of 7/31/91

© VALUE LINE PUB., INC.

| | 1981 | 1982 | 1983 | 1984 | 1985 | 1986 | 1987 | 1988 | 1989 | 1990 | 1991 | 1992 | 94-96 |
|---|---|---|---|---|---|---|---|---|---|---|---|---|---|
| Revenues per sh A | -- | -- | -- | 19.55 | 19.79 | 20.85 | 21.38 | 22.64 | 23.94 | 24.32 | 25.15 | 26.10 | 30.80 |
| "Cash Flow" per sh | -- | -- | -- | 4.78 | 5.05 | 6.02 | 6.22 | 7.24 | 7.69 | 7.37 | 7.65 | 8.30 | 11.10 |
| Earnings per sh B | -- | -- | -- | 2.12 | 2.27 | 2.51 | 2.21 | 2.81 | 3.02 | 2.77 | 2.85 | 3.05 | 4.00 |
| Div'ds Decl'd per sh D | -- | -- | -- | 1.35 | 1.43 | 1.52 | 1.64 | 1.76 | 1.88 | 2.02 | 2.14 | 2.25 | 2.60 |
| Cap'l Spending per sh | -- | -- | -- | 5.20 | 5.26 | 4.89 | 4.75 | 3.58 | 4.22 | 4.85 | 6.05 | 6.30 | 6.60 |
| Book Value per sh | -- | -- | -- | 16.20 | 17.04 | 18.01 | 18.47 | 19.30 | 19.68 | 18.53 | 19.30 | 20.15 | 22.70 |
| Common Shs Outst'g E | -- | -- | -- | 400.14 | 429.41 | 430.55 | 427.12 | 418.91 | 400.79 | 399.46 | 398.00 | 396.75 | 378.10 |
| Avg Ann'l P/E Ratio | -- | -- | -- | 7.1 | 6.6 | 6.8 | 10.1 | 12.4 | 10.4 | 13.4 | 17.1 | *Bold figures are Value Line estimates* | 15.0 |
| Relative P/E Ratio | -- | -- | -- | .66 | .66 | .68 | .83 | .86 | 1.01 | 1.26 | | | 1.25 |
| Avg Ann'l Div'd Yield | -- | -- | -- | 9.0% | 7.8% | 6.0% | 6.0% | 6.0% | 4.6% | 4.6% | | | 4.3% |
| Revenues ($mill) A | 6818.9 | 7973.9 | 8132.6 | 7824.3 | 8498.6 | 8977.3 | 9131.0 | 9463.0 | 9593.0 | 9716.0 | 10000 | 10250 | 11640 |
| Net Profit ($mill) C | 438.8 | 580.6 | 631.2 | 828.5 | 929.1 | 1079.4 | 950.0 | 1188.0 | 1242.0 | 1030.0 | 1135 | 1210 | 1540 |
| Income Tax Rate | 56.3% | 40.4% | 39.5% | 41.5% | 44.7% | 44.3% | 40.2% | 38.7% | 37.4% | 36.6% | 38.5% | 38.5% | 38.5% |
| Net Profit Margin | 6.4% | 7.3% | 7.8% | 10.6% | 10.9% | 12.0% | 10.4% | 12.5% | 12.9% | 10.6% | 11.4% | 11.7% | 13.2% |
| Long-Term Debt Ratio | -- | 47.4% | 47.2% | 44.1% | 43.5% | 41.4% | 40.2% | 40.3% | 40.1% | 42.8% | 41.0% | 42.0% | 40.5% |
| Common Equity Ratio | -- | 48.8% | 48.6% | 52.0% | 54.9% | 58.2% | 59.6% | 59.5% | 59.4% | 56.5% | 58.0% | 57.0% | 58.0% |
| Total Capital ($mill) F | -- | 13716 | 12202 | 12456 | 13339 | 13318 | 13233 | 13597 | 13279 | 13205 | 14050 | 14050 | 14600 |
| Net Plant ($mill) | -- | 15129 | 16000 | 16968 | 17245 | 17192 | 17155 | 17079 | 17160 | 17150 | 17200 | 17200 | 17700 |
| % Earned Total Cap'l | -- | 4.4% | 8.1% | 9.2% | 9.2% | 9.2% | 10.1% | 10.7% | 11.3% | 10.1% | 11.0% | 10.5% | 12.5% |
| % Earned Net Worth | -- | 8.7% | 10.6% | 12.8% | 12.7% | 13.9% | 12.0% | 14.7% | 15.7% | 13.9% | 15.0% | 15.0% | 18.0% |
| % Earned Comm Equity | -- | 8.7% | 10.6% | 12.8% | 12.7% | 13.9% | 12.0% | 14.7% | 15.7% | 13.9% | 15.0% | 15.0% | 18.0% |
| % Retained to Comm Eq | -- | 3.6% | 2.4% | 4.6% | 4.6% | 5.5% | 3.1% | 6.4% | 6.9% | 3.9% | 3.5% | 4.0% | 6.0% |
| % All Div'ds to Net Prof | -- | | | 64% | 64% | 61% | 74% | 56% | 57% | 72% | 75% | 74% | 65% |

| CURRENT POSITION ($MILL.) | 1989 | 1990 | 6/30/91 |
|---|---|---|---|
| Cash Assets | -- | 110 | 90 |
| Other | 2085 | 2366 | 2319 |
| Current Assets | 2085 | 2476 | 2409 |
| Debt Due | 1853 | 1970 | 1617 |
| Other | 665 | 446 | 663 |
| Current Liab. | 2797 | 3536 | 3446 |
| Fix. Chg. Cov. | 460% | 343% | 322% |

| ANNUAL RATES of change (persh) | Past 10 Yrs. | Past 5 Yrs. | Est'd '88-'90 to '94-'96 |
|---|---|---|---|
| Revenues | -- | 3.5% | 4.5% |
| "Cash Flow" | -- | 9.0% | 6.5% |
| Earnings | -- | 5.5% | 6.0% |
| Dividends | -- | 6.5% | 5.5% |
| Book Value | -- | 3.0% | 3.0% |

| Cal-endar | QUARTERLY REVENUES ($ mill.) | | | | Full Year |
|---|---|---|---|---|---|
| | Mar.31 | Jun.30 | Sep.30 | Dec.31 | |
| 1988 | 2308 | 2366 | 2381 | 2428 | 9483.0 |
| 1989 | 2343 | 2407 | 2368 | 2475 | 9593.0 |
| 1990 | 2373 | 2434 | 2468 | 2441 | 9716.0 |
| 1991 | 2410 | 2520 | 2530 | 2540 | 10000 |
| 1992 | 2480 | 2600 | 2620 | 2650 | 10350 |

| Cal-endar | EARNINGS PER SHARE | | | | Full Year |
|---|---|---|---|---|---|
| | Mar.31 | Jun.30 | Sep.30 | Dec.31 | |
| 1988 | .71 | .76 | .75 | .59 | 2.81 |
| 1989 | .76 | .79 | .68 | .79 | 3.02 |
| 1990 | .65 | .72 | .72 | .68 | 2.77 |
| 1991 | .68 | .75 | .75 | .69 | 2.85 |
| 1992 | .70 | .75 | .82 | .78 | 3.05 |

| Cal-endar | QUARTERLY DIVIDENDS PAID | | | | Full Year |
|---|---|---|---|---|---|
| | Mar.31 | Jun.30 | Sep.30 | Dec.31 | |
| 1987 | .38 | .41 | .41 | .41 | 1.61 |
| 1988 | .41 | .44 | .44 | .44 | 1.73 |
| 1989 | .44 | .47 | .47 | .47 | 1.85 |
| 1990 | .47 | 505 | 505 | 505 | 1.99 |
| 1991 | 505 | 535 | 535 | | |

(A) Historical figures (pre-1984) are not comparable to cost-divestiture estimates and results. (B) Based on weighted average shares outstanding. Next earnings report due late Oct. | Excludes nonrecurring gain (loss) in '90, (17¢); in '91, 7¢. (C) Excludes nonrecurring gains in '82, $226.1 mill.; '83, $216.4 mill. (D) Next dividend meeting about Dec. 10. Goes ex about | Jan. 5. Dividend payment dates Feb. 1, May 1, Aug. 1, Nov. 1. ■ Dividend reinvestment plan available. (E) In millions, adjusted for stock splits. (F) Includes minority interest.

**BUSINESS:** Pacific Telesis Group is one of seven regional holding companies previously owned by AT&T. Serves 53 of 58 California counties through Pacific Bell subsidiary (97% of regulated revenues) and about one-third of Nevada through Nevada Bell (3%). Also markets cellular and paging services and business information systems. Has 14.2 million access lines in service. 30.7 million cel-lular POPS of which 1.8% are subscribers. '90 revenue breakdown: local service, 32%; network access, 23%; toll, 23%; unregulated, 22%. Access lines per telco employees: 231. '90 depreciation rate: 7.2%. Has 65,829 employees. 1.1 million shareholders. Chairman & CEO: Sam L. Ginn. Inc. Nevada. Address: 130 Kearny Street, San Francisco, CA 94108. Telephone: 415-394-3000.

**Pacific Telesis will likely post only a nominal earnings gain this year.** The recession in parts of California and some of PacTel's other markets is hurting revenue growth. This trend is especially true for the more elective services such as cellular, where growth in operating costs is outpacing sales so far this year. At the same time, the company is setting up cellular operations in Germany. Since Pac Tel is not yet able to begin cellular service there, it's incurring startup expenses without any corresponding revenues coming in. All told, we're looking for a slim gain in share net for 1991. These shares are untimely.

**Going forward, operating gains should accelerate in the core telephone segment.** The large majority of the company's regulated sales have fallen under price-cap instead of rate-of-return mandates since '89. Thus, PacTel can keep a larger portion of its benefits from cost improvements. In the near-term, headcount reductions are likely to comprise the majority of the telephone subsidiary's gains. Its also likely, though, that breakthroughs in call transmission technology will lower costs. Too, growth in usage of the phone system should rise with the proliferation of new and more profitable add-on services such as voice mail. Finally, the repeal of the ban against providing information services by the Baby Bells also augurs well for increased network usage.

**This top-quality equity looks to be a solid total return vehicle for patient investors.** PacTel's international ventures, though initially dilutive, are likely to boost long-term profit growth. PacTel has been constructing a digital cellular system in Germany (the first in the world) and is building another in Portugal. As a result, the high-growth cellular business is becoming an increasingly larger portion of the company's business mix. In addition, if it establishes its success with such projects, more favorable investment opportunites may appear, as countries increasingly privatize their telecommunications services to stimulate economic growth and raise cash. Therefore, our 3-to 5-year projections may prove to be conservative if PacTel adds more overseas investments to its business portfolio.

*Philip S. Mulqueen*     *October 18, 1991*

| Company's Financial Strength | A+ |
|---|---|
| Stock's Price Stability | 90 |
| Price Growth Persistence | 90 |
| Earnings Predictability | 95 |

# PFIZER INC. NYSE-PFE

| | | |
|---|---|---|
| RECENT PRICE | 71 | |
| PE RATIO | 25.1 (Trailing: 27.4 / Median: 14.0) | |
| RELATIVE PE RATIO | 1.70 | |
| DIV'D YLD | 2.0% | |
| VALUE LINE | 1272 | |

**TIMELINESS 2** Above average (Relative Price Perform- ance Next 12 Mos.)

**SAFETY 1** Highest
(Scale: 1 Highest to 5 Lowest)

**BETA 1.05** (1.00 = Market)

**1994-96 PROJECTIONS**

| | Price | Gain | Ann'l Total Return |
|---|---|---|---|
| High | 110 | (+55%) | 13% |
| Low | 90 | (+25%) | 9% |

Insider Decisions

| | D | J | F | M | A | M | J | J | A |
|---|---|---|---|---|---|---|---|---|---|
| to Buy | 0 | 0 | 0 | 0 | 1 | 0 | 0 | 0 | 2 |
| Options | 0 | 0 | 1 | 2 | 7 | 0 | 0 | 0 | 2 |
| to Sell | 0 | 0 | 1 | 0 | 1 | 0 | 0 | 7 | 3 |

Institutional Decisions

| | 4Q'90 | 1Q'91 | 2Q'91 |
|---|---|---|---|
| to Buy | 208 | 177 | 240 |
| to Sell | 219792 | 240070 | 219974 |
| Hld's(000) | 219792 | 240070 | 219974 |

Percent shares traded — 9.0 / 6.0 / 3.0

**Options: ASE**

Target Price Range 1994 | 1995 | 1996

Relative Price Strength

14.0 x "Cash Flow" p sh

2-for-1 split · 2-for-1 split · 2-for-1 split

Shaded areas indicate recessions

| | 1975 | 1976 | 1977 | 1978 | 1979 | 1980 | 1981 | 1982 | 1983 | 1984 | 1985 | 1986 | 1987 | 1988 | 1989 | 1990 | 1991 | 1992 | © VALUE LINE PUB., INC. | 94-96 |
|---|---|---|---|---|---|---|---|---|---|---|---|---|---|---|---|---|---|---|---|---|
| Sales per sh | 5.93 | 6.72 | 7.23 | 8.39 | 9.39 | 10.31 | 10.84 | 11.22 | 11.75 | 11.99 | 12.27 | 13.56 | 14.95 | 16.28 | 17.15 | 19.40 | 21.40 | 24.20 | | 35.00 |
| "Cash Flow" per sh | .70 | .78 | .86 | .99 | 1.09 | 1.16 | 1.06 | 1.44 | 1.76 | 1.97 | 2.16 | 2.45 | 2.59 | 2.98 | 2.83 | 3.11 | 3.50 | 4.05 | | 6.20 |
| Earnings per sh A | .53 | .57 | .63 | .73 | .82 | .87 | .74 | 1.07 | 1.37 | 1.54 | 1.72 | 1.95 | 2.04 | 2.35 | 2.16 | 2.39 | 2.70 | 3.20 | | 5.25 |
| Div'ds Decl'd per sh B | .20 | .22 | .25 | .29 | .33 | .36 | .40 | .46 | .58 | .66 | .74 | .82 | .90 | 1.00 | 1.10 | 1.20 | 1.32 | 1.50 | | 2.40 |
| Cap'l Spending per sh | .63 | .29 | .32 | .39 | .46 | .56 | .56 | .86 | .67 | .45 | .60 | .59 | .79 | 1.04 | 1.38 | 1.66 | 2.00 | 2.50 | | 4.00 |
| Book Value per sh C | 3.31 | 3.64 | 3.99 | 4.44 | 4.83 | 5.35 | 5.56 | 6.41 | 6.83 | 7.73 | 8.93 | 10.35 | 11.80 | 13.00 | 13.72 | 15.42 | 16.20 | 17.00 | | 23.70 |
| Common Shs Outst'g D | 290.90 | 280.97 | 281.17 | 281.61 | 292.49 | 293.88 | 299.81 | 307.87 | 319.14 | 321.53 | 327.88 | 330.01 | 328.98 | 330.79 | 330.63 | 330.26 | 330.70 | 330.75 | | 331.00 |
| Avg Ann'l P/E Ratio | 14.2 | 12.4 | 10.7 | 10.9 | 10.2 | 12.0 | 16.7 | 14.2 | 14.1 | 11.6 | 13.5 | 15.5 | 16.1 | 11.5 | 14.6 | 14.4 | Bold figures are Value Line estimates | | | 19.0 |
| Relative P/E Ratio | 1.89 | 1.59 | 1.48 | 1.49 | 1.48 | 1.59 | 2.03 | 1.56 | 1.19 | 1.08 | 1.10 | 1.05 | 1.08 | .95 | 1.11 | 1.06 | | | | 1.60 |
| Avg Ann'l Div'd Yield | 2.7% | 3.0% | 3.7% | 3.7% | 4.0% | 3.5% | 3.2% | 3.0% | 3.0% | 3.7% | 3.2% | 2.7% | 2.7% | 3.7% | 3.5% | 3.5% | | | | 2.1% |

| | | | | | | | | | | | | | | | | | | | © VALUE LINE PUB., INC. | 94-96 |
|---|---|---|---|---|---|---|---|---|---|---|---|---|---|---|---|---|---|---|---|---|
| Sales ($mill) | | | | | | | 3249.7 | 3453.6 | 3750.0 | 3854.5 | 4024.5 | 4476.0 | 4919.8 | 5385.4 | 5671.5 | 6406.0 | 7070 | 8000 | | 11500 |
| Operating Margin | | | | | | | 18.7% | 20.6% | 23.3% | 24.9% | 25.1% | 24.7% | 22.4% | 22.4% | 20.7% | 20.0% | 20.5% | 21.0% | | 23.0% |
| Depreciation ($mill) | | | | | | | 96.2 | 109.4 | 114.5 | 126.8 | 129.5 | 147.1 | 162.0 | 194.5 | 207.1 | 224.8 | 250 | 260 | | 400 |
| Net Profit ($mill) | | | | | | | 221.3 | 332.8 | 447.1 | 507.9 | 579.7 | 660.0 | 690.2 | 791.3 | 727.3 | 801.2 | 900 | 1080 | | 1740 |
| Income Tax Rate | | | | | | | 36.1% | 37.9% | 35.3% | 36.3% | 33.6% | 31.2% | 31.4% | 28.0% | 25.9% | 27.0% | 27.0% | 27.0% | | 28.0% |
| Net Profit Margin | | | | | | | 6.8% | 9.6% | 11.9% | 13.2% | 14.4% | 14.7% | 14.0% | 14.7% | 12.8% | 12.5% | 12.7% | 13.3% | | 14.7% |
| Working Cap'l ($mill) | | | | | | | 1136.3 | 1090.0 | 1212.0 | 1354.8 | 1198.3 | 1169.3 | 2144.1 | 1750.5 | 1593.2 | 1319.0 | 1225 | 1050 | | 1750 |
| Long-Term Debt ($mill) | | | | | | | 690.0 | 519.2 | 483.7 | 338.3 | 323.5 | 245.4 | 248.9 | 226.9 | 190.6 | 193.3 | 195 | 200 | | 300 |
| Net Worth ($mill) | | | | | | | 1597.6 | 1973.7 | 2180.8 | 2484.5 | 2927.3 | 3415.2 | 3882.4 | 4301.1 | 4535.8 | 5092.0 | 5295 | 5590 | | 7850 |
| % Earned Total Cap'l | | | | | | | 10.5% | 14.2% | 17.6% | 18.5% | 18.2% | 18.2% | 17.0% | 17.7% | 15.6% | 15.3% | 16.5% | 18.5% | | 21.5% |
| % Earned Net Worth | | | | | | | 13.0% | 16.9% | 20.5% | 20.4% | 19.8% | 19.3% | 17.8% | 18.4% | 16.0% | 15.7% | 17.0% | 19.0% | | 22.0% |
| % Retained to Comm Eq | | | | | | | 7.1% | 9.8% | 12.1% | 11.9% | 11.6% | 11.4% | 10.1% | 10.7% | 8.0% | 7.9% | 9.0% | 10.5% | | 12.0% |
| % All Div'ds to Net Prof | | | | | | | 69% | 42% | 41% | 42% | 42% | 41% | 43% | 42% | 50% | 50% | 47% | 46% | | 46% |

**CAPITAL STRUCTURE as of 6/30/91**

Total Debt $1715.6 mill. Due 5 Yrs $1558.4 mill.
LT Debt $157.2 mill.  LT Interest $15.2 mill.
Incl. $1.3 mill. 4% sub. debs. ('97), callable 102.40
each conv. into 84.20 shs. at $11.875; $35.0 mill.
8¾% sub. debs. ('06), callable 100.00 cv. into
70.80 shs. at $14.125.
(Total interest coverage: 12.8x) (3% of Cap'l)

Leases, Uncapitalized Annual rentals $31.6 mill.
Pension Liability None

Common Stock 330,537,660 shs. (97% of Cap'l)
as of 7/26/91

## CURRENT POSITION

| | 1989 | 1990 | 6/30/91 |
|---|---|---|---|
| Cash Assets | 1057.7 | 1068.2 | 843.7 |
| Receivables | 2064.9 | 1962.1 | 2039.1 |
| Inventory (LIFO) | 1080.5 | 1142.6 | 1202.1 |
| Other | 301.7 | 263.0 | 276.3 |
| Current Assets | 4504.8 | 4435.9 | 4361.2 |
| Accts Payable | 401.4 | 450.3 | 411.0 |
| Debt Due | 1526.3 | 1499.3 | 1558.4 |
| Other | 983.9 | 1167.3 | 1292.3 |
| Current Liab. | 2911.6 | 3116.9 | 3261.7 |

## ANNUAL RATES

| of change (per sh) | Past 10 Yrs. | Past 5 Yrs. | Est'd '88-'90 to '94-'96 |
|---|---|---|---|
| Sales | 6.5% | 8.0% | 13.0% |
| "Cash Flow" | 10.0% | 8.5% | 13.0% |
| Earnings | 11.0% | 8.5% | 15.5% |
| Dividends | 13.0% | 10.0% | 9.0% |
| Book Value | 12.5% | 12.5% | 9.0% |

## QUARTERLY SALES ($ mill.)

| Cal-endar | Mar.31 | Jun.30 | Sep.30 | Dec.31 | Full Year |
|---|---|---|---|---|---|
| 1988 | 1297.9 | 1336.4 | 1382.9 | 1368.2 | 5385.4 |
| 1989 | 1436.3 | 1302.7 | 1438.5 | 1494.0 | 5671.5 |
| 1990 | 1482.0 | 1495.7 | 1643.0 | 1785.3 | 6406.0 |
| 1991 | 1695.7 | 1631.1 | 1773.0 | 1970.2 | 7070 |
| 1992 | 1865 | 1985 | 2020 | 2230 | 8000 |

## EARNINGS PER SHARE

| Cal-endar | Mar.31 | Jun.30 | Sep.30 | Dec.31 | Full Year |
|---|---|---|---|---|---|
| 1988 | .66 | .63 | .65 | .41 | 2.35 |
| 1989 | .72 | .40 | .65 | .39 | 2.16 |
| 1990 | .75 | .45 | .73 | .46 | 2.39 |
| 1991 | .79 | .53 | .81 | .57 | 2.70 |
| 1992 | .92 | .63 | .92 | .73 | 3.20 |

## QUARTERLY DIVIDENDS PAID

| Cal-endar | Mar.31 | Jun.30 | Sep.30 | Dec.31 | Full Year |
|---|---|---|---|---|---|
| 1987 | .225 | .225 | .225 | .225 | .90 |
| 1988 | .25 | .25 | .25 | .25 | 1.00 |
| 1989 | .275 | .275 | .275 | .275 | 1.10 |
| 1990 | .30 | .30 | .30 | .30 | 1.20 |
| 1991 | .33 | .33 | .33 | | |

**Pfizer is reaping the benefits of a greatly expanded R&D effort.** The 1991 research budget of $772 million represents nearly 11% of sales and almost a threefold increase over what it was just five years ago. Such heavy R&D spending has produced several new drugs that are now either in early stages of marketing or in registration in major markets around the world. A trio of recent entries, Procardia XL and Cardura for cardiovascular disease, and Diflucan for treating systemic fungal infections, have been enthusiastically received by the medical community and are well on their way to becoming major commercial successes. We estimate that these new medicines alone will account for nearly half of the drug maker's total pharmaceutical sales in 1991. Since these drugs carry high price tags, that's a big plus for profits.

**Additional promising new pharmaceutical compounds now waiting in the wings should greatly enhance** Pfizer's earning power. The drug maker recently received approvable letters from the FDA for Zithromax, an antibiotic, and for Zoloft, a serotonin re-uptake inhibitor for depression, similar to Lilly's Prozac. Assuming final approval by yearend, these drugs could well generate combined sales of $250-$300 million in 1992 and $1.5-$2 billion when fully established. And by mid-1992, we expect Norvasc, a calcium channel blocker for hypertension and angina, with sales potential of $500 million to $1 billion, to enter Pfizer's sales stream.

**We continue to recommend the purchase of high-quality Pfizer shares.** With new products expected to lift up the bottom line by 13% this year, followed by growth in the 15%-20% range in 1992, this equity should have no difficulty outlegging the year-ahead market. We caution, however, that the stock may exhibit more volatility than usual in this unsettled market, due to ongoing litigation involving the company's Shiley heart valve.

Rudolph C. Carryl          November 8, 1991

Restated Sales (and Pretax Margins) by Business Line

| | 1988 | 1989 | 1990 | 1991 |
|---|---|---|---|---|

# PEPSICO, INC. NYSE-PEP

| RECENT PRICE | P/E RATIO | | DIV'D YLD | VALUE LINE |
|---|---|---|---|---|
| 29 | 18.8 (Trailing: 20.3 Median: 13.0) | RELATIVE P/E RATIO 1.23 | 1.7% | 1541 |

**TIMELINESS 2** Above Average (Relative Price Performance Next 12 Mos.)
**SAFETY 2** Above Average (Scale: 1 Highest to 5 Lowest)
**BETA 1.10** (1.00 = Market)

**1994-96 PROJECTIONS**

| | Price | Gain | Ann'l Total Return |
|---|---|---|---|
| High | 45 | (+55%) | 13% |
| Low | 35 | (+20%) | 7% |

**Insider Decisions**

| | J | F | M | A | M | J | J | A | S |
|---|---|---|---|---|---|---|---|---|---|
| to Buy | 0 | 0 | 0 | 0 | 1 | 0 | 0 | 1 | 1 |
| Options | 0 | 0 | 0 | 1 | 0 | 0 | 1 | 0 | 1 |
| to Sell | 0 | 0 | 0 | 2 | 1 | 0 | 0 | 1 | 1 |

**Institutional Decisions**

| | 4Q90 | 1Q91 | 2Q91 |
|---|---|---|---|
| to Buy | 200 | 229 | 215 |
| to Sell | 219 | 250 | 268 |
| Hld's(000) | 465800 | 465378 | 432784 |

**CAPITAL STRUCTURE as of 9/7/91**
Tot. Debt $8406.0 mill. Due in 5 Yrs $2900.0 mill.
LT Debt $7143.0 mill. LT Interest $550.0 mill.
Incl. $193.8 mill. capitalized leases.
(LT interest earned: 4.1x; total interest coverage: 3.5x)
(58% of Cap'l)

Leases, Uncapitalized Annual rentals $275.1 mill.
Pension Liability None
Pfd Stock None
Common Stock 788,440,204 shs. (42% of Cap'l)

Options: CBOE

Target Price Range 1994 1995 1996
Price scale: 80 50 40 32 24 20 16 12 10 8 6 4

Chart legends: 8.0 x "Cash Flow" p sh — 3-for-1 split — Relative Price Strength — Shaded areas indicate recessions.

**Per-share data** — © VALUE LINE PUB., INC.

| | 1975 | 1976 | 1977 | 1978 | 1979 | 1980 | 1981 | 1982 | 1983 | 1984 | 1985 | 1986 | 1987 | 1988 | 1989 | 1990 | 1991 | 1992 | 94-96 |
|---|---|---|---|---|---|---|---|---|---|---|---|---|---|---|---|---|---|---|---|
| Sales per sh | 3.62 | 4.12 | 4.54 | 5.13 | 6.22 | 7.27 | 8.52 | 8.92 | 9.38 | 9.11 | 10.21 | 11.90 | 14.70 | 16.50 | 19.27 | 22.58 | 24.53 | 27.25 | 36.25 |
| "Cash Flow" per sh | .24 | .30 | .35 | .41 | .50 | .56 | .65 | .64 | .65 | .69 | .90 | 1.10 | 1.47 | 1.76 | 2.10 | 2.45 | 2.70 | 3.15 | 4.55 |
| Earnings per sh | .16 | .21 | .24 | .27 | .32 | .36 | .40 | .36 | .33 | .38 | .50 | .58 | .74 | .97 | 1.12 | 1.31 | 1.50 | 1.75 | 2.60 |
| Div'ds Decl'd per sh | .06 | .07 | .09 | .11 | .14 | .16 | .16 | .18 | .18 | .19 | .20 | .21 | .22 | .27 | .32 | .38 | .46 | .54 | .78 |
| Cap'l Spending per sh | .11 | .18 | .33 | .44 | .47 | .54 | .50 | .57 | .62 | .68 | 1.00 | 1.13 | .99 | .92 | 1.19 | 1.50 | 1.90 | 1.75 | 2.15 |
| Book Value per sh | .98 | 1.14 | 1.24 | 1.39 | 1.54 | 1.74 | 1.99 | 1.96 | 2.13 | 2.19 | 2.33 | 2.64 | 3.21 | 4.01 | 4.92 | 6.22 | 7.40 | 8.60 | 13.40 |
| Common Shs Outst'g | 641.27 | 662.41 | 781.74 | 837.68 | 818.59 | 821.49 | 824.45 | 840.37 | 842.06 | 845.17 | 789.36 | 780.96 | 781.24 | 788.43 | 791.06 | 788.39 | 800.00 | 800.00 | 800.00 |
| Avg Ann'l P/E Ratio | 14.1 | 13.9 | 11.5 | 11.6 | 8.8 | 7.7 | 9.4 | 12.1 | 11.9 | 11.8 | 12.6 | 16.3 | 15.5 | 12.6 | 15.7 | 17.8 | | | 15.0 |
| Relative P/E Ratio | 1.88 | 1.78 | 1.51 | 1.58 | 1.27 | 1.02 | 1.14 | 1.33 | 1.01 | 1.10 | 1.02 | 1.11 | 1.04 | 1.05 | 1.19 | 1.32 | | | 1.25 |
| Avg Ann'l Div'd Yield | 2.4% | 2.5% | 3.3% | 3.5% | 4.4% | 5.1% | 4.2% | 4.1% | 4.5% | 4.1% | 3.1% | 2.2% | 1.9% | 2.2% | 1.8% | 1.6% | | | 1.9% |

Bold figures are Value Line estimates.

**Financial data**

| | 1981 | 1982 | 1983 | 1984 | 1985 | 1986 | 1987 | 1988 | 1989 | 1990 | 1991 | 1992 | 94-96 |
|---|---|---|---|---|---|---|---|---|---|---|---|---|---|
| Sales ($mill) | 7027.4 | 7499.0 | 7895.9 | 7698.7 | 8056.7 | 9290.8 | 11485 | 13007 | 15242 | 17803 | 19650 | 21800 | 29000 |
| Operating Margin | 12.1% | 11.7% | 10.2% | 12.4% | 12.8% | 13.1% | 14.9% | 15.3% | 16.8% | 16.6% | 16.5% | 17.2% | 18.0% |
| Depreciation ($mill) | 203.9 | 230.4 | 260.7 | 256.2 | 290.8 | 400.7 | 563.0 | 629.3 | 772.0 | 884.0 | 970 | 1100 | 1550 |
| Net Profit ($mill) | 333.5 | 303.7 | 284.1 | 327.7 | 420.1 | 457.8 | 586.6 | 762.2 | 886.4 | 1050.0 | 1195 | 1400 | 2075 |
| Income Tax Rate | 38.8% | 42.8% | 43.2% | 43.0% | 36.7% | 32.7% | 37.1% | 33.0% | 33.0% | 33.0% | 35.0% | 35.0% | 35.0% |
| Net Profit Margin | 4.7% | 4.0% | 3.6% | 4.3% | 5.2% | 4.9% | 5.1% | 5.9% | 5.8% | 5.9% | 6.1% | 6.4% | 7.2% |
| Working Cap'l ($mill) | 405.6 | 245.0 | 443.9 | 664.8 | 958.8 | 280.7 | 216.8 | d608.9 | d141.0 | d689.1 | d270 | 255 | 3510 |
| Long-Term Debt ($mill) | 816.1 | 864.2 | 819.2 | 686.3 | 1162.7 | 2632.6 | 2279.8 | 2356.6 | 5777.1 | 5600.1 | 5600 | 5600 | 5600 |
| Net Worth ($mill) | 1640.3 | 1650.5 | 1794.2 | 1853.4 | 1837.7 | 2059.1 | 2508.6 | 3161.0 | 3891.1 | 4904.2 | 5915 | 6680 | 10735 |
| % Earned Total Cap'l | 15.0% | 13.6% | 12.3% | 14.4% | 16.9% | 12.4% | 14.5% | 16.6% | 11.8% | 12.7% | 12.5% | 13.5% | 14.5% |
| % Earned Net Worth | 20.3% | 18.4% | 15.8% | 17.7% | 22.9% | 22.2% | 24.1% | 24.1% | 22.8% | 21.4% | 20.0% | 20.5% | 29.5% |
| % Retained to Comm Eq | 12.6% | 9.8% | 7.4% | 9.3% | 14.1% | 14.3% | 16.4% | 17.8% | 16.6% | 15.4% | 14.0% | 14.0% | 13.5% |
| % All Div'ds to Net Prof | 38% | 47% | 53% | 47% | 38% | 36% | 30% | 26% | 27% | 28% | 31% | 31% | 30% |

**High / Low price range**

| | 1980 | 1981 | 1982 | 1983 | 1984 | 1985 | 1986 | 1987 | 1988 | 1989 | 1990 | 1991 |
|---|---|---|---|---|---|---|---|---|---|---|---|---|
| High | 3.2 | 4.4 | 5.6 | 4.5 | 5.1 | 8.4 | 11.9 | 14.1 | 14.5 | 22.0 | 27.9 | 35.6 |
| Low | 2.2 | 3.0 | 3.5 | 3.6 | 3.8 | 4.5 | 7.3 | 8.5 | 10.0 | 12.6 | 18.0 | 23.5 |

## CURRENT POSITION ($MILL.)

| | 1989 | 1990 | 9/7/91 |
|---|---|---|---|
| Cash Assets | 1533.9 | 1815.7 | 2204.3 |
| Receivables | 1239.7 | 1411.7 | 1656.2 |
| Inventory (FIFO) | 546.1 | 585.8 | 633.6 |
| Other | 231.1 | 265.2 | 375.8 |
| Current Assets | 3550.8 | 4081.4 | 4869.9 |
| Accts Payable | 1054.5 | 1116.3 | 942.1 |
| Debt Due | 866.3 | 1626.5 | 1263.0 |
| Other | 1771.0 | 2027.7 | 2335.5 |
| Current Liab. | 3691.8 | 4770.5 | 4540.6 |

## ANNUAL RATES

| of change (per sh) | Past 10 Yrs. | Past 5 Yrs. | Est'd '88-'90 to '94-'96 |
|---|---|---|---|
| Sales | 15.5% | 15.5% | 11.0% |
| "Cash Flow" | 12.0% | 12.0% | 12.0% |
| Earnings | 13.5% | 23.0% | 12.0% |
| Dividends | 15.5% | 22.5% | 15.0% |
| Book Value | 10.0% | 11.5% | 16.0% |
| | 12.5% | 18.0% | 17.5% |

## QUARTERLY SALES ($ mill.) A

| Cal-endar | Mar.Per | Jun.Per | Sep.30 | Dec.31 | Full Year |
|---|---|---|---|---|---|
| 1988 | 2569 | 3013 | 3241 | 4184 | 13007 |
| 1989 | 2958 | 3592 | 3902 | 4790 | 15242 |
| 1990 | 3677 | 4204 | 4475 | 5447 | 17803 |
| 1991 | 4117 | 4680 | 4881 | 5972 | 19650 |
| 1992 | 4550 | 5150 | 5400 | 6700 | 21800 |

## EARNINGS PER SHARE A B

| Cal-endar | Mar.Per | Jun.Per | Sep.30 | Dec.31 | Full Year |
|---|---|---|---|---|---|
| 1988 | .14 | .28 | .30 | .25 | .97 |
| 1989 | .21 | .31 | .34 | .26 | 1.12 |
| 1990 | .23 | .36 | .38 | .34 | 1.31 |
| 1991 | .26 | .39 | .43 | .42 | 1.50 |
| 1992 | .30 | .45 | .52 | .48 | 1.75 |

## QUARTERLY DIVIDENDS PAID C

| Cal-endar | Mar.31 | Jun.30 | Sep.30 | Dec.31 | Full Year |
|---|---|---|---|---|---|
| 1987 | .053 | .057 | .057 | .057 | .22 |
| 1988 | .057 | .07 | .07 | .07 | .27 |
| 1989 | .07 | .083 | .083 | .083 | .32 |
| 1990 | .083 | .10 | .10 | .10 | .38 |
| 1991 | .10 | .12 | .12 | | |

BUSINESS: PepsiCo, Inc., the world's second largest producer of soft drinks, controls more than 1,000 bottlers throughout the world. Major soft drink products include: *PepsiCola, Diet Pepsi*, and *Mountain Dew*. Operations include: Specialty snack foods: Frito-Lay (major product offerings include *Doritos, Ruffles*, and *Lay's*), Walker Crisps, Smiths Crisps; Quick Service Restaurants: Pizza Hut, KFC (formerly Kentucky Fried Chicken), Taco Bell. Est'd. labor costs: 26% of sales. 1990 depreciation rate: 9.8%. Est'd plant age: 3 yrs. Has about 235,000 employees, 94,000 stockholders. Insiders own less than 1% of common. Chairman & Chief Executive Officer: D.W. Calloway. Incorporated: North Carolina. Address: PepsiCo World Headquarters, Purchase, New York 10577. Tel.: 914-253-2000.

**PepsiCo's fourth quarter looks promising.** Domestic soft drink sales picked up in September after an uncharacteristic falloff in August, and pricing has improved, too. Moreover, results will be helped by lower corporate expenses and declining interest charges. Some benefits should also begin to accrue from a recent restructuring at Frito-Lay that was designed to eventually save $100 million a year in labor costs.

**We think the growth will continue in 1992, with all of the major businesses participating.** Domestic soft drink volume (which accounts for nearly 80% of PepsiCo's total beverage sales) should pick up after showing almost no growth in 1991, when demand was clearly affected by the economy. We also expect somewhat higher prices. Frito-Lay sales are expected to keep rising, with increased volume more than offsetting lower prices and a trend by consumers to purchase smaller-sized packages. Earnings in the snack food area should benefit from the recent restructuring, which resulted in a significant reduction in manpower, and comparisons should benefit from lower potato prices. Growth in the restaurant area will come from a continuing expansion in the number of units. Pizza Hut has been seeing excellent results from its expanded home-delivery business, and good growth should continue there. As in recent years, sales and earnings abroad will grow faster than those in the U.S. and....

**We expect that international growth will be a major objective for many years to come.** Foreign sales now account for just over 20% of the total, and we expect that percentage to grow steadily as PepsiCo expands its overseas activities in soft drinks, snack foods and restaurants. While expansion of Pepsi's soft drink business seems most natural given the expected growth in per-capita consumption of soda abroad, the potential for most of the other businesses is probably just as strong. **The shares in this large, well run company are an attractive holding for the next twelve months.** We do caution though that the stock already has a rich P/E ratio, and unless that ratio expands further, the stock is likely to be a below average performer through 1994-96.
Stephen Sanborn        *November 22, 1991*

| | |
|---|---|
| Company's Financial Strength | A |
| Stock's Price Stability | 80 |
| Price Growth Persistence | 90 |
| Earnings Predictability | 100 |

(A) Quarters are 12, 12, 12 and 16 week periods. (B) Primary earnings. Excl. extra. losses: '78, 1¢; '79, 5¢; '80, 18¢; '81, 13¢; '82, 28¢; '84, 47¢; '91, 7¢. Excl. disc'd op gains (losses): '84, 7¢; '85, 44¢; '87, (4¢); '90, (2¢). Excl nonrecur. gains; '87, 7¢; '89, 4¢; '90, 6¢. Next earn rep due late Jan. (C) Next div'd meeting about Feb 25 Goes ex about Mar 5. Div'd payment dates: March 31, June 30, Sept 30, Dec. 31 ■ Div'd reinvestment plan avail. (D) Includes intangibles. In '90 $5.85 bill. $7.41/sh (E) In millions, adj for stock splits

# US WEST NYSE-USW

| | | | |
|---|---|---|---|
| RECENT PRICE **35** | P/E RATIO **12.2** (Trailing: 11.3 / Median: NMF) | RELATIVE P/E RATIO **0.85** | DIV'D YLD **6.0%** |
| VALUE LINE **773** | | | |

**TIMELINESS 4** Below Average (Relative Price Performance Next 12 Mos.)

**SAFETY 1** Highest (Scale: 1 Highest to 5 Lowest)

**BETA .90** (1.00 = Market)

**1994-96 PROJECTIONS**

| | Price | Gain | Ann'l Total Return |
|---|---|---|---|
| High | 60 | (+70%) | 19% |
| Low | 50 | (+45%) | 14% |

**Insider Decisions**

| | D | J | F | M | A | M | J | J | A |
|---|---|---|---|---|---|---|---|---|---|
| to Buy | 0 | 0 | 0 | 0 | 0 | 0 | 0 | 0 | 0 |
| Options | 0 | 0 | 7 | 0 | 4 | 0 | 0 | 1 | 0 |
| to Sell | 0 | 0 | 2 | 0 | 2 | 0 | 0 | 0 | 0 |

**Institutional Decisions**

| | 4Q90 | 1Q91 | 2Q91 |
|---|---|---|---|
| to Buy | 165 | 148 | 158 |
| to Sell | 129 | 161 | 159 |
| Hld's(000) | 165937 | 166170 | 168932 |

Percent shares traded: 8.0 / 4.0 / 2.0

High: 15.0 Low: 13.8

1.40 x Dividends p.sh divided by Interest Rate

2-for-1 split · 2-for-1 split

Relative Price Strength

Target Price Range 1994 | 1995 | 1996 — scale: 125, 100, 80, 60, 50, 40, 30, 25, 20, 15, 10, 7.5

Shaded areas indicate recessions

Options: ASE

| High: / Low: (price) | 1981 | 1982 | 1983 | 1984 | 1985 | 1986 | 1987 | 1988 | 1989 | 1990 | 1991 | 1992 | ©VALUE LINE PUB., INC. | 94-96 |
|---|---|---|---|---|---|---|---|---|---|---|---|---|---|---|
| | -- | -- | -- | 17.7 / 13.9 | 22.3 / 17.1 | 31.0 / 20.8 | 30.1 / 21.3 | 29.8 / 24.4 | 40.3 / 28.4 | 40.5 / 32.4 | 40.8 / 34.0 | | | |
| Revenues per sh(A) | | | | 18.90 | 20.52 | 21.87 | 22.75 | 25.24 | 25.91 | 25.30 | 24.65 | 26.15 | | 32.50 |
| "Cash Flow" per sh | | | | 5.17 | 5.78 | 6.12 | 7.13 | 7.67 | 7.55 | 7.74 | 7.55 | 8.00 | | 10.00 |
| Earnings per sh(A) | | | | 2.31 | 2.42 | 2.43 | 2.66 | 2.85 | 3.01 | 3.11 | 2.90 | 3.15 | | 4.35 |
| Div'ds Decl'd per sh(C)■ | | | | 1.35 | 1.43 | 1.50 | 1.64 | 1.76 | 1.88 | 2.00 | 2.08 | 2.20 | | 2.60 |
| Cap'l Spending per sh | | | | 4.50 | 5.25 | 4.76 | 4.81 | 6.24 | 5.84 | 6.50 | 6.15 | 6.15 | | 6.75 |
| Book Value per sh | | | | 17.25 | 18.24 | 19.16 | 20.09 | 21.31 | 21.58 | 23.48 | 22.95 | 23.75 | | 28.00 |
| Common Shs Outst'g(D) | | | | 385.31 | 380.65 | 379.95 | 371.16 | 365.28 | 373.99 | 393.49 | 406.00 | 405.00 | | 400.00 |
| Avg Ann'l P/E Ratio | | | | 6.7 | 8.0 | 10.8 | 10.0 | 9.6 | 11.2 | 11.7 | Bold figures are Value Line estimates | | | 12.5 |
| Relative P/E Ratio | | | | .62 | .65 | .73 | .67 | .80 | .85 | .87 | | | | 1.05 |
| Avg Ann'l Div'd Yield | | | | 8.8% | 7.4% | 5.7% | 6.2% | 6.4% | 5.6% | 5.5% | | | | 4.8% |
| Revenues ($mill)(A) | 6855.2 | 7482.0 | 7800.6 | 7280.6 | 7812.6 | 8308.0 | 8445.3 | 9220.6 | 9690.6 | 9957.3 | 10000 | 10600 | | 13000 |
| Net Profit ($mill) | 817.9 | 837.3 | 894.4 | 887.0 | 925.6 | 924.3 | 1005.5 | 1043.0 | 1110.7 | 1198.9 | 1175 | 1275 | | 1740 |
| Income Tax Rate | NMF | NMF | NMF | 41.7% | 42.3% | 41.4% | 36.1% | 29.7% | 28.1% | 31.9% | 32.0% | 32.0% | | 32.0% |
| Net Profit Margin | 11.9% | 11.2% | 11.5% | 12.2% | 11.8% | 11.1% | 11.9% | 11.3% | 11.5% | 12.0% | 11.8% | 12.0% | | 13.4% |
| Long-Term Debt Ratio | NMF | 37.7% | 38.6% | 42.2% | 40.5% | 40.3% | 39.9% | 45.4% | 47.3% | 43.7% | 45.0% | 44.5% | | 41.5% |
| Common Equity Ratio | 11.9% | 62.3% | 61.4% | 57.8% | 59.5% | 59.7% | 60.1% | 54.6% | 52.7% | 56.3% | 55.0% | 55.5% | | 58.5% |
| Total Capital ($mill) | 11721 | 11721 | 11942 | 11502 | 11677 | 12188 | 12405 | 14252 | 15319 | 16415 | 16935 | 17345 | | 19215 |
| Net Plant ($mill) | 15672 | 15672 | 15866 | 14582 | 15242 | 15614 | 15721 | 17007 | 17413 | 18103 | 18725 | 19270 | | 20500 |
| % Earned Total Cap'l | 7.1% | 7.1% | 9.1% | 9.2% | 9.2% | 9.7% | 9.7% | 9.4% | 9.2% | 9.3% | 9.0% | 9.5% | | 11.0% |
| % Earned Net Worth | 11.5% | 11.5% | 12.2% | 13.3% | 13.3% | 12.7% | 13.5% | 13.4% | 13.8% | 13.0% | 12.5% | 13.0% | | 15.5% |
| % Earned Comm Equity | 11.5% | 11.5% | 12.2% | 13.3% | 13.3% | 12.7% | 13.5% | 13.4% | 13.8% | 13.0% | 12.5% | 13.0% | | 15.5% |
| % Retained to Comm Eq | 5% | 5% | 2% | 5.6% | 5.5% | 4.8% | 5.3% | 5.2% | 5.3% | 4.8% | 3.5% | 3.5% | | 6.0% |
| % All Div'ds to Net Prof | 65% | 95% | 98% | 58% | 59% | 63% | 61% | 61% | 61% | 63% | 72% | 70% | | 60% |

US WEST is one of the seven regional holding companies resulting from the breakup of American Telephone & Telegraph Company on January 1, 1984. Each AT&T shareholder received one share of US West common for every 10 shares of AT&T (pre-divestiture) common stock held. The stock began trading on a when-issued basis on November 21, 1983. "Regular" trading of U S West shares began on February 16, 1984.

**CAPITAL STRUCTURE as of 6/30/91**

Total Debt $9876.2 mill. Due in 5 Yrs $4123.6 mill.

LT Debt $7898.3 mill. LT Interest $715.0 mill.

(LT interest earned: 3.3x; total interest coverage: 3.1x)

Leases, Uncapitalized Annual rentals $105.5 mill.

Pension Liability None

Pfd Stock None

Common Stock 395,889,000 shs.

BUSINESS: U S WEST Inc. is one of seven regional phone holding cos. resulting from the AT&T breakup (owns 9.9% of the former AT&T assets). Major subsidiary, U S West Communications (formerly Mountain Bell, Northwestern Bell, and Pacific Northwest Bell) serves Ariz., Colo., Idaho, Iowa, Minn., Montana, Neb., N. Mex., N. Dakota, Ore., S. Dakota, Utah, Wash., and Wyom. Access lines in service: 12.6 million. '90 Telco revenue breakdown: local service, 42%; toll, 18%; access charges, 33%; other, 7%. Telco employees per 10,000 access lines: 42.1. '90 depreciation rate: 6.9%. Est. plant age: 6 yrs. Has 65,859 employees, almost 1.0 million shareholders. Chrmn. & C.E.O.: J.A. MacAllister. Inc.: CO. Address: 7800 E. Orchard Rd, Englewood, CO 80111. Tel.: 303-793-6500.

**U S West continues to expand its telephone system.** Although the its access line growth of 2.8%-3.0% is not as strong as it was a year-ago, it still ranks among the best in the industry. Indeed, the economy in the Northwest has slowed a bit, but is still one of the strongest in the country. Also, we expect access minutes of use to remain at about a strong 7.7% growth rate during the remainder of this year. However, revenue gains are likely to be squeezed because of reductions in interstate and intrastate rates that have been put in place over the past 12 months. In addition, we look for a rate reduction in Oregon by yearend that will likely reduce revenues by about $15 million a quarter. Looking ahead, we think it will take a number of years before the reductions that have been put in place over the last several years will benefit the bottom line.

**Earnings are likely to fall below last year's level.** The reduction in telephone rates are offsetting the increases in access lines, minutes of use, and cost constraint programs. As a result, we have reduced this year's earnings estimate to $2.90 a share. This figure includes the effects of one-time credits associated with incentive rate agreements in Oregon (about 6¢ to 7¢ a share) and in Washington (about 4¢). For next year, we have reduced our share net estimate by 30¢, to $3.15. This figure takes into account the $60 million-$65 million projected rate decrease that is being negotiated in Oregon.

**U S West completed the purchase of the 19% of U S West/NewVector it did not own.** The company issued about 11 million shares in exchange for the 9.7 million shares of NewVector common that U S West did not own. The value of the deal was about $430 million. We expect the purchase to initially dilute earnings, although the effects are likely to be diminished in the years ahead.

**These good-yielding shares offer worthwhile total-return potential to 1994-96,** based on the positive demographic trends that we expect to remain in force during this time span. In addition, the company's expansion into Eastern Europe could lead to earnings growth that is above our expectations.
*Jerome D. Fischer*    *October 18, 1991*

| CURRENT POSITION (\$MILL.) | 1989 | 1990 | 6/30/91 |
|---|---|---|---|
| Cash Assets | 290.5 | 338.2 | 541.5 |
| Other | 2485.3 | 2476.9 | 2525.0 |
| Current Assets | 2775.8 | 2815.1 | 3066.5 |
| Accts Payable | 1098.8 | 981.1 | 714.9 |
| Debt Due | 1408.9 | 1822.3 | 1977.9 |
| Other | 561.5 | 1517.6 | 1488.6 |
| Current Liab. | 4069.2 | 4321.0 | 4181.4 |
| Fix. Chg. Cov. | 306% | 320% | 313% |

| ANNUAL RATES of change (per sh) | Past 10 Yrs. | Past 5 Yrs. | Est'd '88-'90 to '94-'96 |
|---|---|---|---|
| Revenues | -- | -- | 4.5% |
| "Cash Flow" | -- | -- | 6.5% |
| Earnings | -- | -- | 5.5% |
| Dividends | -- | -- | 4.0% |
| Book Value | -- | -- | |

| Cal-endar | QUARTERLY REVENUES (\$ mill.) | | | | Full Year |
|---|---|---|---|---|---|
| | Mar.31 | Jun.30 | Sep.30 | Dec.31 | |
| 1988 | 2193 | 2251 | 2428 | 2349 | 9220.6 |
| 1989 | 2394 | 2435 | 2323 | 2539 | 9690.6 |
| 1990 | 2426 | 2411 | 2482 | 2638 | 9957.3 |
| 1991 | 2450 | 2501 | 2550 | 2409 | 10000 |
| 1992 | 2500 | 2600 | 2700 | 2800 | 10600 |

| Cal-endar | EARNINGS PER SHARE (B) | | | | Full Year |
|---|---|---|---|---|---|
| | Mar.31 | Jun.30 | Sep.30 | Dec.31 | |
| 1988 | .65 | .68 | .78 | .74 | 2.85 |
| 1989 | .68 | .71 | .70 | .92 | 3.01 |
| 1990 | .73 | .72 | .77 | .89 | 3.11 |
| 1991 | .73 | .70 | .65 | .82 | 2.90 |
| 1992 | .70 | .75 | .82 | .88 | 3.15 |

| Cal-endar | QUARTERLY DIVIDENDS PAID (C) ■ | | | | Full Year |
|---|---|---|---|---|---|
| | Mar.31 | Jun.30 | Sep.30 | Dec.31 | |
| 1987 | 38 | 41 | 41 | 41 | 1.61 |
| 1988 | 41 | 44 | 44 | 44 | 1.73 |
| 1989 | 44 | 47 | 47 | 47 | 1.85 |
| 1990 | 47 | 50 | 50 | 50 | 1.97 |
| 1991 | 50 | 52 | | | |

(A) Historical figures (pre-1984) are not comparable to post-divestiture estimates and results. (B) Based on average shs outstanding. Incl. charge of 13¢ in '86. Excl. non-recurring gain: '88, 24¢; '89, 5¢. Next earnings report due late-Oct. (C) Next dividend meeting about Dec. 15. Goes ex-dividend about Dec. 22. | Dividend payment dates: Feb. 1, May 1, Aug. 1, Nov. 1 ■ Dividend reinvestment plan available. (D) In millions, adjusted for stock splits.

| | |
|---|---|
| Company's Financial Strength | A+ |
| Stock's Price Stability | 95 |
| Price Growth Persistence | 95 |
| Earnings Predictability | 100 |

# S.W. BELL NYSE-SBC

| RECENT PRICE | P/E RATIO | | RELATIVE P/E RATIO | DIV'D YLD | VALUE LINE |
|---|---|---|---|---|---|
| 54 | 14.6 | (Trailing: 15.6 / Median: NMF) | 1.02 | 5.3% | 770 |

**TIMELINESS 4** Below Average
(Relative Price Performance Next 12 Mos.)

**SAFETY 1** Highest
(Scale: 1 Highest to 5 Lowest)

**BETA .90** (1.00 = Market)

### 1994-96 PROJECTIONS

| | Price | Gain | Ann'l Total Return |
|---|---|---|---|
| High | 85 | (+55%) | 16% |
| Low | 70 | (+30%) | 11% |

**Insider Decisions**

| | D | J | F | M | A | M | J | J | A |
|---|---|---|---|---|---|---|---|---|---|
| to Buy | 0 | 0 | 1 | 0 | 0 | 0 | 0 | 0 | 0 |
| Options | 0 | 0 | 0 | 0 | 0 | 0 | 0 | 0 | 0 |
| to Sell | 0 | 0 | 0 | 0 | 0 | 0 | 0 | 0 | 0 |

**Institutional Decisions**

| | 4Q90 | 1Q91 | 2Q91 |
|---|---|---|---|
| to Buy | 157 | 159 | 156 |
| to Sell | 131 | 168 | 172 |
| Hld's(000) | 114005 | 113432 | 111536 |

| | Percent shares traded | 6.0 / 4.0 / 2.0 |
|---|---|---|

Southwestern Bell is one of the seven regional holding companies that resulted from the breakup of American Telephone & Telegraph Co. on January 1, 1984. One share of Southwestern Bell stock was issued for each 10 shares of AT&T (pre-divestiture). The stock began trading on a when-issued basis on November 21, 1983. "Regular" trading of SWB shares began on February 16, 1984.

**CAPITAL STRUCTURE as of 6/30/91**
Total Debt $7139.9 mill. Due in 5 Yrs $700.0 mill.
LT Debt $5560.7 mill.   LT Interest $511.3 mill.
Incl. $54.0 mill. capitalized leases.
(LT interest earned: 3.6x; total interest coverage: 2.8x)

Leases, Uncapitalized Annual rentals $59.9 mill.

Pension Liability None

Pfd Stock None

Common Stock 299,843,400 shs.

**Options: PACE**

© VALUE LINE PUB., INC. 94-96

| | 1981 | 1982 | 1983A | 1984 | 1985 | 1986 | 1987 | 1988 | 1989 | 1990 | 1991 | 1992 | 94-96 |
|---|---|---|---|---|---|---|---|---|---|---|---|---|---|
| Revenues per sh A | | | | 24.08 | 26.52 | 26.35 | 26.64 | 28.14 | 29.04 | 30.39 | 30.90 | 32.95 | 41.65 |
| "Cash Flow" per sh B | | | | 6.78 | 7.69 | 8.04 | 8.98 | 9.67 | 9.93 | 9.31 | 9.65 | 11.05 | 14.60 |
| Earnings per sh B | | | | 3.01 | 3.33 | 3.42 | 3.48 | 3.53 | 3.64 | 3.67 | 3.60 | 4.10 | 5.85 |
| Div'ds Decl'd per sh C ■ | | | | 1.87 | 2.00 | 2.13 | 2.32 | 2.48 | 2.60 | 2.76 | 2.84 | 3.00 | 3.65 |
| Cap'l Spending per sh | | | | 6.04 | 6.99 | 6.57 | 4.94 | 4.07 | 4.93 | 5.93 | 6.50 | 6.95 | 8.40 |
| Book Value per sh D | | | | 23.43 | 24.75 | 26.07 | 27.26 | 27.83 | 27.83 | 28.62 | 29.05 | 30.15 | 35.35 |
| Common Shs Outst'g E | | | | 298.60 | 298.86 | 299.88 | 300.45 | 300.41 | 300.58 | 299.87 | 300.00 | 296.00 | 292.00 |
| Avg Ann'l P/E Ratio | | | | 6.8 | 7.8 | 9.8 | 10.9 | 10.8 | 14.0 | 14.8 | *Bold figures are Value Line estimates* | | 13.0 |
| Relative P/E Ratio | | | | .63 | .63 | .66 | .73 | .90 | 1.06 | 1.11 | | | 1.10 |
| Avg Ann'l Div'd Yield | | | | 9.1% | 7.7% | 6.4% | 6.1% | 6.5% | 5.1% | 5.1% | | | 4.8% |
| Revenues ($mill) A | 6782.4 | 7711.1 | 7904.4 | 7191.3 | 7925.0 | 7902.4 | 8002.6 | 8452.7 | 8729.8 | 9112.9 | 9275 | 9750 | 12100 |
| Net Profit ($mill) | 781.2 | 864.0 | 892.7 | 883.1 | 996.2 | 1022.7 | 1047.1 | 1060.1 | 1092.8 | 1101.4 | 1080 | 1220 | 1715 |
| Income Tax Rate | 41.4% | 39.5% | 40.7% | 39.6% | 39.7% | 41.0% | 34.2% | 24.8% | 26.1% | 28.5% | 29.5% | 29.0% | 29.0% |
| Net Profit Margin | 11.5% | 11.2% | 11.3% | 12.3% | 12.6% | 12.9% | 13.1% | 12.5% | 12.5% | 12.1% | 11.6% | 12.5% | 14.2% |
| Long-Term Debt Ratio | 38.9% | 40.0% | 41.4% | 40.3% | 38.6% | 40.8% | 37.2% | 39.5% | 39.0% | 38.5% | 37.5% | | 33.5% |
| Common Equity Ratio | 61.1% | 60.0% | 58.6% | 59.7% | 61.4% | 59.2% | 62.8% | 60.5% | 61.0% | 61.5% | 62.5% | | 66.5% |
| Total Capital ($mill) | 12009 | 12427 | 11929 | 12730 | 13840 | 13543 | 13822 | 14064 | 14110 | 14220 | | | 15470 |
| Net Plant ($mill) | 16072 | 16795 | 15394 | 16140 | 16727 | 16740 | 16304 | 16078 | 16322 | 16570 | 17025 | | 17505 |
| % Earned Total Cap'l | 9.2% | 9.1% | 9.4% | 10.0% | 9.9% | 9.3% | 9.7% | 9.8% | 9.5% | | 10.5% | | 12.5% |
| % Earned Net Worth | 11.8% | 12.0% | 12.6% | 13.5% | 13.1% | 12.8% | 12.5% | 13.1% | 13.1% | 12.8% | 12.5% | 13.5% | 16.5% |
| % Earned Comm Equity | 11.8% | 12.0% | 12.6% | 13.5% | 13.1% | 12.8% | 12.8% | 13.1% | 12.8% | 12.5% | 13.5% | | 16.5% |
| % Retained to Comm Eq | 1.5% | 1.4% | 4.8% | 5.4% | 4.9% | 4.3% | 4.9% | 4.8% | 3.2% | 2.5% | 3.5% | | 6.5% |
| % All Div'ds to Net Prof | 85% | 87% | 88% | 62% | 60% | 62% | 67% | 61% | 63% | 75% | 79% | 73% | 62% |

| | High | Low |
|---|---|---|
| | 20.7 | 19.4 |
| | 23.8 | 18.3 |
| | 29.5 | 22.8 |
| | 38.8 | 26.3 |
| | 45.5 | 28.3 |
| | 42.6 | 33.0 |
| | 64.4 | 38.9 |
| | 64.8 | 47.3 |
| | 57.8 | 49.0 |

### Target Price Range 1994 | 1995 | 1996

160
120
100
80
64
48
40
32
24
20
16
12
8

Shaded areas indicate recessions

1.34 x Dividends p sh divided by Interest Rate

3-for-1 split

Relative Price Strength

**BUSINESS:** Southwestern Bell Corporation is one of the seven regional holding companies formerly owned by the American Telephone & Telegraph Company. Owns 10.2% of the assets of the former AT&T. Provides communications service in most of Arkansas (6.1% of access lines), Kansas (8.9%), Missouri (16.9%), Oklahoma (10.8%), and Texas (57.3%). Access lines in service: 12.1 mill.

1990 revenue breakdown: local service, 39%; access charges, 31%; toll, 12%; directory advertising, 5%; other, 13%. Telco employees per 10,000 access lines: 48.1. '90 depreciation rate: 7.2%. Est'd plant age 5 years. Has 66,690 employees, 1.05 million shareholders. Chairman and C.E.O.: Edward E. Whitacre, Jr. Inc.: DE. Address: 1 Bell Ctr., St. Louis, MO 63101. Phone 314-235-9800.

**Signs of an economic pickup in Southwestern Bell's operating territory are a plus for its telephone business.** With access line growth up to 2.5% in the June period, it seems as though a recovery may be getting underway in the Southwest. We're looking for access line growth to come in at a decent 2.5% for the year, with calling volume expanding by about 8%.

**The cellular unit continues to expand.** Subscribers numbered 799,000 by July and may well top 900,000 at yearend. Also, the Mobile Systems unit's marketing efforts are keeping revenues per user stable, at about $75-$80. We expect a growing contribution to earnings from the already profitable cellular business in the future.

**SWB has exercised its option on Telefonos de Mexico, doubling its stake to 10%.** The additional 5% ownership cost Southwestern approximately $540 million, which includes the $73.5 million option purchase cost. At the current price of a Telmex 'L' share (about $1.86), the value of SWB's Telmex holding exceeds $1.97 billion, over twice the total invested. What's more, we think that Telmex could add between 4¢ and 7¢ a share to

SWB's bottom line this year, and possibly over a dime in 1992. (See our full-page report on Telmex on page 794.)

**Rate recommendations remain an issue.** The Oklahoma Public Utilities Commission recommended that SWB refund $107 million and reduce rates by some $149 million in that state, bringing ROE down to 12.2%. However, we believe that the recommendation is probably based on inflated earnings projections and won't be implemented in its entirety.

**In sum, we think this stock, though not timely now, may be worth a look** for conservative, long-term investors. Although the dividend yield on these top-quality shares is a bit below some of the other regional Bells' (which average 5.5%), SWB's good growth prospects to 1994-96 should fuel above-average earnings gains and enable it to boost dividends by a solid 6% per year out to that time. Finally, acquisitions (possibly in the cellular market) or the passage of legislation allowing the regional Bells to manufacture equipment or enter into information services may further enhance long-term prospects.

*Stuart Novick*     *October 18, 1991*

(A) Historical figures (pre-1984) not comparable to post-divestiture est's and results.
(B) Primary earnings. Next earnings report due late October.
(C) Next dividend meeting about December 15. Goes ex about January 5. Approximate dividend payment dates: Feb. 1, May 1, Aug. 1, Nov. 1. ■ Dividend reinvestment plan available.
(D) Includes intangibles. In '90 $1236.7 million, $4.12/share.
(E) In millions, adjusted for stock split.
(F) Doesn't add due to rounding.

| | |
|---|---|
| Company's Financial Strength | A+ |
| Stock's Price Stability | 90 |
| Price Growth Persistence | 100 |
| Earnings Predictability | 100 |

To receive THE VALUE LINE INVESTMENT SURVEY, please call or write:

> VALUE LINE INVESTMENT SURVEY
> 711 Third Avenue
> New York, NY 10017
> 212/687-3965     800/634-3583

Current rates: 10-week trial: $ 65
                One full year: $525

Other terms and non-U.S. rates available upon request. Prices subject to change without notice. Above rates quoted in U.S. dollars.

# = Appendix B =

## Morningstar Reports

We recommend mutual funds based primarily on the ratings of Morningstar. Where the objective is growth, in general we prefer the 4 to 5 star rated funds. Another consideration is the size of the fund family and therefore an investors ability to swap funds within the family without incurring an additional sales charge. Where the objective is relatively safe income we will use a 3 star rated fund for diversification purposes.

All are alphabetized to simplify your research. The reports are cut in half to keep the type large enough to be legible.

The major information of value to you is set forth in the top half of the report:

- Rating
- Price Chart
- Performance

MORNINGSTAR, INC.

# Alger Small Capitalization

| | OBJECTIVE | LOAD % | YIELD % | ASSETS($MIL) | N.A.V. |
|---|---|---|---|---|---|
| MORNINGSTAR MUTUAL FUNDS | Small Company | 5.00d | 0.0 | 48.3 | 19.61 |

Alger Small Capitalization Portfolio seeks long-term capital appreciation. Income is not a central investment objective.

The fund invests primarily in companies traded in the over-the-counter market. These may be companies still in the developmental stage; older companies that appear to be entering a new stage of growth progress owing to factors such as management changes or development of new technology, products, or markets; or companies providing products or services with a high unit volume growth. The fund may also invest up to 35% of its net assets in companies with market capitalizations of $1 billion and above.

**RATING**

| RETURN | RISK |
|---|---|
| High | Above Avg |

RATING ★★★★
Highest

## TOTAL RETURN %

| | 1st Qtr. | 2nd Qtr. | 3rd Qtr. | 4th Qtr. | TOTAL |
|---|---|---|---|---|---|
| 1987 | 25.64 | 0.74 | 5.86 | -26.52 | -1.54 |
| 1988 | 10.15 | 7.03 | -3.73 | 3.50 | 17.47 |
| 1989 | 20.21 | 18.44 | 19.14 | -3.01 | 64.53 |
| 1990 | 3.02 | 12.92 | -22.41 | 18.20 | 6.69 |
| 1991 | 26.18 | -5.91 | ... | ... | ... |

## INCOME

| | | | | | TOTAL |
|---|---|---|---|---|---|
| 1989 | 0.00 | 0.00 | 0.00 | 0.00 | 0.00 |
| 1990 | 0.00 | 0.00 | 0.00 | 0.00 | 0.00 |
| 1991 | 0.00 | 0.00 | 0.00 | ... | ... |

## CAPITAL GAINS

| | | | | | TOTAL |
|---|---|---|---|---|---|
| 1989 | 0.00 | 0.00 | 0.00 | 0.00 | 0.00 |
| 1990 | 0.00 | 0.00 | 0.00 | 0.00 | 0.00 |
| 1991 | 0.00 | 0.00 | ... | ... | ... |

## PERFORMANCE/RISK — 07/31/91

| | TOTAL RETURN % | +/- S&P 500 | +/- W4500 | PERCENTILE RANK ALL | OBJ |
|---|---|---|---|---|---|
| 3 MONTH | 6.23 | 2.09 | 2.40 | 14 | 28 |
| 6 MONTH | 19.87 | 5.28 | 0.92 | 15 | 57 |
| 1 YEAR | 25.31 | 12.52 | 11.83 | 4 | 14 |
| 3 YEAR AVG. | 31.96 | 15.41 | 20.75 | 1 | 2 |
| 5 YEAR AVG. | ... | ... | ... | ... | ... |
| 10 YEAR AVG. | ... | | | | |
| 15 YEAR AVG. | ... | | | | |

| | ALPHA | BETA | R² | STD. DEV. |
|---|---|---|---|---|
| | 11.4 | 1.35 | 78 | 6.49 |
| PERCENTILE ALL | 1 | 6 | 64 | 8 |
| RANK OBJ. | 2 | 21 | 45 | 23 |

Percentile Ranks: 1 = Highest, 100 = Lowest
Except MMF Risk: 1 = Lowest, 100 = Highest

## HISTORY

| | 1979 | 1980 | 1981 | 1982 | 1983 | 1984 | 1985 | 1986 | 1987 | 1988 | 1989 | 1990 | 07/91 |
|---|---|---|---|---|---|---|---|---|---|---|---|---|---|
| N.A.V. | ... | ... | ... | ... | ... | ... | ... | 9.71 | 9.56 | 11.23 | 14.58 | 15.28 | 19.61 |
| TOTAL RETURN % | ... | ... | ... | ... | ... | ... | ... | ... | -1.54 | 17.47 | 64.53 | 6.69 | 28.34 |
| +/- S&P 500 INDEX | ... | ... | ... | ... | ... | ... | ... | ... | -6.76 | 0.96 | 32.86 | 9.79 | 8.64 |
| +/- WILSHIRE 4500 | ... | ... | ... | ... | ... | ... | ... | ... | 1.97 | -3.07 | 40.59 | 20.24 | 2.34 |
| TOT. RTN % ALL FUNDS | ... | ... | ... | ... | ... | ... | ... | ... | 73 | 25 | 1 | 17 | 14 |
| % RANK OBJECTIVE | ... | ... | ... | ... | ... | ... | ... | ... | 48 | 58 | 2 | 5 | 56 |
| INCOME | ... | ... | ... | ... | ... | ... | ... | 0.00 | 0.00 | 0.00 | 0.00 | 0.00 | 0.00 |
| CAPITAL GAIN | ... | ... | ... | ... | ... | ... | ... | 0.00 | 0.00 | 0.00 | 3.79 | 0.27 | 0.00 |
| EXPENSE % | ... | ... | ... | ... | ... | ... | ... | ... | 3.00 | 3.01 | 3.25 | 2.66 | ... |
| INCOME % | ... | ... | ... | ... | ... | ... | ... | ... | -2.02 | -2.07 | -1.92 | -1.17 | ... |
| TURNOVER % | ... | ... | ... | ... | ... | ... | ... | ... | 268 | 228 | 441 | 253 | ... |
| NET ASSETS ($MIL) | ... | ... | ... | ... | ... | ... | ... | 1.1 | 2.8 | 3.7 | 13.6 | 29.5 | 48.3 |

**M-STAR RISK % RANK**

| | ALL | OBJ. |
|---|---|---|
| 3 YEAR | 86 | 56 |
| 5 YEAR | | |
| 10 YEAR | | |

**MORNINGSTAR RETURN RISK** (1.00 = EQUITY AVG)

| | RETURN | RISK |
|---|---|---|
| 3 YEAR | 2.78 | 1.19 |
| WEIGHTED AVG. | 2.78 | 1.19 |

**MORNINGSTAR RISK-ADJUSTED RATING** ★★★★★

*Source:* Morningstar Reports on pp. 298–353 courtesy of Morningstar Mutual Funds, Chicago, IL.; used by permission.

## ANALYSIS

**Amy C. Arnott**    09/06/91

Alger Small Capitalization Portfolio offers dazzling returns for assertive growth seekers.

Over the trailing three-year period, the fund ranks in the top percentile of our fund universe, buoyed by spectacular years like 1989. And last year, the fund held up remarkably well, earning money in a dismal small-cap market. A focus on earnings growth shielded it from the slings and arrows of recessionary 1990.

So far, manager David Alger's strategy has served the fund well. He aims for an average earnings-growth rate of 35%. This year, he says, the portfolio's growth rate is 41%, led by several restaurant stocks. The fund's largest holding, Spaghetti Warehouse, has skyrocketed 86% in price so far this year. The fund also holds numerous health-care stocks, which have performed well overall. And some have been phenomenal: Healthcare Compare, for example, has tripled this year.

Earnings growth is central on the sell side, too. Alger typically will sell a stock if earnings growth slows or disappoints. He'll also sell when he believes a stock has become relatively overvalued. This part, he concedes, is more difficult to call.

The fund isn't without flaws. Because of a small asset base, its expense ratio remains high. And the fund isn't for the cautious. The portfolio is turned over at breakneck pace, and recent highfliers have plenty of room to fall if earnings don't meet market expectations. It's quite concentrated: nearly one third of net assets are in stocks related to health care, the hottest sector in the market for almost three years running.

Still, we think those who know what they're getting into will be amply rewarded. And despite the fund's feverish style, its risk profile is actually in line with the small-company-fund averages.

## OPERATIONS

**ADDRESS** 75 Maiden Lane
New York, NY 10038
**ADVISOR** Fred Alger Management
**DISTRIBUTOR** Fred Alger
**PORTFOLIO MANAGER** David Alger (1986)
**MANAGEMENT FEE** 0.85% flat fee
**FEES** 5.00%D, 1.00%B
**TICKER** ALSCX

**TELEPHONE NUMBER** 201-547-8320
800-992-3863
**PHONE SWITCH** Yes
**# OF SHAREHOLDERS** 4327
**MINIMUM INITIAL PURCHASE** 1000
**MINIMUM SUBSEQUENT PURCHASE** 100
**DATE OF INCEPTION** 11/11/86
**SHAREHOLDER REPORT RATING** C-

| PORTFOLIO | | TOTAL # STOCKS 43 | TOP 30 EQUITY HOLDINGS AS OF: | 06/28/91 |
|---|---|---|---|---|
| SHARE CHANGE | AMOUNT | STOCK | VALUE $000 | % NET ASSETS |
| 38462 | 85537 | SPAGHETTI WAREHOUSE | 1754 | 3.63 |
| 74000 | 74000 | HEALTHCARE COMPARE | 1610 | 3.33 |
| 72500 | 72500 | XILINX | 1523 | 3.15 |
| 36500 | 56500 | CHAMBERS DEVELOPMENT CL A | 1497 | 3.10 |
| 8000 | 27000 | MEDICAL CARE INTERNATIONAL | 1472 | 3.05 |
| 51750 | 51750 | VENCOR | 1449 | 3.00 |
| 88500 | 88500 | MAXIM INTEGRATED PRODUCTS | 1427 | 2.96 |
| 58000 | 58000 | LIFELINE SYSTEMS | 1421 | 2.94 |
| 71000 | 71000 | INTELLIGENT ELECTRONICS | 1385 | 2.87 |
| 37500 | 37500 | BMC SOFTWARE | 1378 | 2.85 |
| 8000 | 41000 | CRITICAL CARE AMERICA | 1343 | 2.78 |
| -32000 | 100000 | UTILX | 1338 | 2.77 |
| 85000 | 85000 | ALTERA | 1328 | 2.75 |
| 60000 | 106600 | MEDICAL IMAGING CTRS AMERICA | 1293 | 2.68 |
| 41500 | 41500 | FOUNDATION HEALTH | 1209 | 2.50 |
| 65400 | 65400 | ALIAS RESEARCH | 1194 | 2.47 |
| 74000 | 74000 | SYNCOR INTERNATIONAL | 1147 | 2.38 |
| 8500 | 39900 | HEALTHSOUTH REHABILITATION | 1097 | 2.27 |
| 88000 | 88000 | HMO AMERICA | 1078 | 2.23 |
| 94500 | 94500 | DI | 957 | 1.98 |
| 41000 | 41000 | GOOD GUYS | 912 | 1.89 |
| 51000 | 51000 | ISOMEDIX | 893 | 1.85 |
| 90000 | 90000 | BEVERLY ENTERPRISES | 844 | 1.75 |
| 29300 | 29300 | SYNOPTICS COMMUNICATIONS | 842 | 1.74 |
| 26000 | 26000 | CRACKER BARREL OLD COUNTRY | 819 | 1.70 |
| 48000 | 48000 | CIRCUIT CITY STORES | 816 | 1.69 |
| 52600 | 52600 | INTL RECTIFIER | 802 | 1.66 |
| 13500 | 23500 | CENTOCOR | 746 | 1.55 |
| -4000 | 29000 | NATIONAL PIZZA | 740 | 1.53 |
| 17500 | 17500 | EMPLOYEE BENEFIT PLANS | 739 | 1.53 |

### PORTFOLIO STATISTICS 07/31/91

| | PORT-FOLIO | % OF AVG. STOCKS | REL. S&P 500 |
|---|---|---|---|
| PRICE/EARNINGS RATIO | 27.1 | 86 | 1.55 |
| PRKC/BOOK RATIO | 6.6 | 93 | 1.89 |
| 5 YR. EARN. GR. % | 26.4 | 23 | 2.03 |
| RETURN ON ASSETS | 9.8 | 89 | 1.30 |
| DEBT % TOTAL CAP. | 21.1 | 89 | 0.66 |
| MED. MKT. CAP. ($MIL) | 296 | 96 | 0.03 |

### COMPOSITION %

| | | | 06/30/91 |
|---|---|---|---|
| CASH | 16.7 | PREFERREDS | 0.0 |
| STOCKS | 83.3 | CONVERTIBLES | 0.0 |
| BONDS | 0.0 | OTHER | 0.0 |

### SECTOR WEIGHTINGS

| | PORT-FOLIO % | REL. S&P 500 |
|---|---|---|
| NATURAL RESOURCES | 0.0 | 0.00 |
| INDUSTRIAL PRODUCTS | 13.3 | 1.09 |
| CONSUMER DURABLES | 20.3 | 3.55 |
| NON-DURABLES | 4.9 | 0.23 |
| RETAIL TRADE | 7.9 | 1.13 |
| SERVICES | 51.5 | 5.87 |
| UTILITIES | 2.2 | 0.16 |
| TRANSPORTATION | 0.0 | 0.00 |
| FINANCE | 0.0 | 0.00 |
| MULTI-INDUSTRY | 0.0 | 0.00 |

# Alliance Mortgage Sec Inc

| OBJECTIVE | LOAD % | YIELD % | ASSETS($MIL) | N.A.V. |
|---|---|---|---|---|
| Grt Mortgage | 4.75 | 9.5 | 494.9 | 9.05 |

Alliance Mortgage Securities Income Fund seeks a high level of current income consistent with prudent investment risk.

The fund invests at least 65% of its total assets in mortgage-related securities, except when in a temporary defensive posture. These securities directly or indirectly provide funds for residential mortgage loans made to home buyers throughout the United States. These loans are originated primarily by savings and loan institutions, mortgage bankers, commercial banks, and other mortgage lenders and are grouped into pools by various government, government-related, and private organizations.

**TOP LINE:** Adjusted NAV
**BOTTOM LINE:** Relative Strength

| RETURN | RISK |
|---|---|
| High | Below Avg |
| **RATING** | |
| ★ ★ ★ ★ | |
| Above Avg | |

## TOTAL RETURN %

| | 1st Qtr. | 2nd Qtr. | 3rd Qtr. | 4th Qtr. | TOTAL |
|---|---|---|---|---|---|
| 1987 | 2.27 | -1.44 | -2.60 | 5.32 | 3.40 |
| 1988 | 5.39 | 1.50 | 1.63 | -0.06 | 8.64 |
| 1989 | 0.86 | 4.86 | 1.09 | 3.80 | 10.98 |
| 1990 | -0.37 | 3.43 | 1.72 | 5.90 | 11.01 |
| 1991 | 2.72 | 1.99 | 5.62 | … | … |

## INCOME

| | | | | | TOTAL |
|---|---|---|---|---|---|
| 1989 | 0.25 | 0.25 | 0.25 | 0.23 | 0.97 |
| 1990 | 0.22 | 0.22 | 0.22 | 0.22 | 0.87 |
| 1991 | 0.22 | 0.21 | 0.21 | … | 0.64 |

## CAPITAL GAINS

| | | | | | TOTAL |
|---|---|---|---|---|---|
| 1989 | 0.00 | 0.00 | 0.00 | 0.00 | 0.00 |
| 1990 | 0.00 | 0.00 | 0.00 | 0.00 | 0.00 |
| 1991 | 0.00 | 0.00 | 0.00 | … | 0.00 |

## PERFORMANCE/RISK
09/30/91

| | TOTAL RETURN% | +/- LB GVT./CP. | PERCENTILE RANK ALL | PERCENTILE RANK OBJ. |
|---|---|---|---|---|
| 3 MONTH | 5.62 | -0.13 | 54 | 30 |
| 6 MONTH | 7.72 | 0.37 | 28 | 14 |
| 1 YEAR | 17.19 | 1.33 | 66 | 9 |
| 3 YEAR AVG. | 10.86 | -0.39 | 50 | 49 |
| 5 YEAR AVG. | 9.60 | 0.48 | 49 | 20 |
| 10 YEAR AVG. | | | | |
| 15 YEAR AVG. | | | | |

| | ALPHA | BETA | R² | STD. DEV. |
|---|---|---|---|---|
| | 0.5 | 0.76 | 82 | 1.07 |
| PERCENTILE / ALL | 12 | 49 | 36 | 71 |
| RANK OBJ. | 33 | 73 | 90 | 71 |

Percentile Ranks: 1 = Highest, 100 = Lowest
Except M-Star Risk: 1 = Lowest, 100 = Highest

## HISTORY

| | 1979 | 1980 | 1981 | 1982 | 1983 | 1984 | 1985 | 1986 | 1987 | 1988 | 1989 | 1990 | 09/91 |
|---|---|---|---|---|---|---|---|---|---|---|---|---|---|
| N.A.V. | … | … | … | … | … | 9.54 | 9.97 | 9.74 | 9.03 | 8.81 | 8.76 | 8.79 | 9.05 |
| TOTAL RETURN % | … | … | … | … | … | … | 18.36 | 11.16 | 3.40 | 8.64 | 10.98 | 11.01 | 10.65 |
| +/- LB GOVT./CP. | … | … | … | … | … | … | -2.95 | -4.46 | 1.10 | 1.06 | -3.25 | 2.73 | 0.41 |
| TOT. RTN./ALL FUNDS | … | … | … | … | … | … | 83 | 76 | 38 | 71 | 78 | 3 | 71 |
| % RANK OBJECTIVE | … | … | … | … | … | … | 60 | 52 | 20 | 11 | 82 | 6 | 9 |
| INCOME | … | … | … | … | … | 1.02 | 1.22 | 1.06 | 0.99 | 0.98 | 0.97 | 0.87 | 0.64 |
| CAPITAL GAIN | … | … | … | … | … | 0.00 | 0.00 | 0.21 | 0.03 | 0.00 | 0.00 | 0.00 | 0.00 |
| EXPENSE % | … | … | … | … | … | 0.66 | 0.87 | 1.00 | 1.15 | 1.11 | 1.13 | 1.12 | 1.16 |
| INCOME % | … | … | … | … | … | 12.86 | 12.30 | 10.86 | 10.79 | 10.80 | 11.03 | 10.09 | 10.30 |
| TURNOVER % | … | … | … | … | … | … | 164 | 190 | 211 | 239 | 328 | 393 | … |
| NET ASSETS ($MIL) | … | … | … | … | … | 316.6 | 609.6 | 756.7 | 679.6 | 619.5 | 556.1 | 495.3 | 494.9 |

| | M-STAR RISK % RANK | | MORNINGSTAR RETURN RISK | | MORNINGSTAR RISK-ADJUSTED RATING |
|---|---|---|---|---|---|
| | ALL | OBJ | 1.00 = FIXED-INCOME AVG. | | |
| 3 YEAR | 7 | 36 | 1.07 | 0.82 → | ★ ★ ★ ★ |
| 5 YEAR | 6 | 20 | 1.14 | 0.83 → | ★ ★ ★ ★ |
| 10 YEAR | … | … | … | … | … |
| WEIGHTED AVG. | | | 1.11 | 0.83 | ★ ★ ★ |

NET ASSETS: ($MIL)

## ANALYSIS
**Tom Desmond**    10/18/91

Alliance Mortgage Securities Income Fund has a new captain at the helm.

Michael Jones assumed control of the fund in April 1991, taking over for Paul Zoschke, who had run it since inception. However, this change in management does not indicate a change in investment policy. "The fund's strategies will remain intact," Jones insists. "I've just picked up the reins."

Thus far, the transition has been smooth. Despite its premium-coupon bias, the fund has continued to perform in the category's top decile. Its high-income payout has exceeded the Lehman Brothers Mortgage-Backed Index by roughly 100 basis points, preserving its stature as one of the group's highest-yielding funds. Moreover, it has also participated in the recent bond-market rally, boosting its NAV to pre-1987 levels.

The fund is one of the few in its group to couple opposing factors: high yield with capital appreciation. To begin, the fund concentrates primarily on superpremium coupons, locking into their superior payouts. (Coupons of 11% or above occupy a whopping 81% of assets.)

Of course, this approach also aggravates prepayment risk, particularly as interest rates decline. To offset this risk, the fund relies on call options. These options enable the fund to participate in bond-market rallies, by allowing it to call in the price. "Call options and high-premium coupons make a nice match," Jones explains. "When the market jumps, the juice switches to options. When it retreats, high premiums pick up the ball." In addition, the fund's 5% zero-coupon exposure has also flourished.

So far this year, the fund has enjoyed the best of both worlds. But this strategy may lose momentum if interest rates stagnate. Then, it will hang on to its high yield, but its call options will expire worthless.

## OPERATIONS

| | |
|---|---|
| **ADDRESS** | P.O. Box 1520 |
| | Secaucus, NJ 07096 |
| **ADVISOR** | Alliance Capital Management |
| **DISTRIBUTOR** | Alliance Fund Distributors |
| **PORTFOLIO MANAGER** | Michael Jones (1991) |
| **MANAGEMENT FEE** | 0.55% max./0.50% min. |
| **FEES** | 4.75%L, 0.30%B |
| **TICKER** | ALMSX |

| | |
|---|---|
| **TELEPHONE NUMBER** | 201-319-4000 |
| | 800-227-4618 |
| **PHONE SWITCH** | Yes |
| **# OF SHAREHOLDERS** | 25939 |
| **MINIMUM INITIAL PURCHASE** | 250 |
| **MINIMUM SUBSEQUENT PURCHASE** | 50 |
| **DATE OF INCEPTION** | 02/29/84 |
| **SHAREHOLDER REPORT RATING** | B |

© 1991 Morningstar, Inc. • 53 West Jackson Boulevard • Chicago, IL 60604 • (312) 427-1985
Although gathered from reliable sources, data accuracy and completeness cannot be guaranteed.

## PORTFOLIO

**TOTAL # SECURITIES 58** — **TOP 30 SECURITIES AS OF: 06/30/91**

| AMOUNT $000 | SECURITY | MATURITY | VALUE $000 | % NET ASSETS |
|---:|---|---|---:|---:|
| 195453 | GNMA 12% | 04/15/19 | 221039 | 44.47 |
| 54693 | FHLMC 12% | 07/01/20 | 60025 | 12.08 |
| 36713 | GNMA 12.5% | 02/01/18 | 41828 | 8.42 |
| 34308 | GNMA 11% | 10/15/20 | 37170 | 7.48 |
| 29840 | FHLMC 12.5% | 06/15/19 | 33029 | 6.65 |
| 184715 | RESOLUTION FUNDING 0% | 07/15/12 | 33014 | 6.64 |
| 27717 | GNMA 11.5% | 01/01/21 | 30705 | 6.18 |
| 27146 | FHLMC 11.5% | 06/01/20 | 29164 | 5.87 |
| 18110 | GNMA 13.5% | 07/20/15 | 21011 | 4.23 |
| 17192 | FNMA 12.5% | 04/01/19 | 19061 | 3.84 |
| 16383 | FNMA 12% | 07/01/19 | 18041 | 3.63 |
| 78450 | US TREASURY STRIP 0% | 08/15/10 | 15251 | 3.07 |
| 10587 | FHLMC 9.75% | 10/01/14 | 10832 | 2.18 |
| 9267 | GNMA 10% | 06/01/20 | 9676 | 1.95 |
| 8698 | FHLMC 13% | 12/01/18 | 9666 | 1.94 |
| 7240 | GNMA 14% | 02/15/15 | 8455 | 1.70 |
| 6920 | FNMA 9.5% | 07/01/03 | 7084 | 1.43 |
| 5910 | FNMA 13% | 12/01/15 | 6575 | 1.32 |
| 5355 | GNMA 15% | 02/15/13 | 6291 | 1.27 |
| 4688 | GNMA 13% | 02/20/15 | 5387 | 1.08 |
| 5000 | US TREASURY NOTE 7.625% | 12/31/93 | 5047 | 1.02 |
| 4534 | FHLMC 12.25% | 07/01/14 | 4964 | 1.00 |
| 6695 | TRUST P/O-CMO | 05/23/17 | 4491 | 0.90 |
| 2861 | FNMA 14.75% | 08/01/12 | 3190 | 0.64 |
| 2717 | GNMA 13.25% | 12/15/14 | 3087 | 0.62 |
| 2586 | FHLMC 13.5% | 10/01/16 | 2886 | 0.58 |
| 2594 | FHLMC 11.75% | 12/01/15 | 2781 | 0.56 |
| 2476 | FNMA 13.5% | 08/01/15 | 2767 | 0.56 |
| 2447 | FNMA 15.5% | 12/01/12 | 2753 | 0.55 |
| 6695 | TRUST I/O-CMO | 05/23/17 | 2563 | 0.52 |

### PORTFOLIO STATISTICS

| | |
|---|---|
| AVG. WEIGHTED MATURITY | 17.4 YEARS |
| AVG. WEIGHTED COUPON | 11.2% |
| AVG. WEIGHTED PRICE | 105% OF PAR |

### COMPOSITION % 06/30/91

| | | | |
|---|---:|---|---:|
| CASH | -40.0 | PREFERREDS | 0.0 |
| STOCKS | 0.0 | CONVERTIBLES | 0.0 |
| BONDS | 140.0 | OTHER | 0.0 |

### COUPON RANGE

| | % BONDS | REL. OBL. |
|---|---:|---:|
| 0%, PIK | 7.2 | 1.6 |
| 0% to 8% | 0.8 | 0.1 |
| 8% to 9% | 0.0 | 0.0 |
| 9% to 10% | 4.1 | 0.1 |
| over 10% | 87.9 | 2.9 |

### CREDIT ANALYSIS   06/30/91

US T-Bonds
US T-Notes
GNMA 56
FNMA 10
FHLMCs 23
Other 11

Percentage of Net Assets

MORNINGSTAR, INC.

# Calvert T/F Reserves Ltd

| OBJECTIVE | LOAD% | YIELD% | ASSETS($Mil) | N.A.V. |
|---|---|---|---|---|
| Muni General | 2.00 | 6.0 | 220.1 | 10.64 |

Calvert Tax-Free Reserves Limited-Term Portfolio seeks the highest level of tax-exempt interest income as is consistent with prudent investment management and preservation of capital.

The fund invests primarily in a diversified portfolio of medium- and higher-grade municipal obligations. Fixed-rate investments are limited to obligations with remaining maturities of three years or less; variable-rate investments may have longer maturities. The average weighted maturity of the fund is expected to remain between one and two years.

**TOP LINE:** Adjusted N.A.V.
**BOTTOM LINE:** Relative Strength

|  | RISK |
|---|---|
| RETURN | Low |
| Low |  |
| RATING | ★★★★★ |
|  | Highest |

## TOTAL RETURN %

| | 1st Qtr. | 2nd Qtr. | 3rd Qtr. | 4th Qtr. | TOTAL |
|---|---|---|---|---|---|
| 1987 | 1.46 | 0.56 | -0.03 | 1.44 | 3.47 |
| 1988 | 2.49 | 1.47 | 1.31 | 1.36 | 6.80 |
| 1989 | 1.54 | 2.20 | 1.40 | 1.80 | 7.12 |
| 1990 | 1.40 | 1.74 | 1.24 | 1.97 | 6.50 |
| 1991 | 1.48 | 1.54 | 1.69 | --- | --- |

## INCOME

| | | | | | TOTAL |
|---|---|---|---|---|---|
| 1989 | 0.16 | 0.17 | 0.17 | 0.17 | 0.67 |
| 1990 | 0.17 | 0.16 | 0.17 | 0.17 | 0.67 |
| 1991 | 0.16 | 0.15 | 0.16 | 0.05 | 0.52 |

## CAPITAL GAINS

| | | | | | TOTAL |
|---|---|---|---|---|---|
| 1989 | 0.00 | 0.00 | 0.00 | 0.00 | 0.00 |
| 1990 | 0.00 | 0.00 | 0.00 | 0.00 | 0.00 |
| 1991 | 0.00 | 0.00 | 0.00 | --- | --- |

## PERFORMANCE/RISK 09/30/91

| | TOTAL RETURN% | +/- LB GVT./CP. | PERCENTILE RANK ALL | OBL |
|---|---|---|---|---|
| 3 MONTH | 1.69 | -4.06 | 95 | 100 |
| 6 MONTH | 3.26 | -4.09 | 88 | 99 |
| 1 YEAR | 6.85 | -9.01 | 96 | 100 |
| 3 YEAR AVG. | 6.61 | -4.64 | 89 | 98 |
| 5 YEAR AVG. | 6.13 | -2.99 | 89 | 89 |
| 10 YEAR AVG. | 7.56 | -6.66 | 95 | 92 |
| 15 YEAR AVG. | --- | | | |

| | ALPHA | BETA | R² | STD. DEV. |
|---|---|---|---|---|
| | -1.0 | 0.11 | 56 | 0.19 |
| PERCENTILE ALL | 49 | 97 | 80 | 100 |
| RANK OBL | 33 | 98 | 92 | 100 |

Percentile Ranks: 1 = Highest, 100 = Lowest
Except M-Star Risk: 1 = Lowest, 100 = Highest

## HISTORY

| | 1979 | 1980 | 1981 | 1982 | 1983 | 1984 | 1985 | 1986 | 1987 | 1988 | 1989 | 1990 | 09/91 |
|---|---|---|---|---|---|---|---|---|---|---|---|---|---|
| N.A.V. | --- | --- | 9.98 | 10.31 | 10.29 | 10.33 | 10.48 | 10.67 | 10.45 | 10.55 | 10.61 | 10.61 | 10.64 |
| TOTAL RETURN % | --- | --- | --- | 12.45 | 6.35 | 7.35 | 8.33 | 8.53 | 3.47 | 6.80 | 7.12 | 6.50 | 4.78 |
| +/- LB GOVT./CP. | --- | --- | --- | -18.65 | -1.65 | -7.66 | -12.98 | -7.09 | 1.17 | -0.78 | -7.11 | -1.78 | -5.46 |
| TOT. RTN ALL FUNDS | --- | --- | --- | 90 | 94 | 39 | 97 | 88 | 32 | 81 | 92 | 26 | 96 |
| % RANK OBJECTIVE | --- | --- | --- | 92 | 88 | 70 | 95 | 96 | 4 | 91 | 95 | 34 | 100 |
| INCOME | --- | --- | 0.63 | 0.83 | 0.65 | 0.68 | 0.68 | 0.64 | 0.58 | 0.60 | 0.67 | 0.67 | 0.47 |
| CAPITAL GAIN | --- | --- | 0.00 | 0.03 | 0.01 | 0.01 | 0.01 | 0.04 | 0.00 | 0.00 | 0.00 | 0.00 | 0.00 |
| EXPENSE % | --- | --- | 0.47 | 1.00 | 1.00 | 0.96 | 0.88 | 0.81 | 0.76 | 0.81 | 0.78 | 0.77 | 0.75 |
| INCOME % | --- | --- | 9.25 | 7.90 | 6.37 | 6.84 | 6.65 | 6.00 | 5.59 | 5.71 | 6.35 | 6.35 | 6.01 |
| TURNOVER % | --- | --- | --- | 86 | 79 | 155 | 90 | 67 | 52 | 68 | 21 | 12 | --- |
| NET ASSETS ($Mil) | --- | --- | 4.2 | 31.0 | 55.7 | 52.3 | 77.8 | 189.4 | 204.8 | 145.4 | 132.2 | 151.5 | 220.1 |

| | M-STAR RISK % RANK ALL | OBL | MORNINGSTAR RETURN RISK 1.00 = MIN AVG | | MORNINGSTAR RISK-ADJUSTED RATING |
|---|---|---|---|---|---|
| 3 YEAR | 1 | 1 | 0.74 | 0.26 → | ★★★★★ |
| 5 YEAR | 1 | 1 | 0.82 | 0.27 → | ★★★★★ |
| 10 YEAR | 1 | 7 | 0.60 | 0.32 → | ★★★★ |
| WEIGHTED AVG. | | | 0.69 | 0.30 | |

NET ASSETS ($Mil): 200 / 100 / 0

## ANALYSIS

Eileen Sanders     11/01/91

Calvert Tax-Free Reserves Limited-Term Portfolio wants nothing more than to live up to investor expectations.

While not a total-return champ, the fund consistently pays out a yield 50 to 100 basis points higher than the average muni-money-market account's. In this year's rally, for instance, its returns have scraped the bottom of its objective. Moreover, the fund offers one of the least risky rides of its objective; its NAV hasn't fluctuated more than 30 cents since its inception.

The charter precludes most interest-rate volatility by limiting average weighted maturity to three years or less. However, according to comanager Reno Martini, the fund has taken that limitation a step further. Since 1987, the fund's maturity has hovered near the one-year mark, virtually eliminating interest-rate risk.

To achieve the fund's relatively high yield with such a short maturity schedule, Martini must look beyond plain-vanilla securities. For example, a full 70% of the fund's assets are held in option tender bonds. These issues are similar to puts in that they give the holder the right to return the bond in a period shorter than its long-term maturity. While these issues yield more than their nontender equivalents, they are also less liquid because there's less demand for them.

Besides experimenting with less-common securities, Martini is willing to take on some credit risk in the form of nonrated issues. However, he insists that the fund will only hold those issues that have some form of credit enhancement. "If all of these issues were rated," he claims, "the fund's average credit quality would be AA."

The investor who isn't prepared to sacrifice the security of a money-market account, but who still wants a higher tax-free yield, should look closely at this fund.

## OPERATIONS

| | | | |
|---|---|---|---|
| ADDRESS | 4550 Montgomery Avenue Suite 1000N Bethesda, MD 20814 | TELEPHONE NUMBER | 301-951-4820 800-368-2748 |
| ADVISOR | Calvert Asset Management | PHONE SWITCH | Yes |
| DISTRIBUTOR | Calvert Securities | # OF SHAREHOLDERS | 4818 |
| PORTFOLIO MANAGER | Rochat/Martini (81/83) | MINIMUM INITIAL PURCHASE | 2000 |
| MANAGEMENT FEE | 0.60% flat fee | MINIMUM SUBSEQUENT PURCHASE | 250 |
| FEES | 2.00%L | DATE OF INCEPTION | 03/04/81 |
| TICKER | CTFLX | SHAREHOLDER REPORT RATING | C |

## PORTFOLIO

TOTAL # SECURITIES 75    TOP 20 SECURITIES AS OF: 06/30/91

| AMOUNT $000 | SECURITY | MATURITY | VALUE $000 | % NET ASSETS |
|---|---|---|---|---|
| 22670 | AZ PHOENIX INDL DEV AUTH MULTI-FAM 7.5% | 04/15/04 | 22670 | 10.18 |
| 8200 | CA POMONA PUB FIN AUTH VAR% | 10/01/94 | 8200 | 3.68 |
| 7150 | FL DUVAL MULTI-FAM HSG VAR% | 06/01/07 | 7150 | 3.21 |
| 6950 | PR SUGAR 6.6% | 07/01/93 | 6961 | 3.13 |
| 6500 | PA BERKS INDL DEV AUTH 7.5% | 10/15/17 | 6604 | 2.96 |
| 6125 | FL GULF BREEZE REV LOCAL GOVT RFDG 6.8% | 06/15/15 | 6140 | 2.76 |
| 5485 | TX HARRIS REV MULTI-FAM HSG 7% | 12/01/04 | 5464 | 2.45 |
| 5400 | CA VALLEJO HSG FIN AUTH CONST 6.65% | 12/01/97 | 5400 | 2.42 |
| 5000 | VT HSG FIN AUTH SNGL FAM MTG 7.5% | 05/01/25 | 5005 | 2.25 |
| 5000 | AZ TUCSON INDL DEV AUTH VAR% | 12/01/07 | 5000 | 2.24 |
| 5000 | TN MEMPHIS CTR CONST LOAN 8% | 05/01/23 | 4950 | 2.22 |
| 4800 | NV HSG DIV VAR% | 04/01/20 | 4800 | 2.16 |
| 4725 | PA CAMBRIA REV INDL DEV AUTH 6.9% | 12/01/16 | 4690 | 2.11 |
| 4500 | KY OHIO REV POLL CNTRL VAR% | 10/01/15 | 4500 | 2.02 |
| 4400 | TN NASHVILLE & DAVIDSON INDL DEV VAR% | 12/01/08 | 4400 | 1.98 |
| 4000 | TX BEXAR HLTH FAC DEV 7.375% | 06/01/07 | 4039 | 1.81 |
| 4000 | FL JACKSONVILLE PORT AUTH INDL DEV 7.25% | 11/01/12 | 4007 | 1.80 |
| 4000 | CA RIVERSIDE MULTI-FAM HSG VAR% | 03/01/16 | 4000 | 1.80 |
| 3520 | LA REV MTG PUB FAC 9.2% | 10/01/13 | 3643 | 1.64 |
| 3500 | MA STATE GO 7.5% | 06/01/93 | 3572 | 1.60 |

### SECTOR WEIGHTINGS

| | PORT. % | REL MUNI AVG. | | PORT. % | REL MUNI AVG. |
|---|---|---|---|---|---|
| GEN. OBL. | 2.36 | 0.28 | TRANS. R&R | 0.00 | 0.00 |
| UTILITY | 0.00 | 0.00 | TRANS. A&W | 0.48 | 0.10 |
| HEALTH | 2.51 | 0.15 | COP/LEASE | 0.16 | 0.04 |
| WTR./WASTE | 0.30 | 0.05 | PRIVATE | 30.36 | 2.53 |
| HOUSING | 48.92 | 5.53 | MISC.REV. | 4.77 | 1.02 |
| EDUCATION | 2.02 | 0.29 | UNASSIGNED | 8.12 | 1.76 |

### TOP 5 STATES

| | PORT. % |
|---|---|
| California | 18.94 |
| Arizona | 15.49 |
| Florida | 9.34 |
| Pennsylvania | 7.58 |
| Texas | 6.87 |

### COMPOSITION % 06/30/91

| | | | |
|---|---|---|---|
| CASH | 71.0 | PREFERREDS | 0.0 |
| STOCKS | 0.0 | CONVERTIBLES | 0.0 |
| BONDS | 29.0 | OTHER | 0.0 |

### PORTFOLIO STATISTICS

| | |
|---|---|
| AVG. WEIGHTED MATURITY | 0.7 YEARS |
| AVG. WEIGHTED COUPON | 7.54% |
| AVG. WEIGHTED PRICE | 100% OF PAR |

### COUPON RANGE

| | % BONDS | REL OBL. |
|---|---|---|
| 0% | 0.0 | 0.0 |
| 0% to 6.8% | 20.7 | 1.0 |
| 6.8 to 7.5% | 60.5 | 2.4 |
| 7.5 to 8.3% | 7.8 | 0.3 |
| over 8.3% | 11.0 | 0.4 |

### CREDIT ANALYSIS 09/30/91

Rating categories: US Govt, AAA, AA, BBB, B, N/A — Percentage of Bonds

1046

# MORNINGSTAR, INC.

## Dreyfus NY T/E Bond

| OBJECTIVE | LOAD % | YIELD % | ASSETS($MIL) | N.A.V. |
|---|---|---|---|---|
| Muni General | None | 6.9 | 1722.6 | 15.18 |

Dreyfus New York Tax-Exempt Bond Fund seeks the maximum amount of current income exempt from federal, New York State, and New York City income taxes as is consistent with the preservation of capital.

The fund invests at least 80% of assets in municipal obligations rated BBB or better. At least 65% of assets will be invested in New York municipal obligations. For temporary defensive purposes the fund may invest in taxable short-term investments.

**TOP LINE:** Adjusted N.A.V.
**BOTTOM LINE:** Relative Strength

| RETURN | RISK |
|---|---|
| Above Avg | Average |
| RATING | |
| ★ ★ ★ | |
| Neutral | |

### TOTAL RETURN %

| | 1st Qtr. | 2nd Qtr. | 3rd Qtr. | 4th Qtr. | TOTAL |
|---|---|---|---|---|---|
| 1987 | 2.37 | -5.15 | -3.11 | 3.48 | -2.65 |
| 1988 | 2.33 | 2.34 | 2.78 | 2.31 | 10.12 |
| 1989 | 0.21 | 5.60 | -0.05 | 3.00 | 8.93 |
| 1990 | -0.09 | 2.15 | -0.08 | 3.45 | 5.49 |
| 1991 | 2.32 | 2.11 | 4.31 | ... | ... |

### INCOME

| | | | | | TOTAL |
|---|---|---|---|---|---|
| 1989 | 0.27 | 0.27 | 0.26 | 0.26 | 1.06 |
| 1990 | 0.27 | 0.26 | 0.26 | 0.27 | 1.05 |
| 1991 | 0.25 | 0.26 | 0.26 | ... | 0.77 |

### CAPITAL GAINS

| | | | | | TOTAL |
|---|---|---|---|---|---|
| 1989 | 0.00 | 0.00 | 0.00 | 0.00 | 0.00 |
| 1990 | 0.00 | 0.00 | 0.00 | 0.00 | 0.00 |
| 1991 | 0.00 | 0.00 | 0.00 | ... | 0.00 |

### PERFORMANCE/RISK 09/30/91

| | TOTAL RETURN% | +/- LB GVT./CP. | +/- LB OBJ. | PERCENTILE RANK ALL | RANK OBJ. |
|---|---|---|---|---|---|
| 3 MONTH | 4.31 | -1.44 | 0.00 | 66 | 21 |
| 6 MONTH | 6.51 | -0.84 | 0.00 | 43 | 23 |
| 1 YEAR | 12.75 | -3.11 | 0.00 | 77 | 49 |
| 3 YEAR AVG. | 8.61 | -2.64 | 0.00 | 73 | 54 |
| 5 YEAR AVG. | 6.92 | -2.20 | 0.00 | 82 | 69 |
| 10 YEAR AVG. | | | | | |
| 15 YEAR AVG. | | | | | |

| | ALPHA | BETA | R² | STD. DEV. |
|---|---|---|---|---|
| | -1.2 | 0.68 | 71 | 1.02 |
| PERCENTILE / ALL | 57 | 63 | 44 | 76 |
| RANK / OBJ. | 46 | 64 | 25 | 64 |

Percentile Rank: 1 = Highest, 100 = Lowest
Each Mkt. Sq. Rank: 1 = Lowest, 100 = Higher

### HISTORY

| | 1979 | 1980 | 1981 | 1982 | 1983 | 1984 | 1985 | 1986 | 1987 | 1988 | 1989 | 1990 | 09/91 |
|---|---|---|---|---|---|---|---|---|---|---|---|---|---|
| N.A.V. | ... | ... | ... | ... | 13.28 | 13.14 | 14.59 | 15.89 | 14.39 | 14.73 | 14.94 | 14.67 | 15.18 |
| TOTAL RETURN % | ... | ... | ... | ... | | 8.07 | 20.63 | 17.07 | -2.65 | 10.12 | 8.93 | 5.49 | 8.99 |
| +/- LB GOVT./CP. | ... | ... | ... | ... | | -6.95 | -0.68 | 1.46 | -4.95 | 2.54 | -5.31 | -2.79 | -1.25 |
| TOT. RTN./ALL FUNDS | ... | ... | ... | ... | | 36 | 66 | 37 | 78 | 60 | 84 | 36 | 67 |
| % RANK/OBJECTIVE | ... | ... | ... | ... | | 62 | 34 | 51 | 83 | 67 | 69 | 74 | 20 |
| INCOME | ... | ... | ... | ... | 0.49 | 1.15 | 1.16 | 1.12 | 1.08 | 1.07 | 1.06 | 1.05 | 0.77 |
| CAPITAL GAIN | ... | ... | ... | ... | 0.00 | 0.00 | 0.00 | 0.00 | 0.00 | 0.00 | 0.00 | 0.00 | 0.00 |
| EXPENSE % | ... | ... | ... | ... | | 0.77 | 0.76 | 0.71 | 0.71 | 0.72 | 0.69 | 0.70 | 0.70 |
| INCOME % | ... | ... | ... | ... | | 8.61 | 8.74 | 7.83 | 7.04 | 7.41 | 7.34 | 7.12 | 7.08 |
| TURNOVER % | ... | ... | ... | ... | | ... | 29 | 15 | 38 | 57 | 38 | 31 | 26 |
| NET ASSETS ($MIL) | ... | ... | ... | ... | 112.5 | 404.0 | 967.3 | 1646.9 | 1417.4 | 1559.4 | 1686.3 | 1657.1 | 1722.6 |

| | M-STAR RISK % RANK ALL | OBJ. |
|---|---|---|
| 3 YEAR | 18 | 36 |
| 5 YEAR | 21 | 39 |
| 10 YEAR | | |

| | MORNINGSTAR RETURN RISK | | |
|---|---|---|---|
| 3 YEAR | 1.15 | 0.94 | ★★★★ |
| 5 YEAR | 1.05 | 0.98 | ★★★ |
| 10 YEAR | ... | ... | ★★★ |
| WEIGHTED AVG. | 1.09 | 0.97 | |

| MORNINGSTAR RISK-ADJUSTED RATING |
|---|
| ★★★★ |
| ★★★ |
| ★★★ |

**NET ASSETS ($MIL)**

## PORTFOLIO

TOTAL # SECURITIES 169    TOP 29 SECURITIES AS OF 05/31/91

| AMOUNT $000 | SECURITY | MATURITY | VALUE $000 | % NET ASSETS |
|---|---|---|---|---|
| 47680 | NY REV ELEC FAC ENGY RSRCH & DEV AUTH 9% | 08/15/20 | 52848 | 3.02 |
| 35220 | NY LOCAL GOVT ASSISTANCE 7% | 04/01/16 | 33917 | 1.94 |
| 26500 | NY REV MED CARE FAC FIN AGCY FHA 8.875% | 01/15/26 | 28554 | 1.63 |
| 24500 | NY REV DORM AUTH CITY UNIV SYS 10.875% | 07/01/14 | 28175 | 1.61 |
| 24000 | NY TRIBOROUGH REV BRIDGE/TUNNEL CONV 9% | 01/01/11 | 27420 | 1.56 |
| 22000 | NY REV GAS FAC ENGY RSRCH & DEV AUTH 9% | 05/15/15 | 24145 | 1.36 |
| 22560 | NY REV PORT AUTH OF NY/NJ 7.875% | 03/01/24 | 23688 | 1.35 |
| 20500 | NY REV PORT AUTH OF NY/NJ CONSOLID 8.7% | 07/15/20 | 22601 | 1.29 |
| 19500 | NY REV URBAN DEV CRTNL FAC 9.2% | 01/01/16 | 22596 | 1.29 |
| 21700 | NY REV POLL CNTRL ENVIR FAC WTR 7.5% | 06/15/12 | 22321 | 1.27 |
| 20175 | NY NEW YORK CITY REV WTR & SWR SYS 9% | 06/15/17 | 22092 | 1.26 |
| 21660 | NY REV POLL CNTRL ENVIR FAC WTR 7% | 06/15/12 | 21498 | 1.23 |
| 19750 | NY REV GAS FAC ENGY RSRCH & DEV 8.75% | 07/01/15 | 21478 | 1.23 |
| 21220 | NY REV ELEC FAC ENGY RSRCH & DEV 7.25% | 11/01/24 | 21220 | 1.21 |
| 18055 | NY NEW YORK CITY 9.5% | 08/15/95 | 21012 | 1.20 |
| 17850 | NY REV MED CARE FAC FIN AGCY HOSP 10.25% | 02/15/24 | 20438 | 1.17 |
| 16660 | PR REV PWR ELEC AUTH RFDG 9.25% | 07/01/06 | 19992 | 1.14 |
| 19750 | NY REV MED CARE FAC FIN AGCY FHA 7.45% | 02/15/19 | 19972 | 1.14 |
| 19200 | NY REV ELEC FAC ENGY RSRCH & DEV 7.75% | 01/01/24 | 19752 | 1.13 |
| 17000 | NY REV DORM AUTH METRO MUSEUM AP 9.2% | 07/01/15 | 19529 | 1.11 |

### TOP 5 STATES

| | PORT. % |
|---|---|
| New York | 84.28 |
| Puerto Rico | 15.43 |
| Guam | 0.30 |

### SECTOR WEIGHTINGS

| | PORT. MUNI % | REL. MUNI AVG. | | PORT. MUNI % | REL. MUNI AVG. |
|---|---|---|---|---|---|
| GEN. OBL. | 0.00 | 0.00 | TRANS. R.R | 8.56 | 1.51 |
| UTILITY | 17.24 | 1.08 | TRANS. A&W | 5.41 | 1.12 |
| HEALTH | 12.21 | 0.72 | COP/LEASE | 0.25 | 0.06 |
| WTR./WASTE | 5.54 | 0.84 | PRIVATE | 11.20 | 0.93 |
| HOUSING | 6.40 | 0.72 | MISC. REV. | 2.88 | 0.62 |
| EDUCATION | 18.61 | 2.67 | UNASSIGNED | 11.70 | 2.54 |

### PORTFOLIO STATISTICS

| | |
|---|---|
| AVG. WEIGHTED MATURITY | 22.7 YEARS |
| AVG. WEIGHTED COUPON | 8.25% |
| AVG. WEIGHTED PRICE | 105% OF PAR |

### COMPOSITION % 06/30/91

| | | | |
|---|---|---|---|
| CASH | 3.6 | PREFERREDS | 0.0 |
| STOCKS | 0.0 | CONVERTIBLES | 0.0 |
| BONDS | 96.4 | OTHER | 0.0 |

### COUPON RANGE    CREDIT ANALYSIS 05/31/91

| | % BONDS | REL. OBL. |
|---|---|---|
| 0% | 0.3 | 0.1 |
| 0% to 6.8% | 5.2 | 0.3 |
| 6.8 to 7.5% | 31.6 | 1.2 |
| 7.5 to 8.3% | 20.6 | 0.9 |
| over 8.3% | 42.3 | 1.5 |

Credit analysis: US Govt, AAA, AA, A, BBB, BB, B, N/A — Percentage of Bonds

**1057**

---

## ANALYSIS

Helen O'D. Johnstone   11/01/91

Like many of its muni-fund peers, Dreyfus New York Tax-Exempt Bond Fund prefers maintaining a competitive payout to beating its rivals' returns.

Traditionally, the fund has stuck with a high-paying, premium-coupon strategy. This premium bias has typically limited the fund's ability to benefit from interest-rate declines, putting a lid on the portfolio's capital-appreciation potential.

The fund's returns have never been terrible, but they haven't hit many high spots, either, leaving it in the middle of its objective for the trailing three years (and in the bottom quartile over five years). Among New York muni-general funds, though, the fund's three-year returns rate better than average. That's because New York's relatively high taxes make a yield focus all the more inviting, prompting many of these funds to employ yield-enhancing strategies rather than focus on capital growth.

However, in 1991's municipal-bond market, that income bias hasn't prevented the fund from outperforming the majority of its muni-general competitors. Supported by prospects for economic recovery and a balanced City budget, New York issues have enjoyed a significant rebound, so far this year, the state's muni market has outperformed those of all other states. As a result, although this fund hasn't been helped as much by falling interest rates as some of its current- and discount-favoring peers, it ranked in the muni-general group's top quartile through September.

With the notable exception of 1991, this fund's income bias has put something of a damper on its long-term returns. However, its Morningstar risk—although equal to the average muni-general fund's—has ranked consistently below the New York fund average. A good payout and reasonable expenses add to its appeal.

## OPERATIONS

| | |
|---|---|
| ADDRESS | 144 Glenn Curtiss Boulevard, Uniondale, NY 11556 |
| ADVISOR | Dreyfus |
| DISTRIBUTOR | Dreyfus Service |
| PORTFOLIO MANAGER | Monica Wieboldt (1985) |
| MANAGEMENT FEE | 0.60% flat fee |
| FEES | No-load |
| TICKER | DRNYX |
| TELEPHONE NUMBER | 718-895-1206 / 800-645-6561 |
| PHONE SWITCH | Yes |
| # OF SHAREHOLDERS | 41158 |
| MINIMUM INITIAL PURCHASE | 2500 |
| MINIMUM SUBSEQUENT PURCHASE | 100 |
| DATE OF INCEPTION | 07/26/83 |
| SHAREHOLDER REPORT RATING | C- |

© 1991 Morningstar, Inc. • 53 West Jackson Boulevard • Chicago, IL 60604 • (312) 427-1985
Although gathered from reliable sources data accuracy and completeness cannot be guaranteed

# Eaton Vance Govt Obligations

| OBJECTIVE | LOAD % | YIELD % | ASSETS($MIL) | N.A.V. |
|---|---|---|---|---|
| Govt General | 4.75 | 9.6 | 283.8 | 11.52 |

Eaton Vance Government Obligations Trust seeks a high current return.

The fund may invest in all kinds of U.S. government securities, including mortgage-backed securities. The fund may also enter into repurchase agreements concerning these securities. The fund may engage in several active management strategies, including the lending of portfolio securities, forward commitment purchases of securities, leverage through borrowing, and various options transactions.

**TOP LINE:** Adjusted NAV
**BOTTOM LINE:** Relative Strength

| | RETURN | RISK |
|---|---|---|
| | Above Avg | Below Avg |
| RATING | ★★★★ | |
| | Highest | |

**NET ASSETS:** ($MIL)

## TOTAL RETURN %

| | 1st Qtr. | 2nd Qtr. | 3rd Qtr. | 4th Qtr. | TOTAL |
|---|---|---|---|---|---|
| 1987 | 1.72 | -0.31 | -1.29 | 4.05 | 4.16 |
| 1988 | 3.80 | 1.19 | 1.38 | 0.83 | 7.37 |
| 1989 | 0.26 | 7.12 | 1.55 | 3.90 | 13.31 |
| 1990 | -0.28 | 2.98 | 1.60 | 4.44 | 8.97 |
| 1991 | 2.11 | 2.04 | 4.67 | ... | ... |

## INCOME

| | | | | | TOTAL |
|---|---|---|---|---|---|
| 1989 | 0.28 | 0.28 | 0.28 | 0.28 | 1.11 |
| 1990 | 0.28 | 0.28 | 0.28 | 0.28 | 1.11 |
| 1991 | 0.28 | 0.28 | 0.28 | 0.09 | 0.93 |

## CAPITAL GAINS

| | | | | | TOTAL |
|---|---|---|---|---|---|
| 1989 | 0.00 | 0.00 | 0.00 | 0.00 | 0.00 |
| 1990 | 0.00 | 0.00 | 0.00 | 0.00 | 0.00 |
| 1991 | 0.00 | 0.00 | 0.00 | ... | 0.00 |

## PERFORMANCE/RISK

09/30/91

| | TOTAL RETURN% | +/- LB GVT./CP. | PERCENTILE RANK ALL | PERCENTILE RANK OBJ. |
|---|---|---|---|---|
| 3 MONTH | 4.67 | -1.08 | 68 | 83 |
| 6 MONTH | 6.80 | -0.55 | 41 | 49 |
| 1 YEAR | 13.89 | -1.97 | 79 | 74 |
| 3 YEAR AVG. | 10.73 | -0.52 | 52 | 20 |
| 5 YEAR AVG. | 9.24 | 0.12 | 52 | 9 |
| 10 YEAR AVG. | - | | | |
| 15 YEAR AVG. | - | | | |

| | ALPHA | BETA | R² | STD. DEV. |
|---|---|---|---|---|
| | 0.3 | 0.79 | 92 | 1.04 |
| PERCENTILE ALL | 16 | 45 | 20 | 74 |
| RANK OBJ. | 15 | 69 | 47 | 71 |

Percentile Ranks: 1 = Highest; 100 = Lowest
Listed M-Star Risk: 1 = Lowest; 100 = Highest

## HISTORY

| | 1979 | 1980 | 1981 | 1982 | 1983 | 1984 | 1985 | 1986 | 1987 | 1988 | 1989 | 1990 | 09/91 |
|---|---|---|---|---|---|---|---|---|---|---|---|---|---|
| N.A.V. | ... | ... | ... | ... | ... | 12.22 | 12.26 | 12.36 | 11.54 | 11.22 | 11.52 | 11.37 | 11.52 |
| TOTAL RETURN % | ... | ... | ... | ... | ... | ... | 13.20 | 13.37 | 4.16 | 7.37 | 13.31 | 8.97 | 9.06 |
| +/- LB GOVT./CP. | ... | ... | ... | ... | ... | ... | -8.10 | -2.24 | -0.21 | -0.92 | -0.92 | 0.68 | -1.18 |
| TOT. RTN/ALL FUNDS | ... | ... | ... | ... | ... | ... | 94 | 63 | 32 | 78 | 68 | 8 | 79 |
| % RANK/ OBJECTIVE | ... | ... | ... | ... | ... | ... | 95 | 30 | 6 | 32 | 25 | 35 | 54 |
| INCOME | ... | ... | ... | ... | ... | 0.30 | 1.17 | 1.20 | 1.16 | 1.14 | 1.11 | 1.11 | 0.83 |
| CAPITAL GAIN | ... | ... | ... | ... | ... | 0.12 | 0.28 | 0.25 | 0.14 | 0.00 | 0.00 | 0.00 | 0.00 |
| EXPENSE % | ... | ... | ... | ... | ... | ... | 0.28 | 1.46 | 1.41 | 1.85 | 2.33 | 2.41 | 2.11 |
| INCOME % | ... | ... | ... | ... | ... | ... | 1.74 | 9.40 | 9.63 | 9.82 | 10.02 | 9.86 | 9.79 |
| TURNOVER % | ... | ... | ... | ... | ... | ... | 10.12 | 37 | 36 | 53 | 25 | 22 | ... |
| NET ASSETS ($MIL) | ... | ... | ... | ... | ... | 63.4 | 250.3 | 415.0 | 375.5 | 321.7 | 296.9 | 279.8 | 283.8 |

| | M-STAR RISK % RANK ALL / OBJ. | | MORNINGSTAR RETURN 100 + FIXED-INCOME AVG | RISK | MORNINGSTAR RISK-ADJUSTED RATING |
|---|---|---|---|---|---|
| 3 YEAR | 6 | 30 | 1.05 | 0.77 → | ★★★★ |
| 5 YEAR | 3 | 9 | 1.09 | 0.71 → | ★★★★★ |
| 10 YEAR | ... | ... | ... | ... | ★★★★★ |
| WEIGHTED AVG. | | | 1.08 | 0.73 | |

## PORTFOLIO

| | | TOTAL # SECURITIES: 70 | TOP 30 SECURITIES AS OF: 06/30/91 | |
|---|---|---|---|---|
| **AMOUNT $000** | **SECURITY** | **MATURITY** | **VALUE $000** | **% NET ASSETS** |
| 34545 | US TREASURY BOND 12% | 08/15/13 | 44952 | 15.83 |
| 23213 | FHLMC 13.5% | 2015 | 25943 | 9.14 |
| 14229 | FHLMC 6.5% | 2010 | 13138 | 4.63 |
| 13916 | FNMA 6.5% | 2017 | 12869 | 4.53 |
| 11386 | FHLMC 12.5% | 04/15/14 | 12613 | 4.44 |
| 12612 | FHLMC 7% | 2017 | 11857 | 4.18 |
| 9307 | FNMA 12.5% | 2016 | 10385 | 3.66 |
| 10525 | FHLMC 7.5% | 2009 | 10071 | 3.55 |
| 8038 | FNMA 13.5% | 2015 | 9050 | 3.19 |
| 7509 | FNMA 13% | 2015 | 8428 | 2.97 |
| 8939 | FNMA 6% | 2004 | 8284 | 2.92 |
| 8252 | FHLMC 6.75% | 2011 | 7724 | 2.72 |
| 6911 | FHLMC 13% | 2019 | 7701 | 2.71 |
| 5761 | FNMA 14.75% | 08/01/12 | 6626 | 2.33 |
| 5497 | FHLMC 14% | 04/01/16 | 6172 | 2.17 |
| 5843 | FHLMC 5.5% | 2011 | 5396 | 1.90 |
| 4434 | FHLMC 12.75% | 06/15/15 | 4931 | 1.74 |
| 4907 | FHLMC 7.25% | 2003 | 4658 | 1.64 |
| 5016 | FNMA 6.75% | 2008 | 4644 | 1.64 |
| 4987 | FNMA 6.25% | 2007 | 4558 | 1.61 |
| 3713 | FNMA 12.75% | 2014 | 4126 | 1.45 |
| 3437 | FHLMC 13.25% | 2019 | 3858 | 1.36 |
| 4190 | FHLMC 6% | 2013 | 3846 | 1.35 |
| 3193 | FNMA 13.25% | 2014 | 3586 | 1.26 |
| 3799 | FNMA 5.5% | 2006 | 3536 | 1.25 |
| 3070 | FHLMC 15% | 2013 | 3514 | 1.24 |
| 3435 | FHLMC 8% | 2008 | 3335 | 1.17 |
| 2798 | FNMA 14% | 11/01/04 | 3164 | 1.11 |
| 3220 | FNMA 7% | 2009 | 2996 | 1.06 |
| 2992 | FHLMC 8.5% | 2008 | 2959 | 1.04 |

### PORTFOLIO STATISTICS

| | |
|---|---|
| AVG. WEIGHTED MATURITY | 14.1 YEARS |
| AVG. WEIGHTED COUPON | 10.5 % |
| AVG. WEIGHTED PRICE | 108 % OF PAR |

### COMPOSITION % 06/30/91

| | | | |
|---|---|---|---|
| CASH | -8.6 | PREFERREDS | 0.0 |
| STOCKS | 0.0 | CONVERTIBLES | 0.0 |
| BONDS | 108.6 | OTHER | 0.0 |

### COUPON RANGE

| | % BONDS | REL. OBJ. |
|---|---|---|
| 0% | 0.2 | 0.0 |
| 0% to 8% | 37.9 | 3.1 |
| 8% to 9% | 2.1 | 0.1 |
| 9% to 10% | 0.4 | 0.0 |
| over 10% | 59.5 | 2.5 |

### CREDIT ANALYSIS 06/30/91

| | |
|---|---|
| US T-Bonds | 15 |
| US T-Notes | |
| GNMAs | 2 |
| FNMAs | 31 |
| FHLMCs | 49 |
| Other | 4 |

Percentage of Net Assets 0 20 40 60 80 100

## ANALYSIS

Amy C. Arnott    10/18/91

Move over, Frank Sinatra: Eaton Vance Government Obligations Trust really does do things its way.

For one, the fund is one of the few flexibly chartered government funds to heavily favor mortgage-backed securities. Even within that realm, the fund is unique because it doesn't buy ever-popular GNMAs, but favors FHLMCs and FNMAs.

This nonconformity stems in part from manager Mark Venezia's desire for extra yield; these issues typically offer higher payouts than do Ginnies. Venezia attempts to give the fund a boost by barbelling holdings around inefficiently priced mortgage-backeds, with low coupons of 0.25% to 8.75% on one side, and highs of 12.5% to 16.25% on the other. Only a tiny fraction of the portfolio is in the intermediate range, because Venezia finds that these tend to be too sensitive to prepayments.

Interestingly, even the portfolio's premium side has proven resistant to interest-rate-induced prepayments. Anyone with a 13% or 14% mortgage after years of declining rates, contends Venezia, is unlikely to suddenly refinance. Prepayments, therefore, have remained at a relatively constant and predictable level.

In order to further enhance yield, the fund is now borrowing at a level equal to about 11% of net assets, using this technique to purchase more mortgage-backeds. The fund, however, does incur interest charges from this leveraging. That's the culprit in the fund's high expense ratio; without interest charges, expenses would be on par with the average fund in the government group.

Despite this handicap, the fund moves into the elite, 5-star corps this issue. Returns have landed in the top half of the category for five straight years. Moreover, the fund's risk profile is pleasantly low.

## OPERATIONS

**ADDRESS** 24 Federal Street
Boston, MA 02110
**ADVISOR** Eaton Vance Management
**DISTRIBUTOR** Eaton Vance Distributors
**PORTFOLIO MANAGER** Mark S. Venezia (1984)
**MANAGEMENT FEE** 0.75% flat fee
**FEES** 4.75%L, 0.25%B
**TICKER** EVGOX

**TELEPHONE NUMBER** 617-482-8260
800-225-6265
**PHONE SWITCH** Yes
**# OF SHAREHOLDERS** N/A
**MINIMUM INITIAL PURCHASE** 1000
**MINIMUM SUBSEQUENT PURCHASE** 50
**DATE OF INCEPTION** 08/24/84
**SHAREHOLDER REPORT RATING** D

# Fidelity Magellan

| OBJECTIVE | LOAD % | YIELD % | ASSETS($MIL) | N.A.V. |
|---|---|---|---|---|
| Growth | 3.00 | 1.5 | 17276. | 69.40 |

Fidelity Magellan Fund seeks capital appreciation. The fund invests primarily in common stocks and convertible securities; up to 20% of its assets may be invested in debt securities of all types and qualities. The fund features domestic corporations operating primarily in the United States, domestic corporations that have significant activities and interests outside the U.S., and foreign companies. There is no limitation on total foreign investment, but no more than 40% of fund assets will be invested in companies operating exclusively in one foreign country.

Fund shares were not publicly sold until 1981.

| TOP LINE: | RETURN | RISK |
|---|---|---|
| Adjusted NAV | High | Average |
| BOTTOM LINE: | RATING |  |
| Relative Strength | ★ ★ ★ ★ |  |
|  | Highest |  |

## TOTAL RETURN %

|  | 1st Qtr. | 2nd Qtr. | 3rd Qtr. | 4th Qtr. | TOTAL |
|---|---|---|---|---|---|
| 1987 | 22.94 | 2.56 | 6.42 | -24.73 | 1.00 |
| 1988 | 9.98 | 8.46 | 0.23 | 2.69 | 22.76 |
| 1989 | 9.52 | 9.61 | 13.16 | -0.93 | 34.58 |
| 1990 | -2.09 | 6.61 | -16.46 | 9.51 | -4.51 |
| 1991 | 20.23 | -0.14 | 9.06 | --- | --- |

## INCOME

|  |  |  |  |  | TOTAL |
|---|---|---|---|---|---|
| 1989 | 0.00 | 0.09 | 0.00 | 1.15 | 1.24 |
| 1990 | 0.00 | 0.30 | 0.00 | 0.53 | 0.83 |
| 1991 | 0.00 | 0.53 | 0.00 | 0.00 | 0.53 |

## CAPITAL GAINS

|  |  |  |  |  | TOTAL |
|---|---|---|---|---|---|
| 1989 | 0.00 | 0.79 | 0.00 | 3.03 | 3.82 |
| 1990 | 0.00 | 1.93 | 0.00 | 0.49 | 2.42 |
| 1991 | 0.00 | 1.48 | 0.00 | 0.00 | 1.48 |

## PERFORMANCE/RISK                     10/31/91

|  | TOTAL RETURN % | +/- S&P 500 | PERCENTILE RANK ALL | PERCENTILE RANK OBJ. |
|---|---|---|---|---|
| 3 MONTH | 4.06 | 2.08 | 46 | 44 |
| 6 MONTH | 9.96 | 3.76 | 17 | 32 |
| 1 YEAR | 47.17 | 13.73 | 13 | 27 |
| 3 YEAR AVG. | 19.71 | 3.73 | 7 | 19 |
| 5 YEAR AVG. | 16.04 | 2.27 | 7 | 14 |
| 10 YEAR AVG. | 23.08 | 6.16 | 1 | 2 |
| 15 YEAR AVG. | 27.65 | 13.55 | 1 | 1 |

|  | ALPHA | BETA | R² | STD. DEV. |
|---|---|---|---|---|
|  | 2.8 | 1.08 | 95 | 4.58 |
| PERCENTILE ALL | 9 | 16 | 7 | 22 |
| RANK OBJ. | 21 | 33 | 9 | 43 |

Percentile Ranks: 1 = Highest, 100 = Lowest
Except M-Star Risk: 1 = Lowest, 100 = Highest

## HISTORY

|  | 1979 | 1980 | 1981 | 1982 | 1983 | 1984 | 1985 | 1986 | 1987 | 1988 | 1989 | 1990 | 10/91 |
|---|---|---|---|---|---|---|---|---|---|---|---|---|---|
| N.A.V. | 16.30 | 26.83 | 20.76 | 28.50 | 37.33 | 33.69 | 45.21 | 48.69 | 40.10 | 48.32 | 59.85 | 53.93 | 69.40 |
| TOTAL RETURN % | 51.71 | 69.91 | 16.45 | 48.06 | 38.59 | 2.03 | 43.11 | 23.74 | 1.00 | 22.76 | 34.58 | -4.51 | 32.70 |
| +/- S & P 500 INDEX | 33.42 | 37.69 | 21.53 | 26.60 | 16.12 | -4.10 | 11.47 | 5.12 | -4.22 | 6.25 | 2.91 | -1.41 | 10.62 |
| TOT. RTN/ALL FUNDS | 7 | 5 | 4 | 5 | 4 | 59 | 4 | 9 | 49 | 9 | 17 | 67 | 13 |
| % RANK OBJECTIVE | 7 | 5 | 4 | 5 | 4 | 29 | 2 | 7 | 59 | 14 | 17 | 46 | 25 |
| INCOME | 0.17 | 0.39 | 0.58 | 0.33 | 0.26 | 0.37 | 0.65 | 0.46 | 0.72 | 0.90 | 1.24 | 0.83 | 0.53 |
| CAPITAL GAIN | 0.00 | 0.13 | 9.92 | 1.23 | 1.88 | 3.69 | 1.78 | 6.84 | 9.02 | 0.00 | 3.82 | 2.42 | 1.48 |
| EXPENSE % | 1.52 | 1.40 | 1.23 | 1.34 | 0.85 | 1.04 | 1.12 | 1.08 | 1.08 | 1.14 | 1.08 | 1.03 | 1.06 |
| INCOME % | 1.49 | 2.77 | 2.08 | 2.39 | 2.56 | 1.47 | 2.79 | 1.95 | 1.18 | 1.33 | 2.13 | 2.54 | 2.47 |
| TURNOVER % | 249 | 338 | 277 | 194 | 120 | 85 | 126 | 96 | 96 | 101 | 87 | 82 | 135 |
| NET ASSETS ($MIL) | 35.1 | 53.5 | 107.2 | 458.4 | 1606.9 | 1954.3 | 4136.0 | 7405.5 | 7800.1 | 8971.3 | 12699. | 12325. | 17276. |

NET ASSETS ($MIL): 16000 / 8000 / 0

|  | M-STAR RISK % RANK | | MORNINGSTAR RETURN RISK | | MORNINGSTAR RISK-ADJUSTED RATING |
|---|---|---|---|---|---|
|  | ALL | OBJ. | 1.00 = EQUITY AVG. | |  |
| 3 YEAR | 68 | 32 | 1.48 | 0.85 ↑ | ★★★★ |
| 5 YEAR | 71 | 43 | 1.44 | 0.91 ↑ | ★★★★★ |
| 10 YEAR | 61 | 29 | 1.61 | 0.88 ↑ | ★★★★★ |
| WEIGHTED AVG. |  |  | 1.53 | 0.89 | ★★★★★ |

## PORTFOLIO

**TOTAL # STOCKS 665** — **TOP 30 EQUITY HOLDINGS AS OF: 09/30/91**

| SHARE CHANGE | AMOUNT | STOCK | VALUE $000 | % NET ASSETS |
|---|---|---|---|---|
| -191100 | 14092600 | FNMA | 916019 | 5.29 |
| 1236400 | 10843900 | PHILIP MORRIS | 780761 | 4.51 |
| 424700 | 3909633 | EM | 405136 | 2.34 |
| -1127600 | 5383000 | GENERAL ELECTRIC | 373446 | 2.16 |
| 2390100 | 4656100 | PFIZER | 303229 | 1.75 |
| 4543500 | 4543500 | SCHERING-PLOUGH | 255004 | 1.47 |
| 142700 | 2975400 | BRISTOL-MYERS SQUIBB | 246214 | 1.42 |
| 332580 | 3005730 | NATIONALE ELF AQUITAINE | 215092 | 1.24 |
| 1350400 | 3187900 | AMERICAN CYANAMID | 209206 | 1.21 |
| 191500 | 2220700 | ROYAL DUTCH PETROLEUM | 179599 | 1.04 |
| 1068300 | 2017700 | MICROSOFT | 179575 | 1.04 |
| 410100 | 1604400 | FHLMC | 167860 | 0.97 |
| 4174100 | 4174100 | SEARS ROEBUCK | 160703 | 0.93 |
| 4082700 | 6923800 | NATIONAL MEDICAL ENTERPRISES | 147996 | 0.86 |
| 29272100 | 3815900 | TELEFONOS DE MEXICO CL L | 141665 | 0.82 |
| 2104400 | 3421000 | CIRCUS CIRCUS ENTERPRISES | 133419 | 0.77 |
| 204400 | 2037300 | HOUSEHOLD INTERNATIONAL | 119691 | 0.69 |
| -1481200 | 3364000 | PRIMERICA | 119422 | 0.69 |
| 1400200 | 2060600 | AMGEN | 113848 | 0.66 |
| -569500 | 1779700 | TEXACO | 111899 | 0.65 |
| -429900 | 3368600 | REEBOK INTERNATIONAL | 111164 | 0.64 |
| 354700 | 1147700 | THE LIMITED | 107322 | 0.62 |
| 1089100 | 1384100 | NYNEX | 105036 | 0.61 |
| 1106900 | 1828400 | ITT | 100562 | 0.58 |
| 37500 | 843100 | IMCERA GROUP | 95481 | 0.55 |
| 1559400 | 2280000 | K MART | 95475 | 0.55 |
| 220200 | 3100000 | FORD MOTOR | 93000 | 0.54 |
| 1244700 | 2323200 | HOUSTON INDUSTRIES | 92347 | 0.53 |
| 801500 | 801500 | WALT DISNEY | 91371 | 0.53 |
| -466184 | 2726625 | KEMPER | 91342 | 0.53 |

### PORTFOLIO STATISTICS | 10/31/91

| | PORT-FOLIO AVG. | % OF STOCKS | REL S&P 500 |
|---|---|---|---|
| PRICE/EARNINGS RATIO | 17.8 | 80 | 0.97 |
| PRICE/BOOK RATIO | 3.6 | 92 | 0.99 |
| 5 YR. EARN. GR. % | 15.5 | 59 | 1.58 |
| RETURN ON ASSETS | 6.6 | 81 | 0.87 |
| DEBT % TOTAL CAP. | 37.5 | 81 | 1.18 |
| MED. MKT. CAP. ($MIL) | 4582 | 95 | 0.43 |

**COMPOSITION %** — 09/30/91

| CASH | 3.0 | PREFERREDS | 0.0 |
|---|---|---|---|
| STOCKS | 96.5 | CONVERTIBLES | 0.0 |
| BONDS | 0.5 | OTHER | 0.0 |

### SECTOR WEIGHTINGS

| | PORT-FOLIO % | REL S&P 500 |
|---|---|---|
| NATURAL RESOURCES | 14.5 | 0.85 |
| INDUSTRIAL PRODUCTS | 13.0 | 1.21 |
| CONSUMER DURABLES | 7.1 | 1.14 |
| NON-DURABLES | 16.8 | 0.72 |
| RETAIL TRADE | 7.6 | 1.09 |
| SERVICES | 12.8 | 1.33 |
| UTILITIES | 6.9 | 0.50 |
| TRANSPORTATION | 2.9 | 1.52 |
| FINANCE | 16.8 | 2.08 |
| MULTI-INDUSTRY | 1.8 | 0.69 |

## ANALYSIS

John Rekenthaler — 11/29/91

If Fidelity Magellan Fund were permitted to issue junk bonds, it could buy any company on the stock market—or a few countries.

While the fund's size hardly qualifies as news, some things bear repeating: This fund is gigantic. Even without borrowing, it's big enough to swallow all the outstanding stocks of such S&P 500 giants as Sears, Texaco, or Disney. Or, to view it another way, the fund could buy up every nonFidelity entrant in our aggressive-growth and equity-income categories (which account for two thirds of our Issue One) and still receive change.

Such bulk should cause liquidity woes. Like Peter Lynch, though, current manager Morris Smith has been content to ease in and out of major positions, thereby mitigating the fund's effects on stock prices. Happily, Smith has also echoed Lynch in getting his stocks right the first time; with five of its six top year-start holdings scoring big gains, the fund's had the luxury of riding its winners.

That's not to say that the fund has been inactive. Since spring, its exposure to the cyclical computer-hardware and auto sectors has been cut, replaced by faster-growing services and retailers. Consequently, the portfolio's 5-year earnings-growth rate has jumped to 50% above the market's—a very Lynchlike figure, especially when coupled with average P/E and P/B multiples.

Don't be surprised if the fund checks in with a lower earnings-growth rate by next year, though. For one, Smith admits that he's bulked up on growth stocks recently (in both this fund and his previous charge, Fidelity OTC). "I own a lot more higher-P/E stocks" than in the past, he says. Should the economy improve, this trend could reverse. Also, Magellan can't help but to look more like the overall market as it further balloons. As its 1991 results show, however, the fund still retains plenty of its own identity despite its size. If you're in it, stay.

## OPERATIONS

ADDRESS 82 Devonshire Street
Boston, MA 02109
ADVISOR Fidelity Management & Research
DISTRIBUTOR Fidelity Distributors
PORTFOLIO MANAGER Morris J. Smith (1990)
MANAGEMENT FEE 0.30% flat fee+0.52%G+.2%P
FEES 3.00%L
TICKER FMAGX

TELEPHONE NUMBER 800-544-6666
PHONE SWITCH Yes
# OF SHAREHOLDERS N/A
MINIMUM INITIAL PURCHASE 2500
MINIMUM SUBSEQUENT PURCHASE 250
DATE OF INCEPTION 05/02/63
SHAREHOLDER REPORT RATING B-

# Franklin CA Tax-Free Inc

| OBJECTIVE | LOAD % | YIELD % | ASSETS($MIL) | N.A.V. |
|---|---|---|---|---|
| Muni General | 4.00 | 7.1 | 11775 | 7.07 |

Franklin California Tax-Free Income Fund seeks a high level of interest income exempt from federal and California income taxes.

The fund invests in securities rated BBB or better or in unrated securities that are judged to be comparable in quality. It may invest some of its assets in bonds subject to the alternative minimum tax.

The fund charges a load on reinvested income distributions. The effect of this load is reflected in calculations of the fund's total return.

Prior to July 1982, the fund was named Franklin Tax-Free Income Fund.

**RATING**

| | RETURN | RISK |
|---|---|---|
| | Average | Below Avg |
| RATING ★★★★ | Above Avg | |

TOP LINE: Adjusted N.A.V.
BOTTOM LINE: Relative Strength

## TOTAL RETURN %

| | 1st Qtr. | 2nd Qtr. | 3rd Qtr. | 4th Qtr. | TOTAL |
|---|---|---|---|---|---|
| 1987 | 3.20 | -4.81 | -2.12 | 3.16 | -0.80 |
| 1988 | 3.14 | 2.01 | 3.36 | 2.72 | 11.70 |
| 1989 | 0.36 | 5.48 | -0.38 | 2.84 | 8.45 |
| 1990 | 0.78 | 2.83 | -0.43 | 2.98 | 6.27 |
| 1991 | 2.20 | 2.11 | 3.69 | ... | ... |

## INCOME

| | | | | | TOTAL |
|---|---|---|---|---|---|
| 1989 | 0.13 | 0.13 | 0.13 | 0.13 | 0.52 |
| 1990 | 0.13 | 0.13 | 0.13 | 0.13 | 0.51 |
| 1991 | 0.13 | 0.13 | 0.13 | 0.12 | 0.42 |

## CAPITAL GAINS

| | | | | | TOTAL |
|---|---|---|---|---|---|
| 1989 | 0.00 | 0.00 | 0.00 | 0.00 | 0.00 |
| 1990 | 0.00 | 0.00 | 0.00 | 0.00 | 0.00 |
| 1991 | 0.00 | 0.00 | 0.00 | ... | 0.00 |

## PERFORMANCE/RISK  09/30/91

| | TOTAL RETURN % | +/- LB GVT./CP. | PERCENTILE RANK ALL | PERCENTILE RANK OBL. |
|---|---|---|---|---|
| 3 MONTH | 3.69 | -2.06 | 81 | 66 |
| 6 MONTH | 5.88 | -1.47 | 57 | 56 |
| 1 YEAR | 11.43 | -4.43 | 86 | 76 |
| 3 YEAR AVG. | 8.60 | -2.65 | 73 | 55 |
| 5 YEAR AVG. | 7.39 | -1.73 | 75 | 52 |
| 10 YEAR AVG. | 10.98 | -3.24 | 85 | 83 |
| 15 YEAR AVG. | ... | | | |

| | ALPHA | BETA | R² | STD. DEV. |
|---|---|---|---|---|
| | -0.9 | 0.59 | 61 | 0.96 |
| PERCENTILE / ALL | 45 | 75 | 75 | 81 |
| RANK - OBL. | 29 | 79 | 84 | 72 |

Percentile Ranks: 1 = Highest, 100 = Lowest; 100 = Highest
Except M-Star Risk: 1 = Lowest, 100 = Highest

## HISTORY

| | 1979 | 1980 | 1981 | 1982 | 1983 | 1984 | 1985 | 1986 | 1987 | 1988 | 1989 | 1990 | 09/91 |
|---|---|---|---|---|---|---|---|---|---|---|---|---|---|
| N.A.V. | 8.27 | 6.81 | 5.72 | 6.55 | 6.32 | 6.31 | 6.74 | 7.22 | 6.65 | 6.90 | 6.96 | 6.89 | 7.07 |
| TOTAL RETURN % | | -10.05 | -6.32 | 26.39 | 6.23 | 9.95 | 17.01 | 15.37 | -0.80 | 11.70 | 8.45 | 6.27 | |
| +/- LB GOVT./CP. | -4.01 | -13.11 | -13.58 | -4.70 | -1.76 | -5.07 | -4.30 | -0.24 | -3.10 | 4.12 | -5.79 | -2.02 | -2.03 |
| TOT. RTN./ALL FUNDS | 94 | 93 | 75 | 56 | 94 | 26 | 85 | 50 | 65 | 47 | 87 | 28 | 78 |
| % RANK OBJECTIVE | 59 | 26 | 32 | 83 | 90 | 20 | 74 | 76 | 46 | 38 | 78 | 47 | 47 |
| INCOME | 0.59 | 0.64 | 0.68 | 0.61 | 0.63 | 0.60 | 0.60 | 0.54 | 0.53 | 0.52 | 0.52 | 0.51 | 0.37 |
| CAPITAL GAIN | 0.00 | 0.00 | 0.00 | 0.00 | 0.00 | 0.00 | 0.00 | 0.00 | 0.00 | 0.00 | 0.00 | 0.00 | 0.00 |
| EXPENSE % | 1.00 | 1.00 | 0.63 | 0.95 | 0.75 | 0.55 | 0.52 | 0.51 | 0.50 | 0.48 | 0.49 | 0.49 | 0.48 |
| INCOME % | 6.53 | 7.87 | 4.51 | 9.73 | 7.61 | 9.39 | 9.50 | 8.62 | 7.38 | 7.60 | 7.53 | 7.29 | 7.22 |
| TURNOVER % | 118 | 73 | 90 | 65 | 10 | 24 | 26 | 12 | 9 | 23 | 33 | 11 | 16 |
| NET ASSETS ($MIL) | 2.6 | 2.1 | 31.5 | 396.2 | 1552.9 | 2108.1 | 3653.0 | 7667.2 | 7300.0 | 8434.0 | 10216 | 11149 | 11775. |

| M-STAR RISK % RANK | ALL | OBL. |
|---|---|---|
| 3 YEAR | 13 | 21 |
| 5 YEAR | 13 | 21 |
| 10 YEAR | 10 | 23 |

| | MORNINGSTAR RETURN (100 = MUNI AVG) | RISK | | MORNINGSTAR RISK-ADJUSTED RATING |
|---|---|---|---|---|
| 3 YEAR | 0.95 | 0.86 | ↑ | ★★★★ |
| 5 YEAR | 0.99 | 0.88 | ↑ | ★★★★ |
| 10 YEAR | 0.90 | 0.87 | ↑ | ★★★ |
| WEIGHTED AVG. | 0.94 | 0.87 | | ★★★★ |

## PORTFOLIO

| | | | TOTAL # SECURITIES | 1302 | TOP 30 SECURITIES AS OF | 03/31/91 |

| AMOUNT $000 | SECURITY | MATURITY | VALUE $000 | % NET ASSETS |
|---|---|---|---|---|
| 250995 | CA IRVINE RANCH REV WTR DIST AGCY 8.25% | 08/15/23 | 265741 | 2.32 |
| 221265 | CA IRVINE RANCH REV WTR DIST AGCY 7.875% | 02/15/23 | 227350 | 1.98 |
| 156760 | CA SACRAMENTO REV ELEC MUD RFDG 9% | 11/15/09 | 167575 | 1.46 |
| 134770 | CA REV POLL CNTRL FIN AUTH 8.875% | 01/01/10 | 147742 | 1.29 |
| 128715 | CA NORTH REV PUB PWR AGCY HYDROELEC 8% | 07/01/24 | 132737 | 1.16 |
| 121300 | CA REV PUB CAP IMPR FIN AUTH 8.5% | 03/01/18 | 129185 | 1.13 |
| 117800 | CA SOUTH REV TRANSMN PUB PWR AUTH 7.875% | 07/01/18 | 124132 | 1.08 |
| 125600 | CA STATE GO 6.4% | 02/01/06 | 123518 | 1.08 |
| 109675 | CA REV HSG FIN AUTH HOME MTG 7.6% | 08/01/30 | 111183 | 0.97 |
| 103000 | CA REV CCFC FIN AUTH 8.5% | 10/01/22 | 107893 | 0.94 |
| 103250 | CA REV UNIV PARKING SYS 7.8% | 09/01/16 | 104928 | 0.92 |
| 101030 | CA LOS ANGELES COP CONV/EXBTN CTR 7.375% | 08/15/18 | 102672 | 0.90 |
| 92315 | CA SAN JOSE COP PUB FAC FIN CONV 7.875% | 09/01/10 | 96469 | 0.84 |
| 87455 | CA SACRAMENTO REV ELEC MUD 7.875% | 08/15/16 | 90188 | 0.79 |
| 84400 | CA REV HSG FIN AUTH HOME MTG 8% | 08/01/29 | 86616 | 0.76 |
| 73550 | CA REV PUB CAP IMPR FIN AUTH 8.4% | 03/01/08 | 76331 | 0.68 |
| 75880 | CA VACAVILLE REV PUB FIN AUTH 8.65% | 09/02/18 | 77018 | 0.67 |
| 75000 | CA SAN BERNARDINO REV PUB CAP IMPR 8.3% | 09/02/19 | 74719 | 0.65 |
| 70000 | CA COP SPCL DIST FIN AUTH 8.5% | 07/01/18 | 74550 | 0.65 |
| 59200 | CA SAN DIEGO REV INDL DEV GAS & ELEC 10% | 06/01/18 | 64972 | 0.57 |

### SECTOR WEIGHTINGS

| | REL. PORT. MUNI % | PORT. AVG. % | | REL. PORT. MUNI % | PORT. AVG. % |
|---|---|---|---|---|---|
| GEN. OBL. | 4.66 | 0.55 | TRANS. R&R | 1.23 | 0.22 |
| UTILITY | 12.60 | 0.79 | TRANS. A&W | 1.19 | 0.25 |
| HEALTH | 4.84 | 0.28 | COP/LEASE | 17.30 | 4.03 |
| WTR./WASTE | 7.07 | 1.07 | PRIVATE | 12.06 | 1.01 |
| HOUSING | 15.45 | 1.75 | MISC. REV. | 10.94 | 2.34 |
| EDUCATION | 2.64 | 0.38 | UNASSIGNED | 10.01 | 2.17 |

### TOP 5 STATES

California 100.00

### PORTFOLIO STATISTICS

| | | | |
|---|---|---|---|
| AVG. WEIGHTED MATURITY | 23.1 YEARS | | |
| AVG. WEIGHTED COUPON | 7.93 % | | |
| AVG. WEIGHTED PRICE | 102 % OF PAR | | |

### COMPOSITION % 06/30/91

| | | | | | |
|---|---|---|---|---|---|
| CASH | 3.0 | PREFERREDS | 0.0 | | |
| STOCKS | 0.0 | CONVERTIBLES | 0.0 | | |
| BONDS | 97.0 | OTHER | 0.0 | | |

### COUPON RANGE

| | % BONDS | REL. OBL. |
|---|---|---|
| 0% | 1.6 | 0.5 |
| 0% to 6.8% | 4.9 | 0.2 |
| 6.8 to 7.5% | 14.8 | 0.6 |
| 7.5 to 8.3% | 55.6 | 2.3 |
| over 8.3% | 23.2 | 0.8 |

### CREDIT ANALYSIS   06/30/91

---

## ANALYSIS

| Franklin California Tax-Free Income Fund | Amy C. Arnott | 11/01/91 |

Franklin California Tax-Free Income Fund moves up to 4 stars this issue.

In our modified rating system, funds are now given credit for their state tax advantages. Thus, it's now somewhat easier for single-state funds to achieve Morningstar honors. Even so, this mammoth offering has emerged as one of the better California funds, particularly because of its low risk.

The fund has succeeded in part because it makes no attempt to predict interest-rate changes. Instead, it's generally stuck with current and higher coupons—a strategy that muffled gains in rally years like 1985, 1986, and 1989, but has provided big payouts and kept downside risk in check. Lately, though, the fund's beloved high coupons have been harder to come by. "We've had to lower our horizons due to lower interest rates," says manager Bernie Schroer. Thus, he's been adding bonds with considerably

more modest 6.5% and 6.25% coupons.

As a result, although the fund still has an above-average weighting in premium coupons, its performance hasn't been dampened too much by declining interest rates. Nor have tight quality spreads hurt the fund. Although Schroer has been looking to add better-quality and insured bonds, the fund's gargantuan size means that any changes will be slow in coming. Thus, the portfolio's credits still aren't all that high. As of June 30, nearly 20% of its net assets were unrated, mainly because of its large stake in real-estate-backed Mello-Roos bonds.

One final note: Because the fund charges a load on reinvested dividends (a charge reflected in our total-return calculations), we recommend that interested investors elect to take their income payments in cash. After all, throwing off cash is what this fund does best.

## OPERATIONS

| | | | |
|---|---|---|---|
| ADDRESS | 777 Mariners Island Boulevard | TELEPHONE NUMBER | 415-570-3000 |
| | San Mateo, CA 94404 | | 800-342-5236 |
| ADVISOR | Franklin Advisers | PHONE SWITCH | Yes |
| DISTRIBUTOR | Franklin Distributors | # OF SHAREHOLDERS | 198735 |
| PORTFOLIO MANAGER | Bernie Schroer (1987) | MINIMUM INITIAL PURCHASE | 100 |
| MANAGEMENT FEE | 0.63% max./0.40% min. | MINIMUM SUBSEQUENT PURCHASE | 25 |
| FEES | 4.00%L | DATE OF INCEPTION | 03/14/77 |
| TICKER | FKTFX | SHAREHOLDER REPORT RATING | D |

# Fund for U.S. Government Sec

| OBJECTIVE | LOAD % | YIELD % | ASSETS($MIL) | N.A.V. |
|---|---|---|---|---|
| Gvt General | 4.50 | 8.9 | 1180.6 | 8.57 |

Fund for U.S. Government Securities seeks current income.

The fund invests only in securities that are primary or direct obligations of the U.S. government or its instrumentalities or that are guaranteed by the U.S. government or its agencies or instrumentalities. The fund may enter into repurchase agreements regarding these securities.

The fund is part of the Liberty Account, a family of funds sponsored and offered by Federated Securities Corporation.

**TOP LINE:** Adjusted N.A.V
**BOTTOM LINE:** Relative Strength

| RETURN | RISK |
|---|---|
| Above Avg | Below Avg |

RATING ★★★★ Highest

NET ASSETS ($MIL): 1200 / 600 / 0

## TOTAL RETURN %

| | 1st Qtr. | 2nd Qtr. | 3rd Qtr. | 4th Qtr. | TOTAL |
|---|---|---|---|---|---|
| 1987 | 1.61 | 0.76 | -1.07 | 3.98 | 5.31 |
| 1988 | 3.85 | 1.27 | 1.86 | 0.32 | 7.47 |
| 1989 | 0.95 | 7.91 | 0.72 | 3.42 | 13.47 |
| 1990 | 0.17 | 3.12 | 2.00 | 4.09 | 9.67 |
| 1991 | 2.41 | 1.90 | 4.51 | ... | ... |

## INCOME

| | | | | | TOTAL |
|---|---|---|---|---|---|
| 1989 | 0.19 | 0.19 | 0.19 | 0.19 | 0.76 |
| 1990 | 0.19 | 0.19 | 0.20 | 0.20 | 0.78 |
| 1991 | 0.19 | 0.19 | 0.18 | ... | 0.56 |

## CAPITAL GAINS

| | | | | | TOTAL |
|---|---|---|---|---|---|
| 1989 | 0.00 | 0.00 | 0.00 | 0.00 | 0.00 |
| 1990 | 0.00 | 0.00 | 0.00 | 0.00 | 0.00 |
| 1991 | 0.00 | 0.00 | 0.00 | | 0.00 |

## PERFORMANCE/RISK
09/30/91

| | TOTAL RETURN% | +/-LB GVT./CP. | PERCENTILE RANK ALL | OBJ. |
|---|---|---|---|---|
| 3 MONTH | 4.51 | -1.24 | 70 | 88 |
| 6 MONTH | 6.50 | -0.85 | 46 | 71 |
| 1 YEAR | 13.52 | -2.34 | 80 | 81 |
| 3 YEAR AVG. | 10.83 | -0.42 | 51 | 13 |
| 5 YEAR AVG. | 9.46 | 0.34 | 50 | 3 |
| 10 YEAR AVG. | 14.62 | 0.40 | 45 | 17 |
| 15 YEAR AVG. | 8.91 | -1.23 | 93 | 50 |

| | ALPHA | BETA | R² | STD. DEV. |
|---|---|---|---|---|
| | 0.4 | 0.77 | 91 | 1.03 |
| PERCENTILE { ALL | 13 | 47 | 25 | 75 |
| RANK { OBJ. | 10 | 71 | 61 | 74 |

Percentile Ranks: 1 = Highest, 100 = Lowest
Except M-Star Risk: 1 = Lowest, 100 = Highest

## HISTORY

| | 1979 | 1980 | 1981 | 1982 | 1983 | 1984 | 1985 | 1986 | 1987 | 1988 | 1989 | 1990 | 09/91 |
|---|---|---|---|---|---|---|---|---|---|---|---|---|---|
| N.A.V. | 8.40 | 7.39 | 6.53 | 8.36 | 8.43 | 8.44 | 8.77 | 8.62 | 8.29 | 8.12 | 8.41 | 8.40 | 8.57 |
| TOTAL RETURN % | 1.18 | -3.55 | -1.73 | 41.91 | 11.08 | 12.76 | 16.68 | 8.51 | 5.31 | 7.47 | 13.47 | 9.67 | 9.06 |
| +/-LB GOVT./CP. | -1.12 | -6.61 | -8.99 | 10.82 | 3.09 | -2.26 | -4.63 | -7.11 | 3.01 | -0.11 | -0.77 | 1.38 | -1.18 |
| TOT. RTN/ALL FUNDS | 87 | 92 | 59 | 11 | 74 | 13 | 89 | 87 | 26 | 78 | 67 | 6 | 79 |
| % RANK/OBJECTIVE | 75 | 100 | 80 | 17 | 15 | 58 | 73 | 97 | 3 | 30 | 20 | 18 | 52 |
| INCOME | 0.72 | 0.72 | 0.73 | 0.75 | 0.82 | 0.98 | 1.00 | 0.86 | 0.77 | 0.77 | 0.76 | 0.78 | 0.56 |
| CAPITAL GAIN | 0.00 | 0.00 | 0.00 | 0.00 | 0.00 | 0.00 | 0.00 | 0.00 | 0.00 | 0.00 | 0.00 | 0.00 | 0.00 |
| EXPENSE % | 1.05 | 1.16 | 1.39 | 1.50 | 1.29 | 1.15 | 0.89 | 0.91 | 0.95 | 0.96 | 0.96 | 0.96 | 0.97 |
| INCOME % | 7.70 | 8.58 | 9.74 | 11.23 | 9.48 | 11.16 | 12.11 | 10.51 | 9.24 | 9.31 | 9.22 | 9.32 | 9.21 |
| TURNOVER % | 0 | 8 | 3 | 3 | 90 | 117 | 121 | 179 | 135 | 72 | 83 | 98 | 27 |
| NET ASSETS ($MIL) | 84.6 | 71.1 | 52.9 | 50.3 | 54.9 | 47.9 | 156.9 | 1107.6 | 1103.9 | 1112.3 | 1058.0 | 1090.0 | 1180.6 |

| M-STAR RISK % RANK | ALL | OBJ. | MORNINGSTAR RETURN | RISK | MORNINGSTAR RISK-ADJUSTED RATING |
|---|---|---|---|---|---|
| | | | 100 = FIXED-INCOME AVG | | |
| 3 YEAR | 5 | 20 | 1.06 | 0.73 ↑ | ★★★★ |
| 5 YEAR | 3 | 6 | 1.12 | 0.65 ↑ | ★★★★★ |
| 10 YEAR | 4 | 34 | 1.08 | 0.82 ↑ | ★★★★★ |
| WEIGHTED AVG. | | | 1.09 | 0.75 | ★★★★★ |

## PORTFOLIO

TOTAL # SECURITIES: 40    TOP 30 SECURITIES AS OF: 03/28/91

| AMOUNT $000 | SECURITY | MATURITY | VALUE $000 | % NET ASSETS |
|---|---|---|---|---|
| 188400 | US TREASURY NOTE 12.625% | 08/15/94 | 216777 | 19.13 |
| 96079 | GNMA 10.5% | 09/15/19 | 101754 | 8.98 |
| 81105 | GNMA 10% | 10/15/19 | 84915 | 7.50 |
| 51100 | US TREASURY BOND 12.625% | 05/15/95 | 59798 | 5.28 |
| 58300 | GNMA 9.5% | 11/15/19 | 59630 | 5.26 |
| 49840 | FHLMC 11% | 05/01/19 | 52931 | 4.67 |
| 38566 | FHLMC 12.5% | 12/01/15 | 42495 | 3.75 |
| 38600 | US TREASURY NOTE 7.5% | 02/15/01 | 37816 | 3.34 |
| 31600 | US TREASURY NOTE 11.625% | 11/15/94 | 35639 | 3.15 |
| 30704 | FNMA 11% | 01/01/16 | 32816 | 2.90 |
| 28000 | US TREASURY NOTE 8.5% | 09/30/94 | 28875 | 2.55 |
| 20719 | FNMA 9% | 07/01/01 | 20982 | 1.85 |
| 19077 | FHLMC 12% | 07/01/19 | 20841 | 1.84 |
| 20000 | US TREASURY NOTE 7.875% | 02/15/96 | 20087 | 1.77 |
| 20000 | US TREASURY NOTE 0% | 02/29/96 | 19837 | 1.75 |
| 18367 | FHLMC 11.5% | 05/01/19 | 19738 | 1.74 |
| 16916 | GNMA 12% | 07/20/15 | 18898 | 1.67 |
| 17600 | FHLMC 9.2% | 10/15/20 | 17733 | 1.57 |
| 16900 | FNMA 8.75% | 02/25/17 | 16837 | 1.49 |
| 14614 | GNMA 11.5% | 01/15/16 | 16075 | 1.42 |
| 14466 | FNMA 12% | 01/01/16 | 15827 | 1.40 |
| 13732 | FNMA 11.5% | 01/01/16 | 14990 | 1.32 |
| 13300 | FHLMC 9.5% | 06/15/20 | 13505 | 1.19 |
| 12528 | GNMA 11% | 02/15/16 | 13487 | 1.19 |
| 9272 | FNMA 13% | 06/01/15 | 10027 | 0.89 |
| 10000 | FHLMC 9% | 09/15/20 | 9966 | 0.88 |
| 8866 | FNMA 12.5% | 01/01/16 | 9814 | 0.87 |
| 9546 | ML TR-CMO 9% | 03/20/15 | 9595 | 0.85 |
| 7630 | FNMA 9.3% | 01/25/19 | 7778 | 0.69 |
| 6785 | GNMA 12.5% | 05/15/15 | 7650 | 0.68 |

### PORTFOLIO STATISTICS

| | |
|---|---|
| AVG. WEIGHTED MATURITY | 8.5 YEARS |
| AVG. WEIGHTED COUPON | 10.8% |
| AVG. WEIGHTED PRICE | 108% OF PAR |

### COMPOSITION % 06/30/91

| | | | |
|---|---|---|---|
| CASH | 1.7 | PREFERREDS | 0.0 |
| STOCKS | 0.0 | CONVERTIBLES | 0.0 |
| BONDS | 98.3 | OTHER | 0.0 |

### COUPON RANGE

| | % BONDS | REL. OBJ. |
|---|---|---|
| 0% | 1.8 | 0.4 |
| 0% to 8% | 5.4 | 0.4 |
| 8% to 9% | 8.6 | 0.3 |
| 9% to 10% | 18.2 | 0.8 |
| over 10% | 66.0 | 2.8 |

### CREDIT ANALYSIS 03/28/91

| Category | Percentage of Net Assets |
|---|---|
| US T-Bonds | 6 |
| US T-Notes | 32 |
| GNMA | 27 |
| FNMA | 19 |
| FHLMC | 17 |
| Other | 6 |

## ANALYSIS

Jennifer Strickland   10/18/91

They don't make government funds as a whole lot better than Fund for U.S. Government Securities.

Managed conservatively by Gary Madich over the past five years, this fund has consistently produced respectable returns and fine, low-risk ratings. In addition, the fund also is available at a small minimum initial purchase. This is good news to smaller investors, considering that several of Madich's top-rated funds are designed solely for institutional investors.

Except for its fee structure, there's nothing small-time about this fund. Its mix of Treasuries and mortgage securities offers quite a hefty payout. (To date, his older, higher-yielding Treasuries, at one third of assets, have kicked in a good part of this payout, as have a collection of seasoned, large-coupon mortgages.) And to Madich's credit, he has maintained this yield while preserving the fund's NAV; while favoring premiums, he has never let his taste for income hamper the fund's total returns.

Accompanying the fund's high yield is low volatility. Madich insists on a short duration (currently around 3.9 years). To land on the short end of the yield curve, he holds a core of high-coupon mortgages and a few call-protected CMOs, as well as the occasional short Treasury. While this tactic might not seem well suited for bond-market rallies—it certainly wasn't in this year's third quarter—Madich typically has spiced up the fund's bull-market returns through timely purchases of a few long bonds.

We can't recommend this fund highly enough to retail investors. While neither its initial load nor its expenses are especially low, the fund is among the few government vehicles to blend a high-paying/low-risk approach with excellent long-term returns. As indicated by the fund's 5-star rating, that's a winning package.

## OPERATIONS

| | |
|---|---|
| ADDRESS | Liberty Center Federated Inv. Tower Pittsburgh, PA 15222 |
| ADVISOR | Federated Advisers |
| DISTRIBUTOR | Federated Securities |
| PORTFOLIO MANAGER | Gary J. Madich (1986) |
| MANAGEMENT FEE | 0.25% max./0.20% min. +4.5%I |
| FEES | 4.50%L |
| TICKER | FUSGX |

| | |
|---|---|
| TELEPHONE NUMBER | 412-288-1900 / 800-245-5051 |
| PHONE SWITCH | Yes |
| # OF SHAREHOLDERS | 81765 |
| MINIMUM INITIAL PURCHASE | 500 |
| MINIMUM SUBSEQUENT PURCHASE | 100 |
| DATE OF INCEPTION | 10/06/69 |
| SHAREHOLDER REPORT RATING | C |

# Growth Fund of America

| OBJECTIVE | LOAD % | YIELD % | ASSETS($Mil) | N.A.V. |
|---|---|---|---|---|
| Growth | 5.75 | 2.0 | 2954.9 | 22.99 |

Growth Fund of America seeks growth of capital. The realization of current income will not be a consideration.

The fund invests primarily in common stocks, but convertible securities that meet the fund's objective may also be purchased. The fund may invest in a wide range of companies, including growing and profitable companies, turnaround situations, and unseasoned companies.

| TOP LINE: | RETURN | RISK |
|---|---|---|
| Adjusted N.A.V. | Above Avg | Average |
| BOTTOM LINE: | RATING | |
| Relative Strength | ★★★ | |
| | Neutral | |

## TOTAL RETURN %

| | 1st Qtr. | 2nd Qtr. | 3rd Qtr. | 4th Qtr. | TOTAL |
|---|---|---|---|---|---|
| 1987 | 21.76 | 3.02 | 5.91 | -18.71 | 8.00 |
| 1988 | 10.60 | 7.32 | -1.57 | 1.39 | 18.46 |
| 1989 | 9.77 | 10.67 | 10.01 | -2.68 | 30.06 |
| 1990 | -1.34 | 6.28 | -17.64 | 11.01 | -4.12 |
| 1991 | 19.37 | -3.16 | 7.11 | ... | ... |

### INCOME

| | | | | | TOTAL |
|---|---|---|---|---|---|
| 1989 | 0.00 | 0.00 | 0.00 | 0.61 | 0.61 |
| 1990 | 0.00 | 0.00 | 0.00 | 0.48 | 0.48 |
| 1991 | 0.00 | 0.00 | 0.00 | 0.00 | 0.00 |

### CAPITAL GAINS

| | | | | | TOTAL |
|---|---|---|---|---|---|
| 1989 | 0.00 | 0.00 | 0.00 | 1.99 | 1.99 |
| 1990 | 0.00 | 0.00 | 0.00 | 0.82 | 0.82 |
| 1991 | 0.00 | 0.00 | 0.00 | 0.00 | 0.00 |

## PERFORMANCE/RISK

10/31/91

| | TOTAL RETURN % | +/- S&P 500 | PERCENTILE RANK ALL | RANK OBJ. |
|---|---|---|---|---|
| 3 MONTH | 4.17 | 2.19 | 44 | 43 |
| 6 MONTH | 6.78 | 0.57 | 44 | 57 |
| 1 YEAR | 44.03 | 10.59 | 15 | 34 |
| 3 YEAR AVG. | 17.51 | 1.53 | 11 | 30 |
| 5 YEAR AVG. | 15.17 | 1.40 | 8 | 16 |
| 10 YEAR AVG. | 16.56 | -0.36 | 16 | 28 |
| 15 YEAR AVG. | 20.21 | 6.11 | 5 | 11 |

| | ALPHA | BETA | R² | STD. DEV. |
|---|---|---|---|---|
| | 1.1 | 1.06 | 87 | 4.69 |
| PERCENTILE f ALL | 16 | 18 | 29 | 20 |
| RANK f OBJ. | 31 | 37 | 48 | 39 |

Percentile Ranks: 1 = Highest, 100 = Lowest
Except M-Star Risk: 1 = Lowest, 100 = Highest

## HISTORY

| | 1979 | 1980 | 1981 | 1982 | 1983 | 1984 | 1985 | 1986 | 1987 | 1988 | 1989 | 1990 | 10/91 |
|---|---|---|---|---|---|---|---|---|---|---|---|---|---|
| N.A.V. | 7.21 | 9.92 | 9.47 | 11.23 | 13.58 | 12.41 | 14.51 | 15.76 | 15.56 | 17.51 | 20.17 | 18.02 | 22.99 |
| TOTAL RETURN % | 45.77 | 39.89 | 0.66 | 25.08 | 27.11 | -5.58 | 27.08 | 16.16 | 8.00 | 18.46 | 30.06 | -4.12 | 27.58 |
| +/- S & P 500 INDEX | 27.47 | 7.67 | 5.75 | 3.62 | 4.64 | -11.71 | -4.57 | -2.47 | 2.78 | 1.95 | -1.61 | -1.02 | 5.50 |
| TOT. RTN./ALL FUNDS | 10 | 21 | 50 | 61 | 16 | 79 | 36 | 46 | 13 | 17 | 13 | 65 | 20 |
| % RANK OBJECTIVE | 15 | 42 | 42 | 56 | 21 | 66 | 64 | 39 | 18 | 34 | 34 | 43 | 43 |
| INCOME | 0.09 | 0.15 | 0.48 | 0.59 | 0.40 | 0.29 | 0.22 | 0.28 | 0.29 | 0.31 | 0.61 | 0.48 | 0.00 |
| CAPITAL GAIN | 0.00 | 0.00 | 0.00 | 0.00 | 0.27 | 0.11 | 0.87 | 0.79 | 1.10 | 0.59 | 1.99 | 0.82 | 0.00 |
| EXPENSE % | 1.02 | 0.85 | 0.76 | 0.76 | 0.68 | 0.68 | 0.69 | 0.66 | 0.66 | 0.71 | 0.78 | 0.79 | 0.83 |
| INCOME % | 1.62 | 2.19 | 5.07 | 6.89 | 3.85 | 2.57 | 1.66 | 1.84 | 1.50 | 1.56 | 2.82 | 2.67 | 2.13 |
| TURNOVER % | 18 | 15 | 40 | 33 | 26 | 23 | 24 | 24 | 20 | 18 | 30 | 18 | 19 |
| NET ASSETS ($Mil) | 79.2 | 106.5 | 143.4 | 197.5 | 383.0 | 507.9 | 603.0 | 791.9 | 957.9 | 1121.4 | 1806.9 | 2060.6 | 2954.9 |

| | M-STAR RISK % RANK ALL | OBJ. | MORNINGSTAR RETURN | RISK | 1.00 = EQUITY AVG. | MORNINGSTAR RISK-ADJUSTED RATING |
|---|---|---|---|---|---|---|
| 3 YEAR | 75 | 53 | 1.21 | 0.95 ↑ | | ★★★ |
| 5 YEAR | 75 | 53 | 1.30 | 0.94 ↑ | | ★★★★ |
| 10 YEAR | 70 | 46 | 1.13 | 0.95 ↑ | | ★★★ |
| WEIGHTED AVG. | | | 1.20 | 0.95 | | |

NET ASSETS: ($Mil) 3000 / 1500 / 0

## PORTFOLIO

**TOTAL # STOCKS** 109 | **TOP 30 EQUITY HOLDINGS AS OF** 09/30/91

| SHARE CHANGE | AMOUNT | STOCK | VALUE $000 | % NET ASSETS |
|---|---|---|---|---|
| 0 | 2563500 | FNMA | 166628 | 5.64 |
| 482000 | 1192000 | TIME WARNER | 99383 | 3.36 |
| 975000 | 2850000 | MCCAW CELLULAR COMM CL A | 81225 | 2.75 |
| 50000 | 1050000 | PHILIP MORRIS | 75600 | 2.56 |
| 100000 | 4850000 | TELE-COMMUNICATIONS CL A | 74569 | 2.52 |
| 900000 | 1350000 | AMGEN | 74250 | 2.51 |
| 0 | 580000 | EM | 60103 | 2.03 |
| 75000 | 915000 | AMR | 52498 | 1.78 |
| 125000 | 890000 | DIGITAL EQUIPMENT | 50174 | 1.70 |
| 175000 | 665000 | LIN BROADCASTING | 48878 | 1.65 |
| 125000 | 745000 | DELTA AIR LINES | 48425 | 1.64 |
| 80000 | 2500000 | NEWS | 43125 | 1.46 |
| 0 | 650000 | TEXACO | 40869 | 1.38 |
| 0 | 300000 | MERCK | 39038 | 1.32 |
| 250000 | 740000 | APPLE COMPUTER | 36445 | 1.23 |
| 100000 | 1260000 | MCI COMMUNICATIONS | 35595 | 1.20 |
| 21000 | 250000 | UAL | 31594 | 1.07 |
| 250000 | 850000 | WASTE MANAGEMENT | 31556 | 1.07 |
| 25000 | 525000 | PITNEY BOWES | 31434 | 1.06 |
| 0 | 812000 | A SCHULMAN | 30856 | 1.04 |
| 0 | 500000 | SLMA | 29938 | 1.00 |
| 200000 | 790000 | PARAMOUNT COMMUNICATIONS | 29428 | 1.00 |
| 275000 | 825000 | FEDERAL EXPRESS | 28875 | 0.98 |
| 575000 | 575000 | GLAXO | 28175 | 0.95 |
| 415000 | 415000 | PFIZER | 27027 | 0.91 |
| 250000 | 1750000 | UNITED ARTISTS ENTERTNMNT A | 26906 | 0.91 |
| 529600 | 1288800 | US BANCORP (OR) | 26904 | 0.91 |
| 1500 | 825000 | ACUSON | 26813 | 0.91 |
| 0 | 600000 | CATERPILLAR | 26775 | 0.91 |
| 75000 | 375000 | CHIRON | 26156 | 0.89 |

## PORTFOLIO STATISTICS 10/31/91

| | PORT-FOLIO | % OF AVG. STOCKS | REL. S&P 500 |
|---|---|---|---|
| PRICE/EARNINGS RATIO | 18.4 | 58 | 1.00 |
| PRICE/BOOK RATIO | 4.2 | 94 | 1.16 |
| 5 YR. EARN. GR. % | 20.1 | 45 | 2.05 |
| RETURN ON ASSETS | 7.8 | 60 | 1.02 |
| DEBT % TOTAL CAP. | 35.0 | 60 | 1.10 |
| MED. MKT. CAP. ($MIL) | 5025 | 99 | 0.48 |

### COMPOSITION % 09/30/91

| | | | |
|---|---|---|---|
| CASH | 16.0 | PREFERREDS | 0.3 |
| STOCKS | 80.1 | CONVERTIBLES | 2.2 |
| BONDS | 1.4 | OTHER | 0.0 |

## SECTOR WEIGHTINGS

| | PORT-FOLIO % | REL. S&P 500 |
|---|---|---|
| NATURAL RESOURCES | 5.2 | 0.30 |
| INDUSTRIAL PRODUCTS | 17.7 | 1.65 |
| CONSUMER DURABLES | 7.6 | 1.22 |
| NON-DURABLES | 15.7 | 0.67 |
| RETAIL TRADE | 1.7 | 0.24 |
| SERVICES | 25.4 | 2.64 |
| UTILITIES | 6.8 | 0.49 |
| TRANSPORTATION | 8.2 | 4.36 |
| FINANCE | 11.8 | 1.46 |
| MULT-INDUSTRY | 0.0 | 0.00 |

## ANALYSIS

**Eileen Sanders** | 11/29/91

Growth Fund of America's patience has been a virtue.

At first glance, the fund seems like a typical, middle-of-the-road vehicle. Its risk hugs the norm in every ranking period, and its portfolio lists fairly standard large-cap growth fare. But its long-term returns tell a different story; over time, this fund has been consistently fine.

Obviously, management's ability to locate industry-leading companies has keyed the fund's success. By stressing high-quality companies with growth potential, strong balance sheets, and seasoned management, the fund has kept its business risk at a minimum.

It's also done a nice job of mitigating stock-price risk, though, ferreting out businesses that are solid but temporarily unpopular. Thus, although its companies have grown twice as fast as the S&P 500, the portfolio has just a market-level P/E ratio. And, as the fund's low turnover indicates, management is willing to wait until the market recognizes its mistake. Its top holdings, for instance, include unpopular Time Warner and Caterpillar.

Although the fund diversifies across every major sector, it will stress favored areas. Management, however, doesn't follow the latest trends, instead preferring to ease into contrarian positions. Cyclical airlines, for example, dot the fund's top holdings, bringing its transportation weighting to a level four times greater than the market's.

To hedge riskier bets, the fund usually holds a fairly large cash position. Even at its most confident, it generally holds 10%; currently, management has retreated to a 16% cash position. In addition, the fund reduces its individual-company risk by owning about 100 stocks. This doesn't eliminate volatility, but it makes for a fairly steady portfolio by growth-stock standards.

## OPERATIONS

| | |
|---|---|
| **ADDRESS** | 4 Embarcadero Center P.O. Box 7650 San Francisco, CA 94120 |
| **ADVISOR** | Capital Research & Management |
| **DISTRIBUTOR** | American Funds Distributors |
| **PORTFOLIO MANAGER** | Newton/Orasdo/Shanahan |
| **MANAGEMENT FEE** | 0.54% max./0.38% min. |
| **FEES** | 5.75%L, 0.25%B |
| **TICKER** | AGTHX |
| **TELEPHONE NUMBER** | 415-421-9360 t; 800-421-0180 |
| **PHONE SWITCH** | Yes |
| **# OF SHAREHOLDERS** | 237019 |
| **MINIMUM INITIAL PURCHASE** | 1000 |
| **MINIMUM SUBSEQUENT PURCHASE** | 50 |
| **DATE OF INCEPTION** | 01/01/59 |
| **SHAREHOLDER REPORT RATING** | B |

# G.T. International Growth

| OBJECTIVE | LOAD % | YIELD % | ASSETS($MIL) | N.A.V. |
|---|---|---|---|---|
| Intl Stock | 4.75 | 1.2 | 432.4 | 8.97 |

G.T. International Growth Fund seeks long-term capital growth.

Normally, at least 80% of the fund's assets will be invested in a diversified portfolio of non-U.S. equity securities. This fund may invest in all of the countries that the G.T. Pacific Growth Fund, G.T. Japan Growth Fund, and G.T. Europe Growth Fund may select. The fund may also invest in a variety of convertible or fixed-income securities issued by foreign companies, or it may keep funds in U.S. or foreign money-market securities.

The fund may use options and futures strategies to hedge against currency risk.

| | RETURN | RISK |
|---|---|---|
| TOP LINE: Adjusted NAV | Average | Average |
| BOTTOM LINE: Relative Strength | RATING ★★★ | |
| | Neutral | |

## TOTAL RETURN %

| | 1st Qtr. | 2nd Qtr. | 3rd Qtr. | 4th Qtr. | TOTAL |
|---|---|---|---|---|---|
| 1987 | 11.80 | 8.42 | 13.71 | -23.05 | 6.06 |
| 1988 | 9.98 | 0.00 | -0.21 | 8.79 | 19.40 |
| 1989 | 8.81 | 2.27 | 15.70 | 7.63 | 38.57 |
| 1990 | -3.03 | 4.46 | -16.22 | 0.98 | -14.31 |
| 1991 | 10.61 | 0.00 | ... | ... | ... |

## INCOME

| | | | | | TOTAL |
|---|---|---|---|---|---|
| 1989 | 0.00 | 0.00 | 0.00 | 0.02 | 0.02 |
| 1990 | 0.00 | 0.00 | 0.00 | 0.11 | 0.11 |
| 1991 | 0.00 | 0.00 | 0.00 | 0.00 | 0.00 |

## CAPITAL GAINS

| | | | | | TOTAL |
|---|---|---|---|---|---|
| 1989 | 0.00 | 0.00 | 0.00 | 0.11 | 0.11 |
| 1990 | 0.00 | 0.00 | 0.00 | 0.00 | 0.00 |
| 1991 | 0.00 | 0.00 | 0.00 | ... | 0.00 |

## PERFORMANCE/RISK

| | TOTAL RETURN % | +/- S&P 500 | +/- EAFE | PERCENTILE RANK ALL | PERCENTILE RANK OBJ. |
|---|---|---|---|---|---|
| 3 MONTH | 3.34 | -0.80 | 5.12 | 31 | 14 |
| 6 MONTH | 12.27 | -2.32 | 9.05 | 33 | 18 |
| 1 YEAR | -6.17 | -18.96 | 2.31 | 93 | 41 |
| 3 YEAR AVG. | 13.66 | -2.89 | 13.07 | 21 | 12 |
| 5 YEAR AVG. | 12.60 | -1.66 | 2.35 | 16 | 32 |
| 10 YEAR AVG. | ... | ... | ... | ... | ... |
| 15 YEAR AVG. | ... | ... | ... | ... | ... |

| | ALPHA | BETA | R² | STD. DEV. |
|---|---|---|---|---|
| PERCENTILE ALL RANK OBJ. | 0.5 | 0.68 | 46 | 4.24 |
| | 20 | 80 | 87 | 57 |
| | 12 | 83 | 49 | 85 |

Percentile Ranks: 1 = Highest, 100 = Lowest
Except MMF Risk: 1 = Lowest, 100 = Highest

## HISTORY

| | 1979 | 1980 | 1981 | 1982 | 1983 | 1984 | 1985 | 1986 | 1987 | 1988 | 1989 | 1990 | 07/91 |
|---|---|---|---|---|---|---|---|---|---|---|---|---|---|
| N.A.V. | ... | ... | ... | ... | ... | ... | 4.16 | 6.13 | 5.71 | 6.77 | 9.25 | 7.82 | 8.97 |
| TOTAL RETURN % | ... | ... | ... | ... | ... | ... | ... | 53.81 | 6.06 | 19.40 | 38.57 | -14.31 | 14.71 |
| +/- S&P 500 INDEX | ... | ... | ... | ... | ... | ... | ... | 35.18 | 0.84 | 2.89 | 6.90 | -11.21 | -4.99 |
| +/- EAFE INDEX | ... | ... | ... | ... | ... | ... | ... | -15.62 | -18.57 | -8.87 | 28.03 | 9.14 | 8.15 |
| TOT. RTN: ALL FUNDS | ... | ... | ... | ... | ... | ... | ... | 30 | 22 | 19 | 6 | 86 | 55 |
| % RANK: OBJECTIVE | ... | ... | ... | ... | ... | ... | ... | 67 | 67 | 32 | 9 | 67 | 21 |
| INCOME | ... | ... | ... | ... | ... | ... | 0.00 | 0.00 | 0.00 | 0.00 | 0.02 | 0.11 | 0.00 |
| CAPITAL GAIN | ... | ... | ... | ... | ... | ... | 0.20 | 0.20 | 0.75 | 0.05 | 0.11 | 0.00 | 0.00 |
| EXPENSE % | ... | ... | ... | ... | ... | ... | 2.40 | 1.90 | 1.90 | 2.10 | 1.90 | 1.90 | ... |
| INCOME % | ... | ... | ... | ... | ... | ... | -1.10 | -0.90 | -0.30 | -0.20 | 0.10 | 1.40 | ... |
| TURNOVER % | ... | ... | ... | ... | ... | ... | 37 | 122 | 198 | 115 | 82 | 58 | ... |
| NET ASSETS ($MIL) | ... | ... | ... | ... | ... | ... | 1.8 | 12.1 | 17.2 | 29.5 | 136.3 | 343.6 | 432.4 |

| | M-STAR RISK % RANK ALL | M-STAR RISK % RANK OBJ. | MORNINGSTAR RETURN RISK 1.00 = EQUITY AVG. | MORNINGSTAR RISK | MORNINGSTAR RISK-ADJUSTED RATING |
|---|---|---|---|---|---|
| 3 YEAR | 61 | 16 | 1.09 | 0.88 ↑ | ★★★ |
| 5 YEAR | 60 | 27 | 1.17 | 0.88 ↑ | ★★★ |
| 10 YEAR | ... | ... | ... | ... | ... |
| WEIGHTED AVG. | | | 1.13 | 0.88 | ★★★ |

## PORTFOLIO

| | | TOTAL # STOCKS: 135 | | TOP 30 EQUITY HOLDINGS AS OF: 06/28/91 | |
|---|---|---|---|---|---|
| SHARE CHANGE | AMOUNT | STOCK | | VALUE $000 | % NET ASSETS |
| -600000 | 5650000 | HUTCHISON WHAMPOA | | 10773 | 2.49 |
| 3042071 | 3904071 | JARDINE STRATEGIC | | 9003 | 2.08 |
| 310000 | 3291100 | CHINA LIGHT & POWER | | 8310 | 1.92 |
| 750000 | 750000 | SHARP | | 8272 | 1.91 |
| 180000 | 180000 | SONY | | 8229 | 1.90 |
| 265000 | 400000 | ROHM | | 8069 | 1.87 |
| 802000 | 1002000 | HITACHI | | 7998 | 1.85 |
| 1513600 | 8753600 | HONG KONG TELECOMMUNICATIONS | | 7330 | 1.70 |
| 825000 | 825000 | NIKON | | 6825 | 1.58 |
| 100000 | 1525200 | JARDINE MATHESON | | 6779 | 1.57 |
| 600000 | 600000 | CANON | | 6487 | 1.50 |
| 125000 | 225000 | TAIKISHA | | 5992 | 1.39 |
| 21092 | 254092 | CHILE FUND | | 5939 | 1.37 |
| 569000 | 569000 | KAWASAKI ELECTRIC | | 5904 | 1.37 |
| 0 | 1388000 | GENTING | | 5697 | 1.32 |
| 657500 | 657500 | TELEFONICA | | 5682 | 1.31 |
| -817000 | 2303000 | SUN HUNG KAI PROPERTIES | | 5637 | 1.30 |
| 573493 | 573493 | BHP | | 5615 | 1.30 |
| 622000 | 972000 | NATIONAL AUSTRALIA BANK | | 4992 | 1.15 |
| 0 | 200000 | MATSUSHITA COMMUNICATIONS | | 4789 | 1.11 |
| 0 | 13300 | SIEMENS | | 4672 | 1.08 |
| 457000 | 457000 | KANTO NATURAL GAS DEV | | 4643 | 1.07 |
| 400000 | 400000 | NIPPON DENSO | | 4615 | 1.07 |
| 10000 | 10000 | LINDE | | 4543 | 1.05 |
| 0 | 1240333 | RESORTS WORLD | | 4429 | 1.02 |
| -1550 | 10000 | SCHERING | | 4391 | 1.02 |
| 600000 | 600000 | FUJIKURA | | 4332 | 1.00 |
| 0 | 12179 | DEUTSCHE BANK | | 4240 | 0.98 |
| 2000 | 10436 | GENERALE DES EAUX | | 4136 | 0.96 |
| 210000 | 385000 | CRA | | 4021 | 0.93 |

### PORTFOLIO STATISTICS 07/31/91

| | PORT-FOLIO | % OF STOCKS | REL. S&P 500 |
|---|---|---|---|
| PRICE/EARNINGS RATIO | 22.2 | 10 | 1.27 |
| PRICE/BOOK RATIO | 4.2 | 16 | 1.20 |
| 5 YR. EARN. GR. % | 14.0 | 5 | 1.08 |
| RETURN ON ASSETS | 6.1 | 12 | 0.81 |
| DEBT % TOTAL CAP. | 29.7 | 19 | 0.93 |
| MED. MKT. CAP. ($MIL) | 8471 | 19 | 0.72 |

### COMPOSITION % 06/30/91

| | | | |
|---|---|---|---|
| CASH | 3.8 | PREFERREDS | 0.0 |
| STOCKS | 95.7 | CONVERTIBLES | 0.0 |
| BONDS | 0.5 | OTHER | 0.0 |

### REGIONAL EXPOSURE 08/06/91

## ANALYSIS                                    Helen O'D. Johnstone    08/23/91

G.T. International Growth Fund continues to keep a close watch on international monetary trends.

As manager Christian Wignall points out, the fund has traditionally been quick to respond to monetary signals like changing interest rates. Thus, when Japan lowered its discount rate in June, the fund responded by increasing its exposure to Japanese stocks from around 16% in May to 24% in August. (Of course, the fact that these stocks now sell at lower multiples than at any time in recent memory also affected his decision.)

However, while the outlook for Japan seems to be improving overall, says Wignall, there's no raging bull market in sight, either. Thus, the fund will continue to emphasize conservative, stable-growth firms like recent electronic-technology buys Hitachi, Sony, and Sharp, which should aid its down-market resistance. Elsewhere in the Pacific region, Wignall

continues to favor Hong Kong, which now accounts for 12% of assets. This market has provided strong support for the fund recently, allowing it to benefit indirectly from the growing strength of the $U.S. (the fund can't buy U.S. stocks). The fund also favors Australia—currently, about 10% of assets—where interest rates are also heading down, says Wignall.

Overall, Wignall remains committed to blue chips that can grow earnings even during times of economic stress. Though anticipating dull but steady, stock-market gains for the rest of this year, he's not too optimistic about the strength of European currencies. Thus, 50% of the fund's European exposure is hedged into dollars.

While this fund's rating has declined along with its objective's fortunes, it remains among the more reliable overseas portfolios. Over its history, it's kept up with the EAFE, but at considerably less risk.

## OPERATIONS

| | | | |
|---|---|---|---|
| ADDRESS | 50 California Street 27th Floor San Francisco, CA 94111 | TELEPHONE NUMBER | 415-392-6181 800-824-1580 |
| ADVISOR | G.T. Capital Management | PHONE SWITCH | Yes |
| DISTRIBUTOR | G.T. Global Financial Services | # OF SHAREHOLDERS | 38810 |
| PORTFOLIO MANAGER | F.C. Wignall (1986) | MINIMUM INITIAL PURCHASE | 500 |
| MANAGEMENT FEE | 1.00% flat fee | MINIMUM SUBSEQUENT PURCHASE | 100 |
| FEES | 4.75%L, 0.35%B | DATE OF INCEPTION | 07/19/85 |
| TICKER | GINGX | SHAREHOLDER REPORT RATING | B+ |

# Guardian Park Avenue

| OBJECTIVE | LOAD % | YIELD % | ASSETS($Mil.) | N.A.V. |
|---|---|---|---|---|
| Growth | 4.50 | 2.9 | 283.2 | 23.77 |

The Guardian Park Avenue Fund primarily seeks long-term growth of capital. Current income is not an important criterion in investment selection.

The fund invests at least 80% of its assets in common stocks and convertible securities. The fund selects individual securities by analyzing a company's business fundamentals to determine whether the current stock price represents good relative value in the marketplace. The fund uses other quantitative methodologies to identify securities with prospects for superior relative price performance.

| TOP LINE: | Adjusted N.A.V. | | RETURN | RISK |
|---|---|---|---|---|
| BOTTOM LINE: | Relative Strength | | Above Avg | Average |

RATING
★ ★ ★ ★
Above Avg

## TOTAL RETURN %

| | 1st Qtr. | 2nd Qtr. | 3rd Qtr. | 4th Qtr. | TOTAL |
|---|---|---|---|---|---|
| 1987 | 23.77 | -2.13 | 7.05 | -20.60 | 2.96 |
| 1988 | 12.83 | 6.95 | -1.36 | 1.47 | 20.78 |
| 1989 | 9.33 | 5.83 | 9.05 | -1.86 | 23.83 |
| 1990 | -1.39 | 0.64 | -15.65 | 4.74 | -12.33 |
| 1991 | 18.73 | -1.15 | 9.06 | ... | ... |

### INCOME

| | 1st Qtr. | 2nd Qtr. | 3rd Qtr. | 4th Qtr. | TOTAL |
|---|---|---|---|---|---|
| 1989 | 0.00 | 0.35 | 0.00 | 0.63 | 0.98 |
| 1990 | 0.00 | 0.35 | 0.00 | 0.36 | 0.71 |
| 1991 | 0.00 | 0.00 | 0.33 | 0.00 | 0.33 |

### CAPITAL GAINS

| | 1st Qtr. | 2nd Qtr. | 3rd Qtr. | 4th Qtr. | TOTAL |
|---|---|---|---|---|---|
| 1989 | 0.00 | 0.02 | 0.00 | 2.70 | 2.72 |
| 1990 | 0.00 | 0.00 | 0.00 | 0.00 | 0.00 |
| 1991 | 0.00 | 0.00 | 0.00 | 0.00 | 0.00 |

## PERFORMANCE/RISK

10/31/91

| | TOTAL RETURN % | +/- S&P 500 | PERCENTILE RANK ALL | PERCENTILE RANK OBJ. |
|---|---|---|---|---|
| 3 MONTH | 7.07 | 5.09 | 12 | 19 |
| 6 MONTH | 11.72 | 13 | 23 | 23 |
| 1 YEAR | 44.77 | 11.33 | 14 | 32 |
| 3 YEAR AVG. | 13.09 | -2.89 | 25 | 63 |
| 5 YEAR AVG. | 12.30 | -1.46 | 19 | 42 |
| 10 YEAR AVG. | 17.91 | 0.99 | 6 | 12 |
| 15 YEAR AVG. | 17.82 | 3.72 | 14 | 26 |

| | ALPHA | BETA | R² | STD. DEV. |
|---|---|---|---|---|
| | -1.5 | 0.88 | 82 | 4.03 |
| PERCENTILE / ALL | 59 | 38 | 39 | 32 |
| RANK/OBJ. | 60 | 75 | 70 | 71 |

Percentile Ranks: 1 = Highest, 100 = Lowest
Except M-Star Risk: 1 = Lowest, 100 = Highest

NET ASSETS: ($Mil)

## HISTORY

| | 1979 | 1980 | 1981 | 1982 | 1983 | 1984 | 1985 | 1986 | 1987 | 1988 | 1989 | 1990 | 10/91 |
|---|---|---|---|---|---|---|---|---|---|---|---|---|---|
| N.A.V. | 14.83 | 15.31 | 13.87 | 15.84 | 19.20 | 18.17 | 21.20 | 20.74 | 18.63 | 20.47 | 21.59 | 18.26 | 23.77 |
| TOTAL RETURN % | 29.28 | 21.50 | 10.58 | 25.28 | 28.57 | 12.53 | 33.04 | 18.38 | 20.78 | 20.78 | 23.83 | -12.33 | 32.16 |
| +/- S & P 500 INDEX | 10.98 | -10.71 | 3.81 | 5.50 | 6.10 | 6.40 | 1.40 | -0.25 | -2.26 | 4.27 | -7.84 | -9.23 | 10.08 |
| TOT. RTN/ALL FUNDS | 30 | 58 | 28 | 60 | 14 | 14 | 16 | 28 | 35 | 12 | 25 | 87 | 14 |
| % RANK OBJECTIVE | 54 | 89 | 21 | 55 | 15 | 5 | 26 | 25 | 47 | 23 | 62 | 85 | 26 |
| INCOME | 0.57 | 0.83 | 1.14 | 0.72 | 0.54 | 0.60 | 0.49 | 0.33 | 0.60 | 0.55 | 0.98 | 0.71 | 0.33 |
| CAPITAL GAIN | 0.68 | 1.57 | 1.08 | 0.48 | 0.48 | 2.36 | 2.04 | 3.81 | 2.18 | 1.46 | 2.72 | 0.00 | 0.00 |
| EXPENSE % | 0.77 | 0.75 | 0.68 | 0.67 | 0.71 | 0.78 | 0.70 | 0.71 | 0.68 | 0.69 | 0.70 | 0.69 | 0.67 |
| INCOME % | 5.50 | 6.81 | 8.27 | 4.19 | 2.71 | 3.75 | 2.48 | 1.79 | 2.08 | 2.82 | 4.01 | 3.51 | 3.25 |
| TURNOVER % | 58 | 63 | 42 | 63 | 66 | 95 | 80 | 48 | 50 | 58 | 47 | 47 | 46 |
| NET ASSETS ($Mil) | 21.6 | 33.9 | 40.0 | 35.9 | 51.1 | 58.1 | 89.6 | 131.2 | 157.0 | 175.8 | 227.9 | 216.5 | 283.2 |

| M-STAR RISK % RANK | | MORNINGSTAR RETURN RISK | | MORNINGSTAR RISK-ADJUSTED | |
|---|---|---|---|---|---|
| | ALL | OBJ | 1.00 = EQUITY AVG | | RATING |
| 3 YEAR | 72 | 44 | 0.91 | 0.91 ↑ | ★ ★ ★ |
| 5 YEAR | 72 | 46 | 1.06 | 0.92 ↑ | ★ ★ ★ |
| 10 YEAR | 62 | 31 | 1.23 | 0.89 ↑ | ★ ★ ★ ★ |
| WEIGHTED AVG. | | | 1.12 | 0.90 | ★ ★ ★ ★ |

| SHARE CHANGE | AMOUNT | STOCK | VALUE $000 | % NET ASSETS |
|---|---|---|---|---|
| -10000 | 120000 | PHILIP MORRIS | 7620 | 2.94 |
| 0 | 167104 | HOLLY | 5368 | 2.07 |
| 0 | 95000 | MARTIN MARIETTA | 5308 | 2.05 |
| 0 | 80000 | CONSOLIDATED RAIL | 4560 | 1.76 |
| 25000 | 135000 | TEXTRON | 4337 | 1.67 |
| 0 | 108000 | SURGICAL CARE AFFILIATES | 4064 | 1.57 |
| 0 | 130500 | ANDREW | 4062 | 1.57 |
| -10000 | 39000 | IBM | 3788 | 1.46 |
| 104490 | 104490 | FIRSTAR | 3722 | 1.44 |
| 0 | 140000 | ALLIANT TECHSYSTEMS | 3710 | 1.43 |
| 0 | 18709? | CLAYTON HOMES | 3298 | 1.27 |
| 57900 | 115800 | ARNOLD INDUSTRIES | 3242 | 1.25 |
| 0 | 106700 | TRENWICK GROUP | 3001 | 1.16 |
| 1807 | 85607 | TEXAS UTILITIES | 2975 | 1.15 |
| 35000 | 100500 | DETROIT EDISON | 2864 | 1.11 |
| 10000 | 65000 | APPLE COMPUTER | 2706 | 1.04 |
| 0 | 73440 | FREEPORT-MCMORAN | 2681 | 1.04 |
| 0 | 172900 | THIOKOL | 2615 | 1.01 |
| 0 | 50000 | BHC COMMUNICATIONS CL A | 2606 | 1.01 |
| 0 | 30500 | AMERICAN STORES | 2516 | 0.97 |
| 0 | 7370 | ATLANTIC SOUTHEAST AIRLINES | 2497 | 0.96 |
| 0 | 60000 | AMERICAN BRANDS | 2355 | 0.91 |
| 0 | 159600 | ONEOK | 2274 | 0.88 |
| 0 | 200000 | ANALOGIC | 2238 | 0.86 |
| 37500 | 112500 | MICHAEL FOODS | 2102 | 0.81 |
| 0 | 288511 | ADOBE RESOURCES | 2092 | 0.81 |
| 0 | 72200 | AMERICAN ELECTRIC POWER | 2049 | 0.79 |
| 0 | 30000 | SCI-MED LIFE SYSTEMS | 1958 | 0.76 |
| 0 | 30000 | PHELPS DODGE | 1943 | 0.75 |
| -8000 | 50500 | AMERICAN GENERAL | 1913 | 0.74 |

## PORTFOLIO STATISTICS | 10/31/91

| | PORT-FOLIO | % OF AVG. STOCKS | REL. S&P 500 |
|---|---|---|---|
| PRICE/EARNINGS RATIO | 14.9 | 87 | 0.81 |
| PRICE/BOOK RATIO | 2.8 | 98 | 0.79 |
| 5 YR. EARN. GR. % | 14.3 | 52 | 1.46 |
| RETURN ON ASSETS | 7.1 | 89 | 0.94 |
| DEBT % TOTAL CAP. | 32.3 | 90 | 1.01 |
| MED. MKT. CAP. ($MIL) | 1073 | 98 | 0.10 |

## COMPOSITION % | 09/30/91

| CASH | 7.1 | PREFERREDS | 1.0 |
|---|---|---|---|
| STOCKS | 82.3 | CONVERTIBLES | 8.5 |
| BONDS | 1.1 | OTHER | 0.0 |

## SECTOR WEIGHTINGS

| | PORT-FOLIO % | REL. S&P 500 |
|---|---|---|
| NATURAL RESOURCES | 21.6 | 1.27 |
| INDUSTRIAL PRODUCTS | 18.5 | 1.73 |
| CONSUMER DURABLES | 7.0 | 1.13 |
| NON-DURABLES | 8.2 | 0.35 |
| RETAIL TRADE | 4.3 | 0.62 |
| SERVICES | 7.1 | 0.74 |
| UTILITIES | 8.9 | 0.64 |
| TRANSPORTATION | 6.2 | 3.29 |
| FINANCE | 14.0 | 1.73 |
| MULTI-INDUSTRY | 4.3 | 1.70 |

## ANALYSIS

Paul Korngiebel    11/29/91

Guardian Park Avenue Fund is hard to pigeonhole.

Manager Chuck Albers isn't simply a value player. But you can't just call him a momentum player, either. In fact, Albers designed a complex scoring system, which currently tracks 878 stocks, to give equal 40% weightings to value and momentum considerations. The remaining 20% of the system focuses on recurring market patterns, such as the January effect, spin-offs, and insider stock transactions, to add incremental value. After the scoring system crunches its data, the fund buys stocks which rank in the top decile of its investment universe. Albers reviews the portfolio each week with an eye toward weeding out stocks that have fallen into the system's sixth and seventh deciles.

To a certain extent, the portfolio reflects Albers' quest for diversity. After all, few portfolios allow a low-P/E stock like Martin Marietta to rub shoulders with a Surgical Care Affiliates, a momentum story.

Despite the portfolio's odd bedfellows, the fund does have some decided biases. Morningstar's portfolio statistics indicate that the fund has a small- to medium-cap value bias. First, the fund's $1 billion median market cap is a tenth of the S&P 500's, a focus that led to its disastrous double-digit 1990 loss, when investors fled to big, blue-chip stocks. Furthermore, the fund was hurt by cyclical fare, such as rail stocks. Second, at mid year, the portfolio sported below-market P/E and price-to-book ratios, giving the fund a value orientation. Small caps and value stocks have made a dramatic recovery, year to date. Through October, the fund gained a robust 32%.

If the market continues to favor these long-neglected issues, the fund could really soar. Consequently, we still think that this 4-star fund holds promise going forward.

## OPERATIONS

| | | | |
|---|---|---|---|
| ADDRESS | 201 Park Avenue South, New York, NY 10003 | TELEPHONE NUMBER | 212-598-8259 / 800-221-3253 |
| ADVISOR | Guardian Investor Services | PHONE SWITCH | Yes |
| DISTRIBUTOR | Guardian Investor Services | # OF SHAREHOLDERS | 11603 |
| PORTFOLIO MANAGER | Charles Albers (1972) | MINIMUM INITIAL PURCHASE | 1000 |
| MANAGEMENT FEE | 0.50% flat fee | MINIMUM SUBSEQUENT PURCHASE | 100 |
| FEES | 4.50%L | DATE OF INCEPTION | 06/01/72 |
| TICKER | GPAFX | SHAREHOLDER REPORT RATING | C |

# IDEX

| OBJECTIVE | LOAD % | YIELD % | ASSETS($MIL) | N.A.V. |
|---|---|---|---|---|
| Growth | 8.50 | 0.8 | 201.6 | 18.73 |

IDEX Fund's only investment objective is growth of capital.

The fund invests primarily in equity securities that have strong potential for capital growth. Stocks are selected mostly on the basis of an evaluation of factors (such as asset value, cash flow, and earnings per share) that indicate a security's fundamental investment value. The fund also looks at a company's revenues, its earnings and dividend records, and its future prospects when determining whether or not to purchase a particular security.

Janus Capital, the fund's subadvisor, supplies IDEX Management with research and statistical data.

## TOTAL RETURN %

| | 1st Qtr. | 2nd Qtr. | 3rd Qtr. | 4th Qtr. | TOTAL |
|---|---|---|---|---|---|
| 1987 | 24.19 | 4.15 | 6.57 | -22.29 | 7.11 |
| 1988 | 2.84 | 6.25 | 6.04 | 2.24 | 18.46 |
| 1989 | 11.89 | 12.81 | 20.43 | -5.75 | 43.27 |
| 1990 | -2.94 | 14.56 | -16.51 | 6.72 | -0.93 |
| 1991 | 22.15 | -0.70 | 14.06 | --- | --- |

## INCOME

| | | | | | TOTAL |
|---|---|---|---|---|---|
| 1989 | 0.00 | 0.03 | 0.00 | 0.06 | 0.09 |
| 1990 | 0.00 | 0.04 | 0.00 | 0.13 | 0.17 |
| 1991 | 0.00 | 0.04 | 0.00 | 0.00 | 0.04 |

## CAPITAL GAINS

| | | | | | TOTAL |
|---|---|---|---|---|---|
| 1989 | 0.00 | 0.00 | 0.00 | 2.02 | 2.02 |
| 1990 | 0.00 | 0.00 | 0.00 | 1.92 | 1.92 |
| 1991 | 0.00 | 0.00 | 0.00 | 0.00 | 0.00 |

## PERFORMANCE/RISK

as of 10/31/91

| | TOTAL RETURN % | +/- S&P 500 | PERCENTILE RANK ALL | OBJ |
|---|---|---|---|---|
| 3 MONTH | 9.47 | 7.49 | 5 | 7 |
| 6 MONTH | 18.54 | 12.33 | 4 | 5 |
| 1 YEAR | 57.44 | 24.00 | 7 | 14 |
| 3 YEAR AVG. | 27.36 | 11.38 | 2 | 4 |
| 5 YEAR AVG. | 21.20 | 7.43 | 1 | 2 |
| 10 YEAR AVG. | --- | --- | --- | --- |
| 15 YEAR AVG. | --- | --- | --- | --- |

| | ALPHA | BETA | $R^2$ | STD. DEV. |
|---|---|---|---|---|
| | 9.1 | 1.16 | 83 | 5.30 |
| PERCENTILE / ALL | 2 | 11 | 37 | 12 |
| RANK OBJ. | 4 | 19 | 66 | 18 |

Percentile Ranks: 1 = Highest, 100 = Lowest
Except M-Star Risk: 1 = Lowest, 100 = Highest

### RATING

| RETURN | RISK |
|---|---|
| High | Below Avg |

RATING: ★★★★ — Highest

TOP LINE: Adjusted NAV
BOTTOM LINE: Relative Strength

## HISTORY

| | 1979 | 1980 | 1981 | 1982 | 1983 | 1984 | 1985 | 1986 | 1987 | 1988 | 1989 | 1990 | 10/91 |
|---|---|---|---|---|---|---|---|---|---|---|---|---|---|
| N.A.V. | ... | ... | ... | ... | ... | ... | 10.85 | 12.07 | 10.57 | 12.20 | 15.29 | 13.05 | 18.73 |
| TOTAL RETURN % | ... | ... | ... | ... | ... | ... | ... | 18.33 | 7.11 | 18.46 | 43.27 | -0.93 | 43.88 |
| +/- S & P 500 INDEX | ... | ... | ... | ... | ... | ... | ... | -0.30 | 1.90 | 1.95 | 11.60 | 2.17 | 21.80 |
| TOT. RTN / ALL FUNDS | ... | ... | ... | ... | ... | ... | ... | 29 | 15 | 17 | 2 | 55 | 6 |
| % RANK OBJECTIVE | ... | ... | ... | ... | ... | ... | ... | 25 | 23 | 34 | 4 | 23 | 10 |
| INCOME | ... | ... | ... | ... | ... | ... | 0.04 | 0.29 | 0.28 | 0.31 | 0.09 | 0.17 | 0.04 |
| CAPITAL GAIN | ... | ... | ... | ... | ... | ... | 0.00 | 0.48 | 2.29 | 0.00 | 2.02 | 1.92 | 0.00 |
| EXPENSE % | ... | ... | ... | ... | ... | ... | ... | 1.73 | 1.22 | 1.49 | 1.40 | 1.39 | 1.30 |
| INCOME % | ... | ... | ... | ... | ... | ... | ... | 4.50 | 0.55 | 2.61 | 0.49 | 1.23 | 1.59 |
| TURNOVER % | ... | ... | ... | ... | ... | ... | ... | 91 | 185 | 111 | 97 | 159 | ... |
| NET ASSETS ($MIL) | ... | ... | ... | ... | ... | ... | 28.6 | 61.2 | 65.4 | 66.4 | 85.0 | 104.9 | 201.6 |

| | M-STAR RISK % RANK ALL | OBL | MORNINGSTAR RETURN RISK (1.00 = EQUITY AVG) | | MORNINGSTAR RISK-ADJUSTED RATING |
|---|---|---|---|---|---|
| 3 YEAR | 79 | 64 | 1.89 → | 0.98 → | ★★★★★ |
| 5 YEAR | 63 | 26 | 1.79 → | 0.85 → | ★★★★★ |
| 10 YEAR | --- | --- | --- | --- | --- |
| WEIGHTED AVG. | | | 1.83 | 0.90 | ★★★★★ |

| SHARE CHANGE | AMOUNT | STOCK | VALUE $000 | % NET ASSETS |
|---|---|---|---|---|
| 5300 | 62225 | AMGEN | 7347 | 4.57 |
| 15500 | 105650 | PHILIP MORRIS | 6709 | 4.17 |
| 0 | 294025 | KROGER | 6285 | 3.91 |
| 33300 | 147775 | GLAXO | 5985 | 3.72 |
| 0 | 217900 | CHAMBERS DEVELOPMENT CL A | 5774 | 3.59 |
| 85017 | 212543 | TELEFONOS DE MEXICO | 5473 | 3.40 |
| -32225 | 100150 | FNMA | 4957 | 3.08 |
| 36000 | 108000 | HOME DEPOT | 4874 | 3.03 |
| 0 | 41050 | MERCK | 4767 | 2.96 |
| 8175 | 85000 | PFIZER | 4718 | 2.93 |
| 0 | 62778 | CIRCUS CIRCUS ENTERPRISES | 4614 | 2.87 |
| 0 | 90825 | MEDCO CONTAINMENT SERVICES | 4360 | 2.71 |
| 3150 | 29725 | UAL | 4124 | 2.56 |
| 0 | 92850 | WAL-MART STORES | 3961 | 2.46 |
| 0 | 107800 | BANKAMERICA | 3908 | 2.43 |
| 0 | 122750 | THE LIMITED | 3468 | 2.16 |
| 0 | 78825 | SAINT JUDE MEDICAL | 3429 | 2.13 |
| -50000 | 90820 | WASTE MANAGEMENT | 3326 | 2.07 |
| 0 | 168250 | SAFEWAY | 3092 | 1.92 |
| 0 | 48550 | GAP | 2907 | 1.81 |
| 0 | 45025 | BANCORP HAWAII | 2696 | 1.68 |
| 0 | 75000 | NCNB | 2681 | 1.67 |
| 0 | 71025 | NIKE CL B | 2566 | 1.60 |
| 22825 | 22825 | ASTRA CL A | 2251 | 1.40 |
| 0 | 64275 | SYNERGEN | 2177 | 1.35 |
| 10000 | 30000 | MICROSOFT | 2044 | 1.27 |
| 0 | 91050 | DURACELL INTERNATIONAL | 2003 | 1.25 |
| 0 | 53350 | SMITH'S FOOD & DRUG CL B | 1954 | 1.21 |
| 45425 | 91275 | MID-AMERICAN WASTE SYSTEM | 1883 | 1.17 |
| 0 | 73400 | REEBOK INTERNATIONAL | 1789 | 1.11 |

### PORTFOLIO STATISTICS | 10/31/91

| | PORT-FOLIO | % OF AVG. STOCKS | REL S&P 500 |
|---|---|---|---|
| PRICE/EARNINGS RATIO | 23.8 | 78 | 1.30 |
| PRICE/BOOK RATIO | 7.5 | 85 | 2.10 |
| 5 YR. EARN. GR. % | 25.6 | 55 | 2.61 |
| RETURN ON ASSETS | 10.0 | 73 | 1.32 |
| DEBT % TOTAL CAP. | 31.9 | 74 | 1.00 |
| MED. MKT. CAP. ($MIL) | 6665 | 92 | 0.63 |

### COMPOSITION % | 09/30/91

| CASH | 7.0 | PREFERREDS | 0.0 |
|---|---|---|---|
| STOCKS | 88.1 | CONVERTIBLES | 0.0 |
| BONDS | 4.9 | OTHER | 0.0 |

### SECTOR WEIGHTINGS

| | PORT-FOLIO % | REL S&P 500 |
|---|---|---|
| NATURAL RESOURCES | 3.2 | 0.19 |
| INDUSTRIAL PRODUCTS | 1.6 | 0.15 |
| CONSUMER DURABLES | 0.0 | 0.00 |
| NON-DURABLES | 34.1 | 1.46 |
| RETAIL TRADE | 22.9 | 3.30 |
| SERVICES | 21.0 | 2.18 |
| UTILITIES | 0.0 | 0.00 |
| TRANSPORTATION | 3.3 | 1.77 |
| FINANCE | 13.9 | 1.72 |
| MULTI-INDUSTRY | 0.0 | 0.00 |

## ANALYSIS

**Anthony Mayorkas** | 11/29/91

IDEX Fund may be a two-sided coin, but either way you turn it, it's a winner.

The fund has shown its prowess as a growth vehicle, while also demonstrating a clear conservativism. That combination allows the fund to boast all-weather characteristics, which are the true measure of a 5-star fund.

In bear markets, such as those in 1987 and 1990, the fund has performed extremely well, outpacing three fourths of its rivals. Such success owes largely to manager Thomas Marsico's willingness to raise cash. In 1987, he raised cash based on high stock-market valuations. And last year, he raised cash due to concerns about Iraq's invasion of Kuwait.

As for the fund's bull-market abilities, its performances in 1989 and so far this year bespeak much; the fund is in its group's top decile for both periods. Marsico chases after big earnings-growth stories (the fund's five-year earnings-growth rate is over 25%) rather than focusing on price-to-earnings and price-to-book ratios. He also places a high priority on franchise value, new products and structural developments, and cash-flow measures.

Despite Marsico's bottom-up approach, the fund is essentially concentrated in four different sectors: retail, services, finance, and nondurables. The healthcare industry alone accounts for over 20% of assets.

The emphasis on product development underlies why the fund's largest industry weighting is health care. Meanwhile, the importance of franchise value leads the fund to hold an established crew of retailers, including Wal-Mart Stores and Gap. Strong franchises such as these tend to enjoy stable, rather than cyclical, earnings growth.

This fund's success as a growth vehicle, tempered by Marsico's willingness to raise cash, makes it a reliable long-term vehicle.

## OPERATIONS

ADDRESS  201 Highland Avenue
Largo, FL 34640
ADVISOR  IDEX Management
DISTRIBUTOR  IDEX Distributors
PORTFOLIO MANAGER  Thomas F. Marsico (1985)
MANAGEMENT FEE  1.00% flat fee
FEES  8.50%L
TICKER  IDEFX

TELEPHONE NUMBER  813-585-6565
800-624-4339
PHONE SWITCH  Yes
# OF SHAREHOLDERS  19614
MINIMUM INITIAL PURCHASE  50
MINIMUM SUBSEQUENT PURCHASE  50
DATE OF INCEPTION  06/04/85
SHAREHOLDER REPORT RATING  C

©1991 Morningstar, Inc. • 53 West Jackson Boulevard • Chicago, IL 60604 • (312) 427-1985
Although gathered from reliable sources, data accuracy and completeness cannot be guaranteed.

# Kemper U.S. Government Sec

| | OBJECTIVE | LOAD % | YIELD % | ASSETS($MIL) | N.A.V. |
|---|---|---|---|---|---|
| | Gvt Mortgage | 4.50 | 9.1 | 4948.6 | 9.27 |

Kemper U.S. Government Securities Fund seeks high current income, liquidity, and security of principal.

The fund may invest some or all of its assets in Government National Mortgage Association (GNMA) certificates. The balance of fund assets will be invested in obligations issued or guaranteed by the U.S. government or its agencies. These obligations will have maximum maturities of 10 years at the time of purchase.

| | RETURN | RISK |
|---|---|---|
| | Above Avg | Average |
| | RATING | |
| | ★★★★ | |
| | Above Avg | |

TOP LINE: Adjusted N.A.V
BOTTOM LINE: Relative Strength

40
30
20
10
8
6
4
3
2
1

NET ASSETS: ($MIL)
3000
0

## TOTAL RETURN %

| | 1st Qtr. | 2nd Qtr. | 3rd Qtr. | 4th Qtr. | TOTAL |
|---|---|---|---|---|---|
| 1987 | 1.45 | -0.52 | -3.01 | 4.90 | 2.68 |
| 1988 | 3.30 | 1.12 | 1.31 | 0.50 | 6.35 |
| 1989 | 0.98 | 7.91 | 0.94 | 3.64 | 14.00 |
| 1990 | -1.33 | 3.15 | 1.04 | 6.65 | 9.68 |
| 1991 | 2.34 | 1.34 | 6.23 | ... | ... |

## INCOME

| | | | | | TOTAL |
|---|---|---|---|---|---|
| 1989 | 0.22 | 0.22 | 0.22 | 0.22 | 0.90 |
| 1990 | 0.21 | 0.21 | 0.21 | 0.21 | 0.84 |
| 1991 | 0.21 | 0.21 | 0.21 | ... | 0.63 |

## CAPITAL GAINS

| | | | | | TOTAL |
|---|---|---|---|---|---|
| 1989 | 0.00 | 0.00 | 0.00 | 0.00 | 0.00 |
| 1990 | 0.00 | 0.00 | 0.00 | 0.00 | 0.00 |
| 1991 | 0.00 | 0.00 | 0.00 | ... | 0.00 |

## PERFORMANCE/RISK

| | | | 09/30/91 | |
|---|---|---|---|---|
| | TOTAL RETURN% | +/- LB GVT./CP. | PERCENTILE RANK ALL | OBJ. |
| 3 MONTH | 6.23 | 0.48 | 45 | 9 |
| 6 MONTH | 7.66 | 0.31 | 29 | 17 |
| 1 YEAR | 17.51 | 1.65 | 65 | 6 |
| 3 YEAR AVG. | 11.45 | 0.20 | 45 | 22 |
| 5 YEAR AVG. | 9.27 | 0.15 | 52 | 32 |
| 10 YEAR AVG. | 14.36 | 0.14 | 51 | 40 |
| 15 YEAR AVG. | ... | ... | ... | ... |

| | ALPHA | BETA | R² | STD. DEV. |
|---|---|---|---|---|
| | 0.0 | 1.05 | 95 | 1.36 |
| PERCENTILE / ALL | 23 | 10 | 6 | 39 |
| RANK \ OBJ. | 57 | 14 | 3 | 14 |

Percentile Ranks: 1 = highest (100 = lowest)
Lowest M-Star rank: 1 = lowest (100 = highest)

## HISTORY

| | 1979 | 1980 | 1981 | 1982 | 1983 | 1984 | 1985 | 1986 | 1987 | 1988 | 1989 | 1990 | 09/91 |
|---|---|---|---|---|---|---|---|---|---|---|---|---|---|
| N.A.V. | 10.28 | 9.13 | 8.03 | 9.08 | 8.81 | 8.73 | 9.47 | 9.90 | 9.14 | 8.78 | 9.05 | 9.02 | 9.27 |
| TOTAL RETURN % | ... | -0.96 | 0.56 | 28.53 | 8.91 | 12.25 | 22.32 | 16.24 | 2.68 | 6.35 | 14.00 | 9.68 | 10.18 |
| +/- LB GOVT./CP. | ... | -4.02 | -6.70 | -2.57 | 0.91 | -2.77 | 1.01 | 0.63 | 0.38 | -1.23 | -0.24 | 1.39 | -0.06 |
| TOT. RTN./ALL FUNDS | ... | 90 | 52 | 49 | 86 | 15 | 61 | 44 | 43 | 86 | 65 | 5 | 73 |
| % RANK \ OBJECTIVE | ... | 75 | 100 | 60 | 34 | 90 | 15 | 4 | 34 | 84 | 19 | 49 | 25 |
| INCOME | 0.23 | 1.05 | 1.11 | 1.06 | 1.03 | 1.07 | 1.08 | 1.04 | 1.01 | 0.92 | 0.90 | 0.84 | 0.63 |
| CAPITAL GAIN | 0.00 | 0.00 | 0.00 | 0.00 | 0.00 | 0.00 | 0.00 | 0.00 | 0.00 | 0.00 | 0.00 | 0.00 | 0.00 |
| EXPENSE % | 2.46 | 1.60 | 1.33 | 0.85 | 0.64 | 0.63 | 0.59 | 0.48 | 0.51 | 0.50 | 0.49 | 0.53 | ... |
| INCOME % | 6.36 | 9.97 | 12.64 | 11.98 | 12.06 | 12.91 | 12.00 | 10.33 | 9.26 | 10.20 | 9.93 | 9.62 | ... |
| TURNOVER % | ... | ... | ... | 72.2 | | | 556 | 252 | 278 | 203 | 289 | 497 | ... |
| NET ASSETS ($MIL) | 7.0 | 8.4 | 10.3 | 72.2 | 160.6 | 280.5 | 935.7 | 1942.0 | 4216.2 | 4288.1 | 4590.0 | 4740.6 | 4948.6 |

| | M-STAR RISK % RANK | | MORNINGSTAR RETURN RISK | | MORNINGSTAR RISK-ADJUSTED RATING |
|---|---|---|---|---|---|
| | ALL | OBJ. | 1.00 = FIXED INCOME AVG | | |
| 3 YEAR | 15 | 82 | 1.13 | 1.01 → | ★★★ |
| 5 YEAR | 10 | 58 | 1.10 | 0.94 → | ★★★ |
| 10 YEAR | 7 | 60 | 1.06 | 0.95 → | ★★★★ |
| WEIGHTED AVG. | | | 1.09 | 0.96 | ★★★★ |

| AMOUNT $000 | SECURITY | MATURITY | VALUE $000 | % NET ASSETS |
|---|---|---|---|---|
| 1194234 | GNMA 10% | 10/20 | 244989 | 25.16 |
| 1179239 | GNMA 9% | 07/21 | 172606 | 23.70 |
| 961779 | GNMA 9.5% | 06/21 | 979511 | 19.79 |
| 626000 | US TREASURY NOTE 13.125% | 05/15/94 | 719704 | 14.54 |
| 276000 | US TREASURY BOND 8.125% | 08/15/19 | 275997 | 5.58 |
| 49477 | FNMA 10.5% | 07/21 | 52122 | 1.05 |
| 49900 | FNMA STRIP-CMO 0% | 05/17 | 29691 | 0.60 |
| 10000 | US TREASURY NOTE 9.125% | 05/15/99 | 10503 | 0.21 |

## PORTFOLIO STATISTICS

| | |
|---|---|
| AVG. WEIGHTED MATURITY | 10.5 YEARS |
| AVG. WEIGHTED COUPON | 9.95% |
| AVG. WEIGHTED PRICE | 104 % OF PAR |

## COMPOSITION % 06/30/91

| | | | | |
|---|---|---|---|---|
| CASH 6.0 | PREFERREDS 0.0 | | | |
| STOCKS 0.0 | CONVERTIBLES 0.0 | | | |
| BONDS 94.0 | OTHER 0.0 | | | |

## COUPON RANGE

| | % BONDS | REL. OBL. |
|---|---|---|
| 0%, PIK | 0.7 | 0.1 |
| 0% to 8% | 0.0 | 0.0 |
| 8% to 9% | 32.3 | 11 |
| 9% to 10% | 49.8 | 1.6 |
| over 10% | 17.2 | 0.6 |

## CREDIT ANALYSIS 06/30/91

## ANALYSIS

| | Jennifer Strickland | 10/18/91 |
|---|---|---|

Kemper U.S. Government Securities Fund likes to take the straightforward approach.

Comanager Patrick Beimford likes to pick only a few holdings that fit in his target duration range of four to 7.5 years. He tends to neglect Fannie Maes and Freddie Macs, which act as shorter instruments, and restricts derivative investing to only an issue or two. However, Beimford isn't one to buy and hold; his active duration range requires that he shift the portfolio in response to interest-rate conditions. Thus, to facilitate such portfolio movements, he seeks out only the most liquid issues. Mortgage derivatives rarely meet that criteria. However, Treasuries and current-coupon Ginnie Maes are always in demand and thus fit the fund's liquidity requirements.

Good liquidity has come in handy over the past year, as Beimford has repositioned the portfolio along with the changing interest rates. Just before the Gulf War,

Beimford anticipated interest-rate drops and moved the fund to its maximum 7.5 years. Yet, as rates stabilized thereafter, Beimford shortened the portfolio to six years. And again in mid-year, he pulled the fund's duration out to seven years when interest rates slipped back down. The fund has profited greatly from all this aggressive movement, benefiting from both long-Treasury gains and pass-throughs' continued strength.

Beimford concedes that the bulk of the interest-rate drop is over. However, as long as there is stable inflation and a slow economic recovery, he will remain extended to profit from any potential downside. While the fund's total return outlook seems favorable, the same cannot be said for yield. With interest rates falling and mortgage securities selling at a premium, the fund will probably have to cut dividends or else dip into assets to maintain its high yield.

## OPERATIONS

| | | | |
|---|---|---|---|
| ADDRESS | 120 S. LaSalle Street | | |
| | Chicago, IL 60603 | | |
| ADVISOR | Kemper Financial Services | TELEPHONE NUMBER | 312-781-1121 |
| DISTRIBUTOR | Kemper Financial Services | | 800-621-1048 |
| PORTFOLIO MANAGER | Beimford/Schumacher (81/91) | PHONE SWITCH | Yes |
| MANAGEMENT FEE | 0.55% max./0.35% min. | # OF SHAREHOLDERS | 232597 |
| FEES | 4.50%L, 0.15%A | MINIMUM INITIAL PURCHASE | 1000 |
| TICKER | KPGVX | MINIMUM SUBSEQUENT PURCHASE | 100 |
| | | DATE OF INCEPTION | 06/24/77 |
| | | SHAREHOLDER REPORT RATING | C+ |

# Lord Abbett U.S. Govt Sec

| OBJECTIVE | LOAD% | YIELD% | ASSETS($MIL) | N.A.V. |
|---|---|---|---|---|
| Govt Mortgage | 4.75 | 10.1 | 1852.5 | 2.94 |

Lord Abbett U.S. Government Securities Fund seeks high current income with relatively low risk of price decline.

The fund invests in U.S. government securities, including obligations issued by the U.S. Treasury and obligations issued or guaranteed by U.S. government agencies and instrumentalities that are supported by any of the following: the full faith and credit of the United States, the right of the issuer to borrow from the U.S. Treasury, or the credit of the instrumentality.

Prior to October 15, 1985, the fund was known as Lord Abbett Income Fund and had a different investment objective.

TOP LINE: Adjusted NAV
BOTTOM LINE: Relative Strength

| RETURN | RISK |
|---|---|
| Above Avg | Average |

RATING ★★★
Neutral

## TOTAL RETURN %

| | 1st Qtr. | 2nd Qtr. | 3rd Qtr. | 4th Qtr. | TOTAL |
|---|---|---|---|---|---|
| 1987 | 2.04 | -3.19 | -3.79 | 7.36 | 2.03 |
| 1988 | 3.49 | 1.39 | 2.10 | 0.59 | 7.76 |
| 1989 | 0.13 | 7.10 | 1.54 | 3.53 | 12.74 |
| 1990 | -1.79 | 3.80 | 0.18 | 7.02 | 9.28 |
| 1991 | 2.43 | 1.03 | 6.79 | ... | ... |

## INCOME

| | | | | | TOTAL |
|---|---|---|---|---|---|
| 1989 | 0.06 | 0.08 | 0.08 | 0.09 | 0.31 |
| 1990 | 0.06 | 0.08 | 0.08 | 0.09 | 0.30 |
| 1991 | 0.07 | 0.07 | 0.07 | ... | 0.21 |

## CAPITAL GAINS

| | | | | | TOTAL |
|---|---|---|---|---|---|
| 1989 | 0.00 | 0.00 | 0.00 | 0.00 | 0.00 |
| 1990 | 0.00 | 0.00 | 0.00 | 0.00 | 0.00 |
| 1991 | 0.00 | 0.00 | 0.00 | ... | |

## PERFORMANCE/RISK 09/30/91

| | TOTAL RETURN% | +/- LB GVT./CP. | PERCENTILE RANK ALL | OBJ. |
|---|---|---|---|---|
| 3 MONTH | 6.79 | 1.04 | 37 | 3 |
| 6 MONTH | 7.88 | 0.53 | 26 | 6 |
| 1 YEAR | 18.25 | 2.39 | 64 | 3 |
| 3 YEAR AVG. | 11.05 | -0.20 | 48 | 36 |
| 5 YEAR AVG. | 9.10 | -0.02 | 54 | 46 |
| 10 YEAR AVG. | 13.95 | -0.27 | 57 | 60 |
| 15 YEAR AVG. | 10.83 | 0.69 | 77 | 34 |

| | ALPHA | BETA | R² | STD. DEV. |
|---|---|---|---|---|
| | -0.4 | 1.08 | 87 | 1.47 |
| PERCENTILE / ALL | 33 | 8 | 31 | 32 |
| RANK / OBJ. | 82 | 11 | 71 | 6 |

## HISTORY

| | 1979 | 1980 | 1981 | 1982 | 1983 | 1984 | 1985 | 1986 | 1987 | 1988 | 1989 | 1990 | 09/91 |
|---|---|---|---|---|---|---|---|---|---|---|---|---|---|
| N.A.V. | 2.86 | 2.66 | 2.68 | 3.03 | 2.98 | 2.99 | 3.20 | 3.27 | 2.97 | 2.87 | 2.91 | 2.86 | 2.94 |
| TOTAL RETURN % | 3.62 | 3.63 | 13.84 | 28.22 | 10.42 | 13.42 | 22.50 | 14.97 | 2.03 | 7.76 | 12.74 | 9.28 | 10.50 |
| +/- LB GOVT./CP. | 1.32 | 0.57 | 6.58 | -2.87 | 2.43 | -1.60 | 1.19 | -0.65 | -0.27 | 0.18 | -1.50 | 1.00 | 0.26 |
| TOT. RTN/ALL FUNDS | 82 | 82 | 5 | 50 | 78 | 11 | 60 | 52 | 47 | 75 | 70 | 7 | 72 |
| % RANK OBJECTIVE | 34 | 25 | 20 | 80 | 12 | 40 | 10 | 7 | 50 | 28 | 63 | 76 | 11 |
| INCOME | 0.27 | 0.30 | 0.33 | 0.36 | 0.36 | 0.36 | 0.35 | 0.35 | 0.36 | 0.32 | 0.31 | 0.30 | 0.21 |
| CAPITAL GAIN | 0.00 | 0.00 | 0.00 | 0.00 | 0.00 | 0.00 | 0.08 | 0.04 | 0.00 | 0.00 | 0.00 | 0.00 | 0.00 |
| EXPENSE % | 1.13 | 1.22 | 1.22 | 0.94 | 0.90 | 0.90 | 1.01 | 0.82 | 0.89 | 0.88 | 0.88 | 0.89 | ... |
| INCOME % | 8.71 | 10.54 | 11.93 | 12.70 | 11.07 | 12.07 | 11.08 | 10.32 | 10.48 | 11.26 | 10.66 | 10.55 | ... |
| TURNOVER % | 57 | 43 | 40 | 21 | 52 | 86 | 363 | 370 | 429 | 332 | 440 | 578 | ... |
| NET ASSETS ($MIL) | 34.4 | 31.0 | 33.0 | 43.5 | 50.6 | 52.0 | 77.3 | 364.6 | 774.0 | 1008.9 | 1256.6 | 1602.7 | 1852.5 |

NET ASSETS ($MIL): 2000 / 1000 / 0

### M-STAR RISK % RANK

| | ALL | OBJ. |
|---|---|---|
| 3 YEAR | 19 | 92 |
| 5 YEAR | 21 | 98 |
| 10 YEAR | 7 | 40 |

### MORNINGSTAR RETURN RISK (1.00 = FIXED-INCOME AVG)

| | RETURN | RISK |
|---|---|---|
| 3 YEAR | 1.09 | 1.11 → |
| 5 YEAR | 1.08 | 1.21 → |
| 10 YEAR | 1.03 | 0.94 → |
| WEIGHTED AVG. | 1.06 | 1.05 |

### MORNINGSTAR RISK-ADJUSTED RATING

| | |
|---|---|
| 3 YEAR | ★★★ |
| 5 YEAR | ★★ |
| 10 YEAR | ★★★★ |
| WEIGHTED AVG | ★★★ |

Percentile Ranks: 1 = Highest, 100 = Lowest
Except M-Star Risk: 1 = Lowest, 100 = Highest

## PORTFOLIO

**TOTAL # SECURITIES: 21** — **TOP 30 SECURITIES AS OF: 05/31/91**

| AMOUNT $000 | SECURITY | MATURITY | VALUE $000 | % NET ASSETS |
|---|---|---|---|---|
| 530000 | GNMA 8.5% | 2024 | 518294 | 28.39 |
| 284272 | GNMA 10% | 2030 | 298331 | 16.34 |
| 195071 | GNMA 9% | 07/15/09 | 196152 | 10.74 |
| 606000 | RESOLUTION FUNDING STRIP 0% | 07/15/09 | 167546 | 9.18 |
| 100000 | SLMA 16% | 02/14/94 | 121313 | 6.65 |
| 100000 | US TREASURY BOND 8% | 05/15/01 | 99625 | 5.46 |
| 304000 | FICO PRIN STRIP 0% | 2008 | 86008 | 4.71 |
| 65000 | RESOLUTION FUNDING 8.625% | 01/15/21 | 65691 | 3.60 |
| 56054 | GNMA 9.5% | 2024 | 57728 | 3.16 |
| 32809 | GNMA 10.5% | 2024 | 34881 | 1.91 |
| 29600 | FEDERAL FARM CREDIT BK 14.25% | 04/20/94 | 34764 | 1.90 |
| 76000 | FEDERAL HOME LOAN BK STRIP 0% | 02/25/04 | 24762 | 1.36 |
| 25000 | US TREASURY BOND 7.875% | 02/15/21 | 23859 | 1.31 |
| 20000 | FEDERAL FARM CREDIT BK 13.75% | 07/20/92 | 21500 | 1.18 |
| 16614 | GNMA 10.25% | 2024 | 17523 | 0.96 |
| 12036 | FHLMC-CMO 14% | 09/15/07 | 12980 | 0.71 |
| 45000 | US TREASURY STRIP 0% | 05/15/06 | 12846 | 0.70 |
| 10329 | GNMA 8.75% | 2031 | 10226 | 0.56 |
| 9151 | GNMA 9.75% | 2023 | 9483 | 0.52 |
| 8739 | GNMA 9.25% | 2031 | 8867 | 0.49 |
| 13000 | US TREASURY STRIP 0% | 05/15/04 | 4404 | 0.24 |

### PORTFOLIO STATISTICS

| | |
|---|---|
| AVG. WEIGHTED MATURITY | 12.7 YEARS |
| AVG. WEIGHTED COUPON | 8.20% |
| AVG. WEIGHTED PRICE | 90.8% OF PAR |

### COUPON RANGE

| | % BONDS | REL. OBL. |
|---|---|---|
| 0%, PIK | 16.2 | 3.6 |
| 0% to 8% | 6.8 | 0.8 |
| 8% to 9% | 43.3 | 1.5 |
| 9% to 10% | 20.5 | 0.7 |
| over 10% | 13.3 | 0.4 |

### COMPOSITION % 06/30/91

| | | | |
|---|---|---|---|
| CASH | 3.2 | PREFERREDS | 0.0 |
| STOCKS | 0.0 | CONVERTIBLES | 0.0 |
| BONDS | 96.8 | OTHER | 0.0 |

### CREDIT ANALYSIS 05/31/91

Percentage of Net Assets:
- US T-Bonds: 7
- US T-Notes
- GNMA: 63
- FNMA
- FHLMC: 1
- Agency
- Other: 30

---

## ANALYSIS

This year, Lord Abbett U.S. Government Securities Fund's aggressive style is paying off in spades.

Historically, this fund has prospered on an explosive one-two punch, featuring a healthy yield and the ability to ride bond-market rallies. This year, the fund has connected with both gloves. Its distributed yield remains among the group's highest, while its total return has stormed to within a whisker of the category's top decile.

Manager Carroll Coward has roped in both yield and capital appreciation by attacking the market from two directions. To encourage capital appreciation, she has stretched the fund's duration to more than seven years, exceeding the Lehman Brothers Mortgage-Backed Index by roughly two and a half years. Coward has lengthened the portfolio by emphasizing both long, zero-coupon Treasuries and long T-bonds, which excel when interest rates decline.

Likewise, the fund has also gained ground on the strength of its discount Ginnie Maes (many of which are bought on the forward markets). These issues not only feature longer duration, but they offer better call protection than other Ginnies. Consequently, they have flourished in the recent bond-market rally.

However, this approach has not undermined the fund's high-yield emphasis. Coward has reserved roughly 60% of the portfolio for superpremium coupons, which will expire in two to four years. (For accounting purposes, these premiums are left off the portfolio.) These issues are then rolled over into forward contracts, which are purchased at a discount: a swap that will, ideally, erase the principal loss suffered from a premium coupon's redemption.

Coward's strategy has worked wonders so far this year. Of course, the fund does remain vulnerable to interest-rate spikes.

Tom Desmond 10/18/91

## OPERATIONS

ADDRESS General Motors Bldg. 767 Fifth Avenue New York, NY 10153
ADVISOR Lord Abbett
DISTRIBUTOR Lord Abbett
PORTFOLIO MANAGER Carroll Coward (1986)
MANAGEMENT FEE 0.50% flat fee
FEES 4.75%L, 0.25%B
TICKER LAGVX

TELEPHONE NUMBER 212-848-1800 / 800-874-3733
PHONE SWITCH Yes
# OF SHAREHOLDERS 82251
MINIMUM INITIAL PURCHASE 500
MINIMUM SUBSEQUENT PURCHASE None
DATE OF INCEPTION 05/01/32
SHAREHOLDER REPORT RATING B

1001

# Merrill Lynch Federal Sec

MORNINGSTAR MUTUAL FUNDS

| OBJECTIVE | LOAD % | YIELD % | ASSETS($MIL) | N.A.V. |
|---|---|---|---|---|
| Gvt General | 4.00 | 8.1 | 2213.8 | 9.77 |

Merrill Lynch Federal Securities Trust seeks a high current return.

The fund invests in securities of the U.S. government and its agencies, including Government National Mortgage Association (GNMA) certificates and other mortgage-backed government securities. The fund seeks to enhance its return through the use of options and to hedge its portfolio through the use of options and futures.

**RATING**

| | RETURN | RISK |
|---|---|---|
| | Above Avg | Below Avg |
| **RATING** ★★★ | | |
| **Above Avg** | | |

TOP LINE: Adjusted NAV
BOTTOM LINE: Relative Strength

## TOTAL RETURN %

| | 1st Qtr. | 2nd Qtr. | 3rd Qtr. | 4th Qtr. | TOTAL |
|---|---|---|---|---|---|
| 1987 | 1.96 | -1.97 | -2.86 | 5.62 | 2.55 |
| 1988 | 3.53 | 1.31 | 2.34 | 0.31 | 7.68 |
| 1989 | 0.91 | 6.74 | 1.59 | 3.85 | 13.65 |
| 1990 | 0.16 | 3.41 | 1.80 | 4.72 | 10.43 |
| 1991 | 2.55 | 1.70 | 4.83 | … | … |

## INCOME

| | | | | | TOTAL |
|---|---|---|---|---|---|
| 1989 | 0.20 | 0.22 | 0.20 | 0.23 | 0.86 |
| 1990 | 0.20 | 0.21 | 0.21 | 0.22 | 0.83 |
| 1991 | 0.19 | 0.20 | 0.17 | … | 0.57 |

## CAPITAL GAINS

| | | | | | TOTAL |
|---|---|---|---|---|---|
| 1989 | 0.00 | 0.00 | 0.00 | 0.00 | 0.00 |
| 1990 | 0.00 | 0.00 | 0.00 | 0.00 | 0.00 |
| 1991 | 0.00 | 0.00 | 0.00 | … | … |

## PERFORMANCE/RISK 09/30/91

| | TOTAL RETURN% | +/- LB GOVT./CP. | PERCENTILE RANK ALL | OBJ. |
|---|---|---|---|---|
| 3 MONTH | 4.83 | -0.92 | 66 | 79 |
| 6 MONTH | 6.61 | -0.74 | 44 | 61 |
| 1 YEAR | 14.49 | -1.37 | 76 | 61 |
| 3 YEAR AVG. | 11.23 | -0.02 | 46 | 3 |
| 5 YEAR AVG. | 9.22 | 0.10 | 53 | 12 |
| 10 YEAR AVG. | … | | | |
| 15 YEAR AVG. | … | | | |

| | ALPHA | BETA | R² | STD. DEV. |
|---|---|---|---|---|
| | 0.9 | 0.74 | 92 | 0.98 |
| PERCENTILE RANK ALL | 7 | 52 | | 78 |
| RANK OBJ. | 5 | 76 | 52 | 81 |

Percentile Ranks: 1 = Highest 100 = Lowest

## HISTORY

| | 1979 | 1980 | 1981 | 1982 | 1983 | 1984 | 1985 | 1986 | 1987 | 1988 | 1989 | 1990 | 09/91 |
|---|---|---|---|---|---|---|---|---|---|---|---|---|---|
| N.A.V. | … | … | … | … | … | 9.64 | 9.96 | 9.87 | 9.23 | 9.07 | 9.39 | 9.48 | 9.77 |
| TOTAL RETURN % | … | … | … | … | … | … | 19.24 | 12.79 | 2.55 | 7.68 | 13.65 | 10.43 | 9.33 |
| +/-LB GOVT./CP. | … | … | … | … | … | … | -2.06 | -2.82 | 0.25 | 0.10 | -0.59 | 2.14 | -0.91 |
| % RANK ALL FUNDS | … | … | … | … | … | … | 80 | 66 | 44 | 25 | 15 | 3 | 78 |
| % RANK OBJECTIVE | … | … | … | … | … | … | 34 | 34 | 33 | 25 | 15 | 5 | 32 |
| INCOME | … | … | … | … | … | 0.19 | 1.05 | 0.86 | 0.83 | 0.85 | 0.86 | 0.83 | 0.57 |
| CAPITAL GAIN | … | … | … | … | … | 0.02 | 0.35 | 0.44 | 0.04 | 0.00 | 0.00 | 0.00 | 0.00 |
| EXPENSE % | … | … | … | … | … | … | 0.80 | 0.65 | 0.61 | 0.69 | 0.74 | 0.77 | … |
| INCOME % | … | … | … | … | … | … | 10.90 | 8.97 | 8.26 | 9.18 | 9.49 | 9.19 | … |
| TURNOVER % | … | … | … | … | … | … | 284 | 299 | 205 | 293 | 364 | 325 | … |
| NET ASSETS ($MIL) | … | … | … | … | … | 1.6 | 3381.8 | 7016.7 | 4542.7 | 3124.9 | 2637.5 | 2296.7 | 2213.8 |

NET ASSETS ($MIL): 8000 / 4000 / 0

| | M-STAR RISK % RANK ALL | OBJ. | MORNINGSTAR RETURN 1.00 = FIXED INCOME AVG. | RISK | MORNINGSTAR RISK-ADJUSTED RATING |
|---|---|---|---|---|---|
| 3 YEAR | 4 | 13 | 1.10 | 0.71 | ★★★★★ |
| 5 YEAR | 5 | 31 | 1.09 | 0.81 | ★★★★ |
| 10 YEAR | … | | | | |
| WEIGHTED AVG. | | | 1.10 | 0.77 | ★★★ |

Percentile M-Star Risk: 1 = Lowest, 100 = highest

## PORTFOLIO

| AMOUNT $000 | SECURITY | MATURITY | VALUE $000 | % NET ASSETS |
|---|---|---|---|---|
| 155179 | FNMA 9.5% | 05/01/21 | 158670 | 7.06 |
| 143974 | FHLMC 10.5% | 12/01/20 | 150588 | 6.70 |
| 122559 | GNMA 10.5% | 02/15/21 | 130257 | 5.79 |
| 117964 | GNMA 10% | 06/15/21 | 123457 | 5.49 |
| 103702 | FNMA 10% | 05/01/21 | 107906 | 4.80 |
| 101046 | FHLMC-GOLD 9.5% | 04/01/21 | 103572 | 4.61 |
| 93280 | FNMA 9% | 06/01/21 | 93280 | 4.15 |
| 82925 | FNMA 10.5% | 03/01/21 | 87227 | 3.88 |
| 68669 | FNMA-ARM 9.098% | 08/01/29 | 70302 | 3.13 |
| 70000 | US TREASURY NOTE 7.625% | 05/31/96 | 69781 | 3.10 |
| 70258 | FNMA 8.5% | 06/01/21 | 68684 | 3.05 |
| 67683 | FHLMC 9% | 10/01/19 | 67471 | 3.00 |
| 50000 | US TREASURY NOTE 8.5% | 07/15/97 | 51480 | 2.29 |
| 49000 | US TREASURY NOTE 7.75% | 03/31/96 | 49088 | 2.18 |
| 47500 | FHLMC-GOLD 9% | 06/01/21 | 47611 | 2.12 |
| 44690 | FHLMC 10% | 08/01/20 | 46338 | 2.06 |
| 44275 | FNMA-REMIC 8.5% | 09/25/19 | 43267 | 1.92 |
| 41120 | FHLMC-GOLD 10% | 06/01/21 | 42945 | 1.91 |
| 37212 | GNMA 11% | 12/15/20 | 40282 | 1.79 |
| 35203 | GNMA 9% | 12/15/20 | 35535 | 1.57 |
| 33000 | FNMA-REMIC 9% | 02/25/20 | 33190 | 1.48 |
| 29613 | FHLMC 11.5% | 06/01/20 | 31816 | 1.41 |
| 29640 | FHLMC-GOLD 10.5% | 12/01/20 | 31191 | 1.39 |
| 31882 | FHLMC-REMIC GOLD 7.5% | 05/15/15 | 30452 | 1.35 |
| 24527 | FHLMC 9.5% | 02/01/21 | 24971 | 1.11 |
| 25000 | US TREASURY BOND 8% | 05/15/01 | 24898 | 1.11 |
| 24078 | GNMA 9.5% | 09/15/20 | 24702 | 1.10 |
| 25000 | US TREASURY BOND 7.75% | 02/15/01 | 24441 | 1.09 |
| 23660 | FHLMC-15YR 9% | 10/01/05 | 23904 | 1.06 |
| 22957 | GNMA 9.25% | 10/15/23 | 23298 | 1.04 |

### PORTFOLIO STATISTICS

| | |
|---|---|
| AVG. WEIGHTED MATURITY | 11.1 YEARS |
| AVG. WEIGHTED COUPON | 9.41% |
| AVG. WEIGHTED PRICE | 102% OF PAR |

### COMPOSITION % 06/30/91

| | | | |
|---|---|---|---|
| CASH | 0.0 | PREFERREDS | 0.0 |
| STOCKS | 0.0 | CONVERTIBLES | 0.0 |
| BONDS | 100.0 | OTHER | 0.0 |

### COUPON RANGE

| | % BONDS | REL. OBJ. |
|---|---|---|
| 0% | 0.8 | 0.2 |
| 0% to 8% | 12.4 | 1.0 |
| 8% to 9% | 24.5 | 0.9 |
| 9% to 10% | 35.8 | 1.5 |
| over 10% | 26.4 | 1.1 |

### CREDIT ANALYSIS 05/31/91

| Category | Value |
|---|---|
| US T-Bonds | 9 |
| US T-Notes | 7 |
| GNMA | 16 |
| FNMA | 32 |
| FHLMC | 28 |
| Other | 16 |

## ANALYSIS

Jennifer Strickland 10/18/91

Merrill Lynch Federal Securities Trust thinks the real attraction lies with mortgage-backed securities.

Even though the fund falls under the government-general category, it looks more like a mortgage fund. Over the past five years, manager Greg Maunz has downplayed Treasuries, to the tune of 10%, to pursue higher-yielding mortgages.

Latching on to mortgages has proven profitable—as mortgages have outperformed since the mid 1980s, so has this fund.

The fund's primary strategy has been to seek out high-coupon mortgages that fall within the fund's short duration range, but also offer incrementally better yields than Treasuries. However, now that the rally has firmly taken hold and high-coupon mortgages are selling at stiff premiums (along with added repayment risk), the fund has had to look elsewhere. Instead of retreating to Treasuries, though, Maunz jumped into mortgage derivatives. These issues not only conform to the fund's duration range, but also offer higher yields than Treasuries. So far, the fund has been stocking up, with 10% of its assets in ARMs and 20% in REMICs.

These derivative issues offer an element of call protection to the fund (if not as much as Treasuries would provide). As interest rates have declined, the fund's high-coupon mortgages have become potential prepayment targets. The protected derivatives thus soften the portfolio's risk.

Maunz is adamant about his downplay of Treasuries. If spreads between derivatives and Treasuries were to tighten, thus making derivatives less appealing, he would use options to hedge the downside, rather than revert to Treasuries. We're not arguing: Seeking total return by emphasizing mortgages, as opposed to Treasuries, has kept this fund ahead of its pack.

## OPERATIONS

| | | | |
|---|---|---|---|
| ADDRESS | Box 9011, Princeton, NJ 08543 | TELEPHONE NUMBER | 609-282-2800 / 800-637-3863 |
| ADVISOR | Fund Asset Management | PHONE SWITCH | None |
| DISTRIBUTOR | Merrill Lynch Funds Distributor | # OF SHAREHOLDERS | 136450 |
| PORTFOLIO MANAGER | Gregory M. Maunz (1984) | MINIMUM INITIAL PURCHASE | 1000 |
| MANAGEMENT FEE | 0.50% max./0.30% min. | MINIMUM SUBSEQUENT PURCHASE | 50 |
| FEES | 4.00%L, 0.25%B | DATE OF INCEPTION | 09/28/84 |
| TICKER | MLFSX | SHAREHOLDER REPORT RATING | A |

# MetLife Capital Appreciation

| OBJECTIVE | LOAD % | YIELD % | ASSETS($Mil.) | N.A.V. |
|---|---|---|---|---|
| Aggr. Growth | 4.50 | 0.1 | 78.0 | 16.73 |

MetLife-State Street Capital Appreciation Fund seeks maximum capital appreciation. Current income is not a consideration.

The fund invests primarily in common stocks of emerging-growth companies and in special situations that offer the potential for above-average gains. Securities are selected on the basis of the advisor's continuous study of trends in industries and companies, earning power, growth features, and other investment criteria.

The fund may engage in active short-term trading.

| RETURN | RISK |
|---|---|
| High | Above Avg |
| **RATING** | |
| ★★★★ | |
| Above Avg | |

TOP LINE: Adjusted N.A.V.
BOTTOM LINE: Relative Strength

## TOTAL RETURN %

| | 1st Qtr. | 2nd Qtr. | 3rd Qtr. | 4th Qtr. | TOTAL |
|---|---|---|---|---|---|
| 1987 | 28.81 | 3.13 | 8.42 | -27.15 | 4.92 |
| 1988 | 11.11 | 10.04 | -1.55 | 1.02 | 21.59 |
| 1989 | 10.64 | 7.31 | 15.35 | -3.95 | 31.55 |
| 1990 | 0.71 | 5.10 | -23.96 | 7.19 | -13.72 |
| 1991 | 32.11 | -8.70 | 19.91 | ... | ... |

## INCOME

| | | | | | TOTAL |
|---|---|---|---|---|---|
| 1989 | 0.02 | 0.00 | 0.01 | 0.02 | 0.05 |
| 1990 | 0.00 | 0.00 | 0.03 | 0.02 | 0.05 |
| 1991 | 0.00 | 0.00 | 0.00 | 0.00 | 0.00 |

## CAPITAL GAINS

| | | | | | TOTAL |
|---|---|---|---|---|---|
| 1989 | 0.00 | 0.85 | 0.76 | 0.00 | 1.61 |
| 1990 | 0.00 | 0.00 | 0.00 | 0.00 | 0.00 |
| 1991 | 0.00 | 0.00 | 0.00 | 0.00 | 0.00 |

## PERFORMANCE/RISK

| | TOTAL RETURN % | +/- S&P 500 | PERCENTILE RANK ALL | OBJ. |
|---|---|---|---|---|
| 3 MONTH | 18.32 | 16.33 | 4 | ... |
| 6 MONTH | 23.65 | 17.44 | 2 | 7 |
| 1 YEAR | 78.50 | 45.05 | 3 | 18 |
| 3 YEAR AVG. | 20.69 | 4.71 | 6 | 39 |
| 5 YEAR AVG. | 17.20 | 3.43 | 5 | 22 |
| 10 YEAR AVG. | ... | | | |
| 15 YEAR AVG. | ... | | | |

| | ALPHA | BETA | $R^2$ | STD.DEV. |
|---|---|---|---|---|
| | 2.2 | 1.39 | 74 | 6.71 |
| PERCENTILE ALL | 11 | 3 | 50 | 3 |
| RANK OBJ. | 45 | 19 | 66 | 23 |

## HISTORY

| | 1979 | 1980 | 1981 | 1982 | 1983 | 1984 | 1985 | 1986 | 1987 | 1988 | 1989 | 1990 | 10/91 |
|---|---|---|---|---|---|---|---|---|---|---|---|---|---|
| N.A.V. | ... | ... | ... | ... | ... | ... | ... | 8.95 | 9.00 | 10.90 | 12.65 | 10.87 | 16.73 |
| TOTAL RETURN % | ... | ... | ... | ... | ... | ... | ... | ... | 4.92 | 21.59 | 31.55 | -13.72 | 53.91 |
| +/- S & P 500 INDEX | ... | ... | ... | ... | ... | ... | ... | ... | -0.12 | 5.08 | ... | -10.62 | 31.83 |
| TOT. RTN % ALL FUNDS | ... | ... | ... | ... | ... | ... | ... | ... | 23 | 10 | 11 | 90 | 3 |
| % RANK OBJECTIVE | ... | ... | ... | ... | ... | ... | ... | ... | 32 | 28 | 40 | 77 | 23 |
| INCOME | ... | ... | ... | ... | ... | ... | ... | 0.00 | 0.07 | 0.04 | 0.05 | 0.05 | 0.00 |
| CAPITAL GAIN | ... | ... | ... | ... | ... | ... | ... | 0.00 | 0.43 | 1.61 | 1.61 | 0.00 | 0.00 |
| EXPENSE % | ... | ... | ... | ... | ... | ... | ... | ... | 1.50 | 1.50 | 1.50 | 1.50 | ... |
| INCOME % | ... | ... | ... | ... | ... | ... | ... | ... | 0.31 | 0.77 | 0.29 | 0.39 | -0.13 |
| TURNOVER % | ... | ... | ... | ... | ... | ... | ... | ... | ... | 331 | 223 | 239 | 246 |
| NET ASSETS ($Mil) | ... | ... | ... | ... | ... | ... | ... | 7.4 | 25.1 | 27.7 | 42.4 | 49.3 | 78.0 |

| | M-STAR RISK % RANK | | MORNINGSTAR RETURN RISK (1.00=EQUITY AVG) | | MORNINGSTAR RISK-ADJUSTED RATING |
|---|---|---|---|---|---|
| | ALL | OBJ. | | | |
| 3 YEAR | 97 | 88 | 1.51 | 1.50 | ★★★ |
| 5 YEAR | 91 | 56 | 1.53 | 1.24 | ★★★★ |
| 10 YEAR | ... | ... | | | |
| WEIGHTED AVG. | | | 1.52 | 1.34 | ★★★★ |

Percentile Ranks: 1 = Highest, 100 = Lowest
Except M-STAR Risk: 1 = Lowest, 100 = Highest

| SHARE CHANGE | AMOUNT | STOCK | VALUE $000 | % NET ASSETS |
|---|---|---|---|---|
| 33300 | 33300 | US SURGICAL | 2081 | 3.30 |
| 42200 | 42200 | FOREST LABORATORIES CL A | 1519 | 2.41 |
| 18000 | 69825 | KNOWLEDGEWARE | 1519 | 2.41 |
| 20000 | 45000 | BIOGEN | 1215 | 1.93 |
| 21000 | 21000 | TIFFANY | 1113 | 1.77 |
| 25000 | 25000 | BORLAND INTERNATIONAL | 1081 | 1.72 |
| 36900 | 36900 | FOUNDATION HEALTH | 1075 | 1.71 |
| 34000 | 34000 | CISCO SYSTEMS | 1041 | 1.65 |
| 14250 | 14250 | MICROSOFT | 971 | 1.54 |
| 18900 | 18900 | NOVELL | 926 | 1.47 |
| 23800 | 23800 | ALDUS | 898 | 1.43 |
| 61100 | 61100 | BROOKTREE | 886 | 1.41 |
| 16900 | 16900 | CHIRON | 875 | 1.39 |
| 35700 | 35700 | PARAMETRIC TECHNOLOGY | 848 | 1.35 |
| 15600 | 26600 | LOWE'S | 835 | 1.33 |
| 2600 | 2600 | VICOR | 819 | 1.30 |
| 19500 | 19500 | CHIQUITA BRANDS INTL | 819 | 1.30 |
| 0 | 17000 | LIZ CLAIBORNE | 797 | 1.27 |
| -11600 | 17000 | T2 MEDICAL | 774 | 1.23 |
| 34000 | 34000 | DESTEC ENERGY | 774 | 1.23 |
| 4200 | 27150 | GRANITE CONSTRUCTION | 743 | 1.18 |
| 26600 | 26600 | SUN MICROSYSTEMS | 743 | 1.18 |
| 33400 | 33400 | HEALTHCARE COMPARE | 726 | 1.15 |
| 37300 | 37300 | PLATINUM TECHNOLOGY | 718 | 1.14 |
| 15800 | 15800 | HOME DEPOT | 713 | 1.13 |
| 6000 | 6000 | MEDTRONIC | 678 | 1.08 |
| 40000 | 40000 | SIZZLER INTERNATIONAL | 675 | 1.07 |
| -7700 | 20700 | STRUCTURAL DYNAMICS RESEARCH | 673 | 1.07 |
| 22200 | 22200 | APPLIED BIOSCIENCE | 672 | 1.07 |
| 33100 | 33100 | WABAN | 666 | 1.06 |

## PORTFOLIO STATISTICS   10/31/91

| | PORT-FOLIO AVG. | % OF STOCKS | REL. S&P 500 |
|---|---|---|---|
| PRICE/EARNINGS RATIO | 30.5 | 54 | 1.66 |
| PRICE/BOOK RATIO | 7.7 | 75 | 2.17 |
| 5 YR. EARN. GR. % | 20.7 | 30 | 2.12 |
| RETURN ON ASSETS | 10.0 | 65 | 1.32 |
| DEBT % TOTAL CAP. | 24.9 | 65 | 0.78 |
| MED. MKT. CAP. ($MIL) | 712 | 87 | 0.07 |

### COMPOSITION %   09/30/91

| | | | |
|---|---|---|---|
| CASH | 10.5 | PREFERREDS | 0.0 |
| STOCKS | 89.5 | CONVERTIBLES | 0.0 |
| BONDS | 0.0 | OTHER | 0.0 |

### SECTOR WEIGHTINGS

| | PORT-FOLIO % | REL. S&P 500 |
|---|---|---|
| NATURAL RESOURCES | 2.0 | 0.12 |
| INDUSTRIAL PRODUCTS | 18.7 | 1.74 |
| CONSUMER DURABLES | 14.0 | 2.25 |
| NON-DURABLES | 11.6 | 0.50 |
| RETAIL TRADE | 12.9 | 1.85 |
| SERVICES | 29.8 | 3.10 |
| UTILITIES | 2.1 | 0.15 |
| TRANSPORTATION | 3.5 | 1.87 |
| FINANCE | 5.6 | 0.69 |
| MULTI-INDUSTRY | 0.0 | 0.00 |

## ANALYSIS

Helen O'D. Johnstone   11/15/91

Supported by its recently established five-year record, MetLife-State Street Capital Appreciation Fund jumps to 4 stars this issue.

Like its aggressive-growth rivals, the fund carries considerably more risk than the average equity fund (with a correspondingly high beta). Still, patient investors have been well compensated for the fund's volatile tendencies. For example, those who hung on through 1987's fourth quarter—when the fund lost 27%—and last year's third quarter—when it dropped almost 24%—have been rewarded with an average annual return of more than 17% for five years. (However, its risk has crept up in recent years, leading to a less enticing three-year risk/reward profile; the fund earns 3 stars for that period.)

To offset the fund's volatility, manager Fred Kobrick has traditionally held a larger number of individual positions than many of his aggressive-growth peers. However, like his rivals, he has tended to make significant sector bets. Such industry concentrations (notably, an overweighting in technology stocks) have contributed to the fund's above-average long-term risk score.

In 1991, however, Kobrick has broadened the fund's sector bets, supplementing the fund's tech and health-care firms with a variety of specialty retailers, toy makers (e.g., he recently bought Hasbro and Mattel), entertainment firms, and financials— Although he owns a couple of cyclicals— Chrysler and American Airlines—he's focusing for the most part on growth industries in anticipation of continued sluggishness in the economy.

This fund's success depends on its ability to rise high enough in a rally to overcome a negative quarter or two. For investors who can stomach such volatility, it offers exciting capital-growth potential.

## OPERATIONS

ADDRESS   One Financial Center, Boston, MA 02111
ADVISOR   MetLife-State Street Investment
DISTRIBUTOR   MetLife-State Street Investment
PORTFOLIO MANAGER   Frederick Kobrick (1986)
MANAGEMENT FEE   0.75% flat fee.
FEES   4.50%L, 0.50%B
TICKER   MSSCX

TELEPHONE NUMBER   617-348-2000 / 800-882-0052
PHONE SWITCH   Yes
# OF SHAREHOLDERS   12670
MINIMUM INITIAL PURCHASE   250
MINIMUM SUBSEQUENT PURCHASE   25
DATE OF INCEPTION   08/25/86
SHAREHOLDER REPORT RATING   C

# Oppenheimer Global

MORNINGSTAR MUTUAL FUNDS

| OBJECTIVE | LOAD % | YIELD % | ASSETS($MIL) | N.A.V. |
|---|---|---|---|---|
| Intl Stock | 5.75 | 0.3 | 913.0 | 30.14 |

Oppenheimer Global Fund seeks capital appreciation. Current income is not an objective.

Using a global approach, the fund emphasizes investment in common stocks or convertible securities of growth-type companies. The fund may also invest in securities of cyclical industries and special situations.

In its operations, the fund may use special investment techniques, such as hedging, borrowing money for investment in securities, short-term trading, and placement of up to 10% of its assets in restricted securities.

Prior to February 1, 1987, the fund was named Oppenheimer A.I.M. Fund.

**TOP LINE:** Adjusted NAV
**BOTTOM LINE:** Relative Strength

| RETURN | RISK |
|---|---|
| Above Avg | Average |

RATING ★★★
Above Avg

### TOTAL RETURN %

| | 1st Qtr. | 2nd Qtr. | 3rd Qtr. | 4th Qtr. | TOTAL |
|---|---|---|---|---|---|
| 1987 | 16.56 | 6.64 | 14.13 | -31.95 | -3.46 |
| 1988 | 8.82 | 6.08 | -4.73 | 11.84 | 22.99 |
| 1989 | 10.08 | 3.51 | 12.12 | 5.71 | 35.05 |
| 1990 | 4.55 | 8.75 | -16.15 | 4.18 | -0.68 |
| 1991 | 8.71 | -3.72 | ... | ... | ... |

### INCOME

| | | | | | TOTAL |
|---|---|---|---|---|---|
| 1989 | 0.00 | 0.00 | 0.00 | 0.11 | 0.11 |
| 1990 | 0.00 | 0.00 | 0.00 | 0.08 | 0.08 |
| 1991 | 0.00 | 0.00 | 0.00 | 0.00 | 0.00 |

### CAPITAL GAINS

| | | | | | TOTAL |
|---|---|---|---|---|---|
| 1989 | 0.00 | 0.00 | 0.00 | 3.00 | 3.00 |
| 1990 | 0.00 | 0.00 | 0.00 | 1.69 | 1.69 |
| 1991 | 0.00 | 0.00 | 0.00 | 0.00 | 0.00 |

### PERFORMANCE/RISK

07/31/91

| | TOTAL RETURN % | +/- S&P 500 | +/- EAFE | PERCENTILE RANK ALL | PERCENTILE RANK OBJ |
|---|---|---|---|---|---|
| 3 MONTH | 4.25 | 0.11 | 6.03 | 21 | 9 |
| 6 MONTH | 11.42 | -3.17 | 8.20 | 36 | 22 |
| 1 YEAR | -8.63 | -21.42 | -0.15 | 95 | 57 |
| 3 YEAR AVG. | 17.48 | 0.93 | 16.89 | 8 | 3 |
| 5 YEAR AVG. | 14.09 | -0.17 | 3.84 | 10 | 20 |
| 10 YEAR AVG. | 15.00 | -1.02 | -2.70 | 23 | 55 |
| 15 YEAR AVG. | 17.53 | 0.88 | 3.55 | 12 | 8 |

| | ALPHA | BETA | $R^2$ | STD. DEV. |
|---|---|---|---|---|
| | 3.6 | 0.76 | 41 | 5.07 |
| PERCENTILE /ALL | 7 | 70 | 88 | 31 |
| RANK*OBJ. | 6 | 54 | 61 | 40 |

Percentile Ranks 1 = Highest, 100 = Lowest
Except MMF Risk: 1 = Lowest, 100 = Highest

### HISTORY

| | 1979 | 1980 | 1981 | 1982 | 1983 | 1984 | 1985 | 1986 | 1987 | 1988 | 1989 | 1990 | 07/91 |
|---|---|---|---|---|---|---|---|---|---|---|---|---|---|
| N.A.V. | 15.75 | 22.44 | 15.73 | 17.58 | 19.50 | 14.33 | 21.25 | 26.99 | 20.86 | 23.82 | 28.98 | 26.99 | 30.14 |
| TOTAL RETURN % | 56.51 | 55.82 | -11.13 | 14.12 | 26.12 | -21.77 | 49.11 | 46.54 | -3.46 | 22.99 | 35.05 | -0.68 | 11.67 |
| +/- S & P 500 INDEX | 38.21 | 23.60 | -6.05 | -7.34 | 3.66 | -27.90 | 17.47 | 27.91 | -8.68 | 6.48 | 3.38 | 2.42 | -8.03 |
| +/- EAFE INDEX | 51.76 | 33.24 | -8.85 | 15.98 | | -29.16 | -7.05 | -28.09 | -5.28 | 24.51 | 22.77 | 5.11 | |
| TOT. RTN/ALL FUNDS | 4 | 7 | 91 | 87 | 21 | 97 | 2 | 3 | 82 | 11 | 10 | 40 | 61 |
| % RANK OBJECTIVE | 7 | 13 | 95 | 32 | 74 | 100 | 27 | 44 | 88 | 19 | 17 | 6 | 35 |
| INCOME | 0.31 | 0.25 | 0.33 | 0.32 | 0.17 | 0.06 | 0.10 | 0.11 | 0.07 | 0.09 | 0.11 | 0.08 | 0.00 |
| CAPITAL GAIN | 0.00 | 1.64 | 3.73 | 0.33 | 2.50 | 0.93 | 0.00 | 3.87 | 5.62 | 1.73 | 3.00 | 1.69 | 0.00 |
| EXPENSE % | 1.09 | 1.11 | 1.20 | 1.02 | 1.00 | 1.48 | 1.21 | 1.60 | 1.49 | 1.89 | 1.90 | 1.68 | |
| INCOME % | 2.39 | 1.46 | 1.55 | 2.10 | 0.82 | 0.35 | 0.81 | 0.47 | 0.16 | 0.15 | 0.73 | 0.16 | |
| TURNOVER % | 143 | 199 | 150 | 102 | 91 | 50 | 29 | 25 | 37 | 27 | 63 | 27 | |
| NET ASSETS ($MIL) | 164.4 | 220.0 | 190.9 | 189.0 | 285.6 | 245.7 | 231.7 | 387.6 | 370.7 | 414.9 | 566.8 | 805.0 | 913.0 |

NET ASSETS ($MIL) 1000 / 500

### M-STAR RISK % RANK

| | ALL | OBJ |
|---|---|---|
| 3 YEAR | 66 | 24 |
| 5 YEAR | 66 | 45 |
| 10 YEAR | 82 | 74 |

### MORNINGSTAR RETURN RISK (1.00 = EQUITY AVG)

| | RETURN | RISK |
|---|---|---|
| 3 YEAR | 1.39 | 0.92 ↑ |
| 5 YEAR | 1.29 | 0.92 ↑ |
| 10 YEAR | 1.16 | 1.09 ↑ |
| WEIGHTED AVG. | 1.24 | 1.01 |

### MORNINGSTAR RISK-ADJUSTED RATING

| 3 YEAR | ★★★★ |
|---|---|
| 5 YEAR | ★★★★ |
| 10 YEAR | ★★★ |
| 15 YEAR | ★★★★ |

## PORTFOLIO

**TOTAL # STOCKS: 111**  **TOP 38 EQUITY HOLDINGS AS OF: 03/30/91**

| SHARE CHANGE | AMOUNT | STOCK | VALUE $000 | % NET ASSETS |
|---:|---:|---|---:|---:|
| 0 | 330000 | AMGEN | 43313 | 4.69 |
| 74200 | 364000 | ASTRA CL A | 32414 | 3.51 |
| 0 | 1914000 | BOMBARDIER CL B | 28703 | 3.11 |
| 26150 | 395300 | NOVO NORDISK | 24545 | 2.66 |
| 350400 | 791700 | GAMBRO CL B | 23115 | 2.50 |
| -4000 | 1346000 | SAGA PETROLEUM CL A | 21775 | 2.36 |
| 0 | 125000 | CANAL PLUS | 20940 | 2.27 |
| -280 | 34500 | BBC BROWN BOVERI | 19714 | 2.13 |
| 4665 | 44665 | GOLDSCHMIDT | 18572 | 2.01 |
| 0 | 137250 | KONE-OY CL B | 17688 | 1.91 |
| 0 | 169125 | PAKHOED | 17058 | 1.85 |
| -3500 | 604538 | WOLTERS KLUWER | 16500 | 1.79 |
| 0 | 500000 | HAFSLUND NYCOMED | 14673 | 1.59 |
| 0 | 1862700 | ROGERS COMMUNICATIONS CL B | 14670 | 1.59 |
| 193000 | 415500 | GENZYME | 14543 | 1.57 |
| 12007 | 97037 | FLS INDUSTRIES CL B | 13916 | 1.51 |
| 0 | 172000 | BEGEMANN MACHINEFABRIEK | 13771 | 1.49 |
| 304500 | 304500 | VERBUND OEST | 13401 | 1.45 |
| 0 | 250000 | IMMUNO | 13313 | 1.44 |
| 0 | 230000 | T2 MEDICAL | 13053 | 1.41 |
| 600 | 600 | D/S SVENDBORG CL B | 12311 | 1.33 |
| 0 | 185000 | CHIRON | 12118 | 1.31 |
| -180 | 26050 | SCHERING | 11869 | 1.28 |
| 0 | 20000 | UCB | 10776 | 1.17 |
| 20000 | 220000 | SPC ELECTRONICS | 10723 | 1.16 |
| 0 | 301000 | BIOGEN | 10723 | 1.16 |
| 0 | 619000 | SYNCOR INTERNATIONAL | 10523 | 1.14 |
| -20000 | 131500 | BURMEISTER & WAIN CL B | 10231 | 1.11 |
| -85 | 7915 | KRONES | 10198 | 1.10 |
| 100 | 695 | D/S AF 1912 CL B | 9967 | 1.08 |

## PORTFOLIO STATISTICS 07/31/91

| | PORT-FOLIO | % OF AVG. STOCKS | REL. S&P 500 |
|---|---:|---:|---:|
| PRICE/EARNINGS RATIO | 23.7 | 8 | 1.36 |
| PRICE/BOOK RATIO | 5.8 | 21 | 1.66 |
| 5 YR. EARN. GR. % | 9.5 | 7 | 0.73 |
| RETURN ON ASSETS | 5.7 | 10 | 0.76 |
| DEBT % TOTAL CAP. | 22.6 | 10 | 0.70 |
| MED. MKT. CAP. ($MIL) | 728 | 22 | 0.06 |

### COMPOSITION % 06/30/91

| | | | |
|---|---:|---|---:|
| CASH | -2.1 | PREFERREDS | 0.4 |
| STOCKS | 100.2 | CONVERTIBLES | 1.5 |
| BONDS | 0.0 | OTHER | 0.0 |

### REGIONAL EXPOSURE 08/01/91

## ANALYSIS

**Jennifer Strickland**  08/23/91

Oppenheimer Global Fund is betting that blondes have more fun.

This fund long had an unusual affinity for Northern Europe, with close to 60% of it's assets in that area. Scandinavia, a region most fund managers consider too illiquid for comfort, receives equal billing with the U.S. Germany and such Eastern-block neighbors as Austria account for its remaining assets. Meanwhile, the Pacific basin represents but a measly 7.5%.

Fund manager Ken Oberman has been drawn to Northern Europe because of its moderate stock prices and relatively stable interest rates. Given the massive changes sweeping Europe, such as the emergence of the Eastern block and reduced trade barriers in 1992, Oberman sees great, low-priced growth potential, mainly in the capital-spending industries. Due to the need to rebuild the European infrastructure, Oberman identifies pollution control, telecommunications, and construction/engineering as prime investment sectors. In addition, Scandinavia is appealing as an OPEC alternative because of its oil trade with the Soviet Union. The downfall of Soviet hard-liners, he claims, should only accelerate trade and rebuilding.

The fund's trailing 10-year returns have proven that Northern European markets can have worthwhile returns. Even though the fund missed the Japanese bandwagon in the early- to mid-80's, it still realized returns higher than the average equity fund. In fact, the fund's three- and five-year performances merit 4-star ratings.

While the Northern European market has been relatively stable in the past, the Soviet "putsch" reveals that politics and currency fluctuations can flip-flop fortunes in very short periods of time. This fund is fairly stable by international-fund standards, but it still delivers a few jolts.

## OPERATIONS

| | | | |
|---|---|---|---|
| **ADDRESS** | P.O. Box 300 Denver, CO 80201 | **TELEPHONE NUMBER** | 303-671-3200 800-525-7048 |
| **ADVISOR** | Oppenheimer Management | **PHONE SWITCH** | Yes |
| **DISTRIBUTOR** | Oppenheimer Fund Management | **# OF SHAREHOLDERS** | 105622 |
| **PORTFOLIO MANAGER** | Ken Oberman (1981) | **MINIMUM INITIAL PURCHASE** | 1000 |
| **MANAGEMENT FEE** | 0.75% max/0.66% min. | **MINIMUM SUBSEQUENT PURCHASE** | 25 |
| **FEES** | 5.75%L, 0.25%B | **DATE OF INCEPTION** | 12/08/69 |
| **TICKER** | OPPAX | **SHAREHOLDER REPORT RATING** | B- |

# Phoenix Growth

MUTUAL FUND VALUES

| OBJECTIVE | LOAD % | YIELD % | ASSETS($MIL) | N.A.V. |
|---|---|---|---|---|
| Growth | 4.75 | 2.5 | 906.1 | 21.26 |

Phoenix Growth Fund Series seeks long-term appreciation of capital. Any income will be incidental.

The fund invests primarily in common stocks of companies believed to have appreciation potential. However, any amount of its assets may be designated for any type of security, as long as these investments will further the fund's investment objective. The fund may also write covered call options on certain securities in its portfolio.

**TOP LINE:** Adjusted N.A.V.
**BOTTOM LINE:** Relative Strength

| | RETURN | RISK |
|---|---|---|
| | High | Low |
| | RATING | |
| | ★★★★ | |
| | Highest | |

**NET ASSETS:** ($Mil.) 1000 / 500 / 0

## TOTAL RETURN %

| | 1st Qtr. | 2nd Qtr. | 3rd Qtr. | 4th Qtr. | TOTAL |
|---|---|---|---|---|---|
| 1987 | 17.93 | 2.84 | 5.43 | -13.04 | 11.19 |
| 1988 | 1.84 | 2.66 | 1.08 | 1.20 | 6.95 |
| 1989 | 4.99 | 6.38 | 9.12 | 4.59 | 27.47 |
| 1990 | -1.72 | 7.98 | -7.44 | 7.97 | 6.05 |
| 1991 | 15.69 | -1.84 | --- | --- | --- |

## INCOME

| | 1st Qtr. | 2nd Qtr. | 3rd Qtr. | 4th Qtr. | TOTAL |
|---|---|---|---|---|---|
| 1989 | 0.00 | 0.34 | 0.00 | 0.33 | 0.67 |
| 1990 | 0.00 | 0.29 | 0.00 | 0.39 | 0.68 |
| 1991 | 0.00 | 0.16 | --- | --- | 0.16 |

## CAPITAL GAINS

| | 1st Qtr. | 2nd Qtr. | 3rd Qtr. | 4th Qtr. | TOTAL |
|---|---|---|---|---|---|
| 1989 | 0.00 | 0.00 | 0.00 | 0.28 | 0.28 |
| 1990 | 0.00 | 0.00 | 0.00 | 0.77 | 0.77 |
| 1991 | 0.00 | 0.00 | --- | --- | 0.00 |

## PERFORMANCE/RISK

| | TOTAL RETURN % | +/- S&P 500 | PERCENTILE RANK ALL | PERCENTILE RANK OBJ. |
|---|---|---|---|---|
| 3 MONTH | -1.84 | -1.56 | 77 | 66 |
| 6 MONTH | 13.56 | -0.71 | 42 | 70 |
| 1 YEAR | 13.49 | 6.08 | 6 | 6 |
| 3 YEAR AVG. | 16.23 | 1.56 | 7 | 15 |
| 5 YEAR AVG. | 12.62 | 0.71 | 8 | 3 |
| 10 YEAR AVG. | 19.46 | 3.96 | 1 | 3 |
| 15 YEAR AVG. | 17.92 | 4.33 | 9 | 18 |

| | ALPHA | BETA | R² | STD. DEV. |
|---|---|---|---|---|
| | 2.8 | 0.77 | 92 | 3.35 |
| PERCENTILE / ALL | 8 | 69 | 17 | 82 |
| RANK / OBJ. | 9 | 92 | 22 | 94 |

Percentile Ranks: 1 = Highest, 100 = Lowest
Except MFV Risk: 1 = Lowest, 100 = Highest

## HISTORY

| | 1979 | 1980 | 1981 | 1982 | 1983 | 1984 | 1985 | 1986 | 1987 | 1988 | 1989 | 1990 | 06/91 |
|---|---|---|---|---|---|---|---|---|---|---|---|---|---|
| N.A.V. | 9.47 | 9.46 | 9.04 | 12.27 | 12.43 | 13.21 | 16.43 | 16.40 | 15.18 | 15.82 | 19.15 | 18.86 | 21.26 |
| TOTAL RETURN % | 33.05 | 46.24 | 1.79 | 42.51 | 28.41 | 10.15 | 32.32 | 19.24 | 11.19 | 6.95 | 27.47 | 6.05 | 13.56 |
| +/- S & P 500 INDEX | 14.75 | 14.02 | 6.87 | 21.05 | 5.95 | 4.02 | 0.68 | 0.61 | 5.97 | -9.56 | -4.20 | 9.15 | -0.71 |
| TOT. RTN/ALL FUNDS | 22 | 14 | 46 | 10 | 15 | 24 | 18 | 25 | 12 | 82 | 25 | 21 | 42 |
| % RANK / OBJECTIVE | 40 | 24 | 36 | 12 | 18 | 8 | 29 | 20 | 12 | 85 | 46 | 3 | 70 |
| INCOME | 0.27 | 0.78 | 0.59 | 0.62 | 0.49 | 0.42 | 0.62 | 0.34 | 0.57 | 0.41 | 0.67 | 0.68 | 0.16 |
| CAPITAL GAIN | 0.00 | 3.05 | 0.00 | 0.00 | 2.86 | 0.00 | 0.32 | 2.91 | 2.56 | 0.00 | 0.28 | 0.77 | 0.00 |
| EXPENSE % | 0.97 | 0.96 | 0.98 | 1.06 | 0.90 | 0.88 | 0.82 | 0.78 | 0.71 | 0.85 | 1.06 | 1.01 | --- |
| INCOME % | 3.97 | 4.19 | 6.24 | 6.18 | 3.80 | 4.83 | 3.87 | 2.68 | 2.64 | 2.48 | 3.79 | 3.37 | --- |
| TURNOVER % | 56 | 90 | 179 | 213 | 208 | 150 | 151 | 170 | 185 | 221 | 180 | 203 | --- |
| NET ASSETS ($MIL) | 24.1 | 25.2 | 37.6 | 47.1 | 66.1 | 76.2 | 112.3 | 271.9 | 523.4 | 587.2 | 715.8 | 743.5 | 906.1 |

| | MFV RISK % RANK ALL | MFV RISK % RANK OBJ | MFV RETURN 1.00 = EQUITY AVG. | MFV RISK 1.00 = EQUITY AVG. | MFV RISK-ADJUSTED RATING |
|---|---|---|---|---|---|
| 3 YEAR | 35 | 4 | 1.61 | 0.59 ↑ | ★★★★★ |
| 5 YEAR | 45 | 7 | 1.50 | 0.72 ↑ | ★★★★★ |
| 10 YEAR | 38 | 5 | 1.67 | 0.65 ↑ | ★★★★★ |
| WEIGHTED AVG. | | | 1.61 | 0.66 | ★★★★★ |

## PORTFOLIO

**TOTAL # STOCKS** 63    **TOP 30 EQUITY HOLDINGS AS OF:** 03/31/91

| SHARE CHANGE | AMOUNT | STOCK | VALUE $000 | % NET ASSETS |
|---|---|---|---|---|
| 0 | 400000 | PFIZER | 42800 | 4.72 |
| 150000 | 600000 | GENERAL ELECTRIC | 41850 | 4.62 |
| 500000 | 500000 | HEWLETT-PACKARD | 25000 | 2.76 |
| 400000 | 700000 | BAXTER INTERNATIONAL | 23275 | 2.57 |
| 100000 | 300000 | WARNER-LAMBERT | 22388 | 2.47 |
| -25000 | 225000 | AMERICAN INTERNATIONAL GROUP | 21684 | 2.39 |
| -25000 | 275000 | BRISTOL-MYERS SQUIBB | 21484 | 2.37 |
| -90000 | 150000 | AMGEN | 19688 | 2.17 |
| 90000 | 490000 | WASTE MANAGEMENT | 19355 | 2.14 |
| 425000 | 425000 | LIZ CLAIBORNE | 18222 | 2.01 |
| -50000 | 250000 | CHUBB | 17969 | 1.98 |
| 0 | 300000 | MELVILLE | 15863 | 1.75 |
| 0 | 282300 | AMERICAN CYANAMID | 14785 | 1.63 |
| 375000 | 375000 | COMMONWEALTH EDISON | 14766 | 1.63 |
| -100000 | 150000 | JOHNSON & JOHNSON | 14381 | 1.59 |
| 150000 | 150000 | CPC INTERNATIONAL | 12544 | 1.38 |
| 0 | 120000 | LOEWS | 12465 | 1.38 |
| 5000 | 250000 | SCHERING-PLOUGH | 12219 | 1.35 |
| 100000 | 325000 | HOUSTON INDUSTRIES | 11741 | 1.30 |
| 0 | 80000 | UAL | 11560 | 1.28 |
| 0 | 564000 | NORTHEAST UTILITIES | 11421 | 1.26 |
| 10000 | 210000 | H & R BLOCK | 11051 | 1.22 |
| 450700 | 450700 | TRAVELERS | 10648 | 1.18 |
| 100000 | 325000 | COASTAL | 10278 | 1.13 |
| 250000 | 250000 | HJ HEINZ | 9969 | 1.10 |
| 0 | 100000 | GENERAL RE | 9888 | 1.09 |
| 0 | 146000 | NALCO CHEMICAL | 9472 | 1.05 |
| 125000 | 125000 | DELTA AIR LINES | 8703 | 0.96 |
| -150000 | 250000 | PEPSICO | 8531 | 0.94 |
| 100000 | 100000 | AMERICAN STORES | 8450 | 0.93 |

### PORTFOLIO STATISTICS 06/30/91

| | PORT-FOLIO OF AVG. | % OF STOCKS | REL. S&P 500 |
|---|---|---|---|
| PRICE/EARNINGS RATIO | 16.9 | 87 | 1.03 |
| PRICE/BOOK RATIO | 3.7 | 100 | 1.14 |
| 5 YR. EARN. GR. % | 15.2 | 69 | 1.13 |
| RETURN ON ASSETS | 8.4 | 76 | 1.06 |
| DEBT % TOTAL CAP. | 28.9 | 87 | 0.90 |
| MED. MKT. CAP. (SMIL) | 7000 | 100 | 0.59 |

**COMPOSITION %** 03/31/91

| CASH | 24.0 | PREFERREDS | 0.0 |
|---|---|---|---|
| STOCKS | 71.8 | CONVERTIBLES | 1.3 |
| BONDS | 2.9 | OTHER | 0.0 |

### SECTOR WEIGHTINGS

| | PORT-FOLIO % | REL. S&P 500 |
|---|---|---|
| NATURAL RESOURCES | 7.9 | 0.40 |
| INDUSTRIAL PRODUCTS | 15.0 | 1.22 |
| CONSUMER DURABLES | 0.5 | 0.09 |
| NON-DURABLES | 27.8 | 1.31 |
| RETAIL TRADE | 8.2 | 1.32 |
| SERVICES | 13.1 | 1.54 |
| UTILITIES | 10.9 | 0.74 |
| TRANSPORTATION | 4.1 | 2.46 |
| FINANCE | 12.6 | 1.83 |
| MULTI-INDUSTRY | 0.0 | 0.00 |

## ANALYSIS

Strickland/Gillis    07/26/91

It's hard to think up any complaints about Phoenix Growth Fund.

Comanager Robert Chesek has mastered the combination of low risk and high returns. Except in 1988 and 1989, the fund has consistently outperformed the market. In fact, it ranks in the first percentile for all funds over the trailing 10-year period. Even in rough times, like 1990's third quarter, the fund did not suffer as severely as its peers.

Chesek is not counting on an imminent recovery from the recession. Rather, he believes that there was too much optimism in early 1991 that will be dashed by earnings losses in the second half of the year. This pessimistic outlook has kept the fund on the defensive. Its cash position, while normally around 15%, is now at 24% with no immediate plans for reduction. Says Chesek, "I'm having a heck of a time finding stocks I have a passion for." (He looks for stocks with sound fundamentals whose price multiples are cheap relative to their current and projected growth rates.)

As of now, the fund is highly concentrated in large-cap companies from a variety of consumer-spending sectors, whose P/E multiples have risen higher than their current growth. While he has scaled back his exposure to pricey pharmaceuticals, he is watching the economy before deciding on a post-recession direction. He is not, however, just waiting around. Chesek believes that "selling is as important as buying," as evidenced by his high turnover rate of 200%. Any indication of a negative change in fundamentals, excessive growth or of being overpriced and the stock is sold.

A defensive cash position and slow market recovery growth rates may bite at the fund if the market's stock fever continues unabated this year. But the fund's long-term results are unlikely to suffer.

## OPERATIONS

| | | | |
|---|---|---|---|
| **ADDRESS** | 101 Munson Street | **TELEPHONE NUMBER** | 203-253-1000 |
| | Greenfield, MA 01301 | | 800-243-4361 |
| **ADVISOR** | Phoenix Investment Counsel | **PHONE SWITCH** | Yes |
| **DISTRIBUTOR** | Phoenix Equity Planning | **# OF SHAREHOLDERS** | 80066 |
| **PORTFOLIO MANAGER** | Chesek/Dudley (80/90) | **MINIMUM INITIAL PURCHASE** | 500 |
| **MANAGEMENT FEE** | 0.50% max./0.40% min. | **MINIMUM SUBSEQUENT PURCHASE** | 25 |
| **FEES** | 4.75%L, 0.25%B | **DATE OF INCEPTION** | 09/01/58 |
| **TICKER** | PHGRX | **SHAREHOLDER REPORT RATING** | C+ |

# Putnam Global Growth

**PUTNAM, INC.**

| OBJECTIVE | LOAD % | YIELD % | ASSETS($MIL) | N.A.V. |
|---|---|---|---|---|
| Intl Stock | 5.75 | 1.8 | 605.0 | 7.55 |

Putnam Global Growth Fund's objective is to seek capital appreciation.

The fund invests in securities traded in markets located in the United States and in a number of foreign countries. It may invest up to 100% of its assets in securities principally traded in foreign markets or in those principally traded in any one country. The fund may invest in large or small companies with earnings showing strong growth trends, or in non-growth companies with market values per share that are thought to be undervalued.

Prior to August 1, 1990, the fund was named Putnam International Equities Fund.

| TOP LINE: | | RETURN | RISK |
|---|---|---|---|
| Adjusted N.A.V. | | Average | Average |
| BOTTOM LINE: | | RATING | |
| Relative Strength | | ★★★ | |
| | | Neutral | |

## TOTAL RETURN %

| | 1st Qtr. | 2nd Qtr. | 3rd Qtr. | 4th Qtr. | TOTAL |
|---|---|---|---|---|---|
| 1987 | 15.26 | 7.19 | 7.06 | -18.91 | 7.26 |
| 1988 | 3.87 | -0.11 | -2.38 | 7.62 | 9.00 |
| 1989 | 3.52 | 2.60 | 12.21 | 4.54 | 24.58 |
| 1990 | -4.57 | 9.44 | -17.62 | 5.53 | -9.20 |
| 1991 | 11.23 | -1.77 | ... | ... | ... |

### INCOME

| | | | | | TOTAL |
|---|---|---|---|---|---|
| 1989 | 0.00 | 0.00 | 0.00 | 0.14 | 0.14 |
| 1990 | 0.00 | 0.00 | 0.00 | 0.14 | 0.14 |
| 1991 | 0.00 | 0.00 | ... | ... | 0.00 |

### CAPITAL GAINS

| | | | | | TOTAL |
|---|---|---|---|---|---|
| 1989 | 0.00 | 0.00 | 0.00 | 0.07 | 0.08 |
| 1990 | 0.00 | 0.00 | 0.00 | 0.41 | 0.42 |
| 1991 | 0.00 | 0.00 | ... | ... | 0.00 |

## PERFORMANCE/RISK

| | TOTAL RETURN % | +/- S&P 500 | +/- EAFE | PERCENTILE RANK ALL | PERCENTILE RANK OBJ | 07/31/91 |
|---|---|---|---|---|---|---|
| 3 MONTH | 1.75 | -2.39 | 3.53 | 69 | 30 | |
| 6 MONTH | 9.74 | -4.85 | 6.52 | 42 | 28 | |
| 1 YEAR | -2.29 | -15.08 | 6.19 | 91 | 21 | |
| 3 YEAR AVG. | 10.68 | -5.87 | 10.09 | 36 | 27 | |
| 5 YEAR AVG. | 9.93 | -4.33 | -0.32 | 36 | 48 | |
| 10 YEAR AVG. | 16.87 | 0.85 | -0.83 | 7 | 20 | |
| 15 YEAR AVG. | 16.21 | 2.23 | -0.44 | 20 | 39 | |

| | ALPHA | BETA | R² | STD. DEV. |
|---|---|---|---|---|
| | -3.9 | 0.90 | 64 | 4.80 |
| PERCENTILE ALL | 64 | 51 | 78 | 39 |
| RANK OBJ. | 41 | 15 | 18 | 57 |

Percentile Ranks 1 = Highest, 100 = Lowest

## HISTORY

| | 1979 | 1980 | 1981 | 1982 | 1983 | 1984 | 1985 | 1986 | 1987 | 1988 | 1989 | 1990 | 07/91 |
|---|---|---|---|---|---|---|---|---|---|---|---|---|---|
| N.A.V. | 3.62 | 4.44 | 4.12 | 3.92 | 4.93 | 3.94 | 5.88 | 7.60 | 6.07 | 6.50 | 7.88 | 6.59 | 7.55 |
| TOTAL RETURN % | 19.51 | 25.46 | -0.45 | 9.66 | 27.93 | 0.75 | 65.04 | 37.65 | 7.26 | 9.00 | 24.58 | -9.20 | 14.57 |
| +/- S&P 500 INDEX | 1.21 | -6.76 | 4.63 | -11.80 | 5.47 | -5.38 | 33.40 | 19.02 | 2.04 | -7.51 | -7.09 | -6.10 | -5.13 |
| +/- EAFE INDEX | 14.76 | 2.88 | 1.83 | 11.52 | 4.23 | -6.64 | 8.88 | -31.79 | -17.37 | -19.27 | 14.04 | 14.25 | 8.01 |
| TOT. RTN/ALL FUNDS | 53 | 51 | 56 | 93 | 17 | 60 | 9 | 5 | 19 | 68 | 33 | 73 | 55 |
| % RANK OBJECTIVE | 69 | 75 | 53 | 50 | 70 | 20 | 9 | 66 | 57 | 87 | 43 | 38 | 22 |
| INCOME | 0.13 | 0.09 | 0.17 | 0.13 | 0.07 | 0.02 | 0.06 | 0.03 | 0.13 | 0.11 | 0.14 | 0.15 | 0.00 |
| CAPITAL GAIN | 0.00 | 0.00 | 0.00 | 0.38 | 0.38 | 0.99 | 0.34 | 0.38 | 1.91 | 0.00 | 0.08 | 0.42 | 0.00 |
| EXPENSE % | 1.68 | 1.13 | 1.23 | 1.51 | 1.46 | 1.28 | 1.32 | 1.07 | 1.39 | 1.40 | 1.06 | 1.44 | ... |
| INCOME % | 3.55 | 3.94 | 2.82 | 2.31 | 0.62 | 1.52 | 1.04 | 0.85 | 1.03 | 1.34 | 1.52 | 1.56 | ... |
| TURNOVER % | 61 | 88 | 65 | 93 | 132 | 167 | 134 | 176 | 113 | 103 | 67 | 95 | ... |
| NET ASSETS ($MIL) | 38.6 | 42.3 | 38.1 | 38.0 | 44.7 | 47.2 | 90.4 | 411.4 | 524.2 | 479.0 | 534.3 | 561.9 | 605.0 |

| M-STAR RISK % RANK | | MORNINGSTAR RETURN RISK | | MORNINGSTAR RISK-ADJUSTED RATING |
|---|---|---|---|---|
| | ALL | OBJ | 1.00 = EQUITY AVG | |
| 3 YEAR | 75 | 37 | 0.78 1.01 ↑ | ★★ |
| 5 YEAR | 62 | 31 | 0.87 0.89 ↑ | ★★★ |
| 10 YEAR | 56 | 37 | 1.31 0.85 ↑ | ★★★★ |
| WEIGHTED AVG. | | | 1.07 0.89 | ★★★ |

Except MMF Risk: 1 = Lowest, 100 = Highest

| SHARE CHANGE | AMOUNT | STOCK | VALUE $000 | % NET ASSETS |
|---|---|---|---|---|
| 85000 | 190000 | PFIZER | 10545 | 1.74 |
| 59000 | 254000 | MILLIPORE | 10541 | 1.74 |
| 25036 | 59036 | CBS | 9505 | 1.57 |
| 0 | 260000 | BAXTER INTERNATIONAL | 8385 | 1.39 |
| -10000 | 100000 | GENERAL ELECTRIC | 7413 | 1.23 |
| 2000000 | 8000000 | CIFRA CL A | 6962 | 1.15 |
| 232000 | 232000 | UNITED TECHNOLOGIES | 6844 | 1.13 |
| 109000 | 109000 | DIGITAL EQUIPMENT | 6486 | 1.07 |
| 135000 | 360000 | TJX | 6480 | 1.07 |
| 275886 | 275886 | VITRO SOCIEDAD ANONIMA | 6138 | 1.01 |
| 2800 | 62800 | IBM | 6099 | 1.01 |
| 146500 | 266500 | REPSOL | 5996 | 0.99 |
| 1200 | 13200 | CAPITAL CITIES/ABC | 5661 | 0.94 |
| 0 | 210000 | TELEFONICA DE ESPANA | 5460 | 0.90 |
| 98500 | 98500 | RACAL TELECOM | 5454 | 0.90 |
| 200000 | 405555 | BRAMBLES INDUSTRIES | 5292 | 0.87 |
| 129395 | 1297395 | UOB | 5220 | 0.86 |
| 1000000 | 1000000 | NATIONAL AUSTRALIA BANK | 5143 | 0.85 |
| 0 | 50000 | BANCO POPULAR ESPANOL | 5122 | 0.85 |
| 0 | 25000 | SWISS BANK | 5075 | 0.84 |
| 30000 | 115900 | TRIBUNE | 5056 | 0.84 |
| 8500 | 78500 | MOBIL | 5044 | 0.83 |
| 30000 | 121300 | HUNTER DOUGLAS | 5041 | 0.83 |
| 87500 | 222500 | USX-MARATHON GROUP | 5006 | 0.83 |
| 300000 | 300000 | KIMBERLY-CLARK | 4983 | 0.82 |
| -8750 | 191250 | RAYCHEM | 4973 | 0.82 |
| 300000 | 600000 | COLES MYER | 4951 | 0.82 |
| 50000 | 550000 | SIRTI ITALY | 4760 | 0.79 |
| -50000 | 78000 | AMR | 4739 | 0.78 |
| 480357 | 1380357 | WESTPAC BANKING | 4726 | 0.78 |

### PORTFOLIO STATISTICS 07/31/91

| | PORT-FOLIO AVG. | % OF STOCKS | REL S&P 500 |
|---|---|---|---|
| PRICE/EARNINGS RATIO | 17.6 | 28 | 1.01 |
| PRICE/BOOK RATIO | 3.2 | 39 | 0.91 |
| 5 YR. EARN. GR. % | 14.0 | 18 | 1.08 |
| RETURN ON ASSETS | 6.0 | 29 | 0.80 |
| DEBT % TOTAL CAP. | 27.4 | 29 | 0.85 |
| MED. MKT. CAP. ($MIL) | 6457 | 42 | 0.55 |

### COMPOSITION % 06/30/91

| | | | |
|---|---|---|---|
| CASH | 9.3 | PREFERREDS | 0.0 |
| STOCKS | 89.2 | CONVERTIBLES | 0.7 |
| BONDS | 0.8 | OTHER | 0.0 |

### REGIONAL EXPOSURE 07/31/91

Percentage of Net Assets — U.S. 29, Europe 39, Japan 15, Pac R/m 11, Other 6

## ANALYSIS

**Tom Desmond — 08/23/91**

Putnam Global Growth Fund has been riding the strength of the U.S. market.

Beefing up its U.S. exposure to 27% of assets, this fund has enjoyed a 21% gain on its American companies so far this year. Led by a mixed bag of U.S. cyclical and health-care stocks, the portfolio participated nicely in the first-quarter rally, and it has been slowly gaining since.

Comanager Tony Regan is approaching the portfolio from two separate directions. In the U.S., he is emphasizing companies with strong franchises and good prospects following an economic recovery. "We have gone to areas that promise significant earnings recovery in 1992 and 1993," he explains. Relatively inexpensive health-care concerns, such as Pfizer, Baxter International, and Imcera Group offer both stability and growth potential. Meanwhile, a patchwork of economically sensitive issues, such as CBS, TJX, Kimberly-Clark, and AMR, promise attractive gains when the economy recovers.

Overseas, Regan is working from the opposite direction. He is bypassing cyclicals in both Europe and the Far East, which claim roughly 36% and 23% of the portfolio, respectively. "In these regions we are looking for defensive," he says. "We are looking for strong fundamentals and clean balance sheets." He has recently trimmed the fund's exposure to Europe, fearing logistical problems in Germany's reunification. And he is now stressing consumer staples like Britain's Allied Lyons and Tate & Lyle.

Regan is equally cautious about the Pacific Basin. He has pursued mainly blue-chip exporting firms in Japan, and sound financials in Australia. In addition, he has added a sprinkling of conservative issues from both Hong Kong and Singapore.

This conservatism should help temper the fund's aggressive style in the U.S..

## OPERATIONS

ADDRESS One Post Office Square
Boston, MA 02109
ADVISOR Putnam Management
DISTRIBUTOR Putnam Financial Services
PORTFOLIO MANAGER Regan/Beck (1988)
MANAGEMENT FEE 0.75% max./0.50% min.
FEES 5.75%L, 0.25%B
TICKER PEQUX

TELEPHONE NUMBER 617-292-1000
800-225-1581
PHONE SWITCH Yes
# OF SHAREHOLDERS 89852
MINIMUM INITIAL PURCHASE 500
MINIMUM SUBSEQUENT PURCHASE 50
DATE OF INCEPTION 09/01/67
SHAREHOLDER REPORT RATING B-

# Putnam U.S. Government Income

MORNINGSTAR MUTUAL FUNDS

| OBJECTIVE | LOAD % | YIELD % | ASSETS($MIL) | N.A.V. |
|---|---|---|---|---|
| Gvt Mortgage | 4.75 | 9.4 | 2063.3 | 13.89 |

Putnam U.S. Government Income Trust seeks as high a level of current income as is consistent with preservation of capital.

The fund invests exclusively in securities backed by the full faith and credit of the United States and in repurchase agreements with respect to these securities. Suitable investments include U.S. Treasury bills, notes, and bonds, as well as obligations guaranteed by the U.S. Treasury.

|  | RETURN | RISK |
|---|---|---|
| TOP LINE: Adjusted NAV | Above Avg | Low |
| BOTTOM LINE: Relative Strength | RATING ★★★★ Highest | |

| HISTORY | 1979 | 1980 | 1981 | 1982 | 1983 | 1984 | 1985 | 1986 | 1987 | 1988 | 1989 | 1990 | 09/91 |
|---|---|---|---|---|---|---|---|---|---|---|---|---|---|
| N.A.V. | ... | ... | ... | ... | ... | 14.23 | 14.70 | 14.71 | 13.92 | 13.57 | 13.85 | 13.81 | 13.89 |
| TOTAL RETURN % | ... | ... | ... | ... | ... | ... | 15.99 | 11.01 | 4.57 | 7.55 | 12.80 | 9.90 | 8.02 |
| +/- LB GOVT./CP. | ... | ... | ... | ... | ... | ... | -5.32 | -4.61 | 2.27 | -0.03 | -1.44 | 1.62 | -2.22 |
| TOT. RTN/ALL FUNDS | ... | ... | ... | ... | ... | ... | 90 | 77 | 30 | 76 | 69 | 5 | 88 |
| % RANK OBJECTIVE | ... | ... | ... | ... | ... | ... | 95 | 56 | 6 | 38 | 60 | 41 | 90 |
| INCOME | ... | ... | ... | ... | ... | 1.37 | 1.68 | 1.51 | 1.42 | 1.37 | 1.37 | 1.32 | 0.98 |
| CAPITAL GAIN | ... | ... | ... | ... | ... | 0.00 | 0.00 | 0.01 | 0.00 | 0.00 | 0.00 | 0.00 | 0.00 |
| EXPENSE % | ... | ... | ... | ... | ... | ... | 0.60 | 0.56 | 0.58 | 0.61 | 0.65 | 0.75 | ... |
| INCOME % | ... | ... | ... | ... | ... | ... | 9.85 | 10.30 | 9.55 | 9.81 | 9.90 | 9.66 | ... |
| TURNOVER % | ... | ... | ... | ... | ... | ... | 136 | 116 | 43 | 55 | 168 | 63 | ... |
| NET ASSETS ($MIL) | ... | ... | ... | ... | ... | 129.8 | 408.4 | 1058.3 | 1240.7 | 1347.2 | 1446.5 | 1751.1 | 2063.3 |

### TOTAL RETURN %

|  | 1st Qtr. | 2nd Qtr. | 3rd Qtr. | 4th Qtr. | TOTAL |
|---|---|---|---|---|---|
| 1987 | 2.26 | -0.53 | -1.96 | 4.86 | 4.57 |
| 1988 | 3.77 | 1.61 | 1.55 | 0.44 | 7.55 |
| 1989 | 1.21 | 6.45 | 1.25 | 3.40 | 12.80 |
| 1990 | 0.17 | 3.12 | 1.54 | 4.78 | 9.90 |
| 1991 | 2.25 | 1.59 | 3.99 | ... | ... |

### INCOME

|  | 1st Qtr. | 2nd Qtr. | 3rd Qtr. | 4th Qtr. | TOTAL |
|---|---|---|---|---|---|
| 1989 | 0.34 | 0.34 | 0.34 | 0.34 | 1.37 |
| 1990 | 0.34 | 0.33 | 0.33 | 0.33 | 1.32 |
| 1991 | 0.33 | 0.33 | 0.33 | 0.11 | 1.09 |

### CAPITAL GAINS

|  | 1st Qtr. | 2nd Qtr. | 3rd Qtr. | 4th Qtr. | TOTAL |
|---|---|---|---|---|---|
| 1989 | 0.00 | 0.00 | 0.00 | 0.00 | 0.00 |
| 1990 | 0.00 | 0.00 | 0.00 | 0.00 | 0.00 |
| 1991 | 0.00 | 0.00 | 0.00 | ... | ... |

### PERFORMANCE/RISK  09/30/91

|  | TOTAL RETURN% | +/- LB GVT./CP. | PERCENTILE RANK ALL | PERCENTILE RANK OBJ. |
|---|---|---|---|---|
| 3 MONTH | 3.99 | -1.76 | 79 | 87 |
| 6 MONTH | 5.64 | -1.71 | 61 | 92 |
| 1 YEAR | 13.18 | -2.68 | 82 | 79 |
| 3 YEAR AVG. | 10.38 | -0.87 | 55 | 73 |
| 5 YEAR AVG. | 9.23 | 0.11 | 53 | 38 |
| 10 YEAR AVG. | ... | ... | ... | ... |
| 15 YEAR AVG. | ... | ... | ... | ... |

|  | ALPHA | BETA | R² | STD. DEV. |
|---|---|---|---|---|
|  | 0.4 | 0.68 | 94 | 0.89 |

|  | ALPHA | BETA | R² |
|---|---|---|---|
| PERCENTILE / ALL | 14 | 63 | 87 |
| RANK / OBJ. | 38 | 87 | 17 |

Percentile Ranks: 1 = Highest, 100 = Lowest
Except M-Star Risk: 1 = Lowest, 100 = Highest

|  | M-STAR RISK % RANK ALL | M-STAR RISK % RANK OBJ. | MORNINGSTAR RETURN | MORNINGSTAR RISK | MORNINGSTAR RISK-ADJUSTED RATING |
|---|---|---|---|---|---|
| 3 YEAR | 4 | 17 | 1.02 | 0.67 | ★★★★ |
| 5 YEAR | 3 | 9 | 1.09 | 0.69 | ★★★★★ |
| 10 YEAR | ... | ... | ... | ... | |
| WEIGHTED AVG. | | | 1.06 | 0.68 | ★★★★ |

1.00 = FIXED-INCOME AVG.

NET ASSETS: ($MIL) 2000 / 1000 / 0

## ANALYSIS

Anthony Mayorkas 10/18/91

Putnam U.S. Government Income Trust may be trailing its rivals this year, but it's still second to none over the long term.

The fund's bottom-decile year-to-date ranking isn't a big surprise. It's merely a reflection of this fund's premium-coupon emphasis, which leads it to underperform when interest rates are declining. While this stance does eat into the fund's NAV over the long term, it also contributes to the fund's main attraction, its low risk. Indeed, the fund owes its 5-star rating to its tiny risk score.

The fund's average weighted coupon of 11.5% keeps its interest-rate sensitivity to a minimum. At 3.2 years, fund duration now stands at the low end of the portfolio's three-to four-year range, owing to manager Jaclyn Conrad's defensive stance; she expects a modest rise in interest rates.

A 45% Treasury weighting, which is at the high end of the fund's range, generally keeps risk low as well, although Conrad did buy a few longer bonds earlier this year. Conrad raised the fund's Treasuries position (she's barbelling short and longer issues) because she thought that GNMA yields were too close to Treasuries'. A couple of months ago, in fact, she was so dissatisfied with their payouts that she decreased the fund's GNMA position to 35% of net assets. Now, it stands at 55%, which is still lower than the 70% stake the fund held last year.

This fund has excelled in tough interest-rate environments. Moreover, it's held up nicely in circumstances seemingly unfavorable to its premium-coupon strategy, as has been the case this year. That reliability not only keeps the fund sporting our top rating, but brings it new assets at a time when Putnam's other government funds are struggling to retain their monies.

## OPERATIONS

| | |
|---|---|
| ADDRESS | One Post Office Square<br>Boston, MA 02109 |
| ADVISOR | Putnam Management |
| DISTRIBUTOR | Putnam Financial Services |
| PORTFOLIO MANAGER | Jaclyn Conrad (1987) |
| MANAGEMENT FEE | 0.60% max./0.40% min. |
| FEES | 4.75%L, 0.25%B |
| TICKER | PGSIX |

| | |
|---|---|
| TELEPHONE NUMBER | 617-292-1000<br>800-225-1581 |
| PHONE SWITCH | Yes |
| # OF SHAREHOLDERS | 99271 |
| MINIMUM INITIAL PURCHASE | 500 |
| MINIMUM SUBSEQUENT PURCHASE | 50 |
| DATE OF INCEPTION | 02/08/84 |
| SHAREHOLDER REPORT RATING | B- |

## PORTFOLIO

TOTAL # SECURITIES 42  
TOP 30 SECURITIES AS OF: 03/31/91

| AMOUNT $000 | SECURITY | MATURITY | VALUE $000 | % NET ASSETS |
|---|---|---|---|---|
| 163922 | GNMA 12.5% | 11/20/15 | 184986 | 9.82 |
| 110000 | US TREASURY BOND 12% | 08/15/13 | 145063 | 7.70 |
| 120435 | GNMA 12% | 06/15/21 | 134720 | 7.15 |
| 123649 | GNMA 9.5% | 12/15/21 | 126661 | 6.73 |
| 85000 | US TREASURY BOND 13.875% | 05/15/11 | 123888 | 6.58 |
| 110000 | US TREASURY NOTE 11.25% | 02/15/95 | 123166 | 6.54 |
| 90000 | US TREASURY NOTE 13.75% | 05/15/92 | 96750 | 5.14 |
| 78575 | GNMA 13% | 10/20/15 | 89418 | 4.75 |
| 60000 | US TREASURY NOTE 13.125% | 05/15/94 | 69375 | 3.68 |
| 57741 | GNMA 11.5% | 11/15/19 | 63623 | 3.38 |
| 58608 | GNMA 9% | 07/15/21 | 58416 | 3.10 |
| 55000 | US TREASURY NOTE 7.875% | 01/15/98 | 54777 | 2.91 |
| 46373 | GNMA 11% | 12/15/18 | 50054 | 2.66 |
| 40000 | US TREASURY NOTE 12.625% | 08/15/94 | 46025 | 2.44 |
| 35000 | US TREASURY NOTE 11.75% | 11/15/93 | 38653 | 2.05 |
| 36962 | GNMA 8.5% | 01/15/19 | 36019 | 1.91 |
| 26138 | GNMA 13.5% | 06/20/15 | 30007 | 1.59 |
| 250000 | US TREASURY BOND 0% | 05/15/17 | 29531 | 1.57 |
| 16211 | GNMA-GPM 12.75% | 07/20/15 | 18007 | 0.96 |
| 11691 | GNMA-GPM 12.25% | 07/15/15 | 12894 | 0.68 |
| 100000 | US TREASURY BOND 0% | 11/15/19 | 12250 | 0.65 |
| 12238 | GNMA-GPM 9.25% | 02/15/20 | 12249 | 0.65 |
| 10414 | GNMA 9.75% | 04/15/21 | 10596 | 0.56 |
| 9100 | GNMA-GPM 10% | 05/15/10 | 9476 | 0.50 |
| 8539 | GNMA-GPM 11.25% | 01/15/16 | 9131 | 0.48 |
| 6675 | GNMA-GPM 10.75% | 03/15/16 | 7072 | 0.38 |
| 6376 | GNMA 9.25% | 10/15/21 | 6342 | 0.34 |
| 4114 | GNMA 13.25% | 11/15/25 | 4448 | 0.24 |
| 3883 | GNMA 10.5% | 01/15/18 | 4113 | 0.22 |
| 3114 | GNMA 10% | 02/15/18 | 3250 | 0.17 |

### PORTFOLIO STATISTICS

| | |
|---|---|
| AVG. WEIGHTED MATURITY | 10.0 YEARS |
| AVG. WEIGHTED COUPON | 11.5% |
| AVG. WEIGHTED PRICE | 111% OF PAR |

### COUPON RANGE

| | % BONDS | REL. OBL. |
|---|---|---|
| 0%, PIK | 2.6 | 0.6 |
| 0% to 8% | 3.4 | 0.4 |
| 8% to 9% | 5.8 | 0.2 |
| 9% to 10% | 10.4 | 0.3 |
| over 10% | 77.9 | 2.5 |

### COMPOSITION % 06/30/91

| | | | |
|---|---|---|---|
| CASH | 6.8 | PREFERREDS | 0.0 |
| STOCKS | 0.0 | CONVERTIBLES | 0.0 |
| BONDS | 93.2 | OTHER | 0.0 |

### CREDIT ANALYSIS 03/31/91

| | % |
|---|---|
| US T-Bonds | 17 |
| US T-Notes | 23 |
| GNMAs | 47 |
| FNMAs | |
| FHLMCs | |
| Other | 14 |

Percentage of Net Assets

1010

# MORNINGSTAR, INC.

# Quest For Value

| OBJECTIVE | LOAD % | YIELD % | ASSETS($MIL) | N.A.V. |
|---|---|---|---|---|
| Growth | 5.50 | 0.0 | 61.5 | 9.92 |

Quest for Value Fund seeks capital appreciation.

The fund invests primarily in equity securities of companies believed to be undervalued in the marketplace in relation to factors such as the companies' assets, earnings, or growth potential.

The fund may increase its ownership of securities by investing borrowed money. To a limited extent, it may also invest in restricted securities, foreign securities, or small, unseasoned companies.

| RETURN | RISK |
|---|---|
| Above Avg | Below Avg |

**RATING**
★★★★

Above Avg

TOP LINE: Adjusted NAV
BOTTOM LINE: Relative Strength

## TOTAL RETURN %

| | 1st Qtr. | 2nd Qtr. | 3rd Qtr. | 4th Qtr. | TOTAL |
|---|---|---|---|---|---|
| 1987 | 12.63 | 2.53 | 7.37 | -21.07 | -2.13 |
| 1988 | 11.26 | 5.32 | 0.87 | -0.46 | 17.64 |
| 1989 | 6.94 | 2.97 | 8.32 | 0.60 | 19.98 |
| 1990 | -4.20 | 6.71 | -16.73 | 9.41 | -6.86 |
| 1991 | 15.57 | 1.26 | --- | --- | --- |

## INCOME

| | | | | | TOTAL |
|---|---|---|---|---|---|
| 1989 | 0.00 | 0.00 | 0.00 | 0.26 | 0.26 |
| 1990 | 0.00 | 0.00 | 0.00 | 0.00 | 0.00 |
| 1991 | 0.00 | 0.00 | --- | --- | 0.00 |

## CAPITAL GAINS

| | | | | | TOTAL |
|---|---|---|---|---|---|
| 1989 | 0.00 | 0.00 | 0.00 | 0.55 | 0.55 |
| 1990 | 0.00 | 0.00 | 0.00 | 0.16 | 0.16 |
| 1991 | 0.00 | 0.00 | --- | --- | 0.00 |

## PERFORMANCE/RISK

06/30/91

| | TOTAL RETURN % | +/- S&P 500 | PERCENTILE RANK ALL | PERCENTILE RANK OBJ. |
|---|---|---|---|---|
| 3 MONTH | 1.26 | 1.54 | 37 | 13 |
| 6 MONTH | 17.02 | 2.75 | 27 | 40 |
| 1 YEAR | 6.63 | -0.78 | 52 | 36 |
| 3 YEAR AVG. | 9.50 | -5.17 | 44 | 67 |
| 5 YEAR AVG. | 7.67 | -4.24 | 59 | 67 |
| 10 YEAR AVG. | 16.63 | 1.13 | 5 | 9 |
| 15 YEAR AVG. | --- | --- | --- | --- |

| | ALPHA | BETA | R² | STD. DEV. |
|---|---|---|---|---|
| | -4.2 | 0.95 | 93 | 4.13 |

| PERCENTILE RANK | ALL | 64 | 43 | 16 | 59 |
|---|---|---|---|---|---|
| | OBJ. | 70 | 65 | 19 | 70 |

Percentile Ranks: 1 = Highest, 100 = Lowest
Except MFV Risk: 1 = Lowest, 100 = Highest

NET ASSETS: ($MIL)

## HISTORY

| | 1979 | 1980 | 1981 | 1982 | 1983 | 1984 | 1985 | 1986 | 1987 | 1988 | 1989 | 1990 | 06/91 |
|---|---|---|---|---|---|---|---|---|---|---|---|---|---|
| N.A.V. | --- | 4.25 | 5.31 | 7.07 | 7.91 | 6.74 | 8.23 | 8.50 | 7.55 | 8.41 | 9.28 | 8.48 | 9.92 |
| TOTAL RETURN % | --- | --- | 30.42 | 40.75 | 39.02 | 4.51 | 27.42 | 14.27 | -2.13 | 17.64 | 19.98 | -6.86 | 17.02 |
| +/- S & P 500 INDEX | --- | --- | 35.50 | 19.29 | 16.56 | -1.63 | -4.21 | -4.36 | -7.36 | 1.14 | -11.69 | -3.76 | 2.75 |
| TOT. RTN ALL FUNDS | --- | --- | 2 | 13 | 3 | 50 | 38 | 57 | 76 | 25 | 48 | 66 | 27 |
| % RANK OBJECTIVE | --- | --- | 2 | 16 | 3 | 23 | 61 | 52 | 75 | 38 | 78 | 61 | 40 |
| INCOME | --- | 0.00 | 0.02 | 0.10 | 0.17 | 0.11 | 0.09 | 0.07 | 0.14 | 0.10 | 0.26 | 0.00 | 0.00 |
| CAPITAL GAIN | --- | 0.00 | 0.20 | 0.20 | 1.61 | 1.27 | 0.23 | 0.86 | 0.68 | 0.37 | 0.55 | 0.16 | 0.00 |
| EXPENSE % | --- | --- | 4.33 | 2.77 | 2.48 | 2.29 | 2.34 | 2.18 | 2.24 | 2.21 | 1.81 | 1.82 | --- |
| INCOME % | --- | --- | 1.00 | 3.06 | 2.56 | 1.68 | 1.90 | 1.18 | 0.76 | 0.94 | 2.31 | 1.71 | --- |
| TURNOVER % | --- | --- | 79 | 53 | 93 | 74 | 42 | 68 | 21 | 15 | 30 | 51 | --- |
| NET ASSETS ($MIL) | --- | 1.0 | 1.5 | 5.0 | 8.9 | 13.4 | 33.3 | 75.0 | 87.3 | 79.1 | 77.7 | 55.3 | 61.5 |

| | MFV RISK % RANK ALL | MFV RISK % RANK OBJ. | MFV RETURN 1.00 = EQUITY AVG | MFV RISK | MFV RISK-ADJUSTED RATING |
|---|---|---|---|---|---|
| 3 YEAR | 56 | 26 | 0.84 | 0.84 → | ★★★ |
| 5 YEAR | 54 | 19 | 0.84 | 0.83 → | ★★★★ |
| 10 YEAR | 41 | 7 | 1.41 | 0.69 → | ★★★★★ |
| WEIGHTED AVG. | | | 1.13 | 0.76 | ★★★★ |

## ANALYSIS

**Helen O'D. Johnstone** | 07/26/91

Quest For Value Fund reaped some of the fruits of its 1990 labors.

The fund landed in the top half of its objective through June, almost 3 points ahead of the market. Unlike many of its value-oriented rivals, it has traditionally avoided underfollowed stocks. Instead, manager Eileen Rominger looks for value among blue chips, seizing opportunities to increase the fund's exposure when these stocks are temporarily out-of-favor. For example, during 1990's third quarter, she increased some of the fund's existing positions in temporarily downtrodden financial services.

Although strong-balance-sheet stocks like AIG and American Family fared better than most during 1990's harsh environment, they haven't been as lively this year as some of their less credit-conscious peers.

According to management, the common characteristics linking the fund's companies are: solid franchises, strong free cash flow, and solid long-term, but possibly volatile short-term, growth prospects. With a few notable exceptions—Philip Morris doesn't seem to be vulnerable to anything these days—these companies will remain vulnerable to economic downturns, so long as the market continues its love affair with current earnings. In addition, many of them depend heavily on discretionary spending.

Although it held up fairly well last year (for a self-described value fund), the fund's long-term record is somewhat misleading. Its superb 10-year results owe primarily to its small-cap days in the early 1980s, when the fund landed in the top third of its objective for four straight years. However, since the fund switched to larger caps, its performance has been just average.

Note: management voted a 200% stock dividend in June, which cut the fund's NAV to its present level of around $10.

## OPERATIONS

**ADDRESS** One World Financial Center, New York, NY 10281
**ADVISOR** Quest For Value Advisors
**DISTRIBUTOR** Quest For Value Distributors
**PORTFOLIO MANAGER** Eileen Rominger (1989)
**MANAGEMENT FEE** 1.00% flat fee
**FEES** 5.50%L, 0.50%B
**TICKER** QFVFX

**TELEPHONE NUMBER** 212-667-7587 / 800-232-3863
**PHONE SWITCH** Yes
**# OF SHAREHOLDERS** 4821
**MINIMUM INITIAL PURCHASE** 1000
**MINIMUM SUBSEQUENT PURCHASE** 250
**DATE OF INCEPTION** 05/01/80
**SHAREHOLDER REPORT RATING** B-

## PORTFOLIO

**TOTAL # STOCKS 37** — TOP 30 EQUITY HOLDINGS AS OF: 03/28/91

| SHARE CHANGE | AMOUNT | STOCK | VALUE $000 | % NET ASSETS |
|---|---|---|---|---|
| 4000 | 28000 | AMERICAN INTERNATIONAL GROUP | 2699 | 4.39 |
| 8000 | 50000 | MAY DEPARTMENT STORES | 2663 | 4.33 |
| -26000 | 104000 | AMERICAN FAMILY | 2405 | 3.91 |
| 5000 | 35000 | PHILIP MORRIS | 2384 | 3.88 |
| -24000 | 35000 | SMITHKLINE BEECHAM | 2052 | 3.34 |
| 64000 | 64000 | SUNDSTRAND | 2000 | 3.25 |
| 3000 | 37000 | GREAT ATLANTIC & PACIFIC TEA | 1984 | 3.23 |
| 1500 | 4000 | CAPITAL CITIES/ABC | 1858 | 3.02 |
| 32000 | 137000 | FRUIT OF THE LOOM CL A | 1781 | 2.90 |
| 3000 | 29000 | INTL PAPER | 1769 | 2.88 |
| 0 | 40000 | JEFFERSON-PILOT | 1725 | 2.81 |
| 12000 | 30000 | NESTLE | 1714 | 2.79 |
| 80000 | 80000 | ALLIANT TECHSYSTEMS | 1640 | 2.67 |
| -10000 | 15000 | PFIZER | 1605 | 2.61 |
| 44000 | 44000 | TRANSAMERICA | 1595 | 2.59 |
| 40000 | 40000 | UNITRIN | 1540 | 2.50 |
| -40000 | 50000 | PRIMERICA | 1525 | 2.48 |
| 25000 | 52000 | AVNET | 1521 | 2.47 |
| -14000 | 23000 | UNUM | 1449 | 2.36 |
| 57000 | 57000 | UNITED TELECOMMUNICATIONS | 1375 | 2.24 |
| 50000 | 50000 | MCI COMMUNICATIONS | 1281 | 2.08 |
| -21500 | 12500 | GENERAL RE | 1236 | 2.01 |
| -1500 | 27000 | NORFOLK SOUTHERN | 1205 | 1.96 |
| 32000 | 32000 | BURLINGTON RESOURCES | 1200 | 1.95 |
| -10000 | 20000 | AMERICAN HOME PRODUCTS | 1170 | 1.90 |
| 0 | 30000 | EI DUPONT DE NEMOURS | 1114 | 1.81 |
| 0 | 12000 | MINNESOTA MINING & MFG | 1062 | 1.73 |
| 26000 | 26000 | FLEMING | 1011 | 1.64 |
| -25000 | 14000 | GENERAL ELECTRIC | 977 | 1.59 |
| 19000 | 19000 | UNITED TECHNOLOGIES | 922 | 1.50 |

### PORTFOLIO STATISTICS 06/30/91

| | PORT-FOLIO | % OF AVG. STOCKS | REL S&P 500 |
|---|---|---|---|
| PRICE/EARNINGS RATIO | 14.6 | 94 | 0.89 |
| PRICE/BOOK RATIO | 3.0 | 96 | 0.93 |
| 5 YR. EARN. GR. % | 17.8 | 66 | 1.32 |
| RETURN ON ASSETS | 6.6 | 68 | 0.83 |
| DEBT % TOTAL CAP. | 35.5 | 94 | 1.11 |
| MED. MKT. CAP. ($MIL) | 6323 | 96 | 0.54 |

### COMPOSITION % 03/31/91

| | | | |
|---|---|---|---|
| CASH | 13.0 | PREFERREDS | 1.0 |
| STOCKS | 86.0 | CONVERTIBLES | 0.0 |
| BONDS | 0.0 | OTHER | 0.0 |

### SECTOR WEIGHTINGS

| | PORT-FOLIO % | REL S&P 500 |
|---|---|---|
| NATURAL RESOURCES | 10.0 | 0.50 |
| INDUSTRIAL PRODUCTS | 12.2 | 0.99 |
| CONSUMER DURABLES | 4.3 | 0.79 |
| NON-DURABLES | 14.2 | 0.67 |
| RETAIL TRADE | 14.7 | 2.38 |
| SERVICES | 3.7 | 0.43 |
| UTILITIES | 8.5 | 0.57 |
| TRANSPORTATION | 2.4 | 1.43 |
| FINANCE | 24.8 | 3.63 |
| MULTI-INDUSTRY | 5.2 | 1.72 |

298

# Rochester Fund Municipals

| OBJECTIVE | LOAD % | YIELD % | ASSETS($MIL) | N.A.V. |
|---|---|---|---|---|
| Muni General | 4.00 | 7.1 | 367.4 | 16.92 |

Rochester Fund Municipals seeks a high level of interest income exempt from federal, New York State, and New York City income taxes, consistent with preservation of capital.

The fund invests primarily in New York State municipal and public authority debt obligations. Except for temporary defensive purposes, at least 80% of the fund's assets will be invested in municipal securities. The fund may invest more than 25% of its assets in industrial revenue bonds, but no more than 5% of assets will be invested in bonds for which the underlying credit is one business.

**TOP LINE:**
Adjusted N.A.V.
**BOTTOM LINE:**
Relative Strength

| RETURN | RISK |
|---|---|
| High | Low |
| **RATING** | |
| ★★★★ | |
| **Highest** | |

## TOTAL RETURN %

| | 1st Qtr. | 2nd Qtr. | 3rd Qtr. | 4th Qtr. | TOTAL |
|---|---|---|---|---|---|
| 1987 | 0.53 | -0.51 | 1.46 | 2.19 | 3.71 |
| 1988 | 3.97 | 2.77 | 3.26 | 2.97 | 13.61 |
| 1989 | 1.06 | 3.14 | 1.55 | 2.68 | 8.68 |
| 1990 | 1.03 | 2.88 | 0.80 | 2.43 | 7.30 |
| 1991 | 2.54 | 3.17 | 4.01 | ... | ... |

## INCOME

| | | | | | TOTAL |
|---|---|---|---|---|---|
| 1989 | 0.30 | 0.30 | 0.30 | 0.30 | 1.20 |
| 1990 | 0.30 | 0.30 | 0.30 | 0.30 | 1.20 |
| 1991 | 0.30 | 0.30 | 0.30 | ... | 0.90 |

## CAPITAL GAINS

| | | | | | TOTAL |
|---|---|---|---|---|---|
| 1989 | 0.00 | 0.00 | 0.00 | 0.00 | 0.00 |
| 1990 | 0.00 | 0.00 | 0.00 | 0.00 | 0.00 |
| 1991 | 0.00 | 0.00 | 0.00 | ... | 0.00 |

## PERFORMANCE/RISK

| | TOTAL RETURN% | +/- LB GVT./CP. | PERCENTILE RANK ALL | 09/30/91 RANK OBJ. |
|---|---|---|---|---|
| 3 MONTH | 4.01 | -1.74 | 73 | 40 |
| 6 MONTH | 7.31 | -0.04 | 29 | 7 |
| 1 YEAR | 12.71 | -3.15 | 78 | 51 |
| 3 YEAR AVG. | 9.73 | -1.52 | 52 | 11 |
| 5 YEAR AVG. | 9.12 | 0.00 | 46 | 2 |
| 10 YEAR AVG. | ... | ... | ... | - |
| 15 YEAR AVG. | ... | ... | ... | - |

| | ALPHA | BETA | R² | STD. DEV. |
|---|---|---|---|---|
| | 1.1 | 0.33 | 38 | 0.69 |
| PERCENTILE { ALL | 4 | 94 | 84 | 94 |
| RANK { OBJ. | 1 | 93 | 97 | 90 |

Percentile Ranks 1 = Highest, 100 = Lowest

## HISTORY

| | 1979 | 1980 | 1981 | 1982 | 1983 | 1984 | 1985 | 1986 | 1987 | 1988 | 1989 | 1990 | 09/91 |
|---|---|---|---|---|---|---|---|---|---|---|---|---|---|
| N.A.V. | ... | ... | ... | ... | ... | ... | ... | 16.06 | 15.31 | 16.14 | 16.29 | 16.24 | 16.92 |
| TOTAL RETURN % | ... | ... | ... | ... | ... | ... | ... | ... | 3.71 | 13.61 | 8.68 | 7.30 | 10.04 |
| +/- LB GOVT./CP. | ... | ... | ... | ... | ... | ... | ... | ... | 1.41 | 6.03 | -5.56 | -0.98 | -0.20 |
| TOT. RTN./ALL FUNDS | ... | ... | ... | ... | ... | ... | ... | ... | 30 | 86 | 75 | 18 | 58 |
| % RTN/ OBJECTIVE | ... | ... | ... | ... | ... | ... | ... | ... | 4 | 8 | 9 | 9 | 6 |
| INCOME | ... | ... | ... | ... | ... | ... | ... | 1.12 | 1.20 | 1.20 | 1.20 | 1.20 | 0.90 |
| CAPITAL GAIN | ... | ... | ... | ... | ... | ... | ... | 0.00 | 0.11 | 0.00 | 0.00 | 0.00 | 0.00 |
| EXPENSE % | ... | ... | ... | ... | ... | ... | ... | 0.80 | 1.20 | 1.10 | 1.10 | 0.90 | 0.80 |
| INCOME % | ... | ... | ... | ... | ... | ... | ... | 5.50 | 7.30 | 7.40 | 7.20 | 7.20 | 7.30 |
| TURNOVER % | ... | ... | ... | ... | ... | ... | ... | 110 | 73 | 62 | 35 | 52 | 43 |
| NET ASSETS ($MIL) | ... | ... | ... | ... | ... | ... | ... | 7.1 | 16.5 | 39.3 | 98.1 | 260.5 | 367.4 |

| | M-STAR RISK % RANK ALL | OBJ. | MORNINGSTAR RETURN RISK 1.00 = MON AVG. | | MORNINGSTAR RISK-ADJUSTED RATING |
|---|---|---|---|---|---|
| 3 YEAR | 3 | 5 | 1.09 | 0.48 → | ★★★★★ |
| 5 YEAR | 3 | 6 | 1.25 | 0.53 → | ★★★★★ |
| 10 YEAR | | | | | ★★★★★ |
| WEIGHTED AVG. | | | 1.19 | 0.51 | ★★★★★ |

Except M-Star Risk 1 = Lowest, 100 = Highest

NET ASSETS: ($MIL)

## PORTFOLIO

TOTAL # SECURITIES 272 · TOP 20 SECURITIES AS OF: 06/30/91

| AMOUNT $000 | SECURITY | MATURITY | VALUE $000 | % NET ASSETS |
|---|---|---|---|---|
| 15965 | NY WARREN & WASHINGTON INDL DEV 8.2% | 12/15/10 | 16237 | 4.41 |
| 11740 | NY URBAN DEV 7.5% | 04/01/20 | 11567 | 3.14 |
| 10680 | NY MED CARE MENTAL HLTH 7.875% | 08/15/20 | 10785 | 2.93 |
| 9580 | NY HSG FIN AUTH HELP/BRONX 8.05% | 11/01/05 | 9864 | 2.68 |
| 9810 | NY MED CARE MENTAL HLTH 7.5% | 02/15/21 | 9605 | 2.61 |
| 9155 | NY CATTARAUGUS INDL DEV AUTH 8.3% | 12/01/10 | 9228 | 2.51 |
| 9450 | NY ENVIR FAC HUNTINGTON 7.5% | 10/01/12 | 9208 | 2.50 |
| 8355 | NY PORT AUTH OF NY/NJ CONTINENTAL 9.125% | 12/01/15 | 8245 | 2.24 |
| 91000 | NY MTG AGCY 0% | 10/01/23 | 7952 | 2.16 |
| 7500 | NY ENVIR FAC WTR SVC 8.375% | 01/15/20 | 7726 | 2.10 |
| 7500 | NY ERIE INDL DEV AUTH BETHLEHEM VAR% | 09/15/94 | 7313 | 1.99 |
| 6715 | NY INDL DEV AUTH NEKBOH 9.625% | 05/01/11 | 7000 | 1.90 |
| 17075 | NY NEW YORK CITY HSG DEV 0% | 02/15/30 | 6668 | 1.81 |
| 6400 | NY NEW YORK CITY GO 8.25% | 11/15/20 | 6302 | 1.71 |
| 6000 | VI WTR & PWR AUTH 8.5% | 10/01/10 | 6271 | 1.70 |
| 68711 | NY MTG AGCY 0% | 10/01/16 | 6269 | 1.70 |
| 5395 | NY NIAGARA INDL DEV AUTH HOOKER 9.5% | 07/15/04 | 5624 | 1.53 |
| 5225 | NY INDL DEV AUTH AMERICAN YOUTH 8.25% | 01/01/17 | 5413 | 1.47 |
| 4500 | NY INDL DEV AUTH CLG ST VINCENT 10.25% | 05/01/00 | 4865 | 1.32 |
| 4550 | NY MED CARE VASSAR BROTHERS 8.25% | 11/01/13 | 4688 | 1.27 |

### SECTOR WEIGHTINGS

| | PORT. % | REL. MUNI AVG. | | PORT. % | REL. MUNI AVG. |
|---|---|---|---|---|---|
| GEN. OBL. | 2.43 | 0.29 | TRANS. R&R | 0.01 | 0.00 |
| UTILITY | 1.93 | 0.12 | TRANS. A&W | 3.71 | 0.77 |
| HEALTH | 17.56 | 1.03 | COP/LEASE | 0.61 | 0.14 |
| WTR./WASTE | 3.58 | 0.54 | PRIVATE | 38.63 | 3.22 |
| HOUSING | 22.26 | 2.52 | MISC. REV. | 0.00 | 0.00 |
| EDUCATION | 5.05 | 0.72 | UNASSIGNED | 4.22 | 0.91 |

### TOP 5 STATES

| | PORT. % | | PORT. % |
|---|---|---|---|
| New York | 93.98 | Puerto Rico | 1.84 |
| Virgin Islands | 2.44 | Guam | 1.74 |

### PORTFOLIO STATISTICS

| | |
|---|---|
| AVG. WEIGHTED MATURITY | 19.7 YEARS |
| AVG. WEIGHTED COUPON | 7.71% |
| AVG. WEIGHTED PRICE | 92.8% OF PAR |

### COMPOSITION % 06/30/91

| | | | |
|---|---|---|---|
| CASH | 0.2 | PREFERREDS | 0.0 |
| STOCKS | 0.0 | CONVERTIBLES | 0.0 |
| BONDS | 99.8 | OTHER | 0.0 |

### CREDIT ANALYSIS 06/30/91

### COUPON RANGE

| | % BONDS | REL OBL. |
|---|---|---|
| 0% | 10.9 | 3.5 |
| 0% to 6.8% | 0.9 | 0.0 |
| 6.8 to 7.5% | 13.0 | 0.5 |
| 7.5 to 8.3% | 34.0 | 1.4 |
| over 8.3% | 41.3 | 1.5 |

## ANALYSIS

Helen O'D. Johnstone    11/01/91

Rochester Fund Municipals' atypical approach continues to show results.

Of the 41 New York muni-general funds we track (not all are featured in MMF), this fund remains the only 5-star candidate. Not only does it boast the fifth highest three-year returns among all the group's entrants, but it has shown significantly lower risk than its New York muni-general rivals. For example, while second-place entrant Boston Company New York Tax-Free sports a three-year risk score 20% lower than that of the average muni-bond fund, this fund's risk is less than half that average.

On the surface, this fund's premium-laden portfolio—more than 60% of the fund's assets are in bonds with coupons higher than 8%—appears to belie its strong record. Although such a premium bias could be expected to keep interest-rate risk under control, allowing the fund to earn a low Morningstar risk score, it might also have taken its toll on the fund's long-term returns; rich coupons are likely to be called away in a declining-interest-rate environment.

So far, manager Ron Fielding has taken a somewhat unusual approach to offsetting call risk. Unlike many of his competitors, he aims to avoid calls not by paying up for call protection, but by owning small, Upstate New York issuers for whom refinancing is not a practical alternative. For example, almost 39% of assets are in private-activity bonds. Since these bonds' issuers are no longer entitled to float tax-exempt debt, such bonds aren't likely to be called.

Despite the attractiveness of this fund's historic risk/return profile, though, its preference for smaller, private-activity issues opens it up to significant liquidity and credit risk. Because the fund owns many entire issues, pricing is somewhat subjective; if it's ever forced to liquidate its portfolio, shareholders could get burned.

## OPERATIONS

| | |
|---|---|
| ADDRESS | 70 Linden Oaks Rochester, NY 14625 |
| ADVISOR | Fielding Management |
| DISTRIBUTOR | Rochester Fund Distributors |
| PORTFOLIO MANAGER | Ronald Fielding (1983) |
| MANAGEMENT FEE | 0.50% max./0.40% min. |
| FEES | 4.00%L 0.10%B |
| TICKER | RMUNX |
| TELEPHONE NUMBER | 716-383-1300 |
| PHONE SWITCH | Yes |
| # OF SHAREHOLDERS | 11210 |
| MINIMUM INITIAL PURCHASE | 2000 |
| MINIMUM SUBSEQUENT PURCHASE | 100 |
| DATE OF INCEPTION | 05/15/86 |
| SHAREHOLDER REPORT RATING | C- |

# MORNINGSTAR, INC.
# Scudder GNMA

| OBJECTIVE | LOAD % | YIELD % | ASSETS($MIL) | N.A.V. |
|---|---|---|---|---|
| Gvt Mortgage | None | 8.0 | 275.8 | 15.21 |

Scudder GNMA Fund seeks high current income.

The fund invests primarily in mortgage securities issued or backed by the U.S. government or its agencies or instrumentalities. In addition, the fund may invest in bills, notes, and bonds issued by the U.S. Treasury or by various U.S. government agencies or instrumentalities. The fund may purchase or sell options on any of these securities or enter into repurchase agreements secured by U.S. government obligations. For hedging purposes, the fund may use futures contracts and put and call options on such contracts.

The fund used to be named Scudder Government Mortgage Securities Fund.

TOP LINE: Adjusted NAV
BOTTOM LINE: Relative Strength

| RETURN | RISK |
|---|---|
| Average | Average |

RATING: ★★
Neutral

## TOTAL RETURN %

| | 1st Qtr. | 2nd Qtr. | 3rd Qtr. | 4th Qtr. | TOTAL |
|---|---|---|---|---|---|
| 1987 | 1.76 | -2.10 | -2.69 | 4.50 | 1.32 |
| 1988 | 3.54 | 1.40 | -0.13 | 3.67 | 6.76 |
| 1989 | 0.68 | 7.11 | 0.94 | 3.48 | 12.84 |
| 1990 | -0.20 | 3.48 | 1.44 | 5.13 | 10.14 |
| 1991 | 2.63 | 1.58 | 5.33 | ... | ... |

## INCOME

| | | | | | TOTAL |
|---|---|---|---|---|---|
| 1989 | 0.32 | 0.32 | 0.31 | 0.31 | 1.26 |
| 1990 | 0.31 | 0.31 | 0.31 | 0.31 | 1.23 |
| 1991 | 0.30 | 0.30 | 0.30 | ... | 0.91 |

## CAPITAL GAINS

| | | | | | TOTAL |
|---|---|---|---|---|---|
| 1989 | 0.00 | 0.00 | 0.00 | 0.00 | 0.00 |
| 1990 | 0.00 | 0.00 | 0.00 | 0.00 | 0.00 |
| 1991 | 0.00 | 0.00 | 0.00 | ... | 0.00 |

## PERFORMANCE/RISK 09/30/91

| | TOTAL RETURN% | +/- LB GVT./CP. | PERCENTILE RANK ALL | PERCENTILE RANK OBJ. |
|---|---|---|---|---|
| 3 MONTH | 5.33 | -0.42 | 59 | 44 |
| 6 MONTH | 7.00 | -0.35 | 38 | 44 |
| 1 YEAR | 15.44 | -0.42 | 72 | 41 |
| 3 YEAR AVG. | 10.87 | -0.38 | 50 | 44 |
| 5 YEAR AVG. | 8.83 | -0.29 | 58 | 58 |
| 10 YEAR AVG. | | | | |
| 15 YEAR AVG. | | | | |

| | ALPHA | BETA | $R^2$ | STD. DEV. |
|---|---|---|---|---|
| | 0.1 | 0.87 | 92 | 1.15 |
| PERCENTILE ALL | 19 | 31 | 21 | 61 |
| RANK OBJ. | 52 | 49 | 38 | 49 |

Percentile Ranks 1 = Highest, 100 = Lowest
Except M-Star Risk 1 = Lowest, 100 = Highest

## HISTORY

| | 1979 | 1980 | 1981 | 1982 | 1983 | 1984 | 1985 | 1986 | 1987 | 1988 | 1989 | 1990 | 09/91 |
|---|---|---|---|---|---|---|---|---|---|---|---|---|---|
| N.A.V. | ... | ... | ... | ... | ... | ... | 15.34 | 15.50 | 14.43 | 14.09 | 14.56 | 14.72 | 15.21 |
| TOTAL RETURN % | ... | ... | ... | ... | ... | ... | ... | 11.34 | 1.32 | 6.76 | 12.84 | 10.14 | 9.81 |
| +/- LB GOVT./CP. | ... | ... | ... | ... | ... | ... | ... | -4.27 | -0.98 | -0.82 | -1.40 | 1.86 | -0.43 |
| TOT. RTN./ALL FUNDS % RANK | ... | ... | ... | ... | ... | ... | ... | 75 | 53 | 83 | 69 | 4 | 74 |
| OBJECTIVE | ... | ... | ... | ... | ... | ... | ... | 38 | 73 | 76 | 55 | 30 | 36 |
| INCOME | ... | ... | ... | ... | ... | ... | 0.62 | 1.42 | 1.26 | 1.29 | 1.26 | 1.23 | 0.91 |
| CAPITAL GAIN | ... | ... | ... | ... | ... | ... | 0.00 | 0.08 | 0.00 | 0.00 | 0.00 | 0.00 | 0.00 |
| EXPENSE % | ... | ... | ... | ... | ... | ... | ... | 1.02 | 1.05 | 1.04 | 1.04 | 1.05 | 1.04 |
| INCOME % | ... | ... | ... | ... | ... | ... | ... | 10.11 | 8.63 | 8.93 | 8.95 | 8.74 | 8.49 |
| TURNOVER % | ... | ... | ... | ... | ... | ... | ... | 124 | 59 | 92 | 128 | 71 | 52 |
| NET ASSETS ($MIL) | ... | ... | ... | ... | ... | ... | 96.7 | 248.2 | 234.4 | 248.0 | 259.4 | 252.1 | 275.8 |

| | M-STAR RISK % RANK ALL | M-STAR RISK % RANK OBJ. | MORNINGSTAR RETURN (100 = FIXED-INCOME AVG.) | MORNINGSTAR RISK | MORNINGSTAR RISK-ADJUSTED RATING |
|---|---|---|---|---|---|
| 3 YEAR | 11 | 63 | 1.07 | 0.90 | ★★★ |
| 5 YEAR | 9 | 40 | 1.04 | 0.91 | ★★★ |
| 10 YEAR | ... | ... | ↑ | ↑ | ★★★ |
| WEIGHTED AVG. | | | 1.05 | 0.91 | |

NET ASSETS ($MIL)

# PORTFOLIO

TOTAL # SECURITIES: 15 · TOP 10 SECURITIES AS OF: 03/31/91

| AMOUNT $000 | SECURITY | MATURITY | VALUE $000 | % NET ASSETS |
|---|---|---|---|---|
| 74735 | GNMA 9.5% | 10/15/20 | 76510 | 29.11 |
| 45163 | GNMA 9% | 03/15/21 | 45205 | 17.20 |
| 36105 | GNMA 8.5% | 02/15/20 | 35191 | 13.39 |
| 19288 | GNMA 10% | 04/15/19 | 20132 | 7.66 |
| 17620 | GNMA 11% | 02/15/16 | 19018 | 7.24 |
| 14732 | GNMA 12% | 02/20/16 | 16439 | 6.25 |
| 12498 | GNMA 9.25% | 10/15/24 | 12657 | 4.82 |
| 10000 | US TREASURY NOTE 8.625% | 05/15/93 | 10294 | 3.92 |
| 9931 | GNMA 8.75% | 08/15/24 | 9670 | 3.68 |
| 7006 | GNMA 11.5% | 02/15/16 | 7719 | 2.94 |
| 12285 | US TREASURY STRIP 0% | 05/15/98 | 6927 | 2.64 |
| 2996 | GNMA 13% | 09/15/15 | 3412 | 1.30 |
| 1555 | GNMA 12.5% | 10/20/13 | 1717 | 0.65 |
| 697 | GNMA 13.5% | 08/15/14 | 801 | 0.30 |
| 75 | GNMA 15% | 07/15/12 | 87 | 0.03 |

## PORTFOLIO STATISTICS

| | |
|---|---|
| AVG. WEIGHTED MATURITY | 11.6 YEARS |
| AVG. WEIGHTED COUPON | 9.40% |
| AVG. WEIGHTED PRICE | 102% OF PAR |

## COMPOSITION % 06/30/91

| | | | |
|---|---|---|---|
| CASH | 2.0 | PREFERREDS | 0.0 |
| STOCKS | 0.0 | CONVERTIBLES | 0.0 |
| BONDS | 98.0 | OTHER | 0.0 |

## COUPON RANGE / CREDIT ANALYSIS 03/31/91

| COUPON RANGE | % BONDS | REL. OBJ. |
|---|---|---|
| 0% PIK | 2.6 | 0.6 |
| 0% to 8% | 0.0 | 0.0 |
| 8% to 9% | 37.8 | 1.3 |
| 9% to 10% | 41.1 | 1.3 |
| over 10% | 18.5 | 0.6 |

CREDIT ANALYSIS

US T-Bonds
US T-Notes — 4
GNMA — 96
FNMA
FHLMC
Other — 2

(Agency)

# ANALYSIS

Helen O'D. Johnstone · 10/18/91

Coupon selection is the key to negotiating a difficult mortgage-backed environment, says Scudder GNMA manager David Glen.

A declining-interest-rate environment such as this year's usually spells trouble for mortgage- backed investors. As long interest rates drop, homeowners start refinancing their mortgages; when older mortgages are prepaid, investors lose coupons that were significantly higher than those currently available. Thus, although bond funds typically thrive when economic sluggishness prompts the Fed to reduce interest rates, mortgage-backed investors' gains are often diluted by accelerating prepayments.

Indeed, if long rates inch lower as expected, we may see such an acceleration. In anticipation of a heavy rash of prepayments, manager David Glen is emphasizing GNMA 9s and 9.5s, which now account for almost 60% of the portfolio. (He also owns GNMA 8s—16%

of assets—which, he says, are about as low as one can go without sacrificing liquidity). These issues aren't immune to prepayment risk, Glen admits. However, since new FHA regulations have recently made it more difficult for homeowners to refinance, he thinks that prepayments will be concentrated among richer-coupon issues. For example, GNMA 10s and 10.5s (now 6% of assets), he says, will be especially vulnerable.

Meanwhile, the fund has managed to benefit, at least to some degree, from recent interest-rate cuts, because of its 5% stake in long Treasuries. Currently, it has a duration of 4.2 years—a slightly aggressive stance for this fund, says Glen.

This fund is almost a total-return-oriented version of the AARP GNMA and US Treasury Fund Glen also manages. Both are conservative vehicles, but this fund takes on a tad more interest-rate risk to promote capital growth.

# OPERATIONS

| | |
|---|---|
| ADDRESS | 175 Federal Street Boston, MA 02110 |
| ADVISOR | Scudder, Stevens & Clark |
| DISTRIBUTOR | Scudder Investor Services |
| PORTFOLIO MANAGER | David Glen (1985) |
| MANAGEMENT FEE | 0.65% max./0.55% min. |
| FEES | No-load |
| TICKER | SGMSX |
| TELEPHONE NUMBER | 617-439-4640 / 800-225-2470 |
| PHONE SWITCH | Yes |
| # OF SHAREHOLDERS | 17757 |
| MINIMUM INITIAL PURCHASE | 1000 |
| MINIMUM SUBSEQUENT PURCHASE | 100 |
| DATE OF INCEPTION | 07/05/85 |
| SHAREHOLDER REPORT RATING | C+ |

# SunAmerica Aggressive Growth

| OBJECTIVE | LOAD % | YIELD % | ASSETS($MIL) | N.A.V. |
|---|---|---|---|---|
| Aggr. Growth | 5.75 | 0.0 | 31.9 | 14.26 |

SunAmerica Aggressive Growth Portfolio aggressively seeks capital appreciation.

Usually at least 65% of the fund's assets will be invested in equity securities. The fund will generally invest in small, less-well-known companies, but it may also buy well-known and established domestic or foreign companies. The fund may also engage in leveraging, effect short sales, use warrants or rights, invest in special situations, and use options and futures. The fund may trade for either long- or short-term gains without regard to the tax consequences.

Prior to March 1, 1990, the fund was known as Integrated Equity Aggressive Growth Portfolio.

**TOP LINE:** Adjusted N.A.V.
**BOTTOM LINE:** Relative Strength

| | RETURN | RISK |
|---|---|---|
| | Below Avg | High |
| RATING | ★★ | |
| | Below Avg | |

NET ASSETS ($MIL)

## TOTAL RETURN %

| | 1st Qtr. | 2nd Qtr. | 3rd Qtr. | 4th Qtr. | TOTAL |
|---|---|---|---|---|---|
| 1987 | --- | -7.71 | 5.50 | -28.32 | --- |
| 1988 | 31.32 | 15.28 | 0.61 | -2.53 | 48.45 |
| 1989 | 9.22 | 10.89 | 9.24 | -7.00 | 23.05 |
| 1990 | -2.12 | -0.18 | -30.80 | 7.98 | -26.99 |
| 1991 | 27.23 | 6.69 | 9.45 | --- | --- |

## INCOME

| | | | | | TOTAL |
|---|---|---|---|---|---|
| 1989 | 0.00 | 0.00 | 0.00 | 0.00 | 0.00 |
| 1990 | 0.00 | 0.00 | 0.00 | 0.00 | 0.00 |
| 1991 | 0.00 | 0.00 | 0.00 | | 0.00 |

## CAPITAL GAINS

| | | | | | TOTAL |
|---|---|---|---|---|---|
| 1989 | 0.00 | 0.00 | 0.00 | 0.53 | 0.53 |
| 1990 | 0.00 | 0.00 | 0.00 | 2.86 | 2.86 |
| 1991 | 0.00 | 0.00 | 0.00 | | 0.00 |

## PERFORMANCE/RISK 10/31/91

| | TOTAL RETURN % | +/- S&P 500 | PERCENTILE RANK ALL | OBJ. |
|---|---|---|---|---|
| 3 MONTH | 7.87 | 5.88 | 9 | 45 |
| 6 MONTH | 15.28 | 9.07 | 7 | 38 |
| 1 YEAR | 69.77 | 36.32 | 4 | 27 |
| 3 YEAR AVG. | 10.60 | -5.38 | 40 | 80 |
| 5 YEAR AVG. | --- | --- | --- | --- |
| 10 YEAR AVG. | --- | --- | --- | --- |
| 15 YEAR AVG. | --- | --- | --- | --- |

| | ALPHA | BETA | R² | STD. DEV. |
|---|---|---|---|---|
| | -5.2 | 1.23 | 64 | 6.37 |
| PERCENTILE / ALL | 89 | 8 | 72 | 5 |
| RANK / OBJ. | 82 | 45 | 88 | 37 |

Percentile Ranks: 1 = Highest, 100 = Lowest
Except M-STAR Risk: 1 = Lowest, 100 = Highest

## HISTORY

| | 1979 | 1980 | 1981 | 1982 | 1983 | 1984 | 1985 | 1986 | 1987 | 1988 | 1989 | 1990 | 10/91 |
|---|---|---|---|---|---|---|---|---|---|---|---|---|---|
| N.A.V. | ... | ... | ... | ... | ... | ... | ... | ... | 9.77 | 14.21 | 16.95 | 9.51 | 14.26 |
| TOTAL RETURN % | ... | ... | ... | ... | ... | ... | ... | ... | ... | 48.45 | 23.05 | -26.99 | 27.87 |
| +/- S & P 500 INDEX | ... | ... | ... | ... | ... | ... | ... | ... | ... | 31.94 | -8.63 | -23.89 | |
| TOT. RTN/ALL FUNDS | ... | ... | ... | ... | ... | ... | ... | ... | ... | 5 | 27 | 99 | 4 |
| % RANK/ OBJECTIVE | ... | ... | ... | ... | ... | ... | ... | ... | ... | 1 | 61 | 89 | 29 |
| INCOME | ... | ... | ... | ... | ... | ... | ... | ... | 0.00 | 0.00 | 0.00 | 0.00 | 0.00 |
| CAPITAL GAIN | ... | ... | ... | ... | ... | ... | ... | ... | 0.00 | 0.29 | 0.53 | 2.86 | 0.00 |
| EXPENSE % | ... | ... | ... | ... | ... | ... | ... | ... | 1.84 | 2.16 | 1.82 | 2.05 | 2.12 |
| INCOME % | ... | ... | ... | ... | ... | ... | ... | ... | -1.06 | -0.80 | -0.04 | -0.26 | 0.17 |
| TURNOVER % | ... | ... | ... | ... | ... | ... | ... | ... | ... | 54 | 32 | 27 | |
| NET ASSETS ($MIL) | ... | ... | ... | ... | ... | ... | ... | ... | 10.3 | 25.5 | 46.6 | 23.8 | 31.9 |

| M-STAR RISK % RANK | ALL | OBJ. |
|---|---|---|
| 3 YEAR | 96 | 86 |
| 5 YEAR | ... | ... |
| 10 YEAR | ... | ... |

| MORNINGSTAR RETURN RISK | MORNINGSTAR RISK 1.00 = EQUITY AVG | MORNINGSTAR RISK-ADJUSTED RATING |
|---|---|---|
| 0.68 ... 1.44 → | 0.68 ... ... → | ★★ |
| | ... ... → | |
| WEIGHTED AVG. | 0.68 1.44 | ★★ |

## PORTFOLIO

**TOTAL # STOCKS: 39**

| SHARE CHANGE | AMOUNT | STOCK | TOP 30 EQUITY HOLDINGS AS OF 09/30/91 VALUE $000 | % NET ASSETS |
|---|---|---|---|---|
| 0 | 100000 | HELIG-MEYERS | 3388 | 10.61 |
| 0 | 155000 | TELLABS | 2461 | 7.71 |
| 0 | 104500 | WOLOHAN LUMBER | 2168 | 6.79 |
| 50000 | 50000 | VALUE MERCHANTS | 1763 | 5.52 |
| 0 | 179700 | BUILDERS TRANSPORT | 1348 | 4.22 |
| 0 | 47500 | REYNOLDS & REYNOLDS | 1223 | 3.83 |
| 35000 | 35000 | FIRST BRANDS | 1181 | 3.70 |
| 60800 | 60800 | OIL DRI AMERICA CL A | 1125 | 3.52 |
| 0 | 35000 | HEKIN CAN | 1103 | 3.45 |
| 0 | 200000 | JB'S RESTAURANTS | 1000 | 3.13 |
| 0 | 52400 | INTL RECOVERY | 950 | 2.97 |
| 300000 | 300000 | HILLHAVEN | 825 | 2.58 |
| 118200 | 118200 | COLUMBIA LABORATORIES | 813 | 2.55 |
| 40000 | 40000 | ZEBRA TECHNOLOGIES CL A | 705 | 2.21 |
| 30000 | 30000 | NEOZYME | 645 | 2.02 |
| 0 | 151200 | UNIVERSAL MATCHBOX GROUP | 605 | 1.89 |
| 30000 | 30000 | ZEOS INTERNATIONAL | 548 | 1.72 |
| -72418 | 56682 | PIER 1 IMPORTS | 531 | 1.66 |
| 50000 | 50000 | GRAHAM-FIELD HEALTH | 525 | 1.64 |
| 20000 | 20000 | PUGET SOUND BANCORP | 520 | 1.63 |
| 65000 | 65000 | R & B | 463 | 1.45 |
| 0 | 25000 | EGGHEAD | 438 | 1.37 |
| 50000 | 50000 | CANDELA LASER | 400 | 1.25 |
| 200000 | 200000 | STAR TECHNOLOGIES | 400 | 1.25 |
| 10000 | 10000 | SOMATOGEN | 398 | 1.25 |
| 25000 | 25000 | HMO AMERICA | 328 | 1.03 |
| 35700 | 35700 | WORLDCORP | 326 | 1.02 |
| -96600 | 43400 | BALTIMORE BANCORP | 315 | 0.99 |
| 0 | 25000 | LAZARE KAPLAN INTERNATIONAL | 259 | 0.81 |
| 25000 | 25000 | AMERICAN MEDICAL HOLDINGS | 241 | 0.75 |

### PORTFOLIO STATISTICS 10/31/91

| | PORT-FOLIO AVG. | % OF STOCKS | REL S&P 500 |
|---|---|---|---|
| PRICE/EARNINGS RATIO | 18.2 | 57 | 0.99 |
| PRICE/BOOK RATIO | 2.2 | 80 | 0.61 |
| 5 YR. EARN. GR. % | 10.1 | 43 | 1.03 |
| RETURN ON ASSETS | 5.9 | 67 | 0.78 |
| DEBT % TOTAL CAP. | 31.2 | 67 | 0.98 |
| MED. MKT. CAP. ($MIL) | 126 | 84 | 0.01 |

### COMPOSITION %   09/30/91

| | | |
|---|---|---|
| CASH | 11.7 | |
| STOCKS | 88.3 | PREFERREDS 0.0 |
| BONDS | 0.0 | CONVERTIBLES 0.0 |
| | | OTHER 0.0 |

### SECTOR WEIGHTINGS

| | PORT-FOLIO % | REL S&P 500 |
|---|---|---|
| NATURAL RESOURCES | 9.4 | 0.56 |
| INDUSTRIAL PRODUCTS | 3.5 | 0.32 |
| CONSUMER DURABLES | 28.7 | 4.64 |
| NON-DURABLES | 6.2 | 0.26 |
| RETAIL TRADE | 26.9 | 3.87 |
| SERVICES | 14.7 | 1.53 |
| UTILITIES | 0.0 | 0.00 |
| TRANSPORTATION | 7.1 | 3.79 |
| FINANCE | 3.5 | 0.44 |
| MULTI-INDUSTRY | 0.0 | 0.00 |

## ANALYSIS

**Helen O'D. Johnstone    11/15/91**

SunAmerica Aggressive Growth Fund is back in vogue.

Unlike last year, when investors took more than a passing dislike to manager Harvey Eisen's undervalued-asset picks—the fund finished the year 27% in the red—this year's stock market has smiled on Eisen's strategy. That's because his search for growth companies with undervalued assets and market level (or lower) P/E ratios has traditionally led him to overweight the cyclical consumer-durables, industrial-products, and retail industries, sectors that have been regaining popularity this year, as investors anticipate an economic recovery.

Fortunately, though, the fund has also managed to maintain a decent services weighting, despite that sector's often lofty valuations. Anxious to cash in on strong earnings-growth forecasts, Eisen has been willing to pay up for some very small—the fund's median market cap is a tiny fraction of the S&P 500's—HMO, med- tech, and computer firms. Stocks like Graham-Field Health and HMO America have helped the fund stay comfortably inside its objective's top third for the year.

This year's success is indeed impressive, as were the fund's 1988 heroics. Unfortunately, those victories were matched by wretched showings in 1987 and 1990, making this fund an intriguing, but undependable, holding.

In addition to its somewhat unreliable past performance, an upcoming management change makes the fund's future uncertain. Manager Harvey Eisen will leave SunAmerica Asset Management next February. He'll be replaced as president by Colonial's Charlie Mohr, who plans to appoint a new chief investment officer to oversee this fund and its siblings.

## OPERATIONS

| | | | |
|---|---|---|---|
| ADDRESS | 10 Union Square East Second Floor New York, NY 10003 | TELEPHONE NUMBER | 212-353-5125 800-858-8850 |
| ADVISOR | SunAmerica Asset Management | PHONE SWITCH | Yes |
| DISTRIBUTOR | SunAmerica Capital Services | # OF SHAREHOLDERS | 6153 |
| PORTFOLIO MANAGER | Harvey Eisen (1989) | MINIMUM INITIAL PURCHASE | 500 |
| MANAGEMENT FEE | 0.75% max./0.65% min. | MINIMUM SUBSEQUENT PURCHASE | 100 |
| FEES | 5.75%L, 0.35%B | DATE OF INCEPTION | 01/28/87 |
| TICKER | SAGRX | SHAREHOLDER REPORT RATING | C |

# SunAmerica U.S. Government

| OBJECTIVE | LOAD % | YIELD % | ASSETS($MIL) | N.A.V. |
|---|---|---|---|---|
| Gvt General | 5.00d | 9.0 | 512.3 | 8.93 |

SunAmerica U.S. Government Securities seeks to realize high current income consistent with reasonable safety of principal.

The fund intends to invest in obligations issued or guaranteed by the U.S. Treasury and by various agencies and instrumentalities of the U.S. government. Maturities can be less than one year or as long as 30 years. The advisor intends to gradually, rather than dramatically, shift the portfolio's maturity structure to reflect what the advisor believes to be measured interest-rate trends.

The fund's subadvisor is Wellington Management. Prior to June 21, 1991, the fund was named Equitec Siebel U.S. Government Securities Fund.

**TOP LINE:** Adjusted N.A.V.
**BOTTOM LINE:** Relative Strength

| RETURN | RISK |
|---|---|
| Below Avg | Low |

**RATING** ★★★★
Highest

## TOTAL RETURN %

| | 1st Qtr. | 2nd Qtr. | 3rd Qtr. | 4th Qtr. | TOTAL |
|---|---|---|---|---|---|
| 1987 | 1.54 | 0.69 | -0.08 | 1.17 | 3.35 |
| 1988 | 3.76 | 1.56 | 1.31 | 0.87 | 7.69 |
| 1989 | 0.56 | 3.88 | 2.07 | 1.55 | 8.27 |
| 1990 | 1.73 | 1.94 | 2.83 | 2.22 | 9.01 |
| 1991 | 2.77 | 1.41 | 2.57 | ... | ... |

## INCOME

| | | | | | TOTAL |
|---|---|---|---|---|---|
| 1989 | 0.22 | 0.23 | 0.23 | 0.22 | 0.90 |
| 1990 | 0.21 | 0.21 | 0.21 | 0.22 | 0.85 |
| 1991 | 0.21 | 0.19 | 0.20 | ... | 0.59 |

## CAPITAL GAINS

| | | | | | TOTAL |
|---|---|---|---|---|---|
| 1989 | 0.00 | 0.00 | 0.00 | 0.00 | 0.00 |
| 1990 | 0.00 | 0.00 | 0.00 | 0.00 | 0.00 |
| 1991 | 0.00 | 0.00 | 0.00 | ... | 0.00 |

## PERFORMANCE/RISK 09/30/91

| | TOTAL RETURN% | +/- LB GVT./CP. | PERCENTILE RANK ALL | PERCENTILE RANK OBJ. |
|---|---|---|---|---|
| 3 MONTH | 2.57 | -3.18 | 91 | 100 |
| 6 MONTH | 4.02 | -3.33 | 79 | 100 |
| 1 YEAR | 9.27 | -6.59 | 94 | 100 |
| 3 YEAR AVG. | 8.37 | -2.88 | 80 | 100 |
| 5 YEAR AVG. | 7.49 | -1.63 | 78 | 64 |
| 10 YEAR AVG. | ... | ... | | |
| 15 YEAR AVG. | ... | ... | | |

| | ALPHA | BETA | $R^2$ | STD. DEV. |
|---|---|---|---|---|
| PERCENTILE ALL | 0.3 | 0.18 | 30 | 0.43 |
| RANK OBJ. | 15 | 98 | 98 | 97 |
| | 13 | 100 | 98 | 100 |

Percentile Ranks: 1 = Highest, 100 = Lowest
Except M-Star Risk: 1 = Lowest, 100 = Highest

## HISTORY

| | 1979 | 1980 | 1981 | 1982 | 1983 | 1984 | 1985 | 1986 | 1987 | 1988 | 1989 | 1990 | 09/91 |
|---|---|---|---|---|---|---|---|---|---|---|---|---|---|
| N.A.V. | ... | ... | ... | ... | ... | ... | ... | 9.93 | 9.37 | 9.17 | 9.00 | 8.92 | 8.93 |
| TOTAL RETURN % | ... | ... | ... | ... | ... | ... | ... | ... | 3.35 | 7.69 | 8.27 | 9.01 | 6.89 |
| +/-LB GOVT./CP. | ... | ... | ... | ... | ... | ... | ... | ... | 1.05 | 0.11 | -5.96 | 0.73 | -3.35 |
| TOT. RTN/ALL FUNDS | ... | ... | ... | ... | ... | ... | ... | ... | 39 | 76 | 91 | 8 | 94 |
| % RANK OBJECTIVE | ... | ... | ... | ... | ... | ... | ... | ... | 25 | 22 | 100 | 32 | 100 |
| INCOME | ... | ... | ... | ... | ... | ... | ... | 0.54 | 0.88 | 0.90 | 0.90 | 0.85 | 0.59 |
| CAPITAL GAIN | ... | ... | ... | ... | ... | ... | ... | 0.00 | 0.00 | 0.00 | 0.00 | 0.00 | 0.00 |
| EXPENSE % | ... | ... | ... | ... | ... | ... | ... | 2.21 | 2.26 | 2.04 | 2.03 | 1.98 | 1.98 |
| INCOME % | ... | ... | ... | ... | ... | ... | ... | 5.06 | 7.51 | 9.26 | 9.59 | 9.45 | 9.31 |
| TURNOVER % | ... | ... | ... | ... | ... | ... | ... | ... | 120 | 95 | 51 | 31 | 38 |
| NET ASSETS ($MIL) | ... | ... | ... | ... | ... | ... | ... | 40.6 | 124.5 | 261.7 | 380.0 | 440.5 | 512.3 |

| | M-STAR RISK % RANK | | MORNINGSTAR RETURN RISK | | MORNINGSTAR RISK-ADJUSTED RATING |
|---|---|---|---|---|---|
| | ALL | OBJ | 1.00 = FIXED-INCOME AVG | | |
| 3 YEAR | 1 | 5 | 0.82 | 0.32 → | ★★★★★ |
| 5 YEAR | 1 | 3 | 0.89 | 0.34 → | ★★★★★ |
| 10 YEAR | ... | ... | ... | → | |
| WEIGHTED AVG. | | | 0.86 | 0.33 | ★★★★★ |

## PORTFOLIO

**TOTAL # SECURITIES: 42** · **TOP 30 SECURITIES AS OF: 06/30/91**

| AMOUNT $000 | SECURITY | MATURITY | VALUE $000 | % NET ASSETS |
|---|---|---|---|---|
| 95498 | FHLMC 12.5% | 04/15/19 | 105621 | 20.59 |
| 50280 | FHLMC 13% | 10/01/15 | 56037 | 10.92 |
| 34779 | FNMA 13% | 09/01/15 | 38724 | 7.55 |
| 32795 | FHLMC 12% | 06/01/20 | 35992 | 7.02 |
| 27450 | FNMA 12% | 04/01/19 | 30144 | 5.88 |
| 28000 | FNMA 8.5% | 09/25/20 | 26259 | 5.12 |
| 19331 | FHLMC 13.5% | 02/15/19 | 21662 | 4.22 |
| 48608 | FNMA I/O 9% | 01/01/18 | 20631 | 4.02 |
| 49180 | FNMA I/O 9.5% | 01/01/19 | 20407 | 3.98 |
| 12729 | FHLMC 16% | 05/15/18 | 14650 | 2.86 |
| 12802 | FNMA 12.5% | 09/01/15 | 14157 | 2.76 |
| 9800 | GNMA II 13% | 10/20/13 | 10983 | 2.14 |
| 9515 | GNMA 7.5% | 07/15/17 | 8730 | 1.70 |
| 6855 | GNMA 12.25% | 08/15/15 | 7553 | 1.47 |
| 6827 | GNMA 11.75% | 12/15/15 | 7438 | 1.45 |
| 5535 | GNMA 13% | 02/15/15 | 6368 | 1.24 |
| 5644 | FNMA 13.5% | 02/01/17 | 6320 | 1.23 |
| 4099 | GNMA 12.5% | 09/15/15 | 4678 | 0.91 |
| 4099 | FNMA 12.25% | 10/01/15 | 4525 | 0.88 |
| 3890 | FHLMC 12.25% | 06/01/14 | 4291 | 0.84 |
| 5200 | FNMA 17.94% | 10/25/20 | 4264 | 0.83 |
| 5000 | FNMA 17.58% | 02/25/20 | 3950 | 0.77 |
| 3282 | FHLMC 11% | 11/01/15 | 3491 | 0.68 |
| 2726 | FHLMC 13.25% | 12/01/14 | 3051 | 0.59 |
| 2162 | FHLMC 12.75% | 06/01/15 | 2403 | 0.47 |
| 2011 | GNMA 14% | 12/15/14 | 2339 | 0.46 |
| 1777 | FNMA 12.75% | 09/01/15 | 1972 | 0.38 |
| 1794 | FHLMC 11.5% | 06/01/15 | 1933 | 0.38 |
| 1638 | FHLMC 14% | 04/01/16 | 1846 | 0.36 |
| 1206 | GNMA 13.5% | 12/15/14 | 1397 | 0.27 |

### PORTFOLIO STATISTICS

| | |
|---|---|
| AVG. WEIGHTED MATURITY | 11.2 YEARS |
| AVG. WEIGHTED COUPON | 12.2% |
| AVG. WEIGHTED PRICE | 103 % OF PAR |

### COMPOSITION % 06/30/91

| | | | |
|---|---|---|---|
| CASH | 6.4 | PREFERREDS | 0.0 |
| STOCKS | 0.0 | CONVERTIBLES | 0.0 |
| BONDS | 93.6 | OTHER | 0.0 |

### COUPON RANGE

| | % BONDS | REL. OBL. |
|---|---|---|
| 0% | 0.0 | 0.0 |
| 0% to 8% | 1.8 | 0.2 |
| 8% to 9% | 9.8 | 0.4 |
| 9% to 10% | 4.3 | 0.2 |
| over 10% | 84.1 | 3.6 |

### CREDIT ANALYSIS 06/30/91

US T-Bonds
US T-Notes
Agency:
GNMAs 10
FNMAs 34
FHLMCs 49
Other 7

Percentage of Net Assets

## ANALYSIS

Eileen Sanders · 10/18/91

Like a leopard, SunAmerica U.S. Government Securities Fund (née Equitec Seibel U.S. Government Securities) doesn't change its spots.

In the last year, the fund has undergone dramatic surface changes. When its former distributor, Equitec Securities, filed for bankruptcy late in 1990, SunAmerica Capital Management acquired the fund. It promptly named Paul Sullivan interim manager (on November 28, 1990); since then, he has stayed on as manager.

Despite its new trappings, the fund remains basically the same. As usual, it sports an exceptionally high yield. Paradoxically, its expense ratio is still lodged near 2%—extremely high for a government general fund. To maintain its yield, therefore, the fund must, as always, stick to a premium-coupon strategy. As of June, mortgage-backed securities constituted a whopping 93% of the fund's assets. Of these issues, 84% were stashed in coupons greater than 10%: the fund's 12.2% average coupon crowns its group.

These premium antics have one major disadvantage: they erode principal. As premium bonds approach maturity, that portion of their price that was above par slowly erodes. However, the SEC doesn't require that these losses be amortized against income, and with premium-strategy funds, they generally aren't. As a result, the fund slowly suffers capital loss.

Still, the fund does have its advantages. For one thing, its premium strategy does moderate interest-rate risk. Note this fund's low risk ranking. And, although returns fall into its objective's bottom, they aren't bad on an absolute scale. (The fund has only been down one quarter, and that was by a mere eight basis points.) The fund should appeal to the cautious investor who is willing to sacrifice some capital for income.

## OPERATIONS

| | | | |
|---|---|---|---|
| ADDRESS | 10 Union Square East Second Floor New York, NY 10003 | TELEPHONE NUMBER | 212-353-5125 / 800-858-8850 |
| ADVISOR | SunAmerica Asset Management | PHONE SWITCH | Yes |
| DISTRIBUTOR | SunAmerica Capital Services | # JF SHAREHOLDERS | 21451 |
| PORTFOLIO MANAGER | Paul Sullivan (1991) | MINIMUM INITIAL PURCHASE | 2500 |
| MANAGEMENT FEE | 0.75% max./0.55% min. | MINIMUM SUBSEQUENT PURCHASE | None |
| FEES | 5.00%D, 1.00%B | DATE OF INCEPTION | 03/03/86 |
| TICKER | SAGVX | SHAREHOLDER REPORT RATING | D |

# Templeton Foreign

| OBJECTIVE | LOAD % | YIELD % | ASSETS($MIL) | N.A.V. |
|---|---|---|---|---|
| Intl Stock | 8.50 | 3.2 | 1118.7 | 23.69 |

Templeton Foreign Fund's objective is long-term capital growth. Any income realized will be incidental.

The fund has an objective similar to that of Templeton World Fund, but the Foreign Fund will not hold (apart from defensive investments) securities issued by companies or political entities in the United States. The fund maintains a flexible investment policy and can invest in all types of securities; common stocks, however, are the usual form of investment.

**TOP LINE:** Adjusted NAV
**BOTTOM LINE:** Relative Strength

| RETURN | RISK |
|---|---|
| Above Avg | Low |
| RATING | |
| ★★★★ | |
| Highest | |

## TOTAL RETURN %

| | 1st Qtr. | 2nd Qtr. | 3rd Qtr. | 4th Qtr. | TOTAL |
|---|---|---|---|---|---|
| 1987 | 18.88 | 13.70 | 10.90 | -16.80 | 24.72 |
| 1988 | 9.86 | 2.41 | 2.05 | 6.26 | 21.99 |
| 1989 | 5.96 | 1.81 | 13.32 | 6.69 | 30.42 |
| 1990 | 1.89 | 6.94 | -11.65 | 0.75 | -3.01 |
| 1991 | 7.82 | -1.24 | … | … | … |

### INCOME

| | 1st Qtr. | 2nd Qtr. | 3rd Qtr. | 4th Qtr. | TOTAL |
|---|---|---|---|---|---|
| 1989 | 0.00 | 0.00 | 0.00 | 0.75 | 0.75 |
| 1990 | 0.00 | 0.00 | 0.00 | 0.78 | 0.78 |
| 1991 | 0.00 | 0.00 | … | … | 0.00 |

### CAPITAL GAINS

| | 1st Qtr. | 2nd Qtr. | 3rd Qtr. | 4th Qtr. | TOTAL |
|---|---|---|---|---|---|
| 1989 | 0.00 | 0.00 | 0.00 | 0.98 | 0.98 |
| 1990 | 0.00 | 0.00 | 0.00 | 0.90 | 0.90 |
| 1991 | 0.00 | 0.00 | … | … | 0.00 |

## PERFORMANCE/RISK 07/31/91

| | TOTAL RETURN % | +/- S&P 500 | +/- EAFE | PERCENTILE RANK ALL | PERCENTILE RANK OBJ. |
|---|---|---|---|---|---|
| 3 MONTH | 3.04 | -1.10 | 4.82 | 34 | 16 |
| 6 MONTH | 9.63 | -4.96 | 6.41 | 43 | 29 |
| 1 YEAR | -3.47 | -16.26 | 5.01 | 91 | 24 |
| 3 YEAR AVG. | 15.66 | -0.89 | 15.07 | 13 | 6 |
| 5 YEAR AVG. | 19.09 | 4.83 | 8.84 | 2 | 2 |
| 10 YEAR AVG. | … | … | … | | |
| 15 YEAR AVG. | … | … | … | | |

| | ALPHA | BETA | R² | STD. DEV. |
|---|---|---|---|---|
| | 2.0 | 0.69 | 57 | 3.87 |

| PERCENTILE RANK | ALL | 13 | 78 | 81 | 72 |
|---|---|---|---|---|---|
| | OBJ. | 11 | 82 | 26 | 96 |

Percentile Ranks 1 = Highest 100 = Lowest
Except MMF Risk 1 = Lowest 100 = Highest

| HISTORY | 1979 | 1980 | 1981 | 1982 | 1983 | 1984 | 1985 | 1986 | 1987 | 1988 | 1989 | 1990 | 07/91 |
|---|---|---|---|---|---|---|---|---|---|---|---|---|---|
| N.A.V. | … | … | … | 8.34 | 11.18 | 10.70 | 13.15 | 15.41 | 17.35 | 19.28 | 23.32 | 20.97 | 23.69 |
| TOTAL RETURN % | … | … | … | … | 36.45 | -1.25 | 26.88 | 28.77 | 24.72 | 21.99 | 30.42 | -3.01 | 12.97 |
| +/- S & P 500 INDEX | … | … | … | … | 13.99 | -7.38 | -4.76 | 10.14 | 19.50 | 5.48 | -1.25 | 0.09 | -6.73 |
| +/- EAFE INDEX | … | … | … | … | 12.76 | -8.63 | -29.28 | -40.67 | -6.27 | 13 | 19.89 | 20.44 | 6.41 |
| TOT. RTN./ALL FUNDS | … | … | … | … | 6 | 6 | 40 | 8 | 4 | 13 | 18 | 49 | 58 |
| % RANK/ OBJECTIVE | … | … | … | … | 22 | 43 | 92 | 79 | 16 | 20 | 23 | 10 | 29 |
| INCOME | … | … | … | 0.00 | 0.16 | 0.25 | 0.35 | 0.36 | 0.58 | 0.62 | 0.75 | 0.78 | 0.00 |
| CAPITAL GAIN | … | … | … | 0.00 | 0.04 | 0.09 | 0.04 | 1.07 | 1.23 | 1.16 | 0.98 | 0.90 | 0.00 |
| EXPENSE % | … | … | … | … | 1.44 | 0.84 | 0.90 | 0.79 | 0.77 | 0.81 | 0.81 | 0.78 | … |
| INCOME % | … | … | … | … | 3.67 | 3.36 | 3.32 | 2.99 | 2.89 | 3.29 | 3.55 | 2.52 | … |
| TURNOVER % | … | … | … | … | 4 | 4 | 4 | 21 | 14 | 20 | 17 | … | … |
| NET ASSETS ($MIL) | … | … | … | 2.0 | 23.5 | 67.0 | 94.2 | 197.5 | 261.1 | 320.9 | 564.1 | 934.3 | 1118.7 |

| M-STAR RISK % RANK | ALL | OBJ. |
|---|---|---|
| 3 YEAR | 44 | 5 |
| 5 YEAR | 38 | 5 |
| 10 YEAR | … | … |
| WEIGHTED AVG. | | |

| | MORNINGSTAR RETURN RISK | MORNINGSTAR RETURN RISK 1.00 = EQUITY AVG. | |
|---|---|---|---|
| 3 YEAR | 1.13 | 0.70 | → |
| 5 YEAR | 1.72 | 0.61 | → |
| 10 YEAR | … | … | → |
| WEIGHTED AVG. | 1.48 | 0.65 | |

| | MORNINGSTAR RISK-ADJUSTED RATING |
|---|---|
| 3 YEAR | ★★★★★ |
| 5 YEAR | ★★★★★ |
| 10 YEAR | … |
| | ★★★★★ |

### NET ASSETS: ($MIL)

## PORTFOLIO

**TOTAL # STOCKS: 121** — **TOP 30 EQUITY HOLDINGS AS OF: 05/31/91**

| SHARE CHANGE | AMOUNT | STOCK | VALUE $000 | % NET ASSETS |
|---|---|---|---|---|
| 0 | 135100 | BAYER | 22817 | 1.97 |
| 0 | 2865000 | BARCLAYS | 21612 | 1.87 |
| 14972481 | 14972481 | TELEFONOS DE MEXICO CL L | 20292 | 1.75 |
| 10 | 3310 | NESTLE | 19674 | 1.70 |
| 9000 | 2009700 | TELEFONICA DE ESPANA | 19100 | 1.65 |
| 325678 | 3690272 | NATIONAL AUSTRALIA BANK | 18673 | 1.61 |
| 132450 | 602450 | NORSK HYDRO | 18275 | 1.58 |
| 1500000 | 2055000 | SHELL TRANSPORT & TRADING | 17806 | 1.54 |
| 1500000 | 5900000 | BRITISH AIRWAYS | 17241 | 1.49 |
| 8000 | 908000 | CANADIAN PACIFIC | 16155 | 1.39 |
| 10000 | 12140 | TOTAL FRANCAISE DES PETROLES | 16063 | 1.39 |
| 540 | 4630 | HOLDERBANK FINANCIERE GLARIS | 15449 | 1.33 |
| 151433 | 151433 | ALCATEL ALSTHOM | 15381 | 1.33 |
| 0 | 1929758 | NOVA OF ALBERTA | 15376 | 1.33 |
| 0 | 1417000 | SINGAPORE AIRLINES | 14916 | 1.29 |
| 2470000 | 1375436 | CIFRA CL B | 14436 | 1.25 |
| 6703658 | 13300142 | CARTER HOLT HARVEY | 13925 | 1.20 |
| 150000 | 850000 | PHILIPS | 13711 | 1.18 |
| 0 | 9852 | CS HOLDINGS | 13442 | 1.16 |
| 100000 | 399488 | BANK OF MONTREAL | 12689 | 1.10 |
| 0 | 150000 | UNILEVER (NV) | 12596 | 1.09 |
| 9099654 | 9099654 | TELEFONOS DE MEXICO CL A | 12544 | 1.08 |
| 15000 | 215000 | VOLVO CL B | 11949 | 1.03 |
| 2200 | 6000 | ELECTROWATT | 11915 | 1.03 |
| 35000 | 35000 | BMW | 11452 | 0.99 |
| -336000 | 564000 | CHEUNG KONG | 11393 | 0.98 |
| -4476139 | 321812 | HONG KONG & SHANGHAI BANKING | 10945 | 0.94 |
| 0 | 184813 | AKZO | 10745 | 0.93 |
| 0 | 107712 | PAKHOED | 10722 | 0.93 |
| 0 | 508910 | ALCAN ALUMINUM | 10721 | 0.93 |

### PORTFOLIO STATISTICS 07/31/91

| | PORT- FOLIO | % OF AVG. STOCKS | REL. S&P 500 |
|---|---|---|---|
| PRICE/EARNINGS RATIO | 14.4 | 27 | 0.82 |
| PRICE/BOOK RATIO | 1.5 | 30 | 0.43 |
| 5 YR. EARN. GR. % | 9.4 | 11 | 0.72 |
| RETURN ON ASSETS | 4.4 | 27 | 0.58 |
| DEBT % TOTAL CAP. | 32.8 | 27 | 1.02 |
| MED. MKT. CAP. ($MIL) | 6198 | 35 | 0.53 |

### COMPOSITION % 06/30/91

| | | | |
|---|---|---|---|
| CASH | 20.4 | PREFERREDS | 0.1 |
| STOCKS | 78.5 | CONVERTIBLES | 0.9 |
| BONDS | 0.1 | OTHER | 0.0 |

### REGIONAL EXPOSURE 05/31/91

## ANALYSIS

**Helen O'D. Johnstone    08/23/91**

For a fund that can't invest in the U.S., Templeton Foreign Fund is looking good this year.

The U.S. market has been one of the world's strongest, year to date, buoyed by good news from the Gulf, a resurgent dollar, and the prospect of near-term economic recovery. Despite this fund's inability to participate directly in the U.S. market, however, it's in the top third of the international-fund group through July. It's beating the EAFE by a healthy margin, too (although, as we might expect, it's underperforming the S&P 500 by about as much). This performance is all the more impressive, considering that the dollar's strength in the first half of 1991 sabotaged many investors' internationally won spoils. In line with Templeton's habitual style, the fund continues to favor relatively cheap industries like financials (a major boost this year), energy, transportation, and utilities.

(Many of its stocks offer attractive dividend yields—the fund's current yield is high for this category.) It opts for cheaper markets, too, as is illustrated by its habitual neglect of Japan in favor of smaller Pacific-based markets like Hong Kong. The latter was one of the few markets to finish 1990 solidly in the black, gaining more than 8%—and this year, it continues to benefit from the dollar's strength. Although Hong Kong's market advanced by a tiny margin in 1991's first half, the surging dollar turned that seemingly insignificant advance into a 25% gain.

The fund's tendency to spread its country bets—its largest weighting is in the U.K., which accounts for less than 13% of assets—and its patient, value-oriented approach have allowed it to establish an outstanding total-return record. In addition, management's strategic use of cash keeps risk low; the fund currently has a 20% cash buffer.

## OPERATIONS

ADDRESS 700 Central Avenue
St. Petersburg, FL 33701
ADVISOR Templeton, Galbraith Hansberger
DISTRIBUTOR Templeton Funds Distributor
PORTFOLIO MANAGER Mark Holowesko (1987)
MANAGEMENT FEE 0.50% max./0.40% min.
FEES 8.50%L, 0.15%A
TICKER TEMFX

TELEPHONE NUMBER 813-823-8712
800-237-0738
PHONE SWITCH Yes
# OF SHAREHOLDERS 88692
MINIMUM INITIAL PURCHASE 500
MINIMUM SUBSEQUENT PURCHASE 25
DATE OF INCEPTION 10/05/82
SHAREHOLDER REPORT RATING B

# T. Rowe Price T/F H/Y

| OBJECTIVE | LOAD % | YIELD % | ASSETS($MIL) | N.A.V. |
|---|---|---|---|---|
| Muni Hi Yld | None | 7.0 | 546.6 | 11.66 |

T. Rowe Price Tax-Free High-Yield Fund seeks high current income exempt from federal income tax.

The fund invests primarily in medium- to low-quality municipal bonds. The fund has no maturity restrictions, but normally at least 80% of its bonds will have maturities longer than 10 years. It may also purchase bonds that are in default if the advisor believes there is significant capital appreciation potential. Such purchases are not expected to exceed 10% of assets. For temporary, defensive purposes, the fund may invest in higher-quality bonds.

**TOP LINE:** Adjusted NAV
**BOTTOM LINE:** Relative Strength

| RETURN | RISK |
|---|---|
| High | Below Avg |

RATING
★★★★
**Highest**

## TOTAL RETURN %

|  | 1st Qtr. | 2nd Qtr. | 3rd Qtr. | 4th Qtr. | TOTAL |
|---|---|---|---|---|---|
| 1987 | 3.20 | -4.22 | -1.09 | 2.51 | 0.23 |
| 1988 | 3.42 | 2.35 | 2.81 | 2.14 | 11.16 |
| 1989 | 1.71 | 5.04 | 0.42 | 3.00 | 10.51 |
| 1990 | 0.78 | 2.31 | 0.65 | 3.21 | 7.11 |
| 1991 | 1.79 | 2.85 | 3.46 | ... | ... |

## INCOME

|  | 1st Qtr. | 2nd Qtr. | 3rd Qtr. | 4th Qtr. | TOTAL |
|---|---|---|---|---|---|
| 1989 | 0.21 | 0.21 | 0.21 | 0.21 | 0.84 |
| 1990 | 0.21 | 0.21 | 0.20 | 0.21 | 0.83 |
| 1991 | 0.20 | 0.20 | 0.20 | ... | 0.61 |

## CAPITAL GAINS

|  | 1st Qtr. | 2nd Qtr. | 3rd Qtr. | 4th Qtr. | TOTAL |
|---|---|---|---|---|---|
| 1989 | 0.00 | 0.00 | 0.00 | 0.06 | 0.06 |
| 1990 | 0.03 | 0.00 | 0.00 | 0.00 | 0.03 |
| 1991 | 0.02 | 0.00 | 0.00 | ... | 0.02 |

## PERFORMANCE/RISK                    09/30/91

|  | TOTAL RETURN% | +/- LB GVT./CP. | PERCENTILE RANK ALL | PERCENTILE RANK OBJ. |
|---|---|---|---|---|
| 3 MONTH | 3.46 | -2.29 | 84 | 72 |
| 6 MONTH | 6.41 | -0.94 | 46 | 53 |
| 1 YEAR | 11.79 | -4.07 | 84 | 52 |
| 3 YEAR AVG. | 9.41 | -1.84 | 58 | 36 |
| 5 YEAR AVG. | 8.20 | -0.92 | 60 | 19 |
| 10 YEAR AVG. | ... | ... | ... | ... |
| 15 YEAR AVG. | ... | ... | ... | ... |

|  | ALPHA | BETA | R² | STD. DEV. |
|---|---|---|---|---|
|  | 0.0 | 0.53 | 71 | 0.80 |
| PERCENTILE / ALL | 18 | 82 | 41 | 90 |
| RANK-OBJ. | 17 | 79 | 22 | 74 |

Percentile Ranks: 1 = Highest, 100 = Lowest
Except M-Star Risk: 1 = Lowest, 100 = Highest

## HISTORY

| | 1979 | 1980 | 1981 | 1982 | 1983 | 1984 | 1985 | 1986 | 1987 | 1988 | 1989 | 1990 | 09/91 |
|---|---|---|---|---|---|---|---|---|---|---|---|---|---|
| N.A.V. | ... | ... | ... | ... | ... | ... | 10.68 | 11.92 | 10.86 | 11.21 | 11.45 | 11.37 | 11.66 |
| TOTAL RETURN % | ... | ... | ... | ... | ... | ... | ... | 20.40 | 0.23 | 11.16 | 10.51 | 7.11 | 8.31 |
| +/- LB GOVT./CP. | ... | ... | ... | ... | ... | ... | ... | 4.79 | -2.07 | 3.58 | -3.72 | -1.17 | -1.93 |
| TOT. RTN/ALL FUNDS | ... | ... | ... | ... | ... | ... | ... | 18 | 57 | 51 | 68 | 19 | 76 |
| % RANK OBJECTIVE | ... | ... | ... | ... | ... | ... | ... | 9 | 35 | 63 | 29 | 31 | 60 |
| INCOME | ... | ... | ... | ... | ... | ... | 0.72 | 0.88 | 0.84 | 0.83 | 0.84 | 0.83 | 0.61 |
| CAPITAL GAIN | ... | ... | ... | ... | ... | ... | 0.00 | 0.00 | 0.25 | 0.00 | 0.06 | 0.03 | 0.02 |
| EXPENSE % | ... | ... | ... | ... | ... | ... | ... | 1.00 | 0.98 | 0.96 | 0.92 | 0.88 | 0.85 |
| INCOME % | ... | ... | ... | ... | ... | ... | ... | 8.47 | 7.45 | 7.49 | 7.45 | 7.38 | 7.30 |
| TURNOVER % | ... | ... | ... | ... | ... | ... | ... | ... | 111 | 128 | 62 | 72 | 51 |
| NET ASSETS ($MIL) | ... | ... | ... | ... | ... | ... | 129.9 | 274.3 | 250.0 | 312.4 | 431.2 | 490.8 | 546.6 |

|  | M-STAR RISK % RANK ALL | M-STAR RISK % RANK OBJ. | MORNINGSTAR RETURN 1.00 = MUNI AVG | MORNINGSTAR RISK | MORNINGSTAR RISK-ADJUSTED RATING |
|---|---|---|---|---|---|
| 3 YEAR | 5 | 19 | 1.21 | 0.64 ↑ | ★★★★★ |
| 5 YEAR | 8 | 30 | 1.19 | 0.76 ↑ | ★★★★★ |
| 10 YEAR | ... | ... | ... | ... | ★★★★★ |
| WEIGHTED AVG. |  |  | 1.20 | 0.72 |  |

NET ASSETS: ($MIL)

| AMOUNT $000 | SECURITY | MATURITY | VALUE $000 | % NET ASSETS |
|---|---|---|---|---|
| 8500 | LA OFFSHORE TERM AUTH LOOP 7.6% | 09/01/10 | 8927 | 1.52 |
| 7500 | MS CLAIBORNE REV POLL CNTRL 9.875% | 12/01/14 | 8765 | 1.50 |
| 7635 | PR IND MED HIGHER EDUC & ENVIR 9.375% | 12/01/07 | 8033 | 1.37 |
| 7500 | CA LOS ANGELES WTR & PWR DEPT 7.25% | 09/15/30 | 7791 | 1.33 |
| 7225 | MA BAY TRANSP AUTH GENL SYS 7.875% | 03/01/21 | 7591 | 1.30 |
| 7505 | CO DENVER REV ARPT SYS 8% | 11/15/25 | 7464 | 1.27 |
| 5895 | OH HAMILTON EMERSON A NORTH HOSP 9.75% | 07/01/18 | 5945 | 1.02 |
| 5500 | FL BROWARD RESOURCE REC LP NORTH 7.95% | 12/01/08 | 5835 | 1.00 |
| 5600 | DE HLTH FAC AUTH BEEBE MED CTR 8.5% | 06/01/16 | 5748 | 0.98 |
| 5000 | IN EVANSVILLE HOSP AUTH ST MARYS 10.125% | 11/01/15 | 5684 | 0.97 |
| 5250 | AL MARSHALL HLTH CARE AUTH 10.25% | 10/01/13 | 5655 | 0.97 |
| 4900 | OH REV POLL CNTRL WTR DEV AUTH 9.75% | 11/01/22 | 5402 | 0.92 |
| 5480 | MA HLTH & EDUC FAC AUTH DEACONESS 7.2% | 04/01/22 | 5394 | 0.92 |
| 5000 | RI HSG & MTG FIN 8.05% | 04/01/22 | 5174 | 0.88 |
| 5025 | PA JOHNSTOWN PARKING AUTH 8.375% | 10/01/19 | 5167 | 0.88 |
| 4950 | PR ELEC PWR AUTH 7% | 07/01/21 | 4911 | 0.84 |
| 5000 | TX GULF COAST WASTE DISP AUTH 5.1% | 06/01/98 | 4763 | 0.81 |
| 4500 | CO DENVER REV ARPT SYS 8.75% | 11/15/23 | 4725 | 0.81 |
| 4365 | TX WAXAHACHIE INDL DEV AUTH GULF 9.125% | 12/01/02 | 4706 | 0.80 |
| 4700 | IL CHICAGO O'HARE INTL ARPT VAR% | | 4700 | 0.80 |

## SECTOR WEIGHTINGS

| | PORT. % | REL. MUNI AVG. | | PORT. % | REL. MUNI AVG. |
|---|---|---|---|---|---|
| GEN. OBL. | 3.45 | 0.41 | TRANS. R&R | 3.32 | 0.59 |
| UTILITY | 6.66 | 0.42 | TRANS. A&W | 8.98 | 1.86 |
| HEALTH | 30.91 | 1.82 | COP/LEASE | 0.00 | 0.00 |
| WTR./WASTE | 3.08 | 0.47 | PRIVATE | 19.13 | 1.59 |
| HOUSING | 16.79 | 1.90 | MISC. REV. | 0.00 | 0.00 |
| EDUCATION | 2.16 | 0.31 | UNASSIGNED | 5.52 | 1.20 |

## TOP 5 STATES

| | PORT. % |
|---|---|
| Texas | 9.23 |
| Florida | 6.44 |
| Ohio | 5.70 |
| Colorado | 5.56 |
| Pennsylvania | 4.61 |

## PORTFOLIO STATISTICS

| | |
|---|---|
| AVG. WEIGHTED MATURITY | 20.6 YEARS |
| AVG. WEIGHTED COUPON | 8.56% |
| AVG. WEIGHTED PRICE | 103% OF PAR |

## COMPOSITION % 06/30/91

| | | | |
|---|---|---|---|
| CASH | 5.1 | PREFERREDS | 0.0 |
| STOCKS | 0.0 | CONVERTIBLES | 0.0 |
| BONDS | 94.9 | OTHER | 0.0 |

## COUPON RANGE

| | % BONDS | REL. OBL |
|---|---|---|
| 0% | 1.4 | 0.4 |
| 0% to 6.8% | 3.4 | 0.3 |
| 6.8 to 7.5% | 13.8 | 0.9 |
| 7.5 to 8.3% | 24.0 | 1.2 |
| over 8.3% | 57.4 | 1.2 |

## CREDIT ANALYSIS 10/30/91

Rating (US Govt, AAA, AA, BBB, B, N/A) — Percentage of Bonds 0–100

# ANALYSIS

Paul Korngiebel 11/01/91

T. Rowe Price Tax-Free High-Yield Fund's emphasis on credit analysis has certainly paid off.

Although its returns are somewhat lackluster this year, due to fairly muted interest-rate sensitivity during the third quarter, long-term results are impressive. Over the trailing five-year period, the fund has returned 8.2% on an annualized basis, which ranks in its group's top quintile.

Manager William Reynolds attributes this success to intensive credit analysis. Indeed, Reynolds says, the fund tends to err on the side of conservatism, applying more stringent standards than the credit agencies themselves. As a result, the portfolio doesn't contain a single financial default, despite a 27% weighting in bonds rated BB or lower. Extensive credit analysis has allowed the fund to allocate a hefty 30% of assets to high-paying hospital bonds. This sector's historically high default rate and increasing financial woes have scared away many investors. Yet Reynolds has found value in small, rural hospitals. Despite their low occupancy rates and thin coverage ratios, he says, many rural hospitals have the financial support of local governments.

The fund has also been finicky about its housing bonds, which command roughly 15% of its assets. Reynolds avoids multifamily projects because they are structured like limited partnerships. He also stays away from local agencies, where the staff can be less professional than state agencies. Consequently, the fund has avoided the brunt of the real-estate market's woes.

Overall, the fund offers investors a fairly creditworthy portfolio that delivers a fat yield. Obviously, investors agree with our assessment of its merits: fund assets have climbed steadily and now total over $500 million.

# OPERATIONS

| | | | |
|---|---|---|---|
| ADDRESS | 100 E. Pratt Street Baltimore, MD 21202 | TELEPHONE NUMBER | 301-547-2308 800-638-5660 |
| ADVISOR | T. Rowe Price Associates | PHONE SWITCH | Yes |
| DISTRIBUTOR | T. Rowe Price Investment Svcs. | # OF SHAREHOLDERS | 18054 |
| PORTFOLIO MANAGER | William T. Reynolds (1985) | MINIMUM INITIAL PURCHASE | 2500 |
| MANAGEMENT FEE | 0.30% flat fee +0.48%G | MINIMUM SUBSEQUENT PURCHASE | 100 |
| FEES | No-load | DATE OF INCEPTION | 03/01/85 |
| TICKER | PRFHX | SHAREHOLDER REPORT RATING | A- |

MORNINGSTAR, INC.

# Value Line Tax-Exempt H/Y

| | MORNINGSTAR MUTUAL FUNDS | | | | |
|---|---|---|---|---|---|
| OBJECTIVE | LOAD % | YIELD % | ASSETS($MIL) | N.A.V. |
| Muni Hi Yld | None | 6.9 | 280.6 | 10.49 |

Value Line Tax-Exempt High-Yield Fund seeks to provide investors with the maximum income exempt from federal income taxes, while avoiding undue risk to principal. Capital appreciation is its secondary objective.

The fund invests primarily in investment grade municipal bonds. It expects to maintain an average maturity of between 10 and 40 years.

| | RETURN | RISK |
|---|---|---|
| | Above Avg | Below Avg |
| | RATING | |
| | ★ ★ ★ | |
| | **Above Avg** | |

TOP LINE: Adjusted NAV
BOTTOM LINE: Relative Strength

| HISTORY | 1979 | 1980 | 1981 | 1982 | 1983 | 1984 | 1985 | 1986 | 1987 | 1988 | 1989 | 1990 | 09/91 |
|---|---|---|---|---|---|---|---|---|---|---|---|---|---|
| N.A.V. | ... | ... | ... | ... | ... | 9.82 | 10.70 | 10.81 | 9.99 | 10.26 | 10.30 | 10.17 | 10.49 |
| TOTAL RETURN % | ... | ... | ... | ... | ... | ... | 19.76 | 13.66 | 0.71 | 11.10 | 8.36 | 6.55 | 8.55 |
| +/- LB GOVT./CP. | ... | ... | ... | ... | ... | ... | -1.55 | -1.96 | -1.59 | 3.52 | -5.88 | -1.73 | -1.69 |
| TOT. RTN {ALL FUNDS | ... | ... | ... | ... | ... | ... | 73 | 61 | 53 | 52 | 87 | 25 | 73 |
| % RANK {OBJECTIVE | ... | ... | ... | ... | ... | ... | 54 | 83 | 25 | 66 | 85 | 43 | 48 |
| INCOME | ... | ... | ... | ... | ... | 0.75 | 0.98 | 0.91 | 0.82 | 0.81 | 0.79 | 0.77 | 0.53 |
| CAPITAL GAIN | ... | ... | ... | ... | ... | 0.00 | 0.00 | 0.36 | 0.05 | 0.00 | 0.00 | 0.00 | 0.00 |
| EXPENSE % | ... | ... | ... | ... | ... | ... | 0.17 | 0.66 | 0.68 | 0.64 | 0.63 | 0.62 | 0.60 |
| INCOME % | ... | ... | ... | ... | ... | ... | 10.49 | 9.36 | 8.20 | 7.98 | 7.77 | 7.70 | 7.47 |
| TURNOVER % | ... | ... | ... | ... | ... | ... | 187 | 254 | 79 | 76 | 73 | 63 | 122 |
| NET ASSETS ($MIL) | ... | ... | ... | ... | ... | 30.0 | 36.8 | 133.9 | 228.4 | 254.6 | 274.9 | 278.7 | 280.6 |

## TOTAL RETURN %

| | 1st Qtr. | 2nd Qtr. | 3rd Qtr. | 4th Qtr. | TOTAL |
|---|---|---|---|---|---|
| 1987 | 3.33 | -3.41 | -2.11 | 3.07 | 0.71 |
| 1988 | 3.60 | 2.34 | 2.50 | 2.24 | 11.10 |
| 1989 | 1.15 | 4.13 | 0.63 | 2.23 | 8.36 |
| 1990 | 0.67 | 2.02 | -0.20 | 3.96 | 6.55 |
| 1991 | 1.82 | 2.31 | 4.21 | ... | ... |

## INCOME

| | 1st Qtr. | 2nd Qtr. | 3rd Qtr. | 4th Qtr. | TOTAL |
|---|---|---|---|---|---|
| 1989 | 0.20 | 0.20 | 0.20 | 0.20 | 0.79 |
| 1990 | 0.20 | 0.19 | 0.19 | 0.19 | 0.77 |
| 1991 | 0.17 | 0.18 | 0.18 | ... | 0.53 |

## CAPITAL GAINS

| | 1st Qtr. | 2nd Qtr. | 3rd Qtr. | 4th Qtr. | TOTAL |
|---|---|---|---|---|---|
| 1989 | 0.00 | 0.00 | 0.00 | 0.00 | 0.00 |
| 1990 | 0.00 | 0.00 | 0.00 | 0.00 | 0.00 |
| 1991 | 0.00 | 0.00 | 0.00 | ... | 0.00 |

## PERFORMANCE/RISK

09/30/91

| | TOTAL RETURN% | +/- LB GVT./CP. | PERCENTILE RANK ALL | PERCENTILE RANK OBJ. |
|---|---|---|---|---|
| 3 MONTH | 4.21 | -1.54 | 68 | 15 |
| 6 MONTH | 6.61 | -0.74 | 41 | 39 |
| 1 YEAR | 12.85 | -3.01 | 76 | 30 |
| 3 YEAR AVG. | 8.61 | -2.64 | 73 | 73 |
| 5 YEAR AVG. | 7.70 | -1.42 | 68 | 45 |
| 10 YEAR AVG. | ... | ... | | |
| 15 YEAR AVG. | ... | ... | | |

| | ALPHA | BETA | R² | STD. DEV. |
|---|---|---|---|---|
| | -0.8 | 0.57 | 63 | 0.91 |

| PERCENTILE | ALL | 41 | 78 | 71 | 86 |
|---|---|---|---|---|---|
| RANK | OBJ. | 60 | 71 | 63 | 64 |

Percentile Ranks 1 = Highest 100 = Lowest
Except M-Star Risk 1 = Lowest 100 = Highest

| | M-STAR RISK % RANK | | MORNINGSTAR RETURN RISK | | MORNINGSTAR RISK-ADJUSTED RATING |
|---|---|---|---|---|---|
| | ALL | OBJ. | 1.00 = MUNI AVG | | |
| 3 YEAR | 10 | 36 | 1.08 | 0.81 → | ★ ★ ★ ★ |
| 5 YEAR | 10 | 41 | 1.08 | 0.82 → | ★ ★ ★ ★ |
| 10 YEAR | ... | ... | ... | ... | |
| WEIGHTED AVG. | | | 1.08 | 0.82 | ★ ★ ★ ★ |

| AMOUNT $000 | SECURITY | MATURITY | VALUE $000 | % NET ASSETS |
|---|---|---|---|---|
| 7000 | NY NEW YORK CITY GO 8% | 08/01/16 | 6615 | 2.38 |
| 5595 | NJ SALEM REV INDL POLL CNTRL FIN 10.5% | 07/01/14 | 6366 | 2.29 |
| 6000 | IL REV SALES TAX 7.2% | 06/15/14 | 6009 | 2.16 |
| 6000 | AZ REV ELEC SYS SALT RVR PROJ AGRI 6% | 01/01/31 | 5205 | 1.87 |
| 5000 | CA LOS ANGELES REV ELEC PLANT PWR 7.1% | 01/15/31 | 4980 | 1.79 |
| 6000 | FL EVERGLADES REV PORT AUTH IMPR RFDG 5% | 09/01/16 | 4332 | 1.56 |
| 5325 | FL ORLANDO REV WTR & ELEC UTIL COM 5.5% | 10/01/26 | 4300 | 1.55 |
| 4000 | WA REV PUB PWR SPLY SYS PROJ #3 7.5% | 07/01/18 | 4015 | 1.44 |
| 4000 | CA MADERA PUB WKS BRD-DEPT CRTNS 7% | 09/01/09 | 3996 | 1.44 |
| 3500 | WA REV PUB PWR SPLY SYS PROJ #1 7.25% | 07/01/09 | 3553 | 1.28 |
| 3550 | CA REV HOSP HLTH FAC FIN AUTH-KAISER 7% | 12/01/10 | 3531 | 1.27 |
| 3500 | WA REV PUB PWR SPLY SYS PROJ #2 7.875% | 07/01/12 | 3523 | 1.27 |
| 3250 | AK REV INS MTG PROG 7.8% | 12/01/30 | 3315 | 1.19 |
| 3250 | IL REV SALES TAX 6.875% | 06/15/15 | 3140 | 1.13 |
| 3500 | FL JACKSONVILLE REV ELEC AUTH 6% | 10/01/15 | 3099 | 1.11 |
| 3000 | OH FRANKLIN REV HOSP RVRSIDE HOSP 7.6% | 05/15/20 | 3050 | 1.10 |
| 3000 | CA SAN MATEO TRANSIT DIST LTD TAX 6.5% | 06/01/20 | 2853 | 1.03 |
| 3000 | FL ORLANDO REV WTR & ELEC UTIL COM 6.5% | 10/01/20 | 2809 | 1.01 |
| 2575 | OK REV SNGL FAM MTG HSG FIN AGCY 10.75% | 03/01/07 | 2747 | 0.99 |
| 2635 | OK REV SNGL FAM MTG HSG FIN AGCY 9% | 06/01/11 | 2705 | 0.97 |

### SECTOR WEIGHTINGS

| | PORT. % | REL. MUNI AVG. | | PORT. % | REL. MUNI AVG. |
|---|---|---|---|---|---|
| GEN. OBL. | 6.62 | 0.78 | TRANS. R&R | 3.50 | 0.62 |
| UTILITY | 22.58 | 1.42 | TRANS. A&W | 4.71 | 0.98 |
| HEALTH | 18.22 | 1.07 | COP/LEASE | 0.00 | 0.00 |
| WTR./WASTE | 7.40 | 1.12 | PRIVATE | 4.50 | 0.38 |
| HOUSING | 20.31 | 2.30 | MISC. REV. | 7.16 | 1.53 |
| EDUCATION | 2.10 | 0.30 | UNASSIGNED | 2.88 | 0.62 |

### PORTFOLIO STATISTICS

| | |
|---|---|
| AVG. WEIGHTED MATURITY | 23.4 YEARS |
| AVG. WEIGHTED COUPON | 7.86% |
| AVG. WEIGHTED PRICE | 99.7 % OF PAR |

### TOP 5 STATES

| | |
|---|---|
| California | 10.71 |
| Florida | 9.90 |
| Illinois | 9.16 |
| Texas | 8.15 |
| New York | 7.68 |

### COMPOSITION % 06/30/91

| | | | |
|---|---|---|---|
| CASH | 4.6 | PREFERREDS | 0.0 |
| STOCKS | 0.0 | CONVERTIBLES | 0.0 |
| BONDS | 95.4 | OTHER | 0.0 |

### COUPON RANGE

| | % BONDS | REL. OBL. |
|---|---|---|
| 0% | 0.0 | 0.0 |
| 0% to 6.8% | 24.3 | 2.1 |
| 6.8 to 7.5% | 28.3 | 1.8 |
| 7.5 to 8.3% | 17.3 | 0.9 |
| over 8.3% | 30.0 | 0.6 |

### CREDIT ANALYSIS   08/30/91

US Govt, AA, AAA, BBB, B, N/A — Percentage of Bonds

## ANALYSIS

**Value Line Tax-Exempt High-Yield Fund**    Anthony Mayorkas   11/01/91

Value Line Tax-Exempt High-Yield Fund has made all the right moves.

The fund's management has astutely maneuvered the fund to benefit from today's low interest rates. In the process, the fund has shown a promising flexibility.

Its biggest move has been to veer the fund away from its traditional premium-coupon strategy. Over 65% of the portfolio now rests in discount- and current-coupon bonds, a position that has helped the fund perform respectably during the market's rally (it's in its group's top half so far this year). At the same time, the fund kept certain higher-coupon bonds to balance the fund's duration.

Recognizing the risk of premiums in a low interest-rate environment, however, fund management has tried to rein in call risk. When the opportunity exists, fund official James Flood says, the fund has swapped its bonds with 1996 or 1997 calls and has moved into bonds with standard 10-year calls.

Management hasn't had to worry about credit risk; the fund has generally boasted high credit-quality standards (its name merely distinguishes it from Value Line's lower-yielding Money Market Portfolio). At present, over 60% of the portfolio consists of securities rated AA and AAA. With spreads being quite narrow, fund management has increasingly emphasized high-quality holdings. And with municipal-bond insurance as cheap as it is, Flood says, the fund has found another means to upgrade its quality. For instance, the fund recently purchased a Grand Rapids Water and Sewer bond with an underlying single-A credit. But because insurance was so cheap, the fund bought it as well.

Management has reacted successfully to different market conditions, and the fund has thus shown a promising flexibility.

## OPERATIONS

| | | | |
|---|---|---|---|
| **ADDRESS** | 711 Third Avenue<br>New York, NY 10017 | **TELEPHONE NUMBER** | 212-687-3965<br>800-223-0818 |
| **ADVISOR** | Value Line | **PHONE SWITCH** | Yes |
| **DISTRIBUTOR** | Value Line Securities | **# OF SHAREHOLDERS** | 7352 |
| **PORTFOLIO MANAGER** | management team (1990) | **MINIMUM INITIAL PURCHASE** | 1000 |
| **MANAGEMENT FEE** | 0.50% flat fee | **MINIMUM SUBSEQUENT PURCHASE** | 250 |
| **FEES** | No-load | **DATE OF INCEPTION** | 03/23/84 |
| **TICKER** | VLHYX | **SHAREHOLDER REPORT RATING** | B |

# Index